Digital Competition Law in Europe

Digital Competition Law in Europe

Marc Wiggers
Robin Struijlaart
Joost Dibbits

Wolters Kluwer

Published by:
Kluwer Law International B.V.
PO Box 316
2400 AH Alphen aan den Rijn
The Netherlands
E-mail: lrs-sales@wolterskluwer.com
Website: www.wolterskluwer.com/en/solutions/kluwerlawinternational

Sold and distributed by:
Wolters Kluwer Legal & Regulatory U.S.
920 Links Avenue
Landisville, PA 17538
United States of America
E-mail: customer.service@wolterskluwer.com

ISBN 978-94-035-1167-2

e-Book: ISBN 978-94-035-1177-1
web-PDF: ISBN 978-94-035-1187-0

About the Authors

Marc Wiggers (PhD, Nijmegen; LLM Utrecht), is an attorney-at-law, partner in the Competition & Regulatory practice group of Loyens & Loeff (Amsterdam), and founder of the firm's Digital Economy Team. He specialises in EU competition and tech law and advises platforms, business users of platforms and providers and users of digital services and products. Marc is a (head) lecturer at the postgraduate Grotius Academy in the Netherlands and teaches at universities. In 2013, he obtained a PhD with a thesis on competition and regulatory supervision. Chambers Europe 2022 mentions Marc as an 'excellent adviser'. Legal 500 2022 wrote: 'Partner Marc Wiggers is singled out for competition work. Marc is a true super-competition specialist.'

Robin Struijlaart (LLM, College of Europe, Bruges; LLM, Tilburg), is an attorney-at-law and member of the Competition & Regulatory practice group and the Digital Economy Team of Loyens & Loeff (Amsterdam). He specialises in EU and competition law, including competition in digital tech markets. He regularly publishes on competition law-related topics and has lectured on merger control aspects of EU competition law at Utrecht and Nyenrode Universities. Prior to joining Loyens & Loeff, he worked as an associate in the Brussels office of a major US law firm. Chambers Europe has written about Robin: 'Sources affirm that he does "excellent work"'.

Joost Dibbits (LLM, Nijmegen (2012); MA, Nijmegen (2012)) is a competition lawyer and data scientist at Linklaters (Brussels). Before joining Linklaters in 2020, he worked at Loyens & Loeff (Amsterdam) and in the European Parliament.

List of Contributors

Guest Authors

Gareth Shier, director, economics advisory TNT, EY

Tristan Byrne, consultant, Altman Solon

Daniel Mândrescu, PhD, assistant professor, Leiden University

Thibault Schrépel, PhD, associate professor of law at VU Amsterdam, faculty affiliate at Stanford University's Center for Legal Informatics (CodeX)

Giuseppe Colangelo, PhD, Jean Monnet professor of EU Innovation Policy and associate professor of Law and Economics, University of Basilicata; adjunct professor of Markets, Regulations and Law, and of Competition and Markets of Innovation, Luiss; TTLF Fellow, Stanford Law School and University of Vienna

Ai Deng, PhD, principal, Charles River Associates, lecturer, Johns Hopkins University

Wolf Sauter, PhD, coordinating specialist inspector, Autoriteit Consument & Markt, professor of Law Markets and Behaviour, VU Amsterdam

Teodora Groza, PhD candidate, Sciences Po, Paris

Contributors to the chapters credited to the authors

Robert Fröger, senior associate, Competition & Regulatory, Loyens & Loeff N.V., Amsterdam

Boyd Wolffers, senior associate, Competition & Regulatory, Loyens & Loeff N.V., Amsterdam

Marco de Vries, associate, Competition & Regulatory, Loyens & Loeff N.V., Amsterdam

Kirill Ryabtsev, paralegal Competition & Regulatory, Loyens & Loeff N.V., Amsterdam and PhD candidate, VU Amsterdam

Marinus Prakke, associate, Litigation (previously Competition & Regulatory), Loyens & Loeff N.V., Amsterdam

Michiel Krebbers, associate, Finance (previously Competition & Regulatory), Loyens & Loeff N.V., Amsterdam

Table of Contents

Preface to the First Edition

The competition law landscape is changing rapidly under pressure of the development of artificial intelligence (AI). Digital technologies, such as software, algorithms and robots, together with big data and machine learning, are developing at such a pace that it sometimes appears impossible to keep up. Accordingly, numerous associated competition law questions, dilemmas and challenges are facing regulators, academics, policymakers, judges, in-house counsel and lawyers. In our daily law practice and academic work, we also increasingly encounter competition by means of (new) digital technologies. It is certain that this trend will continue to grow in the coming years. Many competition authorities are now making digital competition an explicit area of focus. This means that everyone involved in competition law will soon have to tackle the question, if they are not doing so already, as to how the development of digital technologies will impact competition law and what this will mean for his or her practice. It is in this context that we have set up a Digital Competition Team within our firm. Precedents and views with regard to digital competition are currently in full development, but there is little uniformity so far. Obtaining a broad and thorough overview of recent and expected developments is therefore indispensable for anyone who is active in competition law. This book presen'ts an overview of the (enforcement) practices of six European competition authorities (the European Commission (European Union)), the Competition and Markets Authority (United Kingdom (UK)), Bundeskartellamt (Germany), L'Autorité de la concurrence (France), the Consumer & Market Authority (the Netherlands) and the Belgian Competition Authority (Belgium)). This book takes you on a tour of these European competition authorities and sets out the rapidly changing European competition law landscape. It presents the comparative legal situation to date and on the horizon. It will help you be ready for the new competition law reality, which is here already, whether you like it or not. We hope you will enjoy this book and find it useful.

We would like to thank Loyens & Loeff N.V. and the members of the Digital Competition Team for their support in creating this book. In particular, our thanks go to Marc Custers, Thomas Verstraeten, Bart Terberg, Robert Fröger, Hamza Zourakhti, Joukje Baur, Nick Strous and Marco de Vries. Alex Burrough of Words at Work assisted with translations. We are grateful for his kind and professional assistance. Finally, we would like to thank Kluwer Law International – and in particular Simon Bellamy – for publishing this book.

Amsterdam, 21 May 2019
Joost Dibbits, Robin Struijlaart and Marc Wiggers

Preface to the Second Edition

Less than four years have passed since the first edition of this book was published. If one however looks at the number and magnitude of the developments that have occurred since it seems more like a lifetime. The number of enforcement precedents in the six jurisdictions under review has skyrocketed. This concerns antitrust (the cartel prohibition and the prohibition on the abuse of a dominant position) as well as merger control. The number of pages of this book has approximately tripled, for which reason we no longer deem the subtitle *A Concise Guide* appropriate. It has therefore been dropped for the current volume.

When the first edition appeared, the debate on whether new, sector-specific legislation supplementing or even replacing 'normal' competition law would be required was just getting started. Just over three years later, new legislation has already been introduced in Germany, Belgium, and the EU.

These rapid developments coincide with a profound change in thinking about large tech companies and their impact on society. Roughly, we can distinguish three distinct time periods, which we have observed clearly in the process of drafting both editions of this book.

The first period that can be distinguished lasted up to approximately 2017. There were already certain concerns about the power of tech firms at the time, but the general notion still seemed to be that 'tech was good'. And that notion was not at all surprising. When digital technologies and the companies behind them started to emerge, everyone was very enthusiastic about the many and obvious advantages these new developments brought with them. Just a few of many examples:

- greater access to information;
- easier communication and overall efficiencies;
- easier and greater access to goods and services.

How did this general positive vibe reflect on competition law enforcement? The main aim of the authorities at the time appeared to be not to hinder innovation. To this end, competition authorities conducted a large number of market studies and engaged in a dialogue with tech companies and other stakeholders. Authorities were generally lenient in allowing mergers.

Competition authorities were initially hesitant to interfere in antitrust and abuse cases as well. If at all they interfered, it was through 'nudging'. Almost no fines were imposed.

There was a lively debate on whether the existing competition rules were sufficient to discipline Big Tech or whether new rules would be required. The scene was split between those who feared coming too late to regulate versus those who feared – in line with Schumpeter's theory of creative destruction – that too much regulation would lead to a stifling of innovative markets.

The European Commission's fine for Google in the Shopping case in 2017 marked a clear turning point and the start of the second period. Big Tech was suddenly at the focal point of the authorities' attention and they started hitting hard! Google received more fines in the EU and in France and the other 'members' of 'GAMA' (Google, Apple, Meta and Amazon) also came under great scrutiny in the jurisdictions under review.

Still, this process was gradual and many authorities' initial fining decisions were not addressed to tech companies at large or at GAMA in particular. Many of these fines are related to clear 'classic' infringements – such as resale price maintenance – by 'traditional' (non-tech) companies.

In the course of time, however, authorities started to get bolder and were showing increased preparedness to take up much more complex cases. When we finalised the first edition of this book, we concluded that '*"Big Tech" Is in (Almost) Everyone's Sights*'.

The general stance towards Big Tech in society as a whole, as well as within the competition law community as such, also started to change. It became much more nuanced, and the potentially negative effects of the perceived market and data power of tech giants were gradually becoming evident. A consensus was formed that specific rules were needed to constrain Big Tech and that the general competition rules weren't enough. This seems a direct result of the increase in the number of cases and the lessons learned from these cases. Similar theories of harm started emerging in various cases: self-preferencing, abuse of data power, parity clauses, preventing interoperability and network and lock-in effects arising from digital ecosystems were among the most prominent of these. This led to legislative proposals aimed at regulating or banning such practices.

Where do we stand now? 2021 marked the start of a third period. The swing of the pendulum is complete, and it appears that negative perceptions of Big Tech have become predominant. As technology has become more complex and the power of Big Tech has grown, so has the attention – or even the alarm – in society regarding the darker sides of Big Tech:

- Big Tech penetrates deeper and deeper into our personal lives, often against our own will – we experience a loss of control over our personal data;
- data starts giving Big Tech companies semi-governmental power;
- misleading information/fake news;

- negative influence on democracy because of the two last-mentioned developments;
- network effects and lock-in effects: no alternatives for dominant technologies.

In brief, the second, much-expanded edition of this book comes in time. We have increased the scope of our book by including a set of contextual chapters, written by renowned guest authors who are thought leaders in their fields. Lots of thanks go out to Gareth Shier, Tristan Byrne, Daniel Mândrescu, Thibault Schrépel, Giuseppe Colangelo, Ai Deng, Wolf Sauter and Teodora Groza. We are convinced that their thoughtful and well-written (sub)chapters contribute greatly to the depth of this book and provide significant added value to its readers.

We would like to thank Loyens & Loeff N.V. and the members of the Digital Competition Team for their support in creating this book's second edition. In particular, our thanks go to Boyd Wolffers, Robert Fröger, Marco de Vries, Marinus Prakke, Kiriil Ryabtsev and Michiel Krebbers. Finally, we would like to thank Kluwer Law International – and in particular Simon Bellamy and Niki de Bruin – for publishing the two editions of this book.

Amsterdam, 12 May 2023
Joost Dibbits, Robin Struijlaart and Marc Wiggers

CHAPTER 1
Introduction

There can be no doubt: digital competition law is a hot topic. Its development is accelerating because digital technologies are increasingly influencing the competitive process. This means that important decisions in daily life are ever more being made by artificial intelligence (AI). The term AI is commonly used to refer to a range of digital technologies such as software, algorithms, processes and robots that – contrary to machines only acting on human command – are able to acquire analytical capabilities and perform tasks (often on the basis of 'machine learning' and 'big data' techniques).[1] This may have positive effects on competition by causing an increase in speed, efficiency and objectivity.[2] For example, new services and products are being created and the internet allows clear access to information readily available so that consumers can easily compare products and obtain a quick overview of the best choices on offer. However, such digital technologies may also have the effect of restricting competition. One could, for example, think of pricing algorithms committing a cartel infringement, the creation of dominant positions as a result of a decisive lead in technology or data collection, restriction of choices and services and the abuse of personal data.

Around the world, countries struggle with how to deal with digital competition. The fascinating and diverse ideas that emerge from this struggle are now gradually resulting in sector-specific legislation in various jurisdictions worldwide. As European competition law experts, we raised the question of how competition authorities in Europe deal with and view digital competition. This question culminated in the first edition of this book which was published in late 2019. More than three years later, many new and exciting developments have taken place and it is high time to take stock

1. Definition of AI used by the European Parliament, *see* http://www.europarl.europa.eu/legislative-train/theme-connecteddigital-single-market/file-artificial-intelligence-for-europe.
2. A. Ezrachi and M.E. Stucke, 'Chapter 1: The Promise of a Better Competitive Environment', in A. Ezrachi and M.E. Stucke (eds), *Virtual Competition: The Promise and Perils of the Algorithm-Driven Economy* (Harvard University Press 2016).

once more and examine the state of digital competition in the enforcement practices of the competition authorities in Europe.

This book takes the reader on a 'survey' of six competition authorities through the European landscape: (i) the *European Commission* (Commission); (ii) the *Competition and Markets Authority* (UK competition authority (CMA)) and its predecessor the *Office of Fair Trading* (OFT); (iii) the *Bundeskartellamt* (German competition authority (Bka)); (iv) *L'Autorité de la concurrence* (French competition authority or Autorité); (v) the *Autoriteit Consument & Markt* (Dutch competition authority (ACM)) and (vi) the *Autorité belge de la Concurrence/Belgische Mededingingsautoriteit* (Belgian Competition Authority (BCA)). Ideally, we would like to examine all the European competition authorities, but the presence of language barriers, in particular, has led to the selection of these six competition authorities.

The journey across the European landscape is also a journey in time, as this survey goes back to 1 August 2012 and ends on 30 June 2022 where the cartel prohibition and the prohibition on abuse of a dominant position are concerned and on 31 March 2022 for merger control; with the inclusion of as many landmark cases and other special developments dating from after this date. This implies that the period under investigation does not go back to the very beginning of European digital competition practice, but it does go back to the time when digital competition started to feature more prominently on the agendas of the European competition authorities. Exceptionally, if the investigation gave cause to do so, we have gone further back or forward in time (with an absolute end date of 30 September 2022 save for certain extremely important events in landmark cases).

In this book, 'digital competition' means competition through digital technologies, such as internet platforms and e-commerce, software (self-learning), algorithms[3] and big data.[4] This book therefore only deals with cases in which, in our view, such digital technologies have had a significant impact on the competition law outcome of the case or have at least played a prominent role in the analysis involved.[5] Cases relating to hardware and telecom fall outside the scope of this book. We will discuss not only the decision-making practice of the selected competition authorities and the

3. For the purpose of this book, an algorithm shall mean '*a process or set of rules to be followed in calculations or other problem-solving operations, especially by a computer*' (Oxford English Dictionary).
4. Extremely large data sets that may be analysed computationally to reveal patterns, trends and associations, especially relating to human behaviour and interactions.
5. For this reason, the European Commission's fine of EUR 997 million of 24 January 2018 (*Case AT.40220 (Qualcomm)* (European Commission)) imposed on Qualcomm has not been included, as this decision relates to hardware. Additionally, for this reason, for example, we do discuss the Commission's enforcement practice in the field of consumer electronics, as the role of automatic pricing software (algorithms) has played an important dual role in that case. The Commission's investigation into tour operators (*Case 40308 (Holiday Pricing)* (European Commission)), which was announced in parallel, has not been included. Indeed, the Commission's concerns in that case seem to focus mainly on excluding customers on the basis of their location, and there is no reason to believe that digital technologies play a decisive role in the competition assessment in this procedure. The authors realise that such choices may by necessity be arbitrary.

resulting case law but also the competition authorities' digital competition practice in a broader sense, whereby attention will also be paid to sector-specific regulation, guidance and policy documents, speeches, industry surveys, research reports and annual reports. The aim has been to provide as complete an overview as possible within the scope of our research.

First, this book will kick off with an introductory chapter written by guest authors Gareth Shier and Tristan Byrne on the economic principles of digital markets (Chapter 2). This chapter is followed by a second chapter written by guest author Daniel Mândrescu on the market definition for multisided platforms (Chapter 3). The following chapters contain our actual research and outline the digital competition practices of the Commission (Chapter 4); the CMA (Chapter 5); the Autorité (Chapter 6); the Bka (Chapter 7); the ACM (Chapter 8); and the BCA (Chapter 9). Chapters 4 to 9 have the following structure:

(i) *Introduction*: the digital competition practice of the competition authority with regard to the investigation period is introduced on the basis of an overview of activities and noteworthy facts and achievements.
(ii) *Cartel prohibition:* the (enforcement) practice of the competition authority with regard to the cartel prohibition in relation to digital competition during the investigation period is discussed.
(iii) *Prohibition of abuse of a dominant position:* the (enforcement) practice of the competition authority with regard to the prohibition of abuse of a dominant position in relation to digital competition during the investigation period is discussed.
(iv) *Merger control:* the practice of the competition authority with regard to merger control in relation to digital competition during the investigation period is discussed.
(v) A *sub-conclusion*, which takes stock of the enforcement practice of the authority in the field of digital competition.

The practices and enforcement practices of the various authorities will subsequently be compared and subjected to an analysis (Chapter 10). This analysis will deal *inter alia* with the degree of activity of the various authorities, the focus of the activity, the enforcement styles and the enforcement instruments used, the visible effectiveness of such enforcement, the similarities and differences in the enforcement practices and the positive and negative effects of digital competition in the jurisdictions investigated.

As an outlook to the future, this book contains a chapter dealing with five *game changers* described by guest authors (Chapter 11). This chapter kicks off with a subchapter written by Thibault Schrépel on blockchain and antitrust. It continues with a subchapter on moligopoly and self-preferencing by Giuseppe Colangelo. The next game changer described is machine learning, by Ai Deng. Wolf Sauter is up next with a subchapter dealing with Green Antitrust. Our overview of game changers concludes with a subchapter dealing with computational antitrust, by Teodora Groza. This exercise in comparative law shall be wrapped up with a concluding chapter (Chapter

12). It contains an overview of *bottlenecks* we have identified in our research, and recommendations. As Emile Zola wrote: *'Rien ne développe l'intelligence comme les voyages.'*[6] We wish you a good journey through the burgeoning European digital competitive landscape.

6. Freely translated: 'Nothing develops intelligence as much as travel.'

CHAPTER 2
Economic Principles

Gareth Shier & Tristan Byrne

§2.01 CHARACTERISTICS OF DIGITAL MARKETS

With digital services now touching so many different aspects of our day-to-day lives, the lines between the digital and non-digital economy are becoming increasingly blurred. However, many digital services bring together a series of distinct economic characteristics, including:

- positive and negative externalities;
- direct and indirect network effects;
- economies of scale and scope; and
- barriers to entry.

While these same characteristics can be found in a range of different industries, their combination and strength of application is a defining feature of 'digital disruption'. Furthermore, this combination can lead to several distinctive market outcomes, including:

- tipping markets; and
- ecosystem effects.

In this section, we briefly explain each of these key economic characteristics and market outcomes, while discussing their implications for the assessment of competition in digital markets.

[A] Externalities

In economics, externality effects refer to spillovers – both positive and negative – from the actions of one market participant onto another. A classic example of a negative externality might be that of noise pollution from an industrial manufacturer, spilling over into a residential area, while an example of a positive externality could be the benefit of street lighting enjoyed by all pedestrians.

In the case of digital markets, both positive and negative externalities are common. For example, a developer building apps for a mobile platform may seek to maximise their revenue by including advertising within the app's interface. While this has a positive income effect for the developer, it worsens the experience for the user. Not only that, but it also has a negative externality effect on the platform owner, whose overall ecosystem may be perceived as less high-quality as a result. In another example, an online second-hand marketplace creates value for buyers, sellers and itself by facilitating the exchange of used goods. However, this also creates a *positive* externality for wider society by reducing waste and saving on production inputs.

In fact, scholars examining digital markets have described the important role of platform businesses as an aggregator of positive externality across the economy.[7] In effect, these businesses provide the infrastructure required to enable a large volume of low-value transactions (often with positive spillover effects), that would not otherwise occur in the presence of substantial transaction costs.

By definition, an economic externality will have no positive (or negative) effect on either of the parties directly involved in the transaction. This means that they have no incentive to take the value (or cost) of the externality into account when agreeing to make their trade. A central role for governments (and competition authorities) is to manage these externalities affecting wider society, acting both to minimise the negatives and promote the positives. This is particularly the case for digital markets, where the impact of these externalities can be far-reaching. For example, the free-market interactions between social media platforms, content creators and advertisers have the ability to spill over into societal issues of democracy, freedom of speech and the rule of law.

[B] Network Effects

There are two broad categories of network effects discussed in economics:

(1) ***Direct network effects*** refer to an increasing value for users as more users join the same side of a multi-sided market or platform. These effects were first described in the context of telecoms networks in the 1980s, with the archetypal example being the increased value to everyone using a telephone network as more users join the network and are able to make and receive calls.[8] In a digital context, this is akin to the value of a social media network, which increases for all users as more people contribute content and/or become available to connect with.

7. M. Van Alstyne, 'Two-Sided Network Effects: A Theory of Information Product Design', (2005) 51(10) Management Science 1494–1504.
8. M.L. Katz and C. Shapiro, 'Network Externalities, Competition, and Compatibility', (1985) 75(3) *The American Economic Review* 424–440.

(2) ***Indirect network effects*** refer to an increasing value for users on one side of a platform (or other multi-sided market) as more users join another side. This can be a two-way effect, as is the case for an online marketplace, where more sellers mean more choice for buyers and more buyers means more opportunities for sellers; or asymmetric, as with an advertising-funded content platform, where more users mean more value for advertisers, but more advertising is unlikely to be preferred by users.

While these may appear similar at first, these different effects can create significantly different incentives for operators of digital business models. The example of an advertising-funded content platform neatly demonstrates some of the complexity that arises when trying to analyse platform markets. In this case, different types of network effects occur simultaneously, with each having a different effect on the platform's incentives. For example, we might expect *two-way* indirect network effects between viewers and content creators as more viewers attract more content providers and vice versa, with the platform operator keen to attract more of each. However, we might expect *one-way* indirect network effects between viewers and advertisers, with advertisers valuing a wider audience as more viewers join the platform, but viewers preferring an ad-free experience. The platform must strike an appropriate balance between the funding advertisers provide and the potentially negative effects of ads on the user experience. Finally, depending on the precise nature of the platform, there may even be *direct* network effects between viewers, if social features mean they can connect and share opinions and recommendations for content.

For platform operators, the virtuous circle of growth that network effects create makes it critical for them to engage users on all sides of the market. This is just one example of how the specifics of the digital business model can have a profound impact on the analysis of the market.

[C] Economies of Scale and Scope

Economies of scale are said to occur when a firm's average cost of supplying a given product or service *falls* as its volume of output *increases*. When this is the case, larger firms can offer the same quality of product at a lower cost than smaller rivals.

Economies of scale are common among digital services, given their tendency for high fixed costs, low marginal costs, and strong network effects. For example, while there is a substantial fixed cost to building and running a digital platform – such as a search engine, social media network, or online marketplace – the cost of supplying one additional unit of output (i.e., conducting one more search; connecting one more user; or listing one more product) is negligible. As such, a larger digital platform can spread its fixed costs across a greater volume output, so reducing the average cost of production.

Furthermore, digital service providers can enjoy many of the advantages of scale while avoiding many of the *diseconomies* of scale (i.e., increasing costs) faced by traditional firms. For example, digital firms can serve customers around the world *without* facing the issues of physical distribution and transportation costs that can put a brake on economies of scale for more traditional product manufacturers. At the same time, operating at a greater scale allows digital services to gather more data from a wider variety of users, which they can use to improve products and processes.

Related to economies of scale, economies of scope occur when a firm can supply a range of *different* products and services from a common cost base. As with economies of scale, this allows a larger firm with more product lines to achieve a *lower average cost* than smaller rivals that offer just one or a few products.

Online platforms offer a prime example of how digital firms can benefit from economies of scope. With an established infrastructure and user base, platforms can cost-effectively increase the scope of products and services they offer to users. For example, an online marketplace may expand to include additional product categories, while a social media site may start to offer users access to curated news, job adverts and dating profiles. By spreading the fixed costs of the platform infrastructure over more services and a wider user base, the average cost of provision falls compared to a firm offering just one of these services.

[D] Barriers to Entry

Barriers to entry refer to any advantages that established firms in a market have over-and-above potential entrants, which may act to dissuade competition and allow the incumbents to raise prices above the competitive level (Bain, 1957).[9] Competition authorities typically consider a wide range of factors and market features that can hinder new entry or the growth of competition when conducting an analysis. For example, the European Commission's Horizontal Merger Guidelines identify:[10]

- **legal barriers:** such as regulations, licensing, tariffs and non-tariff barriers;
- **technical barriers:** such as access to essential facilities, resources, R&D capabilities, and intellectual property rights; and
- **other barriers:** such as economies of scale and scope, distribution networks, access to technology, an established market position, branding and promotion, customer loyalty, switching costs, firm reputation and trust, or supply commitments.

As detailed in the section above, economies of scale and scope are common characteristics of digital markets, given their tendency for high fixed costs, low marginal costs, and strong network effects. Added to this, customer lock-in effects (such as content purchases, photo libraries, or social contacts) can make it difficult or costly for users to switch to another service; while the platform's reputation and consumer trust can also play an important role, particularly where users are required

9. J. Bain, *Barriers to New Competition* (Harvard University Press, 1956).
10. European Commission (2004) 'Guidelines on the assessment of horizontal mergers under the Council Regulation on the control of concentrations between undertakings', *OJ C 31 5.2.2004*, pp. 5-18, para. 71.

to provide sensitive information - such as personal data or banking details - in order to access a new service.

In some cases, the data an incumbent has generated may also offer a technical advantage that makes it difficult for new entrants to compete. For example, historic usage data may be used to train machine learning algorithms, while detailed customer profiles allow more targeted recommendations and adverts. This may particularly be the case where data and insights firms can gather through their day-to-day operations (such as popular search queries, consumer trends, or usage statistics) allows firms to continually improve their products or customise their services.

However, this is not always the case. Hagiu and Wright (2020) identify two broad categories of data-enabled learning: (i) within user learning; and (ii) between user learning.[11] Whereas the former relates to *personalisation* improvements that benefit an individual user - such as a video streaming service learning your tastes, or a smart-home device learning your routine - the latter can lead to *general* improvements that benefit all users - such as a navigation app learning traffic conditions, or a search engine learning common search queries.

Importantly, these different types of learning can have different implications for competition and barriers to entry. For example, *between* user learning can generate network effects, given that new users benefit from joining a service with a large existing user base. In contrast, *within* user learning may lead to lock-in effects if the benefits of personalisation are large (i.e., making it costly for consumers to switch services). However, this lock-in effect can be limited if the data required to personalise the service is quick and easy to collect, or changes frequently (meaning the incumbent has no enduring advantage).

[E] Tipping Markets

The common characteristics of digital services discussed so far - economies of scale, network effects and barriers to entry - can combine to create an increased likelihood of markets tipping. Tipping refers to a situation in which all (or most) consumers end up with just one or a few, very large firms. While this means there may be little competition *in* the market, there can be vigorous competition *for* the market as firms vie to gain an advantage and 'tip' the market in their favour. In dynamic markets - such as digital services - this can spur substantial investment in product quality to help entice users. Where this is the case, consumers benefit from incremental improvements to existing products and services, as well as the introduction of complementary new features.

Where tipping does occur, it is not necessarily a problem per se and can be economically efficient. For example, many digital services are characterised by large up-front investments (e.g., technology infrastructure and marketing) followed by low marginal costs for serving an incremental customer. This gives rise to economies of

11. A. Hagiu and J. Wright, 'When Data Creates a Competitive Advantage', (2020) January-February Harvard Business Review Magazine.

scale, as fixed-cost investments are distributed among a greater number of users. In this case, a small number of firms each having a high market share can be both the natural and efficient outcome for the market. In the alternative, a larger number of competitors would need to inefficiently duplicate those investments in order to compete effectively.

However, once a firm has established a leadership position in a tipping market, the network effects and technical advantages they obtain can make them hard to displace. For example, a search engine drawing on many years of accumulated data to improve its algorithm can provide more accurate search results for users, creating a virtuous circle of consumer engagement, data generation, and product improvement. For competition authorities, the lack of contestability as a result of tipping can present a risk to the long-run vitality of a market. With high barriers to entry, the incentives for an established incumbent to invest in innovation may decline while prices can increase, worsening the overall outcomes for consumers.

Despite the advantages that economies of scale, network effects and barriers to entry can offer, there are also numerous factors that can help mitigate the risk of tipping in many digital markets.

First and foremost is the prevalence of multi-homing. A consumer is said to multi-home if they use two or more similar services – such as different messaging and social media apps; different music and video streaming services; or different mapping and navigation apps. The fact that many digital services offer free tiers and integrate seamlessly with other apps and services makes it easier for consumers to use multiple services simultaneously. This can help combat tipping by reducing network effects and lock-in. For example, it is not uncommon for people to use different messaging apps with different sets of friends, while free tiers and interoperability make it easy for people to try out a new photo storage app before making a switch.

In other cases, changing technologies, consumer preferences and social norms can help keep a market contestable. For example, there have been several 'generations' of social media, each with a slightly different focus, including MySpace, Facebook, Twitter, Flickr, Instagram (later purchased by Facebook), Snapchat, TikTok, Clubhouse and many others. Improved mobile connectivity and processing power also helped stimulate change by enabling the growth of photos and video sharing, while changing preferences and social norms around privacy, security and governance have also played a role in encouraging consumers to try new services.

There are also technical considerations that can mitigate tipping. For example, while the accumulation of certain types of data *can* provide incumbents with an advantage, in general data is a non-exhaustible resource. Just because one firm has used someone's data to provide a service (such as product recommendations, or targeted advertising), there is nothing stopping another firm from using that same data to provide a competing service. Diseconomies of scale can also set in if rapid growth leads to services falling in quality, such as network congestion issues for a digital video service or increased wait times for a ride-sharing service. Local laws and regulations may also slow the growth and expansion of some services, such as licensing requirements for financial services providers.

Finally, with rapidly evolving technology, even a tipped market may be contested by a radical innovation – a threat that helps discipline incumbents to remain focused on providing good service to their consumers in order to 'keep' the market. For any digital service, there are generally well-financed players in adjacent markets that can be seen as potential competitors. The evolution of the games console industry in the mid-1990s provides a good example.[12] Despite the strong position held by Nintendo and Sega – a point confirmed by the UK's Monopolies and Mergers Commission – Sony was able to disrupt the market with the launch of the PlayStation console; followed shortly after by Microsoft with the Xbox.[13] A few years later, PlayStation and Xbox had grown to be strong players within the console gaming segment, with Sega having exited completely.

[F] Ecosystem Effects

Over recent years, there has been a growing interest among economics and strategic management scholars in ecosystems as a new form of economic organisation.[14] Jacobides et al. (2018) identify three broad groups of ecosystems described by the literature, including:

- **Business ecosystems:** comprising of a community of firms and organisations whose shared success depends upon their interactions with each other.
- **Innovation ecosystems:** focusing on the interdependence between a focal innovation, its (upstream) components and (downstream) complementor innovations that combine to create value for consumers and make each innovation successful.
- **Platform ecosystems:** describing the interdependence between a platform and the complementary product and service providers that make the platform valuable as the hub of a multi-sided market.

In a later paper, Jacobides et al. (2020) further distinguish between these 'multi-actor' ecosystems – in which the success of each participant depends upon their successful interaction with various complementors, without necessarily having formal contractual arrangements – and the related 'multi-product' ecosystems, in which a single firm offers a collection of complementary products and services, potentially through a series of separate business divisions.[15]

Each of these different forms of ecosystem relationships can be found in digital markets. Indeed, the basis for many digital platforms is a set of standardised core components that can be reused by a variety of peripheral 'complementors' to offer a

---

12. *See* G. Niels, H. Jenkins and J. Kavanagh, *Economics for Competition Lawyers* (2nd ed., Oxford University Press, 2016), para. 3.163.
13. Monopolies and Mergers Commission (1995), 'Video games: A report into the supply of video games in the UK', March.
14. For a summary, *see* M. Jacobides, C. Cennamo and A. Gawer, 'Toward a Theory of Ecosystems', (2018) Strategic Management Journal, 5 June.
15. M. Jacobides, C. Cennamo and A. Gawer, 'Distinguishing Between Platforms and Ecosystems: Complementarities, Value Creation, and Coordination Mechanisms', (2020) Working Paper, 14 October.

variety of different features and services to end users as part of a multi-actor ecosystem. For example, device makers (such as Samsung, LG or Sony) offer a range of different hardware options that all use a standardised mobile operating system (Google's Android), allowing mobile app developers to create a diverse selection of compatible apps for consumers.[16] However, quality, reliability and trust among consumers remain crucial factors in an ecosystem's success and some third-party contributions can be detrimental to the experience of others (e.g., insecure apps or harmful content). As such, digital platform operators and other multi-actor ecosystem coordinators have a role to play as market governors, moderating the activities of third-party contributors to maximise the overall value of the ecosystem for all participants.

A key tool platforms use to manage third-party contributors is the balance between openness and control over the platform environment. For example, an operating system provider might allow third parties to distribute apps through their app store, but may impose quality and security standards to ensure trust, while an online marketplace may allow third-party businesses to sell through their platform, but might impose certain customer service standards and delist businesses that fail to meet them. By being open to third parties, platform operators encourage more diverse innovation that raises the value of the ecosystem as a whole (as the Sun Microsystems co-founder, Bill Joy put it: 'not all the smart people work for you'). However, imposing a degree of governance gives the platform operator control over the strategic direction of the ecosystem, while also allowing them to share in the overall value the ecosystem creates.

In other cases, a single firm (including the notable examples of Google, Apple, Amazon, Facebook and Microsoft) may offer consumers a range of interrelated hardware, software and services, as part of a multi-product ecosystem. Fletcher (2020) describes how several factors make this multi-product strategy more prevalent among digital firms, including: (i) economies of scale and scope; (ii) the ability to apply core competencies and technologies across markets, such as platform design, machine learning and artificial intelligence (AI); (iii) data synergies, in which the data gathered in one setting can be used to provide an advantage in another; and (iv) interoperability benefits, allowing firms to provide better services if they control all aspects of the integrated system.[17] In addition, certain consumer behaviours – such as preferences for a single, trusted operator and lock-in effects for particular services such as photo libraries – can also play a role.

While these ecosystems can be efficient, both for firms and for consumers, they can also give rise to competition concerns. For example, multi-actor ecosystems may be prone to tipping, while their governance role may lead to gatekeeper issues, whereby one or a few large platforms control business users' access to end-consumers. These concerns may be exacerbated in a multi-product ecosystem, where platforms might

16. For further discussion of mobile ecosystems, *see* the UK Competition and Markets Authority (2021) 'Mobile ecosystem market study: statement of scope', June 15.
17. A. Fletcher, 'Digital Competition Policy: Are Ecosystems Different?', (2020) OECD Hearing on Competition Economics of Digital Ecosystems, 3 December.

also be able to leverage their core market position into adjacent markets, at the expense of existing complementary service providers.

§2.02 ECONOMICS OF PLATFORMS BUSINESSES

In this section, we consider some of the specific characteristics of a common digital business model: the online platform.

When considering traditional 'offline' markets, we typically think of a linear supply chain: upstream producers supply products to retailers, who in turn sell those goods to consumers. There is no direct relationship between the upstream suppliers and end-consumers; it is the downstream retailer that sets the price of the goods and terms of sale for their customers. The same can also be true online, such as with online supermarkets, meal delivery services, music streaming services, or any other online retailer selling to consumers directly. In each case, the online service sets its own terms, conditions and prices for consumers as they resell products and services bought from an upstream supplier.

However, a defining feature of many digital services – and one that has attracted much attention from competition authorities – is the platform business model. Loosely speaking, in economics, a platform can be defined as any service that brings together two or more different sides of a market. Unlike the linear resale model, a platform operator does not play an active role in the supply chain. Rather, it simply facilitates an interaction between different user groups. Digital services are particularly well suited to this type of business model, for several reasons:

- First, platform businesses can realise economies of scale and scope by leveraging a core technology to distribute a range of products and services to a large user base, offering low-cost access to wide markets and scaled distribution for third-party suppliers.
- Second, by offering a focal point for a large number of users to come together, platforms can help unlock network benefits for both consumers and businesses.
- Third, by bringing together a wide variety of products and services, platforms can help unlock complementarities in demand, benefiting both consumers and businesses.[18]
- Fourth, the exponential rise in computing power, falling storage costs and advances in machine learning techniques have given digital platforms an unrivalled ability to gather, store and analyse data that can be used to make more effective connections between users and recommend new products and services to them.

18. In economics, two products or services are said to be complements in demand if the value to consumers of each product increases when they are consumed together. For example, uses may value a music recognition service more if they are able to purchase song downloads or gig-tickets directly, and vice versa.

- Fifth, increased mobile interconnectedness combined with changing consumer habits have meant that more and more transactions and interactions are occurring online. This increases the availability of both personal and non-personal data to feed the machine learning processes, and continually improve the platforms' performance.

However, not all digital platforms are the same. There are a wide variety of different digital platforms fulfilling a range of different functions. Some of the key differences that are discussed in the literature include:

- the type of platform (e.g. one-sided, two-sided, multi-sided);
- transaction versus non-transaction platforms (e.g., marketplaces vs. social media); and
- platform versus aggregator functions (e.g., operating systems vs. search engines).

We explore each of these factors in more detail, below.

[A] Types of Platform

The simplest type of platform connects users on one 'side' of a market, such as friends wishing to chat on a private messaging app (e.g., WhatsApp), or consumers sharing their experience of products and services on a user reviews site (e.g., Trustpilot). These one-sided platforms typically create a positive *direct* network effect (*see* section §2.01[B]).

In contrast, a two-sided platform brings together users from opposing sides of a market to facilitate an interaction, such as buyers and sellers; app developers and users; or drivers and riders. Users of these platforms benefit from positive *indirect* network effects (*see* section §2.01[B]).

A more complex type of platform is a multi-sided platform, which brings together three (or more) different groups of users. Advertising-funded content platforms are a good example of this platform type. On one side of the market are viewers, getting free access to content. On the second side are creators, seeking an audience and remuneration for their work. On the third side are advertisers, paying to reach consumers. Platforms such as YouTube or Daily Motion create value by coordinating the interaction between these three user groups.

Platforms may also act as dual-mode operators, offering both their own goods (as a 'linear' retailer) alongside third-party options (as a platform operator). In some cases, a service can start as an online retailer before deciding to open up its platform and become a dual-mode operator.

In the extreme, we can even think of digital ecosystems as highly intricate platform businesses. For example, an operating system allows a range of different device makers, app developers and consumers to come together; while a hardware ecosystem provides both consumers and developers with access to a wide range of interoperable devices, applications and services.

Clearly, the type of platform business model can have a profound effect on both the incentives the platform operator faces and the competition risks associated. These are important differentiators that must be taken into account in any competition assessment, particularly when considering issues such as defining a relevant market and assessing market power.

[B] Transaction Versus Non-transaction Platforms

Even among online platforms, there is a wide variety of different business models being employed, each taking a different approach to sharing in the value they create. Some provide a marketplace or other services that facilitate direct transactions between users, while others facilitate indirect interactions between users, such as video-sharing sites that bring creators, audiences and advertisers together.

For example, an online marketplace could choose to be funded in a variety of ways such as display advertising, listing fees, or by taking a commission on transactions completed; while a content platform or social media provider may choose to adopt a free-to-use model, funded by personalised display advertising.

These differences have led to some discussion among academics and authorities as to the significance of these distinctions: in particular, whether transaction and non-transaction markets should be treated separately.[19] The main distinction that is highlighted between 'transaction' and 'non-transaction' type platforms is the observability of the interaction that the platform facilitates.

In the case of 'transaction' type platforms, such as an online marketplace, payments provider, or dating app, the interaction between the parties is readily identifiable. This gives the platform operator the option to charge both membership fees (e.g., an annual subscription charge) and usage fees (e.g., a transaction fee) since the transaction between the two sides can be observed and regulated by the platform operator – e.g., completing a sale; processing a payment; or providing contact details to arrange a date.

In contrast, a 'non-transaction' type platform, such as ad-funded social media, video sharing, or user reviews sites cannot generally identify transactions between users, making usage fees an impractical strategy. For example, it is not usually possible to accurately identify sales made as a result of online banner advertising, or from favourable user reviews.

The type of platform, and functionality it offers, will undoubtedly impact an operator's business model options. In turn, different business models lead to different concerns that an antitrust – or even consumer protection – agency may have. For example, take an online hotel booking service that is free to use, but earns a commission (i.e., charges a transaction fee) on each booking made. When listing the options available to the consumer, the platform operator may have the incentive to

19. L. Filistrucchi and E. Van Damme, 'Identifying Two-Sided Markets', (2013) 36(1) World Competition and G. Niels, 'Transaction Versus Non-transaction Platforms: A False Dichotomy in Two-Sided Market Definition', (2019) 15(2) Journal of Competition Law & Economics 327–357.

promote the hotels paying it the highest commission first. For the consumer, this may mean higher-cost, or less convenient options are ranked higher in the search results or, in the extreme, that some options are not shown at all. In contrast, a non-transaction platform has no incentive to promote less attractive options or content to consumers. In fact, platforms that rely on advertising have the incentive to attract as much user *attention* as possible, which typically means providing the most relevant and appealing content possible. However, this can lead to alternative consumer protection issues, such as the use of personal data to profile uses and media plurality concerns, as platforms vie for attention with 'click-bait' content.

While the difference between transaction and non-transaction platforms may play a role in the types of concern raised, caution is needed when considering whether and when this distinction may impact the definition of relevant antitrust markets (Niels, 2019).

First, the distinction between transaction and non-transaction platforms is becoming increasingly blurred. There are a wide variety of different monetisation approaches in use by online services, with technological advances making it possible to gain increased insight into the indirect interactions between user groups (e.g., tracking when an advert is clicked on and a purchase made enables affiliate marketing payments to content creators).

Second, the key question for market definition is whether or not a competing product or service can constrain the platform operator. Transactions are just one end of a spectrum of different interventions that platforms facilitate and transaction fees are just one of many monetisation options. Indeed, a transaction platform – such as a restaurant booking service – may find itself constrained by non-transaction platforms (such as user review sites) or even non-platform options (such as direct booking with the restaurant) that may also be considered part of the same relevant market.

Nonetheless, there are examples of where the different types of competition faced by transaction and non-transaction platforms have been informative. For example, in the UK, the Competition and Markets Authority (CMA) considered that non-transaction platforms may face single-sided competitors on either side of the market, while transaction platforms (such as payment service providers) compete only with other platforms that can bring the two sides of the market together.[20]

[C] Platforms Versus Aggregators

Another distinction that some authors have started to make is between digital platforms and content aggregators (Schrepel, 2021).[21] While in competition law and economics the term 'platform' has commonly been applied to both of these types of service interchangeably, it has been argued that a distinction is needed as the

20. CMA (2017), 'Just Eat and Hungryhouse', 16 November, para. 4.11.
21. T. Schrepel, 'Platforms or Aggregators: Implications for Digital Antitrust Law', (2021) 12(1) Oxford Journal of European Competition Law & Practice.

differences between platforms and aggregators result in markedly different incentives and antitrust concerns.

In this context, a platform may be described as a 'backbone' that provides little inherent value to consumers but allows third parties to develop and operate their own products or services. Operating systems such as Microsoft's Windows, or Google's Android are the archetypes of this, while online web development and hosting platforms, such as Wix or WordPress provide additional examples. While platforms may choose to be more open (such as Android and Windows) or less open (such as iOS and macOS), in general, a platform creates value by ensuring users have access to a wide variety of interoperable and complementary products and services.

In contrast, an aggregator provides a valuable service to consumers by helping them discover and decide between a variety of options available to them (Thompson, 2015).[22] Rather than providing a platform on which third parties can build, the aggregator pulls together third-party content, products, or services and presents them in an easily digested manner to the end consumer. For producers, aggregators provide a portal through which they can reach potential audiences and customers. As such, aggregators create value by collecting together as many options as possible, before ranking them and promoting the best options to end consumers.

Thinking about this from a competition standpoint, the concerns raised can be very different. In the case of *platforms*, reducing choice for consumers by restricting access to competing downstream services may be seen as a credible competition concern, particularly if those restrictions favour higher-priced or lower-quality services that benefit the platform operator. However, for *aggregators*, guiding consumers through the sea of choices available toward the most relevant options for them is precisely how they offer benefits. This requires an even more nuanced assessment of harm, raising questions about whether the options presented serve the interests of the consumer, or whether better alternatives were available.

§2.03 DATA AND ALGORITHMS

Much of the discussion and concern around firms' behaviour in digital markets have focused on the accumulation and use of 'big data'. This is not without reason. Digital firms are particularly well placed to benefit from the increased availability of data, as advances in computing power and machine learning techniques allow them to use ever more complex algorithms to optimise their businesses. For example, ready access to a wide variety of user data makes it easier for digital firms to 'match' consumers with existing products or services they may be interested in, while detailed analysis of aggregated data helps them spot new 'white space' opportunities to develop products and services for underserved markets.

In this section, we consider some of the basic principles of data and machine learning that are key to understanding the impact they can have on competition and

22. B. Thompson, 'Aggregation Theory', (2015) *Stratechery*, available at: https://stratechery.com/concept/aggregation-theory/.

market outcomes. We begin by describing the economic characteristics of data, before distinguishing between different types of data and discussing how machine learning algorithms use data to inform business outcomes. Finally, we highlight some benefits and risks to markets from an increased prevalence of data and algorithms.

[A] Economic Characteristics of Data

In recent times, data has been referred to as the 'new oil', reflecting its value to those that can collect and refine it.[23] However, the economic properties of data make it, unlike oil, in a number of important ways.

First, unlike oil, data is non-rivalrous and non-depletable, meaning it can be captured and used in different places simultaneously. Put differently, it is not 'used up' as one firm makes use of it. Many firms can use the *same* pieces of data (such as a user's age and purchase history) to glean insights and improve their products. These insights may be used to deliver competing products and services on a standalone basis, or complementary products and services as part of a digital ecosystem.

Second, unlike oil, the value of data tends to depreciate over time. The value of the data and its rate of decline depends upon a number of factors, such as:

- **Longevity of the data:** (i.e., how frequently it changes) a user's date of birth will never change, their name may change once or twice in a lifetime, but their location is typically out of date within a few minutes or hours of being recorded.
- **Availability of the data:** (i.e., how easy it is to gather) while users are generally happy to share their email addresses, they are far less likely to share sensitive data such as health records or financial information with new service providers.
- **Cost of acquiring the data:** (i.e., the level of investment required) information that required more processing - such as a voice recognition dataset that has been manually recorded and labelled over many years - is more costly to acquire and will hold its value better than data that is a relatively costless by-product of a user's daily interactions with an online service.
- **Usefulness of the data:** (i.e., what can be gained from it) data that helps build a better profile of a user - such as purchase histories, browsing habits, and social networks - can be valuable for recommendations and ad-targeting over the long run. Other data, such as search queries for certain products, can be monetised directly and so have a short-run value.

Third, there also tend to be decreasing returns to the volume of data capture (decreasing economics of scale). With some exceptions, once sufficient data has been gathered to properly train an algorithm (which can be relatively little compared to the

---

23. The Economist, 'The World's Most Valuable Resource Is No Longer Oil, but Data', May 2017, available at: https://www.economist.com/leaders/2017/05/06/the-worlds-most-valuable-resource-is-no-longer-oil-but-data.

vast quantities of data generated online), each incremental data point adds little to meaningfully improve the service quality. However, there are typically *increasing* returns to the combination of *different* datasets (increasing economies of scope). For example, a firm that is able to combine a variety of data points about a user (such as their social group, purchasing history, financial situation, current location, etc.) will be able to build a more comprehensive profile that increases the value of targeted advertising and likelihood of them purchasing a recommended product.

Finally, unlike oil, data is not a homogenous commodity. Different types of data attract different legal requirements and social norms, both of which can play an instrumental role in their value and competitive impact. We briefly contrast some different types of data in the following section.

[B] Different Types of Data

There are several dimensions to consider when thinking about different types of data, many of which can overlap within the same dataset.

First and foremost is the distinction between personal and non-personal data. Importantly for competition assessments, the ways in which firms can use personal data are restricted by privacy regulations (such as the EU's General Data Protection Regulation (GDPR)), which can act to minimise the competitive impact. Personal data can be defined as '*any information relating to an identified or identifiable individual (data subject)*' (OECD, 2013).[24] However, there are different degrees to which data can be personally identifiable, with different implications for the competitive advantages – and associated competition enforcement risks – that the data can bestow on its users (OECD, 2020):[25]

- At one end of the spectrum is fully identifiable data, which is unambiguously associated with an individual. Data of this type – which include a range of identifiers such as names, contact details, or IP addresses – fall within the remit of privacy regulations, placing obligations on businesses (such as obtaining meaningful consent) and giving additional rights and protections to consumers (such as data portability and 'no profiling' rights).[26]
- Next, comes pseudonymised data, in which personal identifiers are replaced with aliases. This may be linked, whereby the aliases can be reversed if the identification key is known, or unlinked, meaning the aliases are irreversible or personal identifiers are simply deleted. Privacy regulations may still play a role for these types of data if there is a risk that the pseudonymisation could be reversed – e.g., by identifying individuals through statistical techniques.

24. OECD, *Recommendation of the Council concerning Guidelines Governing the Protection of Privacy and Transborder Flows of Personal Data* (OECD Publishing, 2013).
25. OECD, 'Consumer Data Rights and Competition: Background Note' (2020).
26. A full treatment of the EU's GDPR is beyond the scope of this book. However, for further details of the rights and obligations it embodies, *see* Regulation (EU) 2016/679 'General Data Protection Regulation'.

- Finally, fully anonymised data removes this risk by modifying the data in such a way as to prevent statistical reversal (e.g., by randomising or generalising certain attributes). Similarly, aggregated data contains no individual-level records. So long as information is combined from numerous different data subjects, there is no prospect of identifying personal information. Without the constraints of privacy regulations firms can use these types of data in a wider variety of ways, which may provide them with some competitive advantages.

In contrast, non-personal data refers to any data that is not concerned with identifiable individuals. Examples can include sales volumes, prices, product trends, transport usage patterns and other market statistics. In fact, much of the data available to firms fall into this category, with advances in connected technologies (the so-called Internet of Things (IoT)) meaning that the number of available smart devices and other data-generating sensors is continuing to grow. As these types of non-personal data are not impacted by privacy regulations, they may present firms with more opportunities to glean a competitive advantage.

However, questions remain as to who should be considered the owner of non-personal data. Take, for example, a connected car sporting a range of sensors for maintenance and self-driving. On the one hand, these may belong to the vehicle maker, which uses the sensors to monitor and improve their product and services to consumers. On the other hand, the data relates to activities undertaken by the vehicle owner, who may also have a legitimate claim to its ownership. They may even be thought to belong to individual component manufacturers that supply parts or sub-systems (such as autonomous driving capabilities) for the vehicle. As this example makes clear, the determination of ownership could have start implications for the use – and usefulness – of the data.

Different data can also be distinguished by its origin, in particular, whether it is volunteered or observed. Volunteered data includes information explicitly provided by consumers as they join or use an online service. This could include sensitive personal data such as medical histories, social data such as friends and contacts, or user-generated content such as photos and videos. In contrast, observed data is not explicitly provided by users, but passively collected by firms as those users engage with their services. This may include behavioural insights such as browsing patterns, biometric data such as health tracking, or location data based on device tracking.

The cost of acquiring these different types of data – and, thus, the competitive advantage they bestow – can vary depending upon several factors. Some data, such as device location, is relatively easy to collect and can be gathered from a wide variety of apps. Other data, such as financial histories, may be hard to collect and/or unique to certain apps and services (such as banking or payment apps). Furthermore, consumers may be reluctant to provide such sensitive data to a new service that lacks an established track record and strong reputation.

A further distinction may be made between processed and unprocessed data. For example, an online search engine may process the raw 'click and query' data generated as users engage with the services to reveal insights into shopping habits or search trends that can be valuable to businesses and advertisers. Importantly for competition policy, while it is desirable to prevent data bottlenecks that create barriers to entry for new firms, the treatment of data can influence incentives to invest in its collection and analysis in the first place. We discuss the benefits that this kind of data collection and processing offer to consumers through the growth of algorithms, AI and machine learning in the following section.

[C] Algorithms, AI and Machine Learning

The efficiency benefits offered by algorithms, AI and machine learning can be found across a wide range of markets, from 'traditional' products like petrol stations and airlines to digital services such as e-commerce and video services. These benefits can include reduced costs, improved products and services, supporting new entry and better matching supply and demand. However, as with other business practices that can boost efficiency, such as information exchange or vertical restraints, the use of data and algorithms by firms can also raise competition concerns. Before considering the benefits and risks that algorithms, AI and machine learning can pose, it is important to have a clear understanding of what these different terms mean.

An algorithm is defined simply as '*a step-by-step procedure for solving a problem or accomplishing some end*', and need not be complex.[27] For example, a simple price matching algorithm could say: '*if my competitor lowers its price, reduce my price to match*'. The algorithm sets out the process steps, such as how and when to change prices, which may even be undertaken by hand; though in practice the term is generally used to refer to more complicated and automated processes.

In contrast, according to IBM, '*[a]rtificial intelligence leverages computers and machines to mimic the problem-solving and decision-making capabilities of the human mind*'.[28] An objective outcome is set by the human operator and the AI uses one-or-more statistical processes to determine the best way to achieve it. These statistical processes can range from relatively simple regression models of the kind commonly used in economics and business to complex machine-learning algorithms trained on large volumes of detailed user data.

Finally, machine learning is a branch of AI that focuses on how machines can 'learn' from data. Different techniques offer different degrees of machine autonomy, ranging from algorithms that seek to replicate human decisions based on historical data, to those that can learn directly from their own experimentation. We can describe four broad types of machine learning, as follows:

- **Supervised learning** refers to a training process based on labelled data (i.e., data where the correct output from the algorithm – such as an object's identity – is included alongside the observed inputs). Since these labels are typically determined manually, it allows some human influence over the training

27. *See* Merriam-Webster definition of algorithm, available at: https://www.merriam-webster.com/dictionary/algorithm.
28. *See* IBM's definition of AI, available at: https://www.ibm.com/uk-en/cloud/learn/what-is-artificial-intelligence.

process. While this offers some control over the machine learning outcomes, it can also be a source of concern. For example, human biases in the input data can be 'learned' and propagated further by the algorithm.

- **Unsupervised learning** occurs when an algorithm achieves its outcome based on unlabelled data alone, such as grouping similar products for a recommendation engine or segmenting customers based on their purchase history. These techniques can provide new insights for firms as the algorithm identifies patterns in the data that humans do not see. However, the rationale for the eventual groupings can be hard to explain – though there are analytical tools that can provide data scientists with insights into machine reasoning.
- **Reinforcement learning** is an advanced form of machine learning, in which an algorithm trains itself by experimenting in a simulated (or sometimes even real-world) environment. These models select an action (such as raising or lowering price) based on a 'policy' for the current state of the world (e.g., price and output of competing firms). Each decision results in either a 'reward' or 'punishment' for the algorithm, which is then used to update the policy going forward. Over many iterations, the algorithm independently learns the optimal action to take in any given state of the world, without ever having been 'instructed' what the correct action is by a human. As a result, while the eventual policy that a model follows may be transparent to the operator, the rationale for that policy may not be, and the model can arrive at a policy which is unlike anything found in historical data.
- **Deep learning** is a particular form of machine learning, that seeks to simulate the learning process of the human brain. To do this, a deep learning model consists of many 'layers' of statistical analysis (known as artificial neural networks), with the results of one layer being passed as an input to the next. These models can be tens, or even hundreds of layers deep, comprising many thousands of modelling parameters that contribute to the overall decision outcome. While this offers a powerful tool to automate learning from vast datasets, it also makes it difficult to say exactly how a deep learning algorithm arrives at any given decision. That is to say, the machine determines how to optimise the model for the objective set making these models 'black boxes', even to the data scientists that create them.

Having trained an algorithm, its decision-making capability can be tested on historical data. At this point, the algorithm can also be tested for adverse outcomes, such as indications of bias. If the algorithm is found to perform well it is ready to be deployed into a real-world production environment. If not, the model will be further refined to improve the results.

As we can see, although the terms algorithm, AI and machine learning are often used interchangeably, they actually refer to quite different concepts with different implications for competition policy. Importantly, while the decisions made by simple algorithms (such as price matching) or less complex AI models (such as supervised learning) can be easily explained and understood, the specific outcomes of more complex AI models (such as unsupervised learning, deep learning and reinforcement learning) can be impossible to explain with certainty.

[D] Benefits and Risks of Data, Algorithms and AI

Now we have a better understanding of the characteristics of data and the various techniques used to process it, we can consider the benefits and risks that these trends present for competition.

First and foremost, the growing use of data and algorithms can improve the efficiency and effectiveness of markets, helping firms make better commercial decisions. Markets are an effective way to allocate efforts and resources, so long as firms are acting upon reliable information. Data-generating technologies, such as user profiling, can help build a deeper understanding of competition and demand in the market; while algorithms, such as load-balancing and repricing software, can help them quickly and cost-effectively respond to these new insights. These tools can also reduce barriers to entry in markets by helping new players identify the prices and features that will make a compelling consumer offer.

Consumers can also benefit from an increased use of data and algorithms by firms. For example, recommendation algorithms help them discover new products and services, while comparison services can help reduce search costs and provide access to a wider variety of options in the market. Furthermore, the ease with which data can be collected and processed – particularly for digital businesses – allows firms to easily update and refine their products and services. This may be in the form of general product improvements, such as mapping services that learn about traffic conditions from driver behaviour; or personalised improvements, such as smart-home devices that learn a family's routines over time.[29]

The choices made by consumers can also be improved through the use of data and algorithms. The term 'choice architecture' was introduced by Thaler and Sunstein in their 2008 book '*Nudge: Improving Decisions about Health, Wealth and Happiness*' to describe the environment in which consumers make a choice.[30] Digital services can use data to shape their choice architecture and help consumers make more informed choices. For example, setting the most appropriate default options or presenting the most appropriate options first can impact the choice consumers make.

However, policymakers and competition authorities have also voiced concerns over the opaque use of data and algorithms to influence choice architecture, with so-called dark patterns online.[31] For example, firms may manipulate ranking algorithms or recommendation engines based on a customer's past purchases to 'nudge'

29. J. Wright and A. Hagiu, 'Is Knowledge Power? Data-Enabled Learning and Competitive Advantage', *Oxera Agenda*, January 2021.
30. R.H. Thaler and C.R. Sunstein, *Nudge: Improving Decisions about Health, Wealth, and Happiness* (Yale University Press, 2008).
31. For example European Commission (2022), 'Behavioural study on unfair commercial practices in the digital environment'; J. Penrose, 'The Penrose Report', *Department for Business, Energy & Industrial Strategy* and *HM Treasury*, 2020, section 7.4.

consumers toward products that are more profitable, rather than those that are most suitable; or they may alter how and when certain information is displayed based on a user's browsing history to maximise the chance that they will make a purchase.

Likewise, the use of data and algorithms in price-setting and shaping consumer offers can also present competition and fairness concerns. In its 2021 report '*Algorithms: How They Can Reduce Competition and Harm Consumers*', the CMA highlights the potential negative consequence for consumers of firms gathering data that helps them assess a customer's willingness to pay.[32] In principle, firms could use these insights to offer customers more personalised prices in order to maximise profitability, based on an algorithmic assessment of their data. While this extreme form of price personalisation appears to be uncommon, there are simpler ways in which firms can personalise consumer offers, such as sending personalised promotions or recommending premium add-ons to certain customers.

From an economic perspective, these kinds of personalised pricing practices are not necessarily harmful. In particular, they can prove to be welfare-enhancing if output is expanded, by reducing prices for consumers that would not otherwise be able to afford the product under uniform pricing. However, these practices can also result in consumer harm if each user is charged the very maximum amount they would be willing to pay for the good, rather than enjoying a 'good deal' by paying a price that is less than the value they get from consuming the product.

Incumbent firms may also use their data advantage to offer 'predatory' personalised prices by charging excessively low (below cost) prices to some (but not all) customers. The aim is to lock in certain key consumers that are most likely to switch to competitors, thus forcing competitors to leave the market. This also serves to protect the dominant firm's position in the market, if it means that new firms are unable to gain the scale needed to compete effectively, discouraging entry into the market.

Other concerns raised in relation to the widespread use of data and algorithms include the possibility that suppliers learn to 'game' ranking algorithms in order to increase their prominence, potentially to the detriment of the underlying product. This has, for example, been seen with the 'hollowing out' of some insurance policies on price comparison websites (PCWs), whereby insurers are incentivised to focus on the key metrics that the PCW considers (such as price) at the expense of other product features (such a range of coverage).

Algorithms and AI are also increasingly used to automatically re-price goods in response to changing market conditions. For example, there are third-party services to dynamically re-price e-commerce offers, or even adjust physical fuel-station prices. After training on historic information, these software services can take account of 'real-time' information (such as competitor prices, weather, traffic, etc.) to optimise sales prices for the sellers. This can, again, benefit consumers as well as sellers if the reduced costs of managing prices and increased market efficiency are passed on to them. However, legitimate competition concerns can also arise: for example, a number

32. CMA (2021), 'Algorithms: How they can reduce competition and harm consumers', January.

of academic papers show how the use of pricing algorithms can reduce competition and increase margins (*see also* §2.04[E] on algorithmic collusion theories of harm).[33]

§2.04 COMMON THEORIES OF HARM

The rapid growth of digital markets through the past decades, along with the central role they have come to play in our economies, has led to increased concerns among academics and antitrust authorities that large operators may be in a position to manipulate markets and distort competition. Furthermore, it is feared that the same economic features that drive many of the benefits of digital platforms (particularly scale, scope and network effects) may also give rise to entrenched positions of market power for the leading digital firms, as markets 'tip' to one or a few large players.

While many of the issues raised are familiar to competition practitioners, a range of new concerns not previously seen – or not seen with such prominence – have also emerged. In this section, we review the economic foundations of some common competition concerns in digital markets, including:

(i) platform envelopment;
(ii) data agglomeration;
(iii) parity clauses and vertical restraints;
(iv) killer and reverse-killer acquisitions; and
(v) algorithmic collusion.

For each, we provide a brief summary of why there may be an issue and highlight what should be considered when assessing the risk.

[A] Platform Envelopment and Exclusionary Conduct

The term 'platform envelopment' is used to describe the practice of a platform operator increasing its scope of services to enter into an adjacent market, such as Microsoft introducing Internet Explorer and Windows Media Player as preinstalled applications on its Windows operating system. This term was coined by Eisemann, Parker and Van Alstyne (2011), who primarily considered this behaviour from a strategic management perspective as a way to capture market share in competitive markets. However, competition economists have also asked whether antitrust issues could arise from platform envelopment, in particular given its association with exclusionary conduct (such as in the Microsoft cases of the 1990s).

Broadly speaking, platform envelopment can have an anticompetitive effect if undertaken by a large operator in a way that excludes competing providers. As

33. A. Ezrachi and M.E. Stucke, *Virtual Competition: The Promise and Perils of the Algorithm-Driven Economy* (Harvard University Press, 2016); J. Harrington, 'Developing Competition Law for Collusion by Autonomous Artificial Agents', (2018) 14(3) Journal of Competition Law & Economics 331-363; E. Calvano et al., 'Algorithmic Pricing: What Implications for Competition Policy?' (2019) 55 *Review of Industrial Organization* 155-171.

Eisemann, Parker and Van Alstyne explain, the enveloping platform can capture a share of the adjacent market by foreclosing the incumbent provider's access to customers over that platform. There are many different exclusionary behaviours that the enveloping platform operator could engage in, including bundling and tying, self-preferencing, and data leveraging. The distinction between these behaviours is not always clear, particularly among digital products where market boundaries can be hard to define. Moreover, platforms may be engaged in a combination of these behaviours at the same time. Nonetheless, we consider each of these in turn, below.

Bundling and tying refer to a group related to practices that see a single firm jointly supply two or more different products or services. 'Pure bundling' describes a strategy in which two (or more goods) are sold *only* as a bundle and are not available for individual purchase. 'Mixed bundling' refers to the case in which two (or more) goods may be purchased *either* in a bundle (often for a discount), or as standalone offers (e.g., as is now common with fixed-line internet and TV services). In contrast, tying refers to a case where one item (the tying product) can only be purchased if the customer also buys another (the tied product), though, unlike a pure bundle, the tied product may still be available for individual purchase. Bundling and tying can be good for consumers, particularly where the bundled products are sold for less than the sum of the individual parts. These practices can also promote new product discovery by consumers and increased overall output. However, they may also be considered exclusionary if used as an entry deterrence, or to induce competitors to exit. For example, consider an incumbent that has a monopoly in one product (product A) but faces potential competition for another product (product B). By bundling these products, anyone buying product A also gets product B – either as part of a pure bundle or at a discount in a mixed bundle. This reduces the rival providers' demand for product B and may make these rivals unprofitable (Whinston, 1990; Nalebuff, 2004; Pietz, 2008). This, in turn, may deter future entry by new firms or even force competitors to close down. This theory of harm was a key consideration in one of the European Commission's cases against Microsoft, with the Commission arguing that preinstalling Windows Media Player on the Windows operating system amounted to anticompetitive bundling.[34]

Self-preferencing can refer to any behaviour by platforms that favours their own products or services over those of third-party competitors. For example, an online search engine could rank its own products and services higher in search results, while an online video provider could give its own content greater prominence on the home screen. Self-preferencing might also encompass behaviours that technologically restrict competing providers, such as limitations for competing software running on a hardware platform, or for competing app providers developing for a mobile operating system. Again, there can be pro-competitive rationales for self-preferencing behaviours, such as to improve quality and promote trust in an ecosystem. For example, a platform may choose to promote its own offerings or restrict competitor access to

34. European Commission Decision (2004), Microsoft, 24 May, Case COMP/C-3/37.792, available at: https://eur-lex.europa.eu/legal-content/EN/ALL/?uri=CELEX%3A32007D0053.

certain parts of the ecosystem to prevent low-quality or even malicious digital services from undermining consumer confidence, ultimately benefitting consumers (Boudreau and Hagiu, 2008; Evans, 2011).[35] However, self-preferencing may also reduce demand for rivals, if the incumbents favour their own products in ranking systems, search engines, or in terms of access to hardware or operating system features. This behaviour may be found to deter potential competitors from entering the market or could induce existing competitors to exit a market (Hagiu et al., 2020).[36] This theory of harm was a key consideration in the European Commission's case regarding the treatment of Google Shopping within general search.[37]

Data leveraging can refer to platforms using data generated by third-party competitors on their platform to gain an advantage for their own products and services. As with the behaviours discussed above, data leveraging by platforms can result in benefits for consumers. In this case, platforms may use third-party data to provide more personalised services, or as a means to identify and invest in new products. For example, Netflix uses data on consumer viewing habits to inform which Netflix Originals to invest in.[38] However, these practices may also be considered exclusionary if an operator uses information about third-party competitors operating over its platform (e.g., user traffic, sales volume or product returns) to decide whether they should compete with a given product. An extreme case would be a platform that uses third-party data to identify hot and new products before launching copycats that compete directly with that third party, a behaviour which may deter future innovation and entry on the platform (Hagiu, Teh and Wright, 2020).

When weighing these concerns, it is important to consider the potential effects from a dynamic competition perspective. Indirect entry (rather than direct, head-to-head competition) is a common characteristic in digital markets (Petit, 2020).[39] For example, Google's entry into mobile operating systems with the purchase of Android introduced indirect competition to Apple's iPhone. There may also be synergies in the planning and ongoing operations of the platform if adjacent products share the same inputs of human and physical capital (Gawer, 2014; Zook and Allen, 2003).[40] That is to say, platforms may be able to use their institutional expertise, data and computing infrastructure to improve an adjacent product to the benefit of consumers.

---

35. K. Boudreau & A. Hagiu (2008) 'Platform Rules: Multi-Sided Platforms as Regulators'; D.S. Evans, 'Governing Bad Behavior by Users of Multi-sided Platforms', (2012) 27 *Berkeley Technology Law Journal* 1201.
36. A. Haigu, T. Teh & J. Wright, 'Should Platforms Be Allowed to Sell on Their Own Marketplaces?', (May 2020) 53 (2) *Rand Journal of Economics* 297-327.
37. European Commission Decision (2017), Google Search (Shopping), 27 June, Case AT.39740, https://eur-lex.europa.eu/legal-content/EN/TXT/?qid=1516198535804&uri=CELEX:52018XC0112(01).
38. D. Carr, 'Giving Viewers What They Want', *New York Times*, 24 February 2013.
39. N. Petit, 'Big Tech Platforms and Schumpeter's Creative Destruction', *Promarket*, 19 November 2020.
40. A. Gawer (2014) 'Bridging Differing Perspectives on Technological Platforms: Toward an Integrative Framework', (September 2014) 43(7) *Research Policy*; C. Zook and J. Allen, 'Growth Outside the Core' (December 2003) 81(12) *Harvard Business Review*.

Consumers can also benefit from platform envelopment if it avoids the 'double marginalisation' of two complementary products. Double marginalisation occurs when two firms supply complementary goods (i.e., those that are consumed in tandem, such as smartphones and apps) with a markup being applied to each separately. If, instead, the products are both provided by a single firm, the output loss from charging a higher overall price is taken into account and prices are set lower (Nalebuff, 2000).[41] This is clearly beneficial when both products have a monetary price, but is less clear if the goods are provided to consumers for free, as is the case with many digital goods.

[B] Data Agglomeration

One impact of platform envelopment can be data agglomeration. As platforms enter into adjacent markets and offer a growing range of different products, they are able to gather richer data about their users. In some cases this can benefit consumers by enabling innovation, improving personalisation and lowering prices. For example, combining data across multiple products may allow for more relevant targeted adverts and/or better recommendations for users.

However, survey evidence indicates that consumers often find targeted ads intrusive and that they are concerned about how their online data is being used (Gormsen 2019, Turow et al. 2015). Looking at this from a data privacy perspective, platform envelopment may harm consumers if the terms of use require that personal data from the adjacent product is combined with personal data from the core platform. In this scenario, some have suggested that consumers are de facto coerced into accepting privacy policies because the use of the underlying services is contingent upon consent and there are no other realistic alternatives.[42]

At the same time, regulators and academics have raised concerns that data agglomeration by larger platform operators may result in barriers to entry or otherwise harm consumers.[43] For example, the collection of data across multiple products allows platforms to build more detailed profiles of users' online habits, which may be used for 'first-degree' price discrimination, i.e., offering different prices to different consumers based on their inferred willingness to pay (Condorelli and Padilla, 2020). At the same time, data agglomeration may be used to erect barriers to entry that protect the core platform's dominant position (Condorelli and Padilla, 2020; Prufer and Schottmüller,

41. Nalebuff, 'Competing Against Bundles', Yale School of Management Working Paper Series H, 2000, August 20. Available at: https://papers.ssrn.com/sol3/papers.cfm?abstract_id = 239684.
42. D. Condorelli and J. Padilla, 'Data-Driven Envelopment with Privacy-Policy Tying', Working Paper (2020); and Bundeskartellamt (2019) decision in case B-22/16 'Facebook, Exploitative business terms pursuant to Section 19(1) GWB for inadequate data processing'.
43. Regulators have raised this issue in the UK, EU and US, while academics raising this issue include: D. Condorelli and J. Padilla 'Harnessing Platform Envelopment in the Digital World' (June 2020) 16(2) *Journal of Law & Economics*; J. Prufer and C. Schottmüller, 'Competing with Big Data', TILEC Discussion Paper No. 2017-006 (2017), CentER Discussion Paper 2017-007, available at https://ssrn.com/abstract = 2918726.

2017).[44] The platform may be able to offer an adjacent service for free if it is better able to monetise the combined user data. If this adjacent product requires you to use the core platform service (or steers users towards that platform), it may give the incumbent an advantage and impede other innovative platforms from entering the market – raising the question of whether the benefits of a free product outweigh the harm associated with a loss in competition for the core platform. This theory of harm was considered by the European Commission in the Google Android case, where the commission considered that Google was using the Android platform to entrench the dominant position of its search engine.[45]

[C] Parity Clauses and Other Vertical Restraints

Vertical restraints refer to business practices between firms at different levels of the supply chain that restrict competition. For digital platforms, this usually takes the form of requiring business users to agree to conditions that entrench the platform's dominant position.

One type of vertical restraint that is seen relatively frequently in digital markets is parity clauses, also often known as 'Most-Favoured-Nation' (MFN) clauses.[46] A parity clause is an agreement whereby a platform prevents suppliers from setting lower prices on any rival platform or distribution channel. In an online or vertical supply setting these agreements are often considered to be anticompetitive if they restrict competition between rival platforms. We can distinguish between *wide* parity clauses, which prevent suppliers from setting lower prices on any rival platform as well as the supplier's own distribution channel; and narrow parity clauses, which cover only a supplier's own distribution channel.

Wide parity clauses may restrict competition in at least three different ways: (i) by dampening competition between existing platforms; (ii) by excluding new innovative platforms; and (iii) by softening competition between existing suppliers. For example, consider two suppliers listing their products on two different online marketplaces. The suppliers set retail prices, while the marketplace earns a commission if users make a purchase. Absent a parity clause, the suppliers would be free to set different prices on different marketplaces, depending upon the competition they face. They may also set lower prices on a marketplace that has lower commissions, in order to encourage users to purchase over that platform (as it reduces their cost-of-sales). However, a parity clause would prevent this, meaning marketplaces face less competitive pressure, allowing them to charge higher commissions (Boik and Corts, 2016;

44. D. Condorelli and J. Padilla 'Harnessing Platform Envelopment in the Digital World' (June 2020) 16(2) *Journal of Law & Economics*; J. Prufer and C. Schottmüller, 'Competing with Big Data', TILEC Discussion Paper No. 2017-006 (2017), CentER Discussion Paper 2017-007, Available at https://ssrn.com/abstract=2918726.
45. European Commission (2018), 'Google Android', CASE AT.40099, July.
46. The term 'MFN' originates from international trade agreements, where one party agrees to treat its trading counterparty as favourably as it treats everyone else.

Johnson, 2017).[47] At the same time, parity clauses can reduce innovation incentives for competing marketplaces providers. Since suppliers cannot offer reduced prices on the new platform if they have existing parity clauses with incumbents, the new entrant cannot gain users by offering lower commissions (Boik and Corts, 2016). Finally, parity clauses can mean consumers enjoy less intra-brand competition on the platform. Suppliers cannot react to the competitive environment on one sales platform without affecting others, making isolated offers impossible.[48]

However, parity clauses do not always restrict competition. Research has shown that in markets where inter-brand competition is high, parity clauses may even result in lower commissions and lower prices for consumers (*see* Johansen and Verge, 2017).[49] If inter-brand competition is high, suppliers that refuse to accept parity clauses can undercut their competitors on different platforms and capture a larger share of the market. To compensate for this, platforms seeking to negotiate parity clauses will need to offer suppliers lower commissions, which can be passed to consumers at lower prices. Another justification is that parity clauses can protect platforms from 'free-riding' behaviour, whereby consumers use platforms to browse different offers before buying directly from the supplier at a lower price. Parity clauses prevent suppliers from undercutting the platform, protecting the business model of online platforms such as PCWs and other marketplaces, which can reduce search costs and increase choice for consumers (Buccirossi 2015, Wang and Wright 2016).[50]

Beyond parity clauses, another common vertical restraint in digital markets is exclusive dealing. This arises when a supplier refuses to sell to particular downstream retailers (e.g., retailers who also stock other competitors). The primary concern here is that suppliers may use such agreements to foreclose competitors or prevent market entry (Aghion and Bolton, 1987).[51] Such agreements have been considered in a number of cases brought forward against suppliers who refuse to sell to certain online retailers, for example, the CMA's case against Ping golf clubs.[52] A competitive justification for such behaviour is that selective distribution may be needed in order to protect the brand quality of the supplier. In a CJEU case, Coty, a seller of luxury cosmetics,

47. A. Boik and K. Corts (2016) 'The Effects of Platform Most-Favoured-Nation Clauses on Competition and Entry' (February 2016) 59(1) *Journal of Law and Economics*; Johnson, 'The Agency Model and MFN Clauses' (July 2017) 84(3) *The Review of Economic Studies*.
48. This theory of harm was raised by the Bundeskartellamt in their decision against the online travel agent, HRS. *See* Bundeskartellamt, 'Decision in the administrative proceedings HRS-Hotel Reservation Service', B 9 – 66/10 (2013).
49. Bjørn Olav Johansen and Thibaud Vergé, 'Platform Price Parity Clauses with Direct Sales', Working Papers in Economics 01/17, University of Bergen, Department of Economics (2017).
50. P. Buccirossi, 'Parity Clauses: Economic Incentives, Theories of Harm and Efficiency Justifications', (2015) 1(3) *Competition Law & Policy Debate* 43-52; C. Wang and J. Wright, 'Platform Investment and Price Parity Clauses', 1 September 2016. NET Institute Working Paper No. 16-17, Available at https://ssrn.com/abstract=2848574.
51. P. Aghion and P. Bolton, 'Contracts as a Barrier to Entry', (June 1987) 77(3) *The American Economic Review* 388-401.
52. *See* Decision of the CMA, 'Online sales ban in the golf equipment sector', Case 50230.

successfully argued that their practice of selective distribution to certain online retailers was necessary in order to preserve the luxury image of their goods.[53]

[D] Killer and Reverse-Killer Acquisitions

An important consideration for competition authorities is the impact of digital mergers on innovation. While a majority of digital mergers have likely been neutral – or even beneficial – for consumers,[54] it is also important for regulators to be alert to scenarios when mergers can hamper innovation. A particular concern that has arisen in the digital sector is that incumbent firms might acquire innovative startups solely to discontinue their innovation projects and prevent future competition (Cunningham et al., 2018).[55] Known as 'killer acquisitions', this theory of harm is considered particularly problematic as it means consumers could lose out on new and innovative products or business models that could have otherwise disrupted incumbents.

A platform would only wish to shut down a competing innovation (such as an app or service offering similar functionality) and not a complementary innovation (such as an add-on feature that can be 'bolted on' to the core platform). This means that an acquirer will only have the motive for killer acquisitions if there is some degree of functional overlap with the target (i.e., that the merger is – to at least some degree – horizontal). However, the OECD's 2020 paper on this topic notes that in the case of digital platforms, even if two firms appear to be producing unrelated or complementary products, horizontal concerns may still arise.[56] For instance, in two-sided markets, the products may be unrelated on one side (e.g., search engines and social media), but horizontally competing for the other side of the market (e.g., advertisers). Moreover, the OECD paper argues that it is important to consider whether the innovation project at hand will horizontally compete with the incumbent *in the future*, even if it does not constitute a direct competitor at its early stage of development.

Empirical evidence suggests that killer acquisitions are relatively rare. For example, Cunningham et al. (2018) investigate mergers and acquisitions in the pharmaceutical industry and find that around 6% of deals involve the discontinuation of the target's competing innovation project. Similarly, Gautier and Lamesch (2020) investigate 175 acquisitions completed by GAFAM tech firms over the period 2015-2017[57] and identify only one deal that they consider to be a killer acquisition. Nevertheless, while killer acquisitions may be relatively infrequent, commentators

53. Case C-230/16 *(Coty Germany GmbH v. Parfümerie Akzente GmbH)*, https://eur-lex.europa.eu/legal-content/EN/TXT/?uri=CELEX%3A62016CJ0230.
54. *See, e.g.*, the panel opinion in the Furman Review, para. 3.48.
55. C. Cunningham, F. Ederer and S. Ma, 'Killer Acquisitions', (March 2020) 129(3) *Journal of Political Economy* 649-702, available at: http://dx.doi.org/10.2139/ssrn.3241707.
56. *See* https://www.oecd.org/daf/competition/start-ups-killer-acquisitions-and-merger-control-2020.pdf, section 2.
57. A. Gautier and J. Lamesch, 'Mergers in the Digital Economy'. CESifo Working Paper No. 8056 (2020), available at: https://ssrn.com/abstract=3529012.

have suggested that competition agencies should remain vigilant because of the scale of consumer harm associated with lost innovations.[58]

A broader concern may be the dampening effect on 'incumbents' innovation incentives if they can simply acquire pre-existing innovative startups, once a certain proof-of-concept stage has been reached.[59] Caffara, Crawford and Valletti coin the term 'reverse-killer acquisition' to describe this theory of harm, suggesting incumbents 'kill' their own internal innovation in favour of acquiring proven technologies. The premise is that permitting a merger would be harmful if, in the counterfactual, an incumbent would have developed an original innovation while still facing competition from the innovative start-up. The UK CMA has considered this concern in relation to the *Amazon/Deliveroo* and *PayPal/iZettle* mergers. However, a challenge for competition authorities is that it is difficult to make predictions regarding an incumbent's investment decisions in the counterfactual, and thus this theory of harm may be difficult to prove.

In this context, it is also important to consider how mergers can boost innovation. In their issue paper for CERRE, Bourraeu and de Streel (2020) highlight that tech mergers often boost innovation through the following two mechanisms.[60] First, the prospect of being acquired can encourage innovative startups to enter the market. Empirical evidence suggests that in industries with more M&A activity, small firms invest more in innovative R&D,[61] and it has been shown that this can be welfare-enhancing for consumers.[62] Second, the acquirer may be better placed to develop an innovation and market it to a wide audience. The acquirer will generally provide funding and expertise to enhance the innovation process. In particular, this occurs when there are synergies between the target's innovation and the acquirer's core product (e.g., Apple's acquisition of Siri).[63] A number of empirical studies have shown that mergers between firms with technological linkages tend to boost expenditure in R&D and the number of innovative patents which are filed.[64]

58. For example O. Latham, I. Tecu & N. Bagaria (2020), section IV, https://media.crai.com/wp-content/uploads/2020/09/16164722/CPI-Latham-Tecu-Bagaria.pdf.
59. The investigation of GAFAM mergers by Gautier and Lamesch (2020) suggest that this is much more common than the pure 'killer acquisition' theory of harm.
60. M. Bourraue and A. De Streel, 'Big Tech Acquisitions Competition & Innovation Effects and EU Merger Control', CERRE Issue Paper (February 2020). In his report to the HM Treasury, Prof. Jason Furman highlights the same two mechanisms. *See* J. Furman, Unlocking Digital Competition, Report of the Digital Competition Expert Panel (2019), paras 3.38-3.39. Furman Review, para. 1.102.
61. G. Phillips and A. Zhdanov, 'R&D and the Incentives from Merger and Acquisition Activity', National Bureau of Economic Research, Working Paper (August 2012).
62. R. Mason and H. Weeds, 'Merger Policy, Entry, and Entrepreneurship', University of Essex, Discussion Paper Series, August 2007.
63. For further discussion of synergies in the digital economy, *see* M. Bourreau and A. de Streel (2019), section 2.1.2. Oxera (2021) provide a case study into Apple's acquisition of Siri.
64. J. Bena and K. Li, 'Corporate Innovations and Mergers and Acquisitions' (2014) 69(5) *The Journal of Finance* 1923-1960.

[E] Algorithmic Collusion

Authorities and academics around the world have voiced concerns over the scope of algorithms to support both explicit and tacit collusion.[65] Broadly speaking, we can consider four ways in which algorithms might help firms to coordinate, including:

- algorithmic monitoring and enforcing of explicit coordination;
- hub-and-spoke algorithms;
- tacit coordination by algorithms (predictable agents);
- autonomous machine collusion.

While this list of options may be decreasing in terms of technical feasibility (given current technology standards), it is increasing in terms of concern – with both detection and enforcement becoming more challenging as the complexity increases.

Consider the first of these concerns: algorithmic monitoring and enforcement. A common problem faced by would-be cartelists is the inherent instability of any collusive agreement. In general, each party has the natural incentive to deviate from a cartel arrangement in order to unilaterally profit from selling at the artificially elevated price level. As such, a cartel can only be maintained if there is sufficient scope for monitoring and enforcement of the agreed outcomes. However, monitoring competitor prices for deviations from the agreed level and responding in a timely manner is difficult, particularly in rapidly changing market environments. This is where algorithms can play a role to help stabilise cartel agreements.

The European Commission's 2017 E-commerce Sector Inquiry found that 36% of retailers responding to the consultation used automatic software to track their competitors' prices online,[66] with 78% of those going on to adjust their own prices in response. While in many cases this will benefit consumers – as firms reduce their prices to remain competitive – it is also possible that the same monitoring tools and repricing software could be used to automatically *enact* a collusive strategy. One example of this was found by the CMA, in its 2016 *Online Sales of Posters and Frames* case (*see* §3.01[D] of 1st edn.).

A second way in which algorithms may support collusion is as the centre of a 'hub-and-spoke' cartel. In this case, a pricing algorithm provider would act as a 'hub', and coordinate the prices offered by competing 'spokes' (sellers). This may be intentional, as the result of sellers agreeing to use a common algorithm, or inadvertent,

---

65. A. Ezrachi and M.E. Stucke, 'Artificial Intelligence & Collusion: When Computers Inhibit Competition' (2017) *University of Illinois Law Review* 1775; the Netherlands' ACM (2020), 'Position Paper: Oversight on Algorithms'; the Norwegian Competition Authority (2021), 'What Effect Can Algorithms Have On Competition?'; the UK's CMA (2021), 'Algorithms: How they can reduce competition and harm consumers', January; European Commission (2021), 'Evaluation support study on the EU competition rules applicable to horizontal cooperation agreements in the HBERs and the Guidelines', Final Report.
66. The European Commission found that 53% of retailers responding to its consultation tracked competitors' prices online; of which, 67% used automated software programmes to do so. European Commission (2017), 'Final report on the E-commerce Sector Inquiry', SWD(2017) 154 final, para. 149.

if a number of sellers independently choose to use the same third-party algorithm to support them with price-setting. Indeed, there are a number of providers offering automatic competitor monitoring and repricing solutions for online and offline retailers (such as Price2spy, or PAARLY) and even for petrol stations (e.g., A2i's PriceCast Fuel).

Authorities – such as the CMA – and academics have highlighted that a dominant provider of such a repricing tool could have both the ability and incentive to increase prices for consumers. One example of this was in a 2016 US class action lawsuit (eventually dropped) that alleged Uber's surge pricing had the effect of coordinating increased prices by cab drivers.[67] Furthermore, nascent research has shown that the use of third-party pricing algorithms can lead to price increases, even when a small number of firms adopt them.[68]

Third, consider how algorithms might increase the risk of tacit coordination in certain markets. Tacit coordination is said to occur when firms arrive at a pricing strategy that is above the competitive level, *without* any explicit communication or agreement. However, reaching and sustaining such an outcome is typically complicated by a number of factors, particularly in markets with differentiated products and rapidly changing demand.

Once again, this provides scope for algorithms to support coordination. For example, firms may have the *unilateral* incentive to implement algorithms that factor in a wide range of data points in an attempt to prevent costly price responses (some third-party algorithm providers even advertise that their software can help prevent price wars). Similarly, recent operational research literature has shown that algorithms can be trained to spot when other market participants are using the same tools and maximise joint profits in those cases, while still optimising for individual profits where that is not the case.[69] In this way, algorithms can help overcome some of the practical challenges that prevent tacit coordination.

The fourth – and perhaps most troubling – way in which algorithms could facilitate coordination is through autonomous machine collusion. This refers to the hypothetical situation in which the price-setting algorithms of several firms reach a collusive outcome *without* explicit instruction or programming to do so. *Reinforcement learning* is an AI technique that allows the machine to 'learn' through trial-and-error actions, as it seeks to maximise its total 'reward' (in this case, profit). Recent research has shown that by using these tools an algorithm can, in principle, autonomously arrive at a strategy of keeping prices high *unless* the competitor deviates – in effect, 'learning' to implement a cartel.[70]

---

67. *Spencer Meyer v. Travis Kalanick and Uber Technologies, Inc.*, 291 F.Supp.3d 526 (2018).
68. J. Harrington, 'Third Party Pricing Algorithms and the Intensity of Competition', unpublished working paper (2020).
69. J.M. Meylahn and A. Den Boer, 'Learning to Collude in a Pricing Duopoly' (2021), available at: https://papers.ssrn.com/sol3/papers.cfm?abstract_id=3741385.
70. T. Klein (2020), 'Autonomous Algorithmic Collusion: Q-Learning under Sequential Competition', *Amsterdam Center for Law & Economics*, Working Paper No. 2018-05, available at: https://papers.ssrn.com/sol3/papers.cfm?abstract_id=3195812; and E. Calvano et al., 'Artificial Intelligence, Algorithmic Pricing, and Collusion' (2020) 110(10) *American Economic Review*.

However, questions remain about how likely this type of autonomous machine collusion is in practice. A number of barriers remain in the real world, such as disturbances to the market caused by human interactions or less sophisticated algorithms that can undermine the learning process – though technical advances are likely to erode these inhibitors.

Finally, in some cases, errors in the specification of algorithms may lead to higher prices. For example, recent research has shown that if an algorithm fails to properly account for competitor prices, it can underestimate the loss in demand from price increases – leading it to set prices above the optimal level.[71]

§2.05 THE FUTURE OF DIGITAL MARKETS

The business models employed by digital firms will continue to rapidly evolve over the coming years and decades. As our lives become ever more digitised the distinction between, 'digital' business models and 'traditional' businesses will also continue to blur. Likewise, our understanding of the economic principles driving these trends will adapt and become more nuanced.

One development that is set to pose further competition policy questions is the rise of blockchain technologies. This is a broad term for digital systems that are characterised by distributed ledgers synchronised across multiple decentralised servers – thus negating the need for a centralised administrator. Prominent examples of blockchain technologies include cryptocurrencies and Non-Fungible Tokens (NTFs), which are both forms of digital assets. Other applications that are of particular interest to antitrust economists are smart contracts and Decentralised Autonomous Organisations (DAOs). These new digital tools claim to offer decentralised solutions to contract enforcement and organisation governance, respectively.

Another is the recent rise of Large Language Models (LLMs) and Generative AI (GAI). These technologies use sophisticated machine learning to create bespoke text and visual responses to user prompts that can be indistinguishable from human-generated content. There are myriad applications of these fast-evolving technologies, from improved online search and virtual assistants to interactive chat-bots and digital content creation.

As with the existing digital technologies, this wave of developments has the potential to reduce anticompetitive behaviour in some areas, while also raising new theories of harm in others. For example, DAOs (and blockchain code more generally) offer an alternative infrastructure to that provided by today's centralised platforms. The decentralised nature of blockchain platforms may make them less subject to anticompetitive behaviour such as exclusionary behaviour or self-preferencing.[72] On the other hand, some commentators raise questions about smart contracts being used

71. W. Cooper, T. Homem-de-Mello and A. Kleywegt, 'Learning and Pricing with Models that do not Explicitly Incorporate Competition' (2015) *Operations Research*.
72. T. Schrepel and V. Buterin, 'Blockchain Code as Antitrust' (2020) Berkeley Technology Law Journal Commentaries.

as an enforcement mechanism in a price-setting cartel,[73] while widespread adoption of blockchain is still uncertain and may be hampered by challenges ranging from data security, energy consumption or the risks of speculative bubbles.[74]

Similarly, LLMs and GAI offer a range of pro-competitive advantages, as well as new risks. On the one hand, these emerging tools exemplify how a radical innovation can unseat established incumbents. Since the launch of Open-AI's ChatGPT in late 2022, there has been a race to incorporate this new functionality into online search tools, for fear of being displaced by rival upstarts. On the other hand, they neatly demonstrate how new technologies continue to create new challenges. While LLMs are effective at creating *plausible*-sounding text, they do not necessarily create *accurate* answers. Moreover, as GAI technology advances to the next stage of audio and video generation, it is expected to make the creation of 'deep fake' content – that is, lifelike portrayals of people saying things they never said, or events that never happened – significantly easier, raising fresh issues around truth and democracy.

In both cases, these are nascent technologies – with the policy debate even more so – but regulators and policymakers should keep abreast of the new economic issues being raised in digital markets, decentralised or otherwise if they are to maximise the benefits of these technologies while avoiding new competition issues.

73. T. Schrepel, 'Collusion by Blockchain and Smart Contracts', (2019) 33(117) Harvard Journal of Law & Technology.

74. Financial Times, 'Web3 for Beginners: A New Realm with Endless Possibilities', 9 May 2022, available at: https://www.ft.com/content/f5e3bdb1-0ef3-4923-abd8-00e9297d3508.

CHAPTER 3

Market Definition and Digital Platforms

Daniel Mândrescu

§3.01 INTRODUCTION

Developments in online markets since the early 2000s have demonstrated the potential for digital or online platforms to create new markets, as well as to disrupt established ones. The success of platforms run by big tech companies such as Facebook, Amazon, Google and Apple has resulted in unprecedented market valuations in relatively short periods of time. Such rapid growth and success have not been the privilege of solely the great and mighty, as the viral growth of digital platform enterprises of the past decade can be witnessed across all corners of the economy. Along with this growth and success came the attention from competition authorities that wish to understand the nature of the commercial practices implemented by these digital platforms, which allows them to become key players in their respective markets.[75] Their inquiries into the business practices of digital platforms commonly aim at identifying the (potential or actual) competitive concerns associated with such practices that should ideally be tackled before they materialise. Otherwise, they should effectively be brought to an end.[76] In the EU, the concerns covered in such inquires involve the frameworks of

75. *See* a compilation of all the main inquiries conducted so far worldwide at https://www.chicagobooth.edu/research/stigler/events/antitrust-competition-conference/world-reports-on-digital-markets, accessed 20 April 2022.

76. *See, e.g.*, Commission, Staff Working Document on Online Platforms Accompanying the document Communication of Online Platforms and the Digital Single Market, COM(2016) 288; Joint report of the Bundeskartellamt and Autorite de la concurrence, Competition law and data (10 May 2016) at 11-25, http://www.autoritedelaconcurrence.fr/doc/reportcompetitionlawanddatafinal.pdf; MonopolKommission, 'Competition policy: The challenge of digital markets', special Report No. 68. http://www.monopolkommission.de/images/PDF/SG/s68_fulltext_eng.pdf; Directorate General for Internal Policies, 'Challenges for Competition Policy in a Digitalized Economy', IP/A/ECON/2014-12, PE 542.235; House of Lords Select Committee on European Union, 'Online Platforms and the Digital Single Market', 10th Report of Session

Articles 101 and 102 TFEU as well as the European merger control regulation (EUMR) and the future Digital Markets Act (DMA). At the core of these inquiries lies, however, one central aspect of analysis which significantly influences the outcome of the analysis as well as the eventual scope of required remedies under these three frameworks, namely the market definition.

In the case of digital platforms, the market definition entails, however, an exceptionally cumbersome process due to the challenges posed by their multisided nature. This chapter will discuss three main challenges that have been identified with respect to the market definition process for digital platforms.

The first challenge identified with regard to the market definition process in the case of digital platforms concerns the decision of how many markets need to be defined in each case with respect to a platform or one (or more) of the services it provides.[77] The manner in which the relevant market is delineated in each case and the number of relevant markets resulting from such process can have significant implications for the outcome of the legal analysis that commonly follows this process. Although there is currently some consensus about the fact that the legal assessment of pro- and anticompetitive effects should not be restricted to one side of a multisided platform,[78] such consensus has not extended to the approach which is best followed when defining the relevant market in each respective case.[79] In this respect, two main approaches still remain the subject of many debates, namely the multimarket and single-market approaches.[80] According to the multimarket approach, cases dealing with multisided digital platforms should always involve the delineation of multiple relevant markets encompassing the various sides of the respective platform. The single-market approach, which also encapsulates the multimarket approach, indicates that under special circumstances, cases dealing with multisided digital platforms may entail the definition of a single relevant market which covers all the sides of the concerned platform. Despite the theoretical and practical merit of both approaches, which have been implemented in practice, there is still no clear guidance on how and when each respective approach should be implemented in practice.

The second identified challenge pertaining to the market definition that remains to be resolved relates to the tools used in the process of the market definition. This challenge concerns predominantly the use of the SSNIP (Small, but Significant, Non-transitory Increase in Price) test when defining the relevant market for the

---

2015-16, HL paper 129 (20 April 2016); For more *see* a complication of all the main inquiries conducted so far worldwide at https://www.chicagobooth.edu/research/stigler/events/antitrust-competition-conference/world-reports-on-digital-markets, accessed 20 April 2022.

77. *See* by analogy the same requirement in *Ohio et al. v. American Express Co. et al.* 585 U. S. (2018), at 2-8 due to the two-sided nature of credit card schemes.
78. European Commission, Support study accompanying the evaluation of the Commission Notice on the definition of the relevant market for purposes of community competition law (2021) (hereinafter 'Support study') at 41-51 https://ec.europa.eu/competition-policy/system/files/2021-06/kd0221712enn_market_definition_notice_2021_1.pdf, accessed 10 September 2021.
79. *Ibid.*
80. Jens-Uwe Franck and Martin Peitz, 'Market Definition and Market Power in the Platform Economy' (2019) Cerre report, at 22-38 https://www.cerre.eu/sites/cerre/files/2019_cerre_market_definition_market_power_platform_economy.pdf, accessed 10 September 2021.

services provided by multisided digital platforms. The essence of this challenge concerns the incompatibility of the SSNIP test, which simulates relative price increases, with situations where it would have to be applied to services that are offered free of charge (commonly referred to as zero-priced). The current solutions for this challenge can also be generally said to encompass two main options, namely converting the price-centred SSNIP test into a costs-oriented SSNIC (Small, but Significant, Non-transitory Increase in Cost) test or a quality-oriented SSNDQ (Small, but Significant, Non-transitory Decrease in Quality) test.[81] Although both alternatives offered for the SSNIP test are theoretically sound, their application in practice entails overcoming multiple practical challenges associated with the creation of an accompanying procedural framework, which for the time being appears to be unaddressed by current practice.

Finally, the third identified challenge concerning the market definition process that will be addressed by this chapter relates to the matter of market shares. Following the delineation of the relevant market, the calculation of the market share(s) of the concerned undertaking(s) is commonly the next step. The calculation of market shares is an important aspect of many analyses under EU competition law. In the context of Article 102 TFEU, it provides a first impression on whether the concerned undertaking under investigation is dominant. In the case of Article 101 TFEU market shares are useful for assessing the potential effects of investigated practice of the concerned undertakings as well as the applicability of various exemptions and exceptions. In the context of the EUMR, market share data provides an insight into how the market structure may evolve post-transaction, thus determining whether notified concentrations may be allowed or not. In the case of digital platforms, however, the ability to calculate market shares as well as their evidentiary value has been called into question due to the limits of the current proxies used for such calculations, as well as due to the limited temporal value that market share data may have. Although such calculations have been made on multiple occasions under the mentioned frameworks, the manner in which some of the theoretical objections are addressed appears to be casuistic and often implicit as decisions on such matters are often taken ad hoc rather than being part of a detailed pre-defined assessment framework.

Against this backdrop, this chapter will explore the above-mentioned challenges from both a theoretical and practical perspective. Accordingly, the theoretical background behind these challenges will be addressed in tandem with the current practice where these matters have been addressed in cases concerning digital platforms. For

81. *See, e.g.*, John M. Newman, 'Antitrust in Zero-Price Markets: Applications' (2016) 94(29) Washington University Law Review 51; John M. Newman, 'Antitrust in Zero-Price Markets: Foundations' (2015) 164(149) University of Pennsylvania Law Review 150; OECD, 'Policy Roundtable – The Role and Measurement of Quality in Competition Analysis' DAF/COMP(2013) http://www.oecd.org/competition/Quality-in-competition-analysis-2013.pdf; Michal S. Gal and Daniel L. Rubinfeld, 'The Hidden Costs of Free Goods: Implications for Antitrust Enforcement' (UC Berkeley Public Law Research Paper No 2529425, 2015), https://ssrn.com/abstract=2529425, accessed 12 September 2021.

this purpose, the chapter will be divided as follows. First, the role of the market definition in EU competition law will be shortly discussed to crystallise the relevance of the market definition (even) in the case of digital platforms. Second, a description of the distinguishing characteristics of digital platforms that may impact the market definition process will be provided so as to clarify the source of the challenges these may cause and the nature of the solutions that would be required to develop. Third, an extensive section will zoom into each of the three challenges mentioned above from a theoretical and practical perspective and attempt to provide some preliminary commentary on the significance of such challenges and manner in which they have been addressed in practice. The final section will provide some concussions and final remarks.

§3.02 MARKET DEFINITION AND EU COMPETITION LAW: PURPOSE AND PRACTICE

[A] The Substantive Legal Relevance of the Market Definition

The concept of market definition in the context of EU competition law is often discussed from an instrumental perspective. It is thus treated as a practical exercise that needs to be performed in order to move on to the elements of the legal analysis that deal with the business practices of the undertaking(s) concerned. Although the market definition certainly has multiple instrumental functions, which will also be discussed in this section, it is important to first mention the legal theoretic importance of market definition that is often overlooked. The central role of market definition in a variety of procedures in EU (but also national) competition law means, in practice, that this procedure is a prerequisite for legal interventions on the basis of (EU) competition law. At their core, many (EU) competition law frameworks limit the economic freedom that would otherwise be enjoyed by the undertakings to which it applies. The intervention in this freedom, which is commonly also protected by fundamental rights in the EU and its Member States, requires however an objective assessment framework through which it can be justified. The market definition provides precisely that. It offers a reference framework in which the market position and the effects of the commercial practices of undertakings can be assessed systematically so as to determine whether the (enforcement) objectives and protected interests of EU competition policy prevail over the restriction of the commercial rights of the undertakings concerned. Performing this balancing act in the absence of such a framework would involve a significant degree of legal uncertainty as the case-by-case approach common in competition law practice may result in adopting diverging reference frameworks across different cases. This in turn would risk undermining the legitimacy of legal interventions on the basis of competition law.

In the context of the digital economy and digital platforms, this role of the market definition can be said to be even more important than before, contrary to calls in favour of limiting the relevance of this process in such cases.[82] The increasing complexity of commercial practices and their novelty can only benefit from a consistent, objective and predictable framework for the purpose of their assessment. Doing away with the market definition in this context would do little to enhance the assessment framework needed to establish the permissibility of business practices in such context. Doing so may indeed make the current scopes of analysis under EU competition law more flexible; however, such flexibility will come with a steep price in terms of legal certainty and potentially even diminished legitimacy. In essence, it would turn back the wheels of time to the period when market definition was a far less important part of the European Commissions' or EU Courts' practice and undertakings were complaining about the unpredictable nature of procedures.[83] Nevertheless, the importance of the market definition should not be mistaken for an objective indispensability in each and every case. The introduction of the market definition concept into practice as a legal prerequisite was a policy choice similar to many other concepts in the context of EU competition law. Consequently, replacing the market definition with a different procedure that aims at serving the same purpose is not unthinkable. It is important, however, to realise the magnitude of this task given the core role played by market definition in competition law enforcement. This realisation is particularly important in the context of the digital economy in general and digital platforms in particular, as their challenging nature intensified calls for reforming the market definition or abandoning it in this context.[84] In this regard, it is important to distinguish between the critique addressed at the market definition as a legal concept at the core of EU competition law and the critique addressed at its instrumental application in practice. The challenges associated with market definition in the digital context do not necessarily mean that market definition as a legal concept is no longer apt to fulfil the core role it currently plays in the framework of EU competition law.

The critique associated with such challenges, some of which are also covered in this chapter, concerns predominately the instrumental functions fulfilled by the market definition and the manner in which these should account for the peculiarities of digital platforms. It is only when such challenges cannot be overcome and thus causing the market definition process to fail in fulfilling these instrumental functions, that its core role in EU competition law could and should be questioned. Therefore for the purpose of this chapter, the focus will be on exploring such challenges and seeing whether these

82. Jacques Crémer, Yves-Alexandre de Montjoye and Heike Schweitzer, 'Competition Policy for the Digital Era' (2019), at 3, 46, https://ec.europa.eu/competition/publications/reports/kd0419345enn.pdf.
83. Miguel Sousa Ferro, *Market Definition in EU Competition Law* (Edward Elgar Publishing 2019) at 8-18.
84. In practice, the market definition has been identified as a challenge to the application of (EU) competition law in the scope of almost any rapport covering competition policy in digital markets. To some extent, it can be said that the peak of such calls was reached once the European Commission itself admitted that the challenges posed by digital platforms in this regard have driven it to revaluate its notice on the definition on the relevant market. *See* European Commission staff working document – the evaluation of the Commission Notice on the definition of the relevant market for the purposes of Community competition law of 9 December 1997, SWD(2021) 119 final, at 24-56.

have been or at least could be overcome. Before doing that, however, it is worth mapping out some of the main practical functions of the market definition that necessitate resolving the challenges covered in this chapter.

[B] The Practical and Procedural Function of the Market Definition

The market definition is generally considered a procedural requirement for the application of various legal frameworks within EU competition law. In situations potentially falling under Article 101 TFEU, the market definition may be required for multiple reasons. The most commonly referred to role is that of helping to evaluate the restrictive nature of the investigated practices, which may qualify as a restriction by object or effect. Practices that do not qualify as restrictions by object must be thoroughly assessed with regard to their effects that need to be appreciable in order to be considered as a potential infringement of Article 101(1) TFEU. Performing this task inevitably necessitates the definition of the relevant market(s) in each case.[85] In such cases, the definition of the relevant market is also crucial to determine whether, for example, the *de minimis* exception or the Vertical Block Exemption Regulation (VBER) may be of relevance.[86]

When dealing with restrictions by object, market definition may be a less important part of the assessment of such restrictions, as object restrictions are considered to have an appreciable effect on competition as these are by their very nature harmful to competition.[87] For this same reason, cases concerning restrictions by object do not require an extensive effects analysis. In fact, performing an effects analysis in such cases may even risk blurring the lines between restrictions by object and those by effect, which would go against the explicit differentiation formulated in Article 101 TFEU.[88] Nevertheless, that is not to say that the market definition is entirely disposable in cases concerning restrictions by object. While an effects analysis may not be needed, arriving at the conclusion that a practice constitutes a restriction by object requires taking into account the entire legal and economic context which it concerns, including the markets involved in the respective case.[89] Thus, some form of market delineation appears to be always required. This need to identify the potentially affected market(s) in question only grows in importance in the case of platforms, as their multisided nature makes the distinction between restrictions by object or effect far more complex. Qualifying a practice as a restriction by object means such a practice is

85. Case C-234/89 *Stergios Delimitis v. Henninger Bräu AG* ECLI:EU:C:1991:91, paras 16-18.
86. Commission Notice on agreements of minor importance which do not appreciably restrict competition under Article 101(1) of the Treaty on the Functioning of the European Union (*De Minimis* Notice) [2014] OJ C291/1, paras 8-11; Commission Regulation (EU) 2022/720 of 10 May 2022 on the application of Article 101(3) of the Treaty on the Functioning of the European Union to categories of vertical agreements and concerted practices [2022] OJ L134/4, Article 2.
87. Case C-67/13P *Groupement des cartes bancaires (CB) v. Commission* ECLI:EU:C:2014:2204, paras 49-53.
88. *See* Case C-8/08 *T-Mobile Netherlands BV and Others* ECLI:EU:C:2009:110, Opinion of AG Kokot, paras 41-49.
89. *Ibid.*, paras 53-57.

evidently harmful to competition. The most common example used for such practices is a price-fixing agreement as included in the text of Article 101(1) TFEU. However, when such practices are implemented in the context of multisided platforms, this commonly assumed evident harmful character may become less evident and require some form of market definition, at least in a provisional from, to prove such character. This can be seen to some degree in *Cartes Bancaires*, where the commission defined the relevant market in the context of credit card schemes despite claiming that the price-fixing agreement in the respective case constituted a restriction by object.[90] When the decision was appealed and reached the CJEU, the Court disagreed with the Commission on the finding of a restriction by object since it found that the Commission failed to take into account the entire legal and economic context when deciding on the matter. According to the Court of Justice, the General Court (GC) nor the Commission could reach such a finding while only focusing on one of the (relevant) markets it identified in its investigation after observing that the identified markets display network effects.[91] Accordingly, in the case of online platforms, the market definition will be an indispensable part of the entire legal and economic context which the Commission (or NCA (national competition authority)) is required to take into account when applying this provision. This is because the complexities created by the multi-sided nature of platform prevent practices from being identified as inherently harmful to competition without first observing the relation between such practices and the various (relevant) markets they may concern. Finally, any attempt by the undertaking in question to rely on the justification possibility of Article 101(3) TFEU will inevitably require defining the relevant market(s) as any efficiencies claimed must be assigned to the customers of the concerted undertakings in specific markets.[92]

In the context of Article 102 TFEU, defining the market constitutes one of the two main steps of establishing dominance,[93] which in turn determines whether legal intervention on the basis of this provision is justified. Once dominance is established, market definition is further required for assessing the effects of the investigated practices of the dominant undertaking.[94] In this regard, it is also important to note that the manner in which the market is defined in a specific case will often also determine to a great extent the manner in which the legal assessment of the business practices under investigation will be performed. This role of the market definition in Article 102 TFEU cases is often overlooked but its importance in practice cannot be overstated. For example, in cases concerning tying or bundling practices, the manner in which the market is defined also determines both whether there is dominance or not as well as the existence of tying or bundling practices which require the identification of at least two

90. *GROUPEMENT DES CARTES BANCAIRES* (Case COMP/D1/38606) Commission decision of 17 October 2007 paras 162-188, 193-251.
91. Case C-67/13P *Groupement des cartes bancaires (CB) v. Commission* ECLI:EU:C:2014:2204, paras 74-79.
92. *See* Commission Guidelines on the application of Article 81(3) of the Treaty [2004] OJ C 101/97, paras 88-104.
93. Robert O'Donoghue and Jorge Padilla, *The Law and Economics of Article 102 TFEU* (2nd ed., Hart, 2013) at 94. The second step being the assessment of market power.
94. Case 322/81 *Michelin v. Commission* ECLI:EU:C:1983:313, para. 37.

separate relevant (product) markets. In cases concerning price-related abuses such as predatory or excessive pricing, the market definition will have a similarly decisive impact as it will determine the manner in which the cost-price assessments in such cases should be performed, which is particularly important when dealing with multi-product companies as many platforms commonly are or will inevitably become so for strategic and commercial reasons.[95] Similarly, in the case of Article 101 TFEU, any attempts to rely on efficiency creation arguments to escape legal scrutiny will require delineating the impacted markets in each case. The manner in which this is done will also determine the way in which such arguments will be accounted for by competition authorities or courts.[96] Consequently, when dealing with multisided online platforms under the scope of Article 102 TFEU, the market definition will determine how dominance should be established, the manner in which the practices of the concerned undertaking should be qualified as well as how the pro- and anticompetitive effects of such practices should be assessed.

In the process of merger review, the market definition is required predominantly in order to assess the future effects of the transaction and the conditions subject to which it can be cleared by the Commission.[97] Under the EUMR, the Commission is endowed with the task of assessing the concentration that may result in a significant impediment to effective competition.[98] In order to do so, the Commission must assess the impact of concentration on the various markets in which the concerned undertakings are active. The first step in this process entails, therefore, delineating the various markets in which the concerned undertakings are active. This first step often entails a general overview of the key activities of the concerned undertakings and a general identification of the sectors where these take place. Past this stage, the Commission will search for potential horizontal overlaps, vertical links or conglomerate relationships so as predict the potential concerns following the eventual market structure changes that may occur following the envisaged concentration. In this second stage, the delineation of markets becomes more detailed and the borders of the respective markets are described with more precision. Generally speaking, it is common practice for the Commission to leave the exact scope of the relevant product and geographic market(s) open, as the absolute majority of concentrations reviewed by it do not pose any significant competitive concerns.[99] Nevertheless, the more competitive concerns the concentration under review is expected to create, the more scrutiny will be applied to

95. *See, e.g.*, Kalina S. Staykova and Jan Damsgaard, 'Platform Expansion Design as Strategic Choice: The Case of WeChat and Kakaotalk' (2016), Research Papers 78, https://aisel.aisnet.org/ecis2016_rp/78/; Thomas Eisenmann, Geoffrey Parker and Marshall van Alstyne, 'Platform Envelopment' (2011) 32(12) Strategic Management Journal 1270.
96. *See* Commission Guidelines on the application of Article 81(3) of the Treaty [2004] OJ C 101/97. Although the guidelines are drafted for the application of Article 101(3) TFEU, these apply by analogy to situations covered by Article 102 TFEU involving efficiencies and arguments put forward by the concerned dominant undertaking with respect to its behaviour.
97. Case T-399/16, *CK Telecoms UK investments Ltd v. Commission* ECLI:EU:T:2020:217, para. 144.
98. Council Regulation (EC) No. 139/2004 of 20 January 2004 on the control of concentrations between undertakings (the EC Merger Regulation) [2004] OJ L24/1, Article 2(2).
99. *See* the statistics of the European Commission in the clearance of concentrations under the EUMR, https://ec.europa.eu/competition-policy/mergers/statistics_en.

the concentration which means the more specific the market definition will need to be. This is most evident in cases where concentrations are cleared subject to commitments which need to address specific competitive concerns in clearly defined markets and even more so in situations where concentrations are blocked by the Commission which almost inherently entail an even more detailed legal analysis.

In light of the briefly described role of the market definition in this section, it becomes clear that it is essential that the market definition process be carried out adequately to prevent erroneous applications and incorrect findings under the various frameworks of EU competition law. In order to do so, also in the case of online platforms, it is important to first understand the distinguishing characteristics of platforms that may complicate the market definition process.

§3.03 ONLINE PLATFORMS: CHARACTERISTICS OF MULTISIDEDNESS

The concept of a platform is not new; markets and newspapers are common examples of more traditional platforms. Nevertheless, the definition of an online platform as a legal concept has proven to be more challenging than one might expect given the wide use of this term in business discourse. This difficulty is mostly a result of a lack of consensus on clear guidelines indicating the existence of an online platform.[100] Over the past ten years, the topic of platforms has been studied predominantly from an economic perspective where they are commonly also referred to as two or multisided markets. Such studies of platforms have come up with different formulas to establish the existence of a platform that vary in their degrees of strictness and inclusiveness.[101] Despite the different definitions of two- (or multi-) sided markets found in economic literature, some common core characteristics that such markets or platforms must exhibit, which are also observable in the case of online platforms, can be distilled. Accordingly, there must be (i) an interaction between two or more separate customer groups on the platform (ii) which exhibit indirect network effects (iii) and the platform is necessary for internalising such cross-group externalities.[102] The materialisation of these characteristics in practice, as in the case of online platforms, places such actors in a different commercial reality compared to non-platform or single-sided undertakings which is an aspect that needs to be taken into account in the context of competition policy.[103]

The fact that platforms facilitate some form of interaction between two separate customer groups does not sound very complex on the face of it; however, the

100. Commission staff working document on online platforms accompanying the document Communication on online platforms and the digital single market {COM(2016) 288}, SWD(2016) 172, at 1-9.
101. Bertin Martens, 'An Economic Policy Perspective on Online Platforms', Institute for Prospective Technological Studies Digital Economy working paper 2016/05, at 12 https://ec.europa.eu/jrc/sites/jrcsh/files/JRC101501.pdf.
102. Martens (2016) *supra* n. 101, at 10-18; Commission staff working document on online platforms {COM(2016) 288}, SWD(2016) 172, at 1-9; OECD Round table on two-sided markets (2009) DAF/COMP/WD(2009) 69, at 3.
103. Martens (2016) *supra* n. 101, at 12.

implications of this aspect entail many consequences that are relevant from a competition law policy perspective. This interaction-facilitating aspect of platforms means they create value for their respective customers in a very different manner than non-platform entities. Where the latter create value in a linear way, the value creation by platforms is based on the triangular relationship where the added value of the platform lies in enabling the interaction between two (or more) of its separate customer groups.[104] This in turn requires that platforms must be able to get all the needed customer groups for their value creation 'on-board'.

Bringing multiple customer groups on board in order to facilitate an interaction between them means in practice that platforms compete on multiple fronts at the same time. This competition can be in relation to one or more services it offers such customer groups in order to bring them on board. Such competition can at times consist of different actors that may also compete for (some of) the same customer groups. For example, an online marketplace must attract both buyers (consumers) and sellers (commercial parties) in order to deliver the value it is supposed to create, namely to facilitate transactions between the two. Doing so means the marketplace will compete for sellers with other marketplaces and for consumers with other marketplaces as well as perhaps non-platform retailers or even producers to which consumers can turn for acquiring goods. In other instances, platforms may compete with similar players, namely other platforms, across their various customer groups, however, in different proportions. This can occur because the concerned customer groups view the range of substitution differently and make use of such substitution in different proportions. In the example of marketplaces, it can occur that both sellers and buyers consider that a specific marketplace may only be substitutable with other marketplaces but such groups may have differing views on which those marketplaces may be. Furthermore, buyers and sellers may adopt different homing patterns as platform customer groups commonly can choose to either single or multi-home. Such patterns can therefore result in three outcomes: (i) multisided single homing; (ii) single homing with respect to one group and multi-homing by the other; (iii) multisided multi-homing.[105] Accordingly, platforms will often experience different competitive constraints with respect to the different customer groups they intend to attract that need to be accounted for in the context of defining the market.

Successfully bringing and keeping different customer groups on board in optimal proportions is by no means an easy task. This is particularly so at the launch phase of the platform when it is not able to offer either of the groups the desired matchmaking service it intends to facilitate. This early stage in the existence of every platform revolves predominately around resolving the coordination problem all such platforms face, commonly referred to as the 'chicken-and-egg' problem. To overcome this

104. Jean-Chalres Rochet and Jean Tirole, 'Two-Sided Markets: A Progress Report' (2006) 37(3) The RAND Journal of Economics 645.
105. Daniel Mândrescu, 'Abusive Pricing Practices by Online Platforms: A Framework Review of Article 102 TFEU for Future Cases' (2022) Journal of Antitrust Enforcement at 12, https://doi.org/10.1093/jaenfo/jnac001; Richard Schmalensee and David S. Evans, 'Industrial Organization of Markets with Two-Sided Platforms' (2007) 3(1) Competition Policy International 166.

problem, a platform must first convince (at least) one customer group to join the platform before members of the other customer group(s) necessary for the interaction also join. Once one group of customers joins the platform, it will form part of the value proposition offered by the platform to attract the other needed customer group(s) to join.[106] As mentioned, because each customer group may often have a different degree of demand and views on substitution for the (matchmaking) service offered by the platform, the platform often has to make different value propositions for such customer groups to join the platform.[107] This commercial reality manifests in the adoption of a skewed pricing structure where (at least) one customer group of the platform (the subsidising group) pays more for participating on the platform than another group (the subsidised group).[108]

In practice, it is often the case that such skewness reaches a state where one customer group (often consisting of consumers) is not subjected to any fee requirements while other customer groups (consisting of commercial parties) are subject to various pricing rules that result in significant fees. Such skewed pricing structures can be observed throughout the many monetisation possibilities that are implemented by online platforms.[109]

Once the coordination problem is overcome, the prevailing argument is that the network effects at play on the platform will propel the respective platforms to a viable state, commonly referred to as 'critical mass', and managed properly even to a 'winner-takes-all' scenario.[110] In this regard, network effects represent a key aspect of the commercial reality of multisided platforms.[111] Indirect network effects are present when the (matchmaking) service offered by the respective platform increases in value for a group of customers when it is used simultaneously by a different group of customers.[112] For example, the more hotels place their room offers on Booking.com, the more valuable the (matchmaking) service of Booking.com is for consumers and vice versa. Direct network effects are present when the value of a platform service for

106. The value proposition refers to the value that an undertaking promises to deliver to its customers if they choose to acquire its service and/or products.
107. Marc Rysman, 'The Economics of Two-Sided Markets' (2009) 23(3) Journal of Economic Perspectives 125, 129-131.
108. Bernard Caillaud and Bruno Jullien, 'Chicken & Egg: Competition among Intermediation Service Providers' (2003) 34(2) The RAND Journal of Economics 309.
109. For example, pay-per-click, membership and transaction fees as well as a combination thereof. Similar to the pricing structure, the monetisation mechanism is also important for enabling different kinds of customer groups to get on board. For example, in the case of app stores, by expanding the monetisation possibilities of the app stores, both Apple and Google enabled the emergence of new kinds of apps such as subscription-based apps (e.g., news, music and movie streaming). In the absence of such monetisation tools, such apps would perhaps not exists as neither company would be interested to invest extensively in their app store tools in the absence of prospective profits from such activities
110. David S. Evans and Richard Schmalensee, 'The Antitrust Analysis of Multi-sided Platform Businesses' in Roger Blair and Daniel Sokol (eds), *Oxford Handbook on International Antitrust Economics* (Oxford University Press 2014); David S. Evans and Richard Schmalensee, 'Failure to Launch: Critical Mass in Platform Businesses' (2010), https://ssrn.com/abstract=1353502.
111. Jean-Chalres Rochet and Jean Tirole, 'Two-Sided Markets: An Overview' (2004), at 5-6, https://pdfs.semanticscholar.org/1181/ee3b92b2d6c1107a5c899bd94575b0099c32.pdf.
112. *Ibid.*

a group of customers increases as more members of the same customer group use it. For example, the more users join TikTok, the more attractive it becomes for its existing users. The presence of both kinds of (positive) network effects will, at least theoretically, enable platforms to grow at a high pace,[113] as displayed by the success of the currently prominent platforms. In this respect, indirect network effects are perceived to represent the most important aspect behind their growth potential.[114] It is important to note, however, that network effects on platforms are not inherently positive and if not managed well and harnessed, these same effects may prevent the platform from ever succeeding, or even worse, make it fail.[115] Thus when assessing the competitive constraints of a particular platform, it is imperative that such aspects are accounted for, given their implications for its survival.

With the overview of the key characteristics of platforms in mind, the following sections will address the main challenges that arise as a result thereof for the process of market definition and discuss the various ways such challenges can and have been tackled in practice.

§3.04 ONLINE PLATFORMS AND MARKET DEFINITION CHALLENGES

[A] How Many Markets Need to Be Defined?

[1] Theoretical Approach

The most difficult and most debated challenge when it comes to the definition of the relevant market in case of online platforms concerns the question of how many markets need to be defined when dealing with such actors. As mentioned, the multisided nature of online platforms means they bring two or more different customer groups on board and meet the demands of these groups by facilitating an interaction between them. The core product or service they provide is, in essence, the interaction between those distinct customer groups in some form of matchmaking.[116] From the perspective of the market definition, this interaction will commonly constitute the focal product for which the market will need to be defined. Since this focal product is offered to different customer groups simultaneously, identifying the competitive constraints experienced by the platform entails assessing the demand-side substitution for it from the perspective of such different groups.[117]

For example, Uber facilitates a matchmaking interaction between consumers and drivers via its platform. Uber does not own the cars that can be booked for a ride; it only enables both parties to find each other and conclude a financial transaction via the

113. Evans and Schmalensee, *supra* n. 110.
114. Sangeet Paul Choudary, *Platform Scale: How an Emerging Business Model Helps Start-Ups Build Large Empires with Minimum Investment* (1st ed., Platform Thinking Labs Publishing 2015).
115. *Ibid.*; Evans and Schmalensee (2010), *supra* n. 110.
116. Pieter Ballon and Eric Van Heesvelde, 'ICT Platforms and Regulatory Concerns in Europe' (2011) 35(8) Telecommunications Policy at 702-708.
117. Daniel Mândrescu, 'Applying (EU) Competition Law to Online Platforms: Reflections on the Definition of the Relevant Market(s)' (2018) 41(3) World Competition at 453-459.

platform. Accordingly, when defining the market for an undertaking like Uber, the demand-side substitution analysis would have to be done with respect to this matchmaking service it offers. When doing so, several scenarios can manifest. In the simplest scenario, both consumers and drivers have an (almost) identical view with respect to substitution, which is limited to an overlapping set of platforms that offer the same matchmaking functionality as Uber does. In a more complex scenario, both customer groups have noticeably different views on substitution in the sense that substitution is still limited to other platform entities that offer a similar matchmaking interaction as Uber; however, the scope of such substitution differs significantly. In an even more difficult scenario, the two customer groups no longer consider substitution to be limited to other platform entities but also include (overlapping and non-overlapping) non-platform entities (e.g., regular taxis). These scenarios and other variations thereof can be expected with respect to any of the matchmaking interactions offered by platforms. Evidently, the more complex the platform and its matchmaking interaction are, the more potential scenarios can be constructed and the more difficult it is to decide how to account for competitive constraint experiences by the respective platform.[118] These various scenarios concerning the different views that platform customer groups may have with respect to the substitutability of a platform matchmaking interaction support, in essence, different outcomes for the market definition and in particular with respect to the questions of how many markets need to be defined.

Generally speaking, practice and academia have produced two main approaches to answer the question of how many markets need to be defined when dealing with a platform. These approaches are commonly referred to as single and multimarket approaches.[119] According to the single-market approach, a single relevant market may at times be defined which will include solely other (platform-based) options, which cater a similar service to the same customer groups as the concerned platform. The rationale behind this approach is based on the demand interdependency between the

118. For example, Deliveroo facilitates the interaction between restaurants, self-employed delivery cyclists and consumers. Deliveroo does not own a restaurant or delivery service that consumers access via the platform. The product or service offered by Deliveroo is facilitating and managing the three-sided interaction between these distinct customer groups. The perspective and demand of the three customer groups with regard to the interaction service provided by Deliveroo may, however, differ. Consumers may not care whether the food is delivered by a self-employed delivery cyclist or by one hired by the restaurant. Restaurants may equally not care whether the delivery cyclists are self-employed. Self-employed delivery cyclists may not care whether they are hired to deliver food orders or documents. Accordingly, the interaction may prove to be more than one product due to such different perspectives by the customer groups of the platform. If that is the case, the demand-side substitutability assessment for each of these groups might offer different results leading to different kinds of competitive constraints with respect to each of these customer groups.

119. Franck and Peitz (2019), *supra* n. 80, at 22-28; Magali Eben and Viktoria H.S.E. Robertson, 'The Relevant Market Concept in Competition Law and Its Application in Digital Markets: A Comparative Analysis of the EU, US and Brazil' (2021) Graz Law Working Papers Series, Working paper No. 01-2021, at 10-13.

platform customer groups that make use of the matchmaking functionality. Accordingly, if a matchmaking functionality can only exist if two or more separate customer groups are brought on board, any realistic substitute for such functionality will have to do the same thing, i.e., potential substitutes can only be those which are substitutes for all the platform customer groups *simultaneously*. This approach was developed in the literature concerning the market definition of payment card schemes, where a distinction was made between transaction and non-transaction platforms.[120] In this context, it has been argued by some that platforms that facilitate a transaction between two groups justify the definition of a single market since any substitutes for the transaction facilitation service would have to include the same parties (customers) as a transaction service inherently requires at least two customer groups. By contrast, in the case of non-transaction platforms which do not facilitate such an interaction, the substitution does not need to be simultaneous for all the concerned customer groups which means separate, yet related, markets can be defined with respect to such groups.[121] In practice, this approach to the market definition has been followed extensively by the Supreme Court of the United States in the recent case of *Ohio v. Amex*,[122] where the market definition resulted in a single relevant market leading to much debate and critique on the outcome of the market definition and its consequences for the entire legal analysis in the case.[123]

In the context of digital platforms, this approach to deciding on how many markets need to be defined has yet to gain substantial traction in practice. Despite the fact that this approach has been developed for credit card payment systems which share a great deal of their economic fundamentals with online platforms, the decisive element for distinction in this approach, namely an observable transaction, is not entirely suitable in the context of these latter actors. Although there are plenty of examples of online platforms that facilitate monetary transactions, such as online marketplaces, it is hard to make the argument that the only substitute for these players is other online marketplaces. The reason behind this (at least partial) incompatibility is that, unlike credit card schemes which have the purpose of enabling transactions *as such*, regardless of the nature of the transaction, the transactions facilitated by online platforms often concern an integral or secondary part of a more complex service or product which can at times also be obtained through other channels. Accordingly, in the latter case, the substitutability analysis may concern products or services that can

120. Lapo Filistrucchi et al., 'Market Definition in Two-Sided Markets: Theory and Practice' (2014) 10(2) Journal of Competition Law & Economics at 293-339.
121. *Ibid.*
122. US Supreme Court case *Ohio et al. v. American Express Co. et al.* 585 US (2018). In this case, the US Supreme Court explicitly endorsed the theory put forward by Lapo Filistrucchi et al., 'Market Definition in Two-Sided Markets: Theory and Practice' (2014) 10(2) Journal of Competition Law & Economics 293, meaning that in 'transaction markets' (which includes credit cards, the subject of the case), a single market has to be defined.
123. *See, e.g.*, Michael L. Katz and A. Douglas Melamed, 'Competition Law and Common Law: American Express and the Evolution of Antitrust' (2020) 168 University of Pennsylvania Law Review 2061.

also be obtained outside the structure of a platform at least for one of its customer groups. If that is the case, the scope of substation will extend beyond an array of platform alternatives and differ across the customer groups of the platform, which in turn would sustain the definition of two or more separate yet related relevant markets.

This limited compatibility has also been observed by the Bundeskartellamt, which considered building on the idea of differentiating between transaction and non-transaction platforms for the purpose of market definition.[124] The Bundeskartellamt however chose to opt for a slightly different division of platform types. According to the Bundeskartellamt, in the case of online platforms, a distinction should be made between audience-providing or advertisement platforms and matching platforms.[125] Matching platforms enable the intermediation or interaction between two or more customer groups based on their mutual demand for each other. Such matching platforms can be further divided into platforms that enable transactions and platforms without such functions.[126] For example, vertical search engines such as Trivago.com are matching platforms without the transaction possibility whereas hotel room booking platforms like Booking.com are matching platforms that enable financial transactions. Audience-providing or advertisement platforms facilitate an interaction between consumers brought to the platform by a product or content that meets their interests, and advertisers seeking access to those consumers.[127] Unlike the matching platforms, the interaction facilitated on the advertisement platforms between users and advertisers is not a result of mutual interest in the interaction, as it is generally only the advertisers that are interested in that aspect.[128] For this reason, the demand interdependency between the respective customer groups is commonly one-sided, meaning the demand of one customer group (usually consisting of consumers) can be met even without the presence of the other customer group (consisting of advertisers) in the same platform. These differences have important implications for the purpose of the market definition. Accordingly, when dealing with a matching platform, a single relevant market could be defined when two conditions are met: (i) the matchmaking intermediation service of the platform cannot be provided without the involvement of all the distinct customer groups.[129] In other words, there is a significant demand interdependency between the customer groups served by the platform and (ii) the demand of the served customer groups cannot be met by other means than through intermediation by the platform.[130]

124. Bundeskartellamt, Working Paper – Market Power of Platforms and Networks B6-113/15 (2016).
125. *Ibid.*, at 19-30; *see* similar discussion in OECD, 'Rethinking Antitrust Tools for Multi-Sided Platforms' (2018) at 55-64, www.oecd.org/competition/rethinking-antitrust-tools-for-multi-sided-platforms.htm.
126. *Supra* n. 124, at 21.
127. *Ibid.*, at 21-22.
128. This one-directional interest in the interaction is primarily true with regard to display advertisements that are presented on an unsolicited basis to consumers. Search-based advertisement on the other hand may exhibit a degree of mutual positive indirect network effects between consumers and advertisers; *see* David S. Evans, 'The Economics of the Online Advertising Industry' (2008) 7(3) Review of Network Economics 27.
129. Bundeskartellamt (2016), *supra* n. 124, at 28.
130. *Ibid.*, at 29.

In case these criteria are not met, the approach would be to define separate yet related relevant markets for the respective customer groups of the platform.[131] In the case of audience-providing or advertisement platforms, the market definition will always result in separate markets for the respective customer groups as these will not fulfil the above-mentioned criteria for the definition of a single market.[132]

Although the approach of the Bundeskartellamt is certainly a bold attempt, it can be argued that the proposed distinction between platforms as such is not entirely in line with what occurs in practice. The main drawback of the approach is that it does not foresee the possibility of hybrid platform structures which include both matching (transaction and non-transaction) and advertisement interactions or functionalities. This is unfortunate given that such hybrid structures are observable in practice and it can be expected that these will continue to emerge.[133] Nevertheless, the core rationale behind the approach remains very much true. Accordingly, the greater the mutual demand for interdependency between the platform customer groups, the greater the likelihood that the definition of a single market would be justified.

That being said, a market definition, which has a single relevant market as its outcome, is not supported by all. Critiques of such a single-market outcome argue that, while such an outcome is possible in theory, the situations in which the specific economic circumstances justifying such a finding materialise are extremely rare.[134] According to such critiques, the approach to the market definition in case of platforms should be by default a multimarket one, meaning that two or more separate yet related markets should always be defined.[135] It is then argued that such a default approach would deliver more accuracy and is less likely to miss out on sources of competitive constraints than a single-market approach may. Therefore, the advocates of the multimarket approach see no reason to take any of the potential risks involved in the single-market approach which may erroneously leave out some aspects of the competitive pressure experienced by the undertaking(s) concerned.[136]

Here it is important to note that the result of the market definition is not isolated to just one step of the legal and economic analysis of a respective case. As mentioned, the market definition process plays a central role in EU competition law and determines to a great extent when and how such a system applies. Consequently, while the definition of single or multiple markets may in certain instances be equally fit to identify the applicable market conditions accurately, the choice between the two will have significant implications for other steps in the application of various frameworks of EU competition law as will be discussed.

---

131. *Ibid.*, at 28-29.
132. *Ibid.*, at 29-30.
133. For example, YouTube can be considered both an audience-providing platform for display advertisement purposes and a transaction platform with respect to its premium membership possibilities. Similarly, many OTA platforms offer hotel room booking options as well and flight search options without the possibility to book them directly, i.e., these are both transaction and non-transaction platforms at the same time.
134. Franck and Peitz (2019), *supra* n. 80, at 23-28; OECD, *supra* n. 125, at 37-69.
135. Franck and Peitz (2019), *supra* n. 80.
136. *Ibid.*

[2] Implications of the Outcomes

When looking at situations involving platforms where market definition is necessary, it soon becomes clear that the choice between the definition of a single market or multiple ones may have significant (legal) consequences.

In the context of cases under Article 101 TFEU, the difference between the two outcomes may have several implications. The application of the VBER depends, procedurally, on whether the undertakings concerned do or do not exceed the applicable various thresholds mentioned in it.[137] The manner in which the market is defined will, of course, have an impact on how such market shares are calculated. In this regard having a single relevant market would not be much different than the outcome in cases involving non-platform entities. The definition of two or more relevant markets however will almost inevitably complicate such matters. Multiple markets can result in different market shares across such markets and there is currently no real methodology as to how such market shares should be taken into account for the purpose of determining the applicability of the VBER. Beyond this matter, the market definition outcome will also determine how the potential restriction of competition should be assessed. In case multiple markets are defined, it must also be decided which of those will also need to be considered in the context of the analysis, as the inclusion or omission of a market may impact the assessment of whether or not the practice is allowed significantly.

This can be observed in the case of *Cartes Bancaires* where two separate yet related markets were defined for the credit card scheme of Visa/MasterCard.[138] When the case was handled by the Commission, the Commission chose to focus only on one of the two defined markets since the potential restriction (a price-fixing agreement) only covered that market.[139] Consequently, the conclusion of the Commission was that the practice concerned a restriction of competition by object. The GC supported this approach on appeal, however, when the case reached the Court of Justice (CJEU), the Court noted that given the indirect network effects between the markets, such a finding of a restriction cannot be made by only looking at one of the relevant markets.[140] When assessed in the broader context of the two markets, the practice at issue no longer constituted a restriction by object.[141] Consequently, when assessing a specific practice in the context of Article 101 TFEU, the definition of multiple markets also involves determining which of those should be included in the analysis. Inevitably, this same

137. Commission Regulation (EU) 2022/720 of 10 May 2022 on the application of Article 101(3) of the Treaty on the Functioning of the European Union to categories of vertical agreements and concerted practices OJ L134/4, Article 2.

138. *Visa International – Multilateral Interchange Fees* (Case COMP/29.373) Commission decision of 24 July 2002 para. 43; *MasterCard, EuroCommerce, Commercial Cards* (Case COMP/34.579, Case COMP/36.518, Case COMP/38.580) Commission decision of 19 Dec. 2007 paras 283-329.

139. *MasterCard, EuroCommerce, Commercial Cards* (Case COMP/34.579, Case COMP/36.518, Case COMP/38.580) Commission decision of 19 December 2007 paras 316, 329.

140. Case C-67/13P *Groupement des cartes bancaires (CB) v. Commission* ECLI:EU:C:2014:2204, paras 74-79.

141. Case T-491/07 RENV *Groupement des cartes bancaires (CB) v. Commission* ECLI: EU:T:2016:379, paras 90-91.

logic also applies in the context of potential justifications under Article 101(3) TFEU. This latter matter, however, is to a large extent already decided by the guidelines of the Commission on this provision which have been made binding through the case law of the CJEU in *MasterCard*.[142] Accordingly, when assessing the potential efficiencies generated by the concerned practices, such efficiencies must first and foremost be identified in the market where the alleged restriction of competition took place. Any efficiencies that are generated in separate related markets may also be taken into account, however, such efficiencies on their own will not suffice for fulfilling the criteria of Article 101(3) TFEU. Where one market is defined, all the anti and pro-competitive arguments could theoretically be weighed against each other without having to make the distinction between in and out-of-market efficiencies. Therefore, the manner in which the market is defined also determines the manner in which efficiencies are accounted for and thus may also impact their likelihood to be accepted.

In the context of Article 102 TFEU cases, the importance of the market definition is quite evident as it plays a key role in the finding of dominance. The manner in which the market definition is performed will therefore have a direct impact on how market power will be assessed following this step. Here too, dealing with one relevant market will be not much different than what is done outside the context of platforms. Having to determine the market power of a platform on two or more separate yet interrelated markets is however unknown territory. This issue is most pertinent in situations where such markets display significant mutual positive indirect effects that exclude the possibility of an isolated analysis of only one of the defined markets. In such cases, identifying different degrees of market power across the defined markets will be feasible up to a certain extent, but there is no clear guidance on how to translate such findings into one final conclusion of dominance in the sense of Article 102 TFEU. Beyond this stage, similar to the case of Article 101 TFEU, the outcome of the market definition will also impact the way in which the legal analysis of the potential abuse is performed. Equally, the possibility to rely on efficiency arguments under Article 102 TFEU will most likely entail similar considerations as under Article 101(3) TFEU despite the fact that no decision on this aspect has been taken by the CJEU.[143] Finally, once a finding of abuse is made, the remedy phase commonly includes a remedy that mirrors to a great extent the undesirable behaviour of the concerned undertaking.[144]

142. Case C-382/12P *MasterCard Inc and Others v. Commission*, ECLI:EU:C:2014:2201, paras 236-242.

143. Communication from the Commission - Guidance on the Commission's enforcement priorities in applying Article 82 of the EC Treaty to abusive exclusionary conduct by dominant undertakings [2009] OJ C45/02, para. 30; Case C-209/10 *Post Danmark A/S tegen Konkurrencerådet*, ECLI:EU:C:2012:172, para. 42.

144. For example, in the case of Magill where it was found that ITP, BBC and RTE abused their dominant position by refusing to grant access to their weekly program listings, the Commission required these undertakings to provides such information to any party wishing to use such information commercially. *See Magill TV Guide/ ITP, BBC and RTE* (Case IV/31.851) Commission decision of 21 December 1988, Article 2. In some cases, however, such an approach would not be sufficient to bring the infringement to an end thus requiring additional measures. *See, e.g.*, *Tetra Pak II* (Case IV/31043) Commission decision of 24 July 1991, Articles 1-4.

The manner in which this should be done in practice inevitably depends also on how the market is defined and the alleged anticompetitive effects that have been identified.

In the case of the EUMR, the market definition will predominantly concern the manner in which the respective concentration is assessed. Since, as mentioned, the market definition impacts the way in which market power is assessed, in the context of the EUMR, it will impact the likelihood of a concentration to be approved. The more market power (e.g., through the increase of market shares) can be identified post-transaction, the less likely it is that a concentration will be approved.[145] In this context, the potential increment in market power following the transaction is in some way less cumbersome to assess in the context of the EUMR than in the case of Article 102 TFEU as the conclusions of this matter are less binary and any related concerns can be attempted to be resolved by the concerned parties through various commitments. Of course, as the market definition will determine how the concentration will be assessed, it will equally determine the kind of commitments that are required (if any) in order to clear the concentration. Equally, any merger-specific efficiencies that are claimed by the concerned parties will equally be evaluated in light of the market definition in the case at issue.[146]

With these considerations in mind, it is not hard to understand why market definition has been given a central spot in the discussions on competition policy in digital markets. Choosing an approach that fails to deliver the desired results with respect to the above-mentioned issues is not only undesired in the context of such procedures but also undermines the entire role of market definition in EU competition law as a whole. Despite (or perhaps because of) these implications and risks, there have been no clear-cut attempts to introduce a formal approach to the market definition in the case of multisided (online) platforms. At the same time, a look into existing practice in the EU shows that the Commission has had a chance to apply both the single and the multimarket approaches, albeit at times inexplicitly.

[3] Application in Practice

The experience of the European Commission with the market definition for multisided digital platforms is for the time being, unsurprisingly, rather limited yet at the same time also quite diversified as it covers cases under Articles 101 and 102 TFEU as well as under the EUMR.

In the framework of Article 101 TFEU, the most renown cases are *Cartes Bancaires* and *MasterCard*, where the Commission dealt with the credit card scheme of Visa and Mastercard. In its decision, the Commission distinguished between three

145. Council Regulation (EC) No. 139/2004 of 20 January 2004 on the control of concentrations between undertakings (the EC Merger Regulation) [2004] OJ L24/1, Article 2(2). The most evident threshold in this regard is reaching a position of dominance, post-transaction.
146. *See* discussion on how efficiencies are to be assessed in the context of (EU) competition policy frameworks in OECD, 'The role of efficiency claims in antitrust proceedings' (2012) DAF/COMP(2012)23.

markets: the inter-system market, the card issuing market and the acquiring market.[147] When looking at the practice of the Commission in these cases, one may say these include both a multi and a single-market approach for the market definition. When defining separate markets for the issuing and the acquiring side of the credit card scheme, the Commission can be said to have followed a multimarket approach. When however the Commission brought up the possibility of an inter-system market, which was not defined as a relevant market in the case, the Commission took a single-market approach. This approach to the market definition has been to a great extent also supported by the GC in the appeal.[148]

The CJEU did not address the market definition directly but mostly focused on how the matter of a potential infringement of Article 101 TFEU should be assessed when dealing with multiple related relevant markets that display indirect network effects.[149] Accordingly, the CJEU considers it imperative that the concerned practices are assessed in the greater context of such markets rather than in the isolated scope of only one of them.[150] Furthermore, in the context of the *Mastercard* case, the CJEU also addressed the manner in which the efficiencies provided for the purpose of relying on Article 101(3) TFEU should be evaluated in such contexts. In this respect, the CJEU was more specific in indicating that evidence of efficiency should be present in the market where the restriction of competition took place. Further evidence of efficiency in other related markets can be taken into account when the respective market displays a degree of indirect network effects, however, such evidence alone would not suffice for the purpose of relying on this justification possibility.[151] In this regard, these cases before the EU courts predominantly show the relevance of the difference between the multimarket and single-market outcomes rather than provide guidance on the choice of approach for the market definition.

In the framework of Article 102 TFEU, the Commission had the opportunity to define the relevant market in the case of multisided platforms on a few occasions. The *Microsoft* cases constitute perhaps some of the most important cases in this context. When looking at the decisions of the Commission in these cases, the relevant market in these cases can be said to infer a single-market approach. In both instances when the market was defined for the purpose of assessing or indicating Microsoft's market power, the Commission referred to the (single) market for personal computer (PC) operating systems.[152] The finding of this market was a result of a substitutability assessment based on the views of all parties that determine the viability of an operating system namely, original equipment manufacturers (OEM), software developers and

147. *Visa International – Multilateral Intercharge Fees* (Case COMP/29.373) Commission decision of 24 July 2002 para. 43; *MasterCard, EuroCommerce, Commercial Cards* (Case COMP/34.579, Case COMP/36.518, Case COMP/38.580) Commission decision of 19 December 2007 paras 283-329.
148. Case T-111/08 *MasterCard v. Commission* EU:T:2012:260, paras 174-177.
149. Case C-67/13 P *Groupement de cartes bancaires v. Commission*, EU:C:2014:2204, para. 77; Case C-382/ 12 P *MasterCard v. Commission* EU:C:2014:2201, paras 178-179.
150. *Ibid.*
151. Case C-382/ 12 P *MasterCard v. Commission*, EU:C:2014:2201, paras 236-246.
152. *Microsoft* (Case COMP/C-3/37.792) Commission decision of 24 March 2004, para. 342.

consumers.[153] At the stage of the market power assessment, the narrow nature of this platform market together with limited interoperability between the various existing operating systems available at the time resulted in market shares of over 90% for Microsoft in terms of both volume and revenues.[154]

In the more recent cases against Google, similar outcomes have also been reached. The case of *Google Android* involved the definition of the relevant market for two multisided platforms, namely a smartphone operating system and a corresponding app store.[155] Similarly, and mostly for the same reasons as in *Microsoft*, the market definition for the smartphone operating system resulted in a single platform market that was limited in scope to licensable operating systems.[156] In this market, Google was found to have a market share of over 90% across the world, with the exception of China where it is not active.[157] When the market for app stores needed to be defined, the final finding corresponds with a single-market outcome market, namely the market for Android OS app stores.[158] This is in itself not entirely surprising given the circumstances of the case. As in the Microsoft case, the tying practices in *Google Android* concerned the OEMs. Accordingly, during the phase of establishing dominance, their perspective was the guiding one for the market definition. Consequently, it was highly unlikely that such parties would find any other non-platform alternative as a viable substitute that they would intend to offer their customers, namely consumers and app developers. By contrast, if the perspective of consumers or app developers was the guiding one for the market definition, the possibility of ending up with multiple relevant markets would be more realistic. This is because the distribution channel role fulfilled by the app store, which enables app developers and consumers to buy and sell apps, could in theory be replaced by other single-sided solutions such as direct downloads. Accordingly, for consumers, at least in theory, it would be possible to download apps directly from developers as an alternative to the Android app store resulting in a market definition that is not solely limited to other app stores. Of course, approaching the market definition from this latter perspective in the *Google Android* case would not have been suitable as tying cases require that dominance should be established with respect to those parties which have been subject to the tying practices, in this case, the OEMs.[159]

Therefore, with the above in mind, it can be argued that in the context of Article 102 TFEU perhaps the only case where the Commission truly had the opportunity to make the choice between a single and a multimarket approach was in the *Google Shopping* case.[160] In this case, the Commission embarked on the task of defining a relevant market for comparison-shopping services. This kind of service essentially comes down to a platform entity bringing on board consumers and various types of

153. *Ibid.*, paras 324-349.
154. *Ibid.*, paras 430-435.
155. *Google Android* (Case AT.40099) Commission decision of 17 July 2018.
156. *Ibid.*, paras 235-240.
157. *Ibid.*, paras 442-460.
158. *Ibid.*, paras 268-322.
159. Jonathan Faull and Ali Nikpay (eds), *The EU Law of Competition* (3rd ed., OUP 2014) at 442.
160. Case AT.39740, Google Search (Shopping) (*supra* n. 37).

sellers with the aim of allowing the former to search and compare various offers of consumer goods posted by the latter. Thus, when attempting to define the relevant market for such service, provided by the Google Shopping function of the Google search page, the Commission had to assess substitution from these two perspectives. The outcome of the market definition can also be said to be a single-market outcome, where the identified relevant market was that of comparison-shopping services which consisted solely of online price comparison platforms dedicated to consumer goods. Other potential substitutes that offered some of the functionalities of such platforms for consumers and/or sellers were excluded from its scope.[161] Throughout its substitution analysis which looked at the perspective of both groups, the Commission found that all other potential alternatives could not be considered as substitutes for both groups to a varying degree and for different reasons evidently.[162] As all the potential alternatives were considered unsuitable to constitute substitutes to both groups, it is hard to say in this regard what the overall approach of the Commission towards substitution was. Accordingly, when looking at the analysis in *Google Shopping*, it is hard to say whether the Commission truly assessed substitution per group, which could have resulted in two relevant markets or whether it did so simultaneously for both groups, thereby implementing a single-market approach.

In the context of the EUMR, the Commission had more opportunities to address the market definition for multisided platforms. The outcomes of these exercises are quite mixed and included the finding of single as well as multiple relevant markets for platform entities. In *Google/DoubleClick*, the Commission defined a relevant market for online advertising space.[163] This market was solely defined from the perspective of advertisers; the views of consumers that are attracted to various advertisement-financed platforms were not taken into account in this process. This corresponds to a great extent with the multimarket approach where only the advertisement side of Google's services was addressed. In *Facebook/WhatsApp*, the Commission followed a similar approach and defined a market for social networking services and a market for online advertising.[164] These two separate markets in essence constitute the two principal sides of the Facebook platform and the final outcome corresponds thus with a multimarket approach. In *Randstad Holding/Monster Worldwide*, the Commission identified, but left open, a relevant market for online job board services.[165] Here the parties to the transaction themselves argued for a single-market approach consisting solely of other providers of online job boards as they found that such services could not be substituted by alternatives which do not offer the matchmaking function of such services.[166] The Commission left the market definition open and proceeded with its analysis based on this market delineation.

161. *Ibid.*, paras 191-250.
162. *Ibid.*, paras 281-322.
163. *Google/DoubleClick* (Case COMP/M.4731) Commission decision of 11 March 2008 paras 44-56.
164. *Facebook/WhatsApp* (Case COMP/M.7217) Commission decision of 3 October 2010 paras 45-62 and 69-79.
165. *Randstad Holding/Monster Worldwide* (Case M.8201) Commission decision of 29 October 2016 paras 18-20.
166. *Ibid.*, para. 19.

Later, in *Microsoft/LinkedIn*, the Commission identified multiple relevant markets which in essence entails a multimarket outcome. Accordingly, the Commission defined a market for professional social networking services,[167] which the Commission identified to be a multisided platform for the first time.[168] In its analysis which appears to be based on the answer to its questions, the Commission considered that the market for professional social networking services consisted solely of platforms that reach the same user groups in a horizontal manner, thus defining a separate market for this functionality.[169] Beyond this, the Commission also defined a separate market for online recruitment services which would include LinkedIn and a variety of other online channels;[170] the possibility of further segmenting this market based on the business models implemented by the various parties in the market was mentioned but eventually left open.[171] Finally, the Commission also defined a separate market for online advertising services, leaving open the potential segmentation between search and non-search advertisements as well as a potential segmentation for advertisement on social networking websites.[172] When looking at this decision in its entirety, it can be said that the Commission's findings follow a multimarket approach. The mentioned separate markets constitute in practice the various sides of the LinkedIn platform, namely consumers, businesses, recruiters and advertisers. For illustration, a single-market outcome, in this case, would entail a relevant market consisting of alternatives which offer all the functionalities used by these customer groups simultaneously. Accordingly, by the fact that the Commission took the different functionalities of LinkedIn as separate independent services, it can be said that the Commission followed a multimarket approach as the (potential) interdependencies between the various sides were not considered.[173]

Finally, in the most recent decision of *Google/FitBit*, the Commission also needed to define the relevant market for multiple platform-based products and services.[174] When dealing with the market definition for app stores, the Commission referred back to its finding in *Google Android*, limiting the relevant market to the platform market. In other words, the only substitutes for app stores are other app stores based on the Commission's appraisal of demand-side substitution of both developers and consumers. Other distribution channels were not considered viable substitutes. Furthermore, it was noted that, in principle, app stores that are designed to work with specific *different* operating systems and devices are considered to be part of separate markets.[175] In addition, similar to *Google Shopping*, the Commission defined separate

167. *Microsoft/LinkedIn* (Case COMP/M.8124) Commission decision of 6 December 2016, paras 87-117.
168. *Ibid.*, para. 87.
169. *Ibid.*, para. 117.
170. *Ibid.*, paras 134-147.
171. *Ibid.*, para. 147.
172. *Ibid.*, paras 159-161.
173. Such interdependencies could have at least theoretically existed between the social networking side and its online recruitment side of LinkedIn.
174. *Google/FitBit* (Case M.9660) Commission decision of 17 December 2020.
175. *Ibid.*, paras 117-125.

markets for general search services and for online advertising services.[176] Overall, when looking at these findings in the decision, it becomes evident that both single and multimarket outcomes were reached. The single-market outcome can be observed in Google Android in the case of the app store market, and the multimarket outcome can be seen with respect to the other markets mentioned which essentially correspond to different sides of Google's platform(s).

[4] *Concluding Remarks on the Approach to Market Definition for Digital Platforms*

Against the background of the Commission's past practice in the three areas of competition law mentioned above, it can be concluded that the current decision-making practice provides limited guidance with respect to the market definition for multisided platforms. The definition of markets by the Commission in all the above cases does not include any clear guidance on how future cases will be addressed. Nevertheless, the Commission often tries to be consistent in its decisions, meaning that some of these recurring findings may serve as indications for the future. When it comes to a general approach, however, it can be argued that this is lacking to a great extent in the Commission's practice. The most common element to all the discussed cases in this regard is that the Commission will commonly test demand and supply substitutability on all sides of the respective platform(s). Depending on such assessment, its findings may result in a single or multimarket outcome which the Commission seems willing to accept, albeit implicitly. There is however no preliminary filter for the manner in which the market definition is performed. In other words, the Commission does not determine whether it would define a single market or multiple markets depending on whether the respective platform is a transaction platform, a non-transaction platform, a matchmaking or an advertisement platform according to the above-mentioned theoretical frameworks.

When this reality is considered in the greater context of the central role played by the market definition in competition policy, it can be argued that this situation is not ideal. The lack of legal certainty caused by the absence of any guidance on the approach to the market definition in platform cases can hardly be contested. Undertakings that operate platforms which have not been addressed by the Commission yet will have to take into account multiple scenarios when self-assessing their market position with the aim of implementing a new business practice, terminating an old one or considering being involved in a concentration. Where the various possible scenarios display diverging outcomes, such uncertainty may lead to more cautious (risk-avoiding) business strategies, thus potentially also to less intensified competition. That being said, such uncertainty may not last long as the Commission has taken it upon itself to update its notice on the market definition with the new challenges brought by

176. *Ibid.*, paras 132-142 and 147-155.

online platforms being one of the reasons for this upcoming revision.[177] Accordingly, it is more than reasonable to expect that the updated version of the notice will address the definition of relevant markets in the context of multisided platforms.[178] Therefore, it can be argued that, at least for now, the shortcomings of current practice in the context of platforms are not so grave as to question the suitability of the market definition as a core concept of EU competition law as such.

[B] The Application of the SSNIP Test and Zero-Priced Markets

[1] Theoretical Approach

The definition of the relevant market in cases concerning online platforms inevitably entails that a relevant market may need to be defined with respect to a zero-price product or service. As previously mentioned, the pricing structures of multisided online platforms are non-neutral, meaning that the demand for the platform is not only determined by the level of its prices but also by the manner in which such fees are divided across the various customer groups it serves. The use of zero-pricing does not mean that platforms make zero profits and do not engage in competition, but rather that they compete on other aspects and that profits are made on different but related products or services.[179] In practice, the special nature of platform pricing structures leads to skewed structures based on which some platform customer groups are not (formally) charged any fees for the respective platform service(s). When defining the market, such zero-priced services will be subject to (demand and supply side) substitution analysis which in turn will raise the question of how should the SSNIP test be applied in such a case. Here it is worth noting that the manner in which the market definition is approached will not necessarily impact this challenge. Accordingly, if a single market is defined for a multisided platform (or interaction) the perspective of the customer groups that are not subject to any fees on substitution still needs to be covered. Similarly, if two or more markets are defined for the platform, the same would have to be done.

The use of the SSNIP test with respect to the zero-priced sides of the platform will have no evidentiary value since such pricing (or lack of it) removes the core aspect of the test itself, namely the positive price charged by the undertakings concerned. The SSNIP test, which operationalises the hypothetical monopolist test (HMT), simulates a theoretical nominal increase in the price of the product or service provided by the concerned undertaking. This exercise becomes however mathematically impossible and logically flawed when the price of the product or service is (inherently) zero. From

177. European Commission, 'Commission staff working document- the evaluation of the Commission Notice on the definition of the relevant market for the purposes of Community competition law of 9 December 1997' SWD(2021) 119 final, at 24-56.
178. European Commission, Support study accompanying the evaluation of the Commission Notice on the definition of the relevant market for purposes of community competition law (2021) (hereinafter 'Support study'), https://ec.europa.eu/competition-policy/system/files/2021-06/kd0221712enn_market_definition_notice_2021_1.pdf.
179. Newman (2015), *supra* n. 81, at 153-158.

a mathematical perspective, an increase of 5%-10% from a zero price is still zero and the increase of a price of zero to any positive price is no longer a nominal one. The latter option is not only mathematically unjustifiable but also logically problematic. Online platforms that do not subject some customer groups to any platform usage fees are very unlikely to switch from zero-pricing to positive pricing regardless of their market power.[180] Thus, posing the underlying question of the SSNIP test (or the HMT), even as a thought experiment, is not sensible since the theoretic scenario depicted cannot or at least will not occur in practice. Consequently, the theoretical increase in price as intended in the context of an SSNIP test cannot be performed when defining the market for a zero-priced product or service.[181] This outcome is rather problematic as the SSNIP test is considered one of the main tools used for the purpose of producing (indirect) quantitative evidence of substitution for the purpose of the market definition.[182] Therefore, in the absence of a workable application of the SSNIP test, the market definition will need to rely more heavily on (indirect) qualitative evidence which is generally considered to be less accurate.[183] Legally speaking, this does not constitute an existential challenge for the market definition as there is no legal obligation for the Commission (or NCAs) to rely on the SSNIP test when defining the market.[184] Accordingly, in cases where there is a lack of data that would be needed to conduct the SSNIP test, the test will not be used and qualitative evidence will serve as the main alternative.[185] Nevertheless, such situations are different from the one at hand as the incompatibility of the SSNIP test with the commercial reality of multisided platforms will be almost systematic.[186] Therefore, treating all cases concerning multisided platforms in the same fashion would de facto result in excluding the possibility to use quantitative tools to assess substitution in an entire category of cases.

In order to avoid this outcome and resolve the incompatibility between the SSNIP test and zero-pricing strategies in the case of multisided (online) platforms, alternative approaches for the SSNIP test have been developed which rely on a nominal change in quality (SSNDQ) or cost (SSNIC).[187]

180. *See, e.g., Microsoft/Skype* (Case COMP/M.6281) Commission Decision of 7 November 2011, paras 13, 76, 121. In the context of the merger, it was observed that despite the prominent position of Skype in the relevant markets for consumer communication services, over 75% of its customers would switch if it started charging them for the services that were regularly provided for free; *see also Facebook/WhatsApp* (Case M.7217) Commission decision of 3 October 2014, paras 90-91 where it was noted that zero-pricing is an industry standard.

181. Newman (2016), *supra* n. 81, at 65-66; David S. Evans, 'The Antitrust Economics of Free' (2011) 7(1) Competition Policy International 81-86; Gal and Rubinfeld (2015), *supra* n. 81, pp. 32-35.

182. O'Donoghue and Padilla (2013), *supra* n. 93, 109.

183. *Ibid.*, 110.

184. Case T-699/14 *Topps Europe Ltd v. Commission*, EU:T:2017:2, para. 82.

185. *Ibid.*

186. Although skewed pricing schemes are inherent to multisided platforms, the reliance on zero-pricing with respect to one or more of the customers is not. The degree of price skewedness is simply the outcome of a business model rather than an existential aspect or the respective platform.

187. OECD, *supra* n. 125.

Replacing the SSNIP test with a quality-oriented test means that the core question will concern the effect of an SSNDQ, which from an economic perspective is comparable to an increase in price.[188] The quality of a product or service has long been recognised as one of the main criteria based on which undertakings compete with each other in the context of digital markets, particularly in light of zero-pricing strategies.[189] The alteration of the SSNIP test into a cost-based test would entail assessing whether the concerned undertaking is capable of imposing a small but significant non-transitory increase in cost for customers in a profitable manner (SSNIC).[190] The costs tested in the scope of the SSNIC would entail *information* and *attention costs*.[191] Information costs concern the amount and to some extent the nature of the data that would need to be provided to the platform in return for the use of the zero-priced product or service.[192] Attention costs concern the exposure to advertisements during the use of the zero-priced product or service.[193] Both types of costs can be identified in the case of zero-priced products or services offered by online platforms.[194] From a logical perspective, both types of costs also appear suitable for use as they depict the existence of a certain form of trade or exchange that resembles that of monetary exchanges that covers some of the aspects that are central to platform competition.[195]

The use of such alternative tests in practice requires, however, more than logical and theoretical suitability. In many respects, both test variations share a great deal of the same procedural challenges. Replacing the SSNIP test with a non-price-centred test means more than simply modifying the question which lies at the core of the test; it requires in essence altering the entire framework of the test. Accordingly, in addition to changing the subject of the test from pricing to costs or quality, the degree of nominal increase or decrease of such aspects must be revisited and established. In other words, an equivalent of a 5%-10% increase in price must be found for a decrease in quality or an increase in costs. As the alternative benchmarks may be perceived differently by customers, it is quite likely that the respective nominal changes will have to be different from those under the SSNIP. In the case of quality, it has been found that a decrease in quality would have to be around 25% in order to trigger a similar effect as a 5%-10% increase in price.[196] In the case of information costs, it has not been yet established what the equivalent theoretical increase would be for this purpose. The choice for such benchmarks will inevitably also require setting up a selection procedure for the manner in which the respective elements of quality or cost are selected in each case and how

188. *See* OECD Directorate for Financial and Enterprise Affairs Competition Committee, 'The Role and Measurement of Quality in Competition Analysis' (2013) DAF/COMP (2013)17.
189. *Microsoft/ Skype* (Case COMP/M.6281) Commission decision of 7 November 2011, para. 81.
190. Newman (2016), *supra* n. 81, at 66-70.
191. Newman (2015), *supra* n. 81, at 165-167. Newman (2016), *supra* n. 81, 67.
192. Newman (2015), *supra* n. 81, at 166-169.
193. *Ibid.*, at 169.
194. Many online platforms expose customers to unsolicited display ads that qualify in this regard as attention costs. Similarly, numerous online platforms require a form of registration and acceptance of cookies prior to allowing customers to access the platform, which can qualify as information costs.
195. Newman (2015), *supra* n. 81, at 163-174.
196. *See* OECD, *supra* n. 81, at 15.

these are weighed in the context of an actual calculation. Unlike the benchmark of pricing which is objectively identical across all kinds of products and services, the benchmarks of quality and costs will likely differ across platforms depending on their respective business models and the value they seek to provide to their customers. Accordingly, before either alteration of the SSNIP test can be applied, the relevant criteria of quality or cost in each case must first be selected.

When doing so, it is imperative that the selected criteria are commercially logical in the context of these tests. Accordingly, when testing the ability of a platform to raise information and/or attention costs profitably, it is important that doing so in practice would indeed be commercially profitable; otherwise, the entire exercise is logically flawed. Similarly, when considering various potential decreases in quality, it is important that the decrease of such quality criteria would also make sense for the platform at issue in the absence of sufficient competition. Evidently, some aspects of product quality may, due to internal considerations, not be sensible for the concerned platform to decrease regardless of its market power.[197] Finally, as with the SSNIP test, applying either alternative test in practice must also take into account to what extent the potential pitfalls of the SSNIP test may also extend to such adjusted test and if so how these could be best avoided. In this regard, the 'cellophane fallacy' is perhaps the most famous example of false findings that could be made.[198]

[2] Application in Practice

The experience of the European Commission with the application of the SSNIP test or any of its alternatives to zero-priced products or services market (provided by either platform or non-platform entities) can be said to be very limited. This limited scope of practice can be said to be a result of two reasons, namely the limited number of such cases in general and the non-obligatory character of the SSNIP test.[199] Nevertheless, this limited batch of cases displays quite an interesting approach by the Commission with regard to the incompatibility of the SSNIP to zero-pricing.

The Commission's practice in the context of the EUMR constitutes the main body of cases dealing with free products or services (offered by platform and non-platform entities). In these cases, the relevant market was based entirely on qualitative considerations regarding the various functionalities and uses of the concerned products or services without any mention of the SSNIP or its potential variations. In *Microsoft/Skype*, the Commission noted that competition among consumer communication services (i.e., substitutability) mainly depends on offering several key functionalities in a package that is provided without cost to consumers.[200] The success of the

197. For example, reducing the user friendliness of a platform's transaction processing quality may as such not be profitable as it could reduce the profitability of each transaction made on the platform by making it, for example, less streamlined.
198. O'Donoghue and Padilla (2013), *supra* n. 93, at 145-147.
199. Case T-699/14 *Topps Europe Ltd v. Commission*, EU:T:2017:2, para. 82.
200. *Microsoft/Skype* (Case COMP/M.6281) Commission decision of 7 November 2011, paras 17-19, 21-26, 75-77.

players that provide such offers depends thus on their ability to innovate and improve such services or products.[201] In *Facebook/WhatsApp*, the Commission found that the markets for consumer communication and social networking services were prone to offerings of free services.[202] The competitive relation between Facebook and WhatsApp was therefore assessed in light of the functionalities and size of the networks the two undertakings were offering. These aforementioned aspects were considered to be the most important for consumer choice in the absence of prices.[203] These same functionalities were also the reason why the two undertakings were considered not to be close competitors.[204] This same functionality-focused approach was also followed in *Microsoft/LinkedIn*, when the relevant product market for professional social networks, that are also offered free of monetary charge, was defined.[205] In *Apple/Shazam*, the market for automatic content recognition (ACR) software solutions, which concerns apps like Shazam (often offered for free), was defined solely based on the various functionalities offered by the different types of software identified by the Commission.[206] Interestingly however, in *Google/Fitbit*, the methodology used in defining the relevant market for app stores with respect to OEM producers appears to point to an SSNDQ at least as a thought experiment.[207] This latest development in the context of the EUMR can be said to be a result of the Commission's earlier experience with the *Google Shopping* and *Google Android* cases where the matter of the SSNIP test was tackled head-on.

The *Google Shopping* case is in this regard highly remarkable, as the Commission explicitly refused to use the SSNIP test when defining the relevant markets for general search services and comparison-shopping services because such services are provided for consumers without charge.[208] According to the Commission, it was not required to apply the SSNIP test as it is not a legally binding aspect of the market definition nor is it the only method available to it in this process. Most interestingly, however, the Commission specifically noted that the SSNIP test would not be appropriate in this case as Google offers its services to consumers for free.[209] Despite the demand by Google that the Commission should use the SSNIP test in the administrative procedure,[210] the disagreement on this point did not go so far as to make it into Google's arguments in the

201. *Ibid.*, paras 81-84. While no attempt to use the SSNIP was made, this remark could, to some extent, be said to point in the direction of a quality-based test as an alternative to the SSNIP.
202. *Facebook/WhatsApp* (Case M.7217) Commission decision of 3 October 2014, paras 47, 90-92.
203. *Ibid.*, paras 46-53, 86.
204. *Ibid.*, paras 101-107, 153-158.
205. *Microsoft/LinkedIn* (Case COMP/M.8124) Commission decision of 6 December 2016 paras 87, 95-117.
206. *Apple/Shazam* (Case COMP/M.8788) Decision of 6 September 2018 paras 105-118.
207. *Google/FitBit* (Case M.9660) Commission decision of 17 December 2020 para. 124. The Commission seems to assume that OEMs are not likely to switch across OSs due to a quality degradation of the wearable app store. No clear references to a degree of degradation of the use of a SSNDQ are made.
208. Case AT.39740, Google Search (Shopping) (*supra* n. 37), paras 242-245.
209. *Ibid.*, para. 245.
210. *Ibid.*, para. 227.

appeal procedure.[211] Nevertheless, the Commission appears keen on avoiding such situations where the SSNIP test cannot be applied, as these inevitably also involve more legal quarrelling over the market definition. Consequently, its approach in *Google Android* was entirely different. In this latter case, when defining the market for licensable smart mobile operating systems, the Commission once more explicitly chose not to apply the SSNIP test for similar reasons as in *Google Shopping*.[212] Unlike in *Google Shopping*, however, this time around, the Commission went on to note that the incompatibility of the SSNIP, in this case, has led it to assess to what extent users (consumers) would switch across smart mobile OSs in response to a small but significant, non-transitory quality degradation of the licensable smart mobile OS.[213] In other words, the Commission performed an SSNDQ test as an alternative to the SSNIP test. Furthermore, when defining the relevant market for app stores for Android OS, when looking at the perspective of OEMs, the Commission seems to have applied both an SSNIP and SSNDQ.[214] In performing the SSNDQ to assess substitutability from the perspective of app developers, the quality criteria that were considered relevant for the test interestingly enough came from Google's own internal documents. These documents included an internal survey done by Google with its (potential) developers which listed several performance parameters that were of importance to them.[215] The SSNDQ was further applied when defining the markets for mobile web browsers and general search services;[216] however, there, the decision is less clear about the quality criteria applied for the test and the way in which these were selected.

[3] Concluding Remarks on the Application of the SSNIP Test

When looking at the current state of practice, it can be argued that the challenges involved in applying the SSNIP test in the context of online platforms have been addressed to a large extent. As far as alterations to the SSNIP test go, it would appear that the Commission had opted for the quality-oriented SSNDQ when dealing with zero-price settings. Now that the choice of methodology appears to have been made, what remains is the clarification of the procedural framework for this alteration. Particularly, the question of how the relevant criteria of quality are selected in each case, the degree of nominal decrease and the manner in which such decrease is calculated across a collection of quality criteria in each case. Finally, a matter that still remains to be clarified is the manner in which the SSNIP test or its alterations will be applied. Accordingly, it is still not evident whether such test should be applied to the various sides of a platform simultaneously, sequentially or separately.[217] This extends

211. Case T-612/17 *Google and Alphabet v. Commission (Google Shopping)*, ECLI:EU:T:2021:763, para. 493.
212. *Google Android* (Case AT.40099) Commission decision of 17 July 2018, paras 263-266.
213. *Ibid.*, paras 267 and 479-512 and 552.
214. *Ibid.*, paras 286-300.
215. *Ibid.*, para. 286. *See* footnote 306 in the text of the decision.
216. *Ibid.*, paras 387-399; 722-725.
217. David S. Evans and Richard Schmalensee, 'The Antitrust Analysis of Multi-sided Platform Businesses', in Roger Blair and Daniel Sokol (eds), *Oxford Handbook on International Antitrust*

to all multisided platform cases and has not been touched upon in the current practice of the Commission. Similar to the manner in which the market definition as such is approached, this matter can also, at least for the time being, be resolved by applying the SSNIP test or its alteration(s) in all three modalities. The various outcomes and their (potentially) differences can then be compared and assessed together with other sources of evidence available to determine which outcome on substitutability is most likely to represent reality best. Nevertheless, one would hope this matter too is addressed once the Commission notice on the market definition is revisited.

[C] The Calculation and Use of Market Shares in Platform Markets

[1] The Theoretical Challenges

The calculation of market shares constitutes an essential step throughout all three legal frameworks discussed in this chapter. Generally speaking, the calculation of market shares in practice has been done based on the value and/or volume of sales which are also indicated as key indicators in the Commission's notice on the definition of the relevant market.[218] Nevertheless, as the notice implicitly mentions, the Commission may at times also rely on different metrics to calculate market shares. Which exact metrics these are is however not entirely clear as recently voiced by the business community and various NCAs in the context of the public consultation in relation to the market definition notice.[219] In the specific context of online multisided platforms, the challenges regarding market shares can be said to concern three aspects. These aspects include the proxies used for the calculation of market shares, the relevance of market shares and the use of market shares for the application of various legal constructions.

The general tendency to rely on the value and/or volume of sales can be said to have caused many of the concerns around the manner in which the calculation of market shares for digital platforms should be done.[220] This is because, as mentioned, platforms commonly make use of zero-pricing with regard to some of their services and customer groups. This, in turn, may diminish the possibility to calculate market shares based on the value of sales. Here it is worth noting however that while this is true with respect to the zero-priced side (or service) of the platform, this is not necessarily true to the platform as a whole. The multisided character of platforms inherently means that revenues may be generated unevenly across different customer groups. Therefore, the

---

Economics (Oxford University Press, 2014); University of Chicago Institute for Law & Economics Online Research Paper No. 623, https://ssrn.com/abstract=2185373; OECD, *supra* n. 125, at 45-50.

218. Commission Notice on the definition of the relevant market for the purposes of Community competition law [1997] Official Journal C 372/5, paras 53-55.
219. European Commission staff working document – the evaluation of the Commission Notice on the definition of the relevant market for the purposes of Community competition law of 9 December 1997, SWD(2021) 119 final, at 50.
220. *See, e.g.*, Franck and Peitz (2019), *supra* n. 80, at 70; Crémer, de Montjoye and Schweitzer (2019), *supra* n. 82, at 48.

mere fact that revenue (sales) information with respect to the zero-priced aspect of the platform does not exist, does not mean that the platform as such does not generate any quantifiable revenue which can be benchmarked against its competitors. Depending on market circumstances and the outcome of the market definition, the calculation of market shares based on revenue for the platform as a whole may serve as a meaningful proxy.[221] In this regard, the claimed inability to calculate market shares for digital platforms may not be as severe as it would first appear as market shares can be calculated based on an open-ended category of factors. The essence of the challenge in this regard is not so much the possibility to calculate market shares, but rather to make sure that the selected criteria are indeed suitable for the task of adequately representing an indication of market power. Whether or not the measurement proxies used for this purpose possess this quality will determine the suitability and relevance of the calculation to fulfil the various roles played by market shares in the context of EU competition law.

The importance of selecting adequate data types for the calculation of market shares relates to the second perceived challenge concerning online platforms, namely the relevance of market shares. This second aspect of concern is related to the dynamic nature that competition in digital markets is said to have. Accordingly, as digital markets are considered to be very dynamic, it has been argued on multiple occasions that this character of competition would lead to (relative) fast changes in market shares, making them less reliable as evidence of market power.[222] When looking at the growth patterns of the currently prominent platforms, it is undeniable that their rise to commercial success occurred at a sometimes phenomenal pace.[223] This reality indeed makes it hard to attribute a high degree of reliability to market share figures concerning digital platforms. Nevertheless, this valid critique should also not be taken at face value. The extent to which market shares can indeed change in the foreseeable (near) future should be assessed in light of the specific nature of competition concerning the service and business model of the respective platform(s) in each case. This is because the likelihood of displacement may vary significantly across various kinds of platforms. For example, displacing the Amazon marketplace would very likely entail different efforts compared to displacing Facebook or Google's Play Store. Accordingly, once market shares have been calculated based on proxies that convey a meaningful manifestation of market power, it is important that the dynamic nature of competition with respect to the concerned service is addressed specifically in order to determine the temporal value of such calculation. This in turn will help alleviate the reservations

221. Franck and Peitz (2019), *supra* n. 80, at 70.

222. Special Report by the Monopolies Commission pursuant to section 44(1)(4) of the Act Against Restraints on Competition, 'Competition Policy: the challenge of digital markets', (2015) special report no 68, at 24 http://www.monopolkommission.de/images/PDF/SG/s68_fulltext_eng.pdf.

223. In the early 2000s, Microsoft and IBM were the only two major technology companies who belonged to the world's largest companies. By 2020, the majority of the top ten largest companies (based on market cap) consists of the big tech companies behind today's most prominent online platforms. *See* data on this by Statista at https://www.statista.com/statistics/263264/top-companies-in-the-world-by-market-capitalization/.

associated with the use of such market shares in the context of the various legal frameworks of EU competition law, which constitutes the third aspect of concern.

This third main aspect of concern with market shares in the context of multisided platforms relates to the various presumptions, benchmarks, and thresholds which apply to a given case based on the market share calculation for their respective services. This concern involves an objection towards applying a strict approach to market shares for the purpose of applying (or excluding the application of) certain legal norms.[224] Evidently, this concern is closely connected to the two previously mentioned concerns in the sense that market shares should not be relied upon in a strict manner for legal purposes if these cannot be adequately calculated and/or because their temporal relevance is limited. Although this argument is to some extent valid, the concerns portrayed by it are in practice rather limited. The application of the various presumptions, benchmarks, and thresholds in the context of EU competition rarely depends strictly on market share calculations.

When considering the role of market shares in the context of Article 102 TFEU cases, which commonly serve as the greatest source of concern in this context, the limited strictness of market share data quickly becomes evident. This is because it cannot be argued that dominance can be determined solely based on a market share calculation. The Commission itself indicates that market shares are a good first indication of market power that needs to be supported by other evidence.[225] Admittedly, the CJEU may have raised the importance of market shares in this regard in *Akzo*, where it introduced a presumption or in any case a preliminary indication of dominance in cases where the market shares of the undertaking concerned are above 50%.[226] Nevertheless, this potentially enhanced status does not go so far as to determine dominance in itself.[227] Therefore, if the calculated market shares are not supported by other evidence or are found to have limited temporal value (i.e., the market shares may be volatile), dominance will not be established.[228] These same considerations can also be expected to be relevant in the context of the EUMR.[229] Furthermore, while market shares will certainly play a role in the analysis of a concentration, the forward-looking approach of such analyses that is inherent to the EUMR allows for mitigating a great deal of the potential unfounded concerns caused by an erroneous calculation of market shares. When looking at the track record of the

224. Franck and Peitz (2019), *supra* n. 80, at 81-83.
225. Communication from the Commission – Guidance on the Commission's enforcement priorities in applying Article 82 of the EC Treaty to abusive exclusionary conduct by dominant undertakings [2009] OJ C 45/02, para. 15.
226. Case C-62/86 *AKZO v. Commission* [1991] ECLI:EU:C:1991:286, para. 60.
227. O'Donoghue and Padilla (2013), *supra* n. 93, at 191-193. In cases concerning very high market shares, the indication of dominance may be more substantial; however, it remains reputable based on special market circumstances.
228. *See, e.g.*, Case T-79/12 *Cisco Systems and Messagenet v. Commission*, ECLI:EU:T:2013:635, para. 69.
229. *Ibid.*

Commission concerning concentrations involving multisided platforms, it becomes clear that high market shares alone do not lead to concentrations being blocked.[230]

Admittedly, outside the scope of Article 102 TFEU and the EUMR, the reliance on market shares may at times indeed be stricter. This is predominately the case with respect to the application of the VBER which depends first on whether the concerned undertaking exceeds the market share thresholds laid down in Article 3. In such cases, an erroneous calculation of market shares may lead to erroneous findings with regard to the platform undertakings that may benefit from the VBER. Although such outcomes are certainly undesirable, their gravity should be put into perspective. In this regard, it is important to recall that falling outside the scope of the VBER as such does not in itself determine whether the undertakings concerned infringe on Article 101 TFEU. The matter of infringement is separate from that of the scope of application. The qualification of infringement should be assessed on a case-by-case basis, looking at the nature of the conduct at issue. Therefore, undertakings which are unjustly excluded from the scope of the VBER but do not engage in anticompetitive practices are not more likely to be found to infringe on Article 101 TFEU just because they do not fall under the scope of the VBER. Similarly, platform undertakings that are considered to fall within the scope of the VBER on the basis of a flawed market share calculation will still not be able to benefit from it if these implement practices contrary to Article 4 or 5 of the VBER. Furthermore, based on Article 29(1) of Regulation 1/2003, the Commission may also, depending on the circumstances of the case, decide to lift the benefit of the VBER in a specific case where the respective practices may have effects incompatible with Article 101(3) TFEU. Similar considerations apply also in the context of the block exemption for research and development agreements,[231] as well as the block exemption for specialisation agreements which follow a comparable structure and logic while subject to different market share thresholds.[232] In the case of the *de minimis* notice, market shares certainly play a role. However, that is only to the extent that no restrictions by object are involved.[233] In the case of establishing a potential effect on trade in the internal market, the Commission guidelines indicate that very low market shares may indicate that certain practices are unlikely to affect trade in the internal market; however, such market shares guidelines are also coupled with turnover thresholds that may (a least partially) compensate for any errors of calculation.[234]

---

230. For example, the acquisition of LinkedIn and Skype by Microsoft, the acquisition and WhatsApp by Facebook and the acquisition of DoubleClick by Google all involved transactions where both the acquirers and the targets were established if not dominant players in several, at times related, markets.
231. Commission Regulation (EU) No. 1217/2010 of 14 December 2010 on the application of Article 101(3) of the Treaty on the Functioning of the European Union to certain categories of research and development agreements [2010] OJ L335/36, Article 4.
232. Commission Regulation (EU) No. 1218/2010 of 14 December 2010 on the application of Article 101(3) of the Treaty on the Functioning of the European Union to certain categories of specialisation agreements [2010] OJ L335/43, Article 3.
233. Commission Notice on agreements of minor importance which do not appreciably restrict competition under Article 101(1) of the Treaty on the Functioning of the European Union (De Minimis Notice) [2014] OJ C291/1, paras 8-11.
234. Commission Notice – Guidelines on the effect on trade concept contained in Articles 81 and 82 of the Treaty OJ C101/81, paras 50-57.

[2] The Calculation of Market Shares in Practice

The decision-making practice of the Commission displays a growing range of cases dealing with the calculation of market shares in the context of multisided (online) platforms. These concern predominantly the frameworks of Article 102 TFEU and the EUMR.

In the context of Article 102 TFEU, the first major platform case that has been dealt with by the Commission was *Microsoft*.[235] In this case, the calculation of the market shares of Microsoft in the market for PC operating systems was done based on the volume of shipments and value of sales,[236] as well as based on the installed base (the included past sales of all Windows OS versions).[237] While Microsoft's market shares were well above 50%, thus providing an indication of dominance, the Commission nevertheless proceeded to assess the temporal value of these market shares given the dynamic nature of technology markets.[238] A similar approach, yet less detailed, was also followed in *Microsoft II* which was completed with a commitment decision rather than an official infringement decision under Article 102 TFEU.[239] In the more recent case of *Google Shopping*, the calculation of Google's market shares in the national markets for the general search was based on the volume of search queries, users, page views or number of sessions.[240] In *Google Android* which followed shortly after, Google's market shares in the worldwide market for licensable smart mobile OSs were calculated based on the volume of devices installed with Android OS. Market share calculations based on revenue generated by advertisements run on Android devices as proposed by Google were considered not suitable by the Commission for portraying Google's market power in this market.[241] According to the Commission, such market shares would represent only one perspective of Google's economic strength relating to Android while excluding other important aspects such as the ability that Android OS allows it to collect user data that can then be utilised to improve and capitalise more of Google's other services.[242] Similarly, market shares based on the value of app sales were equally not suitable for this purpose as these were better suited to portray Google's market position at the level of Android app stores and not the level of licensable OSs.[243] When turning to the worldwide market for Android app stores, Google's market shares were calculated based on the volume of the installed base across Android devices and the number of apps downloaded through the respective app store.[244] In this context, market shares based on revenues earned from app sales were not considered suitable as Android app stores can obtain value from the store in

235. *Microsoft* (Case COMP/C-3/37.792) Commission decision of 24 March 2004.
236. *Ibid.*, para. 431.
237. *Ibid.*, para. 433.
238. *Ibid.*, paras 436-447.
239. *Microsoft (tying)* (Case COMP/C-3/39.530) Commission decision of 16 December 2009, para. 24.
240. Case AT.39740, Google Search (Shopping) (*supra* n. 37), paras 276-284.
241. *Ibid.*, paras 456-459.
242. *Ibid.*, para. 458.
243. *Ibid.*, para. 460.
244. *Ibid.*, paras 591-593.

multiple different ways.[245] To complement such market share data, the Commission also considered the total volume of apps offered through the various existing Android app stores and the volume of app developers that each respective app store managed to attract.[246] Furthermore, when calculating the market shares of Google in the national markets for general search, the proxies used were the same as in *Google Shopping*.[247] Finally, in the most recent case of *Google AdSense*, the market shares of Google in the national markets for search advertisements were calculated based on (gross) revenue and volume of search queries.[248]

In the context of the EUMR, the Commission had multiple occasions to calculate the market shares of multisided (online) platforms. In *Google/DoubleClick*,[249] the Commission calculated Google's market shares in the overall market of national online advertisement, the national market for online search advertisement and the national markets for online non-search advertisement based on the revenue generated by Google from its advertisement services.[250] In the case of DoubleClick and its ad-serving tools, its market shares in relation to advertisers and publishers were calculated based on the volume of installed customer base.[251] Interestingly, in this matter, the Commission acknowledged the limited temporal value of such market shares due to the highly dynamic market environment that often leads to significant shifts in market shares from one year to another.[252] In *Microsoft/Yahoo!*, the Commission calculated the market shares of Microsoft and Yahoo in the national market for general search on the basis of the volume of paid search queries,[253] and their market shares on the national markets for online search advertisements based on the value of sales data.[254] In *Microsoft/Skype*, the market shares of Skype in the EEA market for consumer and enterprise communication services were calculated on the volume of unique users.[255] Market shares based on the value of sales were not considered suitable as most communication services were provided to consumers free of charge.[256] When discussing the relevance of market shares in this market, the Commission acknowledged that their evidentiary value with respect to market power may be rather limited. This is because the concerned markets were highly dynamic and displayed a high degree of

245. *Ibid.*, para. 594. Google's position on this matter was to the contrary, *see* paras 603-605.
246. *Ibid.*, paras 606-611.
247. *Ibid.*, paras 677-685.
248. *Google Search (AdSense)* (Case AT.40411) Commission decision of 20 March 2019 paras 231-238. Although Google appeared to question the reliability of these market share calculations, its reasons for this objection were unfortunately not included in the decision. *See* paras 239-240.
249. *Google/DoubleClick* (Case M.4731) Commission decision of 11 March 2008.
250. *Ibid.*, paras 92-109. The data used for this purpose came from Google itself as well as from third party reports and investigations.
251. *Ibid.*, paras 113-133.
252. *Ibid.*, paras 116-118; 146-167.
253. *Microsoft/Yahoo! Search Business* (Case M. 5727) Commission decision of 18 February 2010, paras 112-119.
254. *Ibid.*, paras 120-130.
255. *Microsoft/Skype* (Case COMP/M.6281) Commission decision of 7 November 2011 paras 78-79.
256. *Ibid.*, para. 80.

price sensitivity in combination with strong potential competition from prominent players like Google and Facebook.[257]

In *Facebook/WhatsApp*, the market shares for consumer communications services were calculated, according to the data provided by the merging parties, on the basis of user base.[258] The Commission noted however in this case too that market shares in this market and on this basis of calculation are not very reliable for depicting market power, as the market is very dynamic and may result in quick and significant changes in market shares.[259] This aspect was further strengthened by the Commission's assessment of the ability of consumers to switch between communication services.[260] Regarding the national markets for online advertisement services, Facebook's market share was calculated based on the turnover of sales as commonly done in previous cases covering such markets.[261] In its assessment, the Commission also considered whether WhatsApp's data collection capacity would enable Facebook to strengthen its position in the online advertisement market(s).[262] In *Randstad Holding/Monster Worldwide*, the market shares of Monster in the national market(s) for online job postings were estimated based on the volume of job listings and the value of sales.[263] In *Microsoft/LinkedIn*, the market shares of both parties in the national markets for search and non-search advertisement were calculated based on revenue.[264] Similarly, the market shares of the parties with respect to customer relationship management (CRM) software solutions were based on revenues.[265] In *Apple/Shazam*, the calculation of Apple's market shares in the EEA and the worldwide market for software solution platforms was based on the volume of device shipments.[266] For digital music streaming apps, Apple's market share was calculated based on the number of subscribers and generated revenue.[267] As regards Shazam's position with respect to the supply of dedicated music recognition apps for smart mobile devices, the market shares provided by Apple and Shazam were calculated based on installed customer base.[268] Nevertheless, when assessing these market shares, which were rather modest, the Commission noted that such data does not adequately portray the position of Shazam as an established market player and therefore launched a separate market investigation.[269] According to its own market investigation and reconstruction,

257. *Ibid.*, paras 70-78; 99-131.
258. *Facebook/WhatsApp* (Case M.7217) Commission decision of 3 October 2014, para. 96.
259. *Ibid.*, paras 98-99.
260. *Ibid.*, paras 108-115.
261. *Ibid.*, paras 171-172.
262. *Ibid.*, paras 184-190. As such data was found to be readily available through other sources as well, which were accessible to Facebook's competitors; the Commission did not see significant competitive concerns in this regard.
263. *Randstad Holding/Monster Worldwide* (Case M.8201) Commission Decision of 26 October 2016, para. 36.
264. *Microsoft/LinkedIn* (Case COMP/M.8124) Commission Decision of 6 December 2016, paras 167-180.
265. *Ibid.*, paras 210-223.
266. *Apple/Shazam* (Case COMP/M.8788) Decision of 6 September 2018, paras 147-151.
267. *Ibid.*, paras 152-158.
268. *Ibid.*, paras 159-161.
269. *Ibid.*, paras 163-165.

the Commission found that Shazam's market position would be more significant than the way it was communicated by both Apple and Shazam.[270] This discrepancy was however not sufficiently significant to raise concerns that would prevent the transaction from being cleared. Similar to previous cases, the market shares of both Apple and Shazam in the national markets (within the EEA) for online advertising were based on sales revenue.[271]

In the more recent *Google/Fitbit* case, market share calculations were made for a large number of platform markets.[272] With respect to wearable devices and fitness trackers, the market shares of Fitbit and its competitors were calculated based on volume and value of sales, whereby fluctuations in the market shares of Fitbit were also identified.[273] When dealing with licensable OSs, the market shares of Google for both smart mobile devices and wrist-worn devices were calculated based on sales volumes.[274] When moving on to app stores, the market shares of Google in the market for Android app stores were calculated based on app downloads. In the case of the app stores for Wear OS or FitBit OS, no market shares were calculated as each OS was compatible only with its own proprietary app store.[275] In the case of online (search and display) advertisement, Google's market share was once more calculated based on sales revenue.[276] In the legal assessment, the Commission addressed the fact that Google's position in this market had not changed over the years and although Google challenged the market share calculation method, it did not offer a more reliable proxy.[277] In the case of health and fitness apps, the market shares of Google and Fitbit were calculated based on the number of monthly active users.[278] In the case of mobile payment services, the market shares of both Google and Fitbit were calculated based on the number of users and the value of processed transactions.[279] With regard to virtual assistants, the market shares of Google were calculated based on the sale of devices that incorporate such software.[280]

[3] Concluding Remarks on the Calculation and Use of Market Shares

When considering the above-mentioned cases, it can be argued that the calculation of market shares in the case of digital platforms, while challenging, does not appear to be impossible. Overall, it appears that the Commission still makes use of the volume and value of sales as proxies, in addition to relying on new user-based proxies such as installed customer base, number of downloads, duration of use, volume of unique

270. *Ibid.*
271. *Ibid.*, paras 168-169.
272. *Google/FitBit* (Case M.9660) Commission Decision of 17 December 2020.
273. *Ibid.*, paras 318-327.
274. *Ibid.*, paras 329-330.
275. *Ibid.*, paras 334-335.
276. *Ibid.*, paras 338-346.
277. *Ibid.*, paras 435-443.
278. *Ibid.*, paras 351-354.
279. *Ibid.*, paras 355-359.
280. *Ibid.*, paras 363-372.

uses, volume of search queries and other factors. Accordingly, the idea that market shares calculations are solely limited to volume and value of sales is clearly misguided and thus also the claimed impossibility to calculate shares with respect to zero-price services. That being said, the use of various additional or alternative proxies is at times challenged by the concerned parties for not being sufficiently reliable. Given the relatively limited number of cases and decisions, it is difficult however to assess if such challenges are any different than those raised in non-platform markets. Furthermore, it can also be observed that the Commission tends to look beyond the bare figures when drawing insights from the calculated market shares in each respective case. Accordingly, the Commission does acknowledge the dynamic nature of (digital) markets when evaluating the market share of the undertakings concerned. Therefore, to the extent that market shares are used to indicate a degree of market power and/or market concentration in the frameworks of Article 102 TFEU and the EUMR, the challenges posed by digital platforms can to some extent be accounted for when the calculated market share are evaluated in light of the characteristics of the markets they concern. In such instances, it is important that the Commission continues to look beyond the market share figures and continuously improve that type of assessment.

That being said, such an approach offers less comfort in cases where market shares are predominantly used in order to determine the applicability of the various block exemptions, the *de minimis* notice or for the assessment of a potential effect on trade in the context of Article 101 TFEU procedures. In these instances, there is less room for revaluating the evidentiary value of calculated market shares. Although such frameworks allow the Commission sometimes to look beyond the figures of the market share, this possibility seems to be limited primarily to those situations where the market power of the concerned undertaking(s) is in practice greater than what is portrayed by calculated market shares. In the opposite situation where the calculated market shares give an overestimated view of market power, it does not seem entirely feasible for the Commission to bypass the market share thresholds included in such frameworks. This is because such frameworks do not always include legal provisions that would facilitate such an option. Therefore, in such instances, an erroneous calculation of market shares may at times unnecessarily bring certain practices within the ambit of Article 101(1) TFEU. Of course, if such practices are not anticompetitive, the core of the harm created by such errors is that of legal economy as market shares alone do not determine the legality of a commercial practice but can influence the length of the analysis attached to it.

With the above in mind, it can be said that the calculation of market shares based on relevant proxies other than the volume or value of sales is possible and is in fact part of practice in the case of digital platforms and markets. Furthermore, it would appear that there is a growing awareness at the Commission level that market shares in dynamic market conditions should be evaluated in the context of such conditions rather than being accepted at face value. Accordingly, the risks associated with errors in the calculation of market share are mitigated to a varying extent through the accompanying legal analysis of the concerned practices.

§3.05 CONCLUSIONS

The discussion in this chapter has shown that digital platforms bring about noticeable challenges for the concept and process of market definition in the context of (EU) competition law. Such challenges concern predominantly the instrumental role played by the market definition within the frameworks of Articles 101 and 102 TFEU as well as the EUMR. While the theoretical background of the challenges covered in this chapter concerns highly pressing matters, it would appear that the practical manifestation of the corresponding legal concerns is less troublesome than portrayed. When looking at current practice, both the European Commission and the EU courts have managed to navigate rather well around many of the challenges that have often been portrayed as crucial for market definition. Furthermore, it is apparent that the current frameworks of EU competition law covered in this chapter offer a considerable degree of flexibility that allows addressing such challenges on a case-by-case basis depending on how they manifest themselves, thus providing some reassurance that the mentioned challenges are not insurmountable. With this in mind, it would appear that the fundamental role played by market definition in the context of EU competition law does not seem to be compromised due to the instrumental challenges discussed above.

Nevertheless, while the current frameworks and practices allow for ad hoc solutions to the challenges posed by digital platforms, such solutions are not optimal. The solutions implemented in practice by the European Commission can be said to come at the cost of legal certainty to some extent. This is particularly so with respect to the approach to market definition and the adjustment of the SSNIP test to zero-priced settings. Although it can be regarded as a positive development that current practice can handle such challenges while continuing to function, the existing solutions should be framed in a more transparent manner rather than relying on a 'patchwork' approach that still leaves a lot of room for ambiguity. It now remains to be seen whether and if so to what extent the foregoing will be covered in the updated version of the Commission's notice on the definition of the relevant market.

Chapter 4
European Union – European Commission

'Whatever the algorithm, there is still a person or business responsible for it.'[281]

Digital markets do not stop at national borders. It is therefore not surprising that the Commission, as a supranational competition authority, has in the past eight years (and before) regularly dealt with major cases relating to digital competition. It is not without reason that the Commission's Directorate-General for Competition has set up a special Single Digital Market Task Force which published its first report in September 2021.[282] In the investigation period, the Commission carried out a general market investigation into possible infringements of the cartel prohibition in the e-commerce sector,[283] initiated a pan-European conference on competition in the digital age, and published the 'Competition Policy for the Digital Era' report.[284] The Commission is also seeking cooperation with authorities outside the European Union, as digital markets do not stop at the European Union's external borders either. Commission President Ursula von der Leyen and US President Joe Biden agreed at a summit on 15 June 2021 to set up the EU-US Trade and Technology Council (TTC). The purpose of TTC includes US-EU cooperation on regulation and enforcement. The first meeting took place on 29 September 2021 between Commissioner Vestager and her US counterparts, US Secretary of State Antony Blinken, US Secretary of Commerce Gina Raimondo and US Trade Representative Katherine Tai, to launch the TTC's competition stream. The Commission further contributed to market research by the Organisation for Economic

281. Vestager, 'Speech: Clearing the Path for Innovation' https://ec.europa.eu/commission/commissioners/2014-2019/vestager/announcements/clearing-path-innovation (no longer available online).
282. DocsRoom – European Commission (europa.eu).
283. 'Report of the Commission to the Council and the European Parliament', Final Report on e-Commerce Sector Inquiry (European Commission 2017) COM(2017) 229 final http://europa.eu/rapid/press-release_IP-17-1261_en.htm.
284. Crémer, de Montjoye and Schweitzer, *supra* n. 82.

Co-operation and Development (OECD) on restrictive effects on competition and restrictive practices related to big data and algorithms.[285]

During the investigation period, the Commission initiated eighteen enforcement proceedings. Of these proceedings, the Commission's investigations under the prohibition of abuse of a dominant position against Amazon, Apple and Google (as many as six procedures) raised particular attention. The Commission however did not stop at these proceedings. Amazon is currently subject to a (second) investigation into possible abuse of a dominant position and the Commission has launched an investigation into Apple's App Store conditions. Google already received three very hefty fines of EUR 1.49 billion, EUR 2.42 billion and EUR 4.34 billion.[286] The Commission also imposed five fines for similar cartel cases regarding online resale price maintenance[287] and launched seven[288] investigations into geoblocking practices, of which two led to a fine.[289] A joint investigation with the Bundeskartellamt into exclusivity agreements between Audible and Apple with respect to the online sales of audiobooks was discontinued.[290] The Commission also issued eleven notable decisions in the area of digital competition during the investigation period in the field of merger control.[291]

With the adoption of the 'Single Digital Market' strategy[292] in 2015, the Commission set out its agenda for the digital sector in concrete terms. Of course, the

285. OECD, 'Algorithms and Collusion – Note from the European Union' (European Commission 2017) para. 38, https://www.oecd.org/officialdocuments/publicdisplaydocumentpdf/?cote=DAF/COMP/WD(2017)12&docLanguage=En.
286. Case AT.40153 E-book MFNs and Related Matters (Amazon) (European Commission); Case AT.39740, Google Search (Shopping), *supra* n. 37; European Commission, 'Press Release 18 July 2018: Antitrust: Commission Fines Google Euro 4.34 Billion for Illegal Practices Regarding Android Mobile Devices to Strengthen Dominance of Google's Search Engine', http://europa.eu/rapid/press-release_IP-18-4581_en.htm: the decision imposing the fine had not yet been published at the time of writing; Commission, decision Case AT.40411 (Google Search (AdSense)) *supra* n. 248.
287. Case AT.40465 (Asus) (European Commission); Case AT.40469 (Denon & Marantz) (European Commission); Case AT.40181 (Philips) (European Commission); Case AT.40182 (Pioneer) (European Commission).
288. Case AT.40413 (Focus Home) (European Commission); Case AT.40414 (Koch Media) (European Commission); Case AT.40420 (ZeniMax) (European Commission); Case AT.40422 (Bandai Namco) (European Commission); Case AT.40424 (Capcom) (European Commission); Case AT.40428 (Guess) (European Commission).
289. Case AT.40428 (Guess), *supra* n. 288.
290. European Commission, 'Press Release 19 January 2017: Antitrust: Commission Welcomes Steps Taken by Amazon/Audible and Apple to Improve Competition in Audiobook Distribution', https://ec.europa.eu/denmark/node/1695_en.
291. Case No. COMP/M.7047 (Microsoft/Nokia) (European Commission); Case No. COMP/M.7217 (Facebook/WhatsApp) (European Commission); Case No. COMP/M.7290 (Apple/Beats), Case M.7866 (Activision Blizzard/King) (European Commission); Case M.8124 (Microsoft/LinkedIn) (European Commission); Case No. COMP/M.8416 (Priceline/Momondo) Case M.8788 (Apple/Shazam) (European Commission); Case M.8994 (Microsoft/Github) (European Commission), Case No. COMP/M.9538 (Broadcom/Symantec), Case No. COMP/M.9660 (Google/Fitbit), Case No. COMP/M.10262 (Meta/Kustomer).
292. With the 'Single Digital Market', the Commission – in its words – aims to create 'a digital single market where the free movement of goods, persons, services, capital and data is guaranteed – and where citizens and businesses can seamlessly and fairly access online goods and services,

Commission's Directorate-General for Competition also participates in this agenda. The Commission's focus on digitisation in general and algorithms, in particular, is also evident from a number of speeches by Vestager. In her speech on 16 March 2017, for example, she warned about the impact that algorithms can have on competition,[293] and she again drew attention to (the possible dangers of) algorithms during the 2017 Web Summit.[294] Vestager stated that it must always be possible to exercise control in respect of self-learning computers and the algorithms they use. In this context, she noted that the situation should be avoided in which algorithms remain a kind of 'black box' beyond the scrutiny of the competition authorities. Vestager ended her speech – in line with the aforementioned speech of March 2017 – with the following remark: '*Whatever the algorithm, there is still a person or business responsible for it.*'[295] On 9 March 2021, Vestager presented Europe's 2030 Digital Targets.[296] In her speech for that occasion, Vestager emphasised Europe's people-centred approach to digitisation. Vestager states 'that technologies and platforms must respect our rights and values'.[297] On 21 April 2021, the Commission published its artificial intelligence (AI) package, which includes rules and actions to transform Europe into a global hub for trustworthy AI.[298] Europe's approach to AI will help build a resilient Europe for the digital decade, where people and businesses can reap the benefits of AI. The approach focuses on two areas: excellent AI and trusted AI. Promoting excellent AI will strengthen Europe's position against global competitors. As for reliable AI, the Commission plans on creating a secure and innovation-friendly environment for users, developers and clients. The European approach will ensure that all improvements in AI are based on rules that ensure the functioning of markets and the public sector, and the safety and fundamental rights of people.

In its contribution (of June 2017) to the OECD investigation referred to above, the Commission concluded:[299] (i) pricing practices that are illegal when implemented offline will most likely also not be allowed when implemented online; and (ii) companies that engage in illegal pricing behaviour cannot hide behind the argument that the prices are not determined by themselves but by algorithms. The Commission

---

whatever their nationality, and wherever they live', https://ec.europa.eu/commission/priorities/digital-single-market_nl.

293. Vestager, *supra* n. 281: 'The challenges that automated systems create are very real. If they help companies to fix prices, they really could make our economy work less well for everyone else. So as competition enforcers, we need to keep an eye out for cartels that use software to work more effectively. If those tools allow companies to enforce their cartels more strictly, we may need to reflect that in the fines that we impose. And businesses also need to know that when they decide to use an automated system, they will be held responsible for what it does. So they had better know how that system works.'
294. The Web Summit is an annual conference focusing on internet technology and its development. 'You have to teach you algorithm what it can do and what it can do and what it cannot do, because otherwise there is a risk that the algorithms will learn the tricks of the old cartels.'
295. Vestager, *supra* n. 281.
296. https://ec.europa.eu/info/strategy/priorities-2019-2024/europe-fit-digital-age/europes-digital-decade-digital-targets-2030_nl.
297. https://ec.europa.eu/commission/presscorner/detail/en/SPEECH_21_1092.
298. A European approach to artificial intelligence | Shaping Europe's digital future (europa.eu).
299. 'Algorithms and Collusion – Note from the European Union', *supra* n. 285, para. 38.

further indicated in the investigation that the application of a price monitoring algorithm could result in a 'heavy-handed' implementation of a price agreement, which may result in a higher seriousness factor when setting a competition fine, especially if it is horizontal in nature.[300] In short, the Commission has no hesitation to strictly enforce competition law in the event of a digital infringement.

On 28 March 2018, the Commission announced that it had appointed an expert group[301] consisting of individuals who would advise the Commission on the challenges posed to competition law by digital practices. Though the specifics of this expert group's activities have not been disclosed, the Commission hosted an open conference on the consequences of digitisation for competition law on 17 January 2019, and at the end of March 2019 the expert group[302] published its report 'Competition Policy for the Digital Era'.[303] According to the report, digital markets are characterised by extreme economies of scale, network effects and an important role of data, which smoothens the path for the development of digital 'ecosystems' and facilitates a competitive advantage for incumbent market players. One of the main conclusions of the report is that the current framework of competition law is sufficient to address the competitive challenges of digital markets, but that '*the specificities of platforms, digital ecosystems and the data economy require adaptation and refinement of established concepts, doctrines and methodologies, and competition law enforcement itself*'.[304] To this end, the report sets out several suggestions, such as prohibiting certain types of behaviour of dominant platforms in advance, unless such types of behaviour are demonstrably pro-competitive, placing less emphasis on market definitions and applying greater flexibility in determining market power and greater emphasis on theories of harm.

The report has separate chapters on platforms, data and merger control in digital markets. The chapter on platforms suggests banning broad parity clauses and allowing narrow parity clauses (*see* §4.01[D]) only where there is strong competition between platforms, to encourage multi-homing (*see* §4.03[D]) by improving data portability and

300. *Ibid.*, para. 23. 'Price monitoring algorithms can be used to detect deviations from the price agreed among horizontal competitors. In such cases, algorithm-enabled price monitoring could form part of the infringement. Moreover, for the purpose of the fines, the Commission may increase the "gravity" percentage – an element of the calculation of the fine – when the firms "rigorously" implemented their agreement or concerted practices. Algorithm-enabled price monitoring can constitute such "rigorous" implementation.' The Commission refers here to its decision of 15 July 2015 in *Case AT.40098 – Blocktrains* (European Commission) [83]. The latter case had nothing to do with digital competition but concerned a cartel between freight train operators.
301. The expert group consists of Prof. Heike Schweitzer (Law Faculty of Humboldt University in Berlin), Prof. Jacques Crémer (Toulouse School of Economics) and Assistant Prof. Yves-Alexandre de Montjoye (Imperial College London).
302. European Commission, 'Press Release 28 March 2018: Commission Appoints Professors Heike Schweitzer, Jacques Crémer and Assistant Professor Yves-Alexandre de Montjoye as Special Advisers to Commissioner Vestager on Future Challenges of Digitisation for Competition Policy', https://ec.europa.eu/commission/commissioners/2014-2019/vestager/announcements/commission-appoints-professors-heike-schweitzer-jacques-cremer-and-assistant-professor-yves_en.
303. Crémer, de Montjoye and Schweitzer, *supra* n. 82.
304. *Ibid.*, 39. Reference is also made to Chapter 2 of this book by Gareth Shier and Tristan Byrne.

interoperability between different systems, and to hold dominant platforms responsible for fair competition on their own platform and thus encourage self-regulation by platforms.[305] With regard to data, the report considers that, within the framework of competition law, more guidance can be given on the conditions under which data may be shared and the conditions under which dominant companies should give access to their data.[306] Finally, the report states that the EU Merger Regulation is not in need of replacement, but that competition authorities should take a closer look at the strategic relevance of a merger to protect the purchaser's ecosystem. Where there is strategic relevance, the parties to the concentration would have to prove that the concentration is pro-competitive.[307]

On 16 July 2020, the Commission launched a sector inquiry into the use of data by market players active in the field of the *Internet of Things*.[308] In particular, the investigation focuses on the market for devices that connect to a network and can be controlled remotely. It expects these products to play a major role in the daily lives of European consumers. Access to data plays an important role in this market. Among other things, the Commission is investigating data access and data interchangeability and the use of proprietary standards. With this investigation, the Commission is trying to get a better picture of potentially anticompetitive practices in this market. On 20 January 2022, the Commission published its findings. According to Vestager, the investigation confirms previously published concerns: '*This is a market with high barriers to entry, a small number of vertically integrated players and concerns about data access, interoperability and exclusivity practices, among others. We believe the findings of the sector inquiry will provide guidance for the Commission's future enforcement and regulatory activities.*' An important step towards better regulation of the digital economy was taken on 15 December 2020, when the Commission published a proposal to introduce (i) the Digital Services Act and (ii) the Digital Markets Act (DMA). Both proposals contain new rules for digital services, including social media, online marketplaces and other online platforms. These rules should ensure fairer and more transparent digital markets. The new rules should contribute to innovation, growth and increased competition. On 5 July 2022, the European Parliament approved the DMA; on 19 July 2022, the Council adopted the proposal, and on 1 November 2022, the DMA entered into force. With its entry into force, the DMA enters the crucial implementation phase and has entered into force on 2 May 2023. Henceforth, potential gatekeepers (meeting the DMA thresholds) will have to notify their core platform services to the Commission no later than 3 July 2023.[309]

The Digital Services Act contains new rules for providers of (i) '*intermediary services*', (ii) '*hosting services*', (iii) '*online platforms*' and (iv) '*very large platforms*'

305. *Ibid.*, 57.
306. *Ibid.*, 109.
307. *Ibid.*, 124.
308. https://ec.europa.eu/commission/presscorner/detail/en/ip_20_1326.
309. https://ec.europa.eu/commission/presscorner/detail/en/IP_22_6423.

and has a layered structure. The basic rules on '*transparency reporting, requirements on terms of service, cooperation with national authorities, and appointment of a point of contact*' apply to all the above providers. The number of rules that apply increases categorically from services offering 'only' '*intermediary services*' (the 'basic package') to providers of '*very large platforms*', to which the full package of measures applies. Among other things, the Digital Services Act aims to prevent the posting of illegal content, goods and services and to help track providers of illegal activities. '*Very large platforms*' must share essential data with authorities and researchers so that they can track how online risks (may) develop. Insight into '*algorithms used for recommendations*' should also be provided. '*Very large platforms*' should thus conduct risk assessments and independent audits of their algorithms used to moderate the content of online ads. In doing so, '*very large platforms*' must be more transparent about how their '*recommendation systems*' for promoting content actually work. These '*recommendation systems*' are widely used by '*very large platforms*'. Very large platforms must offer alternative recommendation systems that are not based on profiling, and they must explain the criteria by which information is prioritised. The DMA applies only to '*large online platforms*' that are designated by the Commission as '*gatekeepers*'. The DMA contains rules referred to as 'do's and don'ts'. Gatekeepers must offer business users insight into the data they generate on their platforms. In addition, business users should be allowed to promote their products outside the platform. Among other things, gatekeepers may not prohibit their users from uninstalling preinstalled software. In addition, gatekeepers may not place their own products higher or more visible (*ranking*) on the platform than competing products offered by third parties sellers on the platform. The Commission monitors compliance with these do's and don'ts.

In short, the above speeches, reports, investigations and new legislation show that digital competition has continued to feature very prominently on the Commission's agenda.

§4.01 THE CARTEL PROHIBITION

Online shopping allows consumers to purchase products and services from providers across the European Union with a click. Through online price comparison services, consumers can easily find the cheapest option. Over the past five years, the Commission has investigated several parties that have included geoblocking clauses in their contracts to prevent consumers from obtaining products (for a better price) in another Member State. In as many as six cases, the Commission concluded that parties acted in infringement of the cartel prohibition and unlawfully partitioned the internal market, preventing products from being offered across borders. Another focus of the Commission is algorithms. Furthermore, the Commission investigated parity clauses. The Commission's view is clear: classic cartels should not be shaped by modern tools.

[A] Consumer Electronics

In February 2017, the Commission announced that it was investigating four consumer electronics manufacturers (Asus,[310] Denon & Marantz,[311] Philips[312] and Pioneer[313]).[314] In 2018, as a result of this investigation, the Commission imposed fines totalling EUR 111 million on these manufacturers for resale price maintenance.[315] In short, the manufacturers restricted the possibilities for (online) retailers to set their own prices for commonly used consumer electronics, which the Commission qualified as a hardcore infringement of Article 101(1) TFEU. An interesting aspect is the double role that algorithms played in these cases. First, the Commission noted that the use of '*sophisticated price monitoring tools*' *by manufacturers* '*allowed the manufacturers to effectively track resale price setting in the distribution network and to intervene swiftly in case of price decreases*'.[316] In brief, the decisions show that the manufacturers used internal software and price comparison websites to monitor their retailers' prices: '*Price monitoring was conducted via various means, in particular through the observation of price comparison websites and, for some product categories, by way of internal software monitoring tools that allowed Asus to identify the retailers that were selling Asus products below the desired price level which typically equalled the RRP.*'[317] Accordingly, in these cases, software and price comparison websites played an important role in strengthening the effective operation of resale price maintenance. Second, the Commission indicates that the influence exerted by manufacturers on the pricing of the most competitive retailers also had an impact on the prices of other retailers because of the widespread use of pricing algorithms among retailers. The Commission states: '*pricing restrictions imposed on low pricing online retailers typically had a broader impact on overall online prices for the respective consumer electronics products.*'[318] The *Pioneer* decision shows that all retailers closely follow the prices of their competitors and that many retailers even have their prices adjusted automatically by so-called spiders: '*Many dealers used so-called spiders that are software programmes that track the prices online and automatically adjust to match the lowest price available online, often even without the dealer being aware of that price adjustment.*'[319]

310. Case AT.40465 (Asus), *supra* n. 287, fine EUR 63.5 million.
311. Case AT.40469 (Denon & Marantz), *supra* n. 287, fine EUR 7.7 million.
312. Case AT.40181 (Philips), *supra* n. 287, fine EUR 29.8 million.
313. Case AT.40182 (Pioneer), *supra* n. 287, fine EUR 10.2 million.
314. European Commission, 'Press Release 2 February 2017: Antitrust: Commission Opens Three Investigations into Suspected Anticompetitive Practices in e-Commerce', http://europa.eu/rapid/press-release_IP-17-201_en.htm.
315. European Commission, 'Press Release 24 July 2018: Antitrust: Commission Fines Four Consumer Electronics Manufacturers for Fixing Online Resale Prices', https://europa.eu/newsroom/content/antitrust-commission-fines-four-consumer-electronics-manufacturers-fixing-online-resale_en.
316. *Ibid.*
317. Case AT.40465 (Asus), *supra* n. 287, para. 27.
318. European Commission, 'Press Release 24 July 2018: Antitrust: Commission Fines Four Consumer Electronics Manufacturers for Fixing Online Resale Prices', *supra* n. 33.
319. Case AT.40182 (Pioneer), *supra* n. 287, para. 136.

[B] Geoblocking Guess

On 17 December 2018, the Commission imposed a EUR 40 million fine on clothing company Guess for illegally restricting its resellers from using the Guess brand names and trademarks for online search ads and cross-border sales of Guess products.[320] In the accompanying press release, the Commission explicitly mentions that its final report on the e-commerce sector enquiry of 10 May 2017 enabled it to focus its antitrust enforcement on the most common and problematic business practices in e-commerce.

Guess had set up a selective distribution system by which it appointed authorised resellers to sell its products. The Commission concludes that Guess had infringed the cartel prohibition by prohibiting its resellers from (i) using Guess brand names when placing online search ads, (ii) independently setting their own prices, (iii) selling online without prior consent, (iv) selling outside their allocated territories, and (v) reselling to other authorised resellers in the Guess network.[321] The Commission found that this enabled Guess to divide up the European market, allowing it to maintain artificially high retail prices in Central and Eastern Europe. These restrictions applied from 1 January 2014 to 31 October 2017.[322]

According to EU Competition Commissioner Margarete Vestager, the Guess agreements intended '*to prevent EU consumers from shopping in other Member States by blocking retailers from advertising and selling cross-border. This allowed the company to maintain artificially high retail prices, in particular in Central and Eastern European countries. As a result, we have today sanctioned Guess for this behaviour. Our case complements the geoblocking rules that entered into force on 3 December – both address the issue of sales restrictions that are at odds with the Single Market.*'[323] The Commission reduced the fine by 50% because Guess cooperated to a further extent than it was legally obliged to do. In particular, Guess provided important additional evidence, expressly acknowledged the infringements and disclosed on its own initiative the prohibition on the use of Guess trademarks in online search adverts (which the Commission was not yet aware of).[324]

[C] Video Games Platform

In parallel with the above-mentioned consumer electronics investigation, in 2017, the European Commission also announced an investigation into bilateral agreements

320. European Commission, 'Press Release: Antitrust: Commission Fines Guess Euro 40 Million for Anti-Competitive Agreements to Block Cross-Border Sales'.
321. Case AT.40428 (Guess), *supra* n. 288, para. 34.
322. *Ibid.*, para. 171.
323. Mrs Vestager is here referring to Regulation (EU) 2018/302 of the European Parliament and of the Council of 28 February 2018 on addressing unjustified geoblocking and other forms of discrimination based on customers' nationality, place of residence or place of establishment within the internal market and amending Regulations (EC) No. 2006/2004 and (EU) 2017/2394 and Directive 2009/22/EC, OJ L 2018, 60, p. 1. This Regulation entered into force on 3 December 2018.
324. Case AT.40428 (Guess), *supra* n. 288, para. 200.

between Valve Corporation, owner of the online games distribution platform Steam, and five publishers of PC games (Bandai Namco,[325] Capcom,[326] Focus Home,[327] Koch Media[328] and ZeniMax[329]).[330] Valve operates the world's largest video game distribution platform called Steam. On Steam, not only can video games be downloaded, but activation codes can also be obtained for video games purchased on a physical media carrier (such as a DVD or CD-ROM). Without the activation code, the video games on these physical media carriers cannot be played.

On 20 January 2021, the Commission announced that as a result of its investigation, it concluded that Valve and the aforementioned five video game publishers entered into agreements to prevent consumers from being able to purchase video games in other countries, thereby engaging in so-called geoblocking practices. With these geoblocking practices, Valve and the five video game publishers partitioned the European Economic Area (EEA) market in violation of the cartel prohibition, according to the Commission. The Commission imposed a fine on Valve and the five video game publishers of in total EUR 7.8 million.

The geoblocking practices that the Commission found impermissible essentially amounted to the following conduct. First, video game publishers granted a non-exclusive licence to Valve to exploit certain PC video games worldwide (including the EEA). In exchange, the video game publishers obtained a licence from Valve to use Steam activation keys to distribute the PC video games outside of Steam. In this context, the video game publishers requested Valve to impose geographic restrictions – based on the location of users in the EEA – and provide Steam activation keys with a geographic blocking feature. Subsequently, video game publishers provided those activation codes to their distributors for the sale and distribution of PC video games in several Member States. This prevented users located outside a particular Member State for which a geoblocking licence had been issued, from activating a particular PC video game with Steam activation codes.

Second, four of the five video game publishers (i.e., Bandai, Focus Home, Koch Media and ZeniMax) engaged in geoblocking practices by entering into licensing and distribution agreements with each other and with a number of their distributors of PC video games in the EEA that contained clauses restricting (cross-border) sales of the PC video games in question within the EEA.[331]

325. Case AT.40422 (Bandai Namco), *supra* n. 288.
326. Case AT.40424 (Capcom), *supra* n. 288.
327. Case AT.40413 (Focus Home), *supra* n. 288.
328. Case AT.40414 (Koch Media), *supra* n. 288.
329. Case AT.40420 (ZeniMax), *supra* n. 288.
330. European Commission, 'Press Release 2 February 2017: Antitrust: Commission Opens Three Investigations into Suspected Anticompetitive Practices in e-Commerce', *supra* n. 314.
331. European Commission Case AT.40413; Case AT.40414; Case AT.40420; Case AT.40422; and Case AT.40424 (Geo-blocking practices). For the press release of the Commission, please refer to: https://ec.europa.eu/commission/presscorner/detail/en/ip_21_170.

[D] Cooperation via ECN: Online Hotel Reservations

Initially, various competition authorities in the online hotel booking sector adopted different approaches to price parity clauses. However, there now seems to be a consensus among these authorities that such new competition problems should be identified as early as possible through a new warning system within the European Competition Network (ECN), in which all EU competition authorities work together.[332] Moreover, experience shows that enforcement and investigations should be coordinated as much as possible: '*New enforcement actions or market investigations will be coordinated within the ECN. [...] An early warning system has been agreed and introduced within the ECN: it allows discussing ongoing cases that raise novel issues at the earliest possible stage.*'[333]

In line with this joint intention, the Commission and ten national competition authorities published a report on the online hotel booking sector on 10 April 2017.[334] The report contains the results of a joint monitoring of this sector by the relevant authorities in 2016 with the aim of '*to measure the effects of recent changes to the parity clauses used by online travel agents ("**OTAs**") in their contracts with hotels*'.[335] These recent changes concern the removal (under pressure from several competition authorities) of the use of 'broad'[336] parity clauses by Booking.com and Expedia since the summer of 2015 and – since then – the prohibition or removal by commitments of the 'narrow' parity clauses in Germany, France and Austria. In the report, the authors conclude, among other things, that 47% of the hotels did not know that Booking and Expedia have recently had to adjust their parity clauses, that 79% of the hotels do not make use of the possibility to offer different prices through different OTAs and that 90% of the hotels did not perceive any difference in the commissions charged by OTAs between July 2015 and June 2016.[337]

Despite these seemingly rather modest figures, the report states that the fact that 21% of the hotels do offer different prices via different OTAs is not without impact on the market: '*The monitoring working group also carried out a difference-in-differences analysis of room price data obtained from one or major metasearch websites, using hotels in Canada as a control group. This analysis suggests that the switch from wide to narrow parity clauses by Booking.com and Expedia produced a positive effect on room price differentiation between OTAs. The effect is statistically significant in Belgium, the*

332. European Competition Network, 'Outcome of the Meeting of ECN DGs on 17-02-2017'.
333. *Ibid.*
334. 'Report on the Monitoring Exercise Carried out in the Online Hotel Booking Sector by EU Competition Authorities in 2016' (European Commission and the Belgian, British, German, French, Hungarian, Irish, Italian, Dutch, Czech and Swedish competition authorities 2017).
335. '*Ibid.*, 4.
336. In short, 'broad' parity clauses oblige the hotel owner to offer the OTA the lowest room price and the best room availability compared to all other distribution channels, while the 'narrow' parity clauses leave the hotel owner free to offer lower room prices and better room availability to other OTAs or through offline distribution channels, but prohibit the hotel owner from offering lower room prices on its own website.
337. 'Report on the Monitoring Exercise Carried out in the Online Hotel Booking Sector by EU Competition Authorities in 2016', *supra* n. 334, marginal 8-14.

Czech Republic, Germany, Hungary, Ireland, Italy, Sweden, and the UK, and is predominantly driven by chain hotels.'[338] A report of an ECN meeting of 17 February 2017 shows that, based on the results of the report, the competition authorities consider that the measures aimed at eliminating (in any case) 'broad' parity clauses are moving in the right direction.[339]

[E] NBCUniversal

On 30 January 2020, the Commission fined several companies belonging to the entertainment conglomerate Comcast Corporation, including NBCUniversal, EUR 14.3 million for prohibiting merchants from selling licensed merchandise outside their assigned territories and customers.[340] This is the third decision dealing with sales restrictions on licensed products.[341]

In June 2017, the Commission initiated an investigation into certain licensing and distribution practices of NBCUniversal. NBCUniversal had imposed a number of direct measures on its distributors restricting licensees' sales of, among other things, merchandise outside their assigned territory, including clauses that purported to expressly prohibit out-of-territory sales, obligations to report out-of-territory sales to NBCUniversal, restrictions on the use of language for the merchandise, and obligations to pay to NBCUniversal revenues from out-of-territory sales.[342]

NBCUniversal also imposed measures on its licensees to restrict online sales and a series of indirect measures to encourage compliance with the aforementioned royalties. These measures included conducting audits to verify compliance with the sales restrictions and threatening not to renew contracts if licensees did not comply with the sales restrictions.[343]

The Commission concludes that NBCUniversal's illegal practices, which continued for more than 6.5 years (from 1 January 2013 to 25 September 2019) constituted a single and continuous infringement.[344] It also argues that this infringement split the internal market and prevented distributors from selling products across borders and to different customer groups, ultimately to the detriment of European consumers.[345]

NBCUniversal cooperated with the Commission beyond its legal obligation by acknowledging the infringement, providing the Commission with additional evidence that enabled it to strengthen its ability to prove the infringement, and waiving certain procedural rights leading to administrative efficiencies. The Commission granted

338. *Ibid.*, marginal 21.
339. European Competition Network, *supra* n. 332.
340. European Commission Case AT.40433 - *Film merchandise.*
341. For other decisions, *see* European Commission Case AT.40432 - *Character Merchandise* and European Commission Case AT.40436 *Ancillary Sports Merchandise.*
342. European Commission Case AT.40433, *Film merchandise* paras 5.2.1-5.2.1.6.
343. *Ibid.*, paras 5.2.1.3 and 5.2.3.
344. *Ibid.*, paras 6.4.2 and 7.
345. *Ibid.*, para. 6.3.2.

NBCUniversal a 30% reduction of the fine in exchange for this cooperation, bringing the total fine to EUR 14,327,000.[346]

[F] Pay-TV Broadcasters

On 13 January 2014, the Commission initiated competition proceedings against Paramount Pictures, Universal Studios, Warner Bros. and Sky Limited, among others.[347] On 23 July 2015, the Commission set out its competition concerns regarding a number of clauses in licensing agreements with Sky.[348]

Sky was granted exclusive rights to broadcast movies on pay-TV and video-on-demand in the United Kingdom and Ireland.[349] Sky was obliged under the agreement to block content offered through its online pay-TV services and satellite pay-TV services from consumers from other Member States. The geoblocking clauses limited the broadcaster's ability to respond to unsolicited requests from consumers from other Member States (*passive sales*).

In its Statement of Objections of 23 July 2015, the Commission reached the preliminary conclusion that these geoblocking clauses may affect competition and have an anticompetitive objective, because they seek to prohibit or restrict cross-border passive sales of pay-TV services and grant absolute territorial exclusivity with respect to the content of the studios, Fox and Paramount Pictures.[350]

Between 2016 and 2019, the parties offered commitments to address the Commission's competition concerns, including a commitment to discontinue the use of the relevant geoblocking clauses. The Commission concludes that the commitments appropriately address its competition concerns.[351]

In its decision of 7 March 2019, the Commission declared the commitments made by the studios and Sky binding.[352] In light of the commitments, the Commission finds that grounds for action against the studios and Sky no longer exist and that the proceedings against the studios and Sky should therefore be terminated.[353] However, on 9 December 2021, the Court of Justice overturned a similar decision on commitments imposed on Paramount, in proceedings brought by Canal+. The European Court of Justice ruled that the Commission should have taken into account the rights of the film studios' contractors, in that case, Canal+. Since the decisions relating to the other film studios have the same scope, the Commission decided to withdraw them. A summary of the decision was published on 24 August 2022.

346. *Ibid.*, paras 9.3.10-9.3.11.
347. European Commission Case AT.40023, *Cross-border access to pay-TV*
348. European Commission, '*Press Release – Antitrust: Commission sends Statement of Objections on cross-border provision of pay-TV services available in UK and Ireland*'.
349. European Commission Case AT.40023, *Cross-border access to pay-TV*, para. 5.
350. *Ibid.*, para. 6.
351. *Ibid.*, para. 10.
352. *Ibid.*, para. 11.
353. *Ibid.*

[G] Nike

On 25 March 2019, the Commission fined Nike EUR 12.5 million for prohibiting distributors between 2004 and 2017 from selling licensed merchandise (online) in countries within the EEA other than the country where the distributor was located.[354] This ban covered merchandise from some of Europe's best-known football clubs and federations, for which Nike had in turn obtained licences. The ban imposed by Nike resulted in fewer choices and higher prices for consumers.

The Commission's investigation found that Nike's licensing and distribution agreements violated the cartel prohibition. Nike imposed a number of direct measures to restrict sales outside the designated territory by licensees, including clauses expressly prohibiting such sales, obligations to refer orders for sales outside the territory to Nike, and clauses under which double royalties were imposed on sales outside the designated territory.[355]

Nike also enforced extra-contractual restrictions through its conduct, for example, by threatening to terminate the contract if distributors sold outside the assigned territory, refusing to supply official product hologram stickers if Nike feared sales might go to other territories in the EEA, and conducting audits to ensure compliance with the restrictions.[356]

Nike also required licensees to also include these prohibitions in contracts with their own customers, often retailers.[357]

The Commission concludes that Nike's illegal practices, which lasted for approximately thirteen years (from 1 July 2004 to 27 October 2017), constituted a single and continuous infringement.[358]

Nike cooperated with the Commission beyond its legal obligation, in particular by providing the Commission with information that allowed the Commission to expand the scope of the case. In return for this cooperation, the Commission granted Nike a 40% reduction in the fine, bringing the total amount of the fine to EUR 12.55 million.[359]

[H] Meliá Holiday Pricing

On 21 February 2021, the Commission fined Spanish hotel group Meliá EUR 6.678 million for including anticompetitive clauses in agreements with tour operators. Meliá restricted both active and passive sales to consumers from Member States other than the Member State where the contracted tour operator was located. The infringement under investigation lasted for two years and covered the years 2014 and 2015.[360]

354. European Commission Case AT.40436 *Ancillary Sports Merchandise.*
355. *Ibid.*, paras 5.3-5.3.1.6.
356. *Ibid.*, paras 5.3.2-5.3.2.3.
357. *Ibid.*, para. 5.3.4.
358. *Ibid.*, paras 6.4 and 7.
359. *Ibid.*, para. 9.3.11.
360. European Commission, Case AT.40528, *Melia (Holiday Pricing)*, para. 66.

The agreements entered into by Meliá partitioned the European single market by restricting tour operators' ability to sell hotel accommodations freely (online) in all EEA countries and to respond to direct requests from consumers residing outside the defined countries. As a result, consumers could not see full hotel availability or book hotel rooms at the best prices from tour operators in other Member States. The Commission concludes that the clauses provided virtually no benefits to consumers and therefore do not fall within the exceptions of Article 101(3) TFEU.[361]

Meliá cooperated with the Commission's investigation even though it was under no obligation to do so. It explicitly acknowledged the facts and the infringement of EU competition rules and cooperated in providing evidence. In exchange for this cooperation, the Commission granted Meliá a 30% reduction in the fine, reducing the fine to EUR 6.678 million.[362]

§4.02 ABUSE OF A DOMINANT POSITION

The Commission issued eleven decisions and initiated eight new investigations relating to the prohibition of abuse of a dominant position during the period under investigation, including three decisions imposing sanctions. Several new investigations have been confirmed, amongst others against Google, Meta and Microsoft.

[A] Amazon

In June 2015, the Commission launched an investigation into Amazon's online parity clauses for e-books. Amazon had required its suppliers to include parity clauses in all contracts to be concluded with e-book suppliers. These parity clauses required publishers (i) to offer Amazon similar (or better) terms and conditions compared to those offered to Amazon's competitors and/or (ii) to inform Amazon about more favourable or alternative terms and conditions granted to Amazon's competitors. The Commission considered that the effect of these clauses was that Amazon could always offer the same price and conditions as its competitors.[363] The Commission found this problematic as it had found that Amazon held a dominant position in the sale of English-language and German-language e-books. In the English-speaking region, its market share for English-language e-books was 70%-90% and in the EEA as a whole as high as 80%-100%. In the German-speaking region of the EU, its market share for German-language e-books was 40%-60%. In addition, it had risen from 30%-50% in 2011 to more than 50%-70% in 2015.

The Commission concluded (in summary) that the various clauses, both individually and collectively, (i) strengthened Amazon's dominant market position, (ii) reduced the incentives for competitors or e-book suppliers to develop new products, services or business models and (iii) raised barriers to entry into the relevant markets,

361. *Ibid.*, paras 62-65.
362. *Ibid.*, paras 96-97.
363. Case AT.40153 E-book MFNs and Related Matters (Amazon), *supra* n. 286, paras 22–38.

making entry by new competitors (or the expansion of existing competitors) more unlikely.[364] In order to avoid a fining decision, Amazon proposed commitments to the Commission, which the Commission accepted in its decision of 4 May 2017.[365] Essentially, these commitments are that Amazon (i) will no longer apply the existing parity clauses and (ii) will in the future no longer include such clauses in its contracts.[366] The commitments applied for a duration of five years.

[B] Amazon II

On 10 November 2020, in a second proceeding, the Commission notified Amazon of its preliminary view that Amazon infringed Article 102 TFEU by impeding competition in online retail markets. The Commission objects to Amazon's systematic use of non-public business data of independent platform users, for the benefit of its own retail operations.[367]

Amazon has a dual role: (i) Amazon provides a platform on which third parties can sell their products and (ii) Amazon is a retailer (it sells its own products through its website). Amazon continuously collects data on the activities on the platform. The Commission's preliminary findings show that very large amounts of non-public sales data are available to employees of Amazon's own sales force. Large amounts of aggregated data are used for strategic purposes to the detriment of other sellers on Amazon, which compete directly with Amazon's own sales activities.[368]

The Commission also launched an investigation into the selection of 'Buy Box' winners. A key feature of Amazon's website is that the same product can be offered by multiple sellers. Only one vendor gets the position in the so-called 'Buy Box'. When the customer clicks on the 'add-to-cart' button, the customer automatically places the products from that one provider listed in the 'Buy Box' into the shopping cart. In particular, the Commission is examining whether the criteria for determining the winner of the 'Buy Box' favour Amazon's own retail operations or provide an advantage to sellers using Amazon's logistics delivery services. The 'Buy Box' is prominently displayed on Amazon's website and the vast majority of sales are generated through the 'Buy Box'. It also examines the opportunities provided to platform users to reach Prime Users. On 14 July 2022, the *Proposed Commitments* submitted by Amazon were published. Among other things, Amazon proposes to no longer use *non-public Seller Data* for the purpose of retail operations in competition with users of its platform. In addition, Amazon proposes to use non-discriminatory terms and criteria in selecting Buy Box. By decision of 22 December 2022 (i.e. after the

364. *Ibid.*, paras 70-152.
365. *Ibid.*
366. *Ibid.*, para. 159.
367. European Commission Cases AT.40702 (*Prime*) and AT.40703 (*Buy Box*). For the press release of the Commission, please refer to: https://ec.europa.eu/commission/presscorner/detail/en/ip_20_2077.
368. *Ibid.*

end of our research period), the Commission declared these commitments legally binding.[369]

[C] Google I

While Amazon was able to agree to a commitment decision with the Commission in May 2017 in the Amazon I-case, at approximately the same time the Commission's investigation into another tech giant, Google, ended about two months later with a fining decision in which the Commission imposed a fine of as much as EUR 2.42 billion on Google for abuse of a dominant position.[370] The Commission concluded that Google algorithmically demotes the price comparison services of its competitors, making these price comparison services appear relatively low in the search results. The price comparisons of its own Google Shopping service are not downgraded by these algorithms and therefore appear higher in the search results, causing Google Shopping to be favoured over the other price comparison services. The Commission noted that Google holds a very dominant position in the search engine market. In all EU Member States surveyed, its market share for search engines was above 80% in 2016 (and in most countries even above 90%). If only mobile use is considered, Google's dominance is even greater. The Commission found that Google's conduct should be considered abusive because Google: (i) diverts traffic from competing price comparison services to its own comparison service, in the sense that it causes traffic from its general search results pages to competing price comparison services to decrease and increases traffic from its general search results pages to its own price comparison service; and (ii) this behaviour is likely to have anticompetitive effects on the national markets for price comparison services and general internet search services. In addition to the imposition of the fine, the Commission set Google a deadline of ninety days from the date of its decision to bring its conduct to an end.[371]

On 10 November 2021, the General Court of the European Union ruled on Google's appeal against the Commission's decision. The General Court upheld the fine of EUR 2.42 billion imposed on Google.[372] The Court endorses the Commission's findings that Google's conduct was of anticompetitive nature, considering four elements; (i) the high importance of the traffic generated by Google's search engine to price comparison services, (ii) the fact that users of the search engine in general only look at the first few search results and (iii) the high proportion of *diverted traffic* (a large proportion of visitors from other comparison sites arrive at the website in question via Google) and (iv) the fact that there are no alternatives to the traffic via

369. European Commission, press release of 22 December 2023 in cases AT.40462 and AT.40703, *Antitrust: Commission accepts commitments by Amazon barring it from using marketplace seller data, and ensuring equal access to Buy Box and Prime*, https://ec.europa.eu/commission/presscorner/detail/en/ip_22_7777.
370. Case AT.39740, Google Search (Shopping), *supra* n. 37.
371. Case T-612/17 (Google and Alphabet v. Commission) (General Court) 17.
372. Press release no. 197/21, General Court of the European Union, Judgment in Case T-612/17 (Google Shopping), https://curia.europa.eu/jcms/upload/docs/application/pdf/2021-11/cp210197en.pdf, p. 1.

Google. The fact that Google's search engine is generally designed to transparently display content (from third parties) based on relevant search parameters makes the way Google Shopping is promoted atypical. The General Court further concludes that Google's search engine has characteristics similar to an essential facility. However, Google's conduct does not qualify as a refusal to supply. Therefore, the *Bronner* line of jurisprudence does not apply to the case and consequently, contrary to Google's argument, its conduct should not be tested against the criteria set forth in the Bronner judgment. Furthermore, it is considered important that Google favours its own service over competing products, rather than showing the best search result for consumers.

However, with regard to the national markets for general searches, the Court concludes that the Commission's considerations are too vague to even potentially infer anticompetitive effects in this market. The Commission had found anticompetitive effects on this market merely by pointing out that Google could finance its general search engine with the revenues generated by the preferential treatment of its product comparator. Indeed, it would appear from the file that Google feared that other product comparators might take advertising revenue. The Court partially sets aside the decision on this point. However, this conclusion does not affect the amount of the fine. Indeed, the amount of the fine was already based by the Commission on turnover in the *market for specialised product search services.* The finding that Google abused its dominant position on the *market for specialised product search services* is upheld and the level of the fine is maintained.

Google's defence that its conduct also has pro-competitive effects is not accepted by the General Court.[373] First of all, the Court finds that while Google's algorithms for ranking generic search results and its criteria and display and positioning of specialised product results as such may constitute pro-competitive service improvements, those potential pro-competitive effects do not outweigh the anticompetitive effects resulting from Google's strategy.

In short, it is clear from this judgment that Google's conduct was unlawful even according to the Court. Google has appealed the judgment.[374]

[D] Google II

The first mega-fine was not the end for Google. In a press release of 18 July 2018, the Commission indicated that it had imposed a second fine of EUR 4.34 billion on Google for abuse of a dominant position.[375] This is by far the highest fine ever imposed by the Commission on a single company for an infringement of competition law. Its parent

373. Press release no. 197/21, General Court of the European Union, Judgment in Case T-612/17 (Google Shopping) https://curia.europa.eu/jcms/upload/docs/application/pdf/2021-11/cp210197en.pdf, p. 3.

374. *Ibid.*

375. European Commission, decision of 18 July 2018 in case AT.40999 (*Google Android*).

company Alphabet also risked a penalty payment of up to 5% of its daily turnover if Google did not end the allegedly infringing conduct within ninety days.

In this case, the Commission states that Google has committed a threefold abuse of yet as many dominant positions. The Commission considers that Google is abusing its dominant positions in (i) the market for licensable mobile device operating systems (OSs),[376] (ii) the market for search engines and (iii) the market for Android app stores. The Commission considers that the following conduct by Google constitutes an abuse:

- Google requires manufacturers of mobile devices running on Android to preinstall the Google search app and Google's browser Chrome.
- Google is said to have paid certain major manufacturers in order to ensure that they would not instal competing search apps on their devices.
- Google prevents manufacturers wishing to preinstall Google apps in advance from selling even a single device running on alternative versions of Android not approved and marketed by Google (so-called Android forks).

The Commission considers that mobile device users are likely to stick to preinstalled apps and are not inclined to try competing apps if they are satisfied with what has been preinstalled on their device. This effect would prevent developers of other search engines and browsers from competing on an equal footing with Google. Google also publishes the source code of Android online, which, in principle, allows the development of Android forks by competitors since they are at liberty to copy and amend the source code. By doing so, they are technically and legally capable of developing Android forks. However, the Commission considers that Google's refusal to allow preinstallation of Google apps on devices running on Android forks allows Google '*[to use] Android as a vehicle to cement the dominance of its search engine*'.[377] The Commission concludes that Google's behaviour also effectively prevented a number of major manufacturers from developing devices that would run on Amazon's Android fork 'Fire OS'. According to the Commission, this effective barrier to the successful development of Android forks also deprives developers of competing search engines from the opportunity to generate traffic on devices running on Android forks. This, in turn, would supposedly prevent competing search engines from collecting enough data from mobile users to compete effectively with Google. Also, this behaviour of Google was said to limit the development of competing apps by Google's competitors. Google has appealed against this second fine.[378] The hearings in this procedure before the General Court started on 27 September 2021.[379] During this hearing, Google stated that: '*Android has created more choice for everyone, not less, and supports thousands of successful businesses in Europe and around the world. This case*

376. The Commission does not consider Apple's iOS or BlackBerry's operating system to be licensable, as these operating systems are installed only on their developers' devices.
377. According to Commissioner Vestager in: European Commission, 'Press Release 18 July 2018: Antitrust: Commission Fines Google Euro 4.34 Billion for Illegal Practices Regarding Android Mobile Devices to Strengthen Dominance of Google's Search Engine' (*supra* n. 286).
378. Case T-604/18 (Google and Alphabet v Commission) (European General Court).
379. https://www.reuters.com/technology/google-fight-eu-antitrust-fine-court-hearing-sept-27-sources-2021-07-12/.

isn't supported by the facts or the law.'[380] By judgment of 14 September 2022, the General Court largely upheld the Commission's findings but did lower the fine to EUR 4.125 billion, because contrary to the Commission it did not consider certain revenue-sharing agreements between Google and manufacturers to constitute an infringement of the prohibition on abuse of a dominant position.[381]

[E] Google III

On 20 March 2019, the Commission imposed a third fine of EUR 1.49 billion on Google for abuse of a dominant position through AdSense on the market for online search advertising intermediation services.[382] AdSense is a Google application that allows third parties to add a search function to their website. Users of the search function are presented not only with search results but also with adverts from Google. When a user clicks on an ad, both Google and the third party receive a commission from the advertiser.

The Commission considers that Google unnecessarily restricted third parties' ability to deal with Google's competitors. More specifically, Google's abuse of a dominant position was based on the following provisions in its contracts with third parties:

(1) Exclusivity: third parties may not use adverts from Google's competitors.
(2) Premium placement of a minimum number of Google ads: third parties must place a minimum number of Google ads, with the Google ads displayed in the most prominent place. Competing ads may not be displayed above or next to Google ads.
(3) Approval rights: third parties must seek Google's approval before using adverts from Google's competitors.

Google started including exclusivity clauses as mentioned above (1) in 2006 and stopped doing so in March 2009. The Commission found that from March 2009 until mid-2016 Google had implemented a strategy of 'relaxed exclusivity' consisting of the inclusion of the clauses mentioned above under (2) and (3). According to the Commission, Google's conduct affected half of the market in terms of turnover and resulted in website owners being restricted in their ability to make money by selling advertising space. Google had already changed its policy in 2016, a few months after it

380. Google in court to appeal EU's 2018 Android antitrust case – ABC News.
381. General Court, judgment of 14 September 2022 in case T-604/18, *Google and Alphabet v. Commission*, ECLI:EU:T:2022:541, https://curia.europa.eu/juris/document/document.jsf?text=&docid=265421&pageIndex=0&doclang=en&mode=lst&dir=&occ=first&part=1&cid=2637.
382. Case AT.40411 (Google Search (AdSense)) (*supra* n. 248). *See* European Commission, 'Press Release 20 March 2019: Antitrust: Commission Fines Google €1.49 Billion for Abusive Practices in Online Advertising', http://europa.eu/rapid/press-release_IP-19-1770_en.htm.

received the Commission's statement of objections.[383] Google has appealed the Commission's decision.[384]

[F] Google IV

Several holiday rental companies and industry associations sent an open letter to the Commission on 9 February 2020, complaining that Google would be giving its own products a preferential position in general search results.[385] Although Google displays holiday rental opportunities from several partners in its search results, Google has reserved a '*visually-rich OneBox at the top of its general search results pages*' for its own Google Vacation Rental Service, which the complainants say raises competition concerns.[386]

The Commission, in the Google shopping case discussed above,[387] had already established that such more favourable ranking/display of its own services would lead to more attention and clicks, even if rival offers are more relevant to the end user's search query.[388]

The holiday rental companies and industry associations (e.g., TripAdvisor and the Digital Economy Network, z.s. (DEN)) argue that Google (technically) links its general search service to its holiday rental search service and consistently positions its own rental options above all competing rental options. Since Google Search is the first step for most Internet users, almost all specialised search service providers depend on being found in the Google search engine. By giving preference to its own product, according to the complainants, Google is able to give its own services an economic advantage that no other provider can compete with on an equal footing.[389]

Moreover, according to the complainants, Google also acts discriminatorily in admitting content of competitors to Google Vacation Rentals, as only a few large players have been approached by Google to share their content so far. As a result, small- and medium-sized companies would be excluded from the Internet traffic generated by Google's holiday rental service. The complainants therefore urge the Commission to investigate Google's behaviour and consider all possible steps to stop the behaviour, which according to the complainants could also lead to an irreversible

---

383. European Commission, 'Press Release 20 March 2019: Antitrust: Commission Fines Google €1.49 Billion for Abusive Practices in Online Advertising' (*supra* n. 382).
384. Case AT.40411 (Google Search (AdSense)) (*supra* n. 248). *See* European Commission, 'Press Release 20 March 2019: Antitrust: Commission Fines Google €1.49 Billion for Abusive Practices in Online Advertising', http://europa.eu/rapid/press-release_IP-19-1770_en.htm. Appeal pending, case T-334/19.
385. Asociación Española de Plataformas Digitales de Alquiler Temporal, Deutscher Ferienshausverband et al. 10 February 2020, 'Our concerns about Google's preferencing and tying of its new product *Google Vacation Rentals* within general search results pages'.
386. *Ibid.*, p. 2.
387. European Commission, Case AT.39740, Google Search (Shopping), *supra* n. 37.
388. *Ibid.*
389. Asociación Española de Plataformas Digitales de Alquiler Temporal, Deutscher Ferienshausverband et al. 10 February 2020, 'Our concerns about Google's preferencing and tying of its new product *Google Vacation Rentals* within general search results pages', p. 3.

'tipping' of the market.[390] It is not known whether the Commission has actually taken any action in response to this letter.

[G] Google V

The Commission is also conducting a preliminary antitrust investigation into Google's 'Google for Jobs' job posting platform.[391]

In a speech on 27 August 2019, Vestager drew several parallels between Google for Jobs and the conduct in the Google Shopping case, for which Google was fined EUR 2.42 billion in 2017: '*And we're looking right now at whether the same thing may have happened with other parts of Google's business – like the job search business known as Google for Jobs*'.[392]

On 13 August 2019, in an open letter, 23 European e-recruitment services called on Vestager to launch a formal investigation into Google's conduct and to impose temporary measures on Google in the course of that investigation. The signatories of the letter argue that Google is abusing its market dominance as a general search service by favouring its own job posting platform, Google for Jobs, in the general search results pages over its competitors.[393] To date, no further details about this research are known.

[H] Google VI

However, the story still did not end here for Google. On 22 June 2021, the Commission announced that it has launched a formal investigation to determine whether Google has infringed competition law by favouring its own technology services for display advertising, to the detriment of competing providers of ad tech services, advertisers and online publishers. In particular, during its investigation, the Commission will seek to determine whether Google impedes competition by restricting third-party access to user data for advertising purposes on websites and apps while reserving that data for its own use.[394]

[I] Apple's App Store

On 16 June 2020, the Commission announced that it has launched an investigation into the conditions under which app developers may distribute their products through Apple's App Store and Apple's conduct in the market for music streaming services. In particular, the investigation focuses on the obligation to use the built-in payment

390. *Ibid.*, p. 4.
391. European Commission, Case AT.40592, *Google for Jobs.*
392. https://www.reuters.com/article/eu-google-antitrust-idUKL5N25N2TX.
393. European online recruitment services 13 August 2019, 'Open Letter: Call of e-recruitment services for intervention against Google's favouring of Google for Jobs'.
394. European Commission, Case AT.40670 (Google – Display advertising). For the press release of the Commission, please refer to: https://ec.europa.eu/commission/presscorner/detail/en/ip_21_3143.

system (proprietary in-app purchase system) and the prohibition on the ability of developers to inform iPhone and iPad users of alternative cheaper purchasing possibilities outside of apps.

Apple charges a 30% commission on all purchases made through the App Store. In addition, Apple appears to obtain valuable data about its competitors' activities and offers. On 30 April 2021, the Commission issued a Statement of Objections to Apple. The Commission's objections concern (i) the mandatory use of *the in-app purchase system* (IAP) and (ii) *the anti-steering provisions*. Users can only pay for services offered in App Store through the in-app purchase system. Based on *the anti-steering provisions*, developers are also not allowed to inform users about alternative purchase/payment options. As a result, actual all payments for (additional) services in the App Store are made through Apple's payment system.

Also on 16 June 2020, the Commission announced that it had begun a formal investigation into Apple's conduct with respect to Apple Pay.[395] The investigation concerns:

(i) Apple's terms and other measures for integrating Apple Pay into commercial apps and websites on iPhones and iPads'
(ii) limiting access to Near Field Communication (NFC) functionality on iPhones for in-store payments. Apple Pay is the only payment system that has access to NFC 'tap and go'; and
(iii) the alleged denial of access to Apple Pay.

[J] Facebook

On 4 June 2021, the Commission announced that it had commenced a formal investigation to determine whether Facebook (now Meta) had infringed competition rules (both the cartel and abuse of dominance prohibitions) by, among other things, using collected ad data from advertisers to compete with those same advertisers in markets in which Facebook is also active, such as the classified ads market. In addition, the Commission will investigate whether Facebook is tying its online classified ad service, Facebook Marketplace, to its social network (i.e., tying) in violation of competition rules. Thus, the Commission will seek to determine whether Facebook, through its position in social networking and online advertising, may restrict competition in adjacent markets in which Facebook is active thanks to its social network, including in particular the market for online classified ads. In particular, this investigation will focus on the area of online classified ads.

During the Commission's preliminary investigation – which had begun on 4 May 2020 – the Commission sent information requests to Facebook. Facebook refused to provide the requested information, stating that the information requests under this investigation are extremely comprehensive and that the information requested by the

395. European Commission Case AT.40452 Apple – Mobile payments.

Commission includes sensitive medical and financial information of its employees.[396] On 15 July 2020, Facebook initiated proceedings before the General Court and on 24 July 2020, the General Court temporarily suspended Facebook's obligation to cooperate with the information requests.[397] The interim suspension is necessary to ensure that the 'disputed material' is not made public pending the Commission's comments and ruling on Facebook's request for interim measures.[398]

On 19 December 2022, the Commission sent a Statement of Objections to Meta in this case.[399]

The UK Competition and Markets Authority (CMA) has also begun an investigation into Facebook's use of data. The Commission will seek to work closely with the CMA in its investigations as the independent inquiries develop.[400]

[K] Possible new investigation into Microsoft Teams

The Commission has issued a questionnaire to competitors of Microsoft's Teams app in response to a complaint from Slack Technologies. Slack Technology complained to the Commission that Microsoft was allegedly engaging in tying practices because the Microsoft Teams app would be preinstalled on Windows and difficult to uninstall. The questionnaire requests competitors, among other things, to what extent COVID-19 has increased demand for *workplace apps* and how this market will develop after the COVID-19 pandemic.[401]

[L] Meta and Google VII

On 11 March 2022, the Commission initiated an antitrust investigation with regard to the 'Jedi Blue' agreement between Meta and Google for online display advertising services.[402]

Google provides advertising technology services that intermediate between advertisers and publishers through real-time auctioning of online display advertising space on websites/mobile apps, including through its 'Open Bidding programme'. On the other hand, Meta provides online display advertising services and, through its

396. 'Facebook Claims EU Antitrust Questions Go Beyond Scope of Probe', Competition Policy International 27 July 2020.
397. EU General Court Cases T-452/20 and T-451/20 (Facebook Ireland/Commission).
398. 'Facebook gains temporary court reprieve on EU antitrust data demand', Reuters 28 July 2020.
399. European Commission, press release of 19 December 2022, *Antitrust: Commission sends Statement of Objections to Meta over abusive practices benefiting Facebook Marketplace*, https://ec.europa.eu/commission/presscorner/detail/en/ip_22_7728.
400. European Commission, Case AT.40684 (Anticompetitive conduct Facebook). For the press release of the Commission, please refer to: https://ec.europa.eu/commission/presscorner/detail/en/ip_21_2848.
401. https://www.reuters.com/technology/eu-questions-microsoft-rivals-over-teams-integration-office-2021-10-08/.
402. European Commission, 'Press Release – Antitrust: Commission opens investigation into possible anticompetitive conduct by Google and Meta, in online display advertising' (2022) Press Release p. 1.

'Meta Audience Network', participates in auctions for third-party publishers' advertising space using the advertising technology services of Google and rivals.[403] Verstager stated that via this 'Jedi Blue' agreement:

> *a competing technology to Google's Open Bidding may have been targeted with the aim to weaken it and exclude it from the market for displaying ads on publisher websites and apps. If confirmed by our investigation, this would restrict and distort competition in the already concentrated ad tech market, to the detriment of rival ad serving technologies, publishers and ultimately consumers.*[404]

The Commission investigated whether this agreement is part of efforts to exclude ad tech services that compete with Google's Open Bidding Programme. The Commission started an in-depth investigation with priority. However, by press release of 19 December 2022, the Commission announced that it had terminated its investigation.[405] It is worthwhile mentioning that the CMA has initiated a parallel investigation of the Jedi Blue agreement.[406]

§4.03 MERGER CONTROL[407]

In the digital economy sector, the question of whether a concentration may restrict unhindered access to big data concerning users is increasingly relevant in the assessment of concentrations. This was one of the central questions in the analysis of the Commission's assessment of the acquisition of WhatsApp by Facebook (now Meta),[408]

---

403. Antitrust: Commission opens investigation into (europa.eu).
404. *Ibid.*
405. European Commission, press release of 19 December 2022 in case AT.40774 – Google-Meta (Open Bidding) agreement, https://ec.europa.eu/competition/antitrust/cases1/202302/AT_40774_8845087_898_3.pdf.
406. Competition and Market Authority, 'Press Release: CMA Investigates Google and Meta over Ad Tech Concerns' (11 March 2022, *GOV.UK*) https://www.gov.uk/government/news/cma-investigates-google-and-meta-over-ad-tech-concerns; *see also*: Pietro Lombardi, 'EU, UK Open Antitrust Probes into Google, Meta Ad-Services Agreement' (11 March 2022, *Politico*) https://www.politico.eu/article/eu-opens-antitrust-probe-into-google-meta-agreement/.
407. For an overview from the perspective of merger control of the European Commission's decision-making practice on digital competition that goes back further in time, *see*, e.g., Eleonora Ocello and Cristina Sjödin, 'Digital Markets in EU Merger Control: Key Features and Implications' (2018) 9 Competition Policy International. During the investigation period, the Commission reviewed the acquisition of Yahoo by Verizon (Case M.8180 (Verizon/Yahoo) (European Commission)). We will not go into a discussion of the substance of this case here, since the Commission devoted few substantive reflections to the concentration on account of low the combined market shares of the parties and in view of the very small addition of market share. We also refrain from discussing cases affecting the telecommunications and banking industries, which include at least the following concentrations: the creation of a business mobile transaction platform in the United Kingdom by Everything Everywhere, Telefónica UK and Vodafone (Case No. COMP/M.6314, Telefónica UK/Vodafone UK/Everything Everywhere/JV) (European Commission); the creation of a mobile payment platform in Belgium by BNP Paribas Fortis and Belgacom (Case No. COMP/M.6967, BNP Paribas Fortis/Belgacom/Belgian Mobile Wallet) (European Commission); and the creation of a payment platform in Lithuania by Bite, Tele2 and Telia Lietuvia (Case No. COMP/M.6967, BNP Paribas Fortis/Belgacom/Belgian Mobile Wallet).
408. Case No. COMP/M.7217 (Facebook/WhatsApp) (*supra* n. 291).

the acquisitions of LinkedIn and Github by Microsoft[409] and the acquisition of Shazam by Apple.[410] In these cases, the Commission concluded that these acquisitions would not give rise to competition concerns as – in short – sufficient access to valuable data would remain available to third parties after the proposed acquisition. In the latter case, this conclusion was also founded on behavioural remedies offered by the merging parties. Earlier, the Commission came to a similar conclusion in its decision on the acquisition of DoubleClick by Google.[411] The Commission also reviewed, *inter alia*, (i) Operating Systems (OSs) and email and calendar communication protocols in the context of the acquisition of Nokia by Microsoft and the acquisition of Beats by Apple; (ii) price comparison websites in the context of the acquisition of Momondo by the Priceline Group; (iii) the market for gaming applications in the context of the acquisition of King by Activision Blizzard; and (iv) software development platforms and applications for software development in the context of Microsoft's acquisition of Github.

[A] Microsoft/Nokia

Microsoft's acquisition of Nokia's mobile telephony business in 2013, involved only minimal horizontal overlap in the field of mobile devices, as a result of which the Commission's decision focuses mainly on vertical relationships between the parties.[412] Microsoft supplies mobile OSs and holds patents in the field of communication protocols for mobile telephone services, which (can be or) are installed on the mobile devices manufactured by Nokia. The Commission reviewed Microsoft's activities in OSs, mobile applications and relevant patents. The Commission considered that it is unlikely that Microsoft would exclude third-party mobile device operators from Windows OS because Microsoft's market share in mobile OS is limited and Microsoft needs these third parties to compete with Android and Apple OS. The Commission also considered it unlikely that Microsoft would restrict the provision of its mobile applications such as Skype and Microsoft Office to third-party mobile device providers because among other factors there are sufficient alternatives for these applications and Microsoft Office applications were not available outside Windows OS in any case. Consequently, any foreclosure strategy would have no effect on mobile devices using Android or Apple OS. Finally, the Commission concluded that Microsoft's patented communication protocols for synchronisation of e-mail, calendar and contact information with Microsoft systems are not likely to have foreclosure effects, in particular since the main mobile device suppliers are licensed for these communication protocols.

409. Case M.8124 (Microsoft/LinkedIn) (*supra* n. 291) and Case M.8994 (Microsoft/Github) (*supra* n. 291).
410. Case No. COMP/M.8788 (Apple/Shazam) (*supra* n. 291).
411. Case No. COMP/M.4731 (Google/DoubleClick) (European Commission) [364 et seq.].
412. Case No. COMP/M.7047 (Microsoft/Nokia) (*supra* n. 291).

[B] Facebook/WhatsApp

The acquisition of WhatsApp by Facebook in 2014 gave rise to controversy a few years after the Commission gave its approval. In the clearance decision, the Commission first concluded that Facebook Messenger and WhatsApp are not close competitors and that consumers can choose from a wide range of alternative communication apps.[413] Moreover, most consumers use more than one app. Furthermore, the Commission considered that WhatsApp could not (yet) be considered a social network so that there would be no horizontal overlap of the parties' activities in this area. Finally, the Commission examined whether Facebook could introduce adverts on WhatsApp and whether it could use WhatsApp user data to bring Facebook users closer to targeted adverts. The Commission concluded that, given the availability of both alternative internet advertising providers and alternative data sources, neither scenario poses a competition problem, resulting in the unconditional clearance for the transaction. The user data (big data) of Facebook and WhatsApp are thus being assessed under this merger control analysis as a means for being competitive in the market for online advertising.

As mentioned, controversy only arose a few years later. On 17 May 2017, the Commission fined Facebook EUR 110 million for providing misleading information in the context of the WhatsApp merger control notification. At the time of the notification procedure, Facebook had indicated that it would not be technically possible to link Facebook and WhatsApp accounts automatically and reliably. However, in August 2016, Facebook announced a change to its terms of use, which provided for the possibility of such an automatic linkage. The Commission subsequently launched an investigation, which supposedly demonstrated that a link was technically possible already at the time of the notification procedure. The Commission therefore concluded that it had been misled at the time. However, the sanction decision did not affect the clearance decision, since Commission's analysis had already assumed a scenario in which Facebook would link accounts and had concluded that there would remain sufficient competition left in such a scenario too.

[C] Apple/Beats

On 24 July 2014, the Commission unconditionally approved the acquisition of Beats Electronics, a producer of headphones and audio speakers, and Beats Music, an online music streaming provider, by Apple.[414] The Commission considers Beats Music, that was only active in Australia and the United States at the time of the decision, a potential competitor of Apple in Europe. According to the Commission, two conditions must be met for a merger with a potential competitor to give rise to anticompetitive effects.[415]

413. Case No. COMP/M.7217 (Facebook/WhatsApp) (*supra* n. 291).
414. Case No. COMP/M.7290 (Apple/Beats) (European Commission, Decision 25 July 2014).
415. *Ibid.*, para. 35.

First, the potential competitor must exert or become a significant constraining influence. Second, there must be a lack of other potential competitors. The Commission noted the first condition was not met because there were stronger competitors than Beats Music such as Deezer and Spotify, the entry of Beats Music in Europe was not imminent, and Beats Music did not even have a significant constraining influence on Apple in its home market the United States. Also, the second condition was not met according to the Commission, because there were other potential competitors, such as Pandora. The Commission also assessed whether the transaction would give Apple the incentive to use the iOS platform to discriminate against competing music streaming services: '*Apple could potentially use its operating system to disadvantage streaming services that compete with Beats Music or iTunes. For instance, it could reduce the interoperability between iOS and the apps of competitors, withhold important information about iOS to developers of these apps or delay the approval of apps.*'[416] The Commission, however, did not consider it plausible that Apple would employ such a strategy, as Apple would not have sufficient market power to do so with a market share of its iOS of 20%-30% in Western Europe and 10%-20% worldwide. In addition, the merger would not change Apple's ability and incentive to discriminate against its competitors.[417] Consequently, the Commission decided to issue an unconditional phase I clearance.

[D] Activision Blizzard/King

In its assessment of the acquisition of King by Activision Blizzard in 2016, both publishers of games for PC, consoles and mobile devices, the Commission concluded that there are different product markets for the publishing of games for PCs, consoles and mobile devices. However, the Commission does not consider a distinction between games running under the different OSs available per category of mobile device to be justified.[418] Although King is a relatively large player in mobile games (10%-20% in the EEA) as is the case for Activision in PC and console games (10%-20% in the EEA and 20%-30% in the UK), the overlap in the parties' activities is limited. Moreover, there are sufficient alternatives, and the Commission's market investigation confirms that Activision and King are not close competitors. In addition, it is easy to enter the mobile games market, and consumers in the mobile games market can choose from an unlimited range of free available games on various online platforms such as Google Play and the App Store. In view of the above, it is not surprising that the Commission gave its unconditional approval in the first phase.

416. *Ibid.*, para. 43.
417. *Ibid.*, para. 44.
418. Case M.7866 (Activision Blizzard/King) (*supra* n. 291).

[E] Microsoft/LinkedIn

In 2016, in the Microsoft/LinkedIn case, the Commission examined whether Microsoft would be able to use its dominant position in the operating system market to install the LinkedIn business-oriented social networking site on all Windows PCs by default.[419] This could discourage consumers from installing a competing platform themselves, which could hinder the entry of competitors of LinkedIn. The Commission further examined whether Microsoft and LinkedIn could, to the extent permitted under data protection law, bundle their user databases and thereby gain a decisive (big) data lead over the customer relationship management (CRM) software competition. In the end, the Commission did not find this plausible, as competitors would retain sufficient access to alternative data sources. The Commission also examined whether Microsoft might be able to restrict Windows' interoperability (the ability for systems to 'cooperate') with LinkedIn's competitors. In the area of software for managing customer relations and online advertising, the Commission saw no objections after an initial investigation. In order to address the Commission's remaining concerns, Microsoft offered the Commission three behavioural remedies, which the Commission accepted. In short, these are: (i) Microsoft will not oblige PC builders to instal LinkedIn on Windows PCs; (ii) Microsoft will provide competing platforms with LinkedIn with the same level of interoperability as they currently enjoy and (iii) competing developers will be provided with access to Microsoft Graph, an application that – with the user's consent – provides access to data stored in the Microsoft Cloud, which could in turn be used by networks competing with LinkedIn. The commitments were for a period of five years – a majority of respondents considered this to be a sufficiently long period – and an independent trustee would monitor compliance.[420]

[F] Priceline/Momondo

On 17 July 2017, the Commission unconditionally approved the acquisition of Momondo, an operator of two metasearch sites (MSSs), also known as price comparison websites, Cheapflights and Momondo, by the Priceline Group, a provider of online travel and related services such as MSSs (including KAYAK) and online travel agents (OTAs) (including Booking.com and Rentalcars.com).[421] The Commission concluded that there were separate product markets for MSSs and OTAs (and subsegments for flights, hotels and car rentals) and assessed the consequences of the proposed concentration on that basis.[422] Geographically, the Commission left open the question of whether global, EEA-wide or national markets should be taken into account for MSSs and OTAs, but considered the impact of the transaction on the smallest possible

419. Case M.8124 (Microsoft/LinkedIn) (*supra* n. 291).
420. *Ibid.*, para. 424.
421. Case M.8416 (Priceline/Momondo) (European Commission, Decision 17 July 2017).
422. *Ibid.*, para. 51.

geographic market (national markets).[423] The Commission concluded that the transaction would not lead to a significant impediment to effective competition because the parties were small players in the MSS market across Europe, the MSSs of the parties were largely geographically complementary and significant competitive pressure is exercised by other global metasearch operators, such as Skyscanner, Trivago, TripAdvisor and Google.[424] The case therefore cleared the transaction unconditionally in the first phase.

[G] Apple/Shazam

Apple announced its intention to acquire the music recognition app Shazam on 14 March 2018.[425] The Commission obtained the power to assess the case following a request from the competition authorities of Austria, France, Iceland, Italy, Norway, Spain and Sweden (under Article 22 of the European Merger Regulation (EUMR)) to refer the case to the Commission because of its EEA-wide dimension. In a press release dated 23 April 2018, the Commission announced that it would conduct an in-depth second-phase investigation into the effects of the proposed transaction.[426] The Commission expressed concerns about anticompetitive vertical effects resulting from the proposed bundling of Shazam's strong market position in music recognition with Apple's position in digital music streaming. Vestager said in the press release: 'The way people listen to music has changed significantly in recent years, with more and more Europeans using music streaming services. Our investigation aims to ensure that music fans will continue to enjoy attractive music streaming offers and won't face less choice as a result of this proposed merger.' The Commission was said to be concerned, according to the press release, that following the acquisition of Shazam, Apple would have access to commercially sensitive data about customers or its competitors for the purpose of providing music streaming services in the EEA. Access to such data may enable Apple to target its competitors' customers directly and encourage them to switch to Apple Music for music streaming. As a result, competing music streaming services could be put at a competitive disadvantage. In addition, Shazam is an important access point for music streaming services, and the Commission would also investigate whether competitors to Apple Music could be harmed if Apple were to cease referring to them via the Shazam app after the transaction.

Nevertheless, the Commission announced its unconditional clearance of the concentration on 6 September 2018. Commissioner Vestager commented: '*Data is key in the digital economy. We must therefore carefully review transactions which lead to the acquisition of important sets of data, including potentially commercially sensitive ones, to ensure they do not restrict competition. After thoroughly analysing Shazam's user and*

423. *Ibid.*, para. 69.
424. *Ibid.*, paras 112-115.
425. Case M.8788 (Apple/Shazam) (*supra* n. 291).
426. European Commission, 'Press Release 23 April 2018: Mergers: Commission Opens In-Depth Investigation into Apple's Proposed Acquisition of Shazam', http://europa.eu/rapid/press-release_IP-18-3505_en.htm.

music data, we found that their acquisition by Apple would not reduce competition in the digital music streaming market.' The Commission first notes that the merged entity would not be able to foreclose competing providers of digital music streaming services through its access to commercially sensitive information about their customers. In particular, access to Shazam data would not substantially enhance Apple's ability to interest music lovers in its offerings. In this respect, the Commission considers that its market investigation has confirmed Apple's contention that there are several suppliers (including Facebook, Google and Twitter) which specifically target music enthusiasts whose services Apple can also use without the acquisition of Shazam. Furthermore, competitors of Apple Music could also rely on the same third parties following the implementation of the concentration. Thus, any attempt by Apple to induce customers to switch to its own services would have only a negligible effect on competition. Furthermore, the new entity will not be able to foreclose competing providers of digital music streaming services by restricting access to the Shazam app. The Commission's investigation has shown that the app's importance as an entry point to Apple Music's competitors' music streaming services is limited. Finally, the Commission concludes that the integration of Shazam's and Apple's user data sets will not give the merged entity a unique advantage in the markets in which it will operate. All concerns in that respect were allayed, as Shazam's data are not unique and Apple's competitors would still have the ability to access and use similar databases.

[H] Microsoft/Github

On 19 October 2018, the Commission gave clearance in the first phase to Microsoft's acquisition of Github.[427] Both companies offer tools for software developers (what are known as 'DevOps tools'). These tools concern (i) software development platforms and (ii) programs for modifying source codes (code editors) and integrated applications that use a code editor and add additional functionalities to it. The Commission concluded that the horizontal effects of the concentration would not lead to a significant impediment to effective competition because there were sufficient alternative suppliers.

With respect to the vertical relationships between the parties, the Commission looked into Microsoft's ability to use the popularity of the Github platform to stimulate the sale of its own DevOps tools by (i) integrating these tools into the Github platform, (ii) limiting the interoperability of the Github platform with competing DevOps tools and (iii) limiting the integration of competing DevOps tools in the Github platform.[428] However, the Commission concluded that Microsoft would have neither the ability nor the incentive to foreclose suppliers of competing DevOps tools. The Commission based its assessment on internal Microsoft documents showing that such a foreclosure strategy would be inconsistent with the rationale of the transaction, namely improving Microsoft's reputation in the open-source community with the ultimate goal of

427. Case M.8994 (Microsoft/Github) (*supra* n. 291).
428. *Ibid.*, para. 110.

encouraging more developers to use Microsoft's cloud services (Azure). Furthermore, the market investigation showed that if Microsoft would adopt such a foreclosure strategy, Github users would switch to competing platforms such as Gitlab and Bitbucket.

Interestingly, the Commission examined the conglomerate effects of the concentration and, more specifically, whether Microsoft could further integrate its cloud services into Github and exclude alternative cloud service providers.[429] However, the Commission considered that such a foreclosure strategy would also run counter to the rationale of the transaction. In addition, Google, a competing cloud service provider, denied that Microsoft would pursue such a strategy, and Github users indicated that they would not allow Github to impose a cloud service provider on them.

Finally, the Commission took a relatively extensive look at whether Microsoft would be able to foreclose competing DevOps tool providers and competing cloud service providers by not providing them access to Github data.[430] The Commission distinguished between data already available to providers of DevOps tools and cloud services and data that were not yet available but might become available in the future. According to the Commission, access to data already available could only be restricted to a very limited extent, as this would destroy the rationale of the transaction, and moreover, the data would not give Microsoft any significant competitive advantage over its competitors. As regards future data, the Commission noted that there were no indications that Github would have started offering these data in the absence of the concentration and that the merger would therefore not change that situation. The Commission also considered it unlikely that these data would confer a competitive advantage on Microsoft and that, moreover, Github's terms of use restrict Microsoft's use of these data without its competitors having access to them at the same time.

Though there was no EU dimension to this acquisition, it was nevertheless assessed at M's request by the Commission under Article 4(5) of the Merger Regulation. On this basis, a merger without an EU dimension can be assessed by the Commission if it is capable of being reviewed under the competition laws of at least three Member States and the purchaser makes a reasoned request to the Commission to deal with the case. In this case, the merger was notifiable in Cyprus, Germany, Austria and the UK, and Microsoft made a reasoned request to the Commission to deal with the case.

[I] Broadcom/Symantec Enterprise Security Business

On 30 October 2019, the Commission unconditionally approved Broadcom's acquisition of Symantec Enterprise Security Business (SESB).[431]

Broadcom is a manufacturer of semiconductors and infrastructure software solutions. SESB provides its customers with an integrated solution for protecting

429. *Ibid.*, para. 120.
430. *Ibid.*, para. 133.
431. Case M.9538, Broadcom/Symantec Enterprise Security Business *m9538_200_3.pdf (europa.eu).

information from external threats through a combination of cloud services and online activity security. The merger was unconditionally approved after a first-phase review.

After assessing the horizontal, vertical and conglomerate relationships between the parties, the Commission concluded that the merger would not raise competition concerns. Regarding the horizontal relationships, the Commission considered that the provision of enterprise security software and IT Operations Management software (ITOM) were the only overlapping activities of the companies.[432] In doing so, the Commission reiterated that software services markets could potentially be further segmented based on the functionality and end user of the software.[433] However, according to the Commission, it was not necessary to make a final decision on the precise product market delineation, since, according to the Commission, there were no indications that the merger raised competition concerns even if the narrowest market definition was used.[434] The main reason for this conclusion was that in the market segment where the parties had the highest combined market share (ITOM and AD mainframe tools), the parties did not supply the same end users.[435] In the other market segments, the merged entity would not have enough market shares to harm competition.[436]

[J] Google/Fitbit

On 17 December 2021, the Commission conditionally approved the acquisition of Fitbit by Google after a phase II investigation.[437] Fitbit was an American consumer electronics and fitness company. Fitbit produced wireless wearable technology, fitness monitors and activity trackers such as smart watches, pedometers and heart rate monitors. Fitbit also produced technology-related software. During its investigation, the Commission found that the transaction would harm competition in the fields of (i) advertising, (ii) access to web application programming interface (API) in digital healthcare and in (iii) wrist-worn wearable devices. The Commission tested the following theories of harm, relating to potential horizontal effects, vertical effects and conglomerate effects to substantiate its concerns:

- The Commission concludes that the transaction '*does not give rise to any horizontally affected markets in a traditional sense*', but still finds that (absent remedies) the transaction's horizontal effects lead to a significant impediment of effective competition on the market for supply of online search advertising.[438] According to the Commission, the transaction '*would allow Google to*

432. Boundary number 12 of the decision.
433. Boundary number 24 of the decision.
434. Boundary number 25 of the decision.
435. Boundary number 35 of the decision.
436. Boundary number 40 of the decision.
437. Case M.9660 (Google/Fitbit) (European Commission, decision 20 December 2020).
438. *Ibid.*, paras 399 and 468.

combine its already very prominent datasets with those of Fitbit, thus strengthening the Parties' ability to supply relatively better services in certain data-based supply markets and foreclose the competitors' entry and ability to expand in such markets'.[439]

- The Commission also conclude its transaction would lead to a significant impediment to effective competition due to vertical effects. According to the Commission, Google could foreclose digital healthcare players from access to Fitbit data. Pre-transaction, Fitbit made certain health data of Fitbit's users available to third parties through its Web API. The Commission notes that a significant number of companies active in digital healthcare rely on access to this API '*in order to access the user health data they need to develop their services*'.[440] It also finds that if Google were to restrict access to the API post transaction, this '*may impact on the success of those [digital healthcare] start-ups*'.[441]
- The Commission finally tested a theory of harm relating to potential conglomerate effects, assessing '*whether Google could leverage its position in the market for licensable OSs for smart mobile devices to the market for wrist-worn wearables*'.[442] According to the Commission, Google could apply a 'tying' strategy, whereby Google would not allow competing wrist-worn wearable suppliers the same degree of interoperability with the Android Operating System (OS) as it would allow the Fitbit wearables. Google could do this by degrading the APIs that enable Android OS to interact with the wrist-worn wearables of third-party suppliers. The Commission concludes that such a degradation strategy could lead to a reduction of the ability of rival producers to compete and could therefore have a significant detrimental effect on effective competition.[443]

To address the Commission's concerns, Google's final remedies package consisted of three commitments: (i) an ads commitment, (ii) a web API commitment and (iii) an Android API commitment.

- Under the ads commitment, Google shall not use the health and wellness data collected from Fitbit devices for its ads business. Interestingly, some respondents claimed that Google could still benefit from the Fitbit data, because of the risk of so-called *algorithm contamination*. This means that the algorithms that are allowed access to the sealed-off data could contaminate the algorithms used for Google's ads business. Algorithm contamination refers to the potential contamination of algorithms used for advertising purposes with insights gained by (non-advertising) algorithms that are allowed to access the protected data and trained using such protected data. This would be an indirect effect of the use of Fitbit users' data on the quality of Google's advertising

439. *Ibid.*, para. 402.
440. *Ibid.*, para. 527.
441. *Ibid.*, para. 528.
442. *Ibid.*, para. 717.
443. *Ibid.*, para. 816.

offers. The Commission however considered that the potential impact of algorithmic contamination would be extremely limited.[444] The Commission considered that the *Ads Commitment*[445] prevents the use of Fitbit users' health and fitness data.

- Under the web API commitment, Google shall give free access to users' data (subject to user consent) to software of third-party developers through the Fitbit web API.
- Under the Android API commitment, Google shall ensure that equipment manufacturers shall have free access to the Android APIs that are needed to ensure interoperability with an Android smartphone.

The commitments apply for a period of ten years and, for the ads commitment, the Commission may extend this period for another ten years. A monitoring trustee shall supervise Google's compliance with the commitments.

The Commission decided to conditionally approve the transaction, as it believes that the commitments would remove all competition concerns.

[K] Meta/Kustomer

On 12 May 2021, the Commission accepted a request from Austria, Belgium, Bulgaria, France, Iceland, Italy, Ireland, the Netherlands, Portugal and Romania to refer the proposed acquisition of Kustomer by Meta (then Facebook) to the Commission. On 27 January 2022, the Commission conditionally approved this proposed acquisition. This decision followed a second-phase investigation that was initiated on 2 August 2021. Kustomer is an innovative and fast-growing software company, offering, among other services, customer services as well as support CRM. Prior to the transaction, a vertical relationship existed between Meta and Kustomer: Meta's services, including WhatsApp and Facebook, constituted important channels for connection between customer support services and their customers. In particular, the Commission examined whether Kustomer's competitors could be disadvantaged by Meta. The Commission was concerned that the transaction could potentially restrict competition in the markets for the provision of (i) CRM software and (ii) customer service and support CRM software. The Commission found that Meta could (absent remedies) pursue a market foreclosure strategy against existing and new competitors in these markets.

To address the concerns identified by the Commission, Meta has offered two ten-year access commitments: (i) non-discriminatory access to its application programming interfaces (APIs) and (ii) access to future enhanced Messenger, Instagram messaging and WhatsApp functionalities to be used by Kustomer's competitors. A trustee will monitor compliance with these commitments. The Commission concludes that these commitments will not lead to a significant restriction of competition. Also in the market for online display advertising services – a market in which the Commission

444. *Ibid.*, para. 972.

445. It follows from para. 896 that the Ads Commitment means, among other things, that measured body data or health and fitness activities will not be used for advertising purposes.

also saw concerns[446] – after the second-phase investigation, the Commission does not foresee a restriction of competition, as the additional data that Meta may obtain would not result in a significant negative impact on competition. On these grounds, the Commission approves the concentration.

[L] Booking.com/eTraveli

On 10 October 2022, Booking.com notified to the Commission its intention to acquire control of eTraveli.[447] Booking and eTraveli are both active in the provision of OTA services, respectively focusing on accommodation OTA and flight OTA services. Booking is also active in the market of metasearch services (MSS) mainly through its price comparison platform KAYAK.

On 16 November 2022, the Commission decided to initiate a Phase II investigation into the acquisition. According to a press release issued on that day, the investigation in Phase I had provided indication that Booking may hold a dominant position in the market for the provision of accommodation OTA services and that the transaction may significantly reduce competition in this market by combining eTraveli's activities in flight OTA services with Booking's own portfolio of services.

The Commission that the transaction may lead to an increase in barriers to entry and expansion for rival OTAs. In particular, the transaction may limit competitors' ability to acquire new customers. The Commission also expressed concerns that the transaction may reinforce network effects by strengthening barriers to entry. This, in turn, could reduce competition in the market for the provision of OTA services and would raise costs for hotels and other accommodation providers as well as higher prices for end customers.

Moreover, the Commission concluded that Booking may have the ability, as well as a potential economic incentive, to engage in foreclosure strategies vis-à-vis Booking's rival flight OTAs, such as degrading their visibility on its price comparison platform KAYAK and preventing these companies from attracting customers to their services. This could reduce competition in the markets for accommodation OTA services as the sale of flight OTA services may be an important channel to acquire customers.[448]

No phase II decision has been issued yet (situation May 2023).

§4.04 INTERMEDIATE CONCLUSION

The rich harvest of enforcement precedents, policy documents and sector investigations shows that the Commission is serious about being a European forerunner in the

446. The Commission was concerned that Facebook's position in this market would be further strengthened by increasing even further the already very significant amount of data that Facebook possesses.
447. Case M.10615.
448. European Commission, press release of 16 November 2022: IP/22/6578, https://ec.europa.eu/commission/presscorner/detail/en/ip_22_6578.

field of digital competition. The Commission is not only actively investigating the functioning of digital markets but also shows no hesitation in intervening (and intervening hard) when it believes that these markets are distorted.

If we look more closely at the Commission's enforcement action, it is noteworthy that the Commission does not shy away from applying the prohibition of abuse of a dominant position in its enforcement policy. It has imposed three fines under this prohibition and is or was investigating various other cases against Google, Meta, Apple and (possibly) Microsoft. A cartel fine was issued 'only' twice more frequently (i.e., on five undertakings in total). This is noteworthy since the cartel prohibition is applied considerably more frequently in the 'classic' offline competition world than the prohibition on abuse of a dominant position. The former implies that the prohibition on abuse of dominance appears could be a more important enforcement tool in the online world than in the offline world. Moreover, the fines imposed under the prohibition of abuse of a dominant position are considerably more substantial (because the dominant companies involved - and certainly Amazon and Google - have a high relevant turnover, which in general leads to a fine that is high in absolute terms). However, perhaps this observation is more logical than it appears at first sight. The Commission may consider - or at least it does not rule out - that unless there are hardcore cartel agreements (as the Commission has actually imposed fines in the resale price maintenance cases), impediments to competition in rapidly changing, innovative markets often resolve themselves through the rapid innovation process. However, as the Commission has stated (*see* the introduction to this Chapter (4) on the Commission), conduct that is not tolerated offline is usually not tolerated online either.[449] In this sense, it is also perfectly logical that the fining decisions in which the Commission applied the cartel prohibition were classic resale price maintenance agreements and, in the *Guess, Video Games, NBCUniversal, Paytv-broadcasters, Nike and Media Holiday* cases, also geoblocking agreements.

With regard to the eleven abuse cases dealt with by the Commission, it is of course also noteworthy that six of these concern the same company, namely Google. As mentioned, Google may also be confronted with three more decisions. However, it is, at least theoretically, possible that the Commission will conclude that there is insufficient evidence for an infringement in all of these cases. Being as it may, this recalls events of a decade ago when the Commission issued enforcement decisions to Microsoft and/or accepted Microsoft's commitments in no less than five different cases.[450] This may be a double warning to other tech giants: once you have entered the Commission's 'net', it may be difficult to escape additional blows from the Commission.

In merger cases too, the Commission has grown more and more interventionist over time. During the investigation period, it required remedies in three merger cases:

449. 'Algorithms and Collusion - Note from the European Union' (*supra* n. 285), para. 38.
450. Case COMP/C-3/37792 (Microsoft) (European Commission) 79; Case COMP/C-3/37924 (Microsoft/UPC) (European Commission); Case COMP/C-3/37925 (Microsoft/NTL) (European Commission); Case COMP/C-3/39294 (ECIS/Microsoft) (European Court of Justice); Case COMP/C-3/39530 (Microsoft (tying)) (European Commission).

in phase I in *Microsoft/LinkedIn*, and in phase II in *Google/Fitbit* and *Meta/Kustomer*. The *Meta/Kustomer* case is of particular relevance since this case marked the first occasion on which the Commission accepted an Article 22 referral for a case in the digital sector that did not meet the national thresholds in the referring EU Member States. In *Apple/Shazam*, the investigation resulted in a second phase as well, but in the end, the Commission cleared that concentration unconditionally. It is interesting that the Commission expressly devotes more attention to conglomerate effects in its more recent cases *Apple/Shazam, Microsoft/Github*, *Google/Fitbit* and *Broadcom/Enterprise Security Business*. *Facebook/WhatsApp* was a case of its own: Facebook was fined for misleading the Commission about the technical possibilities of linking Facebook accounts with WhatsApp accounts. This case underlines a major challenge for competition authorities: how to avoid a (technical) knowledge gap compared to the companies involved? The Commission appears to have run into this 'trap' in *Facebook/WhatsApp* since it only discovered that it had been misinformed after it had already approved the concentration. No doubt the Commission will be very keen to have all the relevant facts correctly presented in future cases before it takes a merger decision. This will undoubtedly lead the Commission to issue more and more extensive requests for information in future merger cases in the digital sector. This trend is already clearly visible in the current legal practice.

CHAPTER 5

UK: Competition and Markets Authority

> *'I have suggested earlier that the competition tools at our disposal can tackle the competition issues that we face in the new digital world, but perhaps this last issue which I have touched on is one where this proposition is not true.'*[451]

The Competition and Markets Authority (CMA) indicates that it is giving high priority to digital markets, among other actions, by establishing the Digital Markets Unit (DMU) within the CMA.[452] In recent years, the CMA has, among other activities, investigated various possible forms of anticompetitive behaviour by online platforms (in particular with regard to the application of parity clauses), which has led to a commitment decision under the cartel prohibition and an investigation that has since been discontinued (*Hotel Online Booking*).[453] As a result, twenty-five online hotel booking companies, including major brands such as TripAdvisor, Airbnb and Google, as well as major hotel chains, have agreed to change the way they display information where necessary and have endorsed the CMA's industry-wide principles for compliance with consumer protection laws.[454] These principles include not giving a false impression of a room's popularity and always displaying the full cost of a room upfront. Furthermore, the CMA fined a cartel that used an algorithm to implement price-fixing (*Online Sales of Posters and Frames*),[455] fined Ping for imposing a total ban on its resellers in respect

451. David Currie, 'Speech at the Concurrences Innovation Economics Conference, King's College London: David Currie on the Role of Competition in Stimulating Innovation'. With "*this last issue*" Currie was referring to algorithmic collusion.
452. https://www.gov.uk/government/collections/digital-markets-unit.
453. *OFT1514dec: Hotel Online Booking: Decision to Accept Commitments to Remove Certain Discounting Restrictions for Online Travel Agents* (Office of Fair Trading); *CE/9692/12: Amazon Online Retailer: Investigation into Anti-competitive Practices* (Office of Fair Trading). For an overview of this study, *see* the website of the CMA (https://www.gov.uk/cma-cases/amazon-online-retailer-investigation-into-anti-competitive-practices).
454. https://www.gov.uk/government/news/major-overhaul-of-hotel-booking-sector-after-cma-action (13 September 2019).
455. *Case 50223: Online Sales of Posters and Frames* (Competition and Markets Authority).

of online sales of golf clubs[456] and twice accepted commitments terminating possible abuses of a dominant position (*ATG Media*, an auction house site,[457] and *epyx*, a platform for maintenance of vehicles[458]). In addition, the CMA imposed fines in 2020 in the musical instruments and equipment sector for resale price maintenance (RPM).[459]

In a case against Google, relating to the use of 'Privacy Sandbox' browser settings, a number of binding commitments were agreed upon with Google to address competition concerns.[460] Currently, an investigation into Meta's data usage in the advertising market, where the CMA suspects an abuse of a dominant position, is ongoing, and the CMA is also investigating whether Apple's terms and conditions to the App store restrict access for app developers.[461] The CMA has also launched an investigation into agreements between Google and Meta. The investigation concerns an agreement between Google and Meta in relation to Meta's use of Google's header-bidding product. This investigation was however integrated into an ongoing stand-alone investigation into Google's ad tech policy on 10 March 2023.[462]

In the period under investigation, the CMA also dealt with twenty-five relevant merger cases (by far the most of all the authorities under review), including thirteen second-phase cases. Three concentrations were prohibited.

By means of speeches at conferences, press releases, market research and online tools, the CMA also tries to provide guidance to market parties on how they should behave and by doing so deal with digital competition.

The speeches and press releases of the CMA provide an interesting insight into the CMA's digital competition policy and its vision for the enforcement of competition law in the digital economy. It is noteworthy that David Currie, chairman of the CMA until 19 June 2018, had reverted from the position previously taken by the CMA that the competition instruments of the CMA are sufficient to curb collusion between algorithms.[463] Currie indicates that particularly in cases where self-learning algorithms

456. *Case 50230: Ping* (Competition and Markets Authority).
457. *Case 50408: Auction Services* (Competition and Markets Authority).
458. *Case CE/9496-11: Epyx Limited and FleetCor Technologies* (Competition and Markets Authority).
459. *Case 50565-2: Online resale price maintenance in the digital piano and digital keyboard sector*, https://assets.publishing.service.gov.uk/media/5d9c539aed915d399eb2160b/non_conf_decision_arrow.pdf, para. 4.13.
460. *Case 50972: Google Privacy Sandbox* (Competition and Markers Authority).
461. *Meta's use of Data* (Competition and Markets Authority), see: https://www.gov.uk/cma-cases/investigation-into-facebooks-use-of-data.
462. *Case 51134, Suspected anti-competitive agreement between Google and Meta* (Competition and Markets Authority), https://www.gov.uk/cma-cases/investigation-into-suspected-anti-competitive-agreement-between-google-and-meta-and-behaviour-by-google-in-relation-to-header-bidding, *Case 51145, Investigation into suspected anti-competitive conduct by Google in ad tech* (Competition and Markets Authority), https://www.gov.uk/cma-cases/investigation-into-suspected-anti-competitive-conduct-by-google-in-ad-tech
463. 'UK Competition and Markets Authority Response to the European Commission's Consultation on the Regulatory Environment for Platforms, Online Intermediaries, Data and Cloud Computing and the Collaborative Economy' (Competition and Markets Authority 2015) 6; 'CMA Response to the Call for Evidence: Online Platforms and the EU Digital Single Market' (Competition and Markets Authority 2015) 12.

violate competition law without targeted human intervention, the current array of instruments may not be sufficient.[464]

The CMA has published several market investigations, including surveys on the consumer market for motor insurance and the role of price parity clauses in that market,[465] digital comparison tools (DCTs)[466] and the commercial use of consumer data, which are briefly summarised below.[467] These market investigations may prompt investigations into concrete presumptions of competition law infringements. In addition, to provide guidance, the CMA has also published a one-page document that provides online sellers with practical information on (prohibited) price agreements.[468] This document described the concept of price-fixing, guidance for online sellers and the most important do's and don'ts regarding online sales. For example, the CMA prescribes (i) not to agree with competitors not to undercut each other, (ii) not to agree on the prices at which products are sold, (iii) not to discuss pricing strategies with competitors, (iv) to make staff aware of what is and is not allowed and (v) to seek independent legal advice to ensure compliance with the law.[469]

Furthermore, on 26 September 2017, the CMA also published its market investigation on DCTs, which focuses on how these tools work for consumers, businesses and the economy.[470] The CMA notes that these tools make it easier for consumers to shop around and also lead to suppliers competing more strongly on price and quality. The CMA does, however, indicate that the CMA, industry, regulators and government must ensure that the benefits of DCTs are secured for non-users and the vulnerable in society.[471] The CMA also points out that certain agreements, in particular parity clauses, between DCTs and suppliers may have restrictive effects on competition.[472]

464. David Currie, 'Speech at the Concurrences Innovation Economics Conference, King's College London: David Currie on the Role of Competition in Stimulating Innovation': '*But machine learning means that the algorithms may themselves learn that co-ordination is the best way to maximise longer-term business objectives. In that case, no human agent has planned the co-ordination. Does that represent a breach of competition law? Does the law stretch to cover sins of omission as well as sins of commission: the failure to build in sufficient constraints on algorithmic behaviour to ensure that the algorithm does not learn to adopt anticompetitive outcomes? And what if constraints are built in but they are inadequately designed, so that the very clever algorithm learns a way through the constraints? How far can the concept of human agency be stretched to cover these sorts of issues? I have suggested earlier that the competition tools at our disposal can tackle the competition issues that we face in the new digital world, but perhaps this last issue which I have touched on is one where this proposition is not true.*'
465. 'Private Motor Insurance Market Investigation, Final Report' (Competition and Markets Authority 2014).
466. 'Digital Comparison Tools Market Study – Final Report' (Competition and Markets Authority 2017).
467. 'The Commercial Use of Consumer Data: Report on the CMA's Call for Information' (Competition and Markets Authority 2015).
468. '60 Seconds Summary – Price-Fixing: Guidance for Online Sellers' (Competition and Markets Authority 2016).
469. https://www.gov.uk/government/publications/price-fixing-guidance-for-online-sellers/price-fixing-guidance-for-online-sellers.
470. 'Digital Comparison Tools Market Study – Final Report', *supra* n. 466.
471. *Ibid.*, 41.
472. *Ibid.*, 8.

The CMA concludes that DCTs should treat consumers fairly by being '*Clear, Accurate, Responsible and Easy to use*'.[473]

On 14 December 2021, the CMA published an elaborate market study on mobile ecosystems (the combination of mobile devices, mobile operating systems and applications ('apps').[474] The CMA concludes that for mobile ecosystems, there exists a duopoly of Apple and Google with other ecosystems holding only marginal market shares in the UK. This duopoly may, according to the CMA in the study, lead to a number of competition concerns:

- competition concerns in the supply of mobile devices and operating systems;
- competition concerns for the distribution of mobile apps;
- competition concerns regarding the supply of mobile browsers and browser engines;
- competition concerns regarding the role of Apple and Google in competition between app developers.

Where the CMA considers that there is a case for a more detailed examination of a market (or markets), it may refer to the market(s) for an in-depth market investigation. In the case of this study, the CMA has however refrained from doing so, as the CMA believes that the DMU should be best placed to tackle the competition concerns identified by this market study.

On 14 July 2022, the CMA and Ofcom (the UK's communications regulator) published a joint statement on online safety and competition.[475] In this statement, both authorities speak out their intent to coordinate their policies regarding this topic:

- First, the CMA and Ofcom will look for opportunities to realise synergies between the two regimes, where interventions in one policy area will promote better outcomes in the other.
- Second, the CMA and Ofcom will coordinate in those instances where interventions in one policy area can have negative implications for the other. In particular, it will be important for both authorities to coordinate to ensure that interventions to promote competition in digital markets do not undermine the safety of users on the largest platforms.
- Third, the CMA and Ofcom will work together to consider interactions between online safety and competition as the CMA addresses the issues identified in its aforementioned mobile ecosystems market study (the new pro-competition regime will be best suited to addressing many of these issues).
- Finally, both authorities will coordinate with the Information Commissioner's Office (ICO) and Financial Conduct Authority (FCA) to take account of the

473. *Ibid.*, 71.
474. CMA, *Mobile ecosystems Market study interim report*, 14 December 2021, https://assets.publishing.service.gov.uk/government/uploads/system/uploads/attachment_data/file/1048746/MobileEcosystems_InterimReport.pdf.
475. CMA and Ofcom, *Online safety and competition in digital markets: a joint statement between the CMA and Ofcom*, 14 July 2022.

complementary roles of online safety regulation, the enforcement of consumer protection law and data privacy regulation.

On 1 July 2020, the CMA published the final report of its *Market study into online platforms and the digital advertising market in the UK*.[476] In it, the CMA found that competition in these markets is not functioning properly, leading to significant harm to consumers and society as a whole. The CMA therefore recommended that the UK government adopt new legislation for the aforementioned new '*pro-competition regulatory regime*', overseen by a DMU.[477] The UK government went along with this and in July 2021, it published a proposal for a *New regulatory regime for digital markets*.[478]

Andrea Coscelli, then chief executive of the CMA, wrote the following about the UK's proposed new approach: '*The competition law inheritance of the UK regime is reflected in its proposed aim: to promote competition in digital markets for the benefit of consumers. In contrast, the European Commission's proposed Digital Markets Act (DMA) seeks to promote "fairness and contestability" and is explicitly separate from competition law.*'

The regime proposed by the CMA would only apply to the most powerful digital companies, namely those with '*strategic market status*' (SMS) in a given activity. For these companies, the regime has three main pillars:

(1) an enforceable *code of conduct* aimed at preventing companies from abusing their dominant position, for example by exploiting consumers and companies that rely on them or excluding competitors. The principles of the code are based on fair trade, open choices, trust and transparency;
(2) *pro-competitive interventions* (PCIs) – such as giving consumers more control over their data, or requiring third parties to access their data – these *remedies aim to address* the fundaments of the firm's dominance; and
(3) a *merger regime* for SMS companies to ensure that transactions involving SMS companies are more closely scrutinised. The regime involves prior notification of all transactions, mandatory notification of a subset of transactions that meet clearly defined thresholds and have a UK link, and a more cautious standard of proof.

The envisaged regime will be overseen by the new DMU, which was set up in a shadow version within the CMA in April 2021 to begin preparations for the regime, with the expectation that the DMU, and the scheme, will obtain a legal basis in the future.

476. https://www.gov.uk/cma-cases/online-platforms-and-digital-advertising-market-study#full-publication-update-history; https://app.parr-global.com/cases/view/1917528.
477. https://www.gov.uk/cma-cases/online-platforms-and-digital-advertising-market-study#full-publication-update-history.
478. CMA, *A new pro-competition regime for digital markets*, consultation outcome 20 July 2021 (last updated 6 May 2022), https://www.gov.uk/government/consultations/a-new-pro-competition-regime-for-digital-markets.

§5.01 CARTEL PROHIBITION

[A] Parity Clauses: Online Hotel Booking Sector

In September 2010, the Office of Fair Trading (OFT), the legal predecessor of the CMA, started an investigation into alleged (vertical) anticompetitive behaviour in the online hotel booking sector. Skoosh.com, an online discount booking company, complained to the OFT and claimed that bigger rivals were putting pressure on hotel operators to stop doing business with smaller online companies that sell their rooms at lower prices. This investigation led to a Statement of Objections being sent to Booking.com, Expedia and InterContinental Hotels Group plc (IHG) in July 2012, because of agreements between IHG on the one hand and Booking.com and Expedia (both separately) on the other hand, which supposedly limited online travel agencies' ability to give out discounts in the booking of hotel rooms reserved separately (without, e.g., flights or car rental). The OFT closed this investigation in January 2014 following a commitment decision addressing the OFT's competition concerns.[479] The commitments accepted by the OFT on 31 January 2014 can be summarised as follows:[480]

- Online Travel Agents (OTAs, hotel booking sites) have the right to offer discounts (out of their own margin) on the room rate set by the hotel concerned to members of a 'closed group' (e.g., members of a loyalty program);
- hotels may offer discounts to members of such a 'closed group' under similar conditions;
- OTAs may announce that they grant such discounts, but in such a way that the amount and method of calculating the discount are not transparent to non-members of a 'closed group' that can claim the discount.

The commitments were in force for a period of two years. (Broad) parity clauses were not officially the subject of the CMA's investigation,[481] but Booking.com and Expedia decided to remove these 'broad' parity clauses from their agreements following the investigations of various EU competition authorities as discussed above.[482]

The Competition Appeal Tribunal (CAT) subsequently annulled the commitment decision regarding the online hotel booking sector at the request of comparison site Skyscanner and of Skoosh International (which had intervened as a third party) on the ground that, in the CAT's view, the CMA had not sufficiently addressed the concerns

479. *OFT1514dec: Hotel Online Booking: Decision to Accept Commitments to Remove Certain Discounting Restrictions for Online Travel Agents*, *supra* n. 453.
480. *Ibid.*, paras 6.1 et seq.
481. *Ibid.*, para. 1.10.
482. However, the CMA does not seem to have any objections to narrow parity clauses, *see* for example 'Private Motor Insurance Market Investigation, Final Report', *supra* n. 465, paras 8.116 et seq.

of market participants regarding the commitments following rounds of consultations and had not sufficiently investigated the negative effects on competition. On the basis of this judgment, the CMA was obliged to reconsider the commitment decision.[483] The CMA eventually decided to no longer give priority to the case following its review on 16 September 2015 – after Booking.com and Expedia had amended their policies within the European Union as of 1 July and 1 August 2015 respectively[484] – such on the basis of altered market conditions.[485]

However, the CMA's pursuit of hotel booking sites did not end there. On 28 June 2018, the CMA issued a press release stating that it had initiated enforcement action against 'a number of' (unnamed) hotel booking sites as a result of a new investigation initiated on 27 October 2017.[486] As a consequence of this investigation, six online hotel booking sites have provided formal commitments to change practices on their websites due to serious concerns relating to among others pressure selling, misleading discount claims, ranking, and hidden charges[487] and the CMA has published a set of principles that aim to help online hotel booking sites to change their practices to conform with consumer law.[488] However, this investigation did not concern a competition law investigation, but an investigation under consumer protection legislation. For this reason, we will not discuss this investigation any further here. During the period under review, the CMA also undertook enforcement action under consumer law in one other case, which we will not discuss in detail here either for the aforementioned reason.[489]

[B] Parity Clauses: Amazon

On 1 November 2013, the OFT closed an investigation into Amazon, after Amazon announced a change in its policy on price parity for its website Amazon.co.uk and other websites within the European Union.[490] In October 2012, the CMA opened an

483. *Skyscanner Ltd v. CMA* [2014] CAT 16 (Competition Appeal Tribunal) para. 174.
484. *Hotel Online Booking Investigation Case Closure Summary* (Competition and Markets Authority) [5].
485. *Ibid.*, para. 7.
486. Competition and Markets Authority, 'Press Release 28 June 2018: CMA Launches Enforcement Action Against Hotel Booking Sites', https://www.gov.uk/government/news/cma-launches-enforcement-action-against-hotel-booking-sites.
487. Competition and Markets Authority, 'Press Release 6 February 2019: Hotel booking sites to make major changes after CMA probe', https://www.gov.uk/government/news/hotel-booking-sites-to-make-major-changes-after-cma-probe.
488. 'Consumer protection law compliance: Principles for businesses offering online accommodation booking services', https://assets.publishing.service.gov.uk/government/uploads/system/uploads/attachment_data/file/781624/webteam_online_booking_services_principles.pdf. Twenty-five firms have signed up to the CMA's principles for complying with consumer protection law, *see*: Competition and Markets Authority, 'Press Release 13 September 2019: Major overhaul of hotel booking sector after CMA action', https://www.gov.uk/government/news/major-overhaul-of-hotel-booking-sector-after-cma-action.
489. *Undertakings Jumpman and Progress Play (Online Gambling)* (Competition and Markets Authority).
490. For an overview of this study, *see* the website of the CMA (https://www.gov.uk/cma-cases/amazon-online-retailer-investigation-into-anti-competitive-practices).

investigation[491] because Amazon's agreements with third parties trading products through Amazon contained a parity clause, obliging these third parties to charge the same price on other websites as on Amazon's website, which could be in violation of the cartel prohibition. Following the investigation of the OFT, Amazon decided on its own initiative to change its policy (only within Europe), after which the OFT closed the investigation.

[C] Online Real Estate Property Portal(s)

On 21 April 2016, the CMA, in an open letter to estate agents,[492] warned that agreements between competitors determining which online property portals a certain property that is for sale will be posted on could potentially violate competition rules. In the open letter, the CMA explains, first, that competing real estate agents may not agree on which suppliers they will use; the decision whether or not a real estate agent will use the services of a particular property portal must be made by that agent alone (or by its parent company) and may not be jointly determined by and between competitors. Second, the CMA indicates continued oversight of the conduct of estate agents. Finally, the CMA points out the consequences of a possible breach of competition rules. The open letter comes after the CMA learned that some brokers are jointly deciding to join the OnTheMarket portal and remove their business from competing portals, rather than making these decisions independently. Although the CMA indicates that it has also contacted some brokers which it suspects may have been directly involved in such activity, it has taken no further action.

[D] Online RPM in the Bathroom Fittings Sector

On 10 May 2016, the CMA imposed a fine of GBP 786,668 on Ultra Finishing Limited and its ultimate parent company Ultra Finishing Group Limited for an online trading policy and, later, online trading guidelines that contained a 'recommendation' in respect of the online prices, which 'recommendation' was enforced in practice by, e.g., reducing the reseller's wholesale terms of supply, ceasing to supply branded products and/or withdrawing the reseller's right to use images for branded products online. According to the CMA, this effectively restricted the ability of resellers to set their online prices below a specified level. The CMA concluded that this amounts to RPM[493] and that this amounts to an object restriction.[494] Ultra set up a compliance program to

491. *CE/9692/12: Amazon Online Retailer: Investigation into Anti-competitive Practices*, *supra* n. 453.
492. https://assets.publishing.service.gov.uk/government/uploads/system/uploads/attachment_data/file/517834/Open_letter_to_estate_agents.pdf.
493. *CE/9857-14: Online resale price maintenance in the bathroom fittings sector*, para. 6.54.
494. *Ibid.*, para. 6.64.

help ensure compliance with applicable competition law, on the basis of which Ultra received a 5% discount on its (in addition to the 20% discount for the settlement). Following publication of its decision, the CMA has also sent warning letters to other parties active in the sector that it suspects have engaged in similar practices in relation to internet sales.[495]

[E] Online RPM in the Commercial Catering Equipment Sector

On 24 May 2016, the CMA imposed a fine of GBP 2,298,820 on ITW Limited (ITW) for implementing a minimum advertised price (MAP) policy pursuant to which resellers were not allowed to advertise products (online and offline) below a MAP.[496] The CMA focused on the restriction on online sales, because of the importance of the internet, since, i.e., the ability to advertise and sell products against a discount online can intensify price competition, both between online and offline resellers as between online resellers inter se.[497] The CMA finds that the conduct has the object of preventing, restricting or distorting competition (through RPM).[498] Following publication of its decision, the CMA has also sent warning letters to twenty other suppliers and/or dealers of commercial catering equipment which it suspects may have engaged in similar practices, as well as an open letter to business, accompanied by a guide for retailers and case studies.[499]

[F] Online RPM in the Lights Fittings Sector

On 3 May 2017, the CMA imposed a fine of GBP 2,763,491 on Poole Lighting Limited, Saxby Lighting Limited, Endon Lighting Limited, and their ultimate parent company The National Lighting Company Limited for requiring retailers to use a minimum price for online sales. The infringement comprised two separate agreements (one in relation to the Endon brand and one in relation to the Saxby brand) and was increased because an earlier warning letter from the CMA was ignored. It is not surprising that the CMA decided that RPM qualifies as an object restriction and by its very nature restricts competition.[500] Following publication of its decision, the CMA has also sent warning letters to other parties active in the sector where there are reasonable grounds to suspect they may also be engaging in RPM.[501]

---

495. https://www.gov.uk/government/news/cma-issues-bathroom-fittings-infringement-decision-and-fine.
496. *CE/9856/14: Online resale price maintenance in the commercial refrigeration sector.*
497. *Ibid.*, paras 4.30-4.31.
498. *Ibid.*, para. 6.60.
499. https://www.gov.uk/cma-cases/commercial-catering-sector-investigation-into-anti-competitive-practices.
500. *Case 50343: Online resale price maintenance in the light fittings sector*, paras 4.138 and 4.153.
501. https://www.gov.uk/government/news/lighting-company-fined-27-million-for-restricting-online-prices.

[G] Parity Clauses: Comparison Websites for Insurance Products

Following a market investigation into the use of DCTs (*see* above footnote 462), the CMA on 26 September 2017 launched an investigation into a possible infringement of the cartel prohibition through the use of parity clauses (referred to as *most favoured nation clauses* by the CMA) by DCTs for retail insurance products. The CMA indicated that it particularly saw a risk in case the scope of the parity clause used included prices used on other DCTs (so-called broad parity clauses). According to the CMA: *'DCTs want suppliers to set lower prices on their sites than on other DCTs to be more attractive to consumers than their rivals. Absent wide MFNs, they can achieve this by competing with each other on the commissions they charge to suppliers. Wide MFNs effectively stop this competitive process by creating a price floor across DCTs: a DCT cannot gain a competitive advantage by lowering its commissions as any subsequent price reduction would also benefit its rivals with wide MFNs. In addition, DCTs with wide MFNs can increase their commissions without the fear that they become more expensive than their rivals, as any price increase by the suppliers would need to be reflected in price increases on rival DCTs.'*[502] In March 2018, the CMA decided that it would continue the investigation. On 2 November 2018, the CMA published a press release announcing that it had issued a statement of objections.[503] On 19 November 2020, the CMA published a press release announcing that it had imposed a fine on ComparetheMarket of GPB 17,910,062 on the basis of the finding that certain clauses used by ComparetheMarket in its contracts with home insurers breach competition law.

During the period from 1 December 2015 to 1 December 2017, ComparetheMarket (a price comparison website) imposed wide most favoured nations (MFNs) on home insurance providers who offered their services through ComparetheMarket. Under these clauses, home insurance providers were prohibited from offering lower prices on other comparison websites. Violation of this prohibition could result in removal from the price comparison website. The CMA found that home insurance providers covered by the wide MFNs accounted for approximately 40% of home insurance product sales through price comparison websites and that ComparetheMarket had a market share of more than 50% on the market for the provision of PCW Services for Home Insurance in the UK. The network of wide MFNs operated by ComparetheMarket made it difficult in practice for ComparetheMarket's competitors to gain a competitive advantage over ComparetheMarket because home insurance providers who were willing to drop prices for their services were obliged to apply the lower price to ComparetheMarket as well.[504] This prevented other price comparison websites from beating ComparetheMarket on the price of home insurance products among a significant portion of the market. As a result of using the wide MFNs, ComparetheMarket itself also experienced a reduced incentive to compete.

502. 'Digital Comparison Tools Market Study – Final Report', *supra* n. 466, 57, footnote 179.
503. Competition and Markets Authority, 'Press Release 2 November 2018: ComparetheMarket Home Insurance Deals Could Deny People Better Prices', https://www.gov.uk/government/news/comparethemarket-home-insurance-deals-could-deny-people-better-prices.
504. *Case 50505, Price comparison website: use of most favoured nation clauses*, para. 9.B.

Although wide MFNs have been examined before (reference commitments Amazon), this is the first decision imposing a significant fine for a (network of) wide MFN(s). In this decision, the CMA explicitly chooses not to determine whether there is a purpose limitation or an effect limitation,[505] although it does consider that *'it is arguable that CTM's wide MFNs were by their very nature harmful to the proper functioning of normal competition'*. However, given the restrictive effect of the wide MFNs, the CMA does not consider it necessary to reach a conclusion as to whether there was a target restriction.[506] It is also notable that the CMA chose to address the case under the antitrust prohibition, rather than the prohibition of abuse of dominance (despite an alleged 50% market share). Nevertheless, the CMA chose to fine only ComparetheMarket and not the home insurance providers who were contracting parties to ComparetheMarket.

On 8 August 2022, the CAT fully annulled the GPB 17,910,062 fine. The CAT concluded that the market definition in the Decision was materially wrong and the process pursuant to which the CMA arrived at its conclusions in respect of the market definition was flawed. The CAT also found that the CMA failed to establish that the wide MFN clauses had the anti-competitive effects set out in the CMA's decision.[507]

[H] Ping: Ban on Online Sales

On 24 August 2017, the CMA fined Ping Europe Limited (Ping), a manufacturer of golf clubs and related products, a sum of GBP 1.45 million for prohibiting retailers who were members of its selective distribution system from selling golf clubs online.[508] Ping had defended this absolute ban by arguing it was important for its brand image that its golf clubs are custom fitted in a recognised store.

Although the CMA accepted that Ping actually operates a selective distribution system,[509] it nevertheless concluded that the total ban on online sales had an anticompetitive object and was neither necessary nor proportionate to protect the Ping brand image.[510] The CMA referred first to the judgment of the Court of Justice in *Pierre Fabre*,[511] in which an agreement stipulating that cosmetics and personal care products were only allowed to be sold in a physical space in the presence of a pharmacist was regarded as a restriction by object. The court considered that such a restriction was not objectively justified in light of the nature of the products in question.[512]

505. *Ibid.*
506. *Ibid.*, para. 3.5. In its advice regarding the UK Vertical Agreements Block Exemption Order (which is to replace the Vertical Agreements Block Exemption Regulation as of 1 June 2022), the CMA does advise that *wide retail parity obligations* should be treated as *hardcore restrictions* under the UK Order, see *Vertical Block Exemption Regulation*, 3 October 2021 CMA145con, para. 5.90.
507. https://www.catribunal.org.uk/judgments/138011221-bgl-holdings-limited-others-v-competition-and-markets-authority-judgment-2022.
508. *Case 50230: Ping, supra* n. 456.
509. *Ibid.*, para. 4.59.
510. *Ibid.*, para. 4.168.
511. *Ibid.*, para. 4.34; *Case C-439/09 (Pierre Fabre)* (European Court of Justice).
512. *Case C-439/09 (Pierre Fabre), supra* n. 511, para. 47.

However, the CMA did not stop at that reference in its reasoning. First, it observed that Ping does not monitor whether its resellers indeed accompany the sale of golf clubs with custom fitting services.[513] Moreover, it did not consider the custom fitting of golf clubs to be inextricably linked to the protection of Ping's brand image.[514] Nevertheless, it considered a ban on online sales as such to be a suitable means (to a limited extent) for promoting the custom fitting of golf clubs. According to the CMA, however, this may result in customers who do not wish to do so nevertheless having to visit physical shops.[515] The CMA therefore decided that a total sales ban goes beyond what is necessary for promoting custom fitting. The CMA identified four alternative solutions which it considers to be less restrictive of competition: (i) online advertising of the benefits of having golf clubs custom fitted, (ii) an obligation on resellers to describe on their websites all options for custom fitting, (iii) an obligation on resellers to offer interactive advice in cases of online sales, and (iv) an obligation on resellers to have online shoppers tick a box in which they state that they understand the importance of custom fitting.[516] The CMA also took into account that Ping requires its distributors to own a physical store. According to the CMA, this obligation - which is not the subject of the decision imposing the fine - limits the risk of freeriding, as it does not allow a situation to arise in which the customer has a golf club custom fitted in a physical shop and then orders it from a party that only sells online. This means that every seller of Ping golf clubs will need to invest in staff and facilities in order to be able to offer custom fitting.[517]

In addition to this fine, the CMA has also imposed an obligation on Ping to cease the infringement established by the CMA within three months by amending its conditions of sale.[518] Ping is expected to itself determine how it can meet this obligation.[519]

In its judgment of 7 September 2018, the CAT largely confirmed the Ping sanction decision.[520] However, the fine was reduced to GBP 1.25 million, as the CAT ruled that the original fine was not reasonable and proportionate since if all circumstances were considered in the round, there was no 'aggravated' infringement.[521] An interesting observation with regard to this overall conclusion is that the CAT had previously rejected all the individual allegedly mitigating circumstances invoked by Ping to reduce the fine.

From a more legally substantive point of view, it is worth noting that the CAT refers to the *Coty*[522] judgment rendered by the European Court of Justice (ECJ) a few

513. *Case 50230: Ping, supra* n. 456, para. 3.121.
514. *Ibid.*, para. 4.101.
515. *Ibid.*, para. 4.113.
516. *Ibid.*, paras 4.120-4.134.
517. *Ibid.*, para. 4.152.
518. *Ibid.*, para. 5.8.
519. *Ibid.*, para. 5.9.
520. *Ping v. CMA [2018] CAT 13* (Competition Appeal Tribunal).
521. *Ibid.*, para. 254.
522. *Ibid.*, paras 84-91.

months after the decision to impose a sanction on Ping.[523] In that judgment, the ECJ ruled that a prohibition on selling through a third-party online platform in a selective distribution system outside the scope of the vertical block exemption[524] does not necessarily constitute an infringement of the cartel prohibition if such prohibition on selling through online platforms is objectively justified and proportionate. The CAT noted, however, that a total ban on *all* sales via the internet goes beyond a mere ban on the sale of internet platforms belonging to third parties: '*Ping's internet policy is to be distinguished from the clause at issue in Coty. The prohibition on the use of third-party platforms in Coty did not place any significant limitation on retailers' ability to sell to consumers over the internet, since those retailers were permitted to sell via their own websites. The nature of that clause therefore did not reveal a sufficient degree of harm to competition* (*see* the Opinion of Advocate General Wahl in paragraphs 116-118).'[525] The CAT went on to conclude that the prohibition on selling Ping golf clubs via the internet has an anticompetitive object and is potentially capable of restricting competition. The actual effects do not therefore need to be examined, according to the CAT.[526]

On 21 January 2020, the Court of Appeal upheld the CAT's judgment and the GBP 1.25 million fine. When addressing whether Ping's internet sales policy is a restriction of competition by object and the second relating to the penalty, the Court of Appeal, *inter alia*, explicitly referred to paragraph 141 of the CAT's judgment and concluded that '*the CAT was right to conclude that there was nothing in the economic or legal context in which the ISP operated that negated the conclusion that the ISP revealed a sufficient degree of harm to justify being regarded as an object restriction*'.[527]

[I] Online Sales of Posters and Frames

The *Online Sales of Posters and Frames* case also offers an interesting set of facts.[528] In this case, the CMA imposed a fine for an agreement and/or concerted practice between Trod Limited (Trod) and GB eye Limited (GBE), which was ultimately implemented by algorithms – after initially having been implemented by humans. The CMA approved this acquisition on 13 June 2018. This case was triggered by a leniency application from GBE, which makes the evidence available quite extensive.

Trod and GBE are both active in the market for the online sale of posters and frames on Amazon.co.uk.[529] Trod also sourced its posters and frames from GBE, which

523. *Supra* n. 53; in the same way as the authors of this article: Th. Graf and T. Kuhn, 'Implications of the CJEU's Coty Judgment for Vertical Online Restrictions' 4 Competition Law & Policy Debate, 1 June 2018.
524. Commission Regulation (EU) No. 330/2010 of 20 April 2010 on the application of Article 101(3) of the Treaty on the Functioning of the European Union to categories of vertical agreements and concerted practices.
525. *Ping v. CMA [2018] CAT 13*, *supra* n. 520, para. 141.
526. *Ibid.*, para. 142.
527. *Ping v. CMA [2020] EWCA civ 13* (Court of Appeal) para. 107.
528. *Case 50223: Online Sales of Posters and Frames*, *supra* n. 455.
529. Although both parties are also active on their own websites, the CMA defines the market for online sales with reference to Amazon UK, *see Case 50223: Online Sales of Posters and Frames*, *supra* n. 455, paras 4.17-4.20.

was also active as a wholesaler at a higher level of the distribution chain. In summary, the behaviour of Trod and GBE consisted of Trod and GBE employees agreeing not to undercut each other so as to address Trod's complaints about aggressive pricing by GBE.[530] Initially, the implementation of these agreements was frustrated by the algorithms used by the parties.[531] This was 'solved' by programming specific exceptions in the algorithms used for (prices of) the fellow cartelist.[532] A remarkable detail is that the cartelists also contacted GBE's software supplier for this purpose, which moreover lent its cooperation. The CMA concludes in this respect that *'[Employee 1's] (GBE) evidence is that he obtained assistance from [GBE's software provider] in configuring the software to implement GBE's pricing strategy, and in particular the arrangement with Trod.'*[533] Complaints on either side about the non-functioning of the algorithms have also been extensively documented.[534] This case shows how easily an anticompetitive agreement can be implemented using algorithms – simply by including a specific exception for the cartel member in the pricing algorithm. The CMA summarises this in its decision as follows: *'the CMA notes that repricing software used by the Parties to implement the Infringing Agreement is normally used by online sellers to compete with other online sellers by automatically adjusting the prices of their products in response to the live prices of competitors' products. However, in the present case, the repricing software was configured by the Parties to restrict price competition between them in order to give effect to the Infringing Agreement'*.[535] The use of the algorithms was included in the investigation into the economic and legal context of the behaviour. The CMA finally concluded that there had been anticompetitive behaviour and imposed a fine on Trod of GBP 163,371.[536] GBE was granted immunity on the basis of its leniency application.

On 8 October 2018, the CMA published a study on price algorithms, in which the CMA investigated collusion by means of algorithms and the personalisation of prices.[537] According to the CMA, the most imminent risk lies in the hub-and-spoke scenario, where competing operators use the same algorithm or the same data to determine their prices and the hub (e.g., a platform) has the ability and incentive to

530. GBE wished to maintain a good relationship with Trod, as it was also one of its customers, *see Case 50223: Online Sales of Posters and Frames, supra* n. 455, para. 3.46.
531. *See ibid.*, para. 3.56. Furthermore, the parties also considered it logistically difficult to align all prices to the agreement on a daily basis, which is why they started to look into the use of algorithms/software to implement the agreement, *see* para. 3.66 of the above-mentioned decision. The use of software was an effective way of implementing the agreement: once GBE's software was operational, GBE itself had stated that prices were the same as Trod's prices on 99% of listings, *see* para. 3.72 of the decision.
532. *See* for example the considerations about Trod's use of the ignore list in this context: *Case 50223: Online Sales of Posters and Frames, supra* n. 455, paras 3.81-3.93.
533. *Ibid.*, para. 3.76.
534. *Ibid.*, paras 3.98–3.101.
535. *Ibid.*, para. 5.47.
536. *Ibid.*, para. 5.58.
537. 'Pricing Algorithms – Economic Working Paper on the Use of Algorithms to Facilitate Collusion and Personalised Pricing' (Competition and Markets Authority 2018).

raise prices above a competitive level with the objective of the collective maximisation of the profits of the suppliers and the hub. As regards price personalisation, the CMA notes in its study that this makes it more unlikely that the use of algorithms leads to a situation of tacit collusion in the market, as the market becomes less transparent. It is also interesting to take note of the conclusion of the CMA that more research should be done into the possibility of competition authorities conducting algorithm audits and whether specific algorithmic decision rules may be assumed to be restrictive of competition.

[J] RPM in the Musical Instruments and Equipment Sector

In the musical instruments and equipment sector, RPM fines totalling approximately GBP 14 million have been imposed by the CMA. The application of RPM has restricted retailers' freedom to set prices online in these cases (the exact conduct of each fined undertaking is discussed below in this paragraph). Moreover, RPM limits retailers' ability to offer discounts on digital pianos, digital keyboards, guitars, electronic drum kits, hi-tech music equipment and synthesisers, among others, and as a result, consumers looking for musical instruments, for example, are unlikely to find a better deal elsewhere. The CMA approved this acquisition on 17 September 2018. This is the first time the CMA has imposed a fine on resellers for RPM practices.[538]

To help the musical instrument industry and to learn from the CMA's investigations in this sector, the CMA published an open letter to suppliers and retailers,[539] published case studies on the Fender and Casio investigations mentioned below[540] and sent warning letters to about seventy manufacturers and retailers.[541] These letters contain guidance for companies regarding RPM enforcement and, in addition, encourage musical instrument suppliers and retailers to review their business practices to ensure compliance with competition law. In addition, the CMA has also launched its own internal price monitoring tool to deter companies from entering into agreements that restrict online discounting. The CMA plans to use this price monitoring tool, which enables the CMA to monitor price levels and thereby increase its market knowledge, in other sectors as well.[542]

538. https://www.gov.uk/government/news/musical-instrument-firms-to-pay-millions-after-breaking-competition-law.
539. https://www.gov.uk/government/publications/restricting-resale-prices-an-open-letter-to-suppliers-and-retailers-in-the-musical-instruments-sector. Ignoring the warning letter can be an aggravating circumstance (*see, e.g.*, Case 50343 Online resale price maintenance in the light fittings sector, paras 5.37-5.39 and https://www.gov.uk/government/case-studies/dar-lighting-fined-1-5-million-for-illegally-preventing-online-price-discounts).
540. *See* https://www.gov.uk/government/case-studies/45-million-fine-for-fender-for-illegally-preventing-online-price-discounts and https://www.gov.uk/government/case-studies/why-we-fined-casio-37-million-for-breaking-competition-law.
541. https://www.gov.uk/government/news/musical-instrument-firms-to-pay-millions-after-breaking-competition-law.
542. *See* https://competitionandmarkets.blog.gov.uk/2020/06/29/restricting-resale-prices-how-were-using-data-to-protect-customers/.

Casio[543]

On 1 August 2019, the CMA imposed a fine of GBP 3,695,535 on Casio Electronics Co. Limited (Casio UK) and Casio Computer Co. Limited (Casio Japan) (collectively *Casio*). Casio breached competition law between 2013 and 2018 by adopting a policy of restricting retailers' freedom to set prices online, by requiring digital pianos and keyboards to be sold at or above a minimum price.[544]

Casio required retailers to sell digital pianos and keyboards online at or above a specified price. Casio then monitored prices and put pressure on retailers to adjust or increase their prices online when they were below the specified price, specifically by instructing retailers not to sell below a minimum price, monitoring retail prices, contacting retailers who sold products below the minimum price in various ways, and threatening sanctions and once actually imposing sanctions.[545] Casio used software in this practice that makes it easier to monitor online prices in real-time and ensure widespread compliance with pricing policies.[546] As of March 2016, Casio UK is using automated reporting software from Price2Spy. This significantly expanded Casio UK's monitoring capabilities with daily reporting and real-time price changes from individual retailers. As of May 2017, Casio UK's sales team used Google Hangouts in conjunction with Price2Spy to facilitate Price2Spy communication and coordination and accelerate retailers' compliance with the minimum price.[547]

Fender Europe[548]

Fender Musical Instruments Europe Limited (Fender), a supplier of guitars to retailers in the UK, adopted a policy of restricting competitive online pricing by prohibiting guitars from being advertised or sold below a minimum price between 2013 and 2018.

543. *Case 50565-2: Online resale price maintenance in the digital piano and digital keyboard sector*, https://assets.publishing.service.gov.uk/media/5d9c539aed915d399eb2160b/non_conf_decision_arrow.pdf.
544. *Case 50565-2: Online resale price maintenance in the digital piano and digital keyboard sector*, https://assets.publishing.service.gov.uk/media/5d9c539aed915d399eb2160b/non_conf_decision_arrow.pdf, para. 4.13.
545. *Ibid.*, para. 4.28.
546. *Ibid.*, paras 3.92, 3.97-3.110.
547. All in all, Price2Spy appears to have played a fairly central role in the monitoring system, but is not being held accountable under competition law, while the CMA itself notes that Price2Spy is marketing itself in a certain way: '*On its website, Price2Spy states that its services provide the capability to "Analyze which retailer (and exactly when!) started pricing chain-reaction (that was followed by other sites)".*' (*Case 50565-2: Online resale price maintenance in the digital piano and digital keyboard sector*, https://assets.publishing.service.gov.uk/media/5d9c539aed915d399eb2160b/non_conf_decision_arrow.pdf, footnote 173) and '*the CMA infers from this that Price2Spy had facilitated widespread adherence to the Casio Pricing Policy and so Casio UK's monitoring had achieved its goal*'. (*Case 50565-2: Online resale price maintenance in the digital piano and digital keyboard sector*, https://assets.publishing.service.gov.uk/media/5d9c539aed915d399eb2160b/non_conf_decision_arrow.pdf, para. 3.109).
548. *Case 50565-3: Online resale price maintenance in the guitar sector*, https://assets.publishing.service.gov.uk/media/5e79d8aed3bf7f52efedfcad/20200320_50565-3_-_DECISION.pdf.

On 22 January 2020, the CMA imposed a fine of GBP 4,531,185[549] on Fender for infringement of the cartel prohibition through RPM. Fender does not appear to have used similar software to Casio, but the CMA notes that Fender did consider it.[550]

Korg[551]

On 29 June 2020, the CMA imposed a fine of GBP 1,504,707 on Korg, a supplier of electronic music equipment. Korg set minimum prices for the resale of its electronic music equipment between June 2015 and April 2018. Korg also told resellers not to sell below these minimum prices. Korg monitored resellers[552] and used price monitoring software (this software is known as Orange Spider and was created and managed by a Korg reseller)[553] to monitor resellers to ensure that they adhered to Korg's minimum pricing policy. In doing so, Korg threatened (and sometimes applied) sanctions against resellers who sold or offered products below the minimum prices. The CMA notes that the use of automated price monitoring systems can make RPM more effective,[554] but also notes on its website that price monitoring if used correctly, should benefit competition by encouraging companies to undercut competitors' prices.[555] In this case, the software was used by Korg as a tool to keep resellers' prices artificially high.

Roland[556]

On 22 July 2020, the CMA imposed a fine of GBP 4,003,321 on Roland UK Limited and Roland Corporation (collectively Roland), active in the music industry through the sale of electronic drums, electronic pianos, keyboards, DJ and recording equipment, among others. Roland operated a pricing policy between 2011 and 2018, the purpose of which was to ensure that resellers would not advertise or sell the products below a minimum price. Again, there was monitoring by Roland (through price monitoring software) and monitoring by resellers, and the CMA notes that the interplay between these two forms

---

549. In determining the amount of the fine, the CMA took into account that Fender admitted the illegal activities and cooperated with the investigation. As a result, the fine was reduced by 20%.
550. *Case 50565-3: Online resale price maintenance in the guitar sector,* https://assets.publishing.service.gov.uk/media/5e79d8aed3bf7f52efedfcad/20200320_50565-3_-_DECISION.pdf, footnote 209: '*The evidence indicates that in late 2016 to early 2017, Fender Europe considered purchasing automated price monitoring software in order to more effectively and systematically monitor its resellers' resale pricing.*'
551. *Case 50565-4: Synthesizers and hi-tech equipment: anti-competitive practices,* https://www.gov.uk/government/case-studies/korg-fined-15-million-for-illegally-preventing-online-price-discounts.
552. Korg was also aided by the resellers themselves: the resellers reported on each other and let Korg know when other resellers dropped their prices. *Case 50565-4: Synthesizers and hi-tech equipment: anti-competitive practices,* https://www.gov.uk/government/case-studies/korg-fined-15-million-for-illegally-preventing-online-price-discounts, paras 3.86-3.90.
553. *Ibid.*, paras 3.91-3.104.
554. *Ibid.*, para. 4.240.
555. https://www.gov.uk/government/case-studies/korg-fined-15-million-for-illegally-preventing-online-price-discounts.
556. *Case 50565-5: Electronic drum sector: anti-competitive practices,* https://assets.publishing.service.gov.uk/media/5f171ab43a6f40727ebfb440/Non-confidential_infringement_decision.pdf.

amplified the impact of the infringement.[557] On appeal, the CAT concluded that the penalty payable by Roland should have been calculated without a 20% settlement discount and increased the penalty to GBP 5,004,141.[558]

GAK & Yamaha[559]

By decision of 17 July 2020, the CMA found that GAK.co.uk Ltd, The Guitar, Amp & Keyboard Centre Ltd and GAK.co.uk (Holdings) Limited (collectively GAK), as reseller, and Yamaha Music Europe GmbH (hereafter Yamaha), as supplier, had violated the cartel prohibition by engaging in RPM. The CMA imposed a fine of GBP 278,945 on GAK, which had already agreed to pay up to this amount. Yamaha obtained immunity for bringing the conduct to the attention of the CMA. This case specifically concerned monitoring by resellers who used so-called *web rat pricing software* for this purpose and then reported other (non-compliant) resellers to Yamaha.[560] The reason that only GAK, and not the seventeen other retailers listed in the decision, is the subject of the CMA's decision appears to be due to the fact that GAK had already received an advisory letter from the CMA earlier, in October 2015, in respect of similar conduct.[561] This is the only decision so far in which a retailer/reseller has also been fined for RPM.

[K] Online RPM in the Domestic Lighting Sector

On 23 March 2022, the CMA imposed a fine of GBP 1,500,000 on Dar Lighting Limited and its immediate and ultimate parent company, Castlegate 624 Limited (together: DAR) for restricting the discounts resellers could offer online. After its earlier investigation into the lighting industry (please refer to the fine imposed in relation to online RPM in the lights fittings sector), the CMA found that the freedom of retailers to set their own sales prices was restricted between 2017 and 2019, despite warning letters sent in 2012 and 2017 addressing potential RPM.[562] In relation to the selective distribution system implemented by DAR, the CMA cited the European Commission's E-commerce Sector Inquiry – in which the Commission set out that within a selective distribution system, it may be easier for a manufacturer to control pricing, effectively engage in RPM or prohibit (certain forms of) online sales or advertisement – and noted that 'Suppliers who adopt a selective distribution model must therefore take particular care to ensure that the implementation and/or enforcement of any selective distribution arrangement does not lead to any infringement of the [Competition] Act [1998].'

557. *Ibid.*, para. 5.27.
558. https://www.catribunal.org.uk/sites/default/files/2021-04/1365_roland_Judgment_190421-_1.pdf.
559. *Case 50565-6: Digital pianos, digital keyboards and guitars: anti-competitive practices*, https://assets.publishing.service.gov.uk/media/5f5749eae90e070997bc8efa/GAK_decision_-_web_-.pdf.
560. *Ibid.*, paras 3.77 and 3.119-3.121.
561. *Ibid.*, para. 2.11.
562. *Case 50952: Domestic Lighting: anti-competitive practices concerning resale price maintenance.*

Similar to earlier cases in respect of online RPM, the CMA again finds that RPM is a restriction by object.[563]

§5.02 ABUSE OF A DOMINANT POSITION

[A] epyx Limited and FleetCor Technologies

In the case of *epyx Limited and FleetCor Technologies*,[564] the CMA closed an investigation into possible abuse of a dominant position with a commitment decision. epyx – part of FleetCor since October 2013 – has been operating an online platform since 2003 that brings together supply and demand for vehicle maintenance in company fleets. epyx's contract terms included a prohibition on demand-side customers using competing platforms alongside the epyx platform. Supply-side customers also had to commit themselves to the exclusive use of the epyx platform. The CMA concluded that such platforms (Service, Maintenance and Repair; 'SMR' platforms) constitute a separate product market in the UK also in view of the barriers to entry (investment in product development and building networks on both the demand and the supply side). According to the CMA, epyx had significant market power on the markets thus defined. The CMA concludes that the epyx terms discussed above are prima facie restrictive of competition, also in view of the lengthy duration of the contracts (three to five years with a notice period of between three and twenty-four months). Ultimately, the CMA accepted commitments from epyx which included, *inter alia*, that:[565]

- all customers are permitted to engage freely with any party and switch platforms;
- all customers are permitted to develop and/or market alternative systems;
- for future customers on the demand side of the market, the duration of the contracts is to be shortened (offering a possibility to switch after eighteen months and annually thereafter) (current customers on the demand side of the market may switch after the end of their current minimum period and annually thereafter);
- customers on the demand side may also use alternative platforms prior to the expiry of the contract with epyx for '*(a) unlimited dummy testing; (b) a capped volume of live testing; and (c) certain types of transactions (referred to as exclusions)*';
- demand-side customers are allowed to use alternative systems to the epyx platform on an unlimited basis after the expiration of their contracts with epyx for a transitional period of up to twelve months during which the customer will complete its migration to an alternative system;
- customers on the supply side may now also use alternative platforms at the express request of customers on the demand side;

563. *Ibid.*, para. 4.288.
564. *Case CE/9496-11: Epyx Limited and FleetCor Technologies, supra* n. 458.
565. *Ibid.*, para. 4.24.

- customers on the supply side shall be free to work with competing platforms for the benefit of customers on the supply side that are not customers of epyx.

These commitments are in force for a period of five years (2014-2019).

[B] ATG Media

In November 2016, the CMA opened an investigation into ATG Media, the largest provider of live online auction systems in the UK,[566] since the CMA suspected an infringement of the prohibition of abuse of a dominant position and an infringement of the cartel prohibition. ATG Media was found to have behaved anticompetitively in the following three ways:

(1) ATG Media encouraged a substantial number of customers (physical auction houses) to accept ATG Media as its exclusive supplier of live online bidding (LOB) auction platform services for the duration of their agreement with ATG Media.
(2) ATG Media required auction houses that were customers of ATG Media to not offer less favourable terms to bidders trading through its sites with the same physical auction house than bidders trading through competing online auction houses (in particular as regards the commissions to be charged).
(3) ATG Media put pressure on physical auction houses not to advertise for competitors of ATG Media.[567]

The CMA was concerned that this behaviour by ATG Media would result in competitors of ATG Media not being able to compete effectively with ATG Media. On the basis of ATG Media's commitment that it will not engage in any of the three types of behaviour mentioned above in the next five years, the CMA ceased the investigation into ATG Media on 29 June 2017.[568]

[C] Google's Privacy Sandbox

On 8 January 2021, the CMA announced in a press release that it had opened an investigation into Google pursuant to Google's proposals to remove third-party cookies and other functionalities from its Chrome browser (known collectively as the 'Privacy

566. Background: (physical) auction houses use a live online auction system to let interested parties who are not physically present participate in the bidding.
567. It is unclear exactly how ATG Media prevented competitors from being advertised. The CMA's decision merely mentions that there is evidence that ATG Media requested certain customers to remove lower commissions from competitors of those customers' websites, *see Case 50408: Auction Services*, *supra* n. 457, para. 2.30.
568. *Ibid.*

Sandbox' project).[569] The changes announced by Google would disable third-party cookies on the Chrome browser and Chromium browser engine, an open-source software engine on which other browsers are based, and replace them with a new set of tools for targeting advertising and other functionality that, according to Google, aims to protect consumers' privacy to a greater extent. In the CMA's recent market study into online platforms' digital advertising, the CMA had already highlighted a number of concerns about the potential impact of Google's Privacy Sandbox, including that it could undermine the ability of publishers to generate revenue and undermine competition in digital advertising, entrenching Google's market power.[570]

Further to complaints alleging that Google is abusing its dominant position and requests for the CMA to ensure that Google develops its proposals in a way that does not distort competition, the CMA investigated whether the proposals could cause advertising spending to become even more concentrated on Google's ecosystem at the expense of its competitors. After initially publishing an intention to accept binding commitments offered by Google on 11 June 2021,[571] the CMA announced on 26 November 2021 that it had secured improved commitments from Google on Google's Privacy Sandbox. The initial commitments, consulted in June 2021, involved a key role for the CMA which would monitor the design and development of Google's Privacy Sandbox proposals. After having heard over forty third parties, the CMA strengthened the commitments on a number of topics, most notably in relation to transparency and consultation with third parties, certain functionalities that should not be deleted from third-party cookies (mainly functionalities providing access to information and/or IP addresses), self-preferencing and monitoring. The CMA consulted the revised proposed commitments from 26 November 2021 to 17 December 2021.[572]

On 11 February 2022, the CMA accepted the revised remedy offer from Google relating to the Privacy Sandbox project. In the decision, the CMA sets out its concerns in respect of the Privacy Sandbox. These concerns relate to the impact of the Privacy Sandbox if implemented without sufficient regulatory scrutiny and oversight, in terms of unequal access by third parties to the functionalities associated with user tracking, self-preferencing by Google (e.g., its own ad tech providers and owned and operated ad inventory), and the imposition of unfair terms on Google Chrome's browser users.[573] The announcement of the Privacy Sandbox by Google has also, according to the CMA, caused uncertainty in the market (i.e., for publishers and ad tech companies).[574]

569. Competition and Markets Authority, 'Press Release 8 January 2021: CMA to investigate Google's "Privacy Sandbox" browser changes', https://www.gov.uk/government/news/cma-to-investigate-google-s-privacy-sandbox-browser-changes.
570. 'Online Platforms and Digital Advertising Market Study – Final Report', paras 5.322-5.328.
571. Case 50972, Notice of intention to accept commitments offered by Google in relation to its Privacy Sandbox Proposals, https://assets.publishing.service.gov.uk/media/60c21e54d3bf7f4bcc0652cd/Notice_of_intention_to_accept_binding_commitments_offered_by_Google_publication.pdf.
572. https://www.gov.uk/cma-cases/investigation-into-googles-privacy-sandbox-browser-changes.
573. Case 50972, Decision to accept commitments offered by Google in relation to its Privacy Sandbox Proposals, para. 3.99.
574. *Ibid.*, paras 3.100-3.101.

However, the CMA believes that the improved commitments address these competition concerns and also provide sufficient safeguards in case the CMA would consider that one or more of its competition concerns is not addressed.[575] The first quarterly report (relating to 11 February 2022 to 15 May 2022 submitted by Google and the related Monitoring Trustee report do not, according to ING Trustee Services, raise any reportable concerns.[576]

[D] CMA Investigation into Possible App Store and Browser 'Engine' Abuse by Apple and Google

On 4 March 2021, the CMA announced in a press release[577] that it would be investigating Apple in relation to suspected anticompetitive behaviour further to complaints that Apple applies unfair and anticompetitive terms and conditions for app developers and the CMA's own market study into online platforms and digital advertising[578] and its advice on the framework for a new pro-competition digital markets regulatory regime.[579] The investigation seeks to determine (i) whether Apple is dominant in the distribution of apps on Apple devices in the UK, and (ii) whether Apple imposes unfair or anti-competitive terms and conditions on developers, resulting in users having less choice or paying higher prices for apps and add-ons. From the case page, it follows that the CMA decided on 30 March 2022 to proceed with the investigation.[580]

However, in June 2022 the CMA did publish a consultation on the launch of a market investigation into Apple and Google's market power in mobile browsers and Apple's restrictions on cloud gaming through its App Store.[581] In addition, at the same time, the CMA announced that it would be taking enforcement action against Google in relation to its app store payment practices.

Browsers are powered by an 'engine', which is fundamental to browser performance. According to the CMA, 97% of all mobile web browsing in the UK in 2021 happened on browsers powered by either Apple's or Google's browser engine. Unlike Google, Apple bans alternatives to its own browser engine on its mobile devices. The CMA expresses concern that this may severely limit the potential for rival browsers to

575. *Ibid.*, para. 5.66.
576. https://www.gov.uk/cma-cases/investigation-into-googles-privacy-sandbox-browser-changes.
577. https://www.gov.uk/government/news/cma-investigates-apple-over-suspected-anti-competitive-behaviour.
578. CMA Market study final report, *Online platforms and digital advertising*, 1 July 2020, https://assets.publishing.service.gov.uk/media/5fa557668fa8f5788db46efc/Final_report_Digital_ALT_TEXT.pdf.
579. CMA Advice of the Digital Markets Taskforce, *A New pro-competition regime for digital markets*, December 2020, https://assets.publishing.service.gov.uk/media/5fce7567e90e07562f98286c/Digital_Taskforce_-_Advice.pdf.
580. The status of the investigation can be found on the website of the CMA, https://www.gov.uk/cma-cases/investigation-into-apple-appstore.
581. *CMA plans market investigation into mobile browsers and cloud gaming*, CMA press release 22 June 2022, https://www.gov.uk/government/news/cma-plans-market-investigation-into-mobile-browsers-and-cloud-gaming.

differentiate themselves from Safari (e.g., on features such as speed and functionality) and would limit Apple's incentives to invest in its browser engine. Apple and Google both have strong positions in mobile web browsing, with a combined share of supply of around 90% for their browsers.

In addition, the CMA also observed that Apple has blocked the emergence of cloud gaming services on its App Store. During its market study, the CMA mentions that a number of UK businesses and start-ups believe that the restrictions in relation to mobile browsers and cloud gaming make it harder for them to innovate and compete in these markets.

The proposed market investigation will further assess the competition concerns identified to date in both areas and decide what, if any, action is appropriate. This could include making legally binding orders requiring changes to be made to Apple's and Google's practices.

On 22 November 2022, the CMA decided to launch a market investigation reference in relation to this case pursuant to section 131 of the Enterprise Act 2002.[582] Apple however succeeded in obtaining an 18-month suspension of this decision to start a market investigation reference before the CAT.[583]

[E] CMA Investigation into Meta's Use of Advertising Data

On 4 June 2021, the CMA announced in a press release[584] that it would be investigating whether Facebook (currently: Meta) might be, through its collection and use of advertising data, abusing a dominant position in the social media or digital advertising markets. Meta collects data through its digital services, such as its advertising services but also the Facebook Login, the single sign-on option that allows users to sign into other websites using their Facebook account. The CMA assesses whether Meta has used such data to benefit its own services and in particular its services Facebook Marketplace – where users can post classified ads – and Facebook Dating (a dating service). From the case page, it follows that the CMA decided on 7 April 2022 that the term for the initial investigation (for analysis and information gathering) has been extended to the summer of 2023.[585] No investigation results have been published yet.

In its press release, the CMA also indicated that the DMU is looking into the use of codes of conduct separately from this investigation to govern the relationship between digital platforms and groups. Even prior to the DMU being granted its full powers, the CMA will continue to promote competition and consumers' interests in digital markets, including taking enforcement action where necessary.

582. *Mobile browsers and cloud gaming, Decision to make a market investigation reference* (Competition and Markets Authority), https://assets.publishing.service.gov.uk/media/637b65c0d3bf7f7208f6c709/reference_decision__1_.pdf.
583. CAT 31 March 2023, case 1576/6/12/23, *Apple v. CMA*, https://www.catribunal.org.uk/sites/cat/files/2023-03/2023.03.31_1576_Apple%20v%20CMA_Judgment%20%28FINAL%29.pdf.
584. https://www.gov.uk/government/news/cma-investigates-facebook-s-use-of-ad-data.
585. https://www.gov.uk/cma-cases/investigation-into-facebooks-use-of-data.

[F] CMA Investigation into Suspected Anticompetitive Agreement Between Google and Meta and Behaviour by Google in Relation to Header Bidding

On 10 March 2022, the CMA announced in a press release[586] that it would be investigating Google and Meta's conduct in markets for online display advertising services. In particular, the CMA investigates two specific questions. First, the CMA investigates whether Google and Meta restricted or prevented the uptake of header-bidding services.[587] Part of this investigation revolves around the 'Jedi Blue' agreement entered into by Google and Meta. In this respect, Andrea Coscelli, CMA Chief Executive, said: '*We're concerned that Google may have teamed up with Meta to put obstacles in the way of competitors who provide important online display advertising services to publishers.*' Second, the CMA also investigates whether Google affected the ability of other firms to compete with its products in the same area through its conduct in relation to header-bidding services more widely in order to establish whether Google abused a dominant position. In the press release, Andrea Coscelli gives a clear signal to big tech firms: '*We will not shy away from scrutinising the behaviour of big tech firms while we await powers for the Digital Markets Unit*'. This investigation was terminated as a standalone case on 10 March 2023 and was integrated into the investigation into Google's potential abuse of dominance in ad tech (*see* §5.01[g] below).[588]

[G] CMA Investigation into Google's Potential Abuse of Dominance in Ad Tech

On 26 May 2022, the CMA announced in a press release[589] that it would be investigating Google, further to the CMA's own market study into online platforms and digital advertising,[590] relating to a potential restriction of competition in the digital advertising technology market where Google has strong positions on various parts of the value chain. In particular, the CMA assesses three parts of the value chain in which Google is the largest provider of services, being: (i) demand-side platforms that allow advertisers and media agencies to purchase advertising space, (ii) ad exchanges that provide the necessary technology to automate the sale of advertising inventory through

586. https://www.gov.uk/government/news/cma-investigates-google-and-meta-over-ad-tech-concerns?utm_campaign=govuk-notifications-topic&utm_content=immediately&utm_medium=email&utm_source=060aa3b5-16a5-4f12-a516-cee7945758e1.
587. So-called 'header bidding' is a service which allows suppliers of advertising space, such as news publishers, to offer their online advertising space to multiple purchasers, i.e., advertisers, simultaneously, rather than one by one. As a result, advertisers compete against each other for ad space and publishers can compare bids from multiple advertisers simultaneously.
588. https://www.gov.uk/cma-cases/investigation-into-suspected-anti-competitive-agreement-between-google-and-meta-and-behaviour-by-google-in-relation-to-header-bidding.
589. https://www.gov.uk/cma-cases/investigation-into-suspected-anti-competitive-conduct-by-google.
590. CMA Market study final report, *Online platforms and digital advertising*, 1 July 2020, https://assets.publishing.service.gov.uk/media/5fa557668fa8f5788db46efc/Final_report_Digital_ALT_TEXT.pdf.

real-time auctions, and (iii) publisher ad servers that manage the advertising space inventory and determine which ad will be shown, on the basis of the bids received. Part of the investigation is also whether 'Google limited the interoperability of its ad exchange with third-party publisher ad servers and/or contractually tied these services together, making it more difficult for rival ad servers to compete.'[591] The CMA further investigates whether Google's conduct in respect of its published ad server and its demand-side platforms favours its own ad exchange services resulting in foreclosure of other ad exchange services. In the press release in which the investigation was announced, Andrea Coscelli said '*It's vital that we continue to scrutinise the behaviour of the tech firms which loom large over our lives and ensure the best outcomes for people and businesses throughout the UK.*'[592] No investigation results have been published yet.[593]

[H] CMA Investigation into Google's Distribution of Apps on Android Devices

On 10 June 2022, the CMA announced in a press release[594] that it would be investigating Google relating to Google's distribution of apps on Android devices. The CMA focuses on how users can make in-app payments for certain digital products. This investigation follows a market study in respect of the mobile ecosystems of Google and Apple.[595] On 19 April 2023, the CMA opened a one-month consultation period with regard to proposed commitments from Google. Google's proposed commitments would give app developers the freedom to offer a different billing system of their choosing, known as 'Developer-only Billing' (DOB), or offer users a choice between an alternative billing system or Google Play's billing system, known as 'User Choice Billing' (UCB). These proposed commitments relate to *inter alia*:

- a proposed reduction in Google's service fee under each of User Choice Billing (UCB) and Developer-Only Billing (DOB);
- a proposed process for the reporting of in-app purchases turnover to Google either manually or using Application Programming Interfaces (APIs), in order for a service fee to be calculated on in-app transactions;

591. https://www.gov.uk/government/news/google-probed-over-potential-abuse-of-dominance-in-ad-tech.
592. https://www.gov.uk/cma-cases/investigation-into-suspected-anti-competitive-conduct-by-google.
593. https://www.gov.uk/cma-cases/investigation-into-suspected-anti-competitive-conduct-by-google-in-ad-tech.
594. https://www.gov.uk/cma-cases/investigation-into-suspected-anti-competitive-conduct-by-google.
595. *Ibid.* The final report of the market study (https://assets.publishing.service.gov.uk/government/uploads/system/uploads/attachment_data/file/1081885/Mobile_ecosystems_final_report_-_full_draft_-_FINAL_.pdf) identifies a range of potential interventions and the CMA decided to consult on making a market investigation reference into mobile browsers and access to cloud gaming on mobile devices (*see* Chapter 9 of the report). The status of the market investigation can be found on the website of the CMA https://www.gov.uk/cma-cases/mobile-browsers-and-cloud-gaming.

- the use of information screens and, for UCB, a billing choice screen; and
- a proposed process for the CMA to monitor Google's compliance with the commitments, including in particular its commitment not to retaliate against app developers choosing to use UCB or DOB.[596]

[I] CMA Investigation into Amazon for Marketplace Concerns

On 6 July 2022, the CMA announced in a press release[597] that it would be investigating Amazon in relation to suspected anticompetitive practices affecting sellers on its UK Marketplace, following the European Commission's probe into similar behaviour. The CMA will investigate whether Amazon has a dominant position in the UK and whether it abuses its position by giving an unfair advantage to its own retail business or sellers that use its fulfilment services when compared to other sellers that do not use such services. According to the press release, the CMA will focus on three areas: (i) the collection and use of third-party seller data, (ii) the criteria for being the preferred choice for Amazon's 'Buy Box', and (iii) the eligibility criteria for the Amazon Prime label. No investigation results have been published yet.[598]

§5.03 MERGER CONTROL[599]

[A] Priceline/Kayak

On 14 May 2013, the OFT approved the acquisition of Kayak Software Corporation, a price comparison website, by Priceline.com, which is part of the Priceline Group.[600] The Priceline Group comprises online travel agencies (OTAs) such as Booking.com, Agoda.com, Priceline.com and Rentalcars.com that intermediate between customers and travel service providers. The OFT assessed the unilateral effects in the online hotel sector and the online car hire sector but found that the transaction would not raise concerns because of the minimal increment to the share of supply.[601] The OFT also

596. *Open consultation, Proposed commitments regarding changes to Google Play's rules to allow certain app developers to use alternative billing systems for in-app purchases*, Competition and Markets Authority, 19 April 2023, https://www.gov.uk/government/consultations/proposed-commitments-regarding-changes-to-google-plays-rules-to-allow-certain-app-developers-to-use-alternative-billing-systems-for-in-app-purchases.
597. https://www.gov.uk/government/news/cma-investigates-amazon-over-suspected-anti-competitive-practices.
598. The status of the investigation can be found on the website of the CMA, https://www.gov.uk/government/news/cma-investigates-amazon-over-suspected-anti-competitive-practices.
599. For the sake of completeness, we observe that after the cut-off date of our research, the CMA prohibited the acquisition of Activision Blizzard by Microsoft on 24 April 2023, see press release: https://www.gov.uk/government/news/microsoft-activision-deal-prevented-to-protect-innovation-and-choice-in-cloud-gaming. PaRR reported on 9 May 2023 that by contrast, the Commission was intending to clear this concentration after a Phase II investigation on 15 May 2023: https://app.parr-global.com/intelligence/view/intelcms-khcbdb.
600. ME/5882/12: Anticipated acquisition by Priceline.Com Incorporated of Kayak Software Corporation (Office of Fair Trading).
601. *Ibid.*, para. 109.

considered whether the transaction would enhance the conditions for coordination following a complaint by a third party that Kayak's data scraping technology would help Priceline to automate the detection of deviations from (broad) price parity clauses and make enforcement of (broad) price parity clauses easier.[602] The OFT, however, did not find this theory of harm credible, because more effective technology than Kayak's technology was already available in the market. Since the OFT did also not find evidence that Priceline.com would have the ability or the incentive to engage in foreclosure activities and conglomerate bundling or tying, the OFT concluded that the transaction would not lead to a substantial lessening of competition within a market in the United Kingdom. For the aforementioned reasons, the OFT decided to issue an unconditional phase I clearance.

[B] Google/Waze

On 11 June 2013, Google acquired the online *turn-by-turn* navigation services provider Waze.[603] Waze is a direct competitor of Google's own navigation service Google Maps. On 5 September 2013, three months after the acquisition, the OFT opened an investigation into the merger at its own initiative.[604] The transaction was not (voluntarily) notified because the parties were of the opinion that the OFT did not have jurisdiction over the transaction.[605] The turn-by-turn navigation services of Waze and Google Maps were offered free of charge and therefore, according to the parties, did not constitute an economic activity. In addition, in the view of the parties, the transaction did not have any significant nexus with the UK. However, the OFT did not accept this because economic activity also includes activities that are currently offered free of charge but may be offered for payment in the future. In addition, the parties had a market share of over 25% in turn-by-turn navigation services for mobile devices in the UK, thus reaching the share-of-supply threshold for notifying a transaction to the OFT.[606]

In the decision, the OFT concluded that Google and Waze were not each other's closest competitors in the UK for turn-by-turn navigation services for mobile devices.[607] The coverage and accuracy of Waze's navigation services were insufficient for this to be the case. According to the OFT, Waze would not be able to become a significant competitor to Google in the future. Waze had insufficient users in the UK to benefit

602. *Ibid.*, para. 81. In the decision, parity agreements are described as what we would now call broad parity clauses: 'agreements that prevent hotels from offering hotel rooms at lower prices to other websites'.
603. ME/6167/13: Completed Acquisition by Motorola Mobility Holding (Google, Inc.) of Waze Mobile Limited (Office of Fair Trading), para. 4.
604. *Ibid.*, para. 5.
605. *Ibid.*, para. 7.
606. Section 23 Enterprise Act 2002.
607. ME/6167/13: Completed Acquisition by Motorola Mobility Holding (Google, Inc.) of Waze Mobile Limited, supra n. 603, para. 85.

from network effects.[608] In addition, it was uncertain whether Waze would succeed in becoming pre-installed on mobile devices. According to the OFT, Apple Maps (with a market share of around 30%) was Google's strongest competitor (with Google holding a market share of around 50%), followed by TomTom and Navfree. In addition, the OFT found that Apple Maps exerted a strong competitive pressure on Google. According to the OFT, the merger would therefore not lead to a significant restriction of competition.

[C] Web Reservations International/Hostelbookers.com

On 2 August 2013, the OFT approved the acquisition of Hostelbookers.com, an online travel agency, by Web Reservations International, also an online travel agency.[609] Despite the fact that the parties had significant combined market shares in the provision of online hostel accommodation services in the UK (between 40% and 55% with an increment of 15%),[610] the OFT cleared the transaction unconditionally in a first-phase decision. It reasoned that there was significant evidence that the parties operated in a 'dynamic marketplace' that was 'rapidly evolving' because the entry by Expedia and the further expansion of Booking.com (the parties' only significant competitor at the time) was likely.[611] Interestingly, the parties' internal documents showed 'increasing and significant concerns' about the competitive threat from Booking.com, Expedia and Airbnb.[612] This helped the OFT in its conclusion that the transaction would not lead to a substantial lessening of competition within a market in the United Kingdom.

[D] Just Eat/Hungryhouse

On 16 November 2017, the CMA approved the acquisition of Hungryhouse by Just Eat in a second-phase decision. Hungryhouse and Just Eat are both platforms that bring consumers into contact with restaurants and enable consumers to order meals through the platform. For understanding this case, it is relevant that the CMA made a distinction between:

- '*online takeaway ordering (OTO) aggregation platforms*' (such as the Hungryhouse and Just Eat platforms) – these are platforms without their own delivery service;
- '*ordering and logistics specialists*' that distinguish themselves from the first category by having their own delivery service, but do not have physical

608. CMA, Decision 11 November 2013, ME/6167/13: Completed Acquisition by Motorola Mobility Holding (Google, Inc.) of Waze Mobile Limited, supra n. 603, para. 49.
609. OFT, Decision 15 August 2013, *Anticipated acquisition by Web Reservations International (through its parent company Hellman & Friedman) of Hostelbookers.com Limited*, Case ME/6062/13.
610. *Ibid.*, para. 48.
611. *Ibid.*, para. 132.
612. *Ibid.*

restaurants of their own (such as Amazon Restaurants, Deliveroo and Uber Eats);
- vertically integrated restaurant chains with their own delivery service (such as Domino's Pizza Group).

In its first-phase decision, the CMA stated that there were indications that Hungryhouse and Just Eat were each other's closest competitors because these parties had a similar business model and were the only market players operating nationally. The ordering and logistics specialists were also said to focus on different types of restaurants than Hungryhouse and Just Eat, namely restaurants in higher market segments without their own delivery service. The CMA expressed concern in the first-phase decision that restaurants doing business with both proposed merging entities would have to accept more unfavourable terms after the merger. For this reason, the CMA referred the case to its panel of experts in charge of second-phase investigations.[613]

In its second-phase decision, the CMA's panel established that the parties' product is double-sided (offering meals to customers on the one hand and offering a platform to restaurants on the other), as the willingness of restaurants to be included in the portfolio of platforms increases as the number of users grows and vice versa.[614] The CMA panel then discussed the substitutability of the parties' product (OTO aggregation platforms) with the product of the ordering and logistics specialists, direct ordering from consumers and vertically integrated restaurant chains. The panel concluded that only the service of the ordering and logistics specialists was sufficiently substitutable with the service of the parties in order to be considered part of the same market, from both the consumer's and the restaurant's perspective. Given that prices and marketing campaigns are decided on at national level and given the scalability of food-ordering places, the CMA's panel assumed a national market for both OTO aggregation platforms and ordering and logistics specialists, taking into account that demand for the parties' services was local from both the consumer's and the restaurant's perspective. The CMA arrived at this conclusion by distinguishing between areas where only the parties were active and areas where at least one ordering and logistics specialist was active alongside the parties.[615]

Where more than one platform is available, consumers and restaurants may opt for single and multi-homing. According to the CMA's panel, this aspect is an important factor in determining the extent to which two platforms compete (*see* Table 5.1). Multi-homing by consumers occurs in case consumers use more than one platform when making a purchasing decision. Because the restaurants served by the parties made more use of multi-homing than the parties' customers, competition between Just Eat and Hungryhouse should (in theory) be targeted at the consumer side.[616] However,

613. ME/6659/16: Anticipated Acquisition by Just Eat.co.uk Limited of Hungryhouse Holdings Limited.
614. 'Just Eat and Hungryhouse – A Report on the Anticipated Acquisition by JUST EAT Plc of Hungryhouse Holdings Limited' (Competition and Markets Authority 2017).
615. *Ibid.*, paras 4.34 et seq.
616. *Ibid.*, para. 6.98.

the CMA's panel's research indicated that Hungryhouse merely places a limited constraint on Just Eat on both the consumer and the restaurant side.[617] Internal documents and economic research from the CMA showed that in the areas where ordering and logistics specialists were active, they exerted greater competitive pressure on Just Eat and Hungryhouse than Just Eat and Hungryhouse did on each other. With regard to the areas where ordering and logistics specialists were not active, the CMA's panel concluded that there was no evidence that Hungryhouse placed greater competitive pressure on Just Eat than on direct orders. In addition, the market was found to be dynamic, challenged by well-funded competitors, with strong brands and technological and logistics experience and expertise. The CMA therefore concluded that the acquisition would not lead to a significant impediment to competition and approved the concentration unconditionally.

Table 5.1 Single and Multi-homing for Food-Ordering Platforms

		Restaurants	
		Single-homing	*Multi-homing*
Consumers	*Single-homing*	Platforms compete on the consumer side and on the restaurant side	Platforms compete on the consumer side; platforms face little direct competition on the restaurant side, as they provide access to separate sets of consumers
	Multi-homing	Platforms compete on the restaurant side; platforms may face little direct competition on the consumer side, as they provide access to separate sets of restaurants, though this depends on the extent to which consumers consider the different sets of restaurants to be close substitutes	Platforms compete on both sides and may try to push restaurants (or consumers) towards single-homing, e.g., through exclusivity (restaurant side) or loyalty rewards (consumer side)

Source: CMA analysis in the *Hungryhouse/Just Eat* decision.

617. *Ibid.*, para. 6.169.

[E] PayPal/iZettle

On 17 May 2018, PayPal announced the 2.2 billion acquisition of Swedish company iZettle. The US company PayPal offers online and offline payment services. iZettle offers payment services mainly to smaller businesses. iZettle and PayPal are, at the time of the CMA's investigation, the largest market players in Mobile point of sale (mPOS) devices in the United Kingdom. These services allow businesses to make payments offline through a card reader connected to an app on a mobile or tablet. These services are an alternative to traditional point of sale (POS) services. Furthermore, both companies operate in the fledgling market for 'omnichannel' payment services. 'Omnichannel' payment services essentially allow businesses to make both offline and online payments through a single provider.

The CMA had filed an Initial Enforcement Order (IEO) on 19 September 2018, one day before the closing. For a breach of the IEO, PayPal was later fined GBP 250,000.[618]

On 1 October 2018, the CMA officially launched its investigation into PayPal's acquisition of iZettle. After concluding its first-phase investigation, the CMA stated on 26 November 2018 that it had reason to believe that the concentration would significantly impede effective competition in the UK market or part of it.[619] According to the UK authority, the transaction could ensure that PayPal would face insufficient competition in the UK market for mPOS given its high combined market share of [80-90]% and the fact that the next largest competitor had a market share of less than 10%. Moreover, had the transaction not taken place, PayPal would have invested – in what the CMA said was a potentially realistic scenario – in its PayPal Here service to compete more effectively with iZettle. In addition, the competition authority said the merger could also potentially have a negative impact on future competition in the market for 'omnichannel' payment services to small, micro and nano merchants. PayPal is already active in this market and iZettle has recently entered the market. In line with the CMA's Merger Assessment Guidelines,[620] the CMA considered whether (i) iZettle would enter and expand in this market absent the merger, and (ii) whether this would result in increased competition. The CMA tentatively concluded that such a loss of potential competition existed. In the absence of remedy proposals, on 5 December 2018, the CMA referred PayPal's acquisition of iZettle to the second phase.

In the second phase, the CMA examined the above theories of harm and, after an in-depth investigation led by an independent panel, reached the preliminary conclusion on 30 April 2019 that the concentration does not involve a restriction of

618. PayPal conducted cross-selling pilot campaigns (intended to target customers in France and Germany) that led to PayPal contacting UK potential customers in breach of the IEO. ME/6766/18 Completed acquisition by PayPal Holdings, Inc. of iZettle AB, Notice of penalty pursuant to section 94A of the Enterprise Act 2002.
619. ME/6766/18 Completed acquisition by PayPal Holdings, Inc. of iZettle AB, Decision on relevant merger situation and substantial lessening of competition.
620. 2010 Merger Assessment Guidelines, para. 5.4.15. Cf. 2021 (revised) Merger Assessment Guidelines, para. 5.7.

competition.[621] The CMA examined in detail how both companies would move in the market for mPOS and the market for 'omnichannel' payment services in the absence of the transaction. Furthermore, the CMA examined PayPal's rationale for the acquisition and the strategies of PayPal and iZettle in the absence of the merger. In addition, the UK competition authority also looked at consumer choice behaviour regarding the new mPOS devices and traditional POS devices, from which it followed that competitive pressure does exist from traditional devices. The CMA found that the overall market in which payment services are offered to smaller retailers will face enough competition from other market players at present and for the foreseeable future. In addition, the CMA noted that iZettle will slowly build its offering in 'omnichannel' services and will play a minor role in this market in the short term. Finally, the merger was also formally approved on 12 September 2019.

[F] Experian/Credit Laser Holdings (ClearScore)

On 25 May 2018, the CMA launched an investigation into the acquisition of Credit Laser Holdings by Experian Limited (Experian).[622] Experian and Credit Laser Holdings each offer free personal credit scores to people through their websites and mobile apps. These platforms allow consumers to compare different credit products. Experian also operates the most popular fee-based credit check tool in the United Kingdom. This tool includes features that help people improve their credit scores, check their credit scores and prevent identity fraud. Experian also provides a tool that allows lenders to identify which financial products a consumer might qualify for.[623] Based on these activities, the CMA retained the following reference frameworks: (i) the provision of personal credit scoring platforms for (individual) loans, credit cards and mortgages in the United Kingdom; (ii) the provision of credit verification tools (paid and free) in the United Kingdom; and (iii) the provision of pre-qualification services (consisting of services linking customers to financial products without the need for a formal credit check) for lenders to credit comparison platforms.[624] After the merger was referred to the second phase, the CMA in its provisional findings considered that the merger may give rise to substantial lessening of competition due to horizontal unilateral effects in the supply of credit comparison platforms and the supply of credit checking tools.[625] In fact, the

621. ME/6766/18 Completed acquisition by PayPal Holdings, Inc. of iZettle AB Provisional findings report.
622. The CMA bases its jurisdiction on the fact that the parties' activities overlap in the procurement of credit comparison platforms in the UK with a combined share of supply of 25%-40% of revenues and that this may be expected to increase by 5%-10%. The CMA therefore considers that the share-of-supply test is met.
623. ME/6743/18 anticipated acquisition by Experian Limited of Credit Laser Holdings Limited (ClearScore).
624. Zie: ME/6743/18 anticipated acquisition by Experian Limited of Credit Laser Holdings Limited (ClearScore), Decision on relevant merger situation and substantial lessening of competition.
625. ME/6743/18 anticipated acquisition by Experian Limited of Credit Laser Holdings Limited (ClearScore). In its first-phase decision, the CMA had also identified a possible SLC concerns based on possible vertical effects in the context of the provision of pre-qualification services, in particular because the merged entity would have the possibility and the incentive to foreclose

parties engage in extensive marketing and product development to attract users. Both parties' product development efforts make their existing products more user-friendly and informative, and new products are also launched from time to time. Both parties use their free platforms to attract and retain users. Without the merger, the parties would continue to develop their products in various ways to help consumers better understand and improve their creditworthiness, according to the CMA. ClearScore's innovations could lead ClearScore to compete more closely with Experian's CreditExpert in the future, according to the CMA. As a result of the merger, the CMA reasoned, Experian would experience reduced incentive to invest in ClearScore. The CMA also raised concerns that the result of weakened competition among free credit comparison platforms could lead to the slowing, reversal or discontinuation of Experian's free credit check tool. Over time, customers of Experian's free tool could be transferred to ClearScore, leaving CreditExpert the market leader for paid credit check services and ClearScore the market leader for free services.

After announcing the provisional findings, the CMA announced on 27 February 2019, that the merger would be abandoned.

[G] ATG Media/LTMO

On 12 July 2018, the CMA approved the acquisition of LTMO by ATG Media.[626] Both LTMO and ATG Media offer LOB auction platform services to auction houses and participants in auctions in the field of art and antiques. ATG Media was already known to the CMA because of the 2017 commitment decision (*see* §5.02[B]) that the CMA took against it for alleged abuse of a dominant position.[627] The CMA did not see any horizontal competition problems: ATG Media was active in the UK, the United States (US) and Canada, while LTMO was mainly active in Germany, Austria, Switzerland, Belgium, France, Italy, the Netherlands and Spain, and only a negligible part of its turnover in the UK was achieved through UK participants in LTMO's LOB auctions.[628] The CMA also looked at vertical effects, as ATG Media was active in the upstream market for technology for LOB platforms. However, according to the CMA, as a result of the merger, ATG Media would not come in a position in which it would be able to implement an exclusionary strategy, due to the very limited presence of LTMO in the UK. Finally, the CMA also looked at the potential conglomerate effects of the transaction, but here too it found no evidence of a possible substantial lessening of competition.

Moreover, the concentration did not meet the turnover threshold of GBP 70 million for the target company. The CMA assumed jurisdiction over this concentration

competing suppliers of credit comparison platforms. However, in its provisional findings, the CMA concludes that such an incentive is unlikely to be materially increased.

626. ME/6754/18, Completed Acquisition by Auction Technology Group of Softwarepartner (Competition and Markets Authority).

627. *Case 50408: Auction Services, supra* n. 457.

628. ME/6754/18, Completed Acquisition by Auction Technology Group of Softwarepartner, supra n. 628, para. 44.

because the share-of-supply test was met.[629] This is the case when a concentration creates or strengthens a share of supply of more than 25%.[630] According to the decision, ATG Media had a market share of between 30% and 40%.[631]

[H] Moneysupermarket.com/DTL

On 8 August 2018, the CMA approved the acquisition of Decision Technologies Limited (DTL), a digital price comparison tool (DCT) for mobile and fixed telecom subscriptions, by Moneysupermarket.com (MSM), a general DCT.[632] The CMA concluded that the horizontal effects of the concentration would not lead to a substantial lessening of competition since DTL and MSM faced sufficient competition from other operators in the market for digital price comparison services for mobile and fixed telecommunications services and a large proportion of consumers would procure subscriptions through other distribution channels.[633]

The CMA also looked at the vertical relationships between DTL and MSM. DTL is a supplier to digital price comparison companies that do not wish to enter into contracts with the providers of the underlying services themselves (white label supply) or that do not wish to develop and maintain the DCT themselves (application programming interface (API) supply) (*see* Figure 5.1).[634] With the type of services offered by DTL, price comparison websites can therefore relatively easily increase the range of types of products and services that can be compared by consumers. The CMA considered that DTL did have the ability to exclude competitive price comparators, because it was the market leader in the field of white label supply of telecom price comparison services and because developing a white label independently is expensive and takes time.[635] However, the CMA concluded that an exclusionary strategy would not be profitable for DTL/MSM because competing price comparators could switch to another white label provider and because the parties held only a relatively limited share of the downstream market for telecom price comparison services and would therefore benefit only to a limited extent from switching consumers. According to CMA, DTL and MSM would therefore not have any incentive to apply an exclusionary strategy after the implementation of the concentration.

629. *Ibid.*, para. 15.
630. ME/6749/18, Anticipated Acquisition by Moneysupermarket.com Financial Group Limited of Decision Technologies Limited (Competition and Markets Authority) [12].
631. ME/6754/18, Completed Acquisition by Auction Technology Group of Softwarepartner, supra n. 628, para. 44.
632. ME/6749/18, Anticipated Acquisition by Moneysupermarket.com Financial Group Limited of Decision Technologies Limited, supra n. 630.
633. *Ibid.*, para. 106.
634. *Ibid.*, para. 26.
635. *Ibid.*, para. 158.

Figure 5.1 The Functioning of the Market for Price Comparison Tools

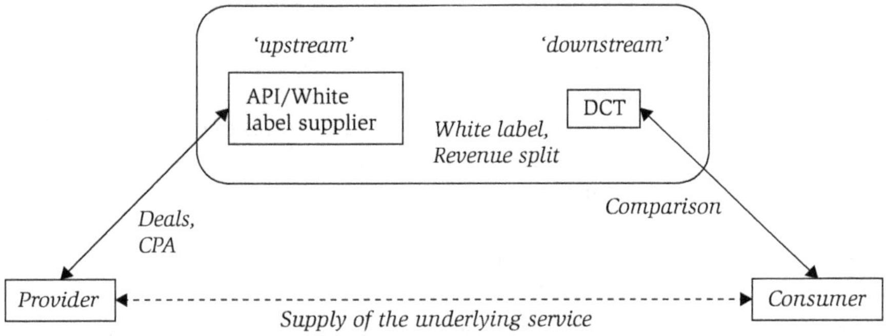

CPA: commission per action.

DTL had a relatively modest turnover of GBP 9.6 million in the UK in 2017, well below the GBP 70 million turnover threshold for reporting to the CMA in this case as well. The CMA assumed jurisdiction over the transaction because the share-of-supply test was passed: the concentration created or reinforced a share of supply of more than 25% (specifically, 25%-30% in home communications; the share of supply for the mobile market remained just below the threshold at 20%-25%).[636]

[I] Sainsbury/Asda

On 23 August 2018, the CMA launched a formal investigation into the proposed merger between J Sainsbury Plc (Sainsbury's) and Asda Group Ltd (Asda).[637] Sainsbury's is the second-largest supermarket chain in the United Kingdom. Asda, a subsidiary of the multinational supermarket chain Walmart Inc. (Walmart), is the third-largest supermarket chain in the United Kingdom. Both Sainsbury's and Asda operate multiple supermarkets, gas stations and an online grocery business in the United Kingdom. In addition to selling food items, both companies also sell various categories of 'general' goods in both their physical stores and online platforms. In addition, both companies also offer financial services.[638]

Both parties, following the commencement of the CMA's formal investigation, requested that the transaction be referred on an expedited basis for an in-depth Phase II investigation. In connection with this request, the CMA focused its Phase I investigation solely on whether the criterion for a referral was met.

636. *Ibid.*, para. 12.
637. ME/6752-18 Anticipated merger between J Sainsbury Plc and Asda Group Ltd, Commencement notice.
638. ME/6752-18 Anticipated merger between J Sainsbury Plc and Asda Group Ltd, Decision on relevant merger situation, substantial lessening of competition and reference.

On 25 April 2018, the CMA published its final report of the Phase II investigation in which it found extensive competition concerns, including in relation to online grocery delivery. Nationally, the concentration of these national operators in in-store groceries would result in a larger share of supply than the UK market leader Tesco. If the merger were to go ahead, it would merge two of the four largest players (also known as the 'Big 4') in the market who are also close competitors to each other. At the local level, the CMA found that Sainsbury's and Asda's stores overlap at more than 100 local locations in the UK. With regard to the online grocery business, the final report concludes, on the basis of, among other things, an extensive survey conducted by the CMA (with 31,404 interviews completed), that the relevant product market is the market for groceries delivered online (although there is some competitive pressure from in-store groceries) and that the geographic market is the delivery area served by each Supply Point, although the CMA also looks at the effects of the merger in the national market.[639] The CMA then concluded that these competition concerns were expected to lead to price increases, deterioration in product quality and online delivery services. In addition, consumers would potentially face worse service, both nationally and locally.[640] The CMA also concludes that possible coordinated effects will occur in 108 local markets for online delivered groceries. Despite far-reaching remedy proposals from Sainsbury's and Asda,[641] the concentration was ultimately prohibited.

[J] Nielsen Holdings/*AdIntel* Division of Ebiquity

The acquisition by Nielsen of the *AdIntel* division of Ebiquity (called 'Bloom') was the second concentration case in the digital sector that entered a second phase in the UK during the period under review. The CMA approved this acquisition on 31 October 2018. What is remarkable is that the case was eventually approved without any problems, because the special panel that assessed the case in the second phase reached diametrically different conclusions on virtually all crucial points in comparison to those of the officials who wrote the first-phase decision.

AdIntel is the (digital) tracking and collection of (digital and analogue) advertising and media data. Buyers of AdIntel services are offered the possibility to search through a large amount of information about the adverts of their competitors or customers.[642] The parties' activities overlapped in respect of (i) *deep dive* and (ii) *international* products. The first category comprises in-depth information at national level (in this case the UK). The second category includes less detailed data on several countries.[643] The CMA found that both deep dive and international data each form a

639. ME/6752-18 Anticipated merger between J Sainsbury Plc and Asda Group Ltd, Final Report, para. 10.56.
640. *Ibid.*
641. Both Sainsbury's and Asda made a number of proposals to meet the CMA's concerns. For example, both parties promised to sell between 125 and 150 supermarkets, along with some petrol stations and other shops, and also promised to make GBP 1 billion worth of price cuts.
642. ME/6733/18, Anticipated Acquisition by Nielsen Holdings PLC of the AdIntel Division of Ebiquity PLC (Competition and Markets Authority) [24].
643. *Ibid.*, para. 3.

separate market.[644] For both products, the geographic market would be national, as customers would value the presence of a sales team at national level.[645] The information offered on both products can also be divided into two categories. On the one hand, there is *ad spend* data (information on format, timing, placement, duration, size, location and costs of the advert, as well as the advertised product and brand). On the other hand, there is *ad creative* data: information on the creative content of the advert (this information may also include a photo, scan or video of the advert as such).

For the UK, the merging parties were (also by their own acknowledgement) the only providers of ad spend and ad creative deep dive data.[646] However, the parties had argued that their products were different and that demand substitution between the two products was therefore limited: Nielsen mainly focused on offering ad spend data, whereas Bloom essentially offered ad creative data. The CMA acknowledged in the first-phase decision that this was indeed the case up to a certain extent but nevertheless observed that both providers offered both ad spend and ad creative data and competed for these. On this basis, the parties would in any case compete for certain customers or groups of customers.[647] The latter was said to also arise from internal documents from both parties which had been reviewed by the CMA.[648] Although the market investigation showed that customers hardly switched from Nielsen to Bloom or vice versa (the CMA was able to identify only two cases), the CMA nevertheless found that customers regularly checked the price of the other supplier in the context of price negotiations.[649] According to the CMA, slightly similar products offered by competitors (such as Kantar, Global AD Source and AdVision) were not complete substitutes for deep dive data relating to the UK (of which, as mentioned, the parties were the only suppliers).[650] The CMA therefore found that the parties were close competitors and on top of that each other's only competitor. Therefore, the proposed acquisition was found to potentially lead to a substantial lessening of competition.

According to the first-phase decision, the parties had a market share of 50%-60% in the field of international products, with the increment being 5%-10%. The main competitors Kantar and Global Ad Source were said to have market shares of 10%-20% and 0%-10%, respectively. In their defence, the parties alluded to the presence of 'various' other competitors with market shares of up to 10%, but the CMA was unable to identify these in its market investigation[651] (and it would appear that the parties themselves did not succeed in doing so either). The parties argued that they were not close competitors with regard to international products either: Nielsen said it did not include any ad creative data in its international products at all, and Bloom said it focused on ad creative data and only offered ad spend data to a limited extent. However, the CMA found that Nielsen possessed raw ad creative data for the UK

644. *Ibid.*, paras 32-66.
645. *Ibid.*, paras 71-73.
646. *Ibid.*, para. 82.
647. *Ibid.*, paras 84-85.
648. *Ibid.*, paras 89-94.
649. *Ibid.*, paras 96-97.
650. *Ibid.*, paras 103-109.
651. *Ibid.*, paras 113-114.

because it collected this data for its deep dive products. Nielsen was further believed to be able to source data for other countries from competitors (although the CMA acknowledged that this would be costly), and, moreover, for some jurisdictions, it would already possess such data at a higher level of abstraction.[652] In addition, the market investigation had shown that at least one customer had actually switched suppliers between the two parties and that in any event, a lack of switching by customers would not preclude the parties from exerting competitive pressure on each other in the same way as they allegedly did (according to the first-phase decision) for deep dive products.[653] The CMA stated that competitors would not be able to sufficiently discipline the merged entity: Kantar was partly dependent on data from both Nielsen and Bloom, and Global Ad Source provided only ad creative data and no ad spend data.[654] The CMA therefore also feared a substantial lessening of competition in respect of international products.

In the first phase already, the CMA did not have any vertical competition concerns: it did not consider it likely that the parties would foreclose (in particular) Kantar from AdIntel information on the UK, as they, in turn, relied on information from Kantar for data on other countries.[655]

As noted above, all competition concerns identified in the first-phase decision disappeared in the second phase.[656]

With regard to deep dive products, the second-phase panel concluded that the parties had hardly any shared customers and rarely tendered to each other's customers. The conclusion from the first phase that customers rarely switched suppliers was confirmed. The panel also interpreted the internal documents of the parties differently from the CMA in the first phase: these were not believed to demonstrate that one party's price level played a role in determining the price level of another party. In addition, the panel found that there was hardly any competition in the field of product innovation. To the extent that the relevant internal documents would indicate that the parties considered each other to be competitors, they evidenced that the competitive pressure that they exerted on each other was weak. Where certain customers had indicated that they considered the other party's product to be to a certain extent a substitute for their supplier's product, the further market investigation showed that, in most cases, these customers had little knowledge of the other product, or that they did not feel that the other product put pressure on the price of the product they purchased.[657] Overall, the panel found that the competitive constraints that the parties exerted on each other were too weak to lead to a substantial reduction in competition,[658] also because the market investigation had shown that such competitive constraints were not likely to increase.[659]

652. *Ibid.*, paras 116-118.
653. *Ibid.*, paras 119-123.
654. *Ibid.*, para. 126.
655. *Ibid.*, paras 129-140.
656. 'Report: Nielsen and Ebiquity' (Competition and Markets Authority 2018).
657. *Ibid.*, para. 54.
658. *Ibid.*, para. 46.
659. *Ibid.*, para. 58.

As regards international products, the panel concluded that the parties exerted – if possible – even less competitive pressure on each other than they did for UK deep dive products and that therefore no competition problem could arise on that market either. The parties' product offerings were very different, and, in addition, their products were very much tailored to the individual needs of the customer, which meant that prices were also highly individualised.[660] Once again, the parties had only a few shared customers, and in practice customers rarely, if ever, switched suppliers between the two parties.[661] Nielsen's internal documents were found not to indicate that it saw Ebiquity/Bloom as a competitor and to the extent that Ebiquity's internal documents did identify Nielsen as a competitor to Bloom, those documents did not address the degree of competitive pressure that Nielsen exerted on Bloom.[662] An examination of correspondence from both parties had shown that only one customer had used the prices of the other party as a benchmark in price negotiations.[663] In addition, customers hardly regarded the parties' products as substitutes also in other respects.[664]

In view of the above, the case was cleared without remedies in the second phase.

[K] Topcashback/Quidco

Top Online Partners Group Limited and Maple Syrup Group Limited both operate cashback websites (Topcashback and Quidco, respectively). These websites are often two-sided in nature. On the one hand, the websites compete for advertisers who promote cashback deals and thus pay the websites for advertising, and on the other hand, the websites compete for consumers, who benefit from money-saving offers.

The CMA opened an investigation into the proposed merger between Topcashback and Quidco on 7 November 2018. Based on its first-phase investigation,[665] the CMA states that Topcashback and Quidco are the two largest cashback websites in the UK and are each other's closest competitors. The parties together have a very high market share (accounting together for [90-100]% share of supply) in the supply of money-saving offers and advertising through cashback websites in the UK. According to the CMA, other parties can exert only minor pressure on Topcashback and Quidco. The CMA is therefore concerned that if the transaction goes ahead, Topcashback could reduce the amount of cashback paid to consumers and also increase advertising prices for businesses. The CMA approved this acquisition on 7 January 2019.

After the first-stage investigation, the parties considered abandoning the transaction, but on 6 February 2019, they informed the CMA that they would proceed with the transaction anyway. The CMA subsequently issued an issues statement on 28

660. *Ibid.*, para. 60.
661. *Ibid.*,. para. 62.
662. *Ibid.*, para. 61.
663. *Ibid.*, para. 63.
664. *Ibid.*, para. 64.
665. https://assets.publishing.service.gov.uk/media/5c5c4bb940f0b676d9455cd2/final_decision_tcb_quidco.pdf.

February 2019, in which it stated it would investigate, among other things, the following theories of harm: '*a. Horizontal unilateral effects in the supply of money-saving offers and advertising via cashback websites in the UK; and b. Horizontal unilateral effects in the supply of white label affiliate marketing services to third parties in the UK*'.[666] In doing so, the CMA also called on the parties to offer remedies, but the parties subsequently decided to abandon the transaction.[667]

[L] Live Nation Gaeity MCD

On 15 May 2019, the CMA announced their investigation into the contemplated acquisition of MCD Productions Unlimited Company (MCD) by LN-Gaiety Holdings Limited (LN-Gaiety).[668] Both MCD and LN-Gaiety operate festivals on the island of Ireland and therefore the CMA investigated the horizontal overlap between the parties' activities. There is also a vertical relationship between the activities of the parties. MCD promotes live music events and uses Ticketmaster, the ticketing business of LN-Gaiety's parent company Live Nation Entertainment, Inc. (Live Nation), to sell tickets to MCD's events and festivals, and it books venue space owned and/or operated by Live Nation to host its live music events. Also, Live Nation manages artists that perform on the island of Ireland some of which are promoted by MCD.

On 11 July 2019, the CMA published the results of its first-phase investigation.[669] Taking into account the limited increment as a result of the merger on the market share for the provision of festivals on the island or Ireland, the CMA particularly assessed the following vertical theories of harm: (a) input foreclosure of rival festivals using Ticketmaster; (b) input foreclosure of rival promoters using Ticketmaster; (c) input foreclosure of rival promoters using Live Nation's venues; (d) input foreclosure of rival promoters using Live Nation's artist management business; (e) customer foreclosure of rival providers of ticketing services using MCD as a promoter or MCD's festivals; and (f) customer foreclosure of venues using MCD. The CMA concluded that the parties would have the ability and may have the incentive to foreclose rival promotors using Ticketmaster (the theory of harm under (b) above). The CMA therefore believed that the concentration would give rise to a realistic prospect of a substantial lessening of competition as a result of vertical effects in relation to the promotion of live music events with over 1,000 tickets capacity on the island of Ireland, and referred the case for a phase two investigation.[670]

---

666. https://assets.publishing.service.gov.uk/media/5c77bc11ed915d3547d50a12/TopCashback_Quidco_Issues_statement.pdf.
667. https://www.gov.uk/government/news/abandonment-of-cashback-websites-merger.
668. ME/6808/18 Anticipated acquisition by LN-Gaiety Holdings Limited of MCD Productions Unlimited Company, Commencement Notice.
669. ME/6808/18 Anticipated acquisition by LN-Gaiety Holdings Limited of MCD Productions Unlimited Company, Decision on relevant merger situation and substantial lessening of competition.
670. ME/6808/18 Anticipated acquisition by LN-Gaiety Holdings Limited of MCD Productions Unlimited Company, Decision to refer.

In the second phase of its investigation, the CMA provisionally found that the merged entity would not have the incentive to harm rival music promoters by making it harder for them to sell tickets through Ticketmaster and also dismissed two specific concerns raised by third parties.[671] On 19 December 2019, the CMA cleared the concentration.[672]

[M] Sabre/Farelogix

Sabre and Farelogix are US-based companies that provide technology and software to the global travel industry. This technology is used for airline ticket booking systems that are distributed through travel agents. Farelogix is primarily developing a merchandising module that allows airlines to offer passengers extras such as an option for extra luggage, seats with more legroom or options for different meals.[673]

On 21 June 2019, the CMA opened an investigation into the proposed concentration between Sabre and Farelogix. On 16 August 2019, the CMA decided to refer the investigation to the second phase. The outcome of the first-phase investigation was that Farelogix, although at that time a much smaller player than top-3 player Sabre, poses a significant threat to Sabre's competitive position and is recognised as a major innovator with a disruptive business model. Because Farelogix is known in the market as a player with new and innovative technologies, one reason the CMA is concerned is that there will be less innovation in the market if the merger goes through.

On 9 April 2020, the CMA[674] blocked Sabre's proposed acquisition of Farelogix. The CMA concluded that the acquisition could lead to less innovation in the companies' services.[675] It is considered unlikely that if Sabre were to buy Farelogix, Sabre itself would develop the technology for a merchandising module. The CMA believes the continued independence of Farelogix will likely help motivate Sabre to further innovate, giving airlines more choices to connect with travel agents, allowing tickets and products to be sold through travel agents in more innovative ways.

Sabre discontinued the acquisition in May 2020. However, on 1 June 2020, Sabre did appeal to the CAT against the CMA's second-stage decision. According to Sabre, the

671. ME/6808/18 Anticipated acquisition by LN-Gaiety Holdings Limited of MCD Productions Unlimited Company, Provisional findings report. The first concern was that Live Nation could threaten music venues that, if they switched away from Ticketmaster, MCD would use its influence over artists to divert events away from the venue concerned. The other concern, already considered by the CMA in its first-phase investigation, was that the concentration would remove the possibility of MCD switching to another provider of ticketing services, thereby foreclosing other providers. The CMA found that these theories of harm do not provide a basis for an SLC.
672. ME/6808/18 Anticipated acquisition by LN-Gaiety Holdings Limited of MCD Productions Unlimited Company, Final report.
673. CMA 9 April 2020, Sabre Corporation/Farelogix Inc. final report, paras 6, 7 & 13.
674. Where jurisdiction is concerned, the CMA assumes that the 25% share-of-supply threshold was deemed to have been reached by looking at the commercial reality of the parties' activities. In the present case, jurisdiction was assumed by suggesting the existence of a complex indirect delivery channel to a single customer in the UK, despite the fact that the Farelogix did not generate any direct revenue in the UK.
675. CMA 9 April 2020, Sabre Corporation/Farelogix Inc. final report, para. 52.

decision was unlawful both in terms of the CMA's jurisdiction and findings. The CMA determined its jurisdiction based on the share-of-supply test. In doing so, three relevant points were decisive in the eyes of the CMA: (i) Sabre and Farelogix each provide services that can be included in the definition of services, (ii) Farelogix provides relevant services in the United Kingdom, and (iii) the share-of-supply test exceeds the ceiling of the 25%.[676] Sabre presents four arguments on the basis of which the decision should be set aside: (i) the CMA erred in law in that its relevant description of services did not provide a legitimate basis for applying the share-of-supply test; (ii) the CMA misconstrued the 'supply in the UK' requirement by confusing direct supply to FLX Services (US airline) with direct supply to British Airways; (iii) the CMA incorrectly relied on an increase in competition that was both hypothetical and insignificant as well as irrationally and incorrectly applied different and inconsistent methodologies; (iv) the CMA erred in its calculation of the total supply of remote desktop services (RDS) services in the UK by failing to apply its own definition of RDS consistently. With respect to the decision that the CMA anticipates a substantial reduction in competition, Sabre raises arguments that involve assessment of the evidence. Sabre argues that if the CMA had correctly assessed the evidence, it could not lead to a decision entailing a substantial lessening of competition.[677] However, on 20 November 2020, Sabre announced that the latter two grounds had been dropped, leaving no substantive ruling by the CAT on whether there was a substantial lessening of competition. In its ruling of 21 May 2021, the CAT also rejected Sabre's arguments contesting the CMA's jurisdiction.[678]

[N] Amazon/Deliveroo

Following the announcement of a substantial investment in Roofoods Ltd (Deliveroo) by Amazon.com, Inc, Amazon NV Investment Holdings LCC and the UK branch of EU SARL (Amazon), the CMA issued an enforcement order to Amazon and Deliveroo on 24 June 2019. As a result of a USD 575 million investment, Amazon would receive certain rights and a minority stake in Deliveroo. Under the enforcement order, Amazon and Deliveroo are in principle not allowed to cooperate with each other for the time being, for example by exchanging company information or transferring staff members.

On 16 October 2019, the CMA announced to formally investigate Amazon's proposed investment in Deliveroo in a Phase I investigation.[679] The first-phase decision shows that the CMA is concerned that Amazon could begin to influence Deliveroo's business strategy through its minority stake. A key factor for this suspicion is that Amazon has substantial expertise in areas such as the operation of online market-places, logistics networks and subscription services. According to the CMA, this

676. Competition Appeal Tribunal 1 June 2020, Case 1345/4/12/20.
677. *Ibid.*
678. Competition Appeal Tribunal 21 May 2021, Case 1345/4/12/20, https://www.catribunal.org.uk/sites/default/files/2021-05/1345_Sabre_Judgment_210521.pdf.
679. *Acquisition by Amazon of certain rights and a minority shareholding in Deliveroo* Commencement notice.

expertise could enable Amazon to exercise substantial influence over Deliveroo's shareholders and board members.

On 11 December 2019, the CMA concluded in the first-phase investigation that Amazon's investment in Deliveroo could adversely affect competition in the United Kingdom in two ways.

(i) First, the CMA noted that the online restaurant food delivery market is highly concentrated with only three major providers in the UK: Deliveroo, Just Eat and Uber Eats. According to the UK regulator, Amazon also competed in the online restaurant food delivery market through its range of online delivery services until November 2018. After 2018, Amazon stopped offering these services. The CMA is concerned that the investment in question will discourage Amazon from re-entering the UK online restaurant food delivery market. The CMA has come across evidence suggesting that Amazon is still interested in this market. Given the small number of providers in the market, Amazon would allow competition in the market to increase significantly. In other words, Amazon's investment in question could have horizontal effects on the market for online restaurant food delivery in the UK.[680]

(ii) In addition, the CMA suspected that the investment could also harm competition in the emerging market for online 'ultrafast' grocery delivery. This market differs from the traditional online food delivery market in that these services often take a day for delivery, rather than minutes/hours. The CMA noted that this market is also highly concentrated, in which, according to the CMA, Amazon and Deliveroo hold the strongest positions due to their installed delivery networks in the UK. The CMA believes through its research that both parties have expansion plans for the future. This would most likely intensify competition in the market, although the CMA also noted slight differences between the companies' services. A collaboration between Amazon and Deliveroo will reduce competition in this market, according to the CMA.[681]

Since the parties offered no remedies, on 27 December 2019, the CMA referred the merger to the second phase. During this second phase, Deliveroo brought forward a failing firm defence. Deliveroo argued that the COVID-19 pandemic had serious financial consequences for its business that would force it to eventually exit the market without investment. Recognising the seriousness and urgency of the situation, the CMA concluded in its 17 April 2020 provisional findings, through a balancing of interests, that the demise of Deliveroo would be more serious for competition and

680. ME/6836/19 Anticipated acquisition by Amazon of a minority shareholding and certain rights in Deliveroo, Decision on relevant merger situation and substantial lessening of competition.
681. *Ibid.*

customers than the potential impact that could occur by allowing Amazon's investment to continue. The transaction was provisionally approved with this in mind.[682]

Following the first provisional findings in April 2020, the CMA monitored and analysed Deliveroo's financial situation. Third parties were also able to comment on the provisional findings. The CMA subsequently revised its provisional findings on 24 June 2020. Due to the changed market situation and financial situation of Deliveroo, on 24 June 2020, the CMA noted in its revised provisional findings that Deliveroo would no longer be likely to exit the market if an investment from Amazon failed to materialise. The CMA stated that the market had recovered unexpectedly quickly.[683] In doing so, the CMA again focused on whether the investment would have negative effects on competition in the market for online restaurant food delivery and the market for online 'ultrafast' grocery delivery in the UK.

Both in the initial provisional findings, the revised provisional findings and its final report, the CMA concluded that Amazon's investment in Deliveroo should be approved. This is the result of an extensive review of internal documents, a survey of consumers and contributions from interested third parties, among other things. The question the CMA focused on was whether a 16% shareholding, would give Amazon enough incentive to compete independently with Deliveroo in online restaurant food delivery and online 'ultrafast' grocery delivery in the future. The CMA ultimately found that this level of investment would not substantially reduce competition in either market, however, the CMA stated that should Amazon acquire more control of Deliveroo, this could trigger further scrutiny.[684]

[O] Salesforce/Tableau

On 22 November 2019, the CMA approved the acquisition of Tableau Software, Inc. (Tableau) by Salesforce.com, Inc. (Salesforce).[685] The parties' activities overlap in the area of business intelligence (BI) tools, in particular in the area of modern BI tools.[686] In addition, a potential vertical relationship exists through Salesforce's activities in customer relationship management (CRM) software. Regarding the horizontal overlap, the CMA concluded that the concentration does not raise competition concerns

682. ME/6836/19 Anticipated acquisition by Amazon of a minority shareholding and certain rights in Deliveroo, Provisional findings report.
683. ME/6836/19 Anticipated acquisition by Amazon of a minority shareholding and certain rights in Deliveroo, Revised provisional findings report.
684. ME/6836/19 Anticipated acquisition by Amazon of a minority shareholding and certain rights in Deliveroo, final report.
685. https://assets.publishing.service.gov.uk/media/5dfa5c69e5274a670091be1a/Publication_version_-_Decision_-_Salesforce-Tableau_.pdf.
686. Modern BI tools refers to '*tools and platforms that (i) allow users in a self-service manner to develop and present the results of data exploration and analysis; (ii) develop interactive management information dashboards and reports; and (iii) may support user development with integrated statistical modelling, machine learning (ML) or natural language processing and require minimal support of IT specialists to integrate and manage new data sources.*' (ME/6841/19, Completed acquisition by Salesforce.com, Inc. of Tableau Software, Inc., para. 17).

because the parties are not close competitors and there are a number of other BI vendors (such as Microsoft, SAP, SAS, IBM, MicroStrategy, Oracle and independent players such as Qlik, Alteryx and Domo) that will continue to exert competitive pressure on the combination of Tableau and Salesforce. The CMA also examined whether the proposed merger could potentially lead to the foreclosure of (i) competing providers of BI tools or (ii) competing providers of CRM software, through technical restrictions, bundling and/or tying. However, the CMA concluded that the parties would have neither the ability nor the incentive to foreclose competing BI and CRM software providers.

[P] Just Eat/Takeaway

On 31 January 2020, Takeaway acquired Just Eat when the bid for Just Eat became unconditional. Both parties are active in providing online takeaway platforms. Just Eat operates these services in thirteen countries worldwide, including the UK. Takeaway operates these services in eleven countries worldwide but has no presence in the UK as Takeaway exited the UK market in 2016. The CMA opened its investigation on 19 March 2020 and considered whether the merger could reduce competition in the supply of online takeaway platforms in the UK. In particular, the CMA considered whether, absent the merger, Takeaway would have re-entered the market, and if so, whether this would have resulted in a more competitive market than was the case before the merger.[687]

The CMA has previously indicated, in its first-phase decision on Amazon/ Deliveroo, that the meal delivery market is characterised by material barriers to entry, including the need for a company to build relationships with restaurants, couriers and consumers and also the need to develop the necessary technology to drive logistics. Although the CMA concludes that Takeaway has the necessary technology and expertise in principle, as it operates in thirteen other countries, Takeaway does not, according to the CMA, have existing relationships with restaurants in the UK, nor does it have an existing customer base, making it unrealistic that Takeaway would enter the market independently.[688] Partly for this reason, the CMA expects no substantial lessening of competition and approved the acquisition on 23 April 2020.

[Q] Google/Looker Data Sciences

On 13 February 2020, in a Phase I decision, the CMA approved the acquisition of Looker Data Sciences Inc. (Looker) by Google LLC (Google). Looker is a US-based provider of BI tools. While Looker's primary focus is on BI tools, Google is a global provider of various software and Internet-based products. Google not only offers BI

687. ME/6881/20 Completed acquisition by Takeaway.com N.V. of Just Eat plc, Decision on relevant merger situation and substantial lessening of competition.
688. *Ibid.*, paras 34-35.

tools but also operates in a number of sectors including Web analytics, online search advertising and cloud computing.

The CMA looked at whether the loss of direct competition between Google and Looker in the provision of BI tools could lead to higher prices or lower quality. The CMA considered this unlikely because Google and Looker are not considered close competitors by companies using BI tools. In addition, companies can still choose from other providers, such as Microsoft, Oracle, Tableu, SAP and IBM.

In addition, the CMA considered whether Google could use its market power in online advertising and Web analytics to drive competing BI providers from the market. The CMA concluded on the basis of an extensive first-phase analysis that while Google had the ability to make it difficult for its competitors to access the necessary data generated by Google from online advertising and web analytics services, there was no compelling evidence that Google would have the incentive to do so.[689] The CMA bases its conclusion on (i) internal Google documents that do not suggest that Google would adopt an exclusionary strategy, (ii) the CMA's analysis of the potential for switching and its (negative) impact on Google's advertising business, (iii) the high costs that any exclusionary strategies would impose against competing BI tool providers, and (iv) the fact that a limited exclusionary strategy would reduce the extent to which customers are steered toward the merged entity's BI tool, thereby limiting the benefits of an exclusionary strategy.[690]

[R] Viagogo/Stubhub

Viagogo acquired competitor StubHub in February 2020 for USD 4.1 billion (GBP 3.1 billion).[691] Both parties are global providers of online exchange platforms for the buying and selling of tickets to live events. They operate on the market for the supply of uncapped secondary ticketing platform services for the resale of tickets to UK events (hereinafter: 'uncapped secondary ticketing market'), on which ticket holders (resellers) can resell tickets to buyers at a price of their choice (with no price limit).

After first inviting third parties to come forward with their views, the CMA announced on 14 April 2020 that it would open an investigation into the concentration.[692] On 25 June 2020, the merger was referred to an in-depth investigation in phase II.[693] In its Provisional findings report of 22 October 2020, the CMA's preliminary assessment was that the acquisition of StubHub by Viagogo will be likely to result in a substantial lessening of competition in the secondary ticketing market through

689. ME/6839/19, Completed acquisition by Google LLC of Looker Data Sciences, Inc., paras 119 ff.
690. *Ibid.*, para. 229.
691. https://www.bbc.com/news/business-55899651.
692. ME/6868/19 Completed acquisition by PUG LLC of StubHub, Inc., StubHub (UK) Limited, StubHub Europe S.à.r.l., StubHub India Private Limited, StubHub International Limited, StubHub Taiwan Co., Ltd., StubHub GmbH, and Todoentradas, S.L., Commencement Notice.
693. ME/6868/19 Completed acquisition by PUG LLC of StubHub, Inc., StubHub (UK) Limited, StubHub Europe S.à.r.l., StubHub India Private Limited, StubHub International Limited, StubHub Taiwan Co., Ltd., StubHub GmbH, and Todoentradas, S.L., Decision to refer.

horizontal unilateral effects.[694] As a result, customers using secondary ticketing platforms could face higher fees or poorer service.

The 2 February 2021 Final Report concludes that Viagogo and StubHub compete closely with each other, have a combined market share of more than 90% and are No. 1 and No. 2 in the UK, respectively.[695] Although the CMA took into account the significant impact of COVID-19 on the live events sector during its investigation, there are still indications that parties will remain significant competitors as the sector recovers. The CMA also concludes that other distribution channels, such as capped price ticket exchanges and social media, exert only limited competitive pressure.[696] Therefore, Viagogo offered to sell all of StubHub's operations outside North America,[697] which has been accepted by the CMA.[698] On 8 September 2021, the CMA announced that case was closed with the divestiture on 3 September 2021.[699]

[S] Taboola/Outbrain

On 29 April 2020, the CMA opened an investigation into the acquisition of Outbrain Inc (Outbrain) by Taboola.com Ltd (Taboola).[700] Taboola is a provider of digital advertising services, including content recommendation through a platform that displays ads on publishers' web pages for external content that users may be interested in. For example, Taboola offers sections such as 'content you may like' or 'recommended for you'. Outbrain is also active in digital advertising services in the UK. Both parties' customers include advertisers such as individual companies, media agencies, digital platforms and publishers.[701]

On 26 June 2020, the CMA completed its first-phase investigation and concluded that the merger will result in the two largest players in the provision of advertising

694. ME/6868/19 Completed acquisition by PUG LLC of StubHub, Inc., StubHub (UK) Limited, StubHub Europe S.à.r.l., StubHub India Private Limited, StubHub International Limited, StubHub Taiwan Co., Ltd., StubHub GmbH, and Todoentradas, S.L., Provisional findings report.
695. ME/6868/19 Completed acquisition by PUG LLC of StubHub, Inc., StubHub (UK) Limited, StubHub Europe S.à.r.l., StubHub India Private Limited, StubHub International Limited, StubHub Taiwan Co., Ltd., StubHub GmbH, and Todoentradas, S.L., Provisional findings report.
696. ME/6868/19 Completed acquisition by PUG LLC of StubHub, Inc., StubHub (UK) Limited, StubHub Europe S.à.r.l., StubHub India Private Limited, StubHub International Limited, StubHub Taiwan Co., Ltd., StubHub GmbH, and Todoentradas, S.L., Final report.
697. ME/6868/19 Completed acquisition by PUG LLC of StubHub, Inc., StubHub (UK) Limited, StubHub Europe S.à.r.l., StubHub India Private Limited, StubHub International Limited, StubHub Taiwan Co., Ltd., StubHub GmbH, and Todoentradas, S.L., Final undertakings.
698. ME/6868/19 Completed acquisition by PUG LLC of StubHub, Inc., StubHub (UK) Limited, StubHub Europe S.à.r.l., StubHub India Private Limited, StubHub International Limited, StubHub Taiwan Co., Ltd., StubHub GmbH, and Todoentradas, S.L., Notice of acceptance of final undertakings.
699. https://assets.publishing.service.gov.uk/media/61379adfe90e07044435c8d0/Viagogo_StubHub_Case_closure_summary.pdf.
700. ME/6877-20 Anticipated acquisition by Taboola.com Ltd. Of Outbrain Inc., Commencement notice.
701. ME/6877-20 Anticipated acquisition by Taboola.com Ltd. Of Outbrain Inc., Decision on relevant merger situation and substantial lessening of competition, paras 1-4.

content recommendation services in the UK having a combined market share of 80%–90%. The parties are each other's closest competitors in the provision of platform recommendation services to UK publishers. The CMA concludes from internal documents that the parties monitor each other's activities and try to win each other's customers. There are no alternative suppliers for the services, according to the CMA. In addition, the majority of publishers at the CMA's enquiry expressed their concerns about the proposed merger. Based on these horizontal unilateral effects, the CMA found that the acquisition raises significant competition concerns due to horizontal unilateral effects in relation to the provision of platform content recommendation services to publishers in the UK.

During the CMA's second-phase investigation, the parties decided to abandon the acquisition, which led to the investigation being cancelled.[702]

[T] Facebook/Giphy

In May 2020, Facebook Inc. (Facebook, now: Meta) announced that GIPHY, Inc. (Giphy) would join Facebook. Giphy is an online database and search engine that allows users to share graphics interchange formats (GIFs) and stickers on social media platforms. As a result of the merger, Giphy's GIF library will be integrated into Instagram and other Facebook apps.[703]

On 9 June 2020, the CMA issued an initial enforcement order (IEO),[704] in which it ordered Facebook and Giphy to remain separate pending the outcome of its competition investigation.[705] In August 2020, Facebook appealed to the CAT regarding the CMA's refusal to grant derogations from the IEO in the interim period. Facebook argued that the IEO would be unreasonable and disproportionate, in part because it was based on a standard template.[706] Then CMA Chairman Andrea Coscelli stated that this case would be important to see if the IEO system can hold up.[707] In November 2020, Facebook lost this appeal,[708] and subsequently also lost the appeal to the review decision in May 2021.[709] On 20 October 2021, the CMA imposed a fine of GBP 50.5

702. CMA: Digital advertising merger to be abandoned by CMA investigation, https://www.gov.uk/government/news/competition-concerns-found-in-digital-advertising-merger.
703. Facebook press release, *Facebook Welcomes GIPHY as Part of Instagram Team*, https://about.fb.com/news/2020/05/welcome-giphy/.
704. ME/6891-20 Completed acquisition by Facebook, Inc. of GIPHY, Inc., Decision on relevant merger situation and substantial lessening of competition.
705. The CMA then also appointed a monitoring trustee and a hold separate manager.
706. Webinar of the Fordham Competition Law Institute's annual International Antitrust Law and Policy Conference. *See also*: Competition Appeal Tribunal, case No. 1366/4/12/20, Summary of Application under Section 120 of the Enterprise Act 2002.
707. Webinar of the Fordham Competition Law Institute's annual International Antitrust Law and Policy Conference.
708. Competition Appeal Tribunal 13 November 2020, Case 1366/4/12/20.
709. Court of Appeal 13 May 2021, [2021] EWCA Civ 701.

million for violation of the IEO[710] and on 4 February 2022, the CMA imposed a second fine of GBP 1.5 million.[711]

On 28 January 2021, the CMA also launched an investigation to assess whether the acquisition could result in a substantial lessening of competition in the UK. The CMA decided to refer the merger to the second phase in view of a possible substantial lessening of competition (SLC) resulting from the following theories of harm: (i) loss of potential competition in display advertising, and (ii) vertical effects through the foreclosure of social media platforms.[712] Based on its second-stage investigation, the CMA concludes in its final report that there is a significant reduction in competition (i) in display advertising provision in the UK due to horizontal unilateral effects arising from a loss of dynamic competition, and (ii) in social media service provision globally due to vertical effects arising from input foreclosure, as a result of which Giphy would have to be fully divested.[713] Facebook brought this conclusion before the CAT, which on 14 June 2022, dismissed Facebook's substantive objections to the decision,[714] but on procedural grounds - specifically, the violation of Facebook's and Giphy's rights since the CMA did not share certain information with the parties - set aside the decision and referred it back to the CMA,[715] which has since begun its remittal inquiry and announced on 29 July 2022, that it is adopting the previously published Final Report in its entirety.[716] On 6 January 2023, the CMA issued its final divestiture order.[717]

[U] Crowdcube/Seedrs

The acquisition of Seedrs Limited (Seedrs) by Crowdcube Limited (Crowdcube) was notified by the parties on 14 and 15 October 2020 with the request for 'a fast track reference of the Merger to an in-depth Phase 2 investigation'. Crowdcube and Seedrs are the two largest equity crowdfunding (ECF) platforms in the UK. The aim of these platforms is to match small- and medium-sized enterprises (SMEs) seeking equity investment with investors willing to provide funding in exchange for a stake in the

710. ME/6891-20 Completed acquisition by Facebook, Inc. of GIPHY, Inc., Decision to impose a penalty on Facebook, Inc., Tabby Acquisition Sub Inc., and Facebook UK Limited under section 94A of the Enterprise Act 2002.
711. ME/6891-20 Completed acquisition by Facebook, Inc. of GIPHY, Inc., Second decision to impose a penalty on Facebook, Inc., Tabby Acquisition Sub Inc., and Facebook UK Limited under section 94A of the Enterprise Act 2002.
712. The CMA also examined the following theories of harm: (iii) raising barriers to entry and expansion by increasing Facebook's data advantage in display advertising and (iv) loss of potential competition in the supply of searchable GIF libraries, but came to the preliminary view that none of these appear to apply. ME/6891-20 Completed acquisition by Facebook, Inc. of GIPHY, Inc., Decision on relevant merger situation and substantial lessening of competition.
713. ME/6891-20 Completed acquisition by Facebook, Inc. of GIPHY, Inc., Final report.
714. Competition Appeal Tribunal 14 June 2022, [2022] CAT 26.
715. https://www.catribunal.org.uk/sites/default/files/2022-07/20220714_1429_Order%20of%20the%20President%20%28Remittal%29.pdf.
716. Zie de case page, https://www.gov.uk/cma-cases/facebook-inc-giphy-inc-merger-inquiry.
717. https://assets.publishing.service.gov.uk/media/63b6a80f8fa8f52732a24662/Final_Order__Remittal_.pdf.

business.[718] Following this request, the CMA referred the merger investigation to the second phase on 12 November 2020.[719]

On 24 March 2021, the CMA reached the preliminary view that the proposed concentration could lead to a substantial lessening of competition (SLC) within the supply of ECF platforms for small- and medium-sized enterprises (SMEs) and investors in the UK.[720] The proposed transaction would result in the joint venture having a market share of at least 90%.[721] The CMA's Phase 2 investigation found that a merger between the two parties could result in small- and medium-sized enterprises (SMEs) and investors in the UK losing out due to higher fees and less innovation.[722] Blocking the merger seemed to be the only way to remove these competition concerns, according to the CMA.[723] A consultation was then launched on these preliminary findings but it never came to that: the parties themselves 'pulled the plug' on the deal a day later.[724]

[V] Adevinta/eBay

On 17 December 2020, the CMA announced its investigation into the contemplated acquisition by Adevinta ASA (Adevinta) of eBay Classifieds Group (eCG) from eBay Inc. (eBay), and eBay's acquisition of a minority stake (33.3% of the voting rights) in Adevinta. Adevinta provides online classified advertising services through Shpock and MB Diffusion. eCG provides online classified advertising services through Gumtree and Motors.co.uk. eBay operates the online marketplace eBay.

The CMA investigated potential horizontal unilateral effects in the field of online generalist classified advertising services and consumer-to-consumer online market-places (i.e., overlap between Adevinta's Shpock, eCG's Gumtree and the consumer-to-consumer segment of eBay's online marketplace),[725] concluding on 16 February 2021 that the concentration gives rise to a realistic prospect of an SLC taking into account that eBay's online market place is the largest platform (with a share of supply of [50-60]%, twice the size of the next largest competitor), Gumtree is the third- or fourth-largest platform, Gumtree and Shpock combined would increase eBay's already large share of supply by a significant increment, and the platforms are or may well be

718. https://assets.publishing.service.gov.uk/media/6059f51ae90e0724c31f720c/PF_Summaryne w-_.pdf, paras 6-8; https://www.gov.uk/government/news/cma-finds-competition-concer ns-in-crowdcube-and-seedrs-merger.
719. ME/6879/20, Anticipated merger between Crowdcube and Seedrs, CMA decision dated 12 November 2020.
720. ME/6879/20, Anticipated merger between Crowdcube and Seedrs, para. 8.2.
721. *Ibid.*, para. 6.50.
722. *Ibid.*, paras 6.294-6.300.
723. *Ibid.*, para. 3.
724. https://assets.publishing.service.gov.uk/media/605ca4b9d3bf7f2f15dd8b2b/Notice_of_canc ellation_of_merger_reference_crowdcube_seedrs.pdf, p. 3.
725. ME/6897/20 Anticipated acquisition by Adevinta ASA of eBay Classifieds Group from eBay Inc., and eBay Inc.'s acquisition of a minority stake in Adevinta ASA, Decision on relevant merger situation and substantial lessening of competition, para. 133.

close competitors.[726] Before the case was referred to Phase 2, the parties offered commitments (a divestment of Adevinta's Shpock and eCG's Gumtree and Motors.co.uk), which were accepted by the CMA[727] and the case was conditionally cleared on 3 December 2021.[728]

[W] Facebook/Kustomer

On 30 July 2021, the CMA initiated an investigation into the acquisition of Kustomer, Inc. (Kustomer) by Facebook, Inc.[729] Facebook is a technology company with a wide range of services, including social media platforms, messaging channels (Messenger, WhatsApp and Instagram Messaging), digital advertising and a range of business tools. Kustomer offers Software as a Service (SaaS) in CRM. Kustomer's CRM software combines multiple communication channels between businesses and consumers, including Messenger, WhatsApp and Instagram Messaging. The CMA explored four theories of harm: (i) whether the merger would raise barriers to entry and expansion by increasing Facebook's data advantage in online display advertising, leading to reduced competition in that market; (ii) whether Facebook could harm the competitiveness of other customer service and support CRM software providers by restricting or worsening their access to Facebook's messaging channels; (iii) whether Facebook could reduce the competitiveness of other B2C messaging service providers by preventing them from integrating their services with Kustomer; and (iv) whether Facebook could rely on cross-subsidisation from its online display advertising business to offer Kustomer for free or on a freemium basis, making it difficult for other CRM service providers to compete, but concluded in its first-phase investigation that the transaction could be approved.[730]

726. ME/6897/20 Anticipated acquisition by Adevinta ASA of eBay Classifieds Group from eBay Inc., and eBay Inc.'s acquisition of a minority stake in Adevinta ASA, Decision on relevant merger situation and substantial lessening of competition. The CMA also investigated two vertical relationships, but did not find SLCs likely, in respect of (i) online classified advertising platforms and online marketplaces for agricultural machinery, construction machinery and trucks (with the relevant vertical relationship between Adevinta's MB Diffusion, eCG's Gumtree, and eBay's online marketplace); and (ii) online classified advertising platforms and online marketplaces for motor vehicles (with the relevant vertical relationship between Adevinta's Shpock, eCG's Gumtree and Motors.co.uk, and eBay's online marketplace).
727. ME/6897/20 Anticipated acquisition by Adevinta ASA of eBay Classifieds Group from eBay Inc., and eBay Inc.'s acquisition of a minority stake in Adevinta ASA, Decision on acceptance of undertakings in lieu of reference.
728. Please refer to the case page: https://www.gov.uk/cma-cases/adevinta-ebay-merger-inquiry.
729. ME/6920/20, Anticipated acquisition by Facebook, Inc. of Kustomer, Inc., Commencement notice.
730. ME/6920/20, Anticipated acquisition by Facebook, Inc. of Kustomer, Inc., Decision on relevant merger situation and substantial lessening of competition.

[X] Anticipated Acquisition by Auction Technology Group Plc of Live Auctioneers, LLC

On 10 August 2021, the CMA announced their investigation into the contemplated acquisition of Live Auctioneers, LLC (Live Auctioneers) by Auction Technology Group plc (ATG).[731] Both Live Auctioneers and ATG operate online auction marketplaces for arts and antiques, two-sided platforms that connect auction houses and bidders. Taking into account that ATG operates by far the largest online auction marketplace for arts and antiques in the UK, the CMA investigated potential horizontal unilateral effects but found that Live Auctioneers is largely focused on the North American market and attracts very few UK bidders and there were alternatives and out-of-market constraints (e.g., white label solutions).

The CMA also assessed whether the concentration could give rise to conglomerate effects, in particular by enabling ATG and Live Auctioneers to leverage the position of Live Auctioneers in the US, where it has a significant number of bidders, to increase the number of auction houses using ATG's services in the UK (e.g., through bundling). However, the CMA found, on the basis of the shares of supply of Live Auctioneers and ATG in the US and UK respectively, that Live Auctioneers is unlikely to have market power in the US and ATG has a pre-existing strong position in the UK. The CMA therefore found it likely that ATG and Live Auctioneer would have limited ability and incentive to implement a leveraging strategy. On 29 September 2021, the CMA therefore decided that the CMA does not believe that it is or may be the case that the Merger may be expected to give rise to an SLC, and cleared the concentration in the first phase.[732]

[Y] Booking Holidays Inc./eTraveli Group

On 23 November 2021, Booking Holdings announced its intention to acquire sole control over the company eTraveli Group.[733] Both of these undertakings are active on the OTA markets in the UK and globally. Booking Holdings' key brand that is present in the UK is Booking.com and it is operating on the accommodation OTA market. eTraveli is primarily active on the flight OTA market but also engages in the accommodation OTA services through a commercial affiliate arrangement with Booking.com. Similarly, Booking.com has a commercial affiliate arrangement with eTraveli to provide flight OTA services.

731. ME/6942/21 Anticipated acquisition by Auction Technology Group plc of Live Auctioneers, LLC, Commencement notice.
732. ME/6942/21 Anticipated acquisition by Auction Technology Group plc of Live Auctioneers, LLC, Decision on relevant merger situation and substantial lessening of competition.
733. Dennis Schaal, 'Booking Holdings to Buy Flights Partner ETraveli Group for $1.8 Billion' (*Skift*, 23 November 2021) https://skift.com/2021/11/23/booking-holdings-to-buy-flights-partner-etraveli-group-for-1-8-billion/.

The CMA opened an investigation into the merger in question as it had doubts regarding whether this transaction can have an adverse impact on competition.[734] The CMA was concerned that the merger might cause a barrier to entry and expansion in the supply of accommodation OTA services.[735] Accordingly, the CMA looked into whether the merger between the parties makes it materially more challenging for the rivals of Booking.com to compete with it by making further strengthening the market power of Booking.com in the accommodation OTA market.[736]

The CMA's assessment was composed of the following three points:[737]

(1) Does Booking.com has a significant market power on the market for supply of accommodation OTA services?
(2) Does the market for supply of accommodation OTA services has any barriers to entry and expansion on that market?
(3) Are the flight OTA services provided by eTraveli an important channel to get and keep consumers of accommodation OTA services in the UK?

With regard to the first point, the CMA concluded that Booking.com clearly has considerable market power on the market for the supply of accommodation OTA services and can even be characterised as a market leader.[738] As to the second point, the CMA observed that, especially as a result of the incumbent position of Booking-.com, there are material barriers to entry and expansion on the accommodation OTA services market.[739] Specifically, the CMA took into account the indirect network effects which are present in the accommodation OTA services market.[740] Indeed, they make it especially difficult for both smaller competitors and new players to join the market. Lastly, with regard to the third point, the CMA noted that eTraveli's flight OTA services cannot be seen as a crucial channel to attract and retain consumers of accommodation OTA services.[741] While conducting the analysis, the CMA checked the behaviour of consumers while purchasing travel online, the flight OTA services' characteristics and possible alternative means for accommodation OTA services providers to attract new clientele.[742]

As a result, the CMA has concluded that the merger in question will not significantly impede effective competition on the market for accommodation OTA

734. Bloomberg Law, 'UK's CMA Starts Merger Probe Into Booking.com Deal for Etraveli' (*Bloomberg Law*, 2 August 2022) https://news.bloomberglaw.com/antitrust/uks-cma-starts-merger-probe-into-booking-com-deal-for-etraveli.
735. CMA, 'Anticipated acquisition by Booking Holdings Inc. of certain activities of eTraveli Group AB: Decision on relevant merger situation and substantial lessening of competition' [2022] ME/6991/22 para. 6.
736. *Ibid.*
737. *Ibid.*, para. 7.
738. *Ibid.*, para. 96.
739. *Ibid.*, para. 105.
740. *Ibid.*, para. 103.
741. *Ibid.*, para. 123.
742. *Ibid.*, para. 106.

services in the UK.[743] It should, however, be noted, that the European Commission has also opened a Phase II investigation into this acquisition and has not yet reached a decision.[744] Similarly to the CMA, the Commission is concerned that the transaction in question will increase barriers to entry and expansion for other competing accommodation OTA service providers in the EU.[745] It remains to be seen what the European competition watchdog decides and whether it will follow the CMA's reasoning in its assessment.

§5.04 INTERMEDIATE CONCLUSION

During the investigation period, the CMA has been very active in the field of digital competition. It would appear that with Brexit, the CMA's level of activity has increased (even) further. This appears logical since matters that were handled by the Commission in the past now come under the CMA's exclusive competence where the UK is concerned. This becomes evident by the fact that in the last few years, the CMA has handled various matters in parallel with the Commission. In particular, the CMA's investigations under the prohibition of abuse of a dominant position in Apple's and Google's app stores and the investigations into Meta's and Google's cooperation agreements run or have run parallel. Since most of these investigations are still pending, it is too soon to tell whether the same will apply to the cases' respective outcomes. It cannot be excluded that these will to (a certain extent) diverge, which could turn out problematic both for the tech companies (that operate internationally) as well as for their customers. Conduct (or mergers) that may be allowed in the UK, could be banned in the EU or vice versa.

If we look specifically at the enforcement practice under the cartel prohibition, it is first noteworthy that in the *Online Frames and Posters* case, a fine was imposed (and immunity granted for a successful leniency application) for algorithmic price-fixing. It should be noted that this case did concern a very specific situation, namely a pricing algorithm that was demonstrably manipulated in order to implement a traditional price-fixing agreement. The algorithm used was also not or hardly self-learning. The fear of an (imminent) enforcement deficit with regard to anticompetitive conduct implemented through algorithms seems to mainly relate to algorithms to which the latter does apply. A striking detail in this respect is that the company that wrote the manipulation into the algorithm on the instructions of the cartelists, was not fined for supporting or facilitating the cartel. The CMA could have seen a reason to do so in view of the very specific and unmistakable instruction that the software supplier received

743. *Ibid.*, para. 128.
744. See §4.3[L] above. Also compare: Foo Yun Chee, 'Booking's Etraveli Deal Faces Full-Scale EU Antitrust Probe, Sources Say' (*Reuters*, 10 November 2022) https://www.reuters.com/business/retail-consumer/bookings-etraveli-deal-faces-full-scale-eu-antitrust-probe-sources-say-2022-11-10/; *Reuters*, 'EU Opens In-Depth Study of Booking Bid for Sweden's Etraveli' (*Reuters*, 16 November 2022) https://www.reuters.com/markets/deals/eu-opens-in-depth-study-booking-bid-swedens-etraveli-2022-11-16/.
745. European Commission, 'Press Release: Mergers: Commission opens in-depth investigation into the proposed acquisition of eTraveli by Booking' (2022) European Commission p. 1.

from the cartelists to modify the algorithm in response to the price-fixing agreement. After all, the facts described in the decision appear to show that the software supplier could not have been unaware of the intentions of the two cartelists. The CMA could, therefore, have issued - even if only symbolically - a clear warning addressed to any subsequent software vendor that would consider helping cartelists achieve their prohibited intentions. It however follows from the CMA's decision that the CMA decided otherwise for reasons of prioritisation.[746] In the *Ping* case, the CMA imposed a fine in combination with an injunction for the imposition of a total ban on online sales. The CMA considered this ban not necessary and proportionate in order to protect the brand image of Ping. These findings were confirmed by the CAT, although the fine imposed was eventually lowered.

Many other cases under the cartel prohibition dealt with parity clauses and RPM and the CMA did not hesitate to impose fines in all of these cases. In total, the CMA imposed no less than ten fines for vertical infringements on individual companies over the research period. However, the highest of these fines (nearly GBP 18 million imposed on ComparetheMarket), was annulled by the CAT as the CMA had failed to carry out a sufficient analysis of the alleged anticompetitive effects of the parity clauses at issue and of the market on which these clauses were enforced.

Looking at the prohibition of abuse of a dominant position, the *epyx* case (relating to an online platform for vehicle maintenance) is interesting because the CMA could apparently also have applied the cartel prohibition in this case (whether or not alongside the prohibition of abuse), but did not do so. After all, there were written contracts between epyx and its customers, which would qualify as agreements between undertakings within the meaning of the (at least European) cartel prohibition. If the CMA would not have issued a commitment decision but instead a sanction decision, the choice of (exclusively) the prohibition of abuse of dominance would have had consequences for the CMA's burden of proof. It then would have had the burden of proving the existence of the dominant position. This makes it all the more remarkable that two years later it did choose to apply the 'double-barrelled' approach (simultaneous prohibition of cartels and prohibition of abuse of a dominant position) in *ATG Media*. The reason for choosing these different approaches is not clear from the two decisions. However, as already touched upon, the most interesting precedents in the field of abuse of a dominant position appear to be still in the making as the CMA is running various investigations against Apple, Google and Meta. The final outcome of all of these investigations is as yet unknown.

In the area of merger control, the CMA's output over the research period was prolific. With twenty-five relevant precedents, it was higher than that of any of the other authorities under review. This may seem somewhat surprising in view of the fact that the UK has a voluntary notification regime (and may thus be expected to receive fewer filings in general than the other jurisdictions under review which all have a mandatory notification system).

746. *Case 50223, Online Sales of Posters and Frames, supra* n. 455, para. 3.76.

Again, Brexit may be part of the explanation since also where mergers are concerned, the CMA has dealt with several cases that were also handled (or are also being handled) by the Commission (e.g., Facebook/Kustomer and – outside the review period- Microsoft/Activision Blizzard). In addition, the fact that it does not need to deal with a steady load of evidently unproblematic cases may make the CMA better placed to track and take on the cases it considers potentially problematic (to the extent that such cases are not notified by the parties themselves). In this respect, it is noteworthy that with the new regime regarding Article 22 EUMR, the EU seems to be moving towards a somewhat similar system (or at least a system that is a hybrid between a mandatory notification system governed by thresholds and a system under which the competition authority has substantial scrutiny over the merger cases it wants to assess. Reference is in this respect made to the chapter on the Commission above.

Also when it comes to the number of prohibition decisions (three), does the CMA achieve the highest 'score' of all the authorities under review? If fact, during the investigation period, the CMA is the only authority under review to have prohibited mergers coming within the scope of this book at all. Just as with regard to antitrust, the CMA is therefore not afraid to be 'tough' when it considers that to be the most appropriate attitude.

All in all, the CMA appears to be well placed to pursue an effective enforcement policy in the field of digital competition and is not scared to 'show its teeth'. Whether the number of precedents would have been (even) greater if the CMA would have had the additional enforcement instruments it insists on getting, is a question that cannot be answered. Assuming that the CMA will indeed be granted these powers, it seems more likely that the number of relevant precedents it will produce in the years to come shall continue to be impressive, also taking into account that several interesting cases under the existing prohibition on the abuse of a dominant position against Apple, Google and Meta are currently pending.

CHAPTER 6
Autorité de la Concurrence

§6.01 INTRODUCTION

> *'Companies need rapid answers. Responsiveness is now a hallmark of our work in all areas [...]; it is clearly essential in the digital arena, where markets and positions change very rapidly, and where there may be a risk of a "fait accompli".'*[747]
>
> – Isabelle de Silva, October 2021

> *'You must have an antitrust discussion with your IT person, because he or she may not know that a decision taken in a pricing algorithm, for example, may expose the company to a big antitrust procedure a few years down the road.'*[748]
>
> – Isabelle de Silva, January 2021

> *'There are two ways we can support the EU: we can identify and bring cases to the commission under the DMA umbrella; but equally important is to maintain our own antitrust work regarding digital platforms in areas not covered by the DMA.'*[749]
>
> – Benoît Cœuré, June 2022

747. Autorité de la Concurrence, speech by Isabelle de Silva, 'A look back at a term: the presidency of the Autorité de la concurrence, 2016-2021', 11 October 2021.
748. MLex, 'Antitrust compliance in digital markets will become especially challenging, EU's Guersent, France's De Silva say', 12 January 2021.
749. GCR, 'An interview with Benoît Cœuré', 24 June 2022.

Digital competition has been a key priority of the Autorité for many years, and it still is. Its first case on account suspension practices by a digital platform dates back to 2010. More than a decade later, this is still a hotly debated topic. The Autorité published its first market study into e-commerce in 2012, five years before the European Commission published the final report on its e-commerce sector inquiry. The Autorité also has an impressive track record of investigations into Google and, more recently, into Apple. Between 2010 and 2021, we count eight[750] (out of thirteen such investigations in total) abuse of dominance investigations against Google (imposing one fine of EUR 150 million)[751] and two[752] against Apple (imposing one fine of EUR 1.1 billion). The Autorité has also fined Apple in relation to a horizontal agreement between Apple and two wholesalers of Apple products (a fine of EUR 662.5 million)[753] and has imposed four[754] fines for online vertical restrictions between 2017 and 2020. The Autorité has also been a front-runner in conducting market studies. It has published studies on e-commerce[755] (2012), on competition law and data[756] (2016, with the Bundeskartellamt), on data processing[757] (2018), on algorithms[758] (2019, together with the Bundeskartellamt) and a second on e-commerce[759] (2020), on payment services[760] (2021) and announced a market study into cloud services (2022).[761] It has also advocated for legislative reforms in merger control (*see* §6.04) and for extending the scope of dominance (*see* §6.03).

In terms of enforcement style, the Autorité calls itself the '*Pionnière en Europe dans l'utilisation des mesures conservatoires*' [freely translated: 'Pioneer in Europe in

750. Autorité de la Concurrence, decision 28 October 2010, 10-D-30 (*Google AdWords I (Navx)*); Autorité de la Concurrence, decision 28 February 2013, 13-D-07 (*Google AdWords II (E-Kanopi)*); Autorité de la Concurrence, decision 19 December 2019, 19-D-26 (*Google AdWords III (Gibmedia)*); Autorité de la Concurrence, decision 23 November 2016, 16-D-25 (*Google AdWords IV (IAH)*); Autorité de la Concurrence, decision 20 July 2018, 18-D-13 (*Google AdWords V (Interactive Labs)*); Autorité de la Concurrence, decision 31 January 2019, 19-MC-01 (*Google AdWords VI (Amadeus)*); Autorité de la Concurrence, decision 18 December 2017, 17-D-24 *(Google AdSense (1PlusV)*); Autorité, decision 9 April 2020, 20-MC-01 (*Google – ancillary rights*).
751. Autorité de la Concurrence, decision 9 April 2020, 20-MC-01 (*Google – ancillary rights*).
752. Autorité de la Concurrence, decision 16 March 2020, 20-D-04 (*Apple/Tech Data/Ingram Micro*); Autorité de la Concurrence, decision 17 March 2021, 21-D-07 (*Apple Targeted advertising*).
753. Autorité de la Concurrence, decision 16 March 2020, 20-D-04 (*Apple/Tech Data/Ingram Micro*).
754. Autorité de la Concurrence, decision 26 January 2017, 17-D-01 (Sanbri); Autorité de la Concurrence, decision 24 October 2018, 18-D-23 (Stihl); Autorité de la Concurrence, decision 1 July 2019, 19-D-14 (Bikeeurope B.V.); Autorité de la Concurrence, decision 16 March 2020, 20-D-04 (*Apple/Tech Data/Ingram Micro*).
755. Autorité de la Concurrence, 'Avis Relatif Au Fonctionnement Concurrentiel Du Commerce Électronique', 12-A-20, 18 September 2012.
756. Autorité de la Concurrence and Bundeskartellamt, 'Competition Law and Data', 10 May 2016.
757. Autorité de la Concurrence, 'Opinion on Data Processing in the Online Advertising Sector', 18-A-03, 6 March 2018.
758. Autorité de la Concurrence & Bundeskartellamt, 'Algorithms and Competition', 6 November 2019.
759. Autorité de la concurrence, 'Competition and e-commerce', 5 June 2020.
760. Autorité de la concurrence, 'Opinion on the sector of new technologies applied to payment activities', 21-A-05, 29 April 2021.
761. Autorité de la concurrence, press release 27 January 2022, 'The Autorité de la concurrence starts proceedings ex officio to analyse competition conditions in the cloud computing sector'.

the use of provisional measures'].[762] It strongly holds the belief that competition authorities must be able to intervene quickly to be effective: '*Pour être pleinement efficace, une autorité de concurrence doit être en mesure d'intervenir rapidement sur le marché, dans l'attente d'une décision au fond.*'[763] [freely translated: '*To be fully effective, a competition authority must be capable of intervening rapidly on the market, pending a decision on the merits.*'] In the field of digital competition law, the Autorité has taken four decisions on provisional measures, each time in relation to abuse of dominance complaints. It granted the requested provisional measures on three occasions (*see* introduction of §6.03).

[A] Presidency

In January 2022, Benoît Cœuré was appointed as President of the Autorité, succeeding Isabelle de Silva after a five-year presidency.[764] He is a former member of the Executive Board and of the Governing Council of the European Central Bank and he chaired the Committee on Payments and Market Infrastructures of the Bank for International Settlements for six years. In an interview in June 2022, he mentioned that there are 'a few more cases' in the Autorité's pipeline, without going into more detail.[765] He also reflected on the role of the Autorité after the entry into force of the Digital Markets Act: '*The text of the DMA is very clear that the commission will be the single enforcer of the regulation and that is correct I think. There are two ways we can support the EU: we can identify and bring cases to the commission under the DMA umbrella; but equally important is to maintain our own antitrust work regarding digital platforms in areas not covered by the DMA. I am firmly convinced we will stay very active with antitrust enforcement and merger control in digital markets as a complement to the DMA. To give an example, I mentioned the Google publishers case and it is not clear to me if that kind of conduct will be covered by the DMA. It's not in the core set of activities that the DMA will regulate. It might be covered by the FRAND clause for search engines that was introduced during the last stages of the DMA negotiations but we do not know yet, so for the foreseeable future we will keep an eye on such behaviour and continue to address it using out national tools.*'[766]

In her farewell address, Isabelle de Silva underlined that digital competition law enforcement during her presidency relied on three pillars.[767] First, developing relevant expertise, for example by studying markets and recruiting new profiles. De Silva: '*To confront the practices of the big platforms (Big Tech or "GAFA"), I had a strong intuition: we must not be system-minded, neither demonising GAFA nor idealising them. Digital businesses have brought a lot of innovation and high-end services. It is therefore not a*

762. Autorité de la Concurrence, 'Bilan de activité, synthèse 2019', 9 July 2020, p. 41.
763. *Ibid.*
764. Autorité de la Concurrence, press release 21 January 2022, 'Benoît Cœuré is appointed President of the Autorité de la concurrence'.
765. GCR, 'An interview with Benoît Cœuré', 24 June 2022.
766. *Ibid.*
767. Autorité de la Concurrence, speech by Isabelle de Silva, 'A look back at a term: the presidency of the Autorité de la concurrence, 2016-2021', 11 October 2021.

question of wanting to eliminate them or break them up "on principle". On the other hand, we need to analyse them "with a cool head", develop incisive and expert knowledge of their operating methods and the way they interact with their ecosystem – customers, distributors, and competitors. A company, however powerful and dominant, is not good or bad in itself. It is on the basis of their actions that the Autorité must intervene, and only when it violates competition law.' Second, there is a need for speed in competition law: '*Companies need rapid answers. Responsiveness is now a hallmark of our work in all areas (e.g., audiovisual rights of the French Ligue 1 and energy); it is clearly essential in the 2021 digital arena, where markets and positions change very rapidly, and where there may be a risk of a "fait accompli."*' Third, a dynamic application of the applicable rules is necessary in digital markets. De Silva: '*We have taken robust and innovative decisions, without affecting current legislation, while simultaneously working to enrich the legislative framework, at both French and European level.*'

[B] International Cooperation

The Autorité is among the first competition authorities that sought international cooperation to face up to the challenges of digital competition, as evidenced by the joint reports with the Bundeskartellamt on data processing and algorithms. And during the G7 meeting in 2019, presided by France, competition law was for the first time a G7 agenda item.[768] This led to the publication of a 'common understanding' in June 2019 by the competition authorities of Italy, France, Germany, the UK, the EU, Canada, the US and Japan.[769] The common understanding acknowledges the benefits of the digital economy, but also states that '*greater international cooperation and convergence in the application of competition laws*' is necessary and that competition authorities should ensure that their '*tools, resources and skills for competition law enforcement should be up to date*'.[770] The joint statement also says: '*Governments should assess whether policies or regulations unnecessarily restrict competition in digital markets or between digital and non-digital players, and should consider procompetitive alternatives where possible.*'[771] The Autorité has advised on abolishing laws that unnecessarily restricted competition, for example in the audiovisual sector (in its capacity of advisor to Parliament) (*see* §6.04).[772] De Silva said on international cooperation: '*This international cooperation is essential, as we need to deal with issues and businesses that are global in nature. All regulators therefore need to come together – in France and abroad – and work together, in a much closer and more interactive way than before, to pursue*

768. Autorité de la Concurrence, 'Bilan de activité, synthèse 2019', 9 July 2020, p. 59.
769. Autorité de la Concurrence and other G7 competition authorities, 'Common Understanding of G7 Competition Authorities on "Competition and the Digital Economy"', 5 June 2019.
770. *Ibid.*
771. *Ibid.*
772. Autorité de la Concurrence, 'Opinion on a request from the Committee on Cultural Affairs and Education of the French National Assembly (Assemblée nationale) for an opinion on the audiovisual sector', 19-A-04, 21 February 2019.

coherent policies and ensure that their respective investigations are even more effective.'[773]

[C] Digital Economy Unit and Cooperation with PEReN

In January 2020, the Autorité set up a dedicated digital economy unit that, at the time of its launch, would include four people.[774] The unit, which will include engineers, lawyers, economists and data scientists, '*will take part in the Autorité's discussions and sector-specific inquiries on new issues related to the development of digital technology, [...]. The new service will also provide support to the Autorité's investigation and inspection units that are handling cases with a significant digital dimension. It will thus contribute to the analysis of the most complex cases regarding company mergers involving actors from the digital sector and litigation procedures that concern compliance with competition law in a digital environment*'. In July 2020, the Autorité appointed Yann Guthman as head of the digital economy unit.[775] Guthman: '*The emergence of systemic players in digital markets with unprecedented power makes it necessary to adjust the tools, [and] also the workforce available to competition authorities.*'[776] In 2021, the Autorité announced a cooperation agreement with Pôle d'Expertise de la Régulation Numérique (PEReN), the French Digital Regulation Expertise Cluster.[777] This cluster was created by the French government in 2020 to support all 'State administrations' that regulate digital platforms. The Autorité notes that the cluster will be '*able to intervene in data analysis, source codes, computer programs, algorithmic processing, and algorithm auditing, and provide its technical expertise in the context of reviews, investigations, dossiers or studies relating to digital platforms*'.

§6.02 CARTEL PROHIBITION

The Autorité has been an active enforcer of the cartel prohibition, with a total number of eight digital competition investigations leading to a total of six decisions.[778] Five

773. Autorité de la Concurrence, speech by Isabelle de Silva, 'A look back at a term: the presidency of the Autorité de la concurrence, 2016-2021', 11 October 2021.
774. Autorité de la Concurrence, press release 9 January 2020, 'The Autorité creates a digital economy unit'.
775. Autorité de la Concurrence, press release 9 July 2020, 'Yann Guthmann appointed head of new Digital Economy Unit'.
776. Mlex, 'We can tackle Big Tech abuses but increasingly need more firepower, says French antitrust official', 2 October 2020.
777. Autorité de la Concurrence, press release 11 May 2021, 'The Autorité de la concurrence and the PEReN sign an agreement on the terms of their cooperation.'
778. The six decisions are: Autorité de la Concurrence, decision 16 March 2020, 20-D-04 (*Apple/Tech Data/Ingram Micro*); Autorité de la Concurrence, decision 10 December 2019, 19-D-23 (*Expedia/HRS*); Autorité de la Concurrence, decision 1 July 2019, 19-D-14 (*Bikeeurope B.V.*); Autorité de la Concurrence, decision 24 October 2018, 18-D-23 (*Stihl*); Autorité de la Concurrence, decision 26 January 2017, 17-D-01 (*Sanbri*); Autorité de la Concurrence, decision

investigations against Adidas,[779] Sanbri,[780] Stihl,[781] Bikeurope[782] and Apple[783] led to four fining decisions between 2017 and 2020 for vertical restrictions. The investigation against Adidas was closed without a decision.[784] Apple got fined an impressive EUR 221.2 million, much higher than the second-highest fine for vertical restrictions (EUR 7.0 million for Stihl). The Apple fining decision also concerns an investigation into a horizontal agreement between Apple and two wholesalers of Apple products, for which Apple received a fine of EUR 662.5 million. Two other decisions concern parity clauses.[785] The Autorité accepted commitments from Booking.com in 2015 and rejected complaints against two other major online hotel booking platforms in 2019. The Autorité conducted dawn raids in the IT and software sector in November 2018 that have not yet led to a decision on the merits of the case.[786]

[A] Policy Documents

[1] E-commerce (2012, 2020)

In its 2012 study on e-commerce, the Autorité concluded that the rise of online stores had led to lower prices and greater choice and warned that it would prevent producers and traditional retailers from entering into agreements that impede the development of online sales. The above-mentioned fining decisions imposed for vertical restrictions show that this warning was not in vain. In its e-commerce study of 2020, the Autorité confirms this line of thinking: '*conducts aiming to limit the gains or earnings associated with online sales, such as imposing resale prices, will continue to require very careful attention*'.[787]

[2] Algorithms (2019)

In its descriptive study on algorithms, carried out jointly with the Bundeskartellamt, the Autorité concludes with regard to algorithmic collusion that it is still too early to

21 April 2015, 15-D-06 (*Booking.com*). The Autorité opened investigations in *Adidas* and *Akka Technologies* (that haven't resulted in a decision (yet)).

779. Autorité de la concurrence, press release 3 December 2015, 'The Autorité de la concurrence has closed an investigation against Adidas.'
780. Autorité de la Concurrence, decision 26 January 2017, 17-D-01 (*Sanbri*).
781. Autorité de la Concurrence, decision 24 October 2018, 18-D-23 (*Stihl*).
782. Autorité de la Concurrence, decision 1 July 2019, 19-D-14 (*Bikeeurope B.V.*).
783. Autorité de la Concurrence, decision 16 March 2020, 20-D-04 (*Apple/Tech Data/Ingram Micro*).
784. Autorité de la concurrence, press release 3 December 2015, 'The Autorité de la concurrence has closed an investigation against Adidas.'
785. Autorité de la Concurrence, decision 10 December 2019, 19-D-23 (*Expedia/HRS*); Autorité de la Concurrence, decision 21 April 2015, 15-D-06 (*Booking.com*).
786. Autorité de la Concurrence, press release 22 May 2019, 'The Akka technologies Group is fined a total of 900 000 euros for obstructing the conduct of inspections made by the Autorité.'
787. Autorité de la concurrence, 'Competition and e-commerce', 5 June 2020, p. 62.

determine whether a revision of the legal framework is necessary.[788] Isabelle de Silva, the then president of the Autorité, gave companies a practical recommendation: '*For example, one of our key recommendations on algorithms was, we told companies "you must have an antitrust discussion with your IT person, because he or she may not know that a decision taken in a pricing algorithm, for example, may expose the company to a big antitrust procedure a few years down the road".*'[789]

[3] Payment Services (2021)

In its opinion on payment services in France, the Autorité flags that the traditional banking players have adapted to the market entry of fintech and big tech players in France by entering into cooperation or partnership agreements with these players.[790] In addition, the Autorité mentions that '*certain agreements concluded at national level between banking groups have enabled the creation of new players, such as Paylib or Lyf Pay, which offer, in particular, contactless payment services. An agreement at European level, the European Payment Initiative or "EPI", should finally make it possible to create a pan-European payment system that could connect banks to each other without using current networks, such as Visa and MasterCard*'. The Autorité also points out the risks of blockchain technology: '*the increased transparency made possible by the use of the blockchain could have restrictive effects on competition, in that it could facilitate coordination among those users and/or enhance the internal stability of an on-going cartel*'.

[B] Enforcement

[1] Adidas (2015)

In 2015, the Autorité investigated Adidas' (selective) distribution agreements, which prohibit distributors from selling Adidas products via online marketplaces such as eBay, Fnac.com or Amazon.[791] After Adidas indicated it would be removing these prohibitions, the Autorité closed the investigation.

788. Autorité de la Concurrence & Bundeskartellamt, 'Algorithms and Competition', 6 November 2019, p. 91. Interestingly, two and a half years earlier, she stated that additional rules were not necessary. *See*: Contexte Numérique, 'La France et l'UE sur la même longueur d'ondes contre les cartels des algorithmes', 17 March 2017, '*Avons-nous besoin de nouvelles lois, de nouveaux régulateurs? Des candidats à l'élection présidentielle l'ont proposé, je ne pense pas que ce soit nécessaire.*'
789. MLex, 'Antitrust compliance in digital markets will become especially challenging, EU's Guersent, France's De Silva say', 12 January 2021.
790. Autorité de la concurrence, 'Opinion on the sector of new technologies applied to payment activities', 21-A-05, 29 April 2021.
791. Autorité de la concurrence, press release 3 December 2015, 'The Autorité de la concurrence has closed an investigation against Adidas.' According to the press release, the Autorité cooperated with the Bundeskartellamt during this investigation. No end decision has (yet) been published on the website of the Autorité.

[2] Booking.com, Expedia and HRS, Parity Clauses (2015-2019)

In its commitment decision of 21 April 2015, the Autorité concluded that it could not be ruled out that Booking.com may have infringed the cartel prohibition by imposing parity clauses on its partners who use the Booking.com internet platform to offer hotel accommodation.[792] In addition, according to the Autorité, it cannot be excluded that Booking.com thereby infringed the prohibition of abuse of an economic dominant position. However, the decision focuses on a possible infringement of the cartel prohibition. The parity clauses in question included, *inter alia*, that Booking.com's partners, the hotels, would not offer lower prices on other internet platforms, would not offer lower prices to consumers via offline channels (e.g., hotel receptions) and would not approach existing customers of the hotel in question. The Autorité argued that the parity clauses were restrictive of competition in so far as they removed the relationship between the amount of the commission charged by Booking.com to its partners and the volume of hotel nights offered since that would in turn lead to the elimination of price competition between the internet platforms.[793] On 11 December 2014, Booking.com offered commitments that in brief came down to the obligation to no longer apply the broad parity clauses at least from 1 July 2015 to 30 June 2020.[794] In the decision, the Autorité does not conclude that Booking.com has violated the cartel prohibition. In February 2017, the Autorité published an interim balance of the effects of the commitments made by Booking.com. This analysis indicated that hotel accommodation prices differ per internet platform, but that no significant changes have occurred in the level of commissions charged by the various Internet platforms.[795] The Autorité indicates that it remains alert and will intervene if the development of competition in the sector so warrants.

On 12 December 2019, the Autorité dismissed complaints about the parity clauses of two other major platforms, Expedia and Hotel Reservation Service (HRS).[796] These complaints dated back to 2015 and were also directed against Booking.com, but were treated separately by the handling general rapporteur once Booking.com showed a willingness to settle. In this context, the Autorité argues that the parity clauses of Expedia and HRS have already been dealt with by other competition authorities in the EU in the meantime.[797] It therefore rejects the complaints.

792. Autorité de la Concurrence, decision 21 April 2015, 15-D-06 (*Booking.com*), paras 134-141.
793. *Ibid.*, para. 140.
794. *Ibid.*, paras 148-157. For an overview in English of the remedies offered by Booking.com, *see* Autorité de la Concurrence, press release 21 April 2015 'The Autorité de la concurrence, in coordination with the European Commission and the Italian and Swedish authorities, has obtained particularly extensive commitments from Booking.com aiming to boost competition between online booking platforms and give hotels more freedom in commercial and pricing matters.'
795. Autorité de la Concurrence, 'The Autorité de la concurrence conducts an initial intermediary assessment of the commitments made by Booking.com', 9 February 2017.
796. Autorité de la Concurrence, decision 10 December 2019, 19-D-23 (*Expedia/HRS*).
797. *Ibid.*, paras 41-48. The national competition authorities of Sweden, Italy, Greece, Poland and the United Kingdom decided to leave the case alone on the basis of the identical set of facts. The German competition authority fined HRS on 20 December 2013 because its parity clauses significantly restricted competition in the market. Expedia and Booking made voluntary

[3] Sanbri (2017)

In a settlement decision dated 26 January 2017, the Autorité imposed a fine of EUR 3,200 on Sanbri, a manufacturer of high-quality table and kitchenware products, for using fixed resale prices in contracts with its internet distributors during the period from March 2011 to March 2016.[798] Sanbri works with various independent distributors for the distribution of its products. Sanbri states that it started imposing fixed resale prices for Internet distributors under pressure from its brick-and-mortar distributors, who feared price reductions by Internet distributors: '*[nos distributeurs exploitant des points de vente physiques] craignaient que les distributeurs Internet, par exemple, cassent les prix*' [freely translated: '*Our distributors operating physical points of sale were concerned that, for example, Internet distributors would undercut prices.*'][799] Sanbri informed its Internet distributors that they should contractually commit to respect and apply Sanbri's recommended prices at all times: '*Je vous informe que je m'engage en tous points à respecter et appliquer au mieux les prix de vente conseillés*' [freely translated: '*I inform you that I commit myself in all points to respect and apply to the best of my ability the recommended selling prices*'].[800] Seven of Sanbri's thirty-five Internet distributors actually complied with Sanbri's request. The Autorité finds that the agreements between Sanbri and some of its internet distributors had the object of restricting competition and infringed the French cartel prohibition and Article 101 TFEU. The maximum fine that the Autorité could have imposed on Sanbri was EUR 750,000.[801] However, the Autorité imposes a relatively low fine on Sanbri because the resale price maintenance (RPM) was not accompanied by other coercive measures and because only seven of the 35 distributors had agreed to the RPM.[802] The distributors were not fined.

[4] Stihl (2018)

On 24 October 2018, the Autorité imposed a fine of EUR 7 million on Stihl, a manufacturer of gardening machines and tools, for restricting online sales through (i) third-party online platforms and (ii) its distributors' own websites between 2006 and 2017.[803] The contract between Stihl and its distributors contained a complete ban on online sales through third-party websites.[804] According to the Autorité, this prohibition is allowed, since it follows from the *Coty* judgment of the ECJ that a prohibition on online sales on platforms can be justified if related to the sale of products of a specific luxury nature but may also be permitted under a selective distribution system for other

commitments to several European competition authorities in August 2020 not to impose 'price parity clauses' on hotels offering room reservations on their own websites.

798. Autorité de la Concurrence, decision 26 January 2017, 17-D-01 (*Sanbri*).
799. *Ibid.*, para. 29.
800. *Ibid.*, para. 32.
801. *Ibid.*, para. 59.
802. *Ibid.*, para. 62.
803. *Ibid.*
804. *Ibid.*, para. 90.

types of products.[805] The Autorité remarks that these in any case include dangerous products: '*S'agissant des produits dits dangereux, il n'apparaît pas illégitime, en premier lieu, d'autoriser Stihl [...] de s'assurer que la commercialisation en ligne a bien été réalisée par l'un d'entre eux*' [freely translated: '*As regards allegedly dangerous products, it does not appear to be illegitimate, in the first place, to authorise Stihl to [...] ensure that the online commercialisation is actually performed by one of them*' – note: 'them' refers to the authorised distributors].[806] In addition, according to the Autorité, a selective distribution system is characterised by the producer's ability to control, *inter alia*, the conditions under which its (dangerous) products are sold (such as demonstration videos and rapid and direct access to advice from skilled professionals). Sales via third platforms could prevent the distributor from exercising this legitimate control, as the producer cannot contractually address these platforms: '*le fournisseur, n'étant contractuellement lié qu'au distributeur, ne peut exiger des plateformes, tierces au contrat de distribution sélective, d'en respecter les dispositions*' [freely translated: '*the supplier, being contractually bound only to the distributor, cannot require the platforms, who are third parties to the selective distribution agreement, to respect the contractual provisions*'].[807]

Stihl furthermore obliged the members of its selective distribution network to physically make Stihl products available to customers via a shop or via personal delivery by the distributor to the customer's home via the distributor's own website in the case of online sales, where the garden tools are assembled and an explanation is given about their safe use. According to the Autorité, this obligation led to a de facto ban on internet sales via the websites of its distributors. The Autorité considered in this context that about one-third of Stihl products have been sold through do-it-yourself (DIY) markets without safety instructions and there were no figures that buyers of Stihl products in DIY markets have had more accidents. According to the Autorité, for these reasons, among others, there is no justification for the obligation of physical delivery in the case of online sales through distributors' own websites.

Interestingly, the maximum fine that the Autorité could have imposed on Stihl in this case was EUR 379 million, but the actual fine was more than fifty times lower (EUR 7 million). The Autorité cites as a reason the fact that, at the beginning of the infringement and for most of the duration of the infringement, there was legal uncertainty about the seriousness of this type of infringement and the fact that the infringement had only a limited harmful effect in that it restricted intra-brand competition, while inter-brand competition between Stihl products and products of fifty other brands was at most affected to a limited extent.

Stihl's appeal against the decision of the Autorité was to no avail. The potentially dangerous nature of the products, which Stihl had invoked as a justification for restricting online sales, did not convince the Paris Court of Appeal (*Cour d'Appel*), nor the Autorité.[808] Confirming that the obligation to physically hand over products went

805. *Ibid.*, para. 278.
806. *Ibid.*, para. 280.
807. *Ibid.*, para. 284.
808. Cour d'Appel de Paris, judgment 17 October 2019, RG 18/24456.

beyond what was necessary to ensure customer safety and had the objective of restricting passive (online) sales within the Stihl distribution network, the Court upheld the Autorité's decision. However, the fine was reduced from EUR 7 million to EUR 6 million, as the Court stated that the Autorité should have taken into account the fact that Stihl had written and oral contact with the Bundeskartellamt about its distribution system and the fact that online sales of the products concerned were limited.[809] Stihl appealed this judgment to the *Court* of *Cassation*, but the appeal was also rejected.[810]

[5] Akka Technologies Group (2018 – Under Investigation)

On 8 November 2018, according to a press release, Autorité conducted dawn raids with a number of companies in the IT and software sectors for alleged anticompetitive behaviour.[811] One of these companies, Akka Technologies Group, was fined on 22 May 2019 for obstructing the Autorité's investigation. Further details on this investigation are not known at the time of writing.

[6] Bikeurope – Trek Bicycles (2019)

In a decision dated 1 July 2019, the Autorité imposes a fine of EUR 250,000 on Bikeurope B.V. and its parent company Trek Bicycle Corporation, a bicycle manufacturer.[812] The Autorité finds that between September 2007 and August 2014, Bikeurope de facto prohibited its French distributors from selling via the Internet through its general terms and conditions. Bikeurope required its distributors to supply Trek products to consumers only in (physical) outlets approved by Bikeurope: '*toute livraison de produit au consommateur doit être effectuée en personne sur le lieu de vente autorisé*' [freely translated: '*any delivery of a product to the consumer must be made in person at the approved point of sale*'].[813] Distributors were also prohibited from advertising Trek products on their websites or the websites of third parties without prior authorisation, and from selling Trek products through auction websites.[814]

Bikeurope argues that the conduct it is accused of is necessary to ensure the safety and quality of its products, citing French legislation that states that bicycles may only be delivered 'fully assembled' and 'fully tuned'.[815] However, the Autorité points out that French law does not require bicycles to be sold in physical shops and that between 2012 and 2015 between 4.5% and 7.5% of bicycles were sold online.[816] The ban on internet sales goes beyond what is necessary to ensure consumer safety and

809. Cour d'Appel de Paris, judgment 17 October 2019, RG 18/24456, paras 361-373.
810. Cour de Cassation, judgment 26 January 2022, 70 FS-D, pourvoi J 19-24.464.
811. Autorité de la Concurrence, press release 22 May 2019, 'The Akka technologies Group is fined a total of 900 000 euros for obstructing the conduct of inspections made by the Autorité.'
812. Autorité de la Concurrence, decision 1 July 2019, 19-D-14 (*Bikeeurope B.V.*).
813. *Ibid.*, paras 32-35.
814. *Ibid.*, paras 33, 35 and 105.
815. *Ibid.*, para. 7.
816. *Ibid.*, paras 127 and 129.

product quality. According to the Autorité, a ban on internet sales has an anticompetitive object as it restricts distributors' sales opportunities and customers' choices.[817] The fact that online sales accounted for only a relatively small proportion of total sales during the infringement period is cited by the Autorité as a factor justifying a reducing the fine (the decision does not say how high the fine would otherwise have been). Bikeurope is fined for being the 'author' of the infringement. No fine is imposed on the distributors.

[7] Apple, Tech Data and Ingram Micro (2020)

Following a complaint by eBizcuss, a distributor of Apple products, on 16 March 2020, the Autorité imposed its highest-ever fine of EUR 1.24 billion on Apple and two wholesalers of Apple products, Tech Data and Ingram Micro.[818] Apple was fined a total of EUR 1.1 billion for entering into anticompetitive agreements relating to the distribution of its products (excluding iPhones) and for abusing a situation of economic dependency vis-à-vis its 'premium' independent distributors.

The Autorité finds three different infringements:

(1) A horizontal customer and product allocation agreement between Apple and two wholesalers of Apple products between December 2005 and March 2013. Apple instructed its wholesalers on the quantities of different products that these wholesalers could allocate to each retailer. These allocations included not only the initial product allocations to the retailers but also reallocations in case of unsold stock. Moreover, these allocation arrangements were combined with frequent and detailed exchanges of information between Apple and its wholesalers. According to the Autorité, this is a hardcore restriction of competition that created an impediment to intra-brand competition for Apple products between the wholesalers and Apple. Apple's justification that the agreement was necessary to prevent product shortages was set aside by the Autorité because Apple did not provide sufficient evidence. Apple, Tech Data and Ingram Micro are fined EUR 662.5 million, EUR 76.1 million and EUR 62.9 million respectively for this infringement.

(2) Vertical agreements on retail prices between Apple and its Apple Premium Resellers (APRs) between October 2012 and April 2017. According to the Autorité, in practice, APRs could not deviate from Apple's recommended prices and were completely restricted in their pricing freedom as they were bound by strict contractual conditions under which they could conduct promotions: '*Apple strictly controls the ability of APRs to implement promotional actions due to the strong restrictions imposed by the various contractual stipulations, for the use of the brand in communication and promotional*

817. *Ibid.*, paras 134-151.
818. Autorité de la Concurrence, decision 16 March 2020, 20-D-04 (*Apple/Tech Data/Ingram Micro*).

materials.'[819] Apple was also able to monitor the prices of its APRs through periodic inspections and mystery shoppers.[820] The Autorité leaves it open whether Apple actually used these means to monitor prices. Apple, as a cartelist, is fined EUR 221.2 million for this infringement. The APRs are not fined.

(3) Abuse of a state of economic dependence[821] by APRs in relation to Apple between November 2009 and April 2013. According to the Autorité, APRs are dependent on Apple because they are allowed near-exclusivity to sell Apple products and because their customers are strongly attached to Apple. APRs have no real option to break with Apple, as this would result in significant costs for APRs to adapt their shops and retrain their staff. According to the Autorité, there was an abuse of economic dependency because Apple made deliveries of its APRs unduly or inadequately compared the APRs to Apple's own distribution channel through the Apple Retail Stores and the Apple Online Store. In addition, according to the Autorité, APRs were kept in uncertainty over the terms of delivery of new Apple products, making it difficult for them to compete with Apple's own distributors.

According to the Autorité, this hindered not only intra-brand competition but also inter-brand competition. Apple, with its network of APRs, had a de facto franchise network without having to assume the obligations of a franchisor, such as the provision of brand names, know-how and other intellectual property rights. The Apple distribution network thus had an advantage over the distribution networks of its competitors, because Apple had almost complete control over its distributors. One of the APRs was quoted as follows: *'les exigences d'Apple s'apparentent à des exigences de franchise sauf que nous ne sommes pas des franchisés! Et pourtant ils agissent comme tel. Nous sommes dans notre société mais n'avons pas le droit de faire comme bon nous semble!'*[822] [freely translated: *'Apple's demands are similar to those of a franchisor, except that we are not franchisees! And yet that is how Apple behaves. We are our own company, but we are not allowed to do what we want!'*].

---

819. *Ibid.*, para. 865.
820. *Ibid.*, paras 872-881.
821. The French provision on abuse of dominant position of Article L. 420-2 has a second paragraph prohibiting the abuse of a state of economic dependence: 'Est en outre prohibée, dès lors qu'elle est susceptible d'affecter le fonctionnement ou la structure de la concurrence, l'exploitation abusive par une entreprise ou un groupe d'entreprises de l'état de dépendance économique dans lequel se trouve à son égard une entreprise cliente ou fournisseur.' The French Court of Cassation (*Cour de cassation*) explained the state of economic dependence for distributors as follows: '*the state of economic dependence, for a distributor, is defined as a situation where a company does not have the ability to replace its supplier(s) with one or more suppliers that can meet its supply needs under equivalent technical and economic conditions; that it deduces that the mere fact that a distributor purchases a significant or even exclusive part of its supplies from a single supplier is not sufficient to characterise its state of economic dependence within the meaning of Article L. 420-2 of the French Commercial Code*'. *See* Court of Cassation, Commercial Chamber of 3 March 2004, No 02-14529.
822. Autorité de la Concurrence, decision 16 March 2020, 20-D-04 (*Apple/Tech Data/Ingram Micro*), para. 379.

The Autorité imposes a fine of EUR 218.3 million on Apple for this third infringement.

All of the above fines result in a total amount of EUR 1,241,050,609. Apple has filed an appeal against this decision.

On 6 October 2022, the Cour d'Appel de Paris limited the fines imposed on Apple, Tech Data and Ingram Micro to EUR 371.6, 24.9 and EUR 19.5 million respectively, representing approximately one-third of the originally imposed fine.[823] Regarding the horizontal customer and product allocation agreement, the court found an infringement but concluded that the infringement only lasted between 2009 and 2013. Regarding the vertical agreements aspect of the case, the court found that the Autorité had not proven beyond doubt that Apple used recommended prices with a binding character and annulled this part of the fine. With respect to abuse of economic dependence, the court found that the APRs are indeed dependent on Apple and the court confirmed the finding of an abusive exploitation. According to the court, the APRs were placed at a disadvantage with respect to the Apple distribution network. Apple has announced to appeal the judgment by the Cour d'Appel, believing that the decision should be fully overturned.[824]

§6.03 ABUSE OF A DOMINANT POSITION

We count fourteen[825] competition investigations relating to abuse of dominance in the digital sector by the Autorité and seventeen[826] decisions. Its track record shows nine[827]

823. Cour d'Appel de Paris, judgment of 6 October 2022, RG 20/08582.
824. Mlex, 'Apple says it wants French antitrust decision fully annulled; promises to appeal', 6 October 2022.
825. Google AdWords II (E-Kanopi) (2013); Vente-privee.com (2014); Google AdWords III (Gibmedia) (2015); Google AdWords IV (IAH) (2016); Google AdSense (1PlusV) (2017); Google AdWords V (Interactive Labs) (2018); APCA (2018); Google AdWords VI (Amadeus) (2019); Amadeus (2019); Apple/Tech Data/Ingram Micro (2020); Google – ancillary rights (2020); Apple Targeted advertising (2021); Meta (2022); Google – Doubleclick for publishers/AdX (2021).
826. 13-D-07, 28 February 2013, Google AdWords II (E-Kanopi); 14-D-18, 28 November 2014, Vente-privee.com; 15-D-23, 9 September 2015, Google AdWords III (Gibmedia); 16-D-25, 23 November 2016, Google AdWords IV (IAH); 17-D-24, 18 December 2017, Google AdSense (1PlusV); 18-D-13, 20 July 2018, Google AdWords V (Interactive Labs); 18-D-20, 5 October 2018, APCA; 19-MC-01, 31 January 2019, Google AdWords VI (Amadeus); 19-D-04, 21 February 2019, Amadeus; 19-D-26, 19 December 2019, Google AdWords III (Gibmedia); 20-D-04, 16 March 2020, Apple/Tech Data/Ingram Micro; 20-MC-01, 9 April 2020, Google – ancillary rights; 21-D-07, 17 March 2021, Apple Targeted advertising; 21-D-17, 12 July 2021, Google – ancillary rights (non-compliance); 22-D-13, 21 June 2022, Google – ancillary rights (commitments); 22-D-12, 16 June 2022, Meta; 21-D-11, 7 June 2021, Google – Doubleclick for publishers/AdX. In three investigations, there were more than two decisions. These decisions are underlined. Outside the investigated period: 10-MC-01, 30 June 2010, Google AdWords I (Navx); 10-D-30, 28 October 2010, Google AdWords I (Navx).
827. Google AdWords II (E-Kanopi) (2013); Google AdWords III (Gibmedia) (2015); Google AdWords IV (IAH) (2016); Google AdSense (1PlusV) (2017); Google AdWords V (Interactive Labs) (2018); Google AdWords VI (Amadeus) (2019); Google – ancillary rights (2020); Google – Doubleclick for publishers/AdX (2021). Outside the investigated period: Google AdWords I (Navx) (2010).

investigations against Google between 2010[828] and 2021, which led to a fine of EUR 150 million in 2019,[829] EUR 500[830] million and EUR 220[831] million in 2021, two commitment decisions dating from 2010[832] (i.e., strictly speaking outside the research period but included for good understating of follow-on cases dating from the research period) and 2021[833] and the imposition of provisional measures on three occasions (in 2010, 2019 and in 2020).[834] The Autorité fined Apple EUR 218.3 million for abuse of a position of economic dependence on APRs[835] (*see* above §6.02). and is currently investigating Apple's iOS14 privacy policy.[836] The Autorité also accepted commitments by Meta in 2022 to end an investigation into abusive practices in the market for non-search-related online advertising.[837] Apart from Google, Apple and Meta, it rejected three abuse of dominance complaints against Vente-privee.com, Amadeus and l'Assemblée permanente des chambres d'agriculture (APCA).

The Autorité has published policy documents on competition law and data (2016, with the Bundeskartellamt), on data processing in the online-advertising sector (2018), on algorithms (2019, again with the Bundeskartellamt) and payment services (2021). It also announced a market study of cloud services (2022).[838]

[A] Policy Documents

[1] Data and Competition Law (2016)

The 2016 '*Competition Law and Data*' report provides guidance on data collection and the associated competition risks. In this report, the Autorité and the Bundeskartellamt indicate that measures that reduce privacy may constitute an abuse of a dominant position: '*data privacy regulations might be a useful benchmark to assess an exploitative conduct, especially in a context where most consumers do not read the conditions and terms of services and privacy policies.*'[839] According to established decision-making

828. This 2010 investigation falls outside the investigated period.
829. Autorité de la Concurrence, decision 19 December 2019, 19-D-26 (Google AdWords III (Gibmedia)).
830. Autorité de la Concurrence, decision 12 July 2021, 21-D-17 (Google – ancillary rights (non-compliance)).
831. Autorité de la Concurrence, decision 7 June 2021, 21-D-11 (Google – Doubleclick for publishers/AdX).
832. Autorité de la Concurrence, decision 30 June 2010, 10-MC-01 (Google AdWords Ia (Navx)).
833. Autorité de la Concurrence, decision 21 June 2022, 22-D-13 (Google – ancillary rights (commitments)).
834. Six of the nine investigations related to Google AdWords, one to Google AdSense, one to Google Doubleclick for publishers/AdX and one to Google's response to the French implementation of the new EU copyright directive.
835. Autorité de la Concurrence, decision 16 March 2020, 20-D-04 (Apple/Tech Data/Ingram Micro).
836. Autorité de la Concurrence, decision 17 March 2021, 21-D-07 (Apple Targeted advertising).
837. Autorité de la Concurrence, decision 16 June 2022, 22-D-12 (Meta).
838. Autorité de la concurrence, press release 27 January 2022, 'The Autorité de la concurrence starts proceedings ex officio to analyse competition conditions in the cloud computing sector.'
839. Autorité de la Concurrence, 'Competition Law and Data', 10 May 2016.

practice of the Autorité in the non-digital sector, the unauthorised use of a data set that cannot be copied by competitors and which provides a significant strategic advantage may, in specific circumstances, constitute an abuse of an economic dominant position.[840] These abuse decisions referred to by the Autorité relate in particular to the use of customer data by former state monopolies.[841]

[2] Data Processing in Online Advertising (2018)

In its 2018 report on data processing in the online advertising sector, the Autorité concludes that having large amounts of high value-added data, as well as expertise and resources to make the best use of that data, provides crucial competitive advantages.[842] The sector enquiry underlying the report shows that several market participants have pointed out to the Autorité that in particular Google and Facebook have such competitively advantageous data at their disposal in combination with their '*advanced computing and algorithmic capabilities [...] for processing large volumes of data in real time*'.[843] The Autorité indicated that it will remain vigilant in this sector and may initiate ex officio proceedings under the prohibition of abuse of a dominant position.[844] However, thus far, the Autorité does not seem to have started proceedings specifically for abusing a data advantage.

[3] Algorithms (2019)

In its 2019 report on algorithms, which mainly focuses on algorithmic collusion (*see* §6.02[A][2] above), the Autorité notes that algorithms may facilitate abuses of market power where: (i) access to information on algorithms is refused, (ii) price-setting is left to algorithms leading to excessive or discriminatory prices, or (iii) (self-) preferencing and ranking of goods and services is left to algorithms leading to the exclusion of certain companies.[845]

840. *Ibid.*, pp. 31-32.
841. Autorité de la Concurrence, decision 9 September 2014, 14-MC-02, paras 164-165: '164. *La promotion par GDF Suez de ses offres de marché en utilisant les moyens commerciaux issus de l'ancien monopole est ainsi susceptible de créer ou de renforcer la confusion pour le consommateur. En exploitant les bases de données, non reproductibles par les concurrents, consacrées aux offres de service public, elle confère à l'opérateur historique un avantage significatif sur les marchés concernés. 165. Cet avantage est susceptible, en l'état de l'instruction, de créer un effet potentiel d'éviction des opérateurs alternatifs nouveaux entrants, qui ne disposent pas des moyens nécessaires pour prospecter la clientèle sur un pied d'égalité.*'
842. Autorité de la Concurrence, 'Opinion on Data Processing in the Online Advertising Sector', 18-A-03, 6 March 2018, para. 10.
843. Autorité de la Concurrence, 'Opinion on Data Processing in the Online Advertising Sector', 18-A-03, 6 March 2018, para. 44.
844. *Ibid.*, para. 10.
845. Autorité de la Concurrence & Bundeskartellamt, 'Algorithms and Competition', 6 November 2019, p. 91.

[4] Digital Economy (2020)

In its contribution to the public debate on competition policy in the light of the challenges arising from the digital economy in 2020, the Autorité states that the development of digital monopolies or 'gatekeepers' – whereby certain market players control market access for multiple users – is of particular concern.[846] The Autorité indicates that this could be solved by expanding the definition of dominance '*à incluire certains acteurs en situation de quasi-dominance ou sur le point de faire basculer le marché*' [freely translated: '*to include market players that are close to dominance or about to tilt the market in their favour*'].[847] This special definition of dominance could, according to the Autorité, be applied to 'key platforms' which have significant market power in the markets in which they operate, but also where this is the case in neighbouring markets due to their status as 'gatekeepers' (*see also* the introduction of Chapter 4, Digital Markets Act).

[5] Payment Services (2021)

In its opinion on payment services, the Autorité earmarks the market power of big tech companies as a point of attention.[848] The Autorité: '*Data collected by BigTechs as part of their core business activities could give them a significant advantage in the payments sector and, conversely, the data collected via the payment services they offer could allow them to further strengthen the attractiveness of their respective platforms.*'[849] The Autorité also flags the preinstallation of mobile contactless payment solutions and effective access to contactless payment technology as potential points of attention.

[6] Cloud Services (2022)

In 2022, the Autorité announced a market study into cloud services (2022) that will be conducted by an investigation team consisting of lawyers, economists and data scientists.[850] The Autorité notes that the study will focus on how competition works in the sector and on '*defining the relevant markets in the cloud sector, assessing the position and competitive advantages of the various players involved and examining the commercial practices that may be put in place*'.

846. Autorité de la Concurrence, 'Contribution to the debate on competition policy and digital challenges', 19 February 2020, p. 4.
847. *Ibid.*
848. Autorité de la concurrence, 'Opinion on the sector of new technologies applied to payment activities', 21-A-05, 29 April 2021.
849. Autorité de la concurrence, press release 29 April 2022, '"FinTech" sector-specific inquiry: The Autorité de la concurrence issues its opinion.'
850. Autorité de la concurrence, press release 27 January 2022, 'The Autorité de la concurrence starts proceedings ex officio to analyse competition conditions in the cloud computing sector.'

[B] Enforcement

[1] Google AdWords I (2010)

To illustrate its enforcement practice, the Autorité regularly refers to its actions in the first *Google AdWords* case of 2010 (i.e., before the investigated period). Although this case dates from before the research period in this book, it is therefore included here to ensure a good comprehension of cases that do date from the research period. The Autorité took provisional measures[851] and subsequently, a commitment decision, which obliged Google to adjust its potentially abusive policy in accordance with competition law.[852] Isabelle de Silva said in 2017: '*L'outil permettant d'obtenir des engagements est aussi très utile: il a permis à l'Autorité d'infléchir la politique de contenus de Google AdWords*' [freely translated: '*The power to impose commitments is also very useful: it allowed the Autorité to influence the Google AdWords content policy*'].[853]

The investigation was launched following a complaint dated 16 February 2010 by Navx, a database vendor for Global Positioning System (GPS) and mobile phones, about the suspension of its Google AdWords account. Google AdWords (currently named Google Ads) is Google's online advertising platform. Google's suspension of Navx followed a restrictive policy change by Google regarding adverts for devices aimed at circumventing speed cameras. In its provisional commitment decision of June 2010, the Autorité found that Google is free to determine its policy with regard to the content of adverts as long as this is done on objective, transparent and non-discriminatory grounds.[854] Since Google had not complied with this obligation according to the provisional opinion of the Autorité, the Autorité imposed on Google, as a provisional measure, the obligation to publish its policy with regard to advertising on the circumvention of speed cameras and the suspension of accounts within four months on an objective, transparent and non-discriminatory basis and to restore Navx's account within five days.[855] In the subsequent commitment decision of October 2010, Google committed to making its policy objective, transparent and non-discriminatory, *inter alia*, by specifying what types of subjects it does not allow, by disclosing any restrictive policy changes at least three months in advance to advertisers who might be affected and by setting out the procedure for suspending an account.[856] The commitment decision states that Google implements the principles of its amended policy in all countries where Google AdWords services are offered.[857]

851. Autorité de la Concurrence, decision 30 June 2010, 10-MC-01 (*Google AdWords I (Navx)*).
852. Autorité de la Concurrence, decision 28 October 2010, 10-D-30 (*Google AdWords I (Navx)*).
853. Le Figaro, 'La France et l'UE sur la même longueur d'ondes contre les cartels des algorithmes', 27 October 2017.
854. Autorité de la Concurrence, decision 30 June 2010, 10-MC-01 (*Google AdWords I (Navx)*).
855. *Ibid.*, paras 47-48.
856. Autorité de la Concurrence, decision 28 October 2010, 10-D-30 (*Google AdWords I (Navx)*), para. 87.
857. *Ibid.*

[2] Google AdWords II (2013)

On 28 February 2013, the Autorité rejected a complaint by E-Kanopi against Google for deactivating its AdWords and AdSense accounts.[858] According to E-Kanopi, Google abused its dominant position in online advertising by excluding E-Kanopi from access to Google's services and by discriminating against E-Kanopi compared to its competitors. E-Kanopi operated the search webpage www.iadah.com (with a Google-powered search function) and several online information services (for, *inter alia*, weather reports and business information). Since January 2010, E-Kanopi had been using AdWords to promote its informative websites and, since April 2010, AdSense, in particular for its search webpage. Users who installed a toolbar application received free access to the information services. In May 2010, Google first terminated the AdWords and AdSense contracts for www.iadah.com and then, in June 2010, those of E-Kanopi's various online information services as well, because, among other reasons, E-Kanopi was using a customer acquisition model that was contrary to Google's rules. From that time onwards, E-Kanopi experienced several suspensions of its accounts and, from May 2011 onwards, its accounts were permanently deactivated.

Referring to its Navx decision, the Autorité reiterates that Google's freedom to define its Adwords and Adsense policies does not release it from the obligation to implement those policies under objective, transparent and non-discriminatory conditions.[859] The evidence in the file shows that Google closed E-Kanopi's accounts because E-Kanopi used a customer acquisition model that was contrary to the Adwords and Adsense contractual arrangements. E-Kanopi would install unsolicited software on users' devices and sell services that are available elsewhere for free: '*It is in fact a departure from the procès-verbal [...] It is clear from the minutes [...] that Google has cut E-Kanopi's Adwords and Adsense accounts following the violation, by E-Kanopi, of the rules aimed at protecting Internet users from the installation of logics not expressly authorised and of the rules concerning the prohibition of selling content which could be obtained free of charge on the* Internet'[860] [Free translation: 'It follows from the minutes [...] that Google closed E-Kanopi's Adwords and Adsense accounts as a result of a breach, by E-Kanopi, of the rules protecting Internet users against the unsolicited installation of software and the rules prohibiting the sale of content that could be obtained for free on the Internet.']. The closure thus followed an individualised and concrete investigation of E-Kanopi's activities and an objective and neutral assessment thereof in the light of Google's general policy, which is permissible. Also, according to the Autorité, E-Kanopi has not demonstrated that Google's conduct was aimed at discriminating against E-Kanopi's information services, as it is unclear whether the competitors mentioned by E-Kanopi are comparable to E-Kanopi. The Autorité therefore rejects E-Kanopi's complaint as insufficiently supported by evidence.

---

858. Autorité de la Concurrence, decision 28 February 2013, 13-D-07 (*Google AdWords II (E-Kanopi)*).
859. *Ibid.*, para. 47.
860. *Ibid.*, para. 60.

[3] Google AdWords III (2015, 2019)

On 19 December 2019, following a complaint from Gibmedia, the Autorité imposed a fine of EUR 150 million on Google for abusing its dominant position in the French online search advertising market through Google Ads between July 2012 and October 2018.[861] Gibmedia operates several websites for paid ad-free information, including telephone number information, weather reports and business information, and had complained that Google had not acted objectively, transparently and non-discriminatorily when suspending its account in January 2015.[862] Only in 2015, the Autorité still rejected a request by Gibmedia in this case to impose interim measures on Google. At that time, the Autorité was unable to establish any serious or immediate harm to the interests of consumers, the industry or Gibmedia as such, but saw sufficient grounds to continue the proceedings in the main case.[863]

Google has rules for access to Google Ads in place that are directed against 'untrustworthy promotions'. These rules, which are amended several times a year, include a prohibition on charging for goods or services that are normally free of charge, a prohibition on non-transparent pricing models and a prohibition on using camouflage techniques (showing website visitors different content from that shown to them via Google).[864] Google also has rules for penalising advertisers who do not comply with the rules against 'untrustworthy promotions'. Thus, Google can reject ads or proceed to suspend websites or accounts of advertisers.

The Autorité notes that Google is 'very dominant' and that the combination of the popularity of the Google search engine and Google's regulatory power over advertisers entails a 'very particular responsibility' on the part of Google towards its customers.[865] Google's rules for advertisers are the 'de facto standard' and Google has a responsibility to set and apply its rules in an objective, transparent and non-discriminatory manner. Google defends itself by arguing that malicious ads pose a threat to its users, to honest advertisers and to the quality of Google services. According to Google, the Google Ads rules are aimed at neutralising these threats and are therefore not restrictive of competition. However, the Autorité reiterates that Google's freedom to define its Adwords and Adsense policies does not release it from the obligation to implement those policies under objective, transparent and non-discriminatory conditions.

The Autorité concludes that Google has not complied with this obligation and is guilty of abusing its dominant position by imposing unfair trading conditions.[866] First, the Autorité states that the Google Ads rules are not unambiguous and are changed frequently, while advertisers are not properly informed about them. According to the

---

861. Autorité de la Concurrence, decision 19 December 2019, 19-D-26 (*Google AdWords III (Gibmedia)*).
862. *Ibid.*, paras 47, 93.
863. Autorité de la Concurrence, decision of 9 September 2015, 15-D-23 (*Google AdWords III (Gibmedia)*).
864. Autorité de la Concurrence, decision 19 December 2019, 19-D-26 (*Google AdWords III (Gibmedia)*), paras 96-134.
865. *Ibid.*, paras 321, 330, 342.
866. *Ibid.*, para. 426.

Autorité, this gives Google policy freedom to treat advertisers unfairly.[867] The Autorité argues that the way Google applies the rules is ambiguous and inconsistent. The enforcement of the rules is carried out by an international 'Trust & Safety' team of about a thousand people. According to the Autorité, that team does not have sufficient capacity: '*Advertisers are not able to speak directly to those in charge of applying the Rules or have their cases and requests handled effectively.*'[868] The Autorité also notes inconsistency in the enforcement of the rules. For example, the accounts of Gibmedia were suspended, but those of its sister company Ecométrie (which has a similar business model and had already committed violations before) were not: '*So even though the business model of the call directory sites published by Ecométrie and Gibmedia is similar and these sites had already violated the "Sale of free items" rule between 2011 and 2014, Google treated them differently in 2015.*' The role of different departments in communicating with customers also contributes to inconsistency in the enforcement of the rules, according to the Autorité. For example, Google's sales teams approached advertisers who had previously been suspended by the Trust & Safety team: '*Whereas Google was complaining to some advertisers that they were not applying its Rules correctly, and was suspending accounts for this reason, at the same time it was offering the same advertisers personalised assistance services designed to maximise coverage of internet users searching for keywords corresponding to these sites' services, through its Google Ads advertising offer.*'[869]

The Autorité imposes a fine of EUR 150 million on Google. The Autorité considers that in 2010 and 2013 (*see* §6.03[B][1] and §6.03[B][2]), it had already pointed out to Google the competition risks of establishing and maintaining Google Ads rules. In addition to this fine, the Autorité requires Google to comply within three months:

(i) clarify the Google Ads rules;
(ii) clarify the suspension procedures; and
(iii) to take measures to improve the detection of violations of Google Ads rules and an obligation to report annually to the Autorité.

Google appealed against the decision, but this was rejected on 7 April 2022.[870] Google has appealed in cassation.

[4] Google AdWords IV (2016)

On 23 November 2016, the Autorité rejected a complaint against Google by Idéal Assistance Habitat (IAH), a provider of repair, plumbing and locksmith services.[871] IAH has been using Google AdWords to advertise its services online since 2010, spending EUR 8,000-EUR 9,000 per month (at an average cost per click of EUR 15-EUR 25). However, as of June 2012, the costs are rising sharply. For July 2012, IAH receives a

867. *Ibid.*, paras 408, 417, 418.
868. *Ibid.*, para. 158.
869. *Ibid.*, para. 247.
870. Cour d'Appel de Paris, judgment 7 April 2022, RG 20/03811.
871. Autorité de la Concurrence, decision 23 November 2016, 16-D-25 (*Google AdWords IV (IAH)*).

Google AdWords invoice of EUR 78,523 and for August 2012 an invoice of EUR 167,466. A dispute develops between Google and IAH, whereby IAH takes the position that the high costs are caused by fraudulent clicks. Google verifies its invoices, admits that some of the clicks were fraudulent and in November 2012 makes a settlement offer in the form of a reduced invoice (the exact terms of the settlement offer are not clear from the decision). IAH had then already stopped paying its invoices since August 2012. The reduced invoice is not paid either. IAH refuses to pay because Google's monitoring system of fraudulent activity would be ineffective and the billing of Google's services would not be transparent. Google closed IAH's account in February 2013. According to IAH, this closure is unjustified and Google is abusing its dominant position with the closure. However, the Autorité rejects IAH's complaint because IAH does not sufficiently substantiate why Google's settlement proposal was unreasonable.

On 20 July 2018, the Autorité dismisses a complaint by Interactive Lab against Google for abuse of dominance.[872] Interactive Lab, an intermediary between website builders and companies wishing to have a website built, used Google AdWords in 2007 and 2008. By means of Google AdWords, it receives 95% of its customer requests. Despite the fact that the overall demand for website building is increasing according to Interactive Lab and its service is 'hyper attractive', in 2008 Interactive Lab received fewer client requests than in 2007.[873] In 2012 and 2017, Interactive Lab also uses AdWords, but the number of client requests continues to decline. Interactive Lab claims that Google discriminates against it by limiting the display of its advertisements. Google would have an interest in directing its users to lesser-quality providers because otherwise, such providers of lesser quality would no longer be interested in buying advertising space. However, the Autorité finds that Interactive Lab has not demonstrated that its services are actually 'hyper attractive' compared to its competitors and that it cannot be established that the decline in customer requests is attributable to Google.[874] Also, according to the Autorité, Interactive Lab has not provided evidence for its complaint that Google would direct users to lesser providers and thus the Autorité rejects the complaint.

[5] Google AdWords VI (2019)

On 31 January 2019, the Autorité imposed provisional measures on Google AdWords for a second time, this time following a complaint from Amadeus, a provider of telephonic enquiry services.[875] Google had suspended the Google AdWords accounts of Amadeus and refused most of its adverts since January 2018. Amadeus subsequently suffered a loss of turnover of approximately 90%.[876] According to Google, Amadeus

872. Autorité de la Concurrence, decision 20 July 2018, 18-D-13 (*Google AdWords V (Interactive Labs)*).
873. *Ibid.*, para. 30.
874. *Ibid.*, para. 50.
875. Autorité de la Concurrence, decision 31 January 2019, 19-MC-01 (*Google AdWords VIa (Amadeus)*).
876. *Ibid.*, para. 172.

had violated Google's rules on 'sale of free items' (defined as charging users for products or services that are normally free), 'misleading statements' and 'circumventing systems'. However, the Autorité found that the sudden termination by Google occurred under conditions that were 'neither objective nor transparent' and constituted a prima facie abuse of dominance by applying dissimilar conditions.[877] Prior to a decision on the merits, the Autorité thus required Google, in its decision imposing interim measures, to clarify the rules it applies to directory enquiry service providers and to review the advert campaigns of Amadeus in light of the clarified rules. On 4 April 2019, the Paris Court of Appeals upheld the decision of the Autorité, ruling that the main provisional measures imposed on Google where necessary and proportional.[878] On 26 October 2020, the Autorité decided to reject the complaint in the main proceedings and not to impose a fine.[879] In this respect, the Authority argues that the decision in the case following Gibmedia's complaint of 19 December 2019 also addresses the behaviour Amadeus complains about (*see* §6.03[B][3]). In the said decision, Google is furthermore forced to change its practices to a greater extent than it would be by the interim measures imposed in response to Amadeus' complaint, the Autorité said in its rejection.[880]

[6] Google AdSense (2017)

On 18 December 2017, the Autorité rejected a complaint by 1PlusV for abuse of dominance by Google.[881] 1PlusV, a developer of website search software, first accuses Google of ad tying and discrimination through *AdSense for Search*. AdSense is a service from Google that allows third-party websites to display ads to their visitors when these visitors use search engines on these websites. The technology for the (internal) search engine on these websites can, when using AdSense, be supplied by Google (the 'Custom Search Engine' formula). Websites can however also opt for an 'Ads-Only' formula where they use their own search technology. According to 1PlusV, however, it has not been able to access this 'Ads-Only' formula. The Autorité notes that Google offered the 'Ads-Only' formula at least from 2010 onwards without linking it to its 'Custom Search Engine' formula. Before that time, the 'Ads-Only' formula was only available to a limited number of companies that could guarantee the safety of using this

877. *Ibid.*, paras 148, 155.
878. Cour d'Appel de Paris, judgment 4 April 2019, RG 19/03274. This does not apply to the obligation to organise a face to face training for support staff in the field of paid electronic directory services. The Paris Court of Appeals declared itself incompetent to rule on whether the Autorité was allowed to publish a 'non-confidential' version of the decision of 31 January 2019 on its webste. Google has appealed this point at the Conseil d'Etat. Op 20 maart 2020 heeft de Conseil d'Etat de zaak verwezen naar het Tribunal des Conflits (Conseil d'Etat, judgment 20 March 2020, 429279). On 5 October 2020, the Tribunal ruled that the Cour d'Appel is competent on this matter and annulled the judgment of the Cour d'Appel to the extent it concerns this particular matter. The case is pending at the Cour d'Appel.
879. Autorité de la Concurrence, decision 26 October 2020, 20-D-14 (*Google AdWords VI (Amadeus)*).
880. *Ibid.*, paras 65-69.
881. Autorité de la Concurrence, decision 18 December 2017, 17-D-24 (*Google AdSense (1PlusV)*).

product. 1PlusV complains that it could not use this option, but cannot prove that it asked Google for an 'Ads-Only' formula.[882] As a result, there is no evidence of discrimination. 1PlusV also argued that Google would discriminate against it because one of its websites would have been guilty of 'pre-popularisation' in the past. This is the practice of filling a website with frequently searched terms in order to attract visitors to a website. Google prohibits this behaviour and desindexes (removes from the Google search engine) websites that make use of pre-popularisation. According to the Autorité, however, it has not been proven that other websites that were also guilty of pre-popularisation were given access to the 'Ads-Only' formula. Thus, the complaints of 1PlusV are dismissed.

[7] Google Doubleclick for Publishers and AdExchange (2021)

On 7 June 2021, the Autorité fined Google EUR 220 million and accepted commitments by Google, for abuse of a dominant position in the market for ad servers for publishers of websites and mobile apps between January 2014 and September 2020.[883] The investigation was triggered by complaints from publishers (or providers of advertising space) that used two distinct Google services: (i) the Doubleclick for publishers (DFP) ad server and (ii) the Doubleclick AdExchange (AdX) advertising space sales platform.

The Autorité describes an ad server as '*a tool that allows the serving of ads on the website or mobile app of the publisher. It also makes it possible to manage the sale of advertising space in a unified manner, in particular by giving the publisher the ability to choose, for the same advertising space, between transactions concluded directly with advertisers (known as "guaranteed campaign elements") and the programmatic sale on multiple platforms which organise auctions (i.e., according to an automated mechanism)*'.[884] Google's AdX platform is a so-called supply-side platform (SSP) for the programmatic sale of advertising space. The Autorité describes this as a marketplace '*where buyers of advertising space and publishers wishing to sell advertising space (or "impressions") come together. They typically solicit bids from advertisers for a given impression, then conduct an auction between the different prices offered by the advertisers, and finally transmit the winning bid to the ad server*'. The Autorité found that publishers normally sell their advertising space through different SSPs simultaneously, but that they only use a single ad server. The interoperability between an ad server and an SSP therefore '*determines both the revenue publishers earn from their advertising space, and their ability to market it, and the attractiveness of the listing [SSP] platforms*'.

According to the Autorité, Google has, with DFP, a dominant position on the market for ad servers for publishers of websites and mobile apps with a growing market share between 60% and 80% on the European market for ad servers. The

882. *Ibid.*, paras 20, 24-30.
883. Autorité de la Concurrence, decision 7 June 2021, 21-D-11 (Google – Doubleclick for publishers/AdX).
884. Autorité de la Concurrence, press release 7 June 2021, 'The Autorité de la concurrence hands out a €220 million fine to Google for favouring its own services in the online advertising sector.'

Autorité notes that this market share has increased significantly since the 2008 clearance decision by the European Commission of the acquisition of Doubleclick by Google when it was only 40%-50%.

The Autorité found that Google abused its dominant position by favouring its own advertising technologies. Firstly, Google's DFP ad server organised 'unfair competition' between AdX and other SSPs. The Autorité notes: '*One of the most notable asymmetries is that DFP indicated, until recently, the price offered by competing platforms to AdX, and that the latter used this information to optimise its bids and maximise its chances to win them against competing SSPs, in particular by varying its commission according to the competitive pressure emanating from other SSPs.*' Second, Google limited the interoperability of AdX with third-party ad servers. According to the Autorité, Google did not offer the same technical and contractual conditions to publishers that used a third-party ad server as to those publishers that used Google's DFP. The Autorité states: '*the AdX platform is only partially interoperable with DFP's competing ad servers, and does not allow the latter to organise a competition between AdX and its competitors – even though AdX itself has a privileged access to a significant portion of advertisers' demand and while all of these competitors have adopted standards allowing for fairer competition*'.

Google offered an interoperability commitment '*allowing competition on the merits between AdX and third-party SSPs for the purchase of inventories from publishers using DFP*'. This commitment includes a right to access information on the auction process, and a commitment by Google not to use data on AdX competitors to optimise AdX bids. In addition, Google will allow publishers using third-party ad servers to access AdX demand in 'real time', enabling them to sell their clients advertising space through AdX. The commitments apply for a period of three years. A monitoring trustee shall monitor Google's compliance with the commitments.

[8] Vente-privee.com (2014)

On 28 November 2014, the Autorité rejected a complaint by Brandalley against Vente-privee.com, a webshop specialising in online 'private sales'.[885] Through online private sales, one can obtain high discounts on online bulk sales by becoming a member of exclusive databases. According to Brandalley, a webshop for textiles, accessories and decoration, Vente-privee.com is abusing its dominant position in the market for online private sales by imposing exclusivity clauses on customers for whom it distributes products since 2005. Vente-privee.com obliged its suppliers not to sell products to third-party websites which, like Vente-privee.com, engage in the sale of discounted products: '*Le Fournisseur s'engage à ne pas vendre ses produits à d'autres sites web marchands, dont l'objet, le mode de fonctionnement [...] seraient identiques ou similaires à celui de Vente-privee.com*'. [Free translation: '*The Supplier undertakes not to sell his products to other commercial websites whose purpose or mode of operation [...] are identical or similar to those of Vente-privee.com*'.] However, the Autorité notes

885. Autorité de la Concurrence, decision 28 November 2014, 14-D-18 (*Vente-privee.com*).

that the existence of a market for online private sales cannot be established, because it is not sufficiently clear to what extent various other distribution channels compete with online private sales. The Autorité is therefore unable to establish whether Vente-privee.com is in a dominant position but nevertheless addresses the alleged abuse. The Autorité considers that exclusivity is justified in so far as it aims to ensure that Vente-privee.com can guarantee the availability of the product to its customers, including during the sixteen-week period in which those customers may return products.[886] The Autorité finds that Vente-privee.com did not respect that period between 2007 and 2011. Any exclusivity clause imposed by a dominant undertaking which goes beyond this period could, in the Autorité's view, potentially be interpreted as an abuse. However, as a dominant position cannot be proven, the Autorité rejects the complaint.

[9] Amadeus (2019)

In early 2019, the Autorité rejected a complaint from Optionizr.[887] According to Optionizr, Amadeus is allegedly abusing its power in the market for ancillary services for 'Passenger Service Systems' (PSS) in the aviation sector. Optionizr, a developer of software for online ticket sales, including airline tickets, argues that Amadeus' PSS is an essential facility for developers of PSS ancillary services and that Amadeus is guilty of denying these developers access to its PSS.

A PSS consists of three modules: (i) an inventory for managing flights and available seats, (ii) a reservation system, and (iii) a system for controlling the boarding and departure of flights. Amadeus' full-service airline PSS is called 'Altea' and is essentially a shared platform for all Amadeus customer airlines. Amadeus allows its customers to develop applications themselves (or with the help of developers such as Optionizr) which use information from Altéa and has made an 'application program interface' (API) available for this purpose. Applications developed by third parties must be certified by Amadeus to ensure the integrity of the system.

However, according to Optionizr, Amadeus refuses to make relevant technical information available, applies unacceptable prices, and causes delays or blockages in the activation of certain functionalities.

The Autorité notes that Amadeus' PSS cannot be an essential facility for Optionizr or other PSS ancillary service providers. There is no commercial relationship between Amadeus and PSS providers; the latter respond to a request from airlines, not from ancillary service providers. Nor does Amadeus constitute an essential facility for airlines, since it is clear from the file that they have a choice of providers. However, the Autorité reiterates that refusal of access may be abusive even in the absence of an essential facility: '*even in the absence of an essential facility, an opposing refusal of access in a discriminatory manner by a dominant company may constitute an abuse of a dominant position, since it jeopardises the competition game*'. [Free translation: '*even*

886. *Ibid.*, paras 125-126.
887. Autorité de la Concurrence, decision 21 February 2019, 19-D-04 (*Amadeus*).

in the absence of an essential facility, a discriminatory refusal of access by a dominant undertaking may constitute an abuse of a dominant position if it significantly distorts competition'].

However, that is not the case in this instance. The Autorité finds that Amadeus did indeed deny Optionizr access to its API documentation after Optionizr requested it. Amadeus provides such access, as explained above, only at the request of its customers, in order to ensure the integrity of the system and to protect the commercial data of its customers. Optionizr can gain access through this route. At least, the Autorité does not consider there to be any evidence to the contrary, nor any unacceptable prices. Optionizr also claims that the functionality of the PSS software it has developed would be obstructed by Amadeus. However, Amadeus demonstrates that Optionizr's software does not make appropriate use of software developed by Amadeus. Therefore, according to the Autorité, Amadeus cannot be held responsible for the problems encountered by the Optionizr software. Amadeus also demonstrates that a security update it performed was not intended to thwart Optionizr, but to ensure the security of its customers' online payments. The Autorité rejected the complaints.

[10] APCA (2018)

On 5 October 2018, the Autorité rejected a complaint by ANELA against l'Assemblée permanente des chambres d'agriculture (APCA).[888] APCA is the umbrella association of the French public law 'chambers of agriculture', which represents the interests of farmers. According to ANELA (l'Association nationale des éditeurs de logiciels agricoles), the national association of producers of agricultural software, APCA abuses its dominant position in the market for advice and assistance to farmers by excluding its competitors in the related market for software for agricultural management. APCA is allegedly offering its software at predatory prices and using public funds for its commercial activities.

The complaint states that a market for agricultural advice or, more precisely, a market for advice and assistance to farmers exists. This market is said to include several services, such as supporting young farmers and representing farmers with the government on subsidies. However, according to the Autorité, the complaint does not contain any indication that would allow measuring the degree of substitutability between these different services, both from a supply and a demand point of view. Nor does the complaint contain any information enabling the local or national dimension of the market(s) concerned to be delineated. The Autorité rejects the complaint as it does not contain sufficient elements indicating the existence of a product market for advice and assistance to farmers.

888. Autorité de la Concurrence, decision 5 October 2018, 18-D-20 (*APCA*).

[11] Google: Ancillary Rights (2020-2022)

Also in 2020, the Autorité will impose (provisional) measures on Google, followed by a fine of EUR 500 million for non-compliance with the measures in 2021 and, finally, a commitment decision in 2022.[889]

Several French publishers had filed a complaint against Google for abuse of dominant position due to Google's conduct around the entry into force of the new French law on neighbouring rights of 24 July 2019, an implementation of Directive 2019/790. The law stipulates that publications of publishers may not be published without their consent by (among others) online platforms and provides guidelines for determining a fee for the use of these publications.

Shortly before the law came into force, Google announced that it would no longer display publishers' publications unless the publishers made it clear to Google what Google was allowed to use: '*we will not show preview in France for a European news publication unless the publisher has taken steps to tell us that's what they want. This applies to search results across Google services*'.[890] Publishers could indicate by means of 'tags' developed by Google in the source code of their website to what extent Google was allowed to display text, photos and videos from their publications. Google simultaneously announced that it did not intend to pay publishers for this: '*When you use the new settings, you agree to the use of previews of your content without payment, both for traffic to and from Google.*' An overwhelming majority of publishers (86.6% according to one study) actually granted Google permission to use their material, without receiving any payment from Google.[891] The publishers who did not use the tags on their websites (in a timely manner) experienced a sharp drop in visitor numbers (between 33% and 50%).[892]

According to the Autorité, it is likely that Google has a dominant position in the French market for general search services and that it has abused that position in three ways:

(1) Imposition of unfair trading conditions: the Autorité considers that Google did not negotiate the new licence conditions with the publishers in the sense as described in the French law, but unilaterally enforced them.[893] According to the Autorité, the terms are unfair because a reasonable interpretation of Directive 2019/790 and French law does not appear to be compatible with Google's 'zero price' policy. According to the Autorité, Google is acting contrary to the spirit of the law. The new licensing terms agreed by Google

889. Autorité de la Concurrence, decision 9 April 2020, 20-MC-01 (Google – ancillary rights); Autorité de la Concurrence, decision 12 July 2021, 21-D-17 (Google – ancillary rights (non-compliance)); Autorité de la Concurrence, decision 21 June 2022, 22-D-13 (Google – ancillary rights (commitments)).
890. Autorité de la Concurrence, decision 9 April 2020, 20-MC-01 (Google – ancillary rights), para. 91.
891. *Ibid.*, paras 103-110, 245.
892. *Ibid.*, paras 120-125.
893. *Ibid.*, paras 196-203.

with publishers and news agencies give Google more rights (to the detriment of the publishers) than was the case prior to the entry into force of the French law.[894]

(2) Imposition of discriminatory conditions: the French law requires Google to take into account, in determining the remuneration, '*human, material and financial investments made by publishers and news agencies, the contribution of press publications to political news and current affairs and the extent of the use of press publications by online public communication services*'. The Autorité considers that Google's 'zero price' policy constitutes discrimination because Google treats different publishers in the same way without taking into account these circumstances and the specific situation of each publisher.

(3) Circumvention of the law: According to the Autorité, Google's actions contrary to the spirit of the applicable French law constitute a third form of abuse. The Autorité considers that the aim of the law is '*to redefine the sharing of value in favour of news publishers within a negotiated framework*', but that Google's zero price policy is precisely contrary to this. As described above, Google even managed to negotiate better conditions than were in place before the French law came into force.

According to the Autorité, Google's conduct causes serious and immediate damage to the press sector and therefore justifies the imposition of interim measures. The Autorité orders Google, inter alia, to negotiate in good faith with publishers on the remuneration for the re-use of their protected content within three months and, in that context, to provide all necessary information enabling the remuneration to be determined in a transparent manner. These negotiations should retroactively cover the fees due since the entry into force of the law.

On 8 October 2020, the Court of Appeal upheld the decision of the Autorité, considering that the measures imposed were proportionate and necessary.[895] In the meantime, in early September 2020, the Autorité received two complaints from two parties involved in the negotiations. These complaints concern Google's non-compliance with the interim measures. Allegedly, Google is trying to sabotage the negotiations in several ways: it is not releasing all the necessary documents, is offering too low fees and is using delaying tactics.[896]

On 12 July 2021, the Autorité imposed a fine of EUR 500 million on Google for non-compliance with the interim measures.[897] According to the Autorité, Google failed

894. *Ibid.*, paras 217, 243-247.
895. Cour d'Appel de Paris, judgment of 8 October, RG 20/08071.
896. Le Monde, 'Le conflit opposant les médias à Facebook et à Google se durcit', 1 September 2020. Google then concludes agreements with a number of parties. For example, on 19 November 2020, Google announced that it had signed agreements with a number of French publishers. And on 21 January 2021, the Alliance de la presse d'information générale (Apig) announced that it had signed an agreement with Google. *See*, Le Figaro, 'Droits voisins: Google a signé un accord pour rémunérer la presse', 21 January 2021.
897. Autorité de la Concurrence, decision 12 July 2021, 21-D-17 (Google – ancillary rights (non-compliance)).

to negotiate in good faith with the publishers, unjustifiably limited the scope of the negotiations and provided insufficient information in the context of the negotiations.[898] Google must also pay a penalty of EUR 900,000 per day if it does not comply with its obligations within two months.

On 21 June 2022, the Autorité announced that it accepted commitments by Google.[899] Google committed to negotiate in good faith '*with press publishers and news agencies that so request, the remuneration for any reproduction of protected content on its services in accordance [...] and according to transparent, objective and non-discriminatory criteria*'.[900] Google has also committed to provide a 'minimum' degree of information to each negotiating party, such as click-through rates of protected content as well as Google revenue data in France. Google has also withdrawn its appeal against the EUR 500 million fine and has to ensure that the negotiations affect the ranking or presentation of the publishers' and news agencies' content. The commitments will be monitored by an independent trustee.

[12] Apple: Targeted Advertising (2021)

On 17 March 2021, the Autorité rejected a request to impose interim measures on Apple.[901] Simultaneously, it announced that it would continue to investigate the data protection policies that Apple uses on its iPhone operating system iOS14 (and later versions).[902]

Apple announced '*as part of its policy to strengthen the privacy protection of its customers, [that] it would implement, in September 2020, a feature called ATT for App Tracking Transparency*'.[903] According to the press release of the Autorité, '*This feature consists, when the holder of an iPhone visits an application downloaded via the App Store, in displaying a pop-up window which then asks for their explicit consent to authorise the sharing of their personal data to third parties for advertising purposes. With consent, third parties can access the Identifier for Advertisers (IDFA), which identifies each Apple device and enables tracking of the owner's advertising, including on third-party sites.*' The investigation was triggered after a complaint by two online advertising trade organisations (IAB France and SRI France) and a trade organisation of buyers and sellers of media (UDECAM). They argued, in essence, that Apple's new

898. Autorité de la Concurrence, press release 13 July 2021, 'Remuneration of related rights for press publishers and agencies: the Autorité fines Google up to 500 million euros for non-compliance with several injunctions.'
899. Autorité de la Concurrence, decision 21 June 2022, 22-D-13 (Google – ancillary rights (commitments)).
900. Autorité de la Concurrence, press release 21 June 2022, 'Related rights: The Autorité accepts Google's commitments.'
901. Autorité de la Concurrence, decision 17 March 2021, 21-D-07 (*Apple Targeted advertising (a)*).
902. Autorité de la Concurrence, press release 17 March 2021, 'Targeted advertising/Apple's implementation of the ATT framework. The Autorité does not issue urgent interim measures against Apple but continues to investigate into the merits of the case.'
903. Autorité de la Concurrence, press release 17 March 2021, 'Targeted advertising/Apple's implementation of the ATT framework. The Autorité does not issue urgent interim measures against Apple but continues to investigate into the merits of the case.'

privacy policy, calls into question the targeted advertising business model of app developers, '*who earn on average twice as much revenue from personalised advertising as from contextual advertising*'.[904]

Interestingly, the decision not to impose interim measures appears to be at least partially motivated by France's data privacy authority, the Commission nationale de l'informatique et des libertés (CNIL). At the Autorité's request, it gave an opinion in favour of Apple's new privacy policy, stating: '*data protection regulation does not prevent Apple from implementing a mechanism to prohibit app developers from tracking the user without the latter's consent, especially when such consent is required by regulation*'.[905]

[13] Meta (2022)

On 16 June 2022, the Autorité accepted commitments by Meta to end an investigation into abusive practices in the market for non-search-related online advertising.[906] The investigation was launched following a complaint in September 2019 by Criteo, a French company that provides optimisation services for ads placement on Facebook and Instagram. Since 2016, Meta provided application programming interfaces (APIs) to companies such as Criteo that could use these APIs to improve bidding for ads space and to measure campaign performance tracking. In 2018, Meta withdrew Criteo's access to the APIs and removed Criteo as a so-called Facebook Marketing Partner (currently called Meta Business Partner (MBP)).

The Autorité finds that Meta is likely to hold a dominant position in the French market for non-search-related online advertising, with a market share of 49% in 2018 and 50% in 2019. On a market for online advertising on social media, Meta's market share is approximately 90%, or 75% if Youtube is included in the market. In its decision, the Autorité flags several practices that raise concerns. In particular, the Autorité notes: '*the conditions under which Criteo was deprived, in July 2018, of access to Meta's former partnership programme, called "Facebook Marketing Partner", were characterised by a lack of objectivity, transparency, predictability and stability in the criteria for accessing this programme, and by differences in treatment in their implementation*'.[907] The Autorité also notes that the withdrawal of Criteo's access to Meta's API 'User Level Bidding' '*raised concerns about the transparency, objectivity and non-discriminatory nature of the criteria for accessing Meta's APIs*'.

Meta has made several commitments to address the competition concerns. It committed to give access to its Meta Business Partner programme subject to '*a quantitative criterion related to the level of expenditure generated on the Advertising APIs [...]*' attributable to the partner. Meta also committed to give free access to a new

904. Autorité de la Concurrence, decision 17 March 2021, 21-D-07 (*Apple Targeted advertising (a)*), para. 88.
905. *Ibid.*, para. 157 and Commission nationale de l'informatique et des libertés (CNIL), opinion 17 December 2020, 2020-137.
906. Autorité de la Concurrence, decision 16 June 2022, 22-D-12 (Meta).
907. Autorité de la Concurrence, press release 16 June 2022.

'Recommendation Functionality' API for advertising service providers, based on criteria that *'are sufficiently justified, objective, transparent and non-discriminatory'*. Interestingly, the remedies apply to advertising service providers that target users on Facebook and Instagram in France, but as soon as a company falls within the quantitative criterion for the Meta Business Partner programme or the criteria for the new 'Recommendation Functionality' API, it can use these *'for all its advertising campaigns, without geographical restrictions'*. The commitments apply for a duration of five years, except for the 'Recommendation Functionality' API commitment. The latter will apply for a duration of five years. A trustee shall monitor Meta's compliance with the commitments.

§6.04 MERGER CONTROL

Isabelle de Silva: *'Les grandes plateformes tirent leur puissance non seulement de leur croissance interne, mais aussi d'une politique active d'acquisitions stratégiques'*[908] [freely translated: 'The big platforms do not only derive their power from internal growth, but also from an active policy of strategic acquisitions.'].

We count eight merger control decisions of the Autorité in the field of digital competition.[909] Important merger cases of the Autorité are the conditional phase 2 clearance of the acquisition of Darty by Fnac in 2016,[910] the unconditional phase 2 clearance of the acquisition of Logic Immo by Axel Springer group in 2018[911] and the conditional approval of the creation of online streaming joint-venture Salto in 2019.[912] In Darty/Fnac, the Autorité set a precedent for assessing the influence of online retail on brick-and-mortar retail markets on the basis of which it has elaborated criteria determining when an online market should be considered as part of the same product market as the brick-and-mortar retail market. Axel Springer/Logic Immo and the creation of Salto are important online platform precedents, in the real estate sector and the online video streaming sector respectively. The Salto decision is particularly interesting for the behavioural remedies package that addresses competition concerns in multiple markets affected by the online video streaming platform. Other noteworthy precedents are Elephant/Webedia in 2019, concerning the market share of influencers on Youtube, La Poste/Softeam in 2019, regarding digital business services and Duval/Blue Green in 2022, regarding the market for online golf course booking platforms.

908. Autorité de la Concurrence, 'Bilan de activité, synthèse 2019', 9 July 2020, p. 6.
909. 16-DCC-111, 27 July 2016 (Fnac/Darty); 18-DCC-18, 1 February 2018 (Axel Springer Group/Logic Immo); 19-DCC-65, 17 April 2019 (Jellej Jouets/Gifram/Luderix International); 19-DCC-94, 24 May 2019 (Webedia/Groupe Elephant); 19-DCC-132, 16 July 2019 (Fnac Darty/Nature et Découvertes); 19-DCC-157, 12 August 2019 (France Télévisions/ TF1/Métropole Télévision/Salto JV); 19-DCC-259, 18 December 2019 (La Poste/Softeam); 22-DCC-111, 24 June 2022 (Duval/Blue Green).
910. Autorité de la Concurrence, decision 27 July 2016, 16-DCC-111 (*Fnac/Darty*).
911. Autorité de la Concurrence, decision 1 February 2018, 18-DCC-18 (*Axel Springer Group/Logic Immo*).
912. Autorité de la Concurrence, decision 12 August 2019, 19-DCC-157 (*France Télévisions/TF1/Métropole Télévision/Salto JV*).

[A] Policy Documents

In their joint report 'Competition Law and Data', the Autorité and the Bundeskartellamt refer to various merger control precedents of the Commission and the US Federal Trade Commission (FTC), which examined the benefits of data collection for companies in digital markets.[913] In each of these precedents, the latter competition authorities concluded that the data advantage that will be obtained as a result of the implementation of the concentration would not lead to any competitive risk in the markets under investigation. According to the Autorité and the Bundeskartellamt, it should be examined on a case-by-case basis whether there will be a data advantage and, if so, what its scope is. The scarcity of the data and the ease with which the data can be copied, on the one hand, and the scale required to enjoy the economic benefit of a data set, on the other hand, must be considered.

In a September 2019 speech, Isabelle de Silva addressed the question 'Should we update our merger control toolkit?'.[914] She mentioned that the issue is not limited to 'killer acquisitions' because '*Facebook certainly didn't "kill" WhatsApp or Instagram.*' She added '*One of the issues at stake, in that kind of case, is whether this type of acquisition, by already very powerful companies, might entrench their position in a way that would significantly lessen the possibilities of entry by other competitors.*' The solution, according to De Silva, is '*that merger watchdogs need to be able to have a look at those specific mergers, even though they would be below the turnover notification threshold. We must be able to check, even if there is no competition concerns in the end*'. How to practically do that is another matter. De Silvia is not a fan of the German and Austrian solution of introducing a deal value threshold, because it creates too much uncertainty. Instead, the Autorité has looked closely into *ex post* merger review systems like in the US and Sweden and has discussed these extensively with the Federal Trade Commission, the Department of Justice and the Swedish competition authority and advocates for application of these new rules to strategic market players only.

[B] Enforcement

[1] Fnac/Darty (2016)

In 2016, the Autorité conditionally approved the acquisition of Darty by Fnac, the two largest physical retailers in France in 'brown' and 'grey' consumer electronics.[915] In its second-phase decision, the Autorité defined, by its own admission for the first time, the relevant market for retail sales of consumer electronics, including online sales, in

913. Autorité de la Concurrence, 'Competition Law and Data', *supra* n. 839.
914. Isabelle de Silva, 'The Future of Competition Law: Time to Change or Time to Adapt?', speech at Fordham Conference, 12 September 2019.
915. Autorité de la Concurrence, decision 27 July 2016, 16-DCC-111 (Fnac/Darty), paras 141 and 148.

Europe.[916] The Autorité's enquiry showed that more than half of the customers of Fnac and Darty were also customers of the exclusive online selling market player Amazon and that if Fnac and Darty would increase their prices by 10%, approximately 30% of their customers would turn to the exclusive online players such as Amazon.[917] Despite the competitive pressure from the online players, Fnac and Darty had a combined market share of more than 50% in nineteen local areas, for nine of which (eight in Paris and one in an area southwest of Paris) the Autorité considered it likely that competition would be significantly impeded by the concentration. Consequently, insufficient alternatives for consumers would remain in these areas, and the merged entity would therefore have insufficient incentives to price its products at competitive prices. To remedy the competition concerns, the Fnac group committed to divest six stores (five in Paris and one in southwest Paris). The Autorité approved the concentration on the condition that Fnac would implement the remedies. If the Autorité continues to follow this line of market definition in the future, which seems plausible, the competitive pressure from online platforms will thus lead to more room for concentration in traditional retail markets.

[2] Axel Springer (Se Loger)/Logic Immo (2018)

In 2018, the Autorité unconditionally approved the acquisition of Logic Immo by Axel Springer Group, marking the first French assessment of a merger between two competing platforms: Logic Immo and SeLoger (part of Axel Springer).[918] For the Autorité, this was a reason to carry out an extensive second-phase investigation into market definition, network effects and the role of possible foreclosure effects due to data ownership. Where it comes to the market definition, the Autorité assumed a single market for online real estate ads, rather than a two-sided market and looked upstream at the relationship between real estate providers and the platform as well as the downstream relationship between consumers looking for real estate and the platform. In its first-phase investigation, the Autorité had concluded that the new entity would reach a market share of more than 50% and would therefore possibly become capable of increasing the prices it charged brokers for online advertising. Ultimately, the Autorité concluded that the concentration did not lead to a significant restriction of competition, partly because one other important platform would remain in the market (Le Bon Coin) to which real estate suppliers could turn in the event of a price increase by the notifying parties. In addition, the Autorité noted that although no real competitive pressure on the merged entity was to be expected from 'GAFA' (Google, Amazon, Facebook, Apple) in the short and medium term, not only Facebook (which had already effectively entered the market on a limited scale) but also Apple, Amazon and Google could well evolve into important competitors of the parties in the long term:

916. Autorité de la Concurrence, 'Rapport annuel 2016', 20 April 2017, Éditorial, p. II.
917. Autorité de la Concurrence, decision 27 July 2016, 16-DCC-111 (Fnac/Darty), paras 141 and 148.
918. Autorité de la Concurrence, decision 1 February 2018, 18-DCC-18 (Axel Springer Group/Logic Immo).

'Compte tenu de l'ensemble de ces éléments, les GAFA, au premier rang desquels Facebook, ne constituent pas une contrainte susceptible de discipliner à court terme le comportement concurrentiel des portails de petites annonces immobilières en ligne de professionnels en France mais il convient d'être prudent sur leur impact à plus long terme tant leur percée dans le secteur des petites annonces immobilières en ligne pourrait être rapide' [freely translated: '*Taking into account all these elements, GAFA, and first and foremost Facebook, are unlikely to constitute a competitive force able to discipline the competitive behavior of portals of online real estate classifieds professionals in France in the short term, but it is appropriate to draw a more cautious conclusion about their longer-term impact as their breakthrough in the online real estate classifieds sector could be swift*']. In view of the above, the Autorité ultimately gave its unconditional approval.

[3] Founding of video platform Salto (2019)

The Autorité has conditionally approved the creation of Salto, a joint venture between TF1, France Télévisions and Métropole Télévision (M6).[919] Salto is a platform which will offer a range of television services to consumers via online streaming, without the intervention of a distributor (*over-the-top*). The Autorité is investigating not only the consumer market on which Salto will operate (the provision of pay-TV) but also the upstream markets (the acquisition of TV rights and the programming and marketing of TV channels, with parent companies holding market shares of up to 80%-90% in France) and the advertising market. The remedy package, which consists of behavioural remedies, addresses all these markets as well as the risk of coordination between the parent companies. It restricts Salto's ability to use its parent companies' content or to purchase broadcasting rights from the parent companies. Also, the parent companies have to offer their TV channels to third-party distributors on objective and non-discriminatory terms and the price paid by Salto for its parent companies' content is set by two independent experts. Finally, the possibility for Salto to advertise on the parent companies' channels is limited and Salto has to pay a market price for advertising space on its parent companies' channels. These remedies are valid for a period of five years and can be renewed for another five years by the Autorité.

Interestingly, the Autorité published an opinion on the audiovisual sector earlier, in 2019, in its capacity as an advisor to the Parliament. The Autorité notes that historical providers of audiovisual content are disadvantaged compared to new entrants (e.g., regarding the possibility for mergers in the sector and to apply personalised ads) such as Netflix by the current legal framework and that the level playing field must be quickly restored.[920] The Autorité: '*In view of the new competitive*

919. Autorité de la Concurrence, decision 12 August 2019, 19-DCC-157 (*France Télévisions/TF1/Métropole Télévision/Salto JV*).
920. Autorité de la Concurrence, 'Opinion on a request from the Committee on Cultural Affairs and Education of the French National Assembly (Assemblée nationale) for an opinion on the audiovisual sector', 19-A-04, 21 February 2019.

landscape emerging at an accelerated pace, these rules do not put all operators on an equal footing and must therefore be rapidly reformed. The Autorité therefore recommends that all rules imposing asymmetric constraints in the field of advertising, production, distribution and anti-concentration mechanisms be amended in the short term.'

[4] Jellej Jouets/Gifram/Luderix (2019)

On 17 April 2019, the Autorité unconditionally approves the acquisition of Luderix International by Jellej Jouets and Gifram.[921] Both Luderix and Jellej Jouets are active in the wholesale and retail of toys. As in Darty/Fnac, the Autorité concludes that the online and physical distribution channels for the retail of toys form one product market. Indeed, the market investigation shows that online toy sales are widely accepted (28.3 % of total toys in France were sold online in 2017), that prices are similar online and offline, and that customers would likely switch to an online outlet in the event of a 5%-10% price increase in the shop. Also, almost all traditional retail chains combine sales through their physical shops with an online sales channel. As in Darty/Fnac, the Autorité examines the effects of the concentration not only on the national market for retail of toys, but also on the local market because '*la grande majorité des ventes sont effectuées en magasin et résultent d'un arbitrage du consommateur realisé notamment en fonction des alternatives qui lui sont géographiquement accessibles*' [free translation: '*the large majority of sales is made in the shop and is the result of a consideration by the consumer based on the alternatives that are geographically available to him*']. The combined market share is less than 20% at national level and does not exceed 50% at any local level. The Autorité approves the concentration unconditionally in the first phase.

[5] Elephant/Webedia (2019)

Following the acquisition of the audiovisual production company Elephant by Webedia, the Autorité has looked at the influencer industry for the first time.[922] Both parties are active in the production of audiovisual content and marketing and communication services. Webedia is also active in talent and influencer management, a market which is vertically linked to the market for audiovisual content production. In none of the markets where the two parties are active, they have a market share in excess of 25%. The Autorité therefore concludes that the horizontal effects of the acquisition do not constitute a competition problem. As regards the vertical effects of the acquisition, the Autorité notes that Webedia has under contract the three French influencers with the most followers on YouTube (between 11.5 and 13.1 million followers). However, the Autorité notes that the market share of these influencers measured by the number of

921. Autorité de la Concurrence, decision 17 April 2019, 19-DCC-65 (Jellej Jouets/Gifram/Luderix International).
922. Autorité de la Concurrence, decision 24 May 2019, 19-DCC-94 (Webedia/Groupe Elephant).

followers and by the number of video views is always less than 25%, even when looking at YouTube segments such as 'sports' or 'beauty'. Also, there are several competitors active in the market that have at least as much diversity as Webedia and Webedia has not agreed on exclusivity with its influencers, so influencers can also work for third-party production companies. On this basis, the Autorité concludes that after the transaction, the parties are not able to implement an input foreclosure strategy harmful to competitors by preventing competitors from accessing Webedia's influencers. The Autorité approves the acquisition unconditionally in the first phase.

[6] Nature & Découvertes/FnacDarty (2019)

On 16 July 2019, the Autorité unconditionally approves the acquisition of Nature & Découvertes by Fnac Darty. In its market investigation, the Autorité focuses on the horizontal overlap on the market for retail of toys and the market for retail of books. The Autorité considers that four criteria are decisive in determining whether the online and offline retail channels belong to the same product market: '*(i) un taux de pénétration important des ventes en ligne dans le secteur concerné; (ii) l'uniformisation tarifaire croissante au sein des différents canaux de distribution; (iii) l'identité des gammes de produits et des services offerts en magasins et en ligne; et (iv) l'adoption, au moins par les parties, d'une organisation interne « omnicanale » et d'une stratégie commerciale et tarifaire tenant compte des acteurs spécialisés dans la vente en ligne et, plus généralement, le développement d'un modèle de distribution « omnicanale » dans le secteur examiné*' [free translation: '*(i) a significant penetration of online sales in the sector concerned; (ii) the increasing uniformity of pricing across the different distribution channels; (iii) the identity of the product ranges and services offered in shops and online; and (iv) the adoption, at least by the parties, of an "omnichannel" internal organisation and commercial and pricing strategy taking into account players specialising in online sales and, more generally, the development of an "omnichannel" distribution model in the sector concerned*']. Like the retail trade in toys (*see* Jellej Jouets/Gifram/Luderix), the retail trade in books meets these criteria. About 20% of new books in France were sold online in 2017, prices and offers online and offline are similar, and the main competitors with physical shops also sell online. The combined market share in book retailing is less than 20% nationally, but more than 80% in some local markets (in terms of sales area). However, in the Autorité's view there is no significant impediment to competition, since the addition of market share is always very small ([0%-5%]), at least one physical competing shop always remains, and the market shares in terms of surface area do not take account of online sales of books. The Autorité approves the concentration unconditionally in the first phase.

[7] La Poste/Softeam (2019)

In its decision of 18 December 2019, the Autorité examines the acquisition of Softeam by La Poste. Softeam and La Poste are both active in the digital services market, but in different segments within that market.[923] La Poste is particularly active in business process outsourcing (managing digital systems for third parties) and Softeam is particularly active in consulting. The Autorité considers that the digital services market may need to be segmented according to the SMACS[924] classification or by technology (e.g., AI, IoT, blockchain, big data, virtual reality, robotics or supercomputers). The Autorité states that these are important developments that should be considered in the market definition. In this case, the combined market share is less than 20% in all possible segments, so there is no significant restriction of competition. La Poste is also active on the market for processing data for third parties and the market for cloud storage. However, La Poste's market share on these markets is consistently below 25%. The Autorité concludes that there are no vertical or conglomerate effects that could require further investigation. The Autorité clears the merger unconditionally in the first phase.

[8] Duval/Blue Green (2022)

On 24 June 2022, the Autorité gave unconditional clearance to the acquisition of Blue Green by Duval.[925] Both Duval and Blue Green operate golf courses in France and the companies use an Internet platform that enables customers to book golf courses. The Autorité defined a national market for '*the operation of online golf course booking platforms*' but ruled that '*the transaction was not likely to raise competition concerns given the presence of competing platforms*'.[926]

§6.05 INTERMEDIATE CONCLUSION

With the counter standing at 31,[927] the number of decisions of the Autorité in the field of digital competition during the investigation period is impressive. The same applies to the total fining amount imposed by the Autorité of more than EUR 2.1 billion,[928] of which EUR 1.1 billion was imposed on Apple and EUR 870 million on Google.

923. Autorité de la Concurrence, decision 18 December 2019, 19-DCC-259 (La Poste/Softeam).
924. SMACS stands for the key drivers of digital transformation: Social, Mobile, Analytics, Cloud and Security.
925. Autorité de la Concurrence, decision 24 June 2022, 22-DCC-111 (Duval/Blue Green). The decision was not published on the day of sending this publication to the publisher.
926. Autorité de la Concurrence, press release 24 June 2022, 'The Autorité de la concurrence unconditionally clears the acquisition of the Blue Green Group by the Duval Group.'
927. The total number of twenty-six decisions consists of six cartel decisions, seventeen abuse of dominance decisions and eight merger control decisions. The 2010 decisions in the Google AdWords I (Navx) investigation dates from before the period under review and is therefore not counted as an investigation of the Autorité for the purposes of this guide.
928. EUR 2,118,303,809.

Figure 6.1 Total Yearly Digital Competition Fines Imposed by the Autorité (2013-2021)[929]

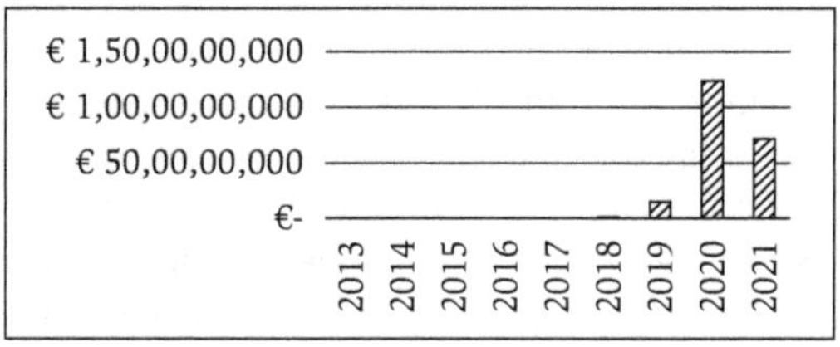

Looking at the enforcement instruments used by the Autorité, it is noteworthy that it did not use the fining instrument until 2017. And against, GAMA, it did not levy its first fine until the end of 2019 (Google), quickly followed by another fine in 2020 (Apple). In the *Adidas* case, Adidas voluntarily ended the violation, and in the *Booking.com* Google (2021) and Meta (2022) cases (and before the investigation period in *Google AdWords I*), the Autorité accepted commitments. The Autorité imposed provisional measures on Google on three occasions, forcing the company to clarify its policy on suspending accounts in 2010, to clarify the rules it applies to directory enquiry service providers in 2019, and, in 2020, to conduct negotiations in good faith with publishers and news agencies on the remuneration for the use of their content. Using this instrument has enabled the Autorité to change the behaviour of a tech giant with great speed, reaching a decision on provisional measures within four to nine months from the date of the complaint. The Autorité has, since 2009, ruled on almost 100 requests for provisional measures, so the use of provisional measures in digital competition cases doesn't appear to be more widespread than in other sectors.[930] Also noteworthy is that the Autorité is more transparent than other authorities in publishing decisions of rejected complaints, with the counter at 10 rejection decisions published in digital competition law cases.[931]

Restrictions on internet sales find no mercy in the eyes of the Autorité. The Autorite acted firmly against broad parity clauses in the Booking.com case in 2015, but refrained from enforcement against HRS and Expedia in 2019, holding that other competition authorities had already dealt with the matter. The Autorité does not seem to have any problems with narrow parity clauses, at least not per se. The application of the abuse of economic independence provision against a tech giant in the Apple case is groundbreaking. Only the appeal will tell whether this provision will prove an effective tool in the Autorité's toolbox. The Autorité's cases against Google address two different aspects of the online search platform: (1) Google's internal rules and procedures for the use of its online advertisement services and (2) Google's use of content of publishers

929. 2017: EUR 3,200; 2018: EUR 7,000,000; 2019: EUR 150,250,000; 2020: EUR 1,241,050,609; 2021: EUR 720,000,000.
930. Autorité de la Concurrence, 'Bilan de activité, synthèse 2019', 9 July 2020, p. 41.
931. *See* decisions 21-D-07, 19-D-23, 19-D-04, 18-D-20, 18-D-13, 17-D-24, 16-D-25, 15-D-23, 14-D-18, 13-D-07.

and news agencies. With respect to the first aspect, the Autorité has, after a decade of investigations, imposed its first fine and imposed behavioural remedies, stating that Google has a very special responsibility to treat the users of its platforms in an objective, transparent and non-discriminatory manner. As to the second aspect, this case is novel as the abuse is grounded in Google's alleged non-compliance with the French (early) implementation of an EU directive that protects publishers and news agencies. It will be interesting to see if similar abuse cases will be pursued in other EU Member States when the EU directive is implemented there. The Autorité has, more recently, addressed self-preferencing by Google in the market for ad servers for publishers of websites and mobile apps. Google's dominance in this market is related to the European Commission's 2008 clearance decision in Google/Doubleclick. It is too early to speculate on whether the January 2022 appointment of Benoît Cœuré will significantly change digital antitrust enforcement in France. The first headline case under his presidency was the acceptance of commitments by Meta to end an investigation into abusive practices in the market for non-search-related online advertising.

In the field of mergers in the digital sector, in the Darty/Fnac case, the Autorité had the courage to definitively answer a question that various competition authorities had been facing for years, by concluding without reservation that physical and online retail markets belong to the same product market. It has since then elaborated general criteria for determining whether offline and online retail channels belong to the same product market in the 2019 cases FnacDarty/Nature & Découvertes and in Jellej Jouets/Gifram/Luderix. An interesting question is whether other European competition authorities will follow this approach or will instead continue to leave open the question of whether or not physical and online sales belong to the same market. An important aspect of the Axel Springer/Logic Immo decision is that the Autorité considered the longer-term competitive pressure from GAMA to be relevant as well, although ultimately the decision to approve the concentration was not based (neither in whole nor in part) on this particular finding. In the subsequent phase I, retail cases FnacDarty/Nature & Découvertes and in Jellej Jouets/Gifram/Luderix a longer-term outlook was not considered. However, the expected market dynamics at a longer time horizon than usually applied in merger control may in future cases play a decisive role in decisions of the Autorité in merger cases in digital markets, especially in the more complex cases. The Salto decision shows that long-term behavioural remedies enable traditional market players, with strong positions in traditional markets, to join forces and compete in a space, in this case, online video streaming, where they have individually lost the race and that is now heavily dominated by technology companies.

CHAPTER 7
Germany: Bundeskartellamt

'[I]f data are collected and exploited illegally, it should be possible to take antitrust action to prevent the abuse of market power.'[932]

The *Bundeskartellamt* has demonstrably paid great attention to competition in the digital economy throughout the review period. In the introduction to its 2017 annual report, the Bundeskartellamt identifies digital competition as one of its spearheads.[933] The focus is placed on consumer protection, and it is from this perspective that the Bundeskartellamt intends to regularly act as amicus curiae in court cases in which digital competition plays a role.[934] The Bundeskartellamt expects that an amendment of the German competition law (of June 2017), which makes it easier to hold direct and indirect parent companies liable for cartel fines of subsidiaries as is the case under the European model, will contribute to the effective enforcement of competition law in digital markets.[935] The Bundeskartellamt's Directorate G.2 is in charge of digital competition.[936] In addition, on the initiative of the Bundeskartellamt, the European Competition Network (ECN) set up a special working group on digital competition in September 2017.[937] In its 2019 annual report, the Bundeskartellamt says about this approach: '*The Bundeskartellamt started looking into this issue at a very early stage and is now one of the internationally leading and most active competition authorities in this area.*'[938]

932. U. Knapp and Douglas Busvine, 'Top German Court Reimposes Data Curbs on Facebook', *Reuters*, https://www.reuters.com/article/us-facebook-germany-idUSKBN23U2P4.
933. Bundeskartellamt, 'Annual Report 2017' (2018) 4-5.
934. *Ibid.*, 10.
935. *Ibid.*
936. *Ibid.*, 46.
937. *Ibid.*, 12-13.
938. Bundeskartellamt, 'Annual Report 2019', https://www.bundeskartellamt.de/SharedDocs/Publikation/EN/Jahresbericht/Jahresbericht_2019.html;jsessionid=A691F64A411F4C9D790FA78FFCABF633.2_cid371?nn=5808430.

During the period under investigation, the Bundeskartellamt carried out five market investigations.[939] The Bundeskartellamt also initiated ten enforcement proceedings: eight proceedings under the cartel prohibition were closed following formal or informal commitments by the undertakings concerned.[940] Three[941] cartel procedures led to enforcement decisions prohibiting narrow and broad parity clauses and a ban on using online marketplaces (although the Bundeskartellamt refrained from imposing fines).[942] Proceedings against Lufthansa under the prohibition of abuse of a dominant position were closed in the investigation stage for lack of evidence.[943] An investigation into the possible abuse of dominance by Amazon was settled through commitments in November 2022.[944] The Bundeskartellamt's investigation into Facebook was closed with a decision prohibiting Facebook to continue to use consumer data collected

939. 'Competition Law and Data', *supra* n. 839; Bundeskartellamt, 'B6-113/15: Working Paper – The Market Power of Platforms and Networks' (2016); Bundeskartellamt, 'Big Data Und Wettbewerb - Schriftenreihe "Wettbewerb Und Verbraucherschutz in Der Digitalen Wirtschaft"' (2017), https://www.bundeskartellamt.de/SharedDocs/Publikation/DE/Schriftenreihe_Digitales/Schriftenreihe_Digitales_1.pdf?__blob=publicationFile&v=3, Autorité de la Concurrence en Bundeskartellamt, *Algorithms and Competition*, November 2019, Bundeskartellamt - Homepage - Working Paper - Algorithms and Competition. Bundeskartellamt. *The effects of narrow price parity clauses on online sales – Investigation results from the Bundeskartellamt's Booking proceeding*, augustus 2020.

940. Bundeskartellamt, 'Case Report - B6-46/12: Amazon Removes Price Parity Obligation for Retailers on Its Marketplace Platform' (2013); Bundeskartellamt, 'Press Release 2 July 2014: Adidas Abandons Ban on Sales via Online Market Places', https://www.bundeskartellamt.de/SharedDocs/Meldung/EN/Pressemitteilungen/2014/02_07_2014_adidas.html; Bundeskartellamt, 'Press Release 3 June 2015: Verivox Vows to Stop Using "Best Price" Clauses' https://www.bundeskartellamt.de/SharedDocs/Meldung/EN/Pressemitteilungen/2015/03_06_2015_Verivox.html; Bundeskartellamt, 'Press Release 19 January 2017: Bundeskartellamt Stelt Verfahren Gegen Audible/Amazon Und Apple Ein', https://www.bundeskartellamt.de/SharedDocs/Meldung/DE/Pressemitteilungen/2017/19_01_2017_Audible_Amazon.html, Bundeskartellamt, persbericht van 5 februari 2020, https://www.bundeskartellamt.de/SharedDocs/Publikation/EN/Pressemitteilungen/2020/05_02_2020_Unamera.html?nn=10160192, Bundeskartellamt, persbericht van 25 juni 2020, https://www.bundeskartellamt.de/SharedDocs/Publikation/EN/Pressemitteilungen/2020/25_06_2020_Intersport.pdf?__blob=publicationFile&v=2., Besluit van 3 december 2019 in zaak B7-25/17, https://www.bundeskartellamt.de/SharedDocs/Entscheidung/DE/Entscheidungen/Missbrauchsaufsicht/2019/B7-25-17.pdf;jsessionid=32E56FB583D305681EECBE838B998B52.2_cid381?__blob=publicationFile&v=2, Bundeskartellamt, persbericht van 8 juli 2020, https://www.bundeskartellamt.de/SharedDocs/Publikation/EN/Pressemitteilungen/2020/08_07_2020_InEK.pdf?__blob=publicationFile&v=3.

941. *Case B9-66/10 (HRS)* (Bundeskartellamt); *Case B9-121/13 (Booking.com/HRS)* (Bundeskartellamt); *Case B2-98/11 (Asics)* (Bundeskartellamt).

942. *Case B2-98/11 (Asics), ibid.*

943. Bundeskartellamt, 'Press Release 29 May 2018: Lufthansa Tickets 25-30 Per Cent More Expensive after Air Berlin Insolvency – "Price Increase Does Not Justify Initiation of Abuse Proceeding"' https://www.bundeskartellamt.de/SharedDocs/Meldung/EN/Pressemitteilungen/2018/29_05_2018_Lufthansa.html.

944. Bundeskartellamt, 'Press Release 2 March 2016: Bundeskartellamt Initiates Proceeding Against Facebook on Suspicion of Having Abused Its Market Power by Infringing Data Protection Rules'https://www.bundeskartellamt.de/SharedDocs/Meldung/EN/Pressemitteilungen/2016/02_03_2016_Facebook.html; press release 22 November 2022: Meta (Facebook) responds to the Bundeskartellamt's concerns – VR headsets can now be used without a Facebook account, https://www.bundeskartellamt.de/SharedDocs/Meldung/EN/Pressemitteilungen/2022/23_11_2022_Facebook_Oculus.html.

through its other applications (notably WhatsApp and Instagram).[945] However, litigation over this decision is still ongoing. A second investigation into Facebook (now called Meta) – aimed at linking the purchase of virtual reality (VR) glasses to the purchase of an account – is also still ongoing, despite commitments offered by Meta that the Bundeskartellamt accepted in late 2022.[946] Finally, the Bundeskartellamt took five[947] relevant merger control decisions.

The Bundeskartellamt explicitly acknowledges that the economy is undergoing major changes as a result of digital technology and that this will affect competition policy and its enforcement.[948] In early 2015, the Bundeskartellamt set up a special think tank to investigate the impact of the digital economy on competition and the enforcement of competition law. This think tank is to pay particular attention to the competition law implications of digital platforms and networks. In the think tank, lawyers and economists work together. The role of the think tank is to further develop existing review tools and also to develop entirely new tools so that concrete cases that arise in digital markets can be analysed and assessed quickly and efficiently.[949] The think tank published a working document on platform and network market power in June 2016 (*see* below under abuse of dominant position; §7.02).[950]

At the end of 2017, the Bundeskartellamt announced that it would publish a series of articles on competition and consumer protection in the digital economy.[951] The first in this series of articles is entitled 'Big Data und Wettbewerb',[952] in which the Bundeskartellamt discusses the role that data can play in competition law analyses. This article is discussed below, in the context of the prohibition of abuse of a dominant position.

945. Bundeskartellamt, 'Case Summary – B6-22/16: Facebook, Exploitative Business Terms Pursuant to Section 19(1) GWB for Inadequate Data Processing' (2019) https://www.bundeskartellamt.de/SharedDocs/Entscheidung/EN/Fallberichte/Missbrauchsaufsicht/2019/B6-22-16.pdf?__blob=publicationFile&v=3. At the time of writing, the full text of the decision had not yet been made available.
946. https://www.bundeskartellamt.de/SharedDocs/Meldung/EN/Pressemitteilungen/2020/10_12_2020_Facebook_Oculus.html?nn=3591568.
947. *Case B6-39/15* (Bundeskartellamt) 15; *Case B8-76/15* (Bundeskartellamt); *Case B6-57/15* (Bundeskartellamt) and https://www.bundeskartellamt.de/SharedDocs/Publikation/EN/Pressemitteilungen/2020/21_12_2020_Gesundheitsplattform.pdf?__blob=publicationFile&v=2 (no case number published), Bundeskartellamt, 'Pressemitteilung: Freigabe der Übernahme von Kustomer durch Meta (ehemals Facebook)' (11 February 2022, *Bundeskartellamt/Digitalwirtschaft*) https://www.bundeskartellamt.de/SharedDocs/Publikation/DE/Pressemitteilungen/2022/11_02_2022_Meta_Kustomer.pdf?__blob=publicationFile&v=2 p. 1.
948. 'Big Data Und Wettbewerb – Schriftenreihe "Wettbewerb Und Verbraucherschutz in Der Digitalen Wirtschaft"', *supra* n. 939.
949. *Ibid.*
950. 'B6-113/15: Working Paper – The Market Power of Platforms and Networks', *supra* n. 939.
951. Bundeskartellamt, 'Press Release 6 October 2017: New Series of Bundeskartellamt Papers on "Competition and Consumer Protection in the Digital Economy"'https://www.bundeskartellamt.de/SharedDocs/Meldung/EN/Pressemitteilungen/2017/06_10_2017_Schriftenreihe%20Digitales.html.
952. 'Big Data Und Wettbewerb – Schriftenreihe "Wettbewerb Und Verbraucherschutz in Der Digitalen Wirtschaft"', *supra* n. 939.

In November 2019, this paper was followed by a joint study with the Autorité on algorithms and competition.[953] This joint study by the Authority and the Bundeskartellamt addresses the potential competition risks associated with the use of algorithms. It takes a closer look at the concept of algorithms as well as the different types and areas of application. The study distinguishes between algorithms whose operation is in principle comprehensible to humans (the strategy and actions resulting from the use of the algorithm can be identified via the code or a description of the algorithm) on the one hand and algorithms whose behaviour is barely comprehensible to humans on the other. In the study, the former are called 'descriptive' algorithms and the latter 'black-box' algorithms. The study then focuses on algorithms and collusion. With a particular focus on pricing algorithms, the study examines the adverse effects of such algorithms on competition and the various ways in which they may influence strategic interactions between companies, leading to horizontal collusion. The study distinguishes between algorithms used to support or facilitate 'traditional' anticompetitive practices on the one hand and algorithm-driven collusion between competitors involving a third party (e.g., a software developer) on the other. The study then deals with collusion that arises from the autonomous but parallel use of the same algorithms by competitors. The study also goes into the legal question of to what extent a user of an autonomously operating algorithm can be held liable for a possible cartel infringement committed with it. The study notes that there are no precedents on this subject yet. Therefore, the study does not draw any conclusions on this point, but propagates – in concurrence with European Commissioner Vestager – that algorithms must be '*compliant by design*'. The study then discusses practical challenges in the investigation of algorithms. According to the study, the biggest challenge for a competition authority is to get to the bottom of the functioning of the algorithm. The study concludes with a preliminary outlook on the future tasks of competition authorities.

In August 2020, the Bundeskartellamt released a study on the results of its approach to Booking.com's narrow price parity clauses, which will be discussed in the section on antitrust.[954]

The Bundeskartellamt is also very active in the discussion about the need for new regulation of digital markets. President Mundt is in favour of this but uttered his regrets in 2021 that the then current European proposals for the *Digital Markets Act (DMA)* and *Digital Services Act (DSA)* do not go far enough. In an interview with the *Financial Times* in July 2021, Mundt said of the DMA: '*I think the DMA is somewhat narrow because it mirrors behaviour from the past and there might be new conduct that might be difficult to catch. (...) The German law is broader and so easier to catch new strategies because the conduct from the past is given just as an example of the type of things that should be prohibited but it leaves space to identify new [anti-competitive] conduct. (...) We have had powerful debates with the EU and have come to a consensus on how to*

953. Autorité de la Concurrence and Bundeskartellamt, *Algorithms and Competition*, November 2019, Bundeskartellamt – Homepage – Working Paper – Algorithms and Competition.
954. Bundeskartellamt. *The effects of narrow price parity clauses on online sales – Investigation results from the Bundeskartellamt's Booking proceeding*, August 2020.

apply competition law. I don't see how we won't do the same in any way within the framework of the DMA.'[955]

Together with the governments of the Netherlands and France, the German government therefore published a *Non-Paper* in May 2021 calling for changes to the proposal of that time.[956] The governments of Germany, France and the Netherlands welcome the arrival of the draft DMA, recognising that digital transformation has changed the global economy and that the COVID-19 pandemic has only increased its importance. The three governments believe that access to the digital market is controlled by a few large suppliers. The governments doubt whether the then proposal for the DMA would be sufficiently equipped to ensure its effectiveness in creating a fair digital market in which users have choice and control. They believed that several elements of the DMA would need to be modified, specified or placed in a broader perspective. These proposals were however ultimately rejected in the definitive text of the DMA as formally adopted.

New enforcement powers

The Bundeskartellamt itself has already been equipped with several new enforcement tools in recent years, which seem to be at least in part tailored to address the specific issues related to digital markets. On 9 June 2017, the German merger thresholds were amended and an additional threshold was introduced, which gives the Bundeskartellamt jurisdiction over mergers with a transaction value exceeding EUR 400 million. Transactions with a value above this threshold are subject to notification if the worldwide turnover of the companies involved exceeds EUR 500 million and the German turnover of at least one company involved exceeds EUR 50 million[957] (provided that the target company operates in Germany to a significant extent). This change of law was motivated by the desire to overcome the risk of innovative start-ups with high market potential being taken over by large established companies without being subject to any kind of merger control.[958] In the tech sector, among other sectors, such transactions occur with above-average frequency.[959]

The previous amendment to merger control did not mark the end of the story. The so-called 'Remondis' provision from the Tenth Amendment to the *Gesetz gegen Wettbewerbsbeschränkungen* (GWB) of 14 January 2021 (named after a waste management company that allegedly bought up small competitors) is intended to prevent the artificial 'chopping up' of transactions and can be applied if the following conditions are satisfied: (i) the addressee must have achieved a worldwide turnover of

955. 'EU draft tech rules too "narrow", says German competition head', *Financial Times*, 14 July 2021.
956. Joint proposal of German Minister Peter Altmaier (Economy and Energy), French Minister Bruno Le Maire (Economy and Finance) and State Secretary Cédric O (Digitalisation), and Dutch State Secretary Mona Keijzer (Economic Affairs and Climate Change), *Strengthening the Digital Markets Act and Its Enforcement*, non-paper-friends-of-an-effective-digital-markets-act.pdf (bmwi.de).
957. At the time the threshold was introduced, the transaction value was still EUR 25 million.
958. *Bundeskartellamt Paper on Platform Market Power – Results and Recommendations*, 2016, p. 4.
959. *Ibid.*, p. 1,

more than EUR 500 million in the last financial year, there are objectively verifiable indications that future concentrations could significantly impede effective competition in Germany in the relevant business sectors, and the addressee supplies or acquires at least 15% of the goods or services in Germany in the relevant business sectors; (ii) the target company must have achieved a turnover of at least EUR 2 million in Germany in the last financial year and generated two-thirds of its turnover in Germany; and (iii) the Bundeskartellamt must have previously carried out a sector enquiry in the relevant industrial sector.

The aforementioned Tenth Amendment also brings changes to antitrust. A *New Competition Tool*, which has been discussed at an EU level but which (at least for the moment) has been replaced by the *DMA* (*see* the introduction on Chapter 4), has meanwhile been introduced in Germany. The new section 19a GWB empowers the Bundeskartellamt to take *ex ante* measures against companies with significant market power. Companies must first be formally designated to be subject to Clause 19a GWB. The Bundeskartellamt has meanwhile determined that (in any event) Google, Meta (Facebook), Apple and Amazon will be designated as such for a period of five years. Once an undertaking has been formally designated as subject to section 19a GWB, the Bundeskartellamt can prohibit such an undertaking (i) from giving preference to its own offers over those of competitors when granting access to purchasing and sales markets (*self-preferencing*); (ii) taking measures that hinder other undertakings in their business activities in purchasing or selling markets if the activities of the undertaking with significant market power are important for access to these markets; (iii) directly or indirectly hindering competitors in a market in which the undertaking could rapidly expand its position; (iv) preventing or hindering market entry, or otherwise hindering other undertakings by processing competitively sensitive information collected by the undertaking, or by imposing conditions which enable such processing; (v) refusing or hindering interoperability of products or services or portability of data, thereby preventing competition; (vi) failing to provide other undertakings with sufficient information on the scope, quality or success of the service provided or commissioned or otherwise making it difficult for them to assess the value of such service; and (vii) requiring benefits for the processing of offers from another undertaking which are disproportionate to the reason for such a requirement. Enforcement proceedings based on this new Article are already underway against Google,[960] Meta (Facebook) and Amazon (for the cases against Amazon and Meta *see* the section on abuse of dominance below, under §7.01[C]).

§7.01 CARTEL PROHIBITION

The Bundeskartellamt has not yet dealt with hardcore cartels in the digital sector. Nevertheless, the Bundeskartellamt has shown a high level of activity during the

960. Bundeskartellamt, press release of 21 June 2022, *Proceeding against Google for possible anti-competitive restrictions of map services (Google Maps Platform)*, https://www.bundeskartellamt.de/SharedDocs/Meldung/EN/Pressemitteilungen/2022/21_06_2022_Google_Maps.html.

investigation period. It investigated price parity clauses in the online hotel booking sector, certain online restrictions in the selective distribution systems of Asics and Adidas, exclusivity clauses between Amazon and Apple relating to the sale of audio-books, an online trading platform for agricultural products, the online sales model of Intersport, agreements between the German association of tax advisors and a software provider, and it is currently investigating agreements between Amazon and manufacturers of branded goods.

[A] Parity Clauses: Online Hotel Booking Sector and Amazon

In the field of the enforcement of cartel prohibition, the Bundeskartellamt made its presence felt in its investigations into the parity clauses used by hotel booking platforms HRS and Booking.com and web retailer Amazon, which received wide international attention.

In 2013, the Bundeskartellamt ruled that HRS,[961] a major German hotel booking site, applied broad parity clauses (on the basis of which hotels were disallowed to offer their rooms more cheaply both on competing platforms as well as through their own sales channels) that infringed the German and European cartel prohibitions. In its decision, the Bundeskartellamt prohibited HRS from continuing to use the clauses in question with immediate effect.[962] The Bundeskartellamt found that the clauses restrict competition between booking sites because they remove the incentive for competing booking sites to lower their commissions in return for offering rooms on their sites at more attractive conditions. This effect would also make the market less attractive to new entrants. HRS, in turn, could increase its commissions without the fear that hotels would pass on this increase by increasing their rates only for bookings made through HRS. This would also reduce competition between hotels. The European block exemption for vertical agreements[963] does not apply in view of the fact that HRS has a market share of more than 30%. In addition, its competitors Booking.com and Expedia apply similar conditions so that broad parity clauses apply to around 90% of the total market and the vast majority of German hotels are tied to such clauses.[964] In 2015, the decision of the Bundeskartellamt in the *HRS* case was confirmed by the Oberlandesgericht Düsseldorf.[965] Following this case, Verivox, an energy price comparison website that at the time was under investigation by the Bundeskartellamt, decided to remove all its price parity clauses in its current and future contracts.[966]

961. *Case B9-66/10 (HRS), supra* n. 941.
962. Under Article 32(1) of the *Gesetz gegen Wettbewerbsbeschränkungen* (GWB), the Bundeskartellamt has the power to impose a commitment to bring to an end an infringement of the German cartel prohibition or of Article 101 or 102 of the TFEU. An undertaking which, despite this obligation, continues the infringement may be fined under Article 81 of the GWB.
963. Regulation No. 330/2010, *OJ* 2010/102/1.
964. *Case B9-66/10 (HRS), supra* n. 941, para. 163.
965. *VI - Kart 1/14 (V)* (Oberlandesgericht Düsseldorf).
966. Bundeskartellamt, 'Press Release 3 June 2015: Verivox Vows to Stop Using "Best Price" Clauses', *supra* n. 940.

In 2015, the Bundeskartellamt adopted a similar decision with regard to Booking.com.[967] Despite the above-mentioned *HRS* judgment of the Oberlandesgericht Düsseldorf, Booking.com continued to apply parity clauses similar to those of HRS on a broad scale. In response to objections raised by various competition authorities, Booking.com amended its terms and conditions in order to comply with commitments accepted by the French, Swedish and Italian competition authorities with effect from 1 July 2015. From then on Booking.com would only apply narrow parity clauses. However, for the Bundeskartellamt, this commitment from Booking.com did not go far enough. The Bundeskartellamt took the view that the fact that hotels had to apply the same conditions on their own website as via Booking.com would remove the incentive to offer more favourable conditions on competing platforms, even though this was no longer formally prohibited to them. The Bundeskartellamt rejected Booking.com's defence that the commitments were supposedly demonstrably effective, as hotels had already started to engage in price differentiation through different channels. In this context, the Bundeskartellamt considered that HRS no longer applied any parity clauses at all, that Booking.com had undertaken to suspend its narrow parity clauses for the duration of the procedure and that hotels were supposedly already anticipating a definitive ban on them. The defence that hotels were free to use their own channels to apply better conditions for participants in their loyalty programmes was also rejected. Since the discount conditions of these programmes are not public, competing hotels would not be able to respond by reducing their loyalty discounts. The Bundeskartellamt therefore prohibited[968] Booking.com from applying the amended terms and conditions (including the narrow parity clauses maintained) even longer and reserved the right to recover any benefits obtained under the parity clauses.[969] The Bundeskartellamt has this power under Article 34 of the GWB.

However, this decision of the Bundeskartellamt was not upheld on appeal by the *Oberlandesgericht* Düsseldorf.[970] The Oberlandesgericht held that the clauses applied by Booking.com at the time of the Bundeskartellamt's decision were indeed permissible under competition law. The Oberlandesgericht therefore annulled the Bundeskartellamt's prohibition decision, holding that the strict parity clauses applied by Booking.com were ancillary to the main contract concluded between Booking.com and the hotels, which concerns the intermediation by Booking.com of hotel reservations made by final consumers.

However, this ruling was overturned the following year in a further appeal before the Bundesgerichtshof (BGH), the highest court in competition cases.[971] According to the BGH, a narrow parity clause does restrict competition in the offering of hotel rooms. The hotels that are subject to such a restriction may not offer more favourable room

967. *Case B9-121/13 (Booking.com/HRS)*, *supra* n. 941.
968. Pursuant to Article 32 GWB, *see Case B9-121/13 (Booking.com/HRS)*, *supra* n. 941, para. 316.
969. *See* Article 34 GWB and Bundeskartellamt, *see Case B9-121/13 (Booking.com/HRS)*, *supra* n. 941, para. 343.
970. Judgment of the Oberlandesgericht Düsseldorf of 4 June 2019 – Kart 2/16 (V), https://openjur.de/u/2176461.html.
971. Judgment of the BGH of 18 May 2021 in Case KVR 54/20, http://juris.bundesgerichtshof.de/cgi-bin/rechtsprechung/document.py?Gericht = bgh&Art = en&nr = 120991&pos = 0&anz = 1.

rates and contract terms through their own online sales channels than through Booking.com. This deprives them of the opportunity to share any agency fee with the customer in whole or in part, by passing it on in the form of price reductions and thus attracting more customers.

Contrary to the view of the Oberlandesgericht, the BGH finds that a narrow parity clause is not an ancillary restraint and therefore the applicability of Article 101(1) TFEU is not excluded beforehand. The BGH further considers the Oberlandesgericht's view to be incompatible with the system established by Article 101 TFEU. The pro-competitive aspects invoked by Booking.com in favour of the narrow parity clauses, such as ensuring appropriate remuneration for the platform service by solving the free-rider problem (guests book directly with the hotel after having informed themselves on Booking.com) or increasing market transparency for consumers, must instead be balanced carefully against their anticompetitive aspects. According to the systemic nature of Article 101 TFEU, this balancing can only take place when examining the conditions for an exemption from the prohibition on cartels under paragraph 3 of that provision, according to the BGH.

Thus, the narrow parity clause could only be exempted if it would be objectively necessary for the performance of the main contract (the mediation contract). According to the BGH, this is not the case. The purpose of the contract between Booking.com and the hotels is the online purchase of hotel rooms. According to the BGH, the narrow parity clause is not an indispensable ancillary restraint for this contractual purpose. Research carried out by the Bundeskartellamt at the request of the Oberlandesgericht (which will be discussed in more detail below) has shown that, after Booking.com had ceased to enforce the narrow parity clauses, it was able to further strengthen its market position in Germany on all relevant parameters of competition, such as turnover, market share, booking volumes, number of hotel partners and number of hotel locations.

According to the BGH, the narrow parity clause of Booking.com also does not qualify for exemption from the cartel prohibition under Article 2(1) of the Block Exemption Regulation for Vertical Agreements,[972] since the market share of Booking-.com on the relevant market for hotel reservation platforms in Germany exceeds 30% (Article 3(1) of the Block Exemption Regulation for Vertical Agreements).

The BGH also ruled that the applicability of Article 101(1) TFEU to the narrow parity clause is not excluded by virtue of an individual exemption under paragraph 3 of that Article. According to the investigation carried out by the Bundeskartellamt and the statements of Booking.com, there are no indications that a free-rider problem – which the BGH acknowledges could occur to a limited extent – could seriously jeopardise the efficiency of the platform's offerings. On the other hand, the narrow parity clause constitutes, in the view of the BGH, a significant obstacle to the platform-independent online distribution of hotel rooms. For that reason, the BGH found that the Oberlandesgericht had decided to set aside the decision of the Bundeskartellamt on incorrect

972. Commission Regulation (EU) No. 330/2010 of 20 April 2010 on the application of Article 101(3) of the Treaty on the Functioning of the European Union to categories of vertical agreements and concerted practices, *OJ* 2010/L 102/1.

grounds. Consequently, the BGH revived the effect of the Bundeskartellamt's prohibition decision.

As already mentioned in the general introduction, the Bundeskartellamt has also issued a market study pursuant to its investigation into Booking.com.[973] The investigation on the basis of which this report was drafted had been carried out (as already mentioned) for the preparation of the replies to questions in the proceedings before the Oberlandesgericht. According to the report, the investigation carried out by the Bundeskartellamt has shown that the abolition of the narrow parity clauses ultimately did not harm Booking.com's market success. Since the Bundeskartellamt's decision had entered into force, Booking.com had become by far the leading online hotel platform in Germany, and even without the narrow parity clauses, the company has been able to further consolidate its market position and achieve huge growth rates. The accommodations contracted by Booking.com use the pricing options currently available to them in a diversified sales mix, without neglecting the online sales channel. According to the study, most consumers do not compare prices, but book where they first find the accommodation. According to the Bundeskartellamt, this finding excludes the possibility of a significant degree of free-riding by the accommodations. The Bundeskartellamt further concludes that an accommodation's own online sales channel is mainly used by consumers who already knew the accommodation before making a booking. In short, the Bundeskartellamt concludes that Booking.com could not have suffered disproportionate damage as a result of the commitments imposed.

The Bundeskartellamt's 'crusade' against parity clauses did not remain confined to hotel booking sites only. Online retailer Amazon was also the subject of an investigation. On the one hand, Amazon sells goods on its website of which it is the owner, and on the other hand, it allows third parties to use its website as a sales platform. These third parties pay a commission for the service provided by Amazon. Amazon is the largest e-commerce platform in Germany with a market share of approximately 30%-40% for the sale of goods over the Internet (in 2012). Pursuant to the litigious clauses, retailers who sold their goods through Amazon were obliged to agree with Amazon that they would not offer their goods cheaper anywhere else online (so this obligation applied both to their own channels and to other platforms). As Amazon also operates as a retailer independently, the Bundeskartellamt found that Amazon and the retailers using its platform are competitors. For this reason, the Bundeskartellamt qualified the broad parity clauses as horizontal price-fixing agreements. Because Amazon had voluntarily announced that it will stop using (broad and narrow) parity clauses, the Bundeskartellamt decided to stop its enquiry into Amazon.[974] No formal (enforcement) action by the Bundeskartellamt against Amazon on the basis of the cartel prohibition has therefore been taken.

973. Bundeskartellamt. *The effects of narrow price parity clauses on online sales – Investigation results from the Bundeskartellamt's Booking proceeding*, August 2020.
974. 'Case Report – B6-46/12: Amazon Removes Price Parity Obligation for Retailers on Its Marketplace Platform', *supra* n. 940.

[B] Asics and Adidas

In a decision of 26 August 2016, the Bundeskartellamt retroactively prohibited three clauses in the contracts that Asics concluded with authorised retailers in its selective distribution system.[975] The first clause concerned a prohibition to use the Asics brand on the website of a third party, such as Amazon. The second clause prohibited retailers from using price comparison sites when selling Asics products. The third ban concerned a total ban on the use of online marketplaces, such as eBay and Amazon. The Bundeskartellamt considers that all the clauses referred to above have an anticompetitive object and are not justified by the selective distribution system operated by Asics. Nor does the Bundeskartellamt see any other justification for the three restrictions. In particular, the Bundeskartellamt rejected Asics' defence that the three restrictions are necessary to protect its brand image. Asics appealed against this decision in two instances,[976] but its appeal was rejected both times.[977]

In a similar case, the Bundeskartellamt ceased its investigation into Adidas' selective distribution system in July 2014, after Adidas announced the complete removal from its distribution agreements of prohibitions on the use of online marketplaces.[978] As in the *Asics* case, the 2012 Adidas distribution terms contain a ban on selling Adidas products through online marketplaces. In this case, the Bundeskartellamt reiterated its view that a complete ban on the use of online marketplaces cannot be justified with reference to an alleged luxury image of the product in question.

[C] Audiobooks

In two press releases on 19 January 2017, the Bundeskartellamt and the Commission each announced separately that they had terminated their ongoing investigations into agreements between Amazon subsidiary Audible.com (Audible) and Apple without the adoption of a formal decision.[979] These investigations were prompted by a complaint from the German Association of Publishers and Book Shops about exclusivity clauses relating to the online sale of audiobooks, as agreed between Audible and Apple. Under these arrangements, Apple purchased the audiobooks sold through its

975. *Case B2-98/11 (Asics), supra* n. 941.
976. *VI-Kart 13/15 (V)* (Oberlandesgericht Düsseldorf) 15; *KVZ 41/17* [2017] Bundesgerichthof ECLI:DE:BGH:2017:121217BKVZ41.17.0.
977. These rulings seem to be stricter than the line chosen by the EU Court of Justice in *Case C-230/16 (Coty Germany GmbH v. Parfümerie Akzente GmbH), supra* n. 53. *See* Graf and Kuhn, *supra* n. 523. Examples of judgments in which a platform ban was allowed within the framework of a selective distribution system are *11 U 84/14 (Kart)* [2015] Oberlandesgericht Frankfurt ECLI:DE:OLGHE:2015:1222.11U84.14KART.0A 14; *ECLI:NL:RBAMS:2017:7282 (Nike/Aktiesport)* (Rechtbank Amsterdam).
978. Bundeskartellamt, 'Press Release 2 July 2014: Adidas Abandons Ban on Sales via Online Market Places', *supra* n. 940; 'Case Summary – B3-137/12: Adidas Abandons Ban on Sales via Online Marketplaces' (Bundeskartellamt 2014).
979. European Commission, 'Press Release 19 January 2017: Antitrust: Commission Welcomes Steps Taken by Amazon/Audible and Apple to Improve Competition in Audiobook Distribution', *supra* n. 290; Bundeskartellamt, 'Press Release 19 January 2017: Bundeskartellamt Stellt Verfahren Gegen Audible/Amazon Und Apple Ein', *supra* n. 940.

iTunes download shop exclusively from Audible and Audible committed itself to Apple not to sell any other music platform similar to iTunes. As both companies have a strong market position in their segment of the distribution column, the Bundeskartellamt and the Commission expressed concerns about these arrangements. In consultation with both competition authorities, Audible and Apple announced that they would be deleting these clauses. Both authorities saw this as a reason to discontinue the investigation. Mundt: '*Durch die Streichung der Exklusivvereinbarung kann Apple nunmehr andere Bezugsquellen für digitale Hörbücher nutzen. Eine größere Angebotsvielfalt und niedrigere Preise für die Verbraucher werden ermöglicht*' [freely translated: '*By terminating the exclusive agreement, Apple can now use other sources for digital audiobooks. Greater product diversity and lower prices for consumers are made possible*'].[980]

[D] Online Trade Platform for Agricultural Products

On 5 February 2020, the Bundeskartellamt issued a press release in which it announced that it had no objections to the establishment of an online trading platform for agricultural products.[981]

The platform in question was Unamera GmbH, founded by the grain trading companies BayWa AG, Getreide AG and ATR Landhandel. Unamera will serve as a platform for the trade of in particular cereals and oilseeds between agricultural trading companies on one side of the platform and farmers and processing companies on the other. In order to avoid an anticompetitive flow of information, the Bundeskartellamt requires that the trading platform remains separate from its partners in terms of personnel, organisation, technology and information. In addition, partners operating on the same market are not allowed to exercise their rights of information and inspection under German company law. As regards the planned publication of market statistics by the platform, the Bundeskartellamt requires that this must only take place on an aggregated level. Trade prices may initially only be displayed anonymously. The contract partner may only be disclosed at the final stage, right before a contract is concluded.

Against this background and within its discretion, the Bundeskartellamt decided not to object to the launch of the Unamera trading platform. In Mundt's words: '*Es ist offensichtlich, dass digitale Plattformen den Handel deutlich effizienter gestalten können. Sie dürfen aber den Wettbewerb nicht beschränken. Unsere Bewertung solcher digitaler Plattformen konzentriert sich auf wesentliche Fragen. Es darf über solche Netzwerke nicht zu Preisabsprachen kommen, sie dürfen nicht diskriminierend wirken, und es darf kein Übermaß an Transparenz geschaffen werden. Besonderes Augenmerk*

980. Bundeskartellamt, 'Press Release 19 January 2017: Bundeskartellamt Stelt Verfahren Gegen Audible/Amazon Und Apple Ein', *supra* n. 940.
981. Bundeskartellamt, press release of 5 February 2020, https://www.bundeskartellamt.de/SharedDocs/Publikation/EN/Pressemitteilungen/2020/05_02_2020_Unamera.html?nn=10160192.

liegt daher regelmäßig auf Art und Umfang des Informationsaustausches, der Gestaltung von "Chinese Walls" zwischen den Beteiligten, der Veröffentlichung von Marktstatistiken sowie der Offenlegung der Identität der Handelspartner.' [Freely translated: *'It is clear that online platforms may make trade much more efficient. However, they must not restrict competition. When assessing online trading platforms, we focus on a number of essential questions. Such networks must not lead to price-fixing, must be non-discriminatory and must not lead to excessive transparency. Important for the assessment are the extent and nature of information exchange, the creation of "Chinese walls" between platform users, the publication of market statistics and the disclosure of the identity of trading partners.'*]

[E] Intersport: Online Sales Model

In a press release of 25 June 2020, the Bundeskartellamt announced that, following an investigation, it saw no competition concerns in a model for an online sales platform set up by Intersport, a (soft) franchise organisation of independent retailers active in the retail of sports goods. Intersport has approximately 900 members who operate a total of 1,500 sports shops in Germany. The Intersport members jointly also operate Intersport Digital GmbH (IDG), an online sales platform.[982]

As of January 2019, IDG has switched to a so-called *drop shipping* model, which means that IDG independently sets prices and sells products to end users. However, Intersport members determine whether and at what price they sell certain items to IDG. IDG selects retailers on the basis of their delivery capacity and geographical proximity to the customer in question. As soon as a customer places an order via the web shop, a contract is established between IDG and the retailer.

According to the Bundeskartellamt, the shared platform affects competition between the participating retailers only to a minimal extent. The Intersport members sell only a small percentage of their products via the online platform. They are mostly active in the area of physical sales. In addition, the members participating in IDG are free to operate their own web shops via third-party platforms or their own homepages and to sell through those channels at prices that they determine entirely by themselves.

The Bundeskartellamt believes that it would be very difficult for many smaller Intersport members to sustainably operate an online sales channel themselves. Individual retailers also find it difficult to compete with the online shops of large online retailers or manufacturers. The use of the shared platform creates an opportunity for these smaller retailers to operate an online sales channel. The Bundeskartellamt therefore concludes that on balance, the Intersport platform enhances rather than restricts competition in the sports retail sector.

The Bundeskartellamt requires, however, that access to the platform must be available to all members on the basis of non-discriminatory access criteria. It must be

982. Bundeskartellamt, press release of 25 June 2020, https://www.bundeskartellamt.de/SharedDocs/Publikation/EN/Pressemitteilungen/2020/25_06_2020_Intersport.pdf?__blob=publicationFile&v=2.

realistic for all members to meet the access criteria and these criteria must not discriminate against smaller retailers who generate less turnover. Bundeskartellamt chairman Mundt says: '*It is especially difficult for smaller retailers to compete alone against major online retailers like Amazon and the manufacturers' online shops. The individual Intersport retailers in Germany face strong competitors, both in the brick-and-mortar business and online. The shared online platform under the Intersport umbrella brand is an attractive sales alternative for the retailers, which are mostly active in the brick-and-mortar business. It strengthens competition in the sports retail business and provides more choice for consumers online.*'

[F] Software for Tax Consultants

By the decision of 3 December 2019, the Bundeskartellamt agreed on commitments with the German trade associations of tax advisors and their software provider Datev eG, to promote competition in the area of software used by tax advisors for communication with tax authorities.[983]

Previously, German tax advisers all used a software package from the same private supplier, Datev, to communicate with the authorities. This software package is still the only one through which it is technically possible to communicate with the authorities. Thus, at present, it is impossible for tax advisors to use other software than Datev for communicating with the authorities. Nevertheless, the Bundeskartellamt believed that the agreement to make exclusive use of the software of a single supplier constituted a possible infringement of the cartel prohibition and the prohibition of abuse of a dominant position and therefore launched an investigation against the industry associations. According to the Bundeskartellamt's preliminary findings, the exclusive use of Datev's software prevented actual competition in the field of software for tax advisors. The infringement procedure ended with the offering of (formal) commitments by the associations of tax advisors and Datev.

The commitments become effective in two phases. In the transition phase, the industry associations themselves operate the software and the involvement of Datev will be limited to a minimum (only what is technically most necessary). With respect to the outside world, Datev will have no role at all. As soon as the government is technically able to communicate through multiple software solutions, the tax consultants will open their databases to interested software developers, enabling the latter to develop competitive solutions. The commitments are valid for a period of six years (until 31 December 2025). The Bundeskartellamt considers it likely that this period will be sufficient to create sustainable competition in the market for software for tax advisors.

983. Decision of 3 December 2019 in Case B7-25/17, https://www.bundeskartellamt.de/SharedDocs/Entscheidung/DE/Entscheidungen/Missbrauchsaufsicht/2019/B7-25-17.pdf;jsessionid=32E56FB583D305681EECBE838B998B52.2_cid381?__blob=publicationFile&v=2.

[G] Amazon: Agreements with Manufacturers of Branded Goods

On 29 October 2020, reports appeared in the press[984] that the Bundeskartellamt was investigating agreements that Amazon would make with manufacturers of branded goods.

Amazon offers manufacturers of branded goods the possibility of exclusivity on its platform by prohibiting third parties from selling that manufacturer's product (the manufacturer thus acquires the exclusive right to sell its own products). To that aim, Amazon concludes so-called *brand gating agreements* with the manufacturers in question. Some brand gating agreements provide full exclusivity for Amazon and the manufacturer to sell the products, in other cases, it is only a matter of excluding certain third-party sellers.

Among the manufacturers with whom Amazon has concluded such agreements is Apple, whose products may only be marketed by authorised retailers - including Amazon itself - from 2019 onwards.

In an interview with the *Frankfurter Allgemeine Zeitung* (*FAZ*), Bundeskartellamt president Mundt stated that such agreements could have the purpose of protecting against product piracy, which Mundt said would be justified in principle. However, in order to be in line with the cartel prohibition, they must '*das Gebot der Verhältnismäßigkeit wahren und dürfen nicht zu einer Ausschaltung des Wettbewerbs führen*' [freely translated: '*uphold the principle of proportionality and [they] must not lead to the elimination of competition*'], Mundt said. Whether this requirement is met must be clarified in further proceedings, just as the question of whether the manufacturers and Amazon could not first have taken other, less far-reaching protective measures. Amazon informed the *FAZ* that it is cooperating fully with the investigation. Amazon would make 'enormous efforts' to: '*[ein] vertrauensvolles Einkaufserlebnis zu bewahren, indem wir unseren Store vor unrechtmäßigen Waren schützen*' '*[a] ensure a reliable shopping experience by protecting our store against illegal products*']. An Apple spokesperson was in turn quoted as saying: '*Unsere Teams arbeiten ständig mit Strafverfolgungsbehörden, Händlern und E-Commerce-Seiten auf der ganzen Welt, um gefälschte Produkte vom Markt zu nehmen. Wir arbeiten mit Amazon, um unsere Kunden vor gefälschten Produkten zu schützen und ihnen die Sicherheit zu geben, dass sie ein echtes Apple-Produkte in ihrem Paket erhalten. (...) In allem, was wir tun, halten wir uns an die Gesetze. Wir freuen uns darauf, dem Bundeskartellamt Informationen zur Verfügung zu stellen.*' [freely translated: '*Our teams are constantly working with public prosecutors' offices, merchants and e-commerce sites around the world to remove counterfeit products from the market. We are working with Amazon to protect our*

984. *Wettbewerbsverfahren gegen Amazon und Apple*, Frankfurter Allgemeine Zeitung, 29 October 2020, https://www.faz.net/aktuell/wirtschaft/unternehmen/bundeskartellamt-wettbewerbsverfahren-gegen-amazon-und-apple-17024712.html and *German agency scrutinising Amazon over 'brand gating'*, PaRR, 29 October 2020, https://app.parr-global.com/intelligence/view/intelcms-7wwkkq?utm_source = Notifications&utm_medium = Email&utm_campaign = Alert&utm_term = 5e98051f9325a10029fac1eb&ssouid = AB918D67-4436-4B13-AE99-7C032BD01A4F.

customers from counterfeit products and to give them peace of mind that they are receiving a genuine Apple product in their package. (...) We abide by the laws in everything we do. We look forward to providing the Bundeskartellamt with information.'

The Bundeskartellamt has not issued any press release or decision following the investigation. It therefore seems likely that the investigation has been abandoned.

§7.02 ABUSE OF A DOMINANT POSITION

In June 2016, the Bundeskartellamt published its working paper '*The Market Power of Platforms and Networks*' (hereinafter 'Working Paper').[985] In this report, the Bundeskartellamt provides an overview of economic literature and domestic and foreign precedents with regard to competition issues relating to platforms and networks. The Working Paper discusses, among other things, how the internet has influenced the way in which the Bundeskartellamt looks at economic activities and thus also the way in which competition law is viewed. From a competition point of view, the special features of platforms are particularly important. Digital platforms and networks are often subject to so-called network effects, with the value of the network for each individual user increasing as the total number of users grows. This can ultimately lead to market dominance. In many cases, the alleged dominant market position of companies active in the digital economy raises concerns. However, in their assessment of cases, competition authorities should take into account the dynamics of the market and the complexity of business models and economic relations in these markets.[986]

In its document '*Big Data und Wettbewerb*', the Bundeskartellamt first concludes that data as such can constitute a source of market power.[987] This may be particularly the case if a specific platform or network has a much larger number of users than its competitors. This means that the provider also has access to the data of a much larger number of users, thus acquiring an irrecoverable 'data advantage'. This effect also seems to occur in practice: the Bundeskartellamt notes that, as a rule, markets where data plays an important role, such as search engines and social networks, are highly concentrated. This may in particular raise a competition problem if the data in question cannot be obtained from third parties. The more difficult it is to reproduce data held by competitors, the sooner there will be reason to enforce competition law. However, the Bundeskartellamt will be reluctant to impose obligations to share data with competitors; this can only be the case under exceptional circumstances (if a database is impossible to duplicate and thus constitutes an 'essential facility').[988] Increased data

985. 'B6-113/15: Working Paper – The Market Power of Platforms and Networks', *supra* n. 939.
986. *Ibid.*, 1.
987. 'Big Data Und Wettbewerb – Schriftenreihe "Wettbewerb Und Verbraucherschutz in Der Digitalen Wirtschaft"', *supra* n. 939.
988. *Ibid.*, 10.

availability can also increase market transparency. On the one hand, this effect can be pro-competitive if it facilitates the entry of new suppliers by giving them a better picture of consumers' wishes and competitors' offerings. On the other hand, increased market transparency may lead to a lessening of price competition, as companies can better monitor each other's pricing and align their prices more quickly with those of competitors. The Bundeskartellamt also points out that the availability of a large amount of data can lead to fully individualised price discrimination. Finally, the Bundeskartellamt discusses the abuse of market power by imposing unfair conditions in the area of the use of personal data. The Bundeskartellamt has investigated this in its enquiry into Facebook, which is discussed below.

[A] Facebook (Privacy)

In a decision of 7 February 2019, the Bundeskartellamt imposed restrictions on Facebook with regard to its processing of user data.[989] Facebook may no longer combine and assign user data of Facebook-owned services such as WhatsApp and Instagram and of third-party websites to Facebook user accounts without the users' voluntary consent. Mr Mundt, president of the Bundeskartellamt has said: '*In view of Facebook's superior market power, an obligatory tick on the box to agree to the company's terms of use is not an adequate basis for such intensive data processing. The only choice the user has is either to accept the comprehensive combination of data or to refrain from using the social network. In such a difficult situation the user's choice cannot be referred to as voluntary consent.*'

According to the Bundeskartellamt, Facebook holds a dominant position in the German market for social networks with a market share of 95% in terms of daily users (23 million daily active users) and more than 80% in terms of monthly users (32 million monthly active users). The abuse is said to be a so-called exploitative abuse, as the Bundeskartellamt concluded that the manner in which and the extent to which Facebook collects and uses data is in violation of the European data protection rules – in particular, the GDPR[990] – to the detriment of users. Interestingly, the Bundeskartellamt took a multidisciplinary approach to deal with the *Facebook* case as it '*closely cooperated with leading data protection authorities in clarifying the data protection issues involved*'. According to the Bundeskartellamt, these authorities 'explicitly' supported the proceeding.[991]

In its decision, the Bundeskartellamt, first of all, discusses the definition of the relevant market. In this context, it considers that Facebook is a multi-sided platform (reference is made to Chapter 3 on market definition in multi-sided markets), which on the one hand provides private users with a free social platform (from private users' perspective) and on the other hand offers online advertising space. The latter activity constitutes Facebook's main source of income. This dual business model leads to

989. Bundeskartellamt, decision of 6 February 2019 in case B6-22/16, Facebook.
990. Regulation (EU) 2016/679, OJ 2016/L 119/1.
991. Bundeskartellamt, 'Background Information on the Bundeskartellamt's Facebook Proceeding'.

indirect network effects: as the number of users increases, Facebook becomes increasingly attractive to advertisers. Nevertheless, the Bundeskartellamt concluded that there is a separate market for the provision of a social platform to private users and that Facebook's activities in the area of advertising are not part of it. The fact that private users do not pay for the services of Facebook does not imply, according to the Bundeskartellamt, that there is (or could be) no market. The Bundeskartellamt considers in this respect that (i) users must conclude an agreement with Facebook in order to be able to use its services and (ii) they provide their private data to Facebook. The Bundeskartellamt also considers that this market is national.[992]

According to the German Bundeskartellamt, since Google+ (a social network similar to Facebook that Google operated on between 2011 and 2019) disappeared from the market, there have been no players active in the German national social network market that compete on an equal footing with Facebook. Messaging services such as WhatsApp and streaming platforms such as YouTube are not fully fledged alternatives, and neither are Snapchat, Twitter, Pinterest and Instagram. The Bundeskartellamt is of the opinion that the market share among daily active users is the most important factor to take into account. Moreover, the Bundeskartellamt considers it unlikely that users would switch to alternative providers in relevant numbers (if at all), as they would only make such a move in case their fellow users would also switch. This effect led to Holtzbrinck, a German competitor of Facebook that was the market leader before Facebook entered the German market, going bankrupt in 2017. Earlier (in 2016), Lokalisten, part of the media group ProSiebenSat.1 had left the market, followed by Google+ in 2018. Moreover, Facebook's success ensures that it has access to a large amount of high-quality data, which enables it to build and increase its lead over the remaining competition.

The Bundeskartellamt subsequently concludes that Facebook's data policy must be regarded as an abuse of the dominant position held by Facebook. On the basis of (German) case law, the Bundeskartellamt concludes that Facebook is practically able to dictate its conditions to its users, thereby abolishing the contractual autonomy of its users. In such a situation, the Bundeskartellamt considers enforcement action necessary. The Bundeskartellamt goes on to argue that the competition law assessment of Facebook's conduct cannot be viewed separately from the outcome of the assessment of Facebook's conduct in the light of the GDPR. In this respect, the Bundeskartellamt first of all observes that the division of powers in the GDPR would not exclude that the Bundeskartellamt is entitled to determine whether the data processing policy of Facebook infringes the GDPR. According to the Bundeskartellamt, the GDPR must be interpreted in such a way that the privacy authorities do not have a monopoly on its enforcement. The Bundeskartellamt is also of the opinion that the prohibition of abuse of dominance under competition law can, in a certain sense, be regarded as a *specialis* of the more general prohibition under the GDPR. Nevertheless, the Bundeskartellamt

992. Again, *see also* Chapter 3 on market definition for multi-sided platforms.

mentions that it kept in regular contact with the umbrella of German privacy authorities in the course of its investigation.

The Bundeskartellamt concluded that the Faceback policy infringes the GDPR. First of all, the Bundeskartellamt found that the combination of Facebook data with data from other sources did not require the users' actual consent (Article 6(1)(a) GDPR). Nor is there any objective justification for processing the data in question (Article 6(1)(b) of the GDPR). The Bundeskartellamt also considers the specific provisions on data processing set out in Article 6(1)(c) to (e) not applicable. Nor, in the opinion of the Bundeskartellamt, do the interests of Facebook outweigh the infringed interests of its users (Article 6(1)(f) GDPR).

The Bundeskartellamt regards Facebook's alleged infringement of the GDPR as a manifestation of Facebook's market power. According to the Bundeskartellamt, in order to conclude that Facebook's conduct is abusive, it is not necessary to show that the contested conduct was only possible because of market dominance and that other market players could not have behaved in a similar manner. It is sufficient that there exists a causal link between the conduct and the dominant position. In this context, the Bundeskartellamt considered that Facebook's dominance makes it impossible for users to decide autonomously about the use of their data. While the Bundeskartellamt recognises that there are efficiencies for consumers associated with a data-driven business model, the degree of data collection by Facebook is excessive and therefore inappropriate and abusive.

The Bundeskartellamt indicates that it did not impose a fine, because it wants to achieve changes in the future behaviour of companies and because the case is complex and involves a number of legal and economic issues.[993]

By judgment of 26 August 2019, the Oberlandesgericht Düsseldorf suspended the effect of the Bundeskartellamt's prohibition decision against Facebook.[994] In its judgment, the Oberlandesgericht expresses serious doubts as to the lawfulness of the Bundeskartellamt's decision, even on the basis of a mere prima facie assessment. The Oberlandesgericht specified that, even if the combination of data such as were at issue would indeed be contrary to the GDPR, that would not mean that there would automatically be a simultaneous infringement of competition law (more specifically, an abuse of a dominant position). According to the Oberlandesgericht, the core of the Bundeskartellamt's reasoning was that the finding of an infringement of the GDPR, which – as the Oberlandesgericht interpreted the Bundeskartellamt's analysis – would necessarily imply that competition law, in particular the prohibition on abuse of a dominant position, would also have been infringed.

The suspension of the Bundeskartellamt's decision by the Oberlandesgericht had as a consequence that Facebook would not have an obligation to implement the Bundeskartellamt's decision for the time being.

993. Bundeskartellamt, 'Background Information on the Bundeskartellamt's Facebook Proceeding', *supra* n. 991.
994. Oberlandesgericht Düsseldorf 26 August 2019, Case VI/Kart1-19.

However, Facebook was able to enjoy this victory only briefly, since the BGH reversed the suspension in an emergency appeal.[995] First of all, the BGH considered that there cannot be any serious doubt that Facebook has a dominant position on the German market for social networks. The BGH does however not agree with the consideration of the Bundeskartellamt in its decision, that for the competition law assessment of Facebook's behaviour, the decisive factor would be whether this behaviour would infringe the GDPR. According to the BGH, the appropriate test is whether Facebook still offers its users a genuine choice with respect to the personalisation of the use of its network and the use of the data provided by the users, in particular with respect to those services which are not part of the Facebook platform proper.

In addition to the finding of a dominant position, the BGH also considers that there is an abuse thereof. In this context, the BGH considered (like the Bundeskartellamt) that Facebook is active on two markets. The first market consists of offering a social platform to its users. The second market consists of offering advertising services to companies. The BGH did observe that both markets overlap to an important extent since Facebook aims to offer its users a largely personalised user experience. The personalisation of advertisements is also part of that experience. The BGH continues with the consideration that Facebook, as operator of the dominant social network, has a special responsibility to maintain the competition that still exists in the market for social networks. Access to data is of great importance in this respect.

The BGH is of the opinion that the lack of options for users to choose which use of their data they allow Facebook to make affects both their personal autonomy and the exercise of their right to self-determination over their information as also guaranteed in the GDPR. Furthermore, network and *lock-in* effects make it very unattractive for users to switch, while the Bundeskartellamt has found in its research that a significant number of users would like to give up less personal data. In a well-functioning market, this should be possible because users would then have the option to switch to a competing provider, according to the BGH.

The BGH concluded, however, that it is not realistic that Facebook users would switch to a competitor in sufficient numbers to make such a competitor an attractive alternative. According to the BGH, Facebook's disposition of a database that is so much larger than that of a competitor (whether imaginary or not) increases the already existing *lock-in* effect. Furthermore, Facebook's large and high-quality database also provides it with a large inflow of advertisements from which income is generated, which, according to the BGH, further increases its lead over the competition. The BGH does not exclude that the latter also leads to a reduction of competition on the market for online advertising. Unlike the Oberlandesgericht, however, the BGH considers that it is not necessary to establish whether there exists a separate market for online

995. Bundesgerichtshof (BGH) 23 June 2020, case KVR 69/19. For the time being, only the text of a press release is public: https://www.bundeskartellamt.de/SharedDocs/Publikation/EN/Pressemitteilungen/2020/23_06_2020_BGH_Facebook.pdf?__blob=publicationFile&v=2.

advertisements for social media and whether Facebook is also dominant on such a market. According to the BGH, the effects of the abuse on one market (the social media market) can also occur on a derived market in which the abusing undertaking is not dominant.

With the BGH judgment, the suspension of the prohibition order has been lifted and Facebook's obligation to adjust its data-sharing policy for Germany has been reinstated. However, this is not the end of the matter. There are still proceedings on the merits before the Oberlandesgericht, which could also result in an appeal to the BGH after the Oberlandesgericht's judgment.

However, contrary to what might have been expected, these proceedings on the merits were not the next step in this unique case. As can be derived from an order of the BGH, the Oberlandesgericht again suspended the decision of the Bundeskartellamt in an as yet unpublished order of 30 November 2020. It follows from the order of the BGH that on 30 November 2020, Facebook again submitted an application to the Oberlandesgericht to order the suspensive effect of the appeal. With a so-called 'pending order' (*Hangbeschluss*) on the same day, the Oberlandesgericht ordered that the appeal against the abuse order of the Bundeskartellamt be provisionally suspended until its decision on Facebook's second application.[996] The Bundeskartellamt in turn appealed to the BGH against that provisional suspension, as a result of which the BGH again delivered a provisional ruling. [997] The BGH confirms in its decision nothing more or less than that the Bundeskartellamt is entitled to request that the suspension be lifted. The question of whether this request is actually justified will be decided by the BGH at a time not yet determined.

The question is, however, whether that ruling will still be forthcoming after the next unexpected development in the saga. This one started on 23 March 2021, when the Oberlandesgericht issued a request for a preliminary ruling to the European Court of Justice.[998] In a nutshell, the Oberlandesgericht wanted the Court of Justice to rule on the relationship between the GDPR and competition law and between German and European law (which the Bundeskartellamt had disapplied). The Oberlandesgericht referred questions to the Court of Justice which (partially in summary) are as follows:

- May the Bundeskartellamt, which has not been designated as the national supervisory authority under Article 51 of the GDPR, nevertheless apply that regulation in the context of the application of the prohibition of abuse of a dominant position? If so, is that compatible with Article 4(3) TEU if, at the same time, the leading supervisory authority in the Member State of the head office of the undertaking under investigation (in the case of Facebook this is Ireland) has examined its contractual data-processing provisions within the meaning of Article 56(1) GDPR?

996. Oberlandesgericht Düsseldorf, decision of 30 November 2020, case Kart 13/20 (V), https://openjur.de/u/2309497.html.
997. BGH, judgment of 15 December in case KVZ 90/20, https://app.parr-global.com//files/cases/1369928/BGH%20decision%20granting%20leave%20to%20appeal%20(German).pdf.
998. Reference for a preliminary ruling from the Oberlandesgericht Düsseldorf by order of that court of 24 March 2021 in Case C-252/21.

- Does the processing of clicks on websites by a user of a service such as Facebook constitute the processing of sensitive personal data within the meaning of Article 9(1) of the GDPR?
- Can a company like Facebook rely on the justification of necessity for the performance of a contract under Article 6(1)(b) of the GDPR or on the justification of the protection of legitimate interests under Article 6(1)(f) of the GDPR?
- In such a case, could:
  - the fact of users being underage;
  - the personalisation of content and advertising, product improvement, network security and other than marketing-related communication with the user;
  - the provision of measurements, analysis and other business services to advertisers, developers and other partners so that they can evaluate and improve their services;
  - the provision of marketing communications with the user, so that the company can improve its products and use direct marketing;
  - research and innovation for the benefit of society, to advance the state of the art or scientific understanding of important social issues, and to have a positive impact on society and the world;
  - the sharing of information with law enforcement agencies and responding to legal requests, responding to court requests in order to prevent, detect and prosecute criminal offences, unlawful use, violation of terms of use and policies, as well as other harmful conduct;
  - constitute legitimate interests within the meaning of Article 6(1)(f) of the GDPR?
- In such a case, can the collection of data from other Facebook group services and from third-party websites and apps be justified under Article 6(1)(c), (d) and (e) of the GDPR?
- Can a dominant company such as Facebook be granted effective voluntary consent within the meaning of Articles 6(1)(a) and 9(2)(a) of the GDPR in accordance with Article 4(11) of the GDPR?
- Can the national competition authority of a Member State, such as the Bundeskartellamt, which is not a supervisory authority within the meaning of Articles 51 et seq. of the GDPR and which examines a breach by a dominant undertaking of the competition-law prohibition on abuse that is not a breach of the GDPR by that undertaking's data processing terms and their implementation, determine, when assessing the balance of interests, whether those data processing terms and their implementation comply with the GDPR? If so, does this also apply if, at the same time, the leading supervisory authority responsible under Article 56(1) GDPR examines that undertaking's data processing conditions?

On 10 May 2022, the hearing at the Court of Justice took place.[999] On 20 September 2022, advocate general Rantos delivered his opinion on the case.[1000] He advised the Court of Justice to rule as follows:

> *"1. Articles 51 to 66 of (...) [the GDPR] must be interpreted as meaning that a competition authority, within the framework of its powers under the competition rules, may examine, as an incidental question, the compliance of the practices investigated with the rules of that regulation, while taking into account any decision or investigation of the competent supervisory authority on the basis of said regulation, informing and, where appropriate, consulting that authority.*
>
> *2. Article 9(1) of (...) [the GDPR] must be interpreted as meaning that the prohibition on processing sensitive personal data may include the processing of data carried out by an operator of an online social network consisting in the collection of the user's data when that user visits other websites or apps or enters such data into those websites or apps, linking the data to the user account on the social network and then using the data, provided that the information processed, considered in isolation or aggregated, allows user profiling based on the categories that emerge from the types of sensitive personal data mentioned in that article.*
>
> *Article 9(2)(e) of (...) [the GDPR] must be interpreted as meaning that a user does not manifestly make public the data revealed by visiting websites and apps or entered into those websites or apps or resulting from having clicked on buttons integrated into those websites or apps.*
>
> *3. Article 6(1)(b), (c), (d), (e) and (f) of (...) [the GDPR] must be interpreted as meaning that the practice consisting in (i) the collection of data from other group services, as well as from third-party websites and apps, by interfaces integrated into the latter or by cookies placed on the user's computer or mobile terminal, (ii) the linking of such data with the user's Facebook account and (iii) the use of said data or some of the activities comprising that practice may be covered by the exemptions laid down in those provisions, as long as each data processing method examined fulfils the conditions provided for by the justification specifically put forward by the controller, and that therefore:*
>
> - *the processing is objectively necessary for the provision of the services relating to the Facebook account;*
> - *the processing is necessary for the purposes of the legitimate interests pursued by the data controller or by the third party or parties to whom the data are disclosed and does not have a disproportionate effect on the fundamental rights and freedoms of the data subject;*
> - *the processing is necessary to respond to a legitimate request for certain data, to combat harmful behaviour and promote security, to conduct research in the public interest and to promote safety, integrity and security.*
>
> *4. Articles 6(1)(a) and 9(2)(a) of (...) [the GDPR]*

999. https://curia.europa.eu/juris/fiche.jsf?id=C%3B252%3B21%3BRP%3B1%3BP%3B1%3BC2021%2F0252%2FP&oqp=&for=&mat=or&lgrec=en&jge=&td=%3BALL&jur=C%2CT%2CF&num=C-252%252F21&dates=&pcs=Oor&lg=&pro=&nat=or&cit=none%252CC%252CCJ%252CR%252C2008E%252C%252C%252C%252C%252C%252C%252C%252C%252C%252Ctrue%252Cfalse%252Cfalse&language=en&GDPR=&cid=10754569.

1000. Opinion of 20 September 2022 in case 252/21, https://curia.europa.eu/juris/document/document.jsf?text=&docid=265901&pageIndex=0&doclang=EN&mode=req&dir=&occ=first&part=1&cid=1992373.

must be interpreted as meaning that the mere fact that an undertaking providing a social network enjoys a dominant position in the domestic market for online social networks for private users cannot, on its own, render invalid the consent of the user of that network to the processing of his or her personal data under Article 4(11) of that regulation. However, that fact does play a role in the assessment of the freedom of consent within the meaning of that provision, which it is for the controller to demonstrate, taking into account, where appropriate, the existence of a clear imbalance of power between the data subject and the controller, any requirement for consent to the processing of personal data other than those strictly necessary for the provision of the services in question, the need for consent to be specific for each purpose of processing and the need to prevent the withdrawal of consent from being detrimental to users who withdraw it."

Although the opinion would appear to be more to the Bundeskartellamt's advantage than Meta's, the outcome of the case is still very uncertain – also because it is far from certain that the Court of Justice will indeed follow the advocate general's advice.

[B] Lufthansa

At the end of 2017, the Bundeskartellamt announced that it had opened an investigation into German national airline Lufthansa.[1001] Following the bankruptcy of Air Berlin in October 2017, the prices of many of Lufthansa's domestic flights showed increases by up to 30%. The rises occurred precisely on the routes where Lufthansa, due to the bankruptcy of Air Berlin, remains the only provider. Lufthansa stated that algorithms had calculated the new rates. The price increases were the result of extra demand combined with less supply, according to Lufthansa. In an interview published on 28 December 2017, Mundt issued a warning to Lufthansa.[1002] According to the interview, Lufthansa had claimed that it had not changed its price-setting algorithms since the bankruptcy of Air Berlin. Mundt stated, however '*Solche Algorithmen werden ja nicht im Himmel vom lieben Gott geschrieben*' [freely translated: '*Such algorithms did not drop from the sky*'] and that Lufthansa '*sich nicht hinter Algorithmen verstecken [könnte]*' [freely translated: '*cannot hide behind algorithms*'].[1003] However, a closer examination by the Bundeskartellamt showed that price levels in February 2018 had returned to the levels from before Air Berlin's bankruptcy after many of Air Berlin's take-off and landing rights were transferred to easyJet.[1004] Mundt went on to state that

1001. Bundeskartellamt, 'Press Release 29 May 2018: Lufthansa Tickets 25-30 Per Cent More Expensive after Air Berlin Insolvency – "Price Increase Does Not Justify Initiation of Abuse Proceeding"', *supra* n. 943.

1002. C. Busse, 'Bundeskartellamt rügt Lufthansa', *Süddeutsche Zeitung*, 28 December 2018, https://www.sueddeutsche.de/wirtschaft/nach-air-berlin-pleite-bundeskartellamt-ruegt-lufthansa-1.3806188.

1003. *Ibid.*

1004. Bundeskartellamt, 'Press Release 29 May 2018: Lufthansa Tickets 25-30 Per Cent More Expensive after Air Berlin Insolvency – "Price Increase Does Not Justify Initiation of Abuse Proceeding"', *supra* n. 943.

the temporary increase in prices did not justify initiating abuse proceedings, which means Lufthansa got off with just Mundt's warning.

[C] Amazon

On 22 November 2018, the Bundeskartellamt issued a press release announcing that it had initiated proceedings against Amazon under the prohibition of abuse of a dominant position.[1005] The investigation was said to cover certain contract terms that Amazon agrees with retailers who sell goods on its platform.

The commercial terms and related practices which, according to the Bundeskartellamt, could potentially be considered abusive are liability clauses to the detriment of merchants, combined with choice of law and jurisdiction clauses, rules for product inspections, non-transparent termination and blocking of merchant accounts, withholding or deferral of payment, clauses granting the right to use information material that a seller must provide in relation to the products offered and finally the commercial terms for the pan-European shipment of products.

According to the Bundeskartellamt, there were indications that Amazon held a dominant position or that the merchants were dependent on Amazon. This is to be further investigated by the Bundeskartellamt. The procedure was initiated by 'numerous' complaints from merchants about Amazon's business practices, received by the Bundeskartellamt in the recent past.

The Bundeskartellamt also confirmed that the European Commission had launched its own investigation into Amazon's European marketplaces (reference is made to the chapter on the European Commission), in particular regarding the collection and use of transaction data by Amazon. According to the Bundeskartellamt, in the summer of 2018, the Commission sent extensive questionnaires to several hundreds of German retailers for this purpose. According to the press release, the activities of the Bundeskartellamt and the Commission would complement each other. While the Commission's investigation focuses on Amazon's use of data to the detriment of merchants in the market, the Bundeskartellamt examines in particular the company's trading conditions and practices vis-à-vis merchants on its German platform. Mundt stated in the press release about the enquiry: '*Amazon is the largest online retailer and operates by far the largest online marketplace in Germany. Many retailers and manufacturers depend on the reach of Amazon's marketplace for their online sales. Amazon functions as a kind of "gatekeeper" for customers. Its double role as the largest retailer and largest marketplace has the potential to hinder other sellers on its platform. Because of the many complaints we have received we will examine whether Amazon is abusing its market position to the detriment of sellers active on its marketplace. We will scrutinize its terms of business and practices towards sellers.*'[1006]

1005. Bundeskartellamt, 'Press Release 29 November 2018: Bundeskartellamt Initiates Abuse Proceeding Against Amazon'.
1006. *Ibid.*

On 17 July 2019, the Bundeskartellamt announced that it had terminated its proceedings against Amazon, as Amazon had voluntarily amended its general terms and conditions on the points to which the Bundeskartellamt objected.[1007] Amazon promised to implement the changes not only in Germany but also worldwide. Specifically, Amazon had indicated that it would amend its terms and conditions on the following points:

- The contract terms would become more transparent and be made available to sellers via a link.
- For sellers, there would be a choice of law, whereas the general terms and conditions previously mandatorily prescribed Luxembourg law.
- The liability and exoneration terms would be amended so that they would be less in favour of Amazon.
- Unilateral cancellation or blocking of third-party seller accounts by Amazon would be subject to a thirty-day notice period. Furthermore, Amazon would be obliged to provide reasons for this and sellers would be given the opportunity to defend themselves.
- The obligation for third-party sellers to give Amazon access to the same (quality) images and product information as the sellers used on their own sites would be curtailed.
- While Amazon's favourable return conditions for consumers would remain in full force, third-party sellers would now be entitled to demand that returns be sent to them directly instead of Amazon and to object within thirty days to Amazon's decision to refund the customer.
- Third-party sellers would gain access to Amazon's *Vine* application for seller and item reviews by customers.
- Amazon promised to remove the obligation of third-party sellers to submit public statements to it in advance.

However, also after the termination of the Bundeskartellamt's investigation, there were rumours in the press that Amazon was still under the Bundeskartellamt's scrutiny. On 18 and 19 August 2020, various online media reported[1008] that the Bundeskartellamt was investigating Amazon's pricing policy. The investigation would focus on the alleged banning of third-party sellers from its website who, in Amazon's opinion, were charging too high prices for their products. In particular, significant price increases were said to have occurred at the height of the coronavirus crisis. Although Amazon seems to take the view that by banning overpricing sellers it would be acting in the interests of consumers, the Bundeskartellamt was said to have regarded this as a possible abuse of Amazon's dominant position. President Mundt is quoted on the internet as saying: '*Wir untersuchen derzeit, ob und wie Amazon die Preisgestaltung*

1007. Bundeskartellamt, Case report B2-88/18 17 July 2019.
1008. *See*, among others, 'Amazon Action: Das wird narrow', https://www.finanztrends.info/amazon-aktie-das-wird-eng/, 18 August 2020 and 'Amazon: Kundenfreundlichkeit oder Missbrauch der Marktmacht?', https://www.futurezone.de/digital-life/article230203962/Amazon-Droht-eine-Klage-wegen-zu-viel-Kundenfreundlichkeit.html, 19 August 2020.

von Dritthändlern auf dem Marktplatz beeinflusst. (...) Amazon darf kein Preiskontrolleur sein.' Freely translated: '*We are currently investigating whether and how Amazon has influenced the pricing of third-party merchants. (...) Amazon should not be a price controller.*'][1009]

In a press release dated 18 May 2021, the Bundeskartellamt announced that it had initiated proceedings under the new section 19a GWB against Amazon.[1010] It seems that this is the same investigation that was reported in the press earlier. Parallel to the investigation under section 19a GWB, the investigation under the abuse prohibition would also continue in any case. Mundt says about this in the English version of her press release:

> *'In the past few years we have had to deal with Amazon on several occasions and also obtained far-reaching improvements for sellers on Amazon Marketplace. Two other proceedings are still ongoing. Parallel to these proceedings we are now also applying our extended competences in abuse control. In this particular case we are first of all examining whether Amazon is of paramount significance for competition across markets. An ecosystem which extends across various markets and thus constitutes an almost unchallengeable position of economic power is particularly characteristic in this respect. This could apply to Amazon with its online marketplaces and many other, above all digital offers. If we find that the company does have such a market position, we could take early action against and prohibit possible anti-competitive practices by Amazon.'*

[D] Meta (Facebook)/Meta Quest (Oculus)

According to a press release from the Bundeskartellamt dated 10 December 2020,[1011] the Bundeskartellamt on that date initiated abuse proceedings against Facebook (now Meta) to investigate the integration of Oculus (now: Meta Quest) VR products and Facebook's social network.

The Bundeskartellamt observes that Meta has begun to integrate its VR activities into its social network Facebook.com. The Quest platform, which was bought by Facebook in 2014 and previously operated separately from Facebook.com, will be offered as an additional feature on Meta's social network under the name *Facebook Reality Labs*. The use of the latest *Quest 2* VR glasses requires the user to register with a Facebook.com account. Existing Oculus accounts (now Meta Quest accounts) can no longer be used for new registrations and for upgrades to this new hardware. According

1009. 'Message: Bundeskartellamt leitet Untersuchung gegen Amazon ein', https://pressfrom.info/de/nachrichten/digital/-481577-bericht-bundeskartellamt-leitet-untersuchung-gegen-amazon-ein.html, 18 augustis 2020.

1010. Bundeskartellamt, press release of 18 May 2021: Bundeskartellamt – Homepage – Proceedings against Amazon based on new rules for large digital companies (section 1, https://www.bundeskartellamt.de/SharedDocs/Meldung/EN/Pressemitteilungen/2021/18_05_2021_Amazon_19a.html9a GWB).

1011. https://www.bundeskartellamt.de/SharedDocs/Meldung/EN/Pressemitteilungen/2020/10_12_2020_Facebook_Oculus.html?nn = 3591568.

to the press release, distribution of the new VR glasses outside Germany had already started on the date of publication.

The purpose of VR products is to create a virtual world that the user can experience while using digital content. A three-dimensional vision that allows the human eye to perceive its surroundings in 3D is made possible by special technology. This VR technology requires the use of VR glasses. More hardware is also needed, usually a personal computer (PC), a game console or a smartphone. Some VR glasses, including Meta's *Quest 2* glasses, already have the required hardware integrated, allowing them to function as standalone devices. Finally, VR software is necessary to access and use VR content. Currently, VR applications are mainly used in the gaming and video sectors. However, their use is not limited to these areas. The number of users and revenue generated by such applications is constantly increasing.

Mundt says in the press release: '*Die Nutzung der neuen Oculus-Brillen soll künftig nur unter der Voraussetzung möglich sein, dass man auch ein Facebook-Konto hat. Diese Verknüpfung zwischen Virtual-Reality-Produkten und dem sozialen Netzwerk des Konzerns könnte einen verbotenen Missbrauch einer marktbeherrschenden Stellung durch Facebook darstellen. Facebook ist mit seinem sozialen Netzwerk marktbeherrschend in Deutschland und auch in dem noch jungen, größer werdenden VR-Markt bereits ein bedeutender Player. Wir wollen untersuchen, ob und inwieweit die Kopplung den Wettbewerb in den beiden Bereichen beeinträchtigt.*' [freely translated: '*In the future, the use of the new Oculus glasses will always require the user to also have a Facebook account. Such tying of virtual reality products and the group's social network in this way could constitute a prohibited abuse of a dominant position by Facebook. Facebook has a dominant position with its social network in Germany and is already a major player in the emerging but growing VR market. We intend to investigate whether and to what extent this tying will affect competition in both areas of activity.*']

On 27 January 2021, the Bundeskartellamt issued an additional press release[1012] announcing that the investigation has been expanded and that the Bundeskartellamt is now also investigating whether Facebook is subject to the new regulations for companies with significant market power (section 19a GWB) and whether the tying of services should be assessed under these rules. The Bundeskartellamt has not yet published any further information on the nature, content and progress of its investigation.

On 23 November 2022, the Bundeskartellamt issued another press release in which it announced that Meta had decided to change its conduct.[1013] The Bundeskartellamt informed the public that users who want to use the Quest 2 VR headset no longer need a Facebook account to do so. Meta was reported to have created a separate account, the Meta account, which could be used with the headset. The Bundeskartellamt declared that with this commitment, sale of the headsets in Germany can go ahead. This would also apply to the new Quest Pro headset.

1012. https://www.bundeskartellamt.de/SharedDocs/Meldung/DE/Pressemitteilungen/2021/28_01_2021_Facebook_Oculus.html.

1013. https://www.bundeskartellamt.de/SharedDocs/Meldung/EN/Pressemitteilungen/2022/23_11_2022_Facebook_Oculus.html.

However, this does mean that the Bundeskartellamt's investigation against Meta is now over. According to the press release, in addition to the specific choice architecture, the Bundeskartellamt is also examining whether and how data processed in the context of different Meta services are combined. As described above under [A], this case is currently pending before the European Court of Justice. The press release concludes by stating that until this matter has been clarified, Meta will, subject to certain exceptions, keep the data of users with a separate Meta account which is generated during their use of the Meta Quest headsets separate from the data gathered from other Meta services.

In the aforementioned press release, Mundt is quoted as saying: '*The digital ecosystem created by Meta with a very large user base makes the company the key player in social media. Meta is also an important player in the growing VR market. Competition in these two sectors could be severely impeded if only Facebook or Instagram members were able to use the VR headsets. Meta has responded to our concerns and has offered to give users of Quest glasses the option to create a separate Meta account as a solution to the problem. While we welcome this development, we will not terminate the proceeding today. We will now continue to monitor the actual design of users' options as well as issues regarding the combination and processing of user data from the various Meta services. This case shows that Section 19a of the German Competition Act (GWB), the new instrument to monitor large digital companies more effectively, allows us to efficiently address competition problems in practice.*'

[E] Software for Hospital Services

On 8 July 2020, the Bundeskartellamt announced in a press release that it had mediated on behalf of the *Institut für das Entgeltsystem im Krankenhaus* (InEK).[1014]

German health insurance companies pay for hospital services on the basis of case-specific flat rates. Hospitals and health insurance companies use special software to correctly identify and bill patients. This software is based on an algorithm that automatically classifies case-specific data and classifies individual patients by relevant reimbursement categories. A licence from InEK is required for use of the algorithm. In case the software is used for billing purposes, it must also be certified by InEK. The Bundeskartellamt states that it mediated the negotiations on licensing the software by ensuring that the licensing conditions complied with competition law. The solution found ensures a level playing field for incumbents and new suppliers and promotes competition for innovative software solutions.

Over time, both hospitals and health insurers developed a need for innovative functionalities that would support not only the actual billing process but also the identification and documentation of patients in a way that would optimise revenues

1014. Bundeskartellamt, press release of 8 July 2020, https://www.bundeskartellamt.de/SharedDocs/Publikation/EN/Pressemitteilungen/2020/08_07_2020_InEK.pdf?__blob=publicationFile&v=3.

and allow for efficient retrospective evaluation of reimbursements paid. While incumbents were increasingly adding such functionalities to their software, InEK refused to license the algorithm to vendors who wanted to use it primarily to develop such new functionalities. This put new market entrants at a particular disadvantage, according to the Bundeskartellamt. The proceedings were triggered by a number of complaints from software manufacturers who had initially been denied a licence by InEK. After a compromise was found, the investigation was stopped.

President Andreas Mundt stated in the press release: '*Bei der Gestaltung der Lizenzierungsbedingungen kam es uns vor allem darauf an, dass es zu keiner ungerechtfertigten Ungleichbehandlung verschiedener Softwareanbieter kommt und der Markt insbesondere auch für innovative Neueinsteiger offengehalten wird. Durch unsere Begleitung ist es gelungen, eine praktikable Lösung zu finden, die einerseits keine unnötigen Marktzutrittshürden errichtet, andererseits aber auch Anliegen der InEK Rechnung trägt.*' [Freely translated: '*When drawing up the licence conditions, we focused on ensuring that there would be no unjustified discrimination between different software suppliers and that the market would remain open, especially for innovative newcomers. Our help has made it possible to find a practical solution that does not create unnecessary barriers to market entry, but also takes into account the concerns of InEK.*']

Further details on the content of the compromise found were not disclosed by the Bundeskartellamt.

[F] Google/Alphabet Subject to Article 19(a) GWB

On 5 January 2022, the Bundeskartellamt decided that Google's parent company Alphabet must be subject to the new regime of *ex ante* measures that can be imposed on undertakings with considerable market power.[1015] This landmark decision is the first one to be based on this new German competition law provision. As a result, due to the decision in question, it is now possible for the Bundeskartellamt to step in and investigate Google's practices.[1016] It should be noted that this decision is valid for a period of five years and that Google announced that it will refrain from appealing it.[1017]

The main points of Bundeskartellamt's reasoning are the following. Due to the 'paramount significance' Google has across the markets and its economic position of power, its activities fall within the scope of section 19a(1) German Competition Act.[1018] Additionally, the Bundeskartellamt stated that Google holds a dominant position when it comes to the provision of search and advertising services in Germany.[1019] This is specifically the case when it comes to the amount of daily and monthly users' activities

1015. Bundeskartellamt, Press Release: Alphabet/Google subject to new abuse control applicable to large digital companies – Bundeskartellamt determines 'paramount significance across markets' (2022) Press Office (Bundeskartellamt Press Release) p. 1; Bundeskartellamt, 'Case Summary: Bundeskartellamt determines Google's paramount significance for competition across markets B7 – 61/21 [2021] (Bundeskartellamt Case Summary) p. 1.
1016. Bundeskartellamt Press Release p. 1.
1017. *Ibid.*, p. 2.
1018. Bundeskartellamt Case Summary p. 3.
1019. *Ibid.*

Google attracts to its platform. Its significant market power also allows Google to have an influence on other companies as the services it provides are exclusive and form an integral part of other market participants' infrastructure.[1020] Similarly, Google can impose terms on its users and customers and can influence the access of third parties to them.[1021] The broad range of these services also allows Google to benefit from the economies of scope and to effectively cross-promote its services.[1022]

Another factor that played a large role in the Bundeskartellamt's decision, is the high level of vertical integration and interconnectivity of the services Google provides across the various markets on which Google operates.[1023] The Bundeskartellamt further noted that the data to which Google has access are pivotal for the competition and provide Google with a serious competitive advantage when it comes to expansion and enhancement of Google's services.[1024] This database, combined with Google's financial resources and flexibility, permits the company to foster its research and development practices and improve its business strategies.[1025] Last but not least, the Bundeskartellamt underlined that due to the fact that Google Search is currently seen as the most significant and widespread search engine, it has a paramount influence on German and global social life and societal participation.[1026]

As a consequence, all of the above made the Bundeskartellamt conclude that Alphabet is one of the most powerful economic players on the German market and thus must be subject to a more strict competition control.

After the end of the research period, the Bundeskartellamt took similar decisions with regard to Apple and Amazon.

§7.03 MERGER CONTROL

The Bundeskartellamt addresses merger control in its report '*Competition Law and Data*', jointly published by the Bundeskartelamt and the Autorité on 10 May 2016, which has already been discussed in the chapter above.[1027] In the report, both authorities point out, among other findings, that the possession of a large quantity of privacy-sensitive data can also lead to a dominant position. In addition to this report, the Bundeskartellamt has also dealt with merger control in the digital sector in practice as becomes clear from the below case reviews. During the period under review, the Bundeskartellamt has dealt with in total six merger cases in the digital sector, all of which were cleared unconditionally. Meta (Facebook)/Kustomer was the case that received the closest scrutiny. That case is also interesting because it was reviewed simultaneously by the Bundeskartellamt and (pursuant to an Article 22 referral that

1020. Bundeskartellamt Press Release p. 2.
1021. Bundeskartellamt Case Summary p. 4.
1022. *Ibid.*, pp. 3-4.
1023. *Ibid.*, p. 3.
1024. Bundeskartellamt Press Release p. 3; Bundeskartellamt Case Summary p. 5.
1025. *Ibid.*, p. 5.
1026. *Ibid.*, p. 6.
1027. 'Competition Law and Data', *supra* n. 839.

was not supported by the Bundeskartellamt) by the Commission, thus creating a notable exception to the *one-stop-shop* rule.

[A] Immonet/Immowelt

In the '*Immonet/Immowelt*' case (2015),[1028] a merger of two real estate platforms, the Bundeskartellamt once again found that online (property) platforms are characterised by pronounced indirect network effects: a large number of property advertisers leads to more consumers joining the platform, which in turn has a positive impact on the group of property providers. The Bundeskartellamt finally ruled that the risks for competition, in particular, '*tipping*' of the market (whereby network effects become so strong that only one platform remains or at least becomes dominant), were unlikely. In this respect, the Bundeskartellamt concluded that the likelihood of tipping would be reduced rather than increased by the merger: '*Der Zusammenschluss wirkt vielmehr auf einem engen Markt für Online-Immobilienplattformen dem sogenannten Markt-Tipping entgegen*' [freely translated: '*Rather than facilitating so-called market tipping in a concentrated market for online real estate platforms, the merger actually works as a counterweight against such an effect*'].[1029] The Bundeskartellamt concluded that the combination of the numbers two and three in the market would have a disciplining effect on the market leader Immoscout. The Bundeskartellamt also considered coordinated and uncoordinated effects between Immoscout and the new entity to be unlikely. In view of the above, the concentration was approved by the Bundeskartellamt in the first phase.

[B] ProSiebenSat.1/Verivox

ProSiebenSat.1/Verivox (2015)[1030] concerned a merger of the 'new' and the 'old' economies: the target company – Verivox – was a consumer comparison platform (for energy among other things) and the acquirer, ProSiebenSat.1, operated a television channel. Accordingly, the vertical effects of the concentration stood central in the assessment. Together with its main competitor CHECK24, Verivox had a market share of approximately 95% in the field of energy comparison sites in Germany. The Bundeskartellamt investigated whether the merger with ProSiebenSat.1 could result in the tipping of the market in Verivox's favour, as television advertising would be one of the two main ways for comparison sites to acquire customers. The Bundeskartellamt considered this unlikely, as CHECK24 had a much stronger market position. In addition, there are numerous other ways (not explicitly identified by the Bundeskartellamt) to acquire customers besides television advertising. The concentration was therefore cleared in the first phase without conditions.

1028. *Case B6-39/15*, *supra* n. 947.
1029. *Ibid.*
1030. *Ibid.*

[C] Online Dating Sites

A third online platform-centred merger case in 2015 concerns *Oakley Capital/EliteMedianet.*[1031] Oakley Capital already owned the online dating site Parship and wanted to acquire the competing EliteMedianet. The parties to the concentration were both clear market leaders in the field of online dating in Germany, but given the large number of players in the market, it was not possible to determine their market shares. The Bundeskartellamt again investigated the risk of tipping. This was considered unlikely as the market supply is very heterogeneous: '*Die Beteiligten erreichen nach dem Zusammenschluss keine Marktposition, die im Hinblick auf die wirkenden indirekten Netzwerkeffekte eine zunehmende Konzentrations – oder Monopolisierungstendenz verbunden mit Marktaustritten der Wettbewerber gerade zugunsten der Beteiligten erwarten lässt. Den Wettbewerb erheblich behindernde unilaterale oder koordinierte Effekte sind ebenfalls nicht zu erwarten*' [freely translated: '*The parties do not achieve a market position after the merger, which, with regard to the likelihood of indirect network effects, would give rise to the expectation of an increasing tendency towards concentration or monopoly combined with competitors leaving the market in favour of the parties. Likewise, unilateral or coordinated effects that significantly hinder competition are not to be expected*'].[1032] Moreover, users generally use multiple sites, which made it unlikely that users would leave competing platforms in great numbers. Nor did the Bundeskartellamt see any risk of coordinated effects. Users were said to be very sensitive to price and switch to smaller suppliers if the duopoly were to increase prices. Finally, the Bundeskartellamt pointed to the emergence of Tinder as a relatively new, innovative competitor. The foregoing analysis resulted in a first phase clearance.

A subsequent acquisition by the merged entity also received unconditional approval from the Bundeskartellamt in the first phase. Parship-Elitemedianet, since 2016 no longer owned by Oakley Capital but by ProSiebenSat.1, had requested the Bundeskartellamt in 2020 for permission to acquire its competitor TheMeetGroup, which operated several dating platforms of which Lovoo was the only one also active in Germany.[1033] Clearance was granted on 6 July 2020. Based on similar considerations as the merger of Parship and EliteMedianet five years earlier, the Bundeskartellamt again gave its blessing. President Mundt said: '*Eine erhebliche Beeinträchtigung des Wettbewerbs bei den Online Dating Plattformen durch den Zusammenschluss ist trotz der Marktstärke der beteiligten Unternehmen nicht zu erwarten. Durch den Zusammenschluss kommt es zu einer weiteren Konzentration im Bereich des Online-Dating, die Beteiligten gehören zu den größten Online-Dating Plattformen in Deutschland. Der Markt des Online-Dating ist aber durch dynamisches Wachstum, Marktzutritte und Wettbewerb gekennzeichnet. Zuletzt hat sich insbesondere das Segment der Dating Apps, zu denen neben dem Zielunternehmen Lovoo auch die konkurrierenden Plattformen Tinder oder Badoo gehören, stark entwickelt.*' [Freely translated: '*Despite the*

1031. *Ibid.*
1032. *Ibid.*, para. 3.
1033. Press release of 6 July 2020, *Parship und Elite Partner dürfen Lovoo übernehmen*, Bundeskartellamt – Homepage – Pressemitteilung (pdf).

companies' market power, it is not to be expected that the merger will hamper competition in the field of online dating platforms. As a result of the merger, there will be further consolidation in the field of online dating; the companies involved are among the largest online dating platforms in Germany. However, the market for online dating is characterised by dynamic growth, market entry and competition. The market for online dating apps, which includes not the target undertaking Lovoo, but also the competing platforms Tinder and Badoo, has recently experienced strong growth.'] Mundt in this respect refers to the Match Group, which in addition to Tinder and Badoo also operates the platforms Lovescout24, OKCupid, neu.de and Zweisam.de. The Bundeskartellamt concluded that users still generally use multiple platforms and platforms constantly need to attract new customers, which makes market entry relatively easy. The recent entry of Bumble and LemonSwan, the growth of the market share of Tinder and other competitors of the merged entity, as well as Facebook's intention to enter the European market was said to illustrate the above. The strong position of ProSiebenSat.1 in the TV advertising market would also not give rise to competition problems, according to the Bundeskartellamt. In this context, the Bundeskartellamt noted that TV advertising is losing importance, especially among younger users.

[D] Digital Platform in the Pharmacy Sector

According to a press release dated 21 December 2020,[1034] the Bundeskartellamt approved the contemplated establishment of a joint venture between the Phoenix Group's subsidiary ADG Pharmacies and Noventi Health, an operator of pharmacies. The aim of the joint venture is to operate a comprehensive digital platform for health services and products, which in addition to the purchase and reservation of prescription and over-the-counter medicines from pharmacies may in the medium term also be able to offer other functionalities, such as online video consultations with a doctor.

Phoenix is one of the leading German pharmaceutical wholesalers, with branches all over Germany. Noventi is a wholly (100%) owned subsidiary of the pharmacy association FSA e.V. and provides industry-specific software and billing services for pharmacies and other healthcare providers.

Prior to the establishment of the platform, Phoenix and Noventi already offered their own apps *deine Apotheke* and *callmyApo* through which patients can pre-order medicines at a pharmacy of their choice. The apps *Ihre Apotheken* of the pharmacists' cooperative Noweda, Pro AvO's *apora* and *Meine Apotheke* offer a competitive service. Large online pharmacies such as DocMorris and Shop Apotheke have also facilitated the purchase of medicines over the Internet in Germany for a long time. According to media reports, these parties are also planning to integrate physical pharmacies into their distribution systems. Furthermore, the Bundeskartellamt envisages that in the

1034. Bundeskartellamt, 'Bundeskartellamt allows Phoenix and Noventi to launch digital health platform' (*Bundeskartellamt*, 21 December 2020) https://www.bundeskartellamt.de/SharedDocs/Meldung/EN/Pressemitteilungen/2020/21_12_2020_Gesundheitsplattform.html?nn=3599398.

future, general online marketplaces could also distribute medicines if they meet the necessary legal requirements. In short, sufficient competition for the planned platform seems to be ensured.

According to the Bundeskartellamt, it is too early to definitively assess these and other pharmacy and health platforms under competition law. The eventual assessment will also depend on the actual design that the platforms shall have and on the way in which these shall operate in practice. However, the fact that the healthcare providers on the platform, i.e., the pharmacies, operate a joint platform through Noventi does not, in the opinion of the Bundeskartellamt, raise any competition concerns as such. In fact, experiences with online marketplaces in other sectors show that it can be useful for suppliers of products and services to keep control over electronic contact with their customers in their own hands in order to avoid dependencies.

[E] Meta (Facebook)/Kustomer

In a press release dated 9 December 2021, the Bundeskartellamt announced that it considers the proposed acquisition of Kustomer by Meta (formerly Facebook) to be notifiable in Germany.[1035] The Bundeskartellamt has established that the proposed acquisition reached the transaction value threshold of EUR 400 million under German merger control. This conclusion is remarkable since at the time the acquisition of Kustomer by Meta was also being investigated by the Commission in a parallel second-phase procedure (reference is made to the chapter on the Commission, §4.03[K]). This Commission investigation was initiated after the case had been referred to the Commission by the Austrian competition authority (*see* the section on the European Commission, §4.03[K]). Germany did not join the request for referral to the Commission as, according to its established practice, the Bundeskartellamt only refers cases to the Commission that meet the German notification thresholds. According to the press release, at the time of the Austrian referral request, it was still unclear whether this was the case for this intended acquisition. Therefore, parallel proceedings were initiated in Germany and at an EU level, which means that there was no *one-stop shop* for this concentration.

In the aforementioned press release, Mundt says about the course of events: '*Die geplante Übernahme fällt nach unserer Ansicht in den Geltungsbereich der deutschen Fusionskontrolle und muss beim Bundeskartellamt angemeldet werden. Unsere Vorprüfung hat gezeigt, dass Kustomer auch in Deutschland tätig ist und die Übernahme Auswirkungen in Deutschland hat. Meta sollte nun unverzüglich entsprechende Unterlagen für eine Prüfung des Vorhabens im Rahmen der Fusionskontrolle einreichen. Eine effektive Fusionskontrolle ist das schlagkräftigste Instrument, das wir haben, um zu verhindern, dass zu viel Marktmacht in die Hände weniger Unternehmen fällt. Besonders in der Digitalwirtschaft sind viele Märkte bereits heute stark konzentriert.*

1035. Bundeskartellamt, 'Bundeskartellamt sieht Anmeldepflicht der Fusion Meta/Kustomer' (*Bundeskartellamt*, 9 December 2021), https://www.bundeskartellamt.de/SharedDocs/Meldung/DE/Pressemitteilungen/2021/09_12_2021_Meta_Kustomer.html.

Deshalb ist eine stringente Kontrolle unverzichtbar' [freely translated: '*In our opinion, the proposed acquisition falls within the scope of German merger control and must be notified to the Bundeskartellamt. Our preliminary investigation showed that Kustomer is also active in Germany and that the acquisition will have effects in Germany. Meta must now immediately submit the relevant documents for a merger control examination of the transaction. Effective merger control is the most powerful tool at our disposal to prevent too much market power from falling into the hands of a few companies. In the digital economy in particular, many markets are already highly concentrated. That is why strict control is indispensable.*'].

After the review process had been conducted, the Bundeskartellamt concluded relatively quickly that the merger between Meta and Kustomer would not lead to any competitive issues in Germany and should thus be cleared.[1036] The significance of this deal for the overall strategy for Meta lay at the heart of this decision.[1037] Accordingly, the Bundeskartellamt has observed that the merger indeed has the potential to play a pivotal role in Meta's business.[1038] By contrast, no anticompetitive effects which could have potentially justified a prohibition have been established.[1039]

Notably, the Bundeskartellamt took into consideration the results of the earlier Commission's assessment, which also, even though conditionally, allowed the Kustomer acquisition by Meta.[1040] This decision, however, has already been discussed in Chapter 4, §4.03[K] of this book.

§7.04 INTERMEDIATE CONCLUSION

The Bundeskartellamt has shown an impressive track record in the field of digital competition during the period under investigation. During this period, the Bundeskartellamt has been rather strict and – despite the highly volatile nature of innovative markets – has clearly shown no hesitation to intervene when it believes it has spotted a restriction of competition in a digital market.

On par with its strict policy on 'traditional' markets, the Bundeskartellamt pursues a strict policy on vertical agreements in the digital sector. In the digital sector, this policy translates into a dislike of both broad and narrow parity clauses. The Bundeskartellamt also shows no mercy when it concerns prohibitions on the use of online marketplaces by customers. What is noteworthy about the decisions under the cartel prohibition is that the Bundeskartellamt has systematically refrained from

1036. Bundeskartellamt, 'Pressemitteilung: Freigabe der Übernahme von Kustomer durch Meta (ehemals Facebook)' (11 February 2022, *Bundeskartellamt/Digitalwirtschaft*) https://www.bundeskartellamt.de/SharedDocs/Publikation/DE/Pressemitteilungen/2022/11_02_2022_Meta_Kustomer.pdf?__blob=publicationFile&v=2 p. 1.
1037. *Ibid.*; Aoife White, 'Meta's Deal Nod Gives German Antitrust Chief: A Stomach Ache' (*Bloomberg*, 11 February 2022) https://www.bloomberg.com/news/articles/2022-02-11/meta-s-deal-approval-gives-german-antitrust-chief-a-stomach-ache.
1038. *Ibid.*
1039. *Ibid.*
1040. European Commission, 'Press Release: Mergers: Commission clears acquisition of Kustomer by Meta (formerly Facebook), subject to conditions' (Jan. 27, 2022, *European Commission*) https://ec.europa.eu/commission/presscorner/detail/en/ip_22_652 p. 2.

imposing fines or other sanctions. The Bundeskartellamt has always confined itself to prohibiting the conduct at issue.

The Bundeskartellamt did the same under the prohibition of abuse of a dominant position in the *Facebook* case, where it prohibited Facebook to continue to collect user data from other applications and combine these with Facebook user data, but did not impose a fine. In particular, if it is upheld in appeal, the *Facebook* case can be considered a landmark case of international importance in view of the Bundeskartellamt's finding that the possession of large amounts of privacy-sensitive data can lead to a dominant position and abuse thereof and its application of privacy law in the context of a competition law proceeding. The case therefore also attracted wide interest outside Germany.

It is interesting to note that this interventionalist approach has been subject to a critical approach by the Oberlandesgericht Düsseldorf (the court of first instance in cartel cases) but has thus far found approval in the eyes of the BGH as the court of final instance.

The Bundeskartellamt only assessed clearly unproblematic cases in the area of merger control during the investigation period. Nevertheless, it is clear from these precedents that the Bundeskartellamt considers the 'tipping' of markets where network effects occur to be a serious problem. However, in the cases dealt with during the investigation period, the Bundeskartellamt did not see any risk of tipping. It seems realistic to expect that where appropriate the Bundeskartellamt will apply significantly stricter assessments in more concentrated markets.

CHAPTER 8
The Netherlands: Consumer & Markets Authority

§8.01 INTRODUCTION

> *'We are ... a little bit behind the development[s]. I don't think that is bad. I think it's good to let market forces and the markets develop first freely and then see whether there is a need for intervention into the market rather than the other way around.'*[1041]

> *'Moreover, we are the referee responsible for enforcing the rules of the game. If that referee blows the whistle too early, he kills the game. In a developing market, you have to operate carefully, you must not blow the whistle too quickly. We are a little cautious, but that is also to avoid ruining the game.'*[1042]

> *'Naturally, in a marketplace as large as the app stores, mistakes can be made, and therefore it is necessary to investigate whether certain conduct is done systematically.'*[1043]

1041. MLex, 'Algorithmic collusion 'biggest concern' for Dutch competition enforcer, Snoep says', speech of M. Snoep at 'Blockchain + The Law' conference, Amsterdam Law & Technology Institute, 3 February 2022.
1042. NRC, 18 January 2019, 'Eerst had ik een handvol cliënten, nu heb ik er 17 miljoen' (interview Martijn Snoep). Free translation from original Dutch text: *'Daar komt bij dat wij de scheidsrechter zijn die de spelregels moet handhaven. Als die scheidsrechter te vroeg fluit, maakt hij het spel dood. In een ontwikkelende markt moet je voorzichtig opereren, je moet niet te snel aan de bel trekken. We zijn wat voorzichtig, maar dat is ook om het spel niet kapot te maken.'*
1043. ACM, report, 'Market Study into Mobile App Stores', 11 April 2019, p. 108.

Until the third quarter of 2018, the Dutch competition authority (ACM) had a rather limited track record when it came to its enforcement practice in the field of digital competition, having only taken enforcement action in a single case.[1044] This was somewhat surprising for an authority that likes to claim to be one of Europe's most 'active' enforcers.[1045] The ACM, however, has shaken off its reticence, as evidenced by two digital competition cartel decisions in December 2018[1046] and 2021,[1047] three[1048] digital competition abuse of dominance investigations, leading to two decisions in 2021[1049] and three merger decisions in 2019[1050] and 2020.[1051] Under the cartel prohibition, an investigation into the parity clauses of Thuisbezorgd.nl, an online platform, led to a rejection of the enforcement request pursuant to which the ACM had initiated proceedings.[1052] The ACM also imposed a fine of EUR 39.9 million fine on Samsung for vertical sales restrictions by exercising undue influence on the online retail prices of television sets.[1053] Additionally, an investigation into online sales restrictions by the Dutch bar association led to the bar association changing its market behaviour.[1054] The three abuse of dominance investigations are investigations into Apple and Google for imposing unfair trading conditions on providers of dating apps[1055] and an investigation of a refusal to supply Dutch registered (.nl) domain name data.[1056] These investigations have led to a EUR 50 million fine on Apple[1057] and a decision rejecting an enforcement request.[1058] The Google investigation is ongoing.

1044. ACM, decision 18 November 2016, ACM/DM/2016/207286 (*Thuisbezorgd.nl*). After an initial investigation of Thuisbezorgd.nl, an online food delivery marketplace, the ACM decided not to take any further action.
1045. C. Fonteijn, 'Speech at the Congress Developments Competition Law 2015: Chris Fonteijn Speaks about Recent Competition Cases and Developments in Competition Practice'.
1046. ACM, decision 14 December 2018, ACM/17/012061 (*handhavingsverzoek Legal Dutch*).
1047. ACM, decision 14 September 2021, ACM/20/040569 (*Samsung*).
1048. Stichting Internet Domeinregistratie Nederland (2021); Apple (2021); Google (2022).
1049. ACM, decision 19 April 2021, ACM/21/049853 (*SIDN*); ACM, summary of decision 24 August 2021 (*Apple*), ACM/19/035630.
1050. ACM, decision 28 August 2019, ACM/19/035555 (*Sanoma Learning B.V./Iddink Holding B.V.*).
1051. ACM, decision 20 May 2020, ACM/20/038614 (*NS Groep N.V./Pon Netherlands B.V./JV*); ACM, decision 9 July 2020, ACM/20/039644 (*GVB Holding N.V./HTM Personenvervoer N.V./NS Groep N.V./Rotterdamse Electrische Tram N.V.*).
1052. ACM, decision 18 November 2016, ACM/DM/2016/207286 (*Thuisbezorgd.nl*); Reuters, 'With Apple fight ongoing, Dutch watchdog ACM to investigate Google Play store practices', 4 May 2022.
1053. ACM, decision 14 September 2021, ACM/20/040569 (*Samsung*).
1054. ACM decision 14 December 2018, ACM/17/012061 (*handhavingsverzoek Legal Dutch*).
1055. ACM, summary of decision 24 August 2021, ACM/19/035630 (*Apple*); NOS, 'ACM start vooronderzoek naar Google na klacht over machtsmisbruik', 4 May 2022; Reuters, 'With Apple fight ongoing, Dutch watchdog ACM to investigate Google Play store practices', 4 May 2022.
1056. ACM, decision 19 April 2021, ACM/21/049853 (*SIDN*).
1057. ACM, summary of decision 24 August 2021, ACM/19/035630 (*Apple*). This fine flows from Apple's non-compliance with an order of the ACM subject to penalty payments. The ACM has said that it may impose '*another order subject to periodic penalty payments (with possibly higher penalties this time around) in order to stimulate Apple to comply with the order*'. *See*: ACM, press release 28 March 2022, 'ACM to assess adjusted proposal of Apple regarding its conditions for dating apps'.
1058. ACM, decision 19 April 2021, ACM/21/049853 (*SIDN*).

The ACM also published a number of policy documents concerning cartels in digital markets: new vertical guidelines, including guidance on parity clauses (2015),[1059] a publication on algorithmic collusion (2018)[1060] and a position paper on guidelines for enforcement against infringements where algorithms play a role (2020).[1061] The ACM also published various policy documents concerning abuse of a dominant position in digital markets: a report on online platforms (2016),[1062] a report on online video services (2016),[1063] a market study into mobile app stores (2019),[1064] a market study on the Dutch (online) payment market (2020),[1065] a study into payment apps' access to Near-Field Communication (NFC) communication (2021),[1066] a market study on sponsored internet rankings (2021),[1067] a market study into Internet Protocol (IP) interconnection[1068] and a market study into Mobility as a Service (MaaS) (2021).[1069] The ACM also started a market investigation into cloud services in 2021.[1070]

Already in 2017, the parties making up the Dutch coalition government requested the ACM to set up a special team in the field of digital competition and to organise itself in such a way that '*effectiever en doelgerichter opgetreden* [kan] *worden tegen misbruik van marktmacht door dominante spelers in de interneteconomie*' [freely translated: '*more effective and targeted action can be taken against abuse of market power by dominant players in the internet economy*'].[1071] In 2019, the ACM had no dedicated team in place, but it had created a team wherein approximately eight people from different ACM directorates participated on a flexible basis. According to Michiel Denkers, Director at the Competition Directorate of the ACM, putting together such a team is not an easy task ('*It is not sufficient to take some people that were working on construction or mushrooms and ask them to look at digital issues, but you have to for example have expertise to understand how an algorithm works or to understand how you make large amounts of data manageable*' and '*Obviously, we are also investing in those capabilities*').[1072] The ACM invests in data science capacity, having introduced a

1059. ACM, guidelines, 'Leidraad afspraken tussen leveranciers en afnemers', 20 April 2015 and ACM, policy document, 'Het toezicht van ACM op verticale overeenkomsten: inzicht in strategie & prioritering', 20 April 2015.
1060. ACM, policy document, 'Het Signaal 2018', 11 April 2018.
1061. ACM, position paper, 'Toezicht op algoritmes', 10 December 2020.
1062. ACM, publication, 'Grote platforms, grote Problemen? Een Beschouwing van Online Platforms Vanuit Mededingingsperspectief', 21 September 2016.
1063. ACM, report, 'Online video platforms onder de loep', 22 August 2017.
1064. ACM, report, 'Market study into mobile app stores', 11 April 2019.
1065. ACM, report, 'Big Techs in the payment system', 16 November 2020.
1066. ACM, press release 2 July 2021, 'Closure of the investigation into payment apps confirms need for new rules'.
1067. ACM, press release 2 February 2021, 'ACM sees risks associated with paid ranking for consumers and competition'.
1068. ACM, press release 13 July 2021, 'ACM onderzoekt markt voor digitale infrastructuur: Nederland is nog altijd goed verbonden'.
1069. ACM, press release 8 March 2021, 'Mobility as a Service is still evolving – ACM is positive, but keeps a close watch on bottlenecks'.
1070. ACM, press release 18 May 2021, 'ACM launches market study into cloud services'.
1071. VVD, CDA, D66 and ChristenUnie, coalition agreement, 'Vertrouwen in de toekomst', 10 October 2017.
1072. PaRR, 'Digital Issues Key Focus for Dutch Agency Agenda' (Interview with Michiel Denkers), 28 August 2018.

recruitment programme in 2018[1073] and highlighted the importance of data science in case work in 2020: [Free translation: '*Traditionally only lawyers, economists (including econometrists) and behavioral scientists work on a case or a project. You see that data specialists are increasingly claiming a more important role, as a fourth wheel on the wagon. Data specialists have the ability to collect more and better data and to combine datasets. This can be a great help for project managers, especially at the beginning of the project.*'].[1074]

The ACM has initially been struggling with the issue of whether '*er daadwerkelijk sprake is van een probleem*' [freely translated: '*there is actually a problem*'].[1075] In 2017, the ACM suggested that the potential damage caused by internet conglomerates is offset by benefits such as freedom of choice, fair prices, opportunities for entrepreneurs and consumers and innovation.[1076] An additional problem for the ACM was that the dynamics of online markets, where companies are emerging and growing rapidly but can also disappear quickly, make it difficult to properly assess the counterfactual: is it possible to establish what would have happened in the event that it would not have intervened?[1077] This reluctance translated originally into a supervisory practice that can be described as contemplative rather than active. Whether or not by way of compensation, the ACM emphasised its track record in the enforcement of consumer law in digital markets and did not shy away from the language of threats.[1078] It is noteworthy that the ACM was reluctant to act too quickly in rapidly developing markets '*Als je te vroeg ingrijpt, heb je de kans dat je innovatie smoort*' [freely translated: '*If you intervene too early, you might stifle innovation*'], according to the ACM chairman Chris Fonteijn.[1079]

1073. ACM, press release 19 June 2018, 'Vacature: Data science traineeship'.

1074. ACM, press release 19 March 2020, 'Toezichthouden ondergaat een digitale transformatie'. Original Dutch text: '*Traditioneel werken alleen juristen, economen (inclusief econometristen) en gedragswetenschappers inhoudelijk aan een zaak of een project. Je ziet dat dataspecialisten daarin een steeds grotere rol krijgen, als het vierde wiel van de wagen. Dataspecialisten kunnen sneller en beter informatie verzamelen en aan elkaar koppelen. Dat kan projectleiders enorm helpen, vooral in de beginfase van het project.*'

1075. ACM, publication, 'Grote platforms, grote Problemen? Een Beschouwing van Online Platforms Vanuit Mededingingsperspectief', 21 September 2016.

1076. ACM, policy document, 'Het Signaal 2017', 29 March 2017 and F. Bruggert and J. Tichem, 'Een Algemene Verplichting Tot Datadeling Is Niet Wenselijk', ESB, 2018.

1077. ACM, publication, 'Grote platforms, grote Problemen? Een Beschouwing van Online Platforms Vanuit Mededingingsperspectief', 21 September 2016.

1078. PaRR, 'Digital Issues Key Focus for Dutch Agency Agenda' (Interview with Michiel Denkers), 28 August 2018 and ACM, press release 6 September 2018, 'Digitaal misbruiken van voorspelbaar consumentengedrag moet stoppen'.

1079. Het Financieele Dagblad, 'De ACM Moet Niet Angstig Zijn, Moet Durven Experimenteren' (Interview with Chris Fonteijn), 25 April 2018. In this interview, which was published at the end of his term as ACM chairman, Fonteijn also issued a warning to businesses active in the digital economy: '*Techbedrijven blijken in staat om in korte tijd gehele sectoren te ontwrichten. Met hun algoritmes kunnen ze markten naar hun hand zetten. De beschikking over enorme hoeveelheden gebruikersdata kan ze immense concurrentievoordelen opleveren, dan wel misbruik in de hand werken, zoals de Facebook-affaire de afgelopen maand liet zien. De toezichthouder moet daarom andere paden betreden. Het risico op de koop toe nemen, dat er zaken verloren gaan. "We moeten niet angstig zijn," geeft hij mee aan de organisatie die hij verlaat. "We moeten durven experimenteren. De reactie mag er niet één zijn van: laten we maar geen enge zaken doen"*' [freely translated: '*Tech companies appear to be able to disrupt entire*

However, in recent years, the ACM has clearly become more active, a trend coinciding with the appointment of its new chairman, Martijn Snoep, as of 1 September 2018. In his first newspaper interview since he took office, Snoep indicated that he indeed wants to break with the often informal enforcement style of his predecessor Fonteijn and impose fines more often. Since his appointment, the ACM has issued four[1080] of its total of five[1081] digital competition law antitrust decisions, including a decision against one of the big tech companies.[1082] Nonetheless, the ACM has only found two[1083] infringements and ACM's cautious attitude has not disappeared, as the ACM is (still) strongly focused on studying how digital markets work through market studies and reports. This for example is evidenced by a recent position paper on guidelines for enforcement against infringements where algorithms play a role (2020),[1084] a market study on the Dutch (online) payment market (2020),[1085] a market study on sponsored internet rankings (2021)[1086] and the launch of a market investigation into cloud services in 2021.[1087] The policy of not acting too quickly so as not to stifle innovation is also maintained under Snoep's chairmanship: [freely translated: '*Moreover, we are the referee responsible for enforcing the rules of the game. If that referee blows the whistle too early, he kills the game. In a developing market you have to operate carefully, you must not blow the whistle too quickly. We are a little cautious, but that is also to avoid ruining the game*'].[1088]

Already at the beginning of 2018, the ACM indicated that additional regulations are desirable for new situations, specifically with regard to the use of algorithms, the regulation of sustainable market power where there is no abuse and an ongoing personalisation of supply and prices: [freely translated: '*The current toolbox does not*

---

industries in a short period of time. They can manipulate markets with their algorithms. Access to enormous amounts of user data can give them immense competitive advantages or encourage abuse, as the Facebook affair last month showed. The regulator must therefore take other paths. Accept the risk that things may be lost. "We should not be anxious," he imparts to the organisation he is leaving. "We have to dare to experiment. The response may not be: let's not do anything scary"'].

1080. ACM decision 14 December 2018, ACM/17/012061 (*handhavingsverzoek Legal Dutch*), ACM, decision 14 September 2021, ACM/20/040569 (*Samsung*), ACM, decision 19 April 2021, ACM/21/049853 (*SIDN*) and ACM, summary of decision 24 August 2021 (*Apple*), ACM/19/035630.

1081. ACM, decision 18 November 2016 (*Thuisbezorgd.nl*), ACM/DM/2016/207286; ACM, decision 14 December 2018, ACM/17/012061 (*handhavingsverzoek Legal Dutch*); ACM, decision 14 September 2021, ACM/20/040569 (*Samsung*); ACM, decision 19 April 2021, ACM/21/049853 (*SIDN*) and ACM, summary of decision 24 August 2021 (*Apple*), ACM/19/035630.

1082. ACM, summary of decision 24 August 2021 (*Apple*), ACM/19/035630.

1083. ACM, decision 14 September 2021, ACM/20/040569 (*Samsung*) and ACM, summary of decision 24 August 2021 (*Apple*), ACM/19/035630.

1084. ACM, Position paper, 'Toezicht op algoritmes', 10 December 2020.

1085. ACM, report, 'Big Techs in the payment system', 16 November 2020.

1086. ACM, press release 2 February 2021, 'ACM sees risks associated with paid ranking for consumers and competition'.

1087. ACM, press release 18 May 2021, 'ACM launches market study into cloud services'.

1088. NRC, 18 January 2019, 'Eerst had ik een handvol cliënten, nu heb ik er 17 miljoen' (interview Martijn Snoep). Original Dutch text: '*Daar komt bij dat wij de scheidsrechter zijn die de spelregels moet handhaven. Als die scheidsrechter te vroeg fluit, maakt hij het spel dood. In een ontwikkelende markt moet je voorzichtig opereren, je moet niet te snel aan de bel trekken. We zijn wat voorzichtig, maar dat is ook om het spel niet kapot te maken.*'

offer many possibilities to prevent undesirable forms of personalisation. From a consumer perspective, a basic condition is that the consumer is clearly informed about the price to be paid. For example, he should not suddenly have to pay more in retrospect and offers must be real offers. As long as consumers are clearly informed of the price they are paying, even if it is different from the price paid by their neighbours, the requirements of current consumer legislation will be met. In addition, in the absence of market power, price discrimination is not likely to lead to restrictions of competition. The use of competition enforcement is therefore also unlikely to be fruitful'].[1089] Unsurprisingly, the ACM has generally supported the Digital Markets Act proposed by the European Commission and has advocated for new European *ex ante* measures to maintain a level playing field in digital payment services markets.[1090]

In the Digital Markets Act (DMA) proposal, the role of Member State representatives is limited to the Digital Markets Advisory Committee. This committee will support the Commission by issuing non-binding opinions. However, the Dutch view is that for an effective implementation of the DMA, it is important that the European Commission cooperates sufficiently with the national competition authorities and that it is not clear whether cooperation via the advisory committee is sufficient for this purpose.[1091] The ACM added in 2021: [Free translation: '*For a rapid and effective introduction of the DMA it is important that the Directorate-General for Competition of the European Commission fulfills a central role. The European authority can thereby be supported by national competition authorities, like the ACM. The European Commission and national competition authorities now have considerable experience in enforcement against Big Tech and broad knowledge of digital markets. The national competition authorities can support the European Commission for example by assisting with dawn raids or requests for information.*']1092

1089. 'Het Signaal 2018', *supra* n. 1060. Original Dutch text: '*Het huidige instrumentarium biedt weinig mogelijkheden om ongewenste vormen van personalisering tegen te gaan. Vanuit het consumentenperspectief is een basisvoorwaarde dat de consument duidelijk geïnformeerd wordt over de te betalen prijs. Zo mag hij achteraf niet opeens meer moeten betalen en moeten aanbiedingen ook echt aanbiedingen zijn. Zolang de consument duidelijk geïnformeerd wordt over de prijs die hij betaalt, ook al is die anders dan voor de buurman, is aan de vereisten van de huidige consumentenwetgeving voldaan. Daarnaast is in afwezigheid van marktmacht niet aannemelijk dat prijsdiscriminatie tot concurrentiebeperkingen leidt. Ook de inzet van het mededingingstoezicht is daarom waarschijnlijk niet vruchtbaar.*'

1090. ACM, report, 'Big Techs in the payment system', 16 November 2020 and ACM, press release 2 July 2021, 'Closure of the investigation into payment apps confirms need for new rules'.

1091. Dutch position on the proposal for the Digital Markets Act | Publication | The Netherlands at International Organisations (permanentrepresentations.nl); and non-paper: non-paper-friends-of-an-effective-digital-markets-act.pdf (bmwi.de).

1092. ACM, press release 23 June 2021, 'Nieuwe Europese concurrentieregels voor Big Techbedrijven kunnen nog effectiever'. Original Dutch text: '*Voor een snelle en effectieve introductie van de DMA is het van belang dat het Directoraat-Generaal Mededinging van de Europese Commissie een centrale rol vervult. Deze Europese toezichthouder kan daarbij ondersteund worden door nationale mededingingsautoriteiten, zoals de ACM. Zowel de Europese Commissie als die nationale autoriteiten hebben inmiddels veel ervaring met het toezicht op Big Tech en ruime kennis van digitale markten. De nationale autoriteiten kunnen de Europese Commissie ondersteunen door bijvoorbeeld mee te helpen bij invallen en informatie te verzamelen.*'

§8.02 CARTEL PROHIBITION

'So far, we haven't come across actual algorithmic collusion in the marketplace but [that's] probably the area of biggest concern to us, that that will happen and also because it will be so ... incredibly difficult to detect.'[1093]

The ACM has initiated three investigations under the cartel prohibition: an investigation into the parity clauses of Thuisbezorgd.nl, an online platform;[1094] an investigation into online sales restrictions by the Dutch bar association[1095] and an investigation into vertical online sales restrictions in the consumer electronics sector.[1096] These investigations have led to one rejection of the enforcement request,[1097] a voluntary change of behaviour[1098] and a fine imposed on Samsung of EUR 39.9 million.[1099]

The ACM also published a number of policy documents concerning cartels in digital markets: new vertical guidelines, including guidance on parity clauses (2015),[1100] a publication on algorithmic collusion (2018)[1101] and a position paper on guidelines for enforcement against infringements where algorithms play a role (2020).[1102]

[A] Policy Documents

[1] Vertical Agreements

The ACM published new guidance on its strategy and prioritisation in the supervision of vertical agreements in 2015.[1103] One of the examples cited by the ACM in the guidelines is the use of parity clauses. The ACM believes that parity clauses may in practice be potentially harmful, but also bring about efficiency improvements.[1104] The ACM indicates that broad parity clauses will be more problematic than narrow parity

1093. MLex, 'Algorithmic collusion "biggest concern" for Dutch competition enforcer, Snoep says', speech of M. Snoep at 'Blockchain + The Law' conference, Amsterdam Law & Technology Institute, 3 February 2022.
1094. ACM, decision 18 November 2016, ACM/DM/2016/207286 (*Thuisbezorgd.nl*).
1095. ACM, decision 14 December 2018, ACM/17/012061 (*handhavingsverzoek Legal Dutch*).
1096. ACM, decision 14 September 2021, ACM/20/040569 (*Samsung*).
1097. ACM, decision 18 November 2016, ACM/DM/2016/207286 (*Thuisbezorgd.nl*).
1098. ACM, decision 14 December 2018, ACM/17/012061 (*handhavingsverzoek Legal Dutch*).
1099. ACM, decision 14 September 2021, ACM/20/040569 (Samsung).
1100. ACM, guidelines, 'Leidraad afspraken tussen leveranciers en afnemers', 20 April 2015 and ACM, policy document, 'Het toezicht van ACM op verticale overeenkomsten: inzicht in strategie & prioritering', 20 April 2015.
1101. 'Het Signaal 2018', *supra* n. 1060.
1102. ACM, position paper, 'Toezicht op algoritmes', 10 December 2020.
1103. ACM, guidelines, 'Leidraad afspraken tussen leveranciers en afnemers', 20 April 2015 and ACM, policy document, 'Het toezicht van ACM op verticale overeenkomsten: inzicht in strategie & prioritering', 20 April 2015.
1104. ACM, policy document, 'Het toezicht van ACM op verticale overeenkomsten: inzicht in strategie & prioritering', 20 April 2015, p. 19.

clauses.[1105] The more likely it is that a parity clause permanently impedes entry to the platform market or increases platform prices and the less likely it is that efficiencies will occur, the more reason there is for the ACM to investigate further. Societal attention to parity clauses may also play a role in the consideration of whether or not to initiate a further investigation.

[2] Algorithms

In a publication of April 2018, the ACM stated that an automated cartel between self-learning algorithms is unlikely to infringe current Dutch and European competition law: [freely translated: '*A specific risk is that self-learning algorithms form automated cartels. Due to the amount of data and the ability to adjust prices at high speed, the algorithms can learn from scenarios and converge towards an equilibrium with higher prices. The outcome may be comparable to the damage caused by traditional cartel agreements. This is probably not contrary to current Dutch and European competition law, because there is no underlying agreement and no intention to form a cartel. This makes the situation comparable to tacit collusion or "smart tracking"*'].[1106] In december 2020 publiceerde de ACM een *position paper* over toezicht op algoritmes.[1107] Dit position paper is een startpunt van waaruit de ACM het toezicht op algoritmes verder wil ontwikkelen en geeft algemene richtlijnen voor onderzoek naar overtredingen waarbij algoritmische toepassingen een rol spelen. In 2022, ACM chairman Snoep said that algorithmic collusion was the ACM's biggest concern and that they are behind the pace of developments set by market players: '*So far, we haven't come across actual algorithmic collusion in the marketplace but [that's] probably the area of biggest concern to us, that that will happen and also because it will be so … incredibly difficult to detect* […] *We are … a little bit behind the development[s]. I don't think that is bad. I think it's good to let market forces and the markets develop first freely and then see whether there is a need for intervention into the market rather than the other way around.*'[1108]

1105. *Ibid.*, 20 April 2015, p. 25.
1106. 'Het Signaal 2018', *supra* n. 1060.
1107. ACM, position paper, 'Toezicht op algoritmes', 10 December 2020. Original text in Dutch: '*Een specifiek risico is dat zelflerende algoritmes geautomatiseerde kartels vormen. Dankzij de hoeveelheid data en de mogelijkheid om prijzen in hoog tempo aan te passen kunnen de algoritmes leren van scenario's en convergeren naar een evenwicht met hogere prijzen. De uitkomst daarvan kan vergelijkbaar zijn met de schade van klassieke kartelafspraken. Waarschijnlijk is dit niet in strijd met de huidige Nederlandse en Europese mededingingswetgeving, omdat er geen onderliggende afspraak is en geen intentie om een kartel te vormen. Daarmee is die situatie vergelijkbaar met stilzwijgende afstemming of "slim volggedrag"*'.
1108. MLex, 'Algorithmic collusion "biggest concern" for Dutch competition enforcer, Snoep says', speech of M. Snoep at 'Blockchain + The Law' conference, Amsterdam Law & Technology Institute, 3 February 2022.

[B] Enforcement

[1] Booking.com (2015)

The ACM decided not to start its own investigation of parity clauses used by online hotel booking website Booking.com. In a press release of April 2015, issued after Booking.com had made commitments to competition authorities in France, Italy and Sweden, the ACM announced that Booking.com would also apply the commitments in the Netherlands.[1109] In the press release the ACM stated that it hadn't started its own investigation in the expectation that the European approach would lead to the elimination of any risks on the Dutch market.

[2] Thuisbezorgd.nl (2016)

In 2016, the ACM started its first substantive investigation in the digital sector (into Thuisbezorgd.nl), following an enforcement request by Onder de Linde (OdL), a provider of chips and snacks that consumers can take away or have delivered.[1110] Thuisbezorgd.nl is an online platform that brings consumers into contact with restaurants and enables them to order meals. The enforcement request concerned a specific provision that Thuisbezorgd.nl applied in its general terms and conditions in respect of participating restaurants. These terms contained what is known as a 'narrow' parity clause, on the basis of which OdL had to apply the same prices as on Thuisbezorgd.nl, including discounts, for products on its own website and on its physical menu (equal-price guarantee).[1111] The ACM assessed whether there was a need to act in the case on the basis of three criteria:

(1) the extent to which the behaviour at issue is harmful to consumer welfare;
(2) the interest to society if the ACM were to act; and
(3) the extent to which ACM would be able to act effectively and efficiently.[1112]

In its market research, the ACM found that Thuisbezorgd.nl did not apply exclusivity clauses with the affiliated restaurants. A participating restaurant may switch to another platform if it does not want to accept the equal-price guarantee or is dissatisfied with the level of the commissions. Furthermore, the equal-price guarantee does not extend to the prices of the takeaway meals, which means restaurants can still compete with Thuiszorgbezorgd.nl by using lower prices or discounts for takeaway meals. The participating Thuisbezorgd.nl restaurants also have some room to differentiate the price of delivery meals by means of discounts or not to charge any payment

1109. ACM, press release 21 April 2015, 'ACM positief over Europese oplossing hotelboekingssite Booking.com'.
1110. ACM, decision 18 November 2016, ACM/DM/2016/207286 (*Thuisbezorgd.nl*).
1111. *Ibid.*, para. 2.
1112. *Ibid.*, para. 3.

costs for transactions via the direct sales channel – despite the equal-price guarantee.[1113] Based on the above findings, the ACM considered that the equal-price guarantee would not harm consumer welfare. Moreover, the ACM did not consider it necessary to act, as the market was growing.[1114] Therefore, the ACM decided not to investigate the issue further and to reject OdL's enforcement request.

[3] NOvA (2018)

In 2018, the *Nederlandse Orde van Advocaten* (the Dutch Bar Association) (NOvA) amended the explanatory notes to its Rules of Conduct (*Gedragsregels*) following a complaint filed with the ACM by LegalDutch (an online platform that focuses on linking litigants to suitable lawyers).[1115] This adjustment was made at the insistence of the ACM and was followed by the publication of a formal decision by the ACM, rejecting the complaint by LegalDutch.[1116]

The stumbling block was the so-called ban on lawyers collecting a commission under Rule of Conduct 2(3). This rule read as follows: '*Het is de advocaat niet toegestaan een beloning toe te kennen of te ontvangen voor het verkrijgen of aanbrengen van opdrachten, tenzij de advocaat kan aantonen dat hij daarbij niet handelt in strijd met de kernwaarden en voorts dat hierbij slechts het belang van de rechtzoekende bepalend is*' [freely translated: '*An attorney is not allowed to award or receive any remuneration for obtaining or placing engagements, unless the attorney can demonstrate that he is not acting contrary to the core values and furthermore that only the interest of the person seeking justice is decisive in this respect.*']. The ACM's investigation revealed that the development of comparison websites for lawyers may be restricted due to a lack of clarity about the interpretation of the Rules of Conduct for lawyers.[1117] After the ACM confronted the NOvA with its findings, the NOvA amended the explanatory notes.[1118]

The new explanatory notes provide (in summary) that referrals that take place on the basis of transparent and clear criteria (e.g., expertise, location, hourly rates, referral of remuneration) and against a reasonable remuneration and when compared to the interest and importance of the case, are in accordance with Rule 2(3). The lawyer can demonstrate that the professional standards are not violated by being transparent about the level and type of remuneration so that the client can form an opinion about, among other things, the independent and partisan service provided by the lawyer.[1119] ACM chairman of the board Snoep says about this new interpretation: '*De uitleg van de Nederlandse Orde van Advocaten van de Gedragsregels voor advocaten haalt een belemmering weg voor vergelijkingssites om advocaten en cliënten bij elkaar te brengen*'

1113. *Ibid.*, para. 12.
1114. *Ibid.*, para. 13.
1115. ACM, press release 13 December 2018, 'Gedragsregels advocaten mogen opkomst online platforms advocaten niet belemmeren'.
1116. ACM decision 14 December 2018, ACM/17/012061 (*handhavingsverzoek Legal Dutch*).
1117. *Ibid.*, para. 20.
1118. *Ibid.*, para. 21.
1119. Nederlandse Orde van Advocaten, Toelichting Gedragsregels Advocatuur 2018,

[freely translated: '*The interpretation of the Dutch Bar Association of the Code of Conduct for lawyers removes an obstacle to comparison sites for bringing lawyers and clients together. That's good news for consumers and businesses looking for legal aid.*']. As the clarification of the explanatory notes closed the case for the ACM, the ACM dismissed LegalDutch's complaint.[1120]

[4] Samsung (2021)

On 14 September 2021, the ACM imposed a fine of EUR 39.9 million on Samsung Electronics B.V. for exercising an illegal influence on the online retail prices for television sets of seven retailers from January 2013 to December 2018.[1121] By means of so-called spider software and price comparison sites, Samsung systematically monitored the price movements of its products in the retail sector. When prices fell below the recommended retail price, Samsung contacted the relevant retailer to draw their attention to the recommended retail price once again and to report that other retailers were advised in the same way. The ACM considers that the aforementioned monitoring by Samsung contributes to a climate in which retailers are discouraged in advance from implementing price increases.[1122]

The ACM considers that Samsung's attempts to influence online retail prices constitute a restriction of competition by object: [Free translation] '*Samsung puts pressure on the retailers with its behaviour. Samsung's practice is aimed at protecting its profit margins and those of its retailers and, as such, facilitates a restriction of competition that is disadvantageous to the customer. [...] The behaviour is aimed at restricting competition.*'[1123] The ACM takes into account, among other factors, the systematic nature of Samsung's interventions in the pricing of its retailers and Samsung's high market share in the Dutch television market in its considerations for the determination of the level of the fine.[1124] The fine is lower because Samsung Electronics did not use coercion or sanctions to maintain the recommended retail price and because this was its first infringement of this kind.[1125] Samsung has filed a request for administrative review against the fine decision.[1126] By decision of 21 November 2022, the ACM declared all arguments brought forward by Samsung unfounded and upheld the fine in its entirety.[1127]

1120. ACM decision 14 December 2018, ACM/17/012061 (*handhavingsverzoek Legal Dutch*).
1121. ACM, decision 14 September 2021, ACM/20/040569 (*Samsung*).
1122. *Ibid.*, para. 403.
1123. *Ibid.*, para. 410. Original Dutch text: '*Samsung zet met haar gedrag detailhandelaren onder druk. De praktijk van Samsung is erop gericht de marges van detailhandelaren en die van haarzelf te beschermen en werkt zodanig dat daarmee de mededinging wordt belemmerd ten nadele van de consument. [...] Het gedrag heeft een mededingingsbeperkende strekking.*'
1124. ACM, decision 14 September 2021, ACM/20/040569 (*Samsung*), paras 502-503.
1125. *Ibid.*, para. 505.
1126. NOS, 'Dutch fine of 39 million euros for Samsung because of price influence', 29 September 2019.
1127. ACM, decision 21 November 2022, ACM/21/167383, (*Samsung*), https://www.acm.nl/system/files/documents/besluit-op-bezwaar-samsung-voor-ongeoorloofde-beinvloeding-verkoopprijzen-televisies.pdf.

§8.03 ABUSE OF A DOMINANT POSITION

The ACM has initiated three abuse of dominance investigations: two investigations for imposing unfair trading conditions on providers of dating apps, one into Apple[1128] and one into Google[1129] and an investigation into a refusal to supply Dutch registered (.nl) domain name data.[1130] These investigations have led to an order subject to periodic penalty payments on Apple[1131] and a decision rejecting an enforcement request.[1132] The Google investigation is ongoing.

The ACM also published various policy documents concerning abuse of a dominant position in digital markets: a report on online platforms (2016),[1133] a report on online video services (2016),[1134] a market study into mobile app stores (2019),[1135] a market study on the Dutch (online) payment market (2020),[1136] a study into payment apps' access to NFC communication (2021),[1137] a market study on sponsored internet rankings (2021),[1138] a market study into IP interconnection[1139] and a market study into MaaS (2021).[1140] The ACM also started a market investigation into cloud services in 2021.[1141]

[A] Policy Documents

[1] Big Platforms (2016)

In 2016, the ACM published its report 'Big Platforms, Big Problems', in which the ACM addressed the dominant market position that online platforms can obtain by collecting data and through potential network effects.[1142] The ACM draws two important conclusions in this report: on the one hand, the various characteristic and earning

1128. ACM, summary of decision 24 August 2021 (*Apple*), ACM/19/035630.
1129. NOS, 'ACM start vooronderzoek naar Google na klacht over machtsmisbruik', 4 May 2022 and Reuters, 'With Apple fight ongoing, Dutch watchdog ACM to investigate Google Play store practices', 4 May 2022.
1130. ACM, decision 19 April 2021, ACM/21/049853 (*SIDN*).
1131. ACM, summary of decision 24 August 2021 (*Apple*), ACM/19/035630.
1132. ACM, decision 19 April 2021, ACM/21/049853 (*SIDN*).
1133. ACM, publication, 'Grote platforms, grote Problemen? Een Beschouwing van Online Platforms Vanuit Mededingingsperspectief', 21 September 2016.
1134. ACM, report, 'Online video platforms onder de loep', 22 August 2017.
1135. ACM, report, 'Market Study into Mobile App Stores', 11 April 2019.
1136. ACM, report, 'Big Techs in the payment system', 16 November 2020.
1137. ACM, press release 2 July 2021, 'Closure of the investigation into payment apps confirms need for new rules'.
1138. ACM, press release 2 February 2021, 'ACM sees risks associated with paid ranking for consumers and competition'.
1139. ACM, press release 13 July 2021, 'ACM onderzoekt markt voor digitale infrastructuur: Nederland is nog altijd goed verbonden'.
1140. ACM, press release 8 March 2021, 'Mobility as a Service is still evolving – ACM is positive, but keeps a close watch on bottlenecks'.
1141. ACM, press release 18 May 2021, 'ACM launches market study into cloud services'.
1142. ACM, publication, 'Grote platforms, grote Problemen? Een Beschouwing van Online Platforms Vanuit Mededingingsperspectief', 21 September 2016.

models make it difficult to identify potential competition problems through *ex ante* competition monitoring (i.e., by a single set of regulatory measures). On the other hand, the ACM concludes that *ex post* competition monitoring is not easy with regard to online platforms, as it is difficult to determine whether there is actually a problem: [free translation: '*The effect of companies' behaviour on consumer welfare is the starting point for action by ACM. (...) The potential damage caused by online platforms is often offset by benefits, such as innovations based on consumer data. ACM will have to weigh the pros and cons on a case-by-case basis to assess the impact on consumer welfare. Conceptual challenges, such as being able to define a market, will not be an obstacle to pursuing a case if ACM is convinced that there is a problem.*'].[1143]

[2] Online Video Services (2016)

In 2016, the ACM also reviewed the Dutch market for online video services. Based on this research, it published the report 'online videoplatforms onder de loep' [freely translated: 'online video platforms under the microscope'].[1144] The ACM established that two US companies, Google and Facebook, hold strong positions in the provision of online search, display and video advertising space, and these two companies in particular dominate the field. Nevertheless, according to the ACM, there are indications that the markets in which Google and Facebook are active remain '*zeer dynamisch, innovatief en competitief*' [freely translated: '*very dynamic, innovative and competitive*']. The ACM observed that the prices for online advertising space through Google and Facebook are not significantly higher than those for products offered via other players. The ACM also saw the emergence of several trends that compete with the above markets, such as the emergence of TV ads, the use of authentication services, and the emergence of advertising platforms and data platforms. The ACM concluded that there is currently sufficient competition between market participants and that there is sufficient dynamism in the market. However, it added to this that the likelihood of competition problems and their impact are closely linked to further market developments: '*Die ontwikkelingen blijven we de komende tijd kritisch volgen*' [freely translated: '*We will continue to monitor these developments critically in the coming period*'].

1143. ACM, publication, 'Grote platforms, grote Problemen? Een Beschouwing van Online Platforms Vanuit Mededingingsperspectief', 21 September 2016. Original Dutch text: '*Het effect van gedragingen van ondernemingen op de consumentenwelvaart is het uitgangspunt voor optreden door ACM. (...) Tegenover de potentiële schade die online platforms veroorzaken staan vaak ook voordelen, zoals innovaties op basis van consumentendata. ACM zal per geval een afweging moeten maken van de voor-en nadelen om het effect op de consumentenwelvaart te beoordelen. Conceptuele uitdagingen, zoals het kunnen afbakenen van een markt, zullen geen belemmering zijn om een zaak door te zetten als ACM ervan overtuigd is dat er een probleem bestaat.*'

1144. ACM, report, 'Online video platforms onder de loep', 22 August 2017.

[3] Mobile App Stores (2019)

On 11 April 2019, the ACM published its report *Market Study into Mobile App Stores*, which focuses on the app stores of Apple and Google.[1145] Simultaneously, the ACM announced its intention to start an investigation into the Apple App Store. The ACM considers that the app stores of Apple and Google form a 'bottleneck' for providers of apps and consumers who use the mobile OS of Apple and Google. The main conclusion of the report is that there are three types of behaviour by Apple and Google via their app stores that raise concern, in particular:

(i) *Favouring own apps over apps from other providers*. For example, Apple and Google can pre-install their own apps. Own apps also do not pay any commission for inclusion in the App Store and have 'full hardware interoperability'. According to the ACM, this justifies the question of '*whether there is, in fact, competition on the merits between apps*'.[1146]

(ii) *Unequal treatment of apps in general*. Apple and Google control the extent to which an app can use hardware components of a mobile phone (*hardware interoperability*), access to payment data via apps (*in-app purchase data*) and finally, Apple and Google can control consumer choice. According to the ACM, the app stores therefore influence competition between apps.

(iii) *Lack of transparency*. The report shows that providers of apps complain about the lack of transparency observed by Apple and Google, especially when it comes to the interpretation of the terms and conditions of Apple and Google and about the removal of apps from the app stores. The ACM indicates that these complaints require further attention from the ACM. At this stage however, ACM does not want to prioritise these complaints due to the entry into force of the Platform to Business Regulation, which would oblige Apple and Google to apply greater transparency.[1147]

According to the ACM, it is necessary to examine whether the first two types of behaviour are systematic. The ACM states that Apple and Google may occasionally make 'mistakes' as long as there is no systematically harmful behaviour: '*Naturally, in a market place as large as the app stores, mistakes can be made, and therefore it is necessary to investigate whether certain conduct is done systematically.*'[1148] Interestingly, the ACM already anticipates a possible finding of systematically harmful behaviour: '*On the premise that intervention is needed, it can be debated whether there is a need for ex-ante regulation.*' The ACM observes that under its current powers, it can

1145. ACM, report, 'Market Study into Mobile App Stores', 11 April 2019. In July 2018 the ACM launched this market investigation, *see* ACM, press release 25 July 2018, 'ACM Start Marktstudie Appstores Voor Mobiele Telefoons'.

1146. ACM, report, 'Market Study into Mobile App Stores', 11 April 2019.

1147. Regulation 2019/1150 of the European Parliament and the Council of 20 June 2019 on promoting fairness and transparency for business users of online intermediation services.

1148. ACM, report, 'Market Study into Mobile App Stores', 11 April 2019, p. 108.

address the most problematic behaviour, but *ex ante* regulation '*may increase certainty for app developers, and prevent problems (new or otherwise) from arising*'.[1149]

[4] Online Payment Markets and NFC Communication (2020)

On 1 December 2020, the ACM published a market study on the activities of Apple, Amazon, Ant Group, Facebook, Google and Tencent on the Dutch (online) payment market.[1150] The ACM notes: '*At the moment, the role of Big Tech companies on the Dutch payment market is still limited, but ACM also sees that Big Tech companies are strengthening their positions on the market through acquisitions and collaborations.*'[1151] The ACM notes that the activities of Big Tech on payment markets in the Netherlands and the rest of Europe lag behind the developments in payment markets in the rest of the world, but the ACM expects that Big Tech companies will continue to expand their activities in the Dutch payment market. This expansion will come with risks that '*are related primarily to the fact that Big Techs operate an ecosystem or platform-ecosystem, to which large groups of users are tied to a certain extent*'.[1152] The risks that the ACM sees are: '*refusal to grant access or unreasonable access conditions, bundling, preferential treatment, for example, of their own services and abuse involving (possibly large-scale) data use*'. The tools at the ACM's disposal, competition enforcement or enforcement under the PSD2 Directive, are insufficient to address these risks: '*The use of the current toolkit is too slow in highly dynamic and innovative markets such as the markets for ecosystems. In payment markets there are large direct and indirect network effects, users are inclined to stay loyal for longer and there are high access barriers as a result of data collection that impede a level playing field.*'[1153] The ACM therefore advocates the adoption of new European ex ante measures that can help maintain a level playing field, either through the adoption of the Digital Markets Act or through the expansion of the scope of the PSD2 Directive.

Shortly after the publication of the report, on 4 December 2020, the ACM announced a new study into payment apps' access to Near-Field Communication (NFC) communication. The ACM: '*NFC communication offers the ability to make contactless payments using smartphones in brick-and-mortar stores. The software on some smartphones only allows the software developer's own payment app to connect to NFC communication. This problem may stifle innovation with respect to payment apps, and it reduces the freedom of choice for consumers and businesses.*'[1154] Seven months later, the ACM concluded that market participants with a potential interest in developing applications based on the NFC technology, are not provided with access to the technology and have therefore not even started developing apps on the basis of the

1149. *Ibid.*
1150. ACM, report, 'Big Techs in the payment system', 16 November 2020.
1151. ACM, press release 1 December 2020, 'ACM Study: Big Techs in the Dutch payment system'.
1152. ACM, report, 'Big Techs in the payment system', 16 November 2020, p. 43.
1153. *Ibid.*, p. 61.
1154. ACM, press release 4 December 2020, 'ACM launches an investigation into users' freedom of choice regarding payment apps on smartphones'.

technology.[1155] This raises concern for the ACM, because the Interchange Fee Regulation (IFR), providing a legal basis for intervening in cases where technical service providers act as gatekeepers, can only be relied upon where there is a choice between different payment apps. According to the ACM new European rules are therefore required. Martijn Snoep, ACM chairman: '*This investigation confirms that access to NFC technology is crucial for the development of payments apps from which consumers and retailers are able to choose. These European rules do not give us the tools to mandate such access in the Netherlands. That is only possible if a competitor payment app already exists, but, apparently, that requires access to NFC technology. So this is a classic catch-22 situation. That is why we would welcome amendments to the European rules.*'[1156]

[5] Sponsored Internet Rankings (2021)

On 2 February 2021, the ACM published a market study on sponsored internet rankings, finding that these entail risks for competition and consumers: '*Consumers may be misled by the presented search results, if it is unclear that the ranking is influenced by payments. Moreover, it may restrict competition among providers.*'[1157] The market study has a strong consumer protection law angle, focusing on transparency requirements as a way of mitigating risks for consumers and companies. The ACM however also notes that the prohibition on abuse of dominance can play a role in effective enforcement where it can be shown that "the lack of transparency distorts competition".[1158] In addition, sponsored ranking may, according to the ACM, in itself infringe competition law where it '*significantly restricts competition on the merits between suppliers*'. The ACM does unfortunately not elaborate on these points in the market study.

In 2021, the ACM also published a market study into MaaS in the Netherlands.[1159] MaaS are services that allow travellers '*to plan, book, and pay for trips from doorstep to destination*'.[1160] The report published by the ACM is not only devoted to competition law, but the ACM warns that it will be vigilant in view of a potential 'winner-takes-all' scenario: [free translation '*there is also a concern about an undesired "winner-takes-all" scenario whereby a dominant (tech-) company obtains too much power and thereby is*

1155. ACM, press release 2 July 2021, 'Closure of the investigation into payment apps confirms need for new rules'.
1156. *Ibid.*
1157. ACM, press release 2 February 2021, 'ACM sees risks associated with paid ranking for consumers and competition'.
1158. ACM, market study, 2 February 2021, 'Sponsored Ranking: an exploration of its effect on consumer welfare', para. 11.
1159. ACM, press release 8 March 2021, 'Mobility as a Service is still evolving – ACM is positive, but keeps a close watch on bottlenecks'.
1160. *Ibid.*

able to exclude or exploit other companies. This can subsequently be an impediment to further innovation and/or lead to higher prices'.].[1161]

[6] IP Interconnection (2021)

Still, in 2021, the ACM published a market study into IP interconnection, which is important for well-functioning internet connections.[1162] The market study contains a small section on abuse of dominance issues, where the ACM notes that the market for interconnection has structural features that heighten the risk of abuse of dominance by internet access providers (IAPs), such as VodafoneZiggo and T-mobile. The ACM notes that IAPs in practice have a 100% market share in relation to the end users that depend on a specific IAP. The ACM lists a couple of examples of potential harmful conduct: [free translation '*Examples of conduct of parties with a dominant position that could be harmful for competition on the market for IP interconnection, are unfair (peering- or transit) conditions; quality discrimination; tying and excessive pricing.*'].[1163]

[7] Cloud Services (2021)

Finally, in May 2021, the ACM started a market investigation into cloud services, services providing on-demand availability of computer system resources, in May 2021.[1164] The ACM stated: '*ACM will look into the design (technical or otherwise) of cloud services, and what the implications thereof are on services that function on the basis of cloud services. In addition, ACM will also assess whether there are any market imperfections such as market power, lock-in effects, and information asymmetry.*'

[B] Enforcement

[1] SIDN (2021)

On 19 April 2021, the ACM decided to reject an enforcement request from Dataprovider B.V., a provider of online brand protection services.[1165] According to Dataprovider, the

---

1161. ACM, market study, 8 March 2021, 'Hoofdbevindingen marktstudie MaaS'. Original Dutch text: '*er [is] ook een bezorgdheid over een ongewenst "winner-takes-all" scenario waarbij een dominant (tech-)bedrijf te veel macht naar zich toetrekt en daarmee andere partijen kan uitsluiten of uitbuiten. Dat kan dan vervolgens een rem op verdere innovatie zetten en/of leiden tot hogere prijzen*'.

1162. ACM, press release 13 July 2021, 'ACM onderzoekt markt voor digitale infrastructuur: Nederland is nog altijd goed verbonden' and ACM, report, 'Marktstudie IP interconnectie 2021', 13 July 2021.

1163. ACM, report, 'Marktstudie IP interconnectie 2021', 13 July 2021, p. 39/46. Original Dutch text: '*Voorbeelden van gedragingen van partijen met een machtspositie die schadelijk kunnen zijn voor de mededinging op de IP-interconnectiemarkt zijn onbillijke (peering- of transit)voorwaarden; kwaliteitsdiscriminatie, koppelverkoop en buitensporig hoge tarieven.*'

1164. ACM, press release 18 May 2021, 'ACM launches market study into cloud services'.

1165. ACM, decision 19 April 2021, ACM/21/049853 (*SIDN*).

Stichting Internet Domeinnaam Registratie (SIDN), the administrator of the.nl domain, has abused its dominant position by refusing to provide Dataprovider with a complete list of all.nl domain names. The ACM observes that SIDN has indeed refused to provide this information.[1166] According to Dataprovider, this refusal leads to unfair competition because SIDN offers services that compete with those of Dataprovider.[1167] However, the ACM notes that the.nl domain information of SIDN is not indispensable for the conduct of Dataprovider's business, nor does it eliminate all competition.[1168] Dataprovider itself has (remarkably) stated that the information is indeed not necessary for it to be able to offer its services.[1169] On this basis, the ACM concludes that there are no indications that the refusal to provide the requested information would constitute an abuse of a dominant position.[1170] The ACM consequently rejects the request for enforcement.

[2] Apple (2021)

On 24 August 2021, the ACM imposed an order subject to periodic penalty payments on Apple for imposing unfair trading conditions on providers of dating apps.[1171] Apple only complied with the order in June 2022, after incurring EUR 50 million in penalty payments.[1172] The ACM found that Apple has a dominant position on the market for app store services on the mobile operating system iOS for dating-app providers.[1173] According to the ACM, dating-app providers do not have any substitutes for Apple's app store service, because dating-app providers need to be present in the Apple and Google app stores: '*Consumers that use dating services assume that the reach of their dating app is not limited to the mobile operating system on which the app has been downloaded. Dating-app providers are therefore forced, even more so than the average app provider, to be present in the both the App Store and the Google Play Store.*'[1174]

According to the ACM, Apple limits app providers in their freedom of choice by requiring app providers to use Apple's payment system when they offer digital content or services within the app for a fee: '*the app provider is required to agree to additional contractual conditions set by Apple. These conditions mandate the app provider to use*

1166. *Ibid.*, para. 13.
1167. *Ibid.*, para. 7.
1168. *Ibid.*, para. 26.
1169. *Ibid.*, para. 25.
1170. *Ibid.*, para. 27.
1171. ACM, summary of decision 24 August 2021 (*Apple*), ACM/19/035630. The text of the full decision was not published on the date this publication was sent to the publisher. The ACM has been in frequent contact with the European Commission with regard to the scope of its investigation in light of the EC's own investigation into the Apple App Store (*see* Chapter 4, European Commission). The ACM declared in June 2021 that it would be able to continue its Apple App Store. *See*: ACM, press release 22 June 2021, 'ACM kan onderzoek naar Apple AppStore voortzetten'.
1172. ACM, press release 11 June 2022, 'Apple changes unfair conditions, allows alternative payments methods in dating apps'.
1173. ACM, summary of decision 24 August 2021 (*Apple*), ACM/19/035630, para. 13.
1174. *Ibid.*, para. 11.

Apple's IAP system for the processing of payments.'[1175] The app providers are also not allowed to refer within their own apps to payment options outside the app.[1176] Apple argues that the conditions it imposes on providers of dating apps are necessary to ensure quality, privacy and safety of its services. However, the ACM notes that '*Apple can also achieve these objectives in other less harmful ways*'.[1177] The ACM therefore concludes that the conditions are unreasonable and constitute abuse.

The ACM orders Apple to change its conditions in such a way that dating-app providers are free to choose their payment provider and to refer to other payment systems outside the app.[1178] Pursuant to the decision, the ACM may impose a weekly penalty of EUR 5 million per week if Apple fails to comply with the order, with a maximum of EUR 50 million.

The Rotterdam district court, in a summary relief procedure, largely upheld the ACM's decision in a ruling of 24 December 2021.[1179] In a press release of January 2022, the ACM announced that Apple did not comply with its order: '*Apple has failed to satisfy the requirements on several points. The most important one is that Apple has failed to adjust its conditions, as a result of which dating-app providers are still unable to use other payment systems.*'[1180] The ACM also stated that it would start imposing weekly penalties if Apple's non-compliance continued. In a press release of February 2022, the ACM announced that Apple had changed its conditions, requiring dating-app providers to develop a new app if they wish to use an alternative payment system.[1181] The ACM is not happy with the new conditions: '*App providers cannot adjust their existing apps. ACM finds this to be an unreasonable condition that is at odds with the requirements that Apple had set out.*' According to the ACM, Apple therefore does not comply with its order and Apple must therefore pay the weekly fines of EUR 5 million. At the end of March, the ACM reported that Apple had changed its proposal and that the ACM would consult market participants about the revised proposal.[1182] On the day of this press release, the total fine stood at the maximum of EUR 50 million and the ACM warned that it may impose '*another order subject to periodic penalty payments (with possibly higher penalties this time around) in order to stimulate Apple to comply with the order*'.[1183] In June 2022, the ACM announced that it would no longer need to impose a new order subject to penalty payments because Apple changed its unfair conditions.[1184] The ACM added: '*From now on, dating-app providers are able to let their*

1175. *Ibid.*, para. 3.
1176. *Ibid.*, para. 16.
1177. *Ibid.*, para. 18.
1178. *Ibid.*, para. 20.
1179. Rotterdam district court, judgment of 24 December 2021, ECLI:NL:RBROT:2021:12851.
1180. ACM, press release 24 January 2022, 'Apple voldoet niet aan de eisen van de ACM'.
1181. ACM, Press release 14 February 2022, 'Developing a new app is an unnecessary and unreasonable condition that Apple imposes on dating-app providers'.
1182. ACM, press release 28 March 2022, 'ACM to assess adjusted proposal of Apple regarding its conditions for dating apps'.
1183. *Ibid.*
1184. ACM, press release 11 June 2022, 'Apple changes unfair conditions, allows alternative payments methods in dating apps'.

customers pay in different ways'. An appeal by Apple against the ACM's initial order subject to penalty payments is pending.

[3] Google (2022)

In May 2022, several news sources reported that the ACM had started an investigation into Google after a complaint from Match Group, the parent company of the dating app Tinder.[1185] Allegedly, dating apps are no longer allowed to use another payment system than Google's payment system and or to refer to other payment options. It remains to be seen how this case, that has clear similarities with the Apple case, will play out. At first sight, it is surprising that Google puts in place a new payment system policy precisely at a moment when Apple is fined for a seemingly similar policy.

§8.04 MERGER CONTROL

The ACM has assessed three mergers in the field of digital competition during the period under review.[1186] In each of these cases, the merger was approved subject to a behavioural remedy. The first case concerned a vertical merger, whereby a publisher of learning materials acquired a distributor of learning materials that owned a major platform for e-learning in the Netherlands.[1187] The merger was cleared subject to an access remedy whereby third-party publishers would get access to the platform under FRAND terms. The other two cases were joint ventures in the MaaS sector. The first was a joint venture between two, mostly vertically related, companies: the largest provider of public transport in the Netherlands (NS) and a major supplier of transportation means including shared bicycles (Pon).[1188] The joint venture, aiming to offer mobility services through an app, was approved by the ACM subject to a commitment that the parties shall offer their shared bicycle and train services to third parties under the same conditions as they will offer these services to the JV. The second case concerned a joint venture between virtually all major Dutch public transport companies, aimed at creating a MaaS wholesale platform, connecting providers of mobility services with providers of retail MaaS services.[1189] The ACM cleared this joint venture subject to an access remedy and a supply remedy. The access remedy entails that the parties give third-party mobility providers and MaaS providers access to the platform

1185. NOS, 'ACM start vooronderzoek naar Google na klacht over machtsmisbruik', 4 May 2022 and Reuters, 'With Apple fight ongoing, Dutch watchdog ACM to investigate Google Play store practices', 4 May 2022.

1186. ACM, decision 20 May 2020, ACM/20/038614 (*NS Groep N.V./Pon Netherlands B.V./JV*); ACM, decision 28 August 2019, ACM/19/035555 (*Sanoma Learning B.V./Iddink Holding B.V.*); ACM, decision 9 July 2020, ACM/20/039644 (*GVB Holding N.V./HTM Personenvervoer N.V./NS Groep N.V./Rotterdamse Electrische Tram N.V.*).

1187. ACM, decision 20 May 2020, ACM/20/038614 (NS Groep N.V./Pon Netherlands B.V./JV)

1188. ACM, decision 28 August 2019, ACM/19/035555 (*Sanoma Learning B.V./Iddink Holding B.V.*).

1189. ACM, decision 9 July 2020, ACM/20/039644 (*GVB Holding N.V./HTM Personenvervoer N.V./NS Groep N.V./Rotterdamse Electrische Tram N.V.*).

under FRAND conditions. The supply remedy entails that the parties will supply their mobility services to third-party MaaS providers regardless of whether these MaaS providers are connected to the JV's platform or not, and under equal conditions.

In October 2021, the ACM published new merger control procedure guidelines.[1190] These guidelines include, among other changes, an adaptation to the European Commission's new policy on Article 22 EUMR referrals that was published in March 2021 (*see* Chapter 4).[1191] The ACM has aligned itself with the Commission's policy to claim residual jurisdiction over acquisitions of companies with low turnover but high competitive potential, also called killer acquisitions, that do not meet EU or national thresholds. The new guidelines now clearly state that the ACM may refer non-reportable transactions to the Commission under Article 22.[1192] In addition, a section of the previous 2013 guidelines, stating that the ACM would exercise restraint in the submission of Article 22 requests to the Commission, has been deleted. In the field of digital competition, the ACM has, to date, not submitted any referral requests but it has joined referral requests by Austria in *Facebook (Meta)/Kustomer*[1193] and by France in *Illumina/GRAIL.*[1194]

[A] Sanoma/Iddink (2019)

On 28 August 2019, the ACM approved the takeover of Iddink by Sanoma in Phase 2 subject to an access remedy.[1195] A vertical relationship exists between Sanoma and Iddink. Sanoma, through its subsidiary Malmberg, is a publisher of digital learning materials for high school students. Iddink is a distributor of learning materials and owns Magister, a platform for e-learning. According to the ACM, Magister is an important platform for publishers such as Malmberg, because schools and their students have access to learning materials through Magister.

1190. ACM, policy document, 'Werkwijze bij concentratiezaken', 6 October 2021.

1191. European Commission, Communication, 'Commission Guidance on the application of the referral mechanism set out in Article 22 of the Merger Regulation to certain categories of cases', C(2021) 1959 final, 26 March 2021. In essence, this policy aims at capturing killer acquisitions, or acquisitions of companies with low turnover, but high competitive potential, that are currently not reviewed by the European Commission or by national competition authorities.

1192. ACM, policy document, 'Werkwijze bij concentratiezaken', 6 October 2021, para. 155: '*Op basis van artikel 22 van de Europese Concentratieverordening kan de ACM namens de Minister van Economische Zaken en Klimaat de Europese Commissie verzoeken om een concentratie die niet bij de ACM gemeld hoeft te worden te onderzoeken of de behandeling van een bij de ACM gemelde concentratie over te nemen.*'

1193. ACM, press release 12 May 2021, 'ACM ondersteunt verzoek tot onderzoek overname Kustomer door Facebook' and European Commission, press release 12 May 2021, 'Mergers: Commission to assess proposed acquisition of Kustomer by Facebook'.

1194. ACM, press release 20 April 2021, 'Europese Commissie gaat farma-overname Illumina – GRAIL onderzoeken', https://www.acm.nl/nl/publicaties/europese-commissie-gaat-farma-overname-illumina-grail-onderzoeken, and European Commission, *Daily News*, 20 April 2021, 'Mergers: Commission to assess proposed acquisition of GRAIL by Illumina', https://ec.europa.eu/commission/presscorner/detail/en/mex_21_1846.

1195. ACM, decision 28 August 2019, ACM/19/035555 (*Sanoma Learning B.V./Iddink Holding B.V.*).

The ACM finds that Magister has a share of 50% to 70% on the market for e-learning environments and student information systems.[1196] In addition, 92% of Dutch schools use e-learning environments and 70% use e-learning environments to enable access to digital learning materials. The ACM finds that Sanoma would have the possibility to improve interoperability between Magister and Malmberg learning materials with respect to learning materials of third-party publishers. Sanoma would also have the incentive to improve interoperability because schools are unlikely to switch away from Magister and it would be profitable for Sanoma if it sells more Malmberg learning materials.[1197] Some schools also indicated that they would prefer learning materials from publishers with improved interoperability. The ACM concludes that the merger will put competing publishers of learning materials at a disadvantage and will raise entry barriers for publishers. The merger would therefore lead to a significant impediment to competition on the market for publication of learning materials in the eyes of the ACM.

Sanoma addresses the ACM's concerns by offering access to the Magister application programming interface (API) to third-party publishers under FRAND terms.[1198] Sanoma also commits to providing any data from Magister requested by third-party publishers under FRAND terms, to the extent that Magister provides comparable data to Malmberg. The commitments also include a system of 'Chinese walls' to prevent Malmberg from obtaining competitively sensitive information on third-party publishers that use Magister. This entails, in practice, that Malmberg and Magister operate as separate businesses, separated by technical firewalls and a cooling down obligation for any employee who changes employment from Malmberg to Magister.[1199] An independent accountant will verify whether Sanoma complies with the commitments on an annual basis.[1200] The commitments apply for an unlimited duration but may be amended upon a substantiated request by Sanoma.[1201]

On 4 March 2021, the Rotterdam district court annulled the ACM's decision after an appeal from Noordhoff, a publisher of learning materials.[1202] The court found that the decision is partially insufficiently reasoned. The ACM has appealed the judgment.[1203] Despite the annulment of the decision, Sanoma indicated that it would continue to abide by the commitments until the ACM has made a new decision. The ACM published this new decision on 26 August 2021, in which it cleared the transaction under the same conditions as in 2019.[1204]

1196. *Ibid.*, para. 67.
1197. *Ibid.*, paras 74-75.
1198. *Ibid.*, para. 194.
1199. *Ibid.*, para. 183. The duration of the cooling down period is not disclosed.
1200. *Ibid.*, para. 190.
1201. *Ibid.*, annex 2, remedy proposal.
1202. Rotterdam District Court, judgment 4 March 2021, ECLI:NL:RBROT:2021:1766.
1203. ACM, press release 16 April 2021, 'ACM gaat in hoger beroep tegen de vernietiging van het overnamebesluit Sanoma/Iddink'.
1204. ACM, decision 26 August 2021, ACM/21/050971 (*Sanoma Learning B.V./Iddink Holding B.V.*).

[B] NS/Pon/Mobility Services JV (2020)

On 20 May 2020, the ACM approved a joint venture between NS Groep and Pon Netherlands in Phase 1 subject to a supply remedy.[1205] NS and Pon are both active in the field of transport and mobility. NS is the largest provider of public transport by train in the Netherlands and also offers shared bicycles and cars at train stations. Pon supplies and imports transportation means, such as cars, scooters and bicycles and also offers shared bicycles and public transport subscriptions to consumers. The JV aims to offer mobility services through an app, including transportation services for third parties.

The ACM defines a national 'retail market for the provision of integrated transport and mobility services through an app', also called integrated MaaS.[1206] Interestingly, this market definition is narrower than the definition of the European Commission, which concluded that integrated (multimodal) MaaS services and individual transport services are part of the same product market.[1207] According to the Commission, these services are substitutable to a certain degree. The ACM agrees with the Commission that providers of integrated MaaS are currently in competition with providers of unimodal transport services, but the ACM considers it plausible that the market 'within the foreseeable future' will change into a more narrow market for integrated MaaS only.[1208] The ACM notes that many MaaS concepts are still in the start-up phase and that companies active in integrated MaaS have the same goal of offering a mobility offering that is as complete and integrated as possible. The ACM therefore conservatively uses the narrower market definition and, despite this, finds no competition concerns as the parties only have a limited market share of 0%-5%.[1209]

There is however a number of vertical relationships between the JV and its parent companies that raise concern for the ACM. More specifically, on the markets for train transport and shared bicycles, the parent companies have market shares that are above 70%.[1210] According to the ACM, the parties' shared bicycles and train transport services are 'important, if not essential inputs' for providers of integrated MaaS services.[1211] The ACM finds that the parties have the possibility and the incentive to implement an input foreclosure strategy by offering train and shared bicycle services for higher prices or under less favourable conditions. The parties avoided a Phase 2 investigation by committing that they would offer shared bicycle and train services under the same conditions to third parties as they will offer these services to the JV. These commitments only apply to the extent that the parties make the shared bicycle and train services 'app-enabled'.[1212] When that happens, third parties will be able to

1205. ACM, decision 20 May 2020, ACM/20/038614 (*NS Groep N.V./Pon Netherlands B.V./JV*).
1206. ACM, decision 20 May 2020, ACM/20/038614 (*NS Groep N.V./Pon Netherlands B.V./JV*), paras 177 ff.
1207. *Ibid.*, para. 122.
1208. *Ibid.*, para. 129.
1209. *Ibid.*, para. 138.
1210. *Ibid.*, paras 159, 174.
1211. *Ibid.*, para. 176.
1212. *Ibid.*, para. 217.

access the parties' API for shared bicycles and train services under the supervision of a monitoring trustee. The commitments apply for the lifetime of the joint venture.[1213]

[C] GVB/HTM/NS/RTE/Mobility Services JV (2020)

On 9 July 2020, the ACM cleared a joint venture between GVB Holding, HTM Personenvervoer, NS Groep and Rotterdamse Electrische Tram in Phase 1 subject to platform access and supply of transport services remedy.[1214] The parties are public transport companies with various business activities related to public transport, including train, metro, streetcar and ferry transport. The parties are the largest public transport players in the Netherlands, representing approximately 80%-90% of all kilometres travelled by public transport passengers in the Netherlands.[1215] The joint venture will be aimed at creating a MaaS wholesale platform, connecting providers of mobility services with providers of retail MaaS services.[1216] The joint venture will not provide its services to public transport passengers.

The ACM notes that the JV will become active in the market for providing wholesale MaaS (platform) services and that the parent companies of the JV are active in several vertically related markets. These are (i) the market for public transport services, including train transport, (ii) the retail market for integrated transport and mobility services through an app (or retail MaaS), and (iii) the market for the provision of shared bicycles. According to the ACM's theories of harm, the parties' vertical relationships with the activities of the JV would enable them to significantly impede competition through four types of conduct.

First, the parties could bundle their public transport services with the wholesale MaaS platform services of the JV to exclude competitors in the market for wholesale MaaS platform services.[1217] The parties could do this by selling their public transport services only to other wholesale MaaS platform providers in combination with a connection to the JV's platform. Second, the parties would have the possibility and incentive to use discriminating, untransparent or non-objective criteria for access to the platform, thereby increasing entry barriers and the costs of competing retail MaaS providers.[1218] Thirdly, the parties could foreclose access to the platform to competing mobility providers by using discriminating, untransparent or non-objective criteria for access to the platform. The ACM acknowledges that the JV's platform would normally benefit from accepting as many mobility providers as possible because it would make the offering of the platform more interesting to providers of retail MaaS. Still, the ACM considers it plausible that the parties have an incentive to exclude mobility providers to the extent that these compete with the mobility services of one of the parties. This

1213. *Ibid.*, para. 202.
1214. ACM, decision 9 July 2020, ACM/20/039644 (*GVB Holding N.V./HTM Personenvervoer N.V./NS Groep N.V./Rotterdamse Electrische Tram N.V.*).
1215. *Ibid.*, para. 123.
1216. *Ibid.*, para. 26.
1217. *Ibid.*, para. 117.
1218. *Ibid.*, para. 145.

would particularly be the case in the market for shared bicycles. Fourthly, the ACM is concerned that the parties and the JV could gain access to commercially sensitive information from competitors.

To take away the concerns of the ACM, the parties committed to:

(i) make their mobility services available to MaaS providers regardless of whether these MaaS providers are connected to the JV's platform or not, and under equal conditions;
(ii) not to impose exclusivity obligations on mobility providers or MaaS providers;
(iii) ensure access to the platform for mobility providers and MaaS providers through FRAND conditions. An interesting conundrum was the need for the JV to prioritise certain providers in case of scarcity of capacity. To solve this, the commitments include an 'Assessment Framework' on the basis of which the JV, in the event of scarcity of capacity, determines the order in which third-party providers are given access to the platform on the basis of neutral and objective prioritisation criteria.[1219] Another interesting feature of the FRAND access remedy is that the parties committed to using a neutral scheduling algorithm, in order to avoid the parties would be able to give their own services a higher ranking than their competitors' services. The scheduling algorithm will base the order of available routes based on the wishes of the traveller and shall not adapt this order to the wishes of mobility providers or the JV's shareholders;[1220]
(iv) ensure that mobility providers and MaaS providers (including the Parties themselves) will not have access to competitively sensitive information.

The ACM approved the transaction subject to these commitments, which will be supervised by a monitoring trustee. The commitments apply for the duration of the shareholdings of each of the parents in the joint venture.[1221]

§8.05 INTERMEDIATE CONCLUSION

The ACM's enforcement policy may be characterised as attentive and informed, with an increasing willingness to act, even against big tech companies. Coincidental or not, the appointment of Martijn Snoep as the new chairman as of 1 September 2018 marked a watershed. All but one of the ACM's digital competition decisions followed after that date. Until Snoep took office, the ACM mainly focused on obtaining the best possible knowledge regarding the functioning of digital markets but appears to have limited its actual intervention in those markets. The basis of this policy lies in the desire not to put unnecessary brakes on innovation. Looking at the impressive number of policy documents that have been published after Snoep took the ACM's helm and Snoep's

1219. *Ibid.*, para. 207 and annex 1 (Remedievoorstel).
1220. *Ibid.*, para. 211.
1221. *Ibid.*, annex 1 (Remedievoorstel).

comments on the risk of distorting innovation, this policy of extensive market research has clearly continued. However, importantly, the ACM has shaken off the fear of intervening, especially in areas where it has built up special expertise. For example, the Google and Apple investigations followed after the ACM initiated a market study into app stores in 2018 and a market study on the Dutch online payment market in 2020. At the same time, market studies followed investigations. After the 2020 behavioural remedies imposed in two merger cases between companies in the MaaS, the ACM published a market study into MaaS in 2021. This shows that the ACM is proceeding with deliberation and thoughtfulness, building on its expertise. Under the leadership of Snoep, the ACM has also been willing to accept behavioural access and supply remedies in markets affected by the platform economy. While time must tell how costly and workable monitoring behavioural remedies will be, it shows that the ACM is an authority that is adapting to the zeitgeist and the need for companies of the old economy to adapt and concentrate their activities through platforms. The ACM is active and it looks like we can expect many more from the ACM in the future.

CHAPTER 9
Belgium: BCA

'We do not require additional legislative tools to bring abuse cases, and our lack of resources is not limited to digital cases.'[1222]

– Jacques Steenbergen

'Wij willen (...) zeker ook positieve beslissingen, d.w.z. beslissingen die geen inbreuk vaststellen. Er valt dikwijls veel meer te leren uit die beslissingen dan uit verbodsbeslissingen.'[1223]

– Jacques Steenbergen [freely translated: 'We certainly also want (...) positive decisions, i.e. decisions that do not establish an infringement. Often, there is much more to learn from those decisions than from prohibition decisions.']

Until recently, the Belgian Competition Authority (BCA) was not visibly active in respect of issues surrounding digital competition. To date, the BCA's track record is limited to three decisions, one under the cartel prohibition,[1224] one under the prohibition on abuse of a dominant position[1225] and one under both prohibitions.[1226] The first decision concerned an investigation into parity clauses used by Immoweb, the most popular real estate site in Belgium.[1227] This investigation was discontinued after

1222. OECD, Abuse of Dominance in Digital Markets – Contribution from Belgium by Jacques Steenbergen, 8 December 2020.
1223. K. Marchand, B. Van de Walle de Ghelcke and P. Wytinck, 'De ambitie is: beslissingen, beslissingen, beslissingen; Interview met Jacques Steenbergen, Voorzitter Belgische Mededingingsautoriteit, *Tijdschrift Belgische Mededinging – Revue de la Concurrence Belge*, 2014-1, 3-9.
1224. BCA, decision 6 May 2021, ABC-2021-P/K-09 (*Caudalie*).
1225. BCA, decision 15 February 2019, ABC-2019-V/M-10 (*IRM*).
1226. BCA, decision 7 November 2016, ABC-2016-I/O-31-AUD (*Immoweb*).
1227. *Ibid.*

Immoweb pledged to remove the parity clauses. In 2019, the BCA found no abuse of a dominant position in *IRM*, a case concerning a refusal to supply data. And, in 2021, the BCA fined Caudalie, a French skincare company, EUR 859,310 for resale price maintenance and online sales restrictions. These cases will be discussed in more detail below.

Only since 2021, the BCA has included the digital economy in its priority sectors. In 2021, the BCA stated that it would focus on the use of personal data and algorithms to facilitate antitrust infringements.[1228] In 2022, the BCA stated that it would be alert on potential abuses of dominance or of economic dependence resulting from the digital transformation in different sectors, especially in the media and communications sectors.[1229] It remains to be seen if this new focus on the digital sector will lead to an actual change of course of the BCA. As far as the authors are aware, it has not dedicated a separate department or task force to this subject. The last BCA initiative concerning the digital economy was a 2019 joint paper with the Dutch and Luxembourg Competition Authorities. They advocated for closer scrutiny of mergers in digital markets and the introduction of an *ex ante* instrument allowing to impose remedies in digital and other fast-moving markets without the need to establish an infringement.[1230]

§9.01 CARTEL PROHIBITION

[A] Immoweb 2016

The investigation focused on broad parity clauses in the agreements between Immoweb, a real estate website, and software developers, who develop software for property firms.[1231] With the help of this software, property firms can automatically and immediately place the real estate they hold in their portfolio on real estate sites, such as Immoweb, via the software developers. Immoweb pays the software developers a fixed amount per advert. The parity clauses in question required software developers to offer Immoweb the same terms and conditions as they offered to its competitors if those terms and conditions were financially more advantageous. In its preliminary analysis, the BCA concluded that Immoweb's parity clauses could restrict competition because they increased costs for Immoweb's competitors since the software developers – also in view of Immoweb's high market share – had hardly any incentive to reduce costs for Immoweb's competitors as a result of the clauses.[1232] The BCA also established that Immoweb holds a dominant position on the Belgian national market for real

1228. 'Het prioriteitenbeleid van de Belgische Mededingingsautoriteit voor 2021' (Belgische Mededingingsautoriteit/ Autorité belge de la Concurrence 2021).
1229. BCA, 'De prioriteitennota van de Belgische Mededingingsautoriteit voor 2022', 31 March 2022, p. 6.
1230. 'Joint memorandum of the Belgian, Dutch and Luxembourg competition authorities on challenges faced by competition authorities in a digital world' (Belgische Mededingingsautoriteit/ Autorité belge de la Concurrence 2019).
1231. BCA, decision 6 May 2021, ABC-2021-P/K-09 (*Caudalie*).
1232. Belgische Mededingingsautoriteit/Autorité belge de la Concurrence, 'Press Release 16 November 2016: Het Auditoraat van de Belgische Mededingingsautoriteit Heeft Een Onderzoek

estate sites (this was disputed by Immoweb). For that reason, it came to the preliminary opinion that the inclusion of the clauses by Immoweb also constituted abuse of a dominant position. After having been notified of the above by the BCA, Immoweb committed itself to completely and unilaterally remove its parity clauses and not to include any new parity clauses in its contracts with software developers for five years. Following these commitments, the BCA discontinued its investigation into Immoweb's behaviour.[1233]

[B] Caudalie (2021)

On 6 May 2021, the BCA imposed a fine of EUR 859,310 on Caudalie, a French skincare company, for imposing online sales restrictions on distributors of its products between 2014 and 2017.[1234] According to the BCA, Caudalie did not allow the distributors in its selective distribution system to accept online orders for more than [0-10] copies of the same product and it also did not allow them to deliver products outside the country where the website was hosted.[1235] This did not only restrict passive sales within the context of a selective distribution system but also restricted passive and active sales outside the territory of the selective distribution system. The BCA notes: '*une interdiction de vendre en ligne à des acheteurs établis dans un Etat membre en dehors du territoire du réseau de distribution sélective ne bénéficie d'aucune exception*'.[1236] [Free translation: 'a prohibition to sell online to buyers in other Member States outside the territory of the selective distribution network doesn't benefit from any exemption'.] The BCA concludes that Caudalie's policy of passive and active sales restrictions constitutes a by object restriction of competition and imposes a fine of EUR 859,310.[1237] On 1 December 2022, the Brussels Court of Appeals annulled the BCA's decision on procedural grounds.[1238] The BCA is expected to take a new decision.

§9.02 ABUSE OF A DOMINANT POSITION

[A] The Great Circle/IRM

On 15 February 2019, the BCA rejects a request by Great Circle, a provider of maritime navigation software, to impose provisional measures on the Institut Royal

Tegen Immoweb Stopgezet Gelet Op Verbintenissen Aangeboden Door Immoweb', https://www.BMA-ABC-abc.be/nl/over-ons/actualiteit/persbericht-nr-19-2016.

1233. Belgische Mededingingsautoriteit/Autorité belge de la Concurrence, *supra* n. 1232.
1234. BCA, Decision of 6 May 2021, ABC-2021-P/K-09 (Caudalie). The BCA also found that Caudalie imposed minimum prices on its selective distributors but this didn't seem to involve any digital aspects and is therefore not discussed here, *see* section VI, para. 111.
1235. BCA, Decision of 6 May 2021, ABC-2021-P/K-09 (Caudalie), section VI, para. 116.
1236. *Ibid.*
1237. *Ibid.*, para. 118.
1238. Cour d'appel Bruxelles, Section Cour des marchés, judgment 1 December 2022, 2021/MR/1, 9071.

Méteorologique (IRM).[1239] Great Circle requested IRM to supply the data that the IRM receives from the European Center for Medium Range Weather Forecasts (ECMWF), an intergovernmental organisation. According to Great Circle, IRM, however, refused to give access to the data, thereby depriving Great Circle of an essential input for its maritime navigation software.

The BCA however finds that, on an at least European-wide market for commercial meteorological information, IRM has no dominant position because the ECMWF data obtained in other Member States can also be used in Belgium and vice versa.[1240] The BCA notes that meteorological data packages that are available on the market normally have a global scope. The data that IRM has is as good as any other data provided by the ECMWF to other parties in other Member States.[1241] The BCA therefore finds that there is no prima facie abuse of a dominant position by IRM and rejects the request for the imposition of provisional measures, also noting that the ECMWF is not the only provider of meteorological data that IRM could rely on. Interestingly, the ECMWF, as an intergovernmental organisation, was granted immunity from jurisdiction which explains why Great Circle was prompted to direct its complaint against IRM, rather than against ECMWF.[1242]

§9.03 MERGER CONTROL

To date, the BCA does not have a relevant decision and enforcement practice regarding mergers in relation to digital competition.

§9.04 INTERMEDIATE CONCLUSION

The BCA's track record in the field of digital competition law is very brief. There are just three precedents and only in 2021 has the BCA decided to shift its focus more to the digital economy. These precedents show that the BCA is critical of online sales restrictions, parity clauses and access to data in concentrated markets. The distinction between broad and narrow parity clauses was not relevant in *Immoweb*, the parity clauses case.

It remains to be seen whether the BCA's 2021 and 2022 priorities will effectively change the course of the BCA. It is worth mentioning that during the conference *Competition Policy and Online Markets* in Brussels on 24 October 2018, BCA chairman Steenbergen indicated that he considered new enforcement instruments unnecessary. In 2020, he repeated that additional legislative tools are not necessary to bring abuse

1239. BCA, Decision of 15 February 2019, ABC-2019-V/M-10 (IRM), section VI, para. 51.
1240. *Ibid.*, para. 45-46.
1241. *Ibid.*, para. 37.
1242. *Ibid.*, para. 17.

cases.[1243] In Steenbergen's opinion, the current instruments are adequate, but he recognises that an *ex ante* instrument is necessary for digital markets to prevent *ex post* enforcement from being too late and to keep markets competitive and contestable.[1244]

1243. OECD, Abuse of Dominance in Digital Markets - Contribution from Belgium by Jacques Steenbergen, 8 December 2020.

1244. 'Joint memorandum of the Belgian, Dutch and Luxembourg competition authorities on challenges faced by competition authorities in a digital world' (Belgische Mededingingsautoriteit/ Autorité belge de la Concurrence 2019).

CHAPTER 10
Analysis

§10.01 INTRODUCTION

[A] Antitrust

A comparison of the practices of the six competition authorities under review reveals a pattern of notable similarities and differences. Most interesting in this respect are the practices of the competition authorities in relation to the cartel prohibition and the prohibition of abuse of dominance. A new category of cases is constituted by various forms of *ex ante* or gatekeeper regulation enforcement (notably section 19a German Competition Act (GWB) and the Digital Markets Act (DMA) – which entered into force on 1 November 2022 and applies from 2 May 2023 – in the EU).

Looking at the cartel prohibition, we have distinguished (horizontal) cartels from vertical restrictions. There are relatively few horizontal cartel precedents, while enforcement against vertical restrictions is prevalent among all authorities. In total, seven cartel investigations have led to four decisions and only two fines, one in the UK and one in France (Table 10.1). On the other hand, there were thirty-eight investigations into vertical restrictions and forty-four decisions.

We count fifty-one abuse of dominance investigations that have led to thirty-one decisions. The European Commission started most investigations into possible abuse of dominance (sixteen) but only published five decisions in this field. The Autorité published more than half of all abuse of dominance decisions (eighteen). The Competition and Markets Authority (CMA), the Bundeskartellamt and the Belgian Competition Authority (BCA) did not issue any fines for abuse of dominance.

Table 10.1 Antitrust Enforcement Stats per Authority (January 2013-July 2022)

	EC	*CMA*	*Autorité*	*Bka*	*ACM*	*BCA*
Abuse of dominance investigations	16[1245]	10[1246]	14[1247]	7[1248]	3[1249]	1[1250]
Abuse of dominance decisions	4[1251]	3[1252]	18[1253]	2[1254]	3[1255]	1[1256]

1245. Google Search (AdSense) (2019); Google Android (2018); Google Search (Shopping) (2017); E-book MFNs and related matters (Amazon) (2017); Amazon Marketplace (2019); Amazon Buy Box (2020); Google for Jobs (2019); Google - Adtech and Data-related practices (2021); Google-Facebook (Open Bidding) agreement (2022); Ciao/Google (2013); 1plusV/Google (2013); Apple - App Store Practices (2020); Apple - App Store Practices (music streaming) (2020); Apple - App Store Practices (e-books/audiobooks) (2020); Apple - Mobile payments (2020); Facebook leveraging (2021).
1246. Google - Privacy Sandbox (2022); Online bidding services - ATG Media (2017); Vehicle service, maintenance and repair platforms - Epyx (2014); Amazon Marketplace (2022); Google - Play Store Billing (2022); Google - Ad tech (2022); Google/Meta - header bidding (Jedi Blue) (2022); Apple - App Store (2022); Meta - Use of ad data (2021); Education Software Solutions Limited (2022).
1247. Meta (2022); Google - Doubleclick for publishers/AdX (2021); Apple Targeted advertising (2021); Google - ancillary rights (2020); Apple/Tech Data/Ingram Micro (2020); Amadeus (2019); Google AdWords VI (Amadeus) (2019); APCA (2018); Google AdWords V (Interactive Labs) (2018); Google AdSense (1PlusV) (2017); Google AdWords IV (IAH) (2016); Google AdWords III (Gibmedia) (2015); Vente-privee.com (2014); Google AdWords II (E-Kanopi) (2013).
1248. Tax advisory software (2019); Facebook - privacy (2019); Lufthansa (2017); Amazon (2018); Facebook - Oculus (2020); Hospital services software (2020); Apple - App Tracking Transparency Framework (2022).
1249. Apple (2021); Stichting Internet Domeinregistratie Nederland (2021); Google (2022).
1250. IRM (2019).
1251. AT.40411, 20 March 2019, Google Search (AdSense); AT.40099, 18 July 2018, Google Android; AT.39740, 27 June 2017, Google Search (Shopping); AT.40153, 4 May 2017, E-book MFNs and related matters (Amazon).
1252. 50972, 11 February 2022, Google - Privacy Sandbox; 50408, 29 June 2017, Online bidding services - ATG Media; CE/9496-11, 9 September 2014, Vehicle service, maintenance and repair platforms - Epyx.
1253. 22-D-13, 21 June 2022, Google - ancillary rights (commitments); 22-D-12, 16 June 2022, Meta; 21-D-17, 12 July 2021, Google - ancillary rights (non-compliance); 21-D-11, 7 June 2021, Google - Doubleclick for publishers/AdX; 21-D-07, 17 March 2021, Apple Targeted advertising; 20-D-14, 26 October 2020, Google AdWords VI (Amadeus); 20-MC-01, 9 April 2020, Google - ancillary rights; 20-D-04, 16 March 2020, Apple/Tech Data/Ingram Micro; 19-D-26, 19 December 2019, Google AdWords III (Gibmedia); 19-D-04, 21 February 2019, Amadeus; 19-MC-01, 31 January 2019, Google AdWords VI (Amadeus); 18-D-20, 5 October 2018, APCA; 18-D-13, 20 July 2018, Google AdWords V (Interactive Labs); 17-D-24, 18 December 2017, Google AdSense (1PlusV); 16-D-25, 23 November 2016, Google AdWords IV (IAH); 15-D-13, 9 September 2015, Google AdWords III (Gibmedia); 14-D-18, 28 November 2014, Vente-privee.com; 13-D-07, 28 February 2013, Google AdWords II (E-Kanopi).
1254. B7-25/17, 3 December 2019, Tax advisory software; B6-22/16, 6 February 2019, Facebook - privacy.
1255. ACM/19/035630, 24 August 2021, Apple (order); ACM/21/049853, 19 April 2021, Stichting Internet Domeinregistratie Nederland; ACM/19/035630, 24 January 2022, Apple (non-compliance).
1256. ABC-2019-V/M-10, 15 February 2019, IRM.

	EC	*CMA*	*Autorité*	*Bka*	*ACM*	*BCA*
Abuse of dominance fines	3[1257]	0	4[1258]	0	1[1259]	0
Cartel investigations	1[1260]	2[1261]	2[1262]	1[1263]	1[1264]	0
Cartel decisions	0	1[1265]	1[1266]	1[1267]	1[1268]	0
Cartel fines	0	1[1269]	1[1270]	0	0	0
Vertical restrictions investigations	9[1271]	10[1272]	7[1273]	8[1274]	2[1275]	2[1276]

1257. AT.40411, 20 March 2019, Google Search (AdSense); AT.40099, 18 July 2018, Google Android; AT.39740, 27 June 2017, Google Search (Shopping).
1258. 21-D-17, 12 July 2021, Google - ancillary rights (non-compliance); 21-D-11, 7 June 2021, Google - Doubleclick for publishers/AdX; 20-D-04, 16 March 2020, Apple/Tech Data/Ingram Micro; 19-D-26, 19 December 2019, Google AdWords III (Gibmedia).
1259. ACM/19/035630, 24 January 2022, Apple (non-compliance).
1260. Google-Facebook (Open Bidding) agreement (2022).
1261. Online sales of posters and frames (2016); Google/Meta - header bidding (Jedi Blue) (2022).
1262. Apple/Tech Data/Ingram Micro (2020); Akka Technologies Group (2018).
1263. Tax advisory software (2019).
1264. Nederlandse Orde van Advocaten (2018).
1265. 50223, 12 August 2016, Online sales of posters and frames.
1266. 20-D-04, 16 March 2020, Apple/Tech Data/Ingram Micro.
1267. B7-25/17, 3 December 2019, Tax advisory software.
1268. ACM/17/012061, 14 December 2018, Nederlandse Orde van Advocaten.
1269. 50223, 12 August 2016, Online sales of posters and frames.
1270. 20-D-04, 16 March 2020, Apple/Tech Data/Ingram Micro.
1271. Video Games - Focus Home (2021); Film merchandise - NBCUniversal (2020); Character merchandise - Sanrio (2019); Ancillary Sports Merchandise - Nike (2019); Cross-order access to pay-TV - Disney, NBCUniversal, Sony Pictures, Warner Bros. and Sky (2019); Guess (2018); Vertical restraints - Asus (2018); E-books - Penguin (2013); Amazon/Audible and Apple (2017).
1272. DAR Lighting (2022); Price comparison website: use of most favoured nation clauses (2020); GAK, Yamaha (2020); Ping (2017); Online bidding services - ATG Media (2017); Pool Lighting Ltd (2017); Online RPM - commercial refrigeration (2016); Online RPM - bathroom fittings sector (2016); Booking.com B.V, Expedia, Inc, InterContinental Hotels Group plc and Hotel Inter-Continental London Limited (2014); Amazon (2012).
1273. Apple/Tech Data/Ingram Micro (2020); Expedia/HRS (2019); Bikeeurope B.V. (2019); Stihl (2018); Sanbri (2017); Booking.com (2015); Adidas (2018).
1274. Booking.com (2015); Asics (2015); Adidas (2014); HRS (2013); Amazon (2013); Verivox (2015); Amazon brand gating (2020); Amazon/Audible and Apple (2017).
1275. Samsung (2021); Thuisbezorgd.nl (2016).
1276. Caudalie (2021); Immoweb (2016).

	EC	*CMA*	*Autorité*	*Bka*	*ACM*	*BCA*
Vertical restrictions decisions	16[1277]	13[1278]	6[1279]	5[1280]	2[1281]	2[1282]
Vertical restrictions fines	13[1283]	11[1284]	4[1285]	0	1[1286]	1[1287]

1277. AT.40413, 20 January 2021, Video Games - Focus Home; AT.40414, 20 January 2021, Video Games - Koch Media; AT.40420, 20 January 2021, Video Games - ZeniMax; AT.40422, 20 January 2021, Video Games - Bandai Namco; AT.40424, 20 January 2021, Video Games - Capcom; AT.40433, 30 January 2020, Film merchandise - NBCUniversal; AT.40432, 9 July 2019, Character merchandise - Sanrio; AT.40436, 25 March 2019, Ancillary Sports Merchandise - Nike; AT.40023, 7 March 2019, Cross-order access to pay-TV - Disney, NBCUniversal, Sony Pictures, Warner Bros. and Sky; AT.40428, 17 December 2018, Guess; AT.40465, 24 July 2018, Vertical restraints - Asus; AT.40469, 24 July 2018, Vertical restraints - Denon & Marantz; AT.40181, 24 July 2018, Vertical restraints - Philips; AT.40182, 24 July 2018, Vertical restraints - Pioneer; AT.40023, 26 July 2016, Cross-order access to pay-TV - Paramount; AT.39847, 25 July 2013, E-books - Penguin.
1278. 50952, 23 March 2022, DAR Lighting; 50505, 19 November 2020, Price comparison website: use of most favoured nation clauses; 50565-6, 17 July 2020, GAK, Yamaha; 50565-4, 29 June 2020, Korg; 50565-5, 29 June 2020, Roland; 50565-3, 22 January 2020, Fender; 50565-2, 1 August 2019, Casio; 50230, 24 August 2017, Ping; 50408, 29 June 2017, Online bidding services - ATG Media; 50343, 20 June 2017, Pool Lighting Ltd; CE/9856/14, 24 May 2016, Online RPM - commercial refrigeration; CE/9857-14, 10 May 2016, Online RPM - bathroom fittings sector; CE/9320/10, 31 January 2014, Booking.com B.V, Expedia, Inc, InterContinental Hotels Group plc and Hotel Inter-Continental London Limited.
1279. 20-D-04, 16 March 2020, Apple/Tech Data/Ingram Micro; 19-D-23, 10 December 2019, Expedia/HRS; 19-D-14, 1 July 2019, Bikeeurope B.V.; 18-D-23, 24 October 2018, Stihl; 17-D-01, 26 January 2017, Sanbri; 15-D-06, 21 April 2015, Booking.com.
1280. B9-121/13, 22 December 2015, Booking.com; B2-98/11, 26 August 2015, Asics; B3-137/12, 27 June 2014, Adidas; B9-66/10, 20 December 2013, HRS; B6-46/12, 26 November 2013, Amazon.
1281. ACM/20/040569, 14 September 2021, Samsung; ACM/DM/2016/207286, 18 November 2016, Thuisbezorgd.nl.
1282. ABC-2021-P/K-09, 6 May 2021, Caudalie; ABC-2016-I/O-31-AUD, 7 November 2016, Immoweb.
1283. AT.40413, 20 January 2021, Video Games - Focus Home; AT.40414, 20 January 2021, Video Games - Koch Media; AT.40420, 20 January 2021, Video Games - ZeniMax; AT.40422, 20 January 2021, Video Games - Bandai Namco; AT.40424, 20 January 2021, Video Games - Capcom; AT.40433, 30 January 2020, Film merchandise - NBCUniversal; AT.40432, 9 July 2019, Character merchandise - Sanrio; AT.40436, 25 March 2019, Ancillary Sports Merchandise - Nike; AT.40428, 17 December 2018, Guess; AT.40465, 24 July 2018, Vertical restraints - Asus; AT.40469, 24 July 2018, Vertical restraints - Denon & Marantz; AT.40181, 24 July 2018, Vertical restraints - Philips; AT.40182, 24 July 2018, Vertical restraints - Pioneer.
1284. 50952, 23 March 2022, DAR Lighting; 50505, 19 November 2020, Price comparison website: use of most favoured nation clauses; 50565-6, 17 July 2020, GAK, Yamaha; 50565-4, 29 June 2020, Korg; 50565-5, 29 June 2020, Roland; 50565-3, 22 January 2020, Fender; 50565-2, 1 August 2019, Casio; 50230, 24 August 2017, Ping; 50343, 20 June 2017, Pool Lighting Ltd; CE/9856/14, 24 May 2016, Online RPM - commercial refrigeration; CE/9857-14, 10 May 2016, Online RPM - bathroom fittings sector.
1285. 20-D-04, 16 March 2020, Apple/Tech Data/Ingram Micro; 19-D-14, 1 July 2019, Bikeeurope B.V.; 18-D-23, 24 October 2018, Stihl; 17-D-01, 26 January 2017, Sanbri.
1286. ACM/20/040569, 14 September 2021, Samsung.
1287. ABC-2021-P/K-09, 6 May 2021, Caudalie.

	EC	*CMA*	*Autorité*	*Bka*	*ACM*	*BCA*
Gatekeeper investigations	0	0	0	9[1288]	0	0
Gatekeeper designations	0	0	0	3[1289]	0	0
Gatekeeper decisions	0	0	0	0	0	0
Gatekeeper fines	0	0	0	0	0	0
Total investigations	25	20	21	22	6	3
Total decisions	20	16	22	10	6	3
Total fining decisions	16	12	9	0	2	0
Commitment decisions	4[1290]	4[1291]	4[1292]	0	0	2[1293]
Interim measures imposed	0	0	1[1294]	0	0	0
Antitrust guidance	1[1295]	0	0	3[1296]	0	0

We count eight abuse of dominance fines, two cartel fines and thirty fines for vertical restrictions. The Commission imposed three abuse of dominance fines (on Google on all three counts). At the national level, the Autorité[1297] (three) and the Dutch competition authority (ACM) (one) have also issued fines for abuse of dominance. The

1288. Amazon - Section 19a (2022); Meta - Section 19a (2022); Google - Section 19a (2021); Facebook - Oculus (2020); Apple - Section 19a (2021); Google - Maps Platform (2022); Google - data processing (2021); Google - News Showcase (2021); Apple - App Tracking Transparency Framework (2022).
1289. 6 July 2022, Amazon - Section 19a; 2 May 2022, Meta - Section 19a; B7-61/21, 30 December 2021, Google - Section 19a.
1290. AT.40023, 7 March 2019, Cross-order access to pay-TV - Disney, NBCUniversal, Sony Pictures, Warner Bros. and Sky; AT.40153, 4 May 2017, E-book MFNs and related matters (Amazon); AT.40023, 26 July 2016, Cross-order access to pay-TV - Paramount; AT.39847, 25 July 2013, E-books - Penguin.
1291. 50972, 11 February 2022, Google - Privacy Sandbox; 50408, 29 June 2017, Online bidding services - ATG Media; CE/9496-11, 9 September 2014, Vehicle service, maintenance and repair platforms - Epyx; CE/9320/10, 31 January 2014, Booking.com B.V, Expedia, Inc, InterContinental Hotels Group plc and Hotel Inter-Continental London Limited.
1292. 22-D-13, 21 June 2022, Google - ancillary rights (commitments); 22-D-12, 16 June 2022, Meta; 21-D-11, 7 June 2021, Google - Doubleclick for publishers/AdX; 15-D-06, 21 April 2015, Booking.com.
1293. ABC-2021-P/K-09, 6 May 2021, Caudalie; ABC-2016-I/O-31-AUD, 7 November 2016, Immoweb.
1294. 20-MC-01, 9 April 2020, Google - ancillary rights.
1295. 19 October 2021, GAIA-X, Feedback on the membership criteria and internal working rules of GAIA-X.
1296. Unamera, 5 November 2020, launch of online agricultural trading platform; Klöckner, 28 February 2018, Klöckner allowed to launch digital platform for steel products; Intersport, 25 May 2020, Bundeskartellamt clears Intersport's online platform sales model.
1297. Three times on Google, including once in the form of a fine for a failure to respect interim measures.

Autorité also levied a fine on Apple for abuse of a position of economic dependence.[1298] Thirteen Commission fines, eleven CMA fines, four fines imposed by the Autorité, and one fine imposed by the ACM and the BCA concerned vertical infringements (including geoblocking cases). The Bundeskartellamt is the only authority not to impose fines for vertical infringements in the digital sector, instead applying other solutions (bans of undesirable behaviour, informal or formal commitments).

The Commission has levied by far the largest proportion (80%) of the total fine amount, with a total fining amount of more than EUR 9 billion. The Autorité takes second place, with a total fine amount of more than EUR 2 billion (*see* Table 10.2). Unsurprisingly, the biggest share of the total fine amount has been issued for abuse of dominance infringements (almost EUR 10 billion), followed by cartel fines (EUR 0.8 billion) and fines for vertical restrictions (EUR 0.5 billion). There have been more investigations and decisions relating to vertical restrictions than investigations and decisions relating to horizontal (cartel) conduct, but this is not reflected in the overall fine amount. The total cartel enforcement fine amount is approximately EUR 300 million higher than the total fine amount for vertical restrictions. This, however, is due to a single cartel fine imposed on Apple, which makes it difficult to draw general conclusions about these amounts or to make any meaningful comparisons. Based on the total fining amount, it is safe to conclude that the prohibition on the abuse of dominance is the most important tool in the toolbox of competition authorities. This makes sense, given the strong influence the dominant tech companies have on our daily lives.

Table 10.2 Fine Amounts per Authority in EUR/GBP Million (2013-2022)

	EC	*CMA*	*Autorité*	*Bka*	*ACM*	*BCA*	*Total*
Abuse of dominance	€ 8,823	£ –	€ 1,088	€ –	€ 50	€ 0.9	€ 9,962
Cartels	€ –	£ 0.2	€ 802	€ –	€ –	€ –	€ 802
Vertical restrictions	€ 197	£ 41	€ 228	€ –	€ 40	€ –	€ 514
Total fine amount	€ 9,020	£ 41	€ 2,118	€ –	€ 90	€ 0.9	€ 11,278
Total fine amount (%)	80.0	0.4	18.8	0.0	0.8	0.0	100.0
Total fine amount GAMA	€ 8,262	£ –	€ 1,972	€ –	€ 50	€ –	€ 10,284
Total fine amount GAMA (%)	80.3	0.0	19.2	0.0	0.5%	0.0	100.0

1298. Autorité de la Concurrence, decision 16 March 2020, 20-D-04 (Apple/Tech Data/Ingram Micro).

Interestingly, the annual total fine amount has steadily decreased since 2018 (*see* Figure 10.1). This may however be coincidental and various investigations (also into GAMA (Google, Amazon, Meta and Apple)) are currently pending in various jurisdictions under investigation. However, the introduction of gatekeeper legislation such as the DMA and section 19a GWB may be expected to lead to new cases being brought under such legislation, which may in turn lead to a decrease in dominance cases (and perhaps also in cases under the cartel prohibition). In Germany, such a shift is already becoming visible, as we see no new cases that are based exclusively on the abuse of dominance prohibition since 2020.[1299] It will be interesting to observe whether a similar shift will take place in the EU after the entry into application of the DMA (on 2 May 2023) (*see* Colangelo §11.03). Regarding the relationship between the DMA and section 19a GWB, the two regimes are expected to be applied in parallel in certain cases. Bundeskartellamt chairman Andreas Mundt: '*I expect Section 19a [of the German law] to complement the DMA successfully, because it combines the competition law's flexibility and "future-proofness", with maybe quicker interventions and streamlined judicial review.*'[1300]

Figure 10.1 Annual Fine Amount in EUR (2013-2022)

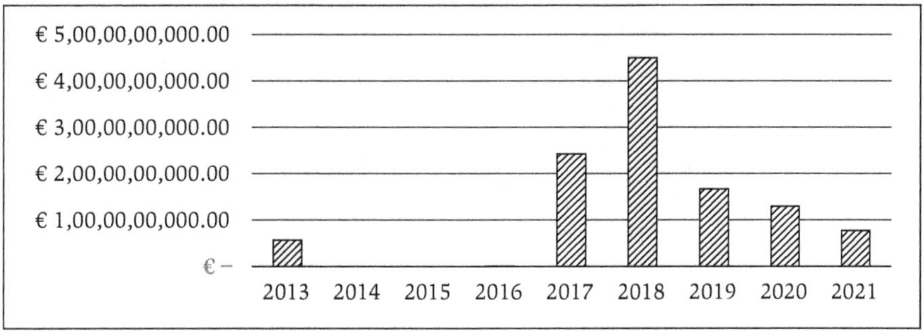

A total of seventeen decisions relate to behaviour by Google, which is more than the number of decisions involving Apple, Meta (previously Facebook) and Amazon combined (*see* Figure 10.2). Looking at the pending investigations against GAMA that have been initiated since 2018, we count ten investigations into Google and eight investigations into Apple. Four investigations are pending into both Amazon and Meta, respectively (*see* Figure 10.3).

1299. The Apple – App Tracking Transparency Framework (2022) investigation is based on both section 19a(2) sentence 1 GWB and Article 102 TFEU. Bundeskartellamt, press release 14 June 2022, 'Bundeskartellamt reviews Apple's tracking rules for third-party apps'.

1300. Mlex, 'EU effort to police digital gatekeepers will need national enforcers' help, Mundt says', 17 March 2022.

Figure 10.2 Decisions Involving GAMA (2013-July 2022)

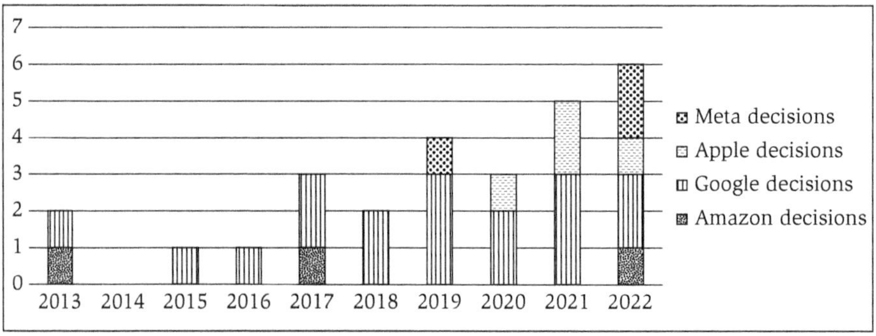

Figure 10.3 Pending Investigations Involving GAMA, by Year of Start of Investigations (2018-July 2022)

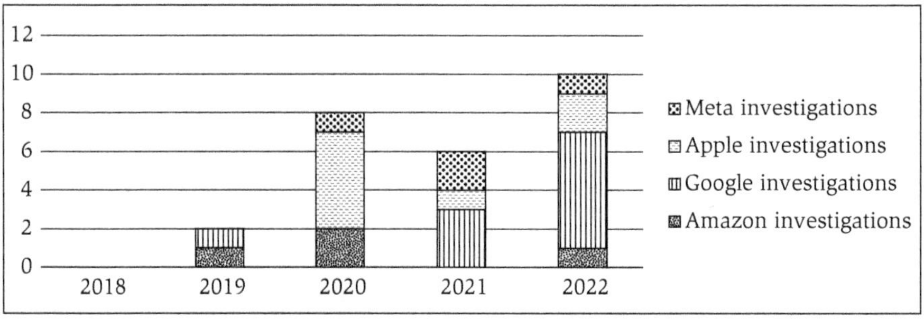

[B] Merger Control

A quantitative comparison of merger practices is less appropriate as the authorities that have a mandatory filing regime are dependent on the mergers that require notification in their jurisdictions. However, it is interesting to observe that the CMA (24) and the Commission (15) handled far more merger cases than any of the other authorities under review (*see* Table 10.3). The BCA is the only authority with no relevant merger decisions.

Table 10.3 Merger Enforcement Statistics per Authority (January 2013-July 2022)

	EC	*CMA*	*Autorité*	*Bka*	*ACM*	*BCA*
Merger decisions	14[1301]	25[1302]	8[1303]	6[1304]	3[1305]	0
GAMA merger decisions	5[1306]	4[1307]	0	1[1308]	0	0

1301. M.10188, 6 September 2022 (Illumina/GRAIL); M.10262, 27 January 2022 (Meta/Kustomer); M.9660, 11 May 2021 (Google/Fitbit); M.9538, 27 November 2019 (Broadcom/Symantec Enterprise Security Business); M.8994, 19 November 2018 (Microsoft/Github); M.8788, 12 November 2018 (Apple/Shazam); M.8416, 2 July 2018 (Priceline/Momondo); M.8124, 20 January 2017 (Microsoft/LinkedIn); M.8180, 22 December 2016 (Verizon/Yahoo); M.8201, 12 December 2016 (Randstad Holding/Monster Worldwide); M.7866, 16 March 2016 (Activision Blizzard/King); M.7217, 3 October 2014 (Facebook/WhatsApp); M.7290, 7 August 2014 (Apple/Beats); M.7047, 4 December 2013 (Microsoft/Nokia).

1302. ME/5882/12: Anticipated acquisition by Priceline.Com Incorporated of Kayak Software Corporation (Office of Fair Trading); ME/6167/13: Completed Acquisition by Motorola Mobility Holding (Google, Inc.) of Waze Mobile Limited (Office of Fair Trading); OFT, Decision 15 August 2013, *Anticipated acquisition by Web Reservations International (through its parent company Hellman & Friedman) of Hostelbookers.com Limited*, Case ME/6062/13; ME/6659/16, 16 November 2017 (Just Eat/Hungryhouse); ME/6754/18, 12 July 2018 (ATG Media/LTMO); ME/6749/18, 7 August 2018 (Moneysupermarket.com/DTL); ME/6841/19, 22 November 2019 (Salesforce/Tableau); ME/6733/18, 22 November 2018 (Nielsen/Ebiquity); ME/6839/19, 13 February 2020 (Google/ Looker Data Sciences); ME/6760/18, 7 January 2019 (Topcashback/Quidco); ME/6806/19, 9 April 2020 (Sabre/Farelogix); ME/6879/20, 25 March 2021 (Crowdcube/Seedrs); ME/6766/18, 12 June 2019 (Paypal/iZettle); ME/6809/19; ME/6810/19; ME6811/19; ME/6812/19; ME/6743/18, 27 February 2019 (Experian/Credit Laser Holdings); ME/6836/19, 4 August 2020 (Amazon/Deliveroo); ME/6752/18, 25 April 2019 (Sainsbury/Asda); ME/6868/19, 2 February 2021 (Viagogo/Stubhub); ME/6891/20, 29 March 2022 (Facebook/Giphy); ME/6920/20, 27 September 2020 (Facebook/Kustomer); ME/6881/20, 7 May 2020 (Just Eat/ Takeaway); ME/6877/20, 14 September 2020 (Taboola/Outbrain); ME/6897/20, 2 June 2020 (Adevinta/eBay); ME/6942/21, 12 November 2021 (Auction Technology Group/Live Auctioneers); ME/6808/18, 19 December 2019 (LN-Gaiety Holdings/MCD Productions); N/A, 29 September 2022 (Booking Holdings/eTraveli).

1303. 22-DCC-111, 24 June 2022 (Duval/Blue Green); 19-DCC-259, 18 December 2019 (La Poste/Softeam); 19-DCC-157, 12 August 2019 (France Télévisions/TF1/Métropole Télévision/Salto JV); 19-DCC-132, 16 July 2019 (Fnac Darty/Nature et Découvertes); 19-DCC-94, 24 May 2019 (Webedia/Groupe Elephant); 19-DCC-65, 17 April 2019 (Jellej Jouets/Gifram/Luderix International); 18-DCC-18, 1 February 2018 (Axel Springer Group/Logic Immo); 16-DCC-111, 27 July 2016 (Fnac/Darty).

1304. B6-57/15, 22 October 2015 (Oakley Capital/EliteMedianet); 6 July 2020 (Parship/Elite Partner/Lovoo); B8-76/15, 24 July 2015 (ProSiebenSat.1/Verivox); B6-39/15, 20 April 2015 (Immonet/Immowelt); 21 December 2020 (Phoenix/Noventi/JV); 11 February 2022 (Meta/Kustomer).

1305. ACM/20/039644, 9 July 2020 (GVB Holding N.V./HTM Personenvervoer N.V./NS Groep N.V./Rotterdamse Electrische Tram N.V.); ACM/20/038614, 20 May 2020 (NS Groep N.V./Pon Netherlands B.V./JV); ACM/19/035555, 28 August 2019 (Sanoma Learning B.V./Iddink Holding B.V.).

1306. M.10262, 27 January 2022 (Facebook/Kustomer); M.9660, 11 May 2021 (Google/Fitbit); M.8788, 12 November 2018 (Apple/Shazam); M.7217, 3 October 2014 (Facebook/Whatsapp); M.7290, 7 August 2014 (Apple/Beats).

1307. ME/6891/20, 29 March 2022 (Facebook/Giphy); ME/6920/20, 27 September 2020 (Facebook/Kustomer); ME/6836/19, 4 August 2020 (Amazon/Deliveroo); ME/6839/19, 13 February 2020 (Google/ Looker Data Sciences).

1308. Decision 11 February 2022, (Facebook/Kustomer).

	EC	*CMA*	*Autorité*	*Bka*	*ACM*	*BCA*
In-depth investigations	5[1309]	13[1310]	2[1311]	0	1[1312]	0
Prohibitions	0	3[1313]	0	0	0	0
Conditional approvals	3[1314]	3[1315]	2[1316]	0	3[1317]	0
Behavioural remedies decisions	3[1318]	1[1319]	1[1320]	0	3[1321]	0

The CMA has taken by far the most merger decisions. The broad scope of the UK merger regime's jurisdictional rules and the CMA's willingness to look at tech mergers appear to be the main factors driving the high number of CMA cases. The UK merger regime's jurisdictional rules have been called 'elastic' and the CMA '*can and has*

1309. M.10262, 27 January 2022 (Facebook/Kustomer); M.9660, 11 May 2021 (Google/Fitbit); M.8788, 12 November 2018 (Apple/Shazam); M.8124, 20 January 2017 (Microsoft/LinkedIn); M.10188, 6 September 2022 (Illumina/GRAIL).
1310. ME/6659/16, 16 November 2017 (Just Eat/Hungryhouse); ME/6733/18, 22 November 2018 (Nielsen/Ebiquity); ME/6760/18, 7 January 2019 (Topcashback/Quidco); ME/6806/19, 9 April 2020 (Sabre/Farelogix); ME/6879/20, 25 March 2021 (Crowdcube/Seedrs); ME/6766/18, 12 June 2019 (Paypl/iZettle); ME/6809/19; ME/6810/19; ME6811/19; ME/6812/19, 1 June 2020 (Bauer Media Group merger inquiry); ME/6743/18, 27 February 2019 (Experian/Credit Laser Holdings); ME/6836/19, 4 August 2020 (Amazon/Deliveroo); ME/6752/18, 25 April 2019 (Sainsbury/Asda); ME/6868/19, 2 February 2021 (Viagogo/Stubhub); ME/6891/20, 29 March 2022 (Facebook/Giphy); ME/6877/20, 14 September 2020 (Taboola/Outbrain); ME/6808/18, 19 December 2019 (LN-Gaiety Holdings/MCD Productions).
1311. 18-DCC-18, 1 February 2018 (Axel Springer Group/Logic Immo); 16-DCC-111, 27 July 2016 (Fnac/Darty).
1312. ACM/19/035555, 28 August 2019 (Sanoma Learning B.V./Iddink Holding B.V.).
1313. ME/6806/19, 9 April 2020 (Sabre/Farelogix); ME/6752/18, 25 April 2019 (Sainsbury/Asda); ME/6891/20, 29 March 2022 (Facebook/Giphy).
1314. M.10262, 27 January 2022 (Meta/Kustomer); M.9660, 11 May 2021 (Google/Fitbit); M.8124, 20 January 2017 (Microsoft/LinkedIn).
1315. ME/6809/19; ME/6810/19; ME6811/19; ME/6812/19, 1 June 2020 (Bauer Media Group merger inquiry); ME/6868/19, 2 February 2021 (Viagogo/Stubhub); ME/6897/20, 2 June 2020 (Adevinta/eBay).
1316. 19-DCC-157, 12 August 2019 (France Télévisions/TF1/Métropole Télévision/Salto JV); 16-DCC-111, 27 July 2016 (Fnac/Darty).
1317. ACM/20/039644, 9 July 2020 (GVB Holding N.V./HTM Personenvervoer N.V./NS Groep N.V./Rotterdamse Electrische Tram N.V.); ACM/20/038614, 20 May 2020 (NS Groep N.V./Pon Netherlands B.V./JV); ACM/19/035555, 28 August 2019 (Sanoma Learning B.V./Iddink Holding B.V.).
1318. M.10262, 27 January 2022 (Meta/Kustomer); M.9660, 11 May 2021 (Google/Fitbit); M.8124, 20 January 2017 (Microsoft/LinkedIn).
1319. ME/6809/19; ME/6810/19; ME6811/19; ME/6812/19, 1 June 2020 (Bauer Media Group merger inquiry).
1320. 19-DCC-157, 12 August 2019 (France Télévisions/TF1/Métropole Télévision/Salto JV).
1321. ACM/20/039644, 9 July 2020 (GVB Holding N.V./HTM Personenvervoer N.V./NS Groep N.V./Rotterdamse Electrische Tram N.V.); ACM/20/038614, 20 May 2020 (NS Groep N.V./Pon Netherlands B.V./JV); ACM/19/035555, 28 August 2019 (Sanoma Learning B.V./Iddink Holding B.V.).

reviewed (and intervened in) mergers with limited nexus to the UK'.[1322] The high number of EU filings can be explained by the fact that major tech deals often reach the EU merger regulation thresholds. This excludes an obligation to notify the concentration in all the other jurisdictions under review save – since Brexit – the UK. In addition, the Apple/Shazam and Meta (Facebook)/Kustomer[1323] cases – which did not meet the EU thresholds in view of Kustomer's and Shazam's turnover respectively – were referred to the Commission under Article 22 EU Merger Regulation (EUMR). The Commission's new Article 22 policy and the duty to notify concentrations under Article 14 DMA may further shift the workload of tech mergers from national authorities to the Commission (*see* Chapter 4 on the Commission). The Meta/Kustomer case is particularly noteworthy since it demonstrates that Article 22 referrals may erode the *one-stop principle*. The Bundeskartellamt made its own assessment of that case after refusing to join a referral to the Commission initiated by the Austrian Bundeswettbewerbsbehörde.[1324]

Of the six authorities under review, the CMA has been the most interventionist when it comes to the substantial assessment of the mergers in the tech sector that came under its jurisdiction during the period under review. It blocked three mergers, opened thirteen in-depth investigations and imposed remedies on three occasions, including one behavioural remedy (*see* Table 10.3). In addition, four mergers were abandoned after the CMA opened an in-depth investigation.[1325] Only the CMA (four) and the Commission (five) have substantially reviewed acquisitions by GAMA companies, leading to three conditional approvals, one prohibition and five unconditional approvals. While the ACM only needed to decide on three mergers, it imposed (behavioural) remedies in all three cases. The Commission had to assess no less than fifteen cases in the period under review but imposed remedies in only three of these (16%). The Autorité imposed remedies twice (of which one was behavioural and the other structural), in the eight cases it needed to assess in total (25%). The Bundeskartellamt cleared all six cases that came under its jurisdiction unconditionally.

Overall, there is no upward trend in interventions under merger control rules. The eight behavioural remedies decisions were issued in 2017, 2019 (2), 2020 (3), 2021 and 2022. The three CMA prohibition decisions were issued in 2019, 2020 and 2022. There are also relatively few in-depth investigations into digital mergers. The CMA has conducted the most (thirteen), which is more than all other authorities combined

1322. S. Pritchard, V. Egerton-Doyle, 'The future is now: Brexit and the end of 30 years of the EUMR One Stop Shop for merger control in the UK', 20 August 2020, LinkingCompetition blog.
1323. Commission decision of 27 January 2022 in case M.10262 (Meta/Kustomer).
1324. Bundeskartellamt, 'Bundeskartellamt sieht Anmeldepflicht der Fusion Meta/Kustomer' (*Bundeskartellamt*, 9 December 2021), https://www.bundeskartellamt.de/SharedDocs/Meldung/DE/Pressemitteilungen/2021/09_12_2021_Meta_Kustomer.htm and Bundeskartellamt, 'Pressemitteilung: Freigabe der Übernahme von Kustomer durch Meta (ehemals Facebook)' (Feb. 11, 2022, *Bundeskartellamt/Digitalwirtschaft*) https://www.bundeskartellamt.de/SharedDocs/Publikation/DE/Pressemitteilungen/2022/11_02_2022_Meta_Kustomer.pdf?__blob=publicationFile&v=2, p. 1.
1325. ME/6760/18, 7 January 2019 (Topcashback/Quidco); ME/6879/20, 25 March 2021 (Crowdcube/Seedrs); ME/6743/18, 27 February 2019 (Experian/Credit Laser Holdings); ME/6877/20, 14 September 2020 (Taboola/Outbrain).

(nine). This suggests that merger control has not been the most appropriate tool to tackle digital competition issues. The figures can even be considered underwhelming, considering the large number of acquisitions that GAMA companies have made during the period under investigation. The Furman Report mentions 400 acquisitions by Amazon, Apple, Meta, Google, and Microsoft between 2010 and 2019.[1326] Bruegel, a think tank, found that these companies did approximately fifty acquisitions per year between 2010 and 2019, with a peak in 2014 (seventy-three acquisitions).[1327]

As indicated, however, any quantitative comparison between the merger control practices of the authorities under review should be made with extreme caution, if at all. Apart from the CMA, which has discretionary power to decide which cases to assess, the authorities under investigation do not have the power to call-in mergers for review. However, national authorities may decide to refer potentially problematic cases over which they do not have jurisdiction themselves to the Commission under Article 22 EUMR under the new Commission policy.

1326. Digital Competition Expert Panel, 'Unlocking Digital Competition' (Furman Report), March 2019.
1327. G. Parker, G. Petropoulos and M. Van Alstyne, 'Platform Mergers and Antitrust', Bruegel Working Paper, 15 June 2021.

§10.02 ENFORCEMENT STYLES

It is undeniable that the authorities under review have displayed a variety of enforcement styles, that in certain cases also changed considerably over time.

Commission hits hard

The Commission has consistently been at one end of the spectrum. During the period under review, the Commission 'dealt hard blows' and handed out no less than eighteen fines,[1328] with Google twice breaking the dubious record for the highest fine imposed on a single undertaking (and afterwards receiving even a third fine). It should also be noted that ten GAMA investigations[1329] are underway, which may lead to intervention by the competition authorities. Vestager has continued to take a critical line towards the big tech companies in her public statements during her second term. Only on four occasions did undertakings (Amazon, Penguin, and the pay-TV broadcasters – twice, in 2016 and 2019) manage to persuade the Commission to accept commitments.[1330]

CMA is balanced, but an aggressive merger control enforcer

The CMA's policy regarding antitrust may in turn be described as balanced. It has stated that innovation should not be stifled. The CMA has nonetheless been quite active with four[1331] commitment decisions and twelve[1332] decisions imposing fines.

1328. AT.40413, 20 January 2021, Video Games – Focus Home; AT.40414, 20 January 2021, Video Games – Koch Media; AT.40420, 20 January 2021, Video Games – ZeniMax; AT.40422, 20 January 2021, Video Games – Bandai Namco; AT.40424, 20 January 2021, Video Games – Capcom; AT.40528, 21 February 2020, Holiday Pricing – Melia; AT.40433, 30 January 2020, Film merchandise – NBCUniversal; AT.40432, 9 July 2019, Character merchandise – Sanrio; AT.40436, 25 March 2019, Ancillary Sports Merchandise – Nike; AT.40411, 20 March 2019, Google Search (AdSense); AT.40428, 17 December 2018, Guess; AT.40465, 24 July 2018, Vertical restraints – Asus; AT.40469, 24 July 2018, Vertical restraints – Denon & Marantz; AT.40181, 24 July 2018, Vertical restraints – Philips; AT.40182, 24 July 2018, Vertical restraints – Pioneer; AT.40099, 18 July 2018, Google Android; AT.39740, 27 June 2017, Google Search (Shopping); AT.39530, 6 March 2013, Microsoft (tying) – non-compliance.

1329. Amazon Marketplace (2019); Amazon Buy Box (2020); Google for Jobs (2019); Google – Adtech and Data-related practices (2021); Google-Facebook (Open Bidding) agreement (2022); Apple – App Store Practices (2020); Apple – App Store Practices (music streaming) (2020); Apple – App Store Practices (e-books/audiobooks) (2020); Apple – Mobile payments (2020); Facebook leveraging (2021).

1330. AT.40023, 7 March 2019, Cross-order access to pay-TV – Disney, NBC, Universal, Sony Pictures, Warner Bros. and Sky; AT.40153, 4 May 2017, E-book MFNs and related matters (Amazon); AT.40023, 26 July 2016, Cross-order access to pay-TV – Paramount; AT.39847, 25 July 2013, E-books – Penguin.

1331. 50972, 11 February 2022, Google – Privacy Sandbox; 50408, 29 June 2017, Online bidding services – ATG Media; CE/9496-11, 9 September 2014, Vehicle service, maintenance and repair platforms – Epyx; CE/9320/10, 31 January 2014, Booking.com B.V, Expedia, Inc, InterContinental Hotels Group plc and Hotel Inter-Continental London Limited.

1332. 50952, 23 March 2022, DAR Lighting; 50505, 19 November 2020, Price comparison website: use of most favoured nation clauses; 50565-6, 17 July 2020, GAK, Yamaha; 50565-4, 29 June 2020, Korg; 50565-5, 29 June 2020, Roland; 50565-3, 22 January 2020, Fender; 50565-2, 1 August 2019, Casio; 50230, 24 August 2017, Ping; 50343, 20 June 2017, Pool Lighting Ltd; 50223, 12 August 2016, Online sales of posters and frames; CE/9856/14, 24 May 2016, Online RPM – commercial refrigeration; CE/9857-14, 10 May 2016, Online RPM – bathroom fittings sector.

None of these fines has been imposed for an abuse of dominance infringement, but this may change soon as six investigations are underway, including five GAMA investigations.[1333] During the investigation period, the CMA has only taken one final decision against GAMA, accepting commitments by Google,[1334] but has displayed with an aggressive merger control policy (*see* Chapter 5, the Introduction above). With twenty-five relevant precedents, the CMA's production far exceeds that of the other authorities under review. During the investigation period, no less than three mergers were prohibited and four mergers were abandoned since the CMA saw concerns for competition. All of this makes the CMA by far the strictest merger control enforcer of the six authorities under review. This may be due to two factors. First, with Brexit, the CMA is often in a position to assess the same merger cases as the Commission. Second, it is possible that the UK's voluntary merger control system makes it possible for the CMA to devote its resources to those cases that really matter for competition.

Autorité is the most aggressive national enforcer in antitrust cases, future policy is however uncertain

The Autorité's enforcement style has evolved. In the first edition of this book, we described the Autorité's enforcement style as balanced and, in certain respects, even restrained. That description is no longer appropriate at present (May 2023). At the time of finishing the first edition of this book in late spring 2019, there was only one fining decision (addressed to Stihl[1335]). By the cut-off date of the investigation for the second edition (July 2022), there were seven[1336] (of which one decision imposed two separate fines on Apple for a customer and market sharing agreement on the one hand and an abuse of a state of economic dependence on the other). Striking are the nine abuse cases (eight[1337] in the investigation period and one[1338] before) against Google, in which three fines were imposed.[1339] The imposition of interim measures in abuse cases, of which the Autorité is the self-proclaimed pioneer, is also characteristic of the Autorité's enforcement style as it is the only authority that has successfully used this instrument

1333. Amazon Marketplace (2022); Google – Play Store Billing (2022); Google – Ad tech (2022); Apple – AppStore (2022); Meta – Use of ad data (2021); Education Software Solutions Limited (2022).
1334. 50972, 11 February 2022, Google – Privacy Sandbox.
1335. Autorité de la Concurrence, decision 24 October 2018, 18-D-23 (*Stihl*).
1336. 21-D-17, 12 July 2021, Google – ancillary rights (non-compliance); 21-D-11, 7 June 2021, Google – Doubleclick for publishers/AdX; 20-D-04, 16 March 2020, Apple/Tech Data/Ingram Micro; 19-D-26, 19 December 2019, Google AdWords III (Gibmedia); 19-D-14, 1 July 2019, Bikeeurope B.V.; 18-D-23, 24 October 2018, Stihl; 17-D-01, 26 January 2017, Sanbri. The Apple decision imposed three separate fines on Apple for a customer and market sharing agreement, an abuse of a state of economic dependence and a fine for resale price maintenance.
1337. Google – Doubleclick for publishers/AdX (2021); Google – ancillary rights (2020); Google AdWords VI (Amadeus) (2019); Google AdWords V (Interactive Labs) (2018); Google AdSense (1PlusV) (2017); Google AdWords IV (IAH) (2016); Google AdWords III (Gibmedia) (2015); Google AdWords II (E-Kanopi) (2013).
1338. Google AdWords I (Navx) (2010).
1339. 21-D-17, 12 July 2021, Google – ancillary rights (non-compliance); 21-D-11, 7 June 2021, Google – Doubleclick for publishers/AdX; 19-D-26, 19 December 2019, Google AdWords III (Gibmedia).

in a digital competition law case (in the definition as used in this book).[1340] The Autorité accepted commitments four times (by Google (twice), Meta and Booking-.com),[1341] and suspended an investigation into Adidas when it voluntarily changed its behaviour. In the field of policy documents and market research, the Autorité frequently cooperates with the Bundeskartellamt.

The question however is to what extent, in due course, our description of the Autorité's supervisory style might be a completely different one once again. Time will tell whether the succession of President Isabelle de Silva by Benoît Cœuré on 21 January 2022 will once more bring a wind of change to the Autorité's enforcement style. In interviews, he has emphasised the need for increased cooperation with data protection authorities: '*The ability of our authorities to act in a coordinated manner is, I am convinced, the condition for an effective response to the challenges posed by the digital economy.*'[1342] He also foresees ample room for French antitrust enforcement in the DMA era: '*There are two ways we can support the EU: we can identify and bring cases to the commission under the DMA umbrella; but equally important is to maintain our own antitrust work regarding digital platforms in areas not covered by the DMA.*'[1343]

Bundeskartellamt is an innovative and active enforcer and is unique in not imposing fines as a matter of policy

The Bundeskartellamt's approach as well can be described as particularly interventionist. Ten cases ended with enforcement action. The Bundeskartellamt has proved itself prepared to take up innovative cases, such as the *Facebook* case.[1344] The Bundeskartellamt stands out in refraining from imposing fines and limiting itself to prohibiting the disputed conduct. This makes the Bundeskartellamt the only authority that establishes and prohibits infringements in the digital sector, but (thus far) systematically does not fine them. Additionally in Germany, on ten occasions, the undertakings concerned made promises to change the conduct of their own accord (without any formal commitment or prohibition decisions), after which these cases were settled informally. The investigation into Lufthansa was terminated by the Bundeskartellamt because no abuse of dominance could be established. However, to this, it must be added that none of the cases investigated by the Bundeskartellamt dealt with hardcore infringements such as resale price maintenance, geoblocking or restrictions of passive sales. It seems plausible that the Bundeskartellamt would also impose fines for such hardcore restrictions if these would come to its attention. Finally, its reluctance to impose fines might have made it easier for the Bundeskartellamt to take up innovative, 'experimental' cases in which it is not evident from prior case law whether the conduct at issue indeed constitutes an infringement.

1340. 20-MC-01, 9 April 2020, Google – ancillary rights; 10-MC-01, 30 June 2010, Google AdWords I (Navx).
1341. 22-D-13, 21 June 2022, Google – ancillary rights (commitments); 22-D-12, 16 June 2022, Meta; 21-D-11, 7 June 2021, Google – Doubleclick for publishers/AdX; 15-D-06, 21 April 2015, Booking.com.
1342. Mlex.
1343. GCR, 'An interview with Benoît Cœuré', 24 June 2022.
1344. Bundeskartellamt, decision of 6 februari 2019 in case B6-22/16, *Facebook*.

The ACM becomes more ambitious and less cautious

Like the Autorité, the ACM, which under the presidency of Mr Fonteijn maintained a rather cautious and investigative approach to digital markets and emphasised that it did not want to act too quickly in order to avoid disrupting innovation, has become a significantly more active enforcer over the past few years. Upon his departure, Fonteijn already hinted that such a change of policy was eminent: '*"We moeten niet angstig zijn", geeft hij mee aan de organisatie die hij verlaat. "We moeten durven experimenteren. De reactie mag er niet één zijn van: laten we maar geen enge zaken doen"*' [freely translated: '*"We should not be anxious", he imparts to the organisation [the ACM] he is leaving. "We have to dare to experiment. The response may not be: let's not do anything scary"*'].[1345] His successor Mr Snoep was even more pronounced when he took office: in his opinion, fines certainly have an absolute added value in certain cases and are even necessary: '*Natuurlijk hoef je er niet altijd met boetes op te slaan, maar als scheidsrechter moet je ook af en toe een gele en rode kaart trekken. (...) Ja, het aantal boetes gaat omhoog.*' [freely translated: '*Of course, you don't always have to hit out with fines, but as a referee you also have to draw a yellow and red card from time to time (...) Yes, the number of fines will go up*'].[1346]

The announcement of a series of dawn raids shortly thereafter in December 2018 was a further omen that the ACM's policy of reluctance was up for a change. As evidenced by the recent fine on Samsung for resale price maintenance that resulted from these raids[1347] and the order under penalty clause imposed on Apple for abuse of dominance,[1348] the above has not turned out to be an empty promise. The transformation of the ACM from a somewhat cautious and consultation-oriented authority to one that does not shy away from enforcement via fines is starting to take form. It may be expected that more fining decisions will follow in the coming years. The ACM also took a disculpatory decision in the *Thuisbezorgd.nl* case and forced a change of behaviour in the *NOvA* case in an informal manner.

Policy of the BCA still needs to take form

The enforcement style of the BCA in the digital sector can be characterised as passive and wait-and-see. Only once during the investigation period (and then at the very end in 2021) did the BCA impose a fine (in the *Caudalie* case[1349] for restricting online sales). Earlier, in 2016, in *Immoweb,*[1350] the BCA ceased its investigation after Immoweb had voluntarily changed its behaviour. Together with the rejection of an abuse of dominance complaint in *The Great Circle/IRM,*[1351] these two cases form the track record of the BCA regarding the application of the cartel and abuse of dominance prohibition.

1345. Het Financieele Dagblad, 'De ACM Moet Niet Angstig Zijn, Moet Durven Experimenteren' (Interview with Chris Fonteijn), 25 April 2018.
1346. NRC, 18 January 2019, 'Eerst had ik een handvol cliënten, nu heb ik er 17 miljoen' (interview Martijn Snoep).
1347. ACM, decision 14 September 2021, ACM/20/040569 (*Samsung*).
1348. ACM, summary of decision 24 August 2021, ACM/19/035630 (*Apple*).
1349. BCA, decision 6 May 2021, ABC-2021-P/K-09 (*Caudalie*).
1350. BCA, decision 7 November 2016, ABC-2016-I/O-31-AUD (*Immoweb*).
1351. BCA, decision 15 February 2019, ABC-2019-V/M-10 (*IRM*).

The BCA also did not conduct any publicly available market studies. As mentioned in the chapter on the BCA, the BCA did label the digital sector as a spearhead of its policy in 2021 and again in 2022. Whether this will also lead to actual enforcement policy changes remains to be seen in the coming years. The BCA appears to be somewhat behind and will have to catch up if it truly wishes to spearhead the digital sector.

Conclusion: substantial differences between enforcement styles; styles change over time

In summary, various patterns can be discerned. The authorities under review have jointly used the full range of possible enforcement instruments (fines, commitments, prohibitions, enforcing behavioural change, provisional measures, and conditional penalty payments), but each authority clearly has its own preferences and styles. What is clear is that the time of study is over and the era of enforcement has begun. The era of the soft approach has come to an end.

Nevertheless, clear differences between the enforcement policies of the various authorities under review can be observed as well as between the policies pursued by a single authority during different periods. Who is president/chair of a competition authority can have a great influence on the policy pursued by that authority. Mundt's (seemingly partly personal) aversion to imposing fines in abuse cases – which shall be discussed in further detail below – forms a good example. The importance of a president's persona becomes even more apparent once that president is succeeded. For example, since Vestager succeeded Joaquin Almunia as Competition Commissioner (just before the start of the research period of this book), the competition policy pursued by the European Commission has clearly become (even) more interventionist. A good example is the *Google Shopping* case. Whereas under Almunia this case was allegedly moving towards a settlement with remedies, under Vestager the Commission eventually decided to impose a hefty fine. Similarly, the ACM has become more active since the appointment of its new chairman, Martijn Snoep, as of 1 September 2018. Since his appointment, the ACM has issued four[1352] of its total of five[1353] digital competition law antitrust decisions, including a decision against one of the big tech companies.[1354] In France and in the UK, it remains to be seen what consequences the succession of President Isabelle de Silva by Benoît Cœuré as of 21 January 2022 and that of Andrea Coscelli by Marcus Bokkerink on 7 September 2022 will have for the enforcement policy pursued by the Autorité and the CMA respectively. The BCA is currently 'decapitated' after Jacques Steenbergen resigned as chairman on 31 January 2023. No successor has been appointed yet (situation May 2023). Before this happens,

1352. ACM decision 14 December 2018, ACM/17/012061 (*handhavingsverzoek Legal Dutch*), ACM, decision 14 September 2021, ACM/20/040569 (*Samsung*), ACM, decision 19 April 2021, ACM/21/049853 (*SIDN*) and ACM, summary of decision 24 August 2021 (*Apple*), ACM/19/035630.
1353. ACM, decision 18 November 2016 (*Thuisbezorgd.nl*), ACM/DM/2016/207286; ACM, decision 14 December 2018, ACM/17/012061 (*handhavingsverzoek Legal Dutch*); ACM, decision 14 September 2021, ACM/20/040569 (*Samsung*); ACM, decision 19 April 2021, ACM/21/049853 (*SIDN*) and ACM, summary of decision 24 August 2021 (*Apple*), ACM/19/035630.
1354. ACM, summary of decision 24 August 2021 (*Apple*), ACM/19/035630.

it appears unlikely that the BCA will change its passive enforcement style that it pursued throughout the investigation period.

Parallel investigations

The authorities under investigation sometimes investigate the same or similar cases in parallel. This may lead to friction. In the hotel booking sector, the CMA (at the time still a member of the European Competition Network (ECN)), the Autorité and the Bundeskartellamt dealt with similar cases which had partially different outcomes (*see* section §5.01[A] on parity clauses). In short, CMA and Autorité approved narrow parity clauses and only saw a problem in broad parity clauses. The Bundeskartellamt however objected (and continues to object) to any form of parity clauses. The Commission tried to play a coordinating role, but – given the diverging results – failed.

At the time of completing the second edition of this book, it is remarkable that three authorities are simultaneously investigating the App Stores of Apple and Google. The ACM has already imposed an order imposing conditional penalty payments on Apple and may also investigate Google. The investigations by the Commission and the CMA into the App Stores of Apple and Google are ongoing. After Brexit, it can be expected that the CMA will increasingly choose its own path. It will be interesting to observe whether the Commission will take a similar approach as the ACM in its investigation of the Apple App Store, or whether once again divergent enforcement policies will emerge within the EU. In a press release from 2021, the ACM suggested that there was at least some alignment between the two authorities and that the investigations would focus on different aspects.[1355] At the time, the ACM was investigating Apple's terms and conditions for the App Store for app providers that offer apps that do not compete with Apple's own apps, particularly in online dating in the Netherlands. The European Commission on the other hand was said to be investigating whether Apple is placing obstacles in the way of apps that do compete directly with Apple's apps, such as music streaming services. As soon as the Commission will also have completed its investigation into Apple, it will become clear whether the investigations are, as expected, complementary and based on the same assessment framework.

In any case, these examples of hotel booking sites and app stores show that the existing coordination mechanisms within the ECN do not always prevent that various competition authorities within the EU are assessing the same or similar conduct either at the same time or consecutively. At least once (in the hotel booking cases), this has led to divergent outcomes. Given both the EU's objective of creating a level playing field within the EU internal market and the inherently cross-border nature of many digital markets, such an outcome can be regarded as undesirable. To conclude, the mistakes of the early online hotel booking cases have not been repeated. This may indicate that cooperation and coordination have improved. However, challenges

1355. ACM, press release 22 June 2021, *ACM can continue investigation into Apple App Store*, https://www.acm.nl/nl/publicaties/acm-kan-onderzoek-naar-apple-appstore-voortzetten.

remain as authorities need to expand their cooperation to, amongst others, gatekeeper legislation enforcement and merger control.

Different opinions regarding the imposition of fines

As becomes clear from the above, there is no consensus among the authorities under investigation regarding the desirability of the imposition of fines. The Bundeskartellamt is unique in, thus far, categorically rejecting the imposition of fines (at least in cases not dealing with hardcore cartel infringements). This decision not to impose fines is based on an explicit policy choice by the Bundeskartellamt. During the Charles River Associates (CRA) conference on Economic Developments in Competition Policy on 5 December 2018, Bundeskartellamt president Andreas Mundt stated during a forum discussion that he was not a strong believer in fines as an enforcement instrument. According to Mundt, a fine only adds value to a prohibition in exceptional cases. In an interview published mid-2021, Mundt was quoted as follows: '*Fines get us nowhere, (…)*'. Instead, the focus should be on the imposition of remedies '*that really correct the conduct of these companies and point them in a better direction*'.[1356] This view would appear to be at odds with the views of (in any event) the Commission, the CMA, the Autorité and – certainly since the entry into office of its current chairman Martijn Snoep – the ACM. This would make Mundt appear to be rather solitary in his policy view of extreme caution in respect of imposing fines. It is likely that the Bundeskartellamt will continue its line of banning agreements and practices, but not imposing fines, at least for the remainder of Mundt's tenure. Consensus also appears to have grown among the other authorities under investigation that in abuse cases, (high) fines may sometimes be required to ensure effective enforcement.[1357] The imposition of fines seems uncontroversial in hardcore cartel cases, even in rapidly developing markets. In simplified terms, all authorities (most likely even including the Bundeskartellamt) appear to be taking the view that classic cartel infringements remain 'classic', also on high-tech markets, and accordingly in principle deserve a 'classic' form of punishment, i.e., a fine. Actual horizontal cartels[1358] were fined only by the Autorité (*Apple/Tech Data/Ingram Micro*[1359]) and the CMA (*Posters and Frames*[1360]). It is likely that the other authorities would not hesitate to impose fines for similar infringements. It is noteworthy that the Autorité – but not the Commission or the CMA – when setting the fine in the *Stihl* case[1361] did take account of the uncertainty of the applicable law at the time of the infringement and therefore mitigated the fine. We expect that authorities will

1356. 'Germans roll out the big guns in antitrust offensive against Big Tech', *Business Day*, 24 June 2021, https://www.businesslive.co.za/bd/life/2021-06-24-germans-roll-out-the-big-guns-in-antitrust-offensive-against-big-tech/.
1357. The BCA labelled the digital sector as a spearhead of its policy in 2021 and again in 2022, but has not yet imposed any fines.
1358. Not including primarily vertical infringements with horizontal elements.
1359. Autorité de la Concurrence, decision 16 March 2020, 20-D-04 (Apple/Tech Data/Ingram Micro).
1360. CMA, decision 12 August 2016, 50223 (Online sales of posters and frames).
1361. Autorité de la Concurrence, decision 24 October 2018, 18-D-23 (Stihl).

continue to apply significantly different fining policies in the absence of any clear movement towards harmonisation of these policies. It will be interesting to see if the Bundeskartellamt will maintain its non-fining policy under the new German gatekeeper legislation.

§10.03 NEW LEGISLATION (ANTITRUST)

[A] Overview of the State of Specific Legislation in the Various Jurisdictions Surveyed

A clearly discernible trend in the jurisdictions surveyed is the introduction of regulation, whether specific to the digital sector or not, aimed at regulating the market in addition to the application of regular competition law. This is an important development, which has also occurred very quickly (in the past three years). At the time of the publication of the first edition of this book in 2019 – except for the French Article L. 420-2 second paragraph of the Code de Commerce, which is not specifically aimed at the digital sector – in all the jurisdictions surveyed, there was still only a rather abstract discussion of whether additional regulation would be necessary. Three years on, additional regulation is already in place in Germany and Belgium, and has been adopted in the EU and also in the UK and the Netherlands, the discussion seems settled in the sense that consensus has emerged that additional regulation is necessary. However, such legislation has yet to be drafted in both jurisdictions.

Below, an overview shall be provided of the different regulatory legislation that has been introduced, will be introduced or is being discussed in the various jurisdictions surveyed and that is aimed (exclusively or *inter alia*) at regulating the digital sector. A more detailed description of legislation already introduced or to be introduced can be found in the various national chapters above.

Next, the similarities and differences between the various regulatory systems chosen or under consideration will be discussed. Since most legislation has yet to be introduced or has come into force fairly recently, it is not possible – except in a theoretical sense – to make any substantiated statements about the effectiveness of the various rules at this point.

[1] EU

On 15 December 2020, the Commission published a proposal to introduce (i) the Digital Services Act (DSA) and (ii) the Digital Markets Act (DMA). Both proposals contain new rules for digital services, including social media, online marketplaces and other online platforms. These rules should ensure fairer and more transparent digital markets. The new rules should contribute to innovation, growth and increased competition.

The DSA contains clear obligations for providers of digital services, such as social media or marketplaces, to tackle the spread of illegal content, online disinformation and other societal risks. The new obligations include (i) new measures to counter illegal online content and obligations for platforms to respond quickly, (ii) better traceability and controls of traders on online marketplaces, (iii) increased transparency and accountability of platforms and (iv) bans on misleading practices and certain forms of targeted advertising.

The DMA imposes certain obligations on large online platforms that act as 'gatekeepers' (platforms whose dominant online position makes them difficult for consumers to circumvent) in the digital market to ensure a fairer business environment and more services for consumers. To prevent unfair trading practices, platforms designated as gatekeepers must, among other things, allow third parties to cooperate with their own services. This allows smaller platforms to ensure that dominant messaging platforms allow their users to exchange messages, voice messages or send files through different messaging apps. In addition, gatekeepers should allow business users access to the data they generate in the gatekeeper's platform to promote their own offers and conclude contracts – even outside the gatekeeper's platforms. Also, the DMA should ensure that gatekeepers can no longer rank their own services or products more favourably than other third parties on their platforms (*self-preferencing*), prevent users from easily uninstalling preinstalled software or apps, and process users' personal data for targeted advertising without explicit consent.[1362]

On 23 November 2021, the European Parliament confirmed that the International Market and Consumer Protection Committee had approved the Commission's proposal for the DMA. On 25 November 2021, the Council of the EU agreed to the European Commission's proposals. On 20 January 2022, the European Parliament finalised its position on the draft DSA, which was adopted in plenary by a large majority. On 5 July 2022, the DMA and DSA were adopted by the European Parliament. The DMA entered into force on 1 November 2022 and has become applicable on 2 May 2023 (after a six-month transition period).[1363] The DSA entered into force on 16 November 2022 and will be directly applicable across the EU and apply fifteen months after entry into force or from 1 January 2024, whichever is later. As regards obligations for very large online platforms and very large online search engines, the DSA will apply from an earlier date, namely four months after their designation.[1364]

[2] France

The French abuse of dominance provision of Article L. 420-2 of the Code de Commerce has a second paragraph prohibiting the abuse of a state of economic dependency.[1365] The French Court of Cassation (Cour de cassation) has defined the state of economic dependency for distributors as follows: '*que l'état de dépendance économique, pour un distributeur, se définit comme la situation d'une entreprise qui ne dispose pas de la possibilité de substituer à son ou ses fournisseurs un ou plusieurs autres fournisseurs répondant à sa demande d'approvisionnement dans des conditions technique et économiques comparables; qu'il s'en déduit que la seule circonstance qu'un distributeur réalise une part très importante voire exclusive de son approvisionnement auprès d'un seul fournisseur ne suffit pas à caractériser son état de dépendance économique au sens*

1362. https://www.europarl.europa.eu/news/en/press-room/20220701IPR34364/digital-services-landmark-rules-adopted-for-a-safer-open-online-environment.
1363. European Commission, press release of 31 October 2022, *Digital Markets Act: rules for digital gatekeepers to ensure open markets enter into force*, https://ec.europa.eu/commission/presscorner/detail/en/ip_22_6423.
1364. https://digital-strategy.ec.europa.eu/en/policies/digital-services-act-package.
1365. *See* Cour de Cassation, chamber commerciale du 3 mars 2004, no. 02-14529.

de l'article L. 420-2 du Code de commerce' [English translation]: '*the state of economic dependence, for a distributor, is defined as a situation where a company does not have the ability to replace its supplier(s) with one or more suppliers that can meet its supply needs under equivalent technical and economic conditions; that it deduces that the mere fact that a distributor purchases a significant or even exclusive part of its supplies from a single supplier is not sufficient to characterise its state of economic dependence within the meaning of Article L. 420-2 of the French Commercial Code*'.[1366]]

The effect of this legislation may be that a business partner on whom the other company is dependent may be held criminally liable in the event of bankruptcy or termination of the contract.

France is (chronologically speaking) a forerunner in terms of new additional regulatory legislation, as the provision on the abuse of a state of economic dependency has been in force for over twenty years. Of course, it should be noted that this French article of law does not specifically target the digital sector.

[3] United Kingdom

New antitrust legislation is hotly debated in the UK. The regime envisioned by the UK government seems to lean towards the German system to be discussed below. In July 2021, at the urging of the CMA, the UK government published a proposal for a *new regulatory regime for digital markets*. The regime proposed by the CMA would only apply to the most powerful digital companies, namely those with 'strategic market status' (SMS) in a given activity. For these companies, the regime has three main pillars:

(1) an enforceable *code of conduct* aimed at preventing companies from abusing their dominant position, for example by exploiting consumers and companies that rely on them or excluding competitors. The principles of the code are based on fair trade, open choices, and trust and transparency;
(2) *pro-competitive interventions* (PCIs) – such as giving consumers more control over their data, or requiring third parties to access their data – these *remedies aim to* address the fundamentals of the firm's dominance; and
(3) a *merger regime* between SMS companies to ensure that transactions involving SMS companies are more closely scrutinised. The regime will involve prior notification of all transactions, mandatory notification of a subset of transactions that meet clearly defined thresholds and have a UK link, and a more cautious standard of proof.

The scheme will be overseen by the new Digital Markets Unit (DMU), which was set up in a shadow version within the CMA in April 2022 to begin preparations for the scheme, with the expectation that the DMU and the scheme will eventually have a statutory basis.

1366. *See ibid.*

[4] Germany

In January 2021, the Tenth Amendment to the German Competition Act (GWB Digitalisation Act) entered into force. The new section 19a GWB empowers the Bundeskartellamt to take *ex ante* measures against companies with significant market power. Companies must first be formally listed by decision of the Bundeskartellamt to be subject to section 19a GWB. It has now been determined by the Bundeskartellamt that (at least) Alphabet (Google),[1367] Meta (Facebook),[1368] Apple[1369] and Amazon[1370] will be subject to the section 19(a) GWB regime for a period of five years. Amazon has since announced that it will challenge its designation under section 19(a) GWB.[1371] Once a company is formally designated as subject to section 19a GWB, the Bundeskartellamt can prohibit such a company from (i) giving preference to its own offers over those of competitors when granting access to purchasing and sales markets (*self-preferencing*); (ii) to take measures which hinder other undertakings in their business activities on purchasing or selling markets if the activities of an undertaking with significant market power (SMP) are important for access to these markets; (iii) to hinder competitors directly or indirectly in a market where the undertaking can rapidly expand its position; (iv) impede or make appreciably more difficult market entry or otherwise hinder other undertakings by processing competitively sensitive data collected by the undertaking, or requiring conditions that allow such processing; (v) refusing or hindering the interoperability of products or services or the portability of data, thereby impeding competition; (vi) failing to provide other undertakings with sufficient information on the scope, quality or success of the service provided or commissioned, or otherwise making it difficult for them to assess the value of that service; and (vii) requiring benefits disproportionate to the reason for that requirement for the treatment of offers from another undertaking.

[5] Netherlands

The need for additional enforcement tools is being discussed in the Netherlands, but there is no legislative proposal or concrete solution direction yet. In early 2018, the ACM indicated that additional regulation is desirable for new situations, specifically with regard to the use of algorithms, the regulation of sustainable market power where

1367. https://www.bundeskartellamt.de/SharedDocs/Meldung/EN/Pressemitteilungen/2022/05_01_2022_Google_19a.html.
1368. https://www.bundeskartellamt.de/SharedDocs/Meldung/EN/Pressemitteilungen/2021/28_01_2021_Facebook_Oculus.html;jsessionid = 9D84548B4F8DB16767E5781E77A9998E.2_cid362?nn = 3591568.
1369. https://www.bundeskartellamt.de/SharedDocs/Meldung/EN/Pressemitteilungen/2021/21_06_2021_Apple.html.
1370. https://www.bundeskartellamt.de/SharedDocs/Meldung/EN/Pressemitteilungen/2021/18_05_2021_Amazon_19a.html.
1371. 'Amazon challenges German 19a designation', *PaRR*, 30 August 2022, https://app.parr-global.com/intelligence/view/intelcms-kjh3r3?utm_source = Notifications&utm_medium = Email&utm_campaign = Alert&utm_term = 5e98051f9325a10029fac1eb&ssouid = AB918D67-4436-4B13-AE99-7C032BD01A4F.

there is no abuse and the ongoing personalisation of offers and prices.[1372] In addition, after concluding its investigation for payment apps to near-field communication (NFC) technology in smartphones, the ACM has been calling for the adaptation of the European payment system rules (PSD2) and the introduction of the DMA. Adjusted and new rules would thus create a level playing field for payment app providers.[1373] It, therefore, seems logical that the ACM supported the DMA when it was first proposed by the European Commission and called for new European *ex ante* measures to maintain a level playing field in the digital payment services markets.[1374]

In the DMA proposal, the role of Member State representatives is limited to the Digital Markets Advisory Committee. This committee will support the Commission by issuing non-binding opinions. However, the Dutch position during the legislative process was that for effective implementation of the DMA, it would be important that the European Commission cooperates sufficiently with national competition authorities and that it is not clear whether cooperation through the advisory committee is sufficient for this purpose. However, this proposal has not been adopted.

[6] Belgium

On 22 August 2020, the prohibition on abuse of economic dependency came into force in Belgium. This prohibition applies in case there is a state of economic dependency, an abuse of that position and the possibility that this abuse affects competition on the Belgian market (or a substantial part of it).[1375] This Belgian legal provision is to a large extent a copy of the French article already mentioned.

For determining the existence of a dominant position vis-à-vis an economically dependent undertaking, the following are particularly relevant: (i) market power; (ii) the dependent firm's significant share of sales; (iii) the firm's technology or know-how; (iv) brand reputation and consumer loyalty to its products; (v) product scarcity and the perishable nature of the product; (vi) access to essential resources or facilities; (vii) the fear of serious economic damage, retaliation or termination of business relationships; (viii) the application of atypical commercial terms; and (ix) whether or not the economic dependency results from the dependent company's conscious choice.[1376]

1372. ACM, policy document, 'The Signal 2018', 11 April 2018. Original Dutch text: '*The current set of instruments offers few possibilities to counter unwanted forms of personalisation. From the consumer perspective, a basic condition is that consumers are clearly informed about the price to be paid. For instance, he should not suddenly have to pay more afterwards and offers should really be offers. As long as the consumer is clearly informed about the price he is paying, even if it is different from the neighbour's, the requirements of current consumer law are met. In addition, in the absence of market power, price discrimination is not likely to lead to restrictions of competition. Therefore, the use of competition law is also unlikely to be fruitful.*'

1373. ACM, press release 2 July 2021, 'Closure of the investigation into payment apps confirms need for new rules'.

1374. ACM, report, 'Big Techs in the payment system', 16 November 2020 and ACM, press release 2 July 2021, 'Closure of the investigation into payment apps confirms need for new rules'.

1375. New Articles I.6 and IV.2/1 of the Economic Code.

1376. *Ibid.*

The rules can be enforced by the Belgian Competition Authority or courts. In enforcing the new rules, the Belgian Competition Authority can conduct an investigation under the standard procedures, by means of requests for information or by conducting dawn raids. For abuses of economic dependency, the Belgian Competition Authority can impose fines (up to a maximum of 2% of the consolidated Belgian turnover of the infringing undertaking), periodic penalty payments (up to a maximum of 2% of daily Belgian turnover) or preliminary measures.

The new rules can also be enforced by commercial courts declaring contracts or clauses null and void or by granting compensation for damages suffered as a result of the abusive practices.

[B] Comparison of the State of Specific Legislation in the Various Jurisdictions Studied

In recent years, the EU and several countries that are the subject of research in this book have introduced (or may or may not have concrete intentions in that direction) new legislation, sector-specific or otherwise, that supplements or even partly (may) replace the classic cartel prohibition and (in particular) the prohibition of abuse of dominance. Looking at the various jurisdictions, the EU, Germany, France and Belgium (in the case of France, for many years) have already introduced such legislation – albeit not sector-specific in the case of France and Belgium. Only the European system and, to a lesser extent, the German system have been written specifically for the digital sector. In the UK, the CMA has presented advanced plans in this direction (although the extent to which these plans will also gain the support of the government and subsequently the legislature is still unclear).

[C] Two Directions for a Solution

Roughly speaking, two lines of solution can be distinguished when introducing new legislation in the jurisdictions studied. The DSA and DMA are highly regulatory in nature. These regulations impose a fixed set of rules and prohibitions and it appears reasonably clear in advance which companies are subject to that regulatory package. The European rules therefore seem to be relatively quick and 'easy' to apply, but the imposition (after entry into force) of a measure not provided for in these draft rules requires a legislative amendment. The German section 19a GWB and the French and Belgian rules on economic dependency have a 'real' *ex ante* character and are therefore vaguer with regard to the measures that can be imposed and thus place a higher burden of proof on the competent competition authority to be entitled to apply the rules in question. On the other hand, once the competition authority has met that burden of proof, it has greater freedom to impose an appropriate measure. The German, French and Belgian systems also do not have an exhaustive list of measures that can be imposed on a company in respect of which section 19a GWB has been declared applicable or to which the French and Belgian provisions on economic dependency can be applied, respectively. At the conference *Digital Antitrust: How to Regulate?* Organized by *Concurrences* on 17 March 2022 in Paris, Bundeskartellamt President Mundt expressed the view that the German model (which he said is based on competition law) would be more future-proof than the EU model (which he referred to as being based on regulation), precisely because the former does not contain an exhaustive list of conduct that is or may be prohibited. An *ex ante* system like the German one would therefore be more responsive to changing market conditions and technological developments.

Moreover, the Commission explicitly leaves open the possibility of coming up with a 'real' *ex ante* instrument at the EU level at a later stage in addition to the DMA and the DSA. At the conference organised by the *Fédération Internationale pour le Droit Européen* (FIDE) in The Hague on 5 November 2021, Commission Director-General Guersent explicitly stated that the DMA is not the so-called *new competition tool* (NCT) that the Commission announced on its website before the actual presentation of its draft for the DMA.[1377] As such, the NCT would likely have resembled the German section 19a GWB had it been introduced. Guersent left open whether the NCT may still be introduced at some point in time or not. One can imagine that the Commission would want to use the NCT – should it ever be proposed again – precisely in those cases where the DMA does not provide for what the Commission regards as an appropriate remedy to a problem identified by the Commission. Should the NCT ever come to the table again, it also seems likely that this would limit the role of Article 102 TFEU in the digital sector. After all, it would appear that the Commission would have a preference for applying for the NCT because the market investigation to be carried out under NCT – should it ever come to be – would be likely to be more limited than what is required under Article 102 TFEU.

It follows that – to apply Mundt's terminology – a competition law instrument and a regulatory instrument are certainly not necessarily mutually exclusive. On several occasions – in addition to the aforementioned conference on 17 March 2022, for example, also at the *CRA Conference* on 30 March 2022 in Brussels – Mundt has therefore indicated that he sees room to apply section 19a GWB at the national level in Germany to cases where the Commission would apply the DMA.

[D] Application of Specific/New Regulations in Practice

Given that most of the specific legislation is still in the draft stage or has been introduced relatively recently, the number of precedents of its application is obviously still very small.

As mentioned above, the French Article L. 420-2 on economic dependence is by far the oldest. Nevertheless, it has only been applied once in the digital sector. That occasion did then immediately mark the imposition of the highest fine ever by the

1377. https://op.europa.eu/en/publication-detail/-/publication/1851d6bb-14d8-11eb-b57e-01aa75ed71a1.

Autorité. It concerned the case of *Apple, Tech Data and Ingram Micro* (2020).[1378] Following a complaint by eBizcuss, a distributor of Apple products, on 16 March 2020, the Autorité imposed its highest-ever fine of EUR 1.24 billion on Apple and two wholesalers of Apple products, Tech Data and Ingram Micro. Apple was fined a total of EUR 1.1 billion for entering into anticompetitive agreements regarding the distribution of its products (excluding iPhones) and for abusing a situation of economic dependency vis-à-vis its 'premium' independent distributors. (For a detailed description of this case, see §6.02[B] above.)

In Germany, no cases under section 19a GWB have yet been concluded, but this may change soon. The first proceedings under section 19a GWB are now pending. The Bundeskartellamt first initiated proceedings under the new section 19a GWB against Amazon. It is notable that parallel to this investigation under section 19a GWB, the investigation under the prohibition on abuse of a dominant was also continued. Mundt says, among other things, that if it can be established that Amazon is indeed '*of paramount significance for competition across markets*', early action can be taken against possible anticompetitive practices by Amazon and such practices can be banned.[1379]

Furthermore, an investigation against Meta (Facebook) under section 19a GWB is now ongoing. The Bundeskartellamt first announced that the investigation, which was already ongoing against Meta (Facebook) regarding *Facebook/Oculus*, would be expanded under section 19a GWB.[1380] On 5 May 2022, the Bundeskartellamt formally confirmed that Meta (formerly Facebook) is indeed subject to regulation under section 19a GWB.[1381]

In Belgium, there are no precedents in the digital sector under the economic dependency legislation yet. The DMA and DSA also have not yet been applied. In other jurisdictions, additional regulatory legislation is not yet in place.

This extremely limited range of precedents (as few as one completed case in France and some pending cases in Germany) makes a comparison between how the various systems work and their effectiveness impossible at the moment. This will undoubtedly be different in a few years' time: developments are moving at lightning speed. For instance, at the time of the previous (first) edition of this book, drafts for the DSA and DMA did not even exist.

[E] Conclusion

Overall, it can be said that in all the jurisdictions covered, there is a growing focus on new regulatory legislation in the digital economy. Additional regulation is already in

1378. *Décision n° 20-D-04 du 16 mars 2020 relative à des pratiques mises en œuvre dans le secteur de la distribution de produits de marque Apple.*
1379. https://www.bundeskartellamt.de/SharedDocs/Meldung/EN/Pressemitteilungen/2022/06_07_2022_Amazon.html.
1380. https://www.bundeskartellamt.de/SharedDocs/Meldung/EN/Pressemitteilungen/2021/28_01_2021_Facebook_Oculus.html.
1381. https://www.bundeskartellamt.de/SharedDocs/Meldung/EN/Pressemitteilungen/2022/04_05_2022_Facebook_19a.html.

place in the EU, Germany, France and Belgium, and a consensus has also emerged in the UK and the Netherlands that additional regulation is needed. Roughly speaking, two directions of solutions by the various legislators can be distinguished when introducing new legislation in the jurisdictions studied, namely, on the one hand, the 'German (*ex ante*) model' (based on competition law) and, on the other hand, the 'EU model' (which is more regulatory in nature). As for precedents of application of the new legislation, there are hardly any yet. However – given the lightning-fast developments – these are bound to emerge in numbers in the coming years.

§10.04 NEW LEGISLATION AND TOOLS (MERGER CONTROL)

[A] Introduction

The rules on merger control are undergoing substantial changes under the influence of new technologies and the impact these have on the functioning of (digital) markets. This section will therefore discuss four current tech-inspired legal developments in merger control, specifically (1) the value-based threshold introduced in Germany, (2) the *Cour d'Appel de Paris'* preliminary reference in the *Towercast* case, (3) the enhanced application of Article 22 of the EU Merger Regulation (EUMR), and (4) the effects of the Article 12 of the Digital Market Act (DMA).

[B] German Transaction Value-Based Threshold

To begin with, it must be recalled that in 2017, in its ninth amendment to the *Gesetz gegen Wettbewerbsbeschränkungen*, Germany introduced a new value-based threshold approach to capture merger cases that would not have been notifiable under the existing thresholds.[1382] Notably, as the Guidance on Transaction Value Thresholds[1383] has been issued jointly by both German and Austrian competition authorities, this approach has also been adopted by the Austrian legislature, which is however not among the jurisdictions under review in this book. Both the German and the Austrian competition authorities have used the aforementioned Guidelines as a justification to implement the transaction value-based thresholds enshrined in their respective competition laws – section 35 of the *Gesetz gegen Wettbewerbsbeschränkungen* in the case of Germany.

Under this provision, a merger must be notified to the Bundeskartellamt in case the transaction value exceeds EUR 400 million.[1384] Through this new approach, the German legislature aims to capture merger cases where it is almost impossible to determine the future market potential of an undertaking in question due to its size and

1382. Bundeskartellamt, 'Bundeskartellamt Paper on Platform Market Power – Results and Recommendations' (2016) Bundeskartellamt p. 4; Bundeskartellamt and Bundeswettbewerbsbehörde, 'Guidance on Transaction Value Thresholds for Mandatory Pre-merger Notification (Section 35 (1a) GWB and Section 9 (4) KartG)' (2018) Bundeskartellamt & Bundeswettbewerbsbehörde p. 9.

1383. Bundeskartellamt and Bundeswettbewerbsbehörde, 'Guidance on Transaction Value Thresholds for Mandatory Pre-merger Notification (Section 35 (1a) GWB and Section 9 (4) KartG)' (2018) Bundeskartellamt & Bundeswettbewerbsbehörde; these Guidelines concern the application of the transaction-based threshold specified in the Gesetz gegen Wettbewerbsbeschränkungen in der Fassung der Bekanntmachung vom 26. Juni 2013 (BGBl. I S. 1750, 3245), das zuletzt durch Artikel 2 des Gesetzes vom 19. Juli 2022 (BGBl. I S. 1214) geändert worden ist.

1384. Gesetz gegen Wettbewerbsbeschränkungen in der Fassung der Bekanntmachung vom 26. Juni 2013 (BGBl. I S. 1750, 3245), das zuletzt durch Artikel 2 des Gesetzes vom 19. Juli 2022 (BGBl. I S. 1214) geändert worden ist Section 35, 1a, 3.

novelty of the market.[1385] Indeed, these cases often involve acquisitions of undertakings with a low turnover, but with the potential to allow the companies involved to rapidly become a dominant party in an emerging market. One can argue that such concentrations are at risk of being detrimental to the competition on the new markets. Already established market participants will be able to buy up their competitors (usually start-ups) which may provide the acquirer with control over (new) markets.[1386] Such a process may have a negative impact on innovation and may prevent new markets from reaching their full potential.

Accordingly, for a merger to fall within the new transaction value threshold, the following four cumulative criteria specified in the Guidance on Transaction Value Thresholds must be satisfied.[1387] First of all, the combined global turnover of the parties must exceed EUR 500 million. Second of all, the revenue in Germany of one concentration party should initially have been more than EUR 25 million, while neither the target undertaking nor any other party's revenues in Germany exceeded EUR 5 million. It should however be noted that in January 2022, with the 10th amendment to the *Gesetz gegen Wettbewerbsbeschränkungen*, the regular turnover-based thresholds were raised. The German legislature raised the threshold for one party's turnover in Germany to EUR 50 million and the other party's turnover in Germany to EUR 17.5 million.[1388] Third of all, as was mentioned earlier, the transaction value in question must exceed EUR 400 million. This latter amount has remained unchanged in the legal review operation of January 2022. Finally, the target undertaking must be active to a significant extent in Germany. It should be further underlined that if a case in question satisfies all of the four aforementioned criteria, the parties involved in a concentration will not be able to invoke the *de minimis* exemption. Accordingly, if the transaction value threshold has been met by the merger in question, but the market share of which is covered by the *de minimis* Notice, the merging parties would not be able to invoke the latter to avoid the transaction from coming under the Bundeskartellamt's jurisdiction. As the *de minimis* Notice of the Commission is only a soft law instrument,[1389] the Bundeskartellamt is free to deviate from it and apply the transaction value base threshold as *lex specialis*.

1385. Martin Sauermann, 'The Transaction Value Threshold in Germany – Experiences with the New Size of Transaction Test in Merger Control' (Competition Policy International, 8 October 2019) https://www.competitionpolicyinternational.com/the-transaction-value-threshold-in-germany-experiences-with-the-new-size-of-transaction-test-in-merger-control/.
1386. OECD, 'Start-ups, killer acquisitions and merger control – Note by Germany' (2020) Directorate For Financial And Enterprise Affairs Competition Committee DAF/COMP/WD(2020)20 p. 4.
1387. Sauermann, *supra* n. 1385.
1388. Bundeskartellamt and Bundeswettbewerbsbehörde, 'Guidance on Transaction Value Thresholds for Mandatory Pre-merger Notification (Section 35 (1a) GWB and Section 9 (4) KartG)' (2022) Bundeskartellamt & Bundeswettbewerbsbehörde p. 26.
1389. Leander Stähler and Mariolina Eliantonio, 'The Legal Effects of EU Competition Soft Law in the Decisions of National Competition Authorities' (2020) 4(4) European Competition and Regulatory Law Review 277; Kirill Ryabtsev, 'The Role of Soft Law in the Development, implementation and Enforcement of EU Competition Law: A Comparative Analysis' (2020) 1 ELSA Law Review 66.

A major drawback of the new transaction value threshold as per the ninth amendment to the *Gesetz gegen Wettbewerbsbeschränkungen* was the fact that it significantly increased the pressure on the Bundeskartellamt resources by resulting in more sector inquiries and a larger number of cases. The aforementioned tenth amendment to the *Gesetz gegen Wettbewerbsbeschränkungen* that increased the turnover thresholds and, consequently, also was partially a reaction to this criticism, was received positively by the stakeholders involved.[1390]

[C] The Cour d'Appel de Paris Preliminary Reference in the Towercast Case

The request for a preliminary ruling from the *Cour d'Appel de Paris* in the *Towercast* case is the second development that should be addressed.[1391] The case originated in 2016, after the undertaking TDF Infrastructure acquired its competitor Itas SAS.[1392] The notification thresholds in France were not met, and neither had the case been referred to the European Commission ('Commission') under Article 22 of the EUMR (*see* below). In 2017, TDF Infrastructure's competitor Towercast filed a complaint with the Autorité and argued that the acquisition in question should be regarded as an abuse of a dominant position by TDF Infrastructure as it would have a detrimental effect on competition on the upstream and downstream wholesale markets for digital terrestrial television broadcasting.[1393] In doing so, Towercast invoked the *Continental Can* judgement of the ECJ. In the *Continental Can* case, the ECJ stated that an undertaking can abuse its dominant position if it strengthens this dominant position by acquiring another undertaking.[1394] Nevertheless, the Autorité disagreed and concluded that no abuse of dominance had occurred as a result of TDF Infrastructure acquiring Itas SAS.[1395] The Autorité found that the *Continental Can* case would be inapplicable to the case at hand and that it would lack the power to use Article 106 TFEU to conduct an *ex post* review of the Itas acquisition by TDF.[1396] In reaction, Towercast brought a case to a French court with the aim of annulling this decision of the Autorité.

As it found that there existed no *acte éclairé* with regard to the question of whether the accomplishment of a concentration under the circumstances at issue could

1390. Lars Mesenbrink and Julius Schradin, 'Good News for Clients from Germany: Increased German Merger Control Thresholds in Force' (*Orrick Antitrust Watch*, 22 January 2021), https://blogs.orrick.com/antitrust/2021/01/22/good-news-for-clients-from-germany-increased-german-merger-control-thresholds-in-force/.

1391. Case C-449/21 *Towercast v. Autorité de la concurrence, Ministère de l'Économie* OJ C 452 [2021].

1392. *Ibid.*, para. 12; TDF, 'Press Release: TDF Buys ITAS' (2016) TDF Infrastructure S.A.S. p. 1.

1393. *Ibid.*, para. 14.

1394. Case C 6-72 *Europemballage Corporation and Continental Can Company v. Commission* ECLI:EU:C:1973:22 [1973] paras 25-26.

1395. Autorité de la Concurrence, 'Rachat d'Itas par TDF: saisie par Towercast, l'Autorité considère que l'abus de position dominante de TDF n'est pas établi' (*Autorité de la Concurrence*, 16 January 2020) https://www.autoritedelaconcurrence.fr/fr/communiques-de-presse/rachat-ditas-par-tdf-saisie-par-towercast-lautorite-considere-que-labus-de.

1396. *Ibid.*

amount to the abuse of a dominant position, the *Cour d'Appel de Paris* decided in 2021 to send a request to the ECJ for a preliminary ruling.[1397] In its preliminary reference, the French court seeks to ascertain whether Article 21(1) of the EUMR precludes a national competition authority from assessing a concentration which: (1) has no EU dimension as per Article 1 EUMR, (2) is below the thresholds for obligatory *ex ante* assessment specified under national law, and (3) was not referred to the Commission under Article 22 EUMR, as constituting an abuse of dominance under Article 102 TFEU, taking into account the structure of competition on a national market in question.[1398]

In here opinion, Advocate General Kokott argued that the non-reportable transactions, such as the one at issue in the Towercast case, can indeed be assessed in light of the rules on abuse of dominant position under Article 102 TFEU.[1399] Kokott supported this opinion with four key arguments.[1400] First, as Article 102 TFEU is a primary law of the EU, its application cannot be precluded by the secondary EU law, such as the EUMR.[1401] Second, Kokott argued that an acquisition of a competitor by a dominant undertaking can sometimes result in the abuse of the latter's dominant position.[1402] Third, she noted that Article 102 TFEU can be seen as an extra instrument capturing killer acquisitions and other mergers which did not meet the national and EU thresholds; thus enhancing the effectiveness of the EUMR enforcement.[1403] Finally, Kokott points out that in order to respect the principle of legal certainty, the earlier cleared mergers cannot be subsequently reassessed under Article 102 TFEU.[1404]

In its judgment of 16 March 2023, the Court of Justice followed Advocate General Kokott's opinion and answered the preliminary questions as follows:

> 'Article 21(1) of Council Regulation (EC) No 139/2004 of 20 January 2004 on the control of concentrations between undertakings must be interpreted as not precluding the competition authority of a Member State from regarding a concentration of undertakings which has no Community dimension within the meaning of Article 1 thereof, is below the thresholds for mandatory ex ante control laid down in national law, and has not been referred to the European Commission under Article 22 of that regulation, as constituting an abuse of a dominant position prohibited under Article 102 TFEU, in the light of the structure of competition on a market which is national in scope.'[1405]

Consequently, national authorities are entitled to apply Article 102 TFEU in cases where no merger control regime applies because the thresholds for notification have not been exceeded but a dominant position is nonetheless strengthened.

1397. Case C-449/21 *Towercast, supra* n. 1391, para. 38.
1398. *Ibid.*, para. 39.
1399. Court of Justice of the European Union, 'Press Release: No 168/22: Advocate General's Opinion in Case C-449/21 | Towercast' (2022) Court of Justice of the European Union p. 1.
1400. Case C-449/21 *Towercast v. Autorité de la concurrence, Ministère de l'Économie* Opinion AG Kokott 13 October 2022.
1401. *Ibid.*, para. 35.
1402. *Ibid.*, para. 45.
1403. *Ibid.*, para. 48.
1404. *Ibid.*, para. 60.
1405. European Court of Justice 16 March 2023, case C-449/21, *Towercast*, ECLI:EU:C:2023:207.

[D] New Approach Towards the Application of the Article 22 of the EUMR

The third development worth mentioning is the new approach of the Commission with regard to the application of Article 22 EUMR. This EUMR provision allows the Commission to take on cases which do not meet the required EU-dimension thresholds, but that have been referred to it by one or more EU Member States, and which adversely affect trade between the EU Member States and significantly distort competition on their territory.[1406] The Commission's policy in the past was to discourage Member States to make case referrals under Article 22 EUMR. Indeed, it generally did not consider cases below the notification threshold to be able to materially influence competition in the EU internal market.[1407] One can argue that one of the key reasons for that was the fact that the Commission does not have enough resources to onboard potentially insignificant cases and had to exclusively focus on those having EU-wide dimensions.[1408]

However, in recent years, the Commission has revised its policy and observes that it sees the use of Article 22 EUMR as vital to secure fair competition on new dynamic markets, specifically those that involve new technology.[1409] As it has also been noted in the Commission Guidelines on Article 22 EUMR application, this notification procedure allowed the Commission to tackle potentially harmful cases below the notification thresholds relating to digital markets.[1410] The Commission observes that in the new emerging markets, smaller players may have the potential to play a major competitive role, regardless of their relatively modest turnover.[1411] Nonetheless, due to their small size, activities of these market players cannot be scrutinised by the Commission under the EUMR notification thresholds. In order to effectively address this potential legislative loophole, the Commission welcomed the value-based thresholds introduced on the national level, such as those in Austria and Germany, and encouraged Member States to make more referrals based on Article 22 EUMR.[1412] Hence, if a merger in question satisfies the two conditions of the Article 22 EUMR – these being (1) affecting trade between the Member States and (2) a potential to significantly distort competition in the Member State that is referring the case to the Commission – such a case may be referred to the Commission.[1413] In order to establish

1406. Council Regulation (EC) No. 139/2004 of 20 January 2004 on the control of concentrations between undertakings (the EC Merger Regulation) OJ L 24 [2004] Article 22.
1407. European Commission, 'Speech by EVP Vestager at the International Bar Association 26th Annual Competition Conference in Florence "Merger control: the goals and limits of competition policy in a changing world' (2022) European Commission p. 2.
1408. Luca Bertuzzi, 'EU Commission set to cut already strained personnel as inflation bites' (*Euractiv*, 1 July 2022) https://www.euractiv.com/section/politics/news/eu-commission-set-to-cut-already-strained-personnel-as-inflation-bites/.
1409. European Commission, *supra* n. 1407.
1410. Commission Guidance on the application of the referral mechanism set out in Article 22 of the Merger Regulation to certain categories of cases C(2021) 1959 [2021] para. 7.
1411. *Ibid.*, para. 9.
1412. *Ibid.*, paras 10-11.
1413. *Ibid.*, paras 13-15.

whether the two criteria are fulfilled, the Commission should take into consideration the prospective nature of the merger control assessment.[1414] Some of the cases referred to the Commission under Article 22 EUMR have already been discussed in this book. For example, the *Meta/Kustomer* acquisition has been referred to the Commission by a large number of EU member states (*see* §4.03[K]). Vestager has emphasised that Article 22 can be used as a targeted tool when it comes to scrutinising the behaviour of smaller digital economy players in niche dynamic markets.[1415] Vestager added that Article 22 EUMR should be applied in synergy with Article 12 of the DMA (*see* below).[1416]

[E] The Notification Procedure under Article 12 of the Digital Market Acts

Finally, the relationship between Article 12 of the DMA and the EUMR must be addressed. The DMA supplements the merger control regime established by the EUMR in Article 12.[1417] According to this Article, an undertaking that qualifies as a gatekeeper pursuant to Article 2(1) of the DMA must notify the Commission of any intended concentration *ex ante*.[1418] In that respect, the DMA explicitly references Article 3 of the Merger Regulation with regard to the definition of a concentration.

Nevertheless, Article 12 DMA procedure does not replace the regular notification procedure under the EUMR.[1419] In this respect, it must be observed that, unlike the EUMR, Article 12 DMA does not provide the Commission with the power to assess, let alone prohibit, concentrations or to impose conditions on concentrations. Instead, this obligation should be perceived as a mechanism for the Commission to stay up-to-date with general developments on digital markets and in particular those involving designated gatekeepers and to enhance the effectiveness of the DMA implementation.[1420] Reference is also made to Recital 31 of the DMA.[1421] This Recital states that the information provided during the notification procedure should be used for classifying a company as a gatekeeper and to assist the Commission with its market investigations specified under the DMA.[1422] It should also be noted that notification under Article 12 DMA is mandatory regardless of whether an acquisition by a gatekeeper exceeds the

1414. *Ibid.*, para. 16.
1415. European Commission, *supra* n. 1407.
1416. *Ibid.*
1417. Regulation of the European Parliament and of the Council on contestable and fair markets in the digital sector (Digital Markets Act) COM/2020/842 final [2020], Article 12.
1418. *Ibid.*, Article 12(1).
1419. Assimakis Komninos, 'Enter the DMA bis! The New Article 22 Guidance and How It Accompanies the DMA' (*Kluwer Competition Law Blog*, 13 April 2021) http://competitionlawblog.kluwercompetitionlaw.com/2021/04/13/enter-the-dma-bis-the-new-article-22-guidance-and-how-it-accompanies-the-dma/.
1420. *Ibid.*
1421. Digital Markets Act, Recital 31.
1422. *Ibid.*

notification thresholds under the Merger Regulation.[1423] In summary, the DMA is meant to complement the merger control regime by allowing the Commission to oversee a broader range of activities of major economic players in the digital market – without granting the Commission the power to interfere directly. It remains to be seen in practice to what extent it will also prove a useful instrument for effective enforcement.

In 2022, ACM Chairman Martijn Snoep argued that national competition authorities need to be actively involved in the enforcement of the DMA by the Commission.[1424] He noted that in case of being successful, such cooperation has the potential to assist the Commission to overcome the challenge of the lack of resources it needs to effectively enforce the DMA.[1425] Effective collaboration, according to Snoep, occurs when the Commission takes the lead in the enforcement of the DMA and the national competition authorities provide it with their civil servants who will be assisting in this process.[1426]

[F] Conclusion

To conclude, technological development has had a considerable impact on merger control legislation and enforcement practice. The competition authorities under review – but also the legislature – have started to focus more on newly emerging markets and on smaller market players in such markets. The introduction of value-based thresholds in Germany forms a good example of this development. Moreover, as illustrated by the preliminary reference in *Towercast*, merger control enforcement in emerging markets may in the future also take place occasionally through the prohibition on abuse of a dominant position.

Merger control legislation itself is also being interpreted differently – and one might say even stretched. The clearest example of this is the new Commission policy in applying Article 2 EUMR. Finally, the notification procedure prescribed by the Article 12 of the DMA strengthens the Commission's oversight powers over the activities of Big Tech and, to some extent, complements the implementation of the EUMR.

1423. Alexander Schmalenberger and Stephan Manuel Nagel, 'The Digital Markets Act – A New Regulation for Digital Markets' (*TaylorWessing*, 4 April 2022), https://www.taylorwessing.com/en/insights-and-events/insights/2022/04/the-digital-markets-act.
1424. Natalie McNelis and Nicholas Hirst, 'Tech Giant "Gatekeepers" Should Face Enforcers Drawn from EU and National Authorities, Snoep Says' (*MLex*, 9 September 2022) https://mlexmarketinsight.com/news/insight/tech-giant-gatekeepers-should-face-enforcers-drawn-from-eu-national-authorities-snoep-says.
1425. *Ibid.*
1426. *Ibid.*, for more information regarding the debate around decentralised DMA enforcement, *see*: Nicholas Hirst and Lewis Crofts, 'Decentralized DMA Gives EU Best Hope of Bringing Big Tech to Heel' (*MLex*, 28 June 2021) https://mlexmarketinsight.com/news-hub/editors-picks/area-of-expertise/antitrust/decentralized-dma-gives-eu-best-hope-of-bringing-big-tech-to-heel.

§10.05 VERTICAL AGREEMENTS

[A] Introduction

The vast majority of investigations and decisions under the cartel prohibition in the digital sector during the period under investigation concern vertical agreements. In total, we count forty-eight examples of vertical restrictions that have been subject to enforcement action (*see* Table 10.4). Most of the restrictions investigated concern resale price maintenance (RPM) (sixteen) and parity clauses (twelve), followed by geoblocking or digital cross-border sales restrictions (ten), platform bans or other restrictions on the use of online distribution channels (seven) and exclusivity agreements (three). The European Commission is the most active authority, accounting for seventeen of the forty-eight restrictions investigated. Among the national competition authorities, the Competition and Markets Authority (CMA) (thirteen) and the Bundeskartellamt (eight) are the most active, followed by the Autorité (six), the Belgian Competition Authority (BCA) (three) and the Dutch competition authority (ACM) (two). Below, we discuss each of these topics and the enforcement practice of the investigated authorities in more detail.

Table 10.4 Vertical Agreements: Investigations and Decisions under the Cartel Prohibition

	European Commission	*CMA*	*Autorité de la Concurrence*	*Bundeskartellamt*	*ACM*	*BCA*	*Total*
Parity clauses	1[1427]	3[1428]	2[1429]	4[1430]	1[1431]	1[1432]	**12**

1427. European Commission, decision 25 July 2013, AT.39847 (E-books – Penguin). Outside the temporary scope: European Commission, decision 12 December 2012, AT.39847 (*E-books – Apple, Hachette, HarperCollins, Holtzbrinck/Macmillan, Simon & Schuster*).
1428. CMA, decision 19 November 2020, 50505 (*Price comparison website: use of most favoured nation clauses*); CMA (OFT), decision 31 January 2014, CE/9320/10 (*Booking.com B.V, Expedia, Inc, InterContinental Hotels Group plc and Hotel Inter-Continental London Limited*); CMA (OFT), investigation closed 1 November 2013, CE/9692/12 (*Amazon*).
1429. Autorité de la Concurrence, decision 21 April 2015, 15-D-06 (*Booking.com*); Autorité de la concurrence, decision 10 December 2019, 19-D-23 (*Expedia, HRS*).
1430. Bundeskartellamt, decision 22 December 2015, B9-121/13 (*Booking.com*); Bundeskartellamt, press release 3 June 2015, 'Verivox vows to stop using 'best price' clauses'; Bundeskartellamt, decision 20 December 2013, B9-66/10 (*HRS*); Bundeskartellamt, decision 26 November 2013, B6-46/12 (*Amazon*).
1431. ACM, decision 18 November 2016, ACM/DM/2016/207286 (*Thuisbezorgd.nl*).
1432. BCA, decision 7 November 2016, ABC-2016-I/O-31-AUD (*Immoweb*).

	European Commission	*CMA*	*Autorité de la Concurrence*	*Bundeska-rtellamt*	*ACM*	*BCA*	*Total*
Platform bans and other restrictions on the use of online distribution channels	2[1433]	1[1434]	3[1435]	2[1436]	0[1437]		**7**
Geoblocking and digital cross-border sales restrictions	9[1438]					1[1439]	**10**
RPM	4[1440]	9[1441]	2[1442]		1[1443]	1[1444]	**16**

1433. European Commission, decision 30 January 2020, AT.40433 (*Film merchandise*); European Commission, decision 9 July 2019, AT.40432 (*Character merchandise*).
1434. CMA, decision 24 August 2017, 50230 (*Ping*).
1435. Autorité de la Concurrence, decision 1 July 2019, 19-D-14 (*Trek*); Autorité de la Concurrence, decision 24 October 2018, 18-D-23 (*Stihl*); Autorité de la Concurrence, press release 18 November 2015, 'L'Autorité de la concurrence clôt une enquête à l'encontre d'Adidas'.
1436. Bundeskartellamt, decision 26 August 2015, B2-98/11 (*Asics*); Bundeskartellamt, decision 27 June 2014, B3-137/12 (*Adidas*).
1437. ACM decision 14 December 2018, ACM/17/012061 (*handhavingsverzoek Legal Dutch*). This case concerned a restriction on the use of comparison websites, although it was not a vertical agreement case. The ACM's investigation revealed that the Rules of Conduct of the Dutch bar association could restrict the development of comparison websites for lawyers.
1438. European Commission, decision 20 January 2021, AT.40413 (*Focus Home – Video Games*); European Commission, decision 20 January 2021, AT.40414 (*Koch Media – Video Games*); European Commission, decision 20 January 2021, AT.40420 (*Zenimax – Video Games*); European Commission, decision 20 January 2021, AT.40422 (*Bandai Namco – Video Games)*; European Commission, decision 20 January 2021, AT.40424 (*Capcom – Video Games*); European Commission, decision 30 January 2020, AT.40433 (*Film merchandise*); European Commission, decision 9 July 2019, AT.40432 (*Character merchandise*); European Commission, decision 25 March 2019, AT.40436 (*Nike*); European Commission, decision 17 December 2018, AT.40428 (*Guess*).
1439. BCA, Decision of 6 May 2021, ABC-2021-P/K-09 (*Caudalie*).
1440. European Commission, decision 24 July 2018, AT.40465 (*Asus*); European Commission, decision 24 July 2018, AT.40469 (*Denon & Marantz*); European Commission, decision 24 July 2018, AT.40181 (*Philips*); European Commission, decision 24 July 2018, AT.40182 (*Pioneer*).
1441. CMA, decision 23 March 2022, 50952 (DAR Lighting); CMA, decision 17 July 2020, 50565-6 (GAK, Yamaha); CMA, decision 29 June 2020, 50565-4 (Korg); CMA, decision 29 June 2020, 50565-5 (Roland); CMA, decision 22 January 2020, 50565-3 (Fender); CMA, decision 1 August 2019, 50565-2 (Casio); CMA, decision 20 June 2017, 50343 (Pool Lighting Ltd); CMA, decision 24 May 2016, CE/9856/14 (Online RPM – commercial refrigeration); CMA, decision 10 May 2016, CE/9857-14 (Online RPM – bathroom fittings sector).
1442. Autorité de la Concurrence, decision 26 January 2017, 17-D-01 (*Sanbri*), Autorité de la Concurrence, decision 16 March 2020, 20-D-04 (*Apple*).
1443. ACM, decision 14 September 2021, ACM/20/040569 (*Samsung*).
1444. BCA, Decision of 6 May 2021, ABC-2021-P/K-09 (*Caudalie*).

	European Commission	CMA	Autorité de la Concurrence	Bundeska-rtellamt	ACM	BCA	Total
Exclusivity agreements	1[1445]			2[1446]			**3**
Total	**17**	**13**	**6**	**8**	**2**	**3**	**48**

[1] Parity Clauses

Table 10.5 Parity Clauses: Investigations and Decisions

	European Commission	CMA	Autorité de la Concurrence	Bundesk-artellamt	ACM	BCA	Total
Parity clauses	1[1447]	3[1448]	2[1449]	4[1450]	1[1451]	1[1452]	**12**

All authorities under investigation have undertaken at least one investigation into parity clauses (*see* Table 10.5).[1453] A distinction should be made between broad and

1445. European Commission, press release 19 January 2017, 'Antitrust: Commission welcomes steps taken by Amazon/Audible and Apple to improve competition in audiobook distribution'.
1446. Frankfurter Allgemeine Zeitung, 29 October 2020, 'Wettbewerbsverfahren gegen Amazon und Apple'; Bundeskartellamt, press release 19 January 2017, 'Bundeskartellamt closes proceedings against Audible/Amazon and Apple'. *See also* (not a vertical agreement): Bundeskartellamt, decision 3 December 2019, B7-25/17 (*Tax advisory software*).
1447. European Commission, decision 25 July 2013, AT.39847 (E-books – Penguin); European Commission. Outside the temporary scope of the period under investigation: decision 12 December 2012, AT.39847 (*E-books – Apple, Hachette, HarperCollins, Holtzbrinck/Macmillan, Simon & Schuster*).
1448. CMA, decision 19 November 2020, 50505 (*Price comparison website: use of most favoured nation clauses*); CMA (OFT), decision 31 January 2014, CE/9320/10 (*Booking.com B.V, Expedia, Inc, InterContinental Hotels Group plc and Hotel Inter-Continental London Limited*); CMA (OFT), investigation closed 1 November 2013, CE/9692/12 (*Amazon*).
1449. Autorité de la Concurrence, decision 21 April 2015, 15-D-06 (*Booking.com*); Autorité de la concurrence, decision 10 December 2019, 19-D-23 (*Expedia, HRS*).
1450. Bundeskartellamt, decision 22 December 2015, B9-121/13 (*Booking.com*); Bundeskartellamt, press release 3 June 2015, 'Verivox vows to stop using 'best price' clauses'; Bundeskartellamt, decision 20 December 2013, B9-66/10 (*HRS*); Bundeskartellamt, decision 26 November 2013, B6-46/12 (*Amazon*).
1451. ACM, decision 18 November 2016, ACM/DM/2016/207286 (*Thuisbezorgd.nl*).
1452. BCA, decision 7 November 2016, ABC-2016-I/O-31-AUD (*Immoweb*).
1453. European Commission, Guidelines on Vertical Restraints, C(2022) 3006 final, 10 May 2022, para. 356: '*Parity obligations, sometimes called Most Favoured Nation clauses ("MFNs") or Across-Platform Parity Agreements ("APPAs"), require a seller of goods or services to offer the goods or services to another party on conditions that are no less favourable than the conditions offered by the seller to certain other parties or via certain other channels. The conditions may concern prices, inventory, availability or any other terms or conditions of offer or sale. The parity obligation may take the form of a contractual clause or it may be the result of other direct*

narrow parity clauses.[1454] The difference between these two types can be explained by giving an example of retail parity clauses applied to the online hotel booking sector. 'Broad' parity clauses would oblige the hotel owner to offer the online travel agent the lowest room price and the best room availability compared to all other distribution channels, including on the platforms of competing online travel agents. 'Narrow' parity clauses leave the hotel owner free to offer lower room prices and better room availability to other online travel agents or through offline distribution channels but prohibit the hotel owner from offering lower room prices on its own website.

Before 2020, there was no common line of policy regarding parity clauses.[1455] The various authorities worked together, or at least coordinated their activities given the cross-border nature of the activities of platforms, but they did not always follow the same principles or reached the same conclusions. The Commission – as a supranational authority – pretty much played second fiddle in the cross-border debate on parity clauses in the hotel booking sector. The Commission didn't go further than to coordinate and summarise the various actions of national authorities that had taken enforcement action (including the CMA, the Autorité and the Bundeskartellamt) and agree with those authorities on joint monitoring.

However, a common line of policy is currently underway: pursuant to the 2022 Vertical Block Exemption Regulation VBER, wide parity clauses used by online platforms[1456] are no longer block exempted.[1457] According to the Commission, these clauses are '*more likely than other types of parity obligation to produce net anti-competitive effects*' because they '*may soften competition and facilitate collusion between suppliers of online intermediation services*' (OIS) and '*may foreclose entry or expansion by new or smaller suppliers of online intermediation services*'.[1458] Narrow parity clauses, on the other hand, are block exempted in the EU under the 2022 guidelines.[1459] The draft UK Vertical Agreements Block Exemption Order takes the same approach to narrow parity clauses but, for wide parity clauses, it goes a step

or indirect measures, such as differential pricing or other incentives whose application depends on the conditions under which the seller offers its goods or services to other parties or via other channels.'

1454. One can also distinguish between retail and wholesale parity clauses. *See* on this distinction: J. Padilla, S. Piccolo and N. Watson, 'The Simple Economics of Wholesale Price-Parity Agreements: The Case of the Airline Tickets Distribution Industry', (June 2021) 17(2) Journal of Competition Law & Economics 364-379, https://doi.org/10.1093/joclec/nhaa028.

1455. Chiara Caccinelli and Joëlle Toledano, 'Assessing Anticompetitive Practices in Two-Sided Markets: A Comparative Analysis of Four Antitrust Proceedings Against Booking.Com' (2018) 14 Journal of Competition Law & Economics 193.

1456. The Commission uses the term 'across-platform retail parity obligations'. *See*: European Commission, Guidelines on Vertical Restraints, C(2022) 3006 final, 10 May 2022, paras 362 ff.

1457. Regulation 2022/720, 10 May 2022.

1458. The report 'Competition Policy for the Digital Era' commissioned by the Commission suggests banning broad parity clauses. The Commission has however opted for a softer approach. *See*: Crémer, de Montjoye and Schweitzer, *supra* n. 82.

1459. Regulation 2022/720, 10 May 2022, para. 16 recitals and European Commission, Guidelines on Vertical Restraints, C(2022) 3006 final, 10 May 2022, para. 254. The report 'Competition Policy for the Digital Era' commissioned by the Commission suggested to allow narrow parity clauses only where there is strong competition between platforms. The Commission has opted for a softer approach. *See*: Crémer, de Montjoye and Schweitzer.

further than the EU's vertical rules.[1460] It not only excludes wide parity clauses from the scope of the block exemption but also considers these to constitute hardcore restrictions.[1461] The thinking behind the UK approach is similar to the Commission's: '*Based on the CMA's experience of scrutinising parity obligations in its casework, the Government is concerned that wide retail parity obligations soften competition between horizontal competitors and reduce the incentives of intermediaries (such as online platforms) to compete on price, to innovate, or to enter markets and expand.*'[1462]

The legal change in the VBER is in line with the enforcement practice of the Commission and the national authorities under investigation during the enforcement period. All authorities concerned already appeared to hold the opinion that broad parity clauses – to the extent that these fell outside the scope of the 2010 vertical block exemption[1463] – constitute an unacceptable restriction of competition and are rarely or never allowed.[1464] The largest fine for the use of wide parity clauses, GBP 17.9 million, was imposed on ComparetheMarket by the CMA.[1465] There is however a slight discrepancy in the imminent draft UK and 2022 EU vertical rules. As mentioned above, the draft UK vertical rules not only exclude wide parity clauses from the scope of the block exemption but also consider these to constitute hardcore restrictions.[1466] This may lead platforms that operate both in continental Europe and the UK to choose between either having different distribution arrangements tailored to both legal regimes or adopting one distribution arrangement that complies with the stricter UK approach.

The Bundeskartellamt is even stricter. It is the only authority under review that seems to categorically reject narrow parity clauses which are not covered by the vertical block exemption. Importantly, the Bundeskartellamt's approach to narrow parity clauses was upheld by Germany's Federal Supreme Court in 2021. The CMA did not act against the narrow parity clauses used by the hotel booking sites and only demanded the deletion of the broad parity clauses. The Autorité acted firmly against broad parity clauses in the Booking.com case in 2015, but refrained from enforcement against Hotel Reservation System (HRS) and Expedia in 2019, taking into account that

1460. The Competition Act 1998 (Vertical Agreements Block Exemption) Order 2022, draft document, February 2022.
1461. The Competition Act 1998 (Vertical Agreements Block Exemption) Order 2022, draft document, February 2022, Article 8(4)(a). However, wide parity obligations that apply to business-to-business markets will not be treated as hardcore restrictions.
1462. Explanatory Memorandum to the Competition Act 1998 (Vertical Agreements Block Exemption) Order 2022, draft document, February 2022, para. 7.36.
1463. Commission Regulation No 330/2010 of 20 April 2010 on the application of Article 101(3) of the Treaty on the Functioning of the European Union to categories of vertical agreements and concerted practices, OJ 2010/L 102/1.
1464. It must however be noted in this respect that, in its *Immoweb* decision, the BCA – given the facts of that case – did not have to distinguish between broad and narrow parity clauses.
1465. Despite a market share of more than 50%, the CMA didn't use the abuse of dominance prohibition, but the cartel prohibition as a legal basis to address the parity clauses.
1466. The Competition Act 1998 (Vertical Agreements Block Exemption) Order 2022, draft document, February 2022, Article 8(4)(a). However, wide parity obligations that apply to business-to-business markets will not be treated as hardcore restrictions.

other competition authorities had already dealt with the matter.[1467] The Autorité does, however, not seem to share the Bundeskartellamt's categorical rejection of narrow parity clauses. Finally, the ACM takes a more or less similar position to the Autorité and does not generally consider narrow parity clauses to be problematic. However, the ACM's only relevant decision appears to leave open the possibility that narrow parity clauses might pose a problem in markets that are less competitive or growing less rapidly than the market for online meal delivery services.[1468]

The discrepancy between the Bundeskartellamt's approach to narrow parity clauses and those of the other authorities is significant, potentially giving rise to serious issues for platforms operating across borders. To take the concrete example of the online hotel booking business, the Bundeskartellamt's win at the Federal Supreme Court means that online hotel booking platforms operating in Germany need to remove their narrow parity clauses or, at least, bring them in line with the judgment. This will quite conceivably also affect the online hotel booking platforms' position outside Germany. After all, the parity clauses in contracts with hotels in Germany will also have to apply to bookings by consumers from other countries. And, even if the hotel is not located in Germany, one could theoretically take the view that there is an impact on the German market if a customer in Germany makes a booking at a hotel located outside Germany. The Bundeskartellamt rightly did not go so far as to include this situation in the scope of its decisions regarding the online hotel booking sector. After all, if the Bundeskartellamt would have done so, Booking.com would, in fact, have been obliged to remove its narrow parity clauses even in those jurisdictions where the local competition authority implicitly or explicitly allows them. In this way, the approach of the strictest authority (in this case the Bundeskartellamt) would also determine the room for manoeuvre in jurisdictions with more 'understanding' authorities. In our opinion, that would really have been a bridge too far. After all, online platforms (for booking or other activities) are often active across Europe and therefore seem to benefit from a clear and unambiguous policy. Although there is much more clarity than before 2020, online platforms operating across borders still need to monitor the different positions of the various competition authorities, even within the EU, and are therefore faced with pluralism and uncertainty.

We expect more fines shall be imposed for (wide) parity clauses in the years to come. It took a long time before authorities started to impose fines for parity clauses. The significant fine of GBP 17.9 million for ComparetheMarket was only the first fine on a total of thirteen investigations. This UK decision, adopted in 2020, is also the most recent decision, setting the tone for future investigations. The Bundeskartellamt's diverging view on narrow parity clauses is a bottleneck for a uniform approach to parity clauses.

1467. Autorité de la Concurrence, decision 21 April 2015, 15-D-06 (*Booking.com*); Autorité de la concurrence, decision 10 December 2019, 19-D-23 (*Expedia, HRS*).
1468. ACM, decision 18 November 2016, ACM/DM/2016/207286 (*Thuisbezorgd.nl*).

[2] Platform Bans and Other Restrictions on Online Sales

Table 10.6 Platform Bans and Other Restrictions of Online Sales: Investigations and Decisions

	European Commission	*CMA*	*Autorité de la Concurrence*	*Bundeskartellamt*	*ACM*	*BCA*	*Total*
Platform bans and other restrictions on online distribution channels	2[1469]	1[1470]	2[1471]	2[1472]	0[1473]		**7**

With the exception of the BCA, all authorities under investigation have dealt with platform bans and other restrictions on online sales (*see* Table 10.6).[1474] Platform bans, or restrictions on the use of online platforms, are clauses where the supplier restricts the use of online platforms by the buyer of its products.[1475] The restriction may range from a total ban on sales through online platforms or may be limited to online platforms that meet certain qualitative criteria. In the landmark *Coty* judgment, the ECJ ruled that a platform ban in the context of a selective distribution system does not necessarily need to constitute a per se infringement of the cartel prohibition, in case there would be an objective justification for such a ban on selling through online platforms.[1476] In its 2022 vertical guidelines, the European Commission confirmed that platform bans are not hardcore restrictions unless the ban aims at preventing online sales altogether.[1477] The Commission notes '*restrictions on the use of online marketplaces may lead to efficiencies, in particular linked to brand protection, a certain level of service quality or reducing opportunities for counterfeiting*'.[1478]

1469. European Commission, decision 30 January 2020, AT.40433 (*Film merchandise*); European Commission, decision 9 July 2019, AT.40432 (*Character merchandise*).
1470. CMA, decision 24 August 2017, 50230 (*Ping*).
1471. Autorité de la Concurrence, decision 1 July 2019, 19-D-14 (*Trek*); Autorité de la Concurrence, decision 24 October 2018, 18-D-23 (*Stihl*); Autorité de la Concurrence, press release 18 November 2015, 'L'Autorité de la concurrence clôt une enquête à l'encontre d'Adidas'.
1472. Bundeskartellamt, decision 26 August 2015, B2-98/11 (*Asics*); Bundeskartellamt, decision 27 June 2014, B3-137/12 (*Adidas*).
1473. ACM decision 14 December 2018, ACM/17/012061 (*handhavingsverzoek Legal Dutch*). This case concerned a restriction on the use of comparison websites, although it was not a vertical agreement case. The ACM's investigation revealed that the Rules of Conduct of the Dutch bar association could restrict the development of comparison websites for lawyers.
1474. Other restrictions can be restrictions on the use of price comparison website or outright bans on online sales.
1475. European Commission, Guidelines on Vertical Restraints, C(2022) 3006 final, 10 May 2022, para. 334.
1476. Case C-230/16 (*Coty Germany GmbH v. Parfümerie Akzente GmbH*), *supra* n. 53.
1477. European Commission, Guidelines on Vertical Restraints, C(2022) 3006 final, 10 May 2022, para. 335.
1478. *Ibid.*, para. 342.

There are different approaches to platform bans among the authorities under investigation. The Bundeskartellamt has so far taken the strictest approach. The *Asics* and *Adidas* cases, for example, appear to show that the Bundeskartellamt has fundamental objections against imposing a ban on the use of online platforms on distributors. The question that is left unanswered is how this view relates to the ECJ's judgment in *Coty* and the 2022 vertical guidelines of the European Commission.[1479] It does not become clear precisely from the decisions to what extent Asics and Adidas used a selective distribution system and whether the use of such a system might have constituted an objective and proportionate justification for the platform bans they imposed. Even in a paper published after *Coty*, the Bundeskartellamt clearly noted: '*the Bundeskartellamt doubts whether restrictions on platforms and other internet distribution channels increase inter-brand competition to the extent that this outweighs the considerable restrictions of intra-brand competition by general prohibitions*'.[1480] Still, it does seem likely that the Bundeskartellamt will eventually be compelled to nuance its rigid position on this doctrine, certainly where it applies Article 101(1) TFEU. In cases where the Bundeskartellamt only applies German law because there is no effect on trade between EU Member States, its policy may however in principle be stricter than European law (Article 3(1) and (2) of Regulation 1/2003). Still, cases involving e-commerce are likely to almost always have a certain effect on trade between EU Member States. Therefore, it can be doubted whether there will ever be a precedent where the Bundeskartellamt would be entitled to apply exclusively German law (although the Bundeskartellamt actually did apply exclusively the German prohibition on abuse of a dominant position in the *Facebook* case, while an effect on trade between Member States was most likely present in that case – this is also one of the points on which the ECJ will need to decide in the pending appeal). The former is irrespective of whether such a situation (where the Bundeskartellamt would be stricter) would be desirable.

The CMA's *Ping*[1481] case concerned a total ban on online sales and not merely a ban on sales via (certain) online platforms belonging to third parties. In the appeal against the decision imposing the fine, the Competition Appeal Tribunal (CAT) stressed the importance of this distinction.[1482] It appears to follow from this judgment that the CAT – like the CMA and the European Commission – will rarely or never consider a total ban on online sales to be permissible. The draft UK Vertical Agreements Block Exemption Order considers any restriction that '*effectively*' prevents online sales (i.e.,

1479. Case C-230/16 (*Coty Germany GmbH v. Parfümerie Akzente GmbH*), *supra* n. 53 and European Commission, Guidelines on Vertical Restraints, C(2022) 3006 final, 10 May 2022. *See* likewise the authors of this article: Graf and Kuhn, *supra* n. 523.

1480. Bundeskartellamt, 'Competition restraints in online sales after Coty and Asics – what's next', October 2018.

1481. Case 50230: *Ping*, *supra* n. 456, 118.

1482. *Ping v. CMA* [2018] CAT 13, *supra* n. 520, para. 141.

a total ban on online sales) a hardcore restriction, thereby leaving space for certain platform bans.[1483] In the Netherlands, the 2019 vertical guidelines state that a platform ban, for example, aimed at protecting the luxury image of a brand, is not a hardcore restriction.[1484]

In France, it is a telling signal that the Autorité gives a broad interpretation of the *Coty* judgment in its decision to impose a fine in the *Stihl* case and takes the firm view that a ban on the use of online platforms cannot only be justified where it concerns the sale of products of a particularly luxurious nature but may also be permitted in the context of a selective distribution system for other products. Partly because Stihl was able to substantiate the need for its ban on the use of online marketplaces by its resellers by relying on the dangerous nature of those products, the Autorité concluded that this ban constituted an authorised restriction. Moreover, the Autorité did not rule out the possibility that, even if it had not concerned dangerous products, a platform ban might still be justified, for example, to prevent the spread of counterfeit products. However, this did not ultimately lead to Stihl escaping the fine, since various other restrictions – including an obligation to physically make the product available to the customer even in the case of online sales, which severely hampered online sales – did not find favour in the eyes of the Autorité.[1485] And in the 2019 *Trek* case, the Autorité found that an obligation to personally deliver each product to the consumer amounted to a de facto online sales ban with an anticompetitive object.[1486] The Autorité, like the CMA, the ACM and the European Commission, draws the line at restrictions that aim at preventing online sales altogether. Similarly, the BCA, in the 2021 *Caudalie* case, considered a restriction that prevented distributors in a selective distribution system to accept online orders for more than ten copies of the same product a hardcore restriction.[1487] Although this Belgian example is not an example of a platform ban, it follows the same logic of those cases that did relate to actual platform bans in that it argues that a tough stance is necessary where a restriction aims at preventing online sales altogether.

All investigated authorities have spoken out on the admissibility of platform bans, albeit in different ways. It is worth mentioning, in addition, that in the Netherlands the district court (*rechtbank*) of Amsterdam ruled in the *Nike v. Aktiesport* case that Nike could terminate its agreement to supply Aktiesport because Aktiesport sold through the unauthorised platform Amazon. In the court's opinion, Nike products could be considered luxury products and the prohibition would serve to maintain Nike's brand image. The court based its judgment on the Opinion of the Advocate

1483. The Competition Act 1998 (Vertical Agreements Block Exemption) Order 2022, draft document, February 2022, Article 8(4)(a).
1484. ACM, Leidraad Afspraken tussen leveranciers en afnemers, 26 February 2019, p. 6.
1485. 'Avis N° 12-A-20 Du 18 Septembre 2012 Relatif Au Fonctionnement Concurrentiel Du Commerce Électronique', *supra* n. 755, 20.
1486. Autorité de la Concurrence, decision 1 July 2019 (*Trek*), 19-D-14.
1487. Decision of 6 May 2021, ABC-2021-P/K-09 (*Caudalie*). The distributors also weren't allowed to deliver products outside the country where the website was hosted in this case.

General in *Coty* (the judgment had not yet been delivered, but the ECJ would follow the Advocate General) and took into account that Nike did allow sales through certain other platforms. For this reason, there was no question of a general platform ban.[1488] In the UK, the CAT ruled, in the context of civil proceedings, that a restriction by an online platform that limited real estate brokers to offer their services on only one other online platform, was not an object restriction: '*the fact that the One Other Portal Rule is not exclusive but permits Members (if they wish) to use or continue to use one other portal appears to create competition between the two established portals*'.[1489]

Restrictions on the use of online platforms will become more ingrained in distribution systems after *Coty* and the more tolerant 2022 EU vertical guidelines. Still, as recent enforcement precedents show, some companies, especially those whose business model suffers from the growth of the platform economy, will continue to be tempted to restrict online sales altogether. This will inevitably trigger new enforcement action. The Bundeskartellamt's approach may constitute, again (*see* §7.01[A] Parity clauses), a bottleneck in reaching a uniform EU approach, although its precedents in *Asics* and *Adidas* are now almost ten years old and may be ripe for an update.

[3] Geoblocking/Digital Cross-Border Sales Restrictions

Table 10.7 Geoblocking/Digital Cross-Border Sales Restrictions: Investigations and Decisions

	European Commission	*CMA*	*Autorité de la Concurrence*	*Bundeskartellamt*	*ACM*	*BCA*	*Total*
Geoblocking/ digital cross-border sales restrictions	9[1490]					1[1491]	**10**

From the authorities under review, the Commission has been a frontrunner in addressing geoblocking practices and digital cross-border sales restrictions, with nine out of ten cases being Commission cases (*see* Table 10.7). The Commission flagged

1488. *ECLI:NL:RBAMS:2017:7282 (Nike/Aktiesport)*, *supra* n. 977.
1489. *Agents' Mutual Limited v. Gascoigne Halman Limited* [2017] CAT 15 (Competition Appeal Tribunal).
1490. European Commission, decision 20 January 2021, AT.40413 (*Focus Home – Video Games*); European Commission, decision 20 January 2021, AT.40414 (*Koch Media – Video Games*); European Commission, decision 20 January 2021, AT.40420 (*Zenimax – Video Games*); European Commission, decision 20 January 2021, AT.40422 (*Bandai Namco – Video Games)*; European Commission, decision 20 January 2021, AT.40424 (*Capcom – Video Games*); European Commission, decision 30 January 2020, AT.40433 (*Film merchandise*); European Commission, decision 9 July 2019, AT.40432 (*Character merchandise*); European Commission, decision 25 March 2019, AT.40436 (*Nike*); European Commission, decision 17 December 2018, AT.40428 (*Guess*).
1491. BCA, Decision of 6 May 2021, ABC-2021-P/K-09 (*Caudalie*).

geoblocking as one of the main competition concerns in its 2017 e-commerce sector inquiry report.[1492] In the report, the Commission defined geoblocking practices as practices where '*retailers refuse to sell to customers abroad, for example by blocking access to websites, re-routing customers to websites targeting other Member States or by simply refusing to deliver cross-border or to accept cross-border payments*'.[1493] Geoblocking practices are, in essence, cross-border (or cross-territory) sales restrictions that can be implemented by digital or non-digital tools.[1494] These practices are a natural concern for the Commission as a supranational competition authority, but they can also be relevant for national authorities in case they relate to sales across territories within the same Member State. Geoblocking practices can be addressed under the cartel prohibition where they are based on an agreement, or instead under the prohibition on abuse of dominance where the company applying the geoblocking practices has a dominant position. For example, the 2018 fine of EUR 39.8 million in *Guess* was an Article 101(1) TFEU decision relying on the agreements between Guess and its distributors.[1495] And the 2021 fine of EUR 7.8 million in *Video Games* was a cartel prohibition decision relying on the bilateral agreements between Valve and five PC video game publishers.[1496] Substantively, the Commission has so far fined digital geoblocking practices, such as geoblocked PC video game activation keys (in *Video Games*), restricting retailers from using brand names and trademarks in online search advertising (in *Guess*), restricting online sales out-of-territory (in *Nike*[1497] and, again, in *Guess*, *see also* section §10.05[A][2] 'Platform bans'). In addition, the Commission has qualified blocking websites, re-routing customers and terminating consumers' online transactions based on credit card data as hardcore restrictions in its 2022 vertical guidelines.[1498]

On the national level, the BCA fined a restriction on product deliveries outside the country where the website was hosted (in *Caudalie*).[1499] There has been no enforcement of digital geoblocking practices under the header of the prohibition on abuse of a dominant position. However, outside the scope of digital competition law, the Commission fined AB InBev EUR 200 million for restricting the possibility of cross-border sales in 2019.[1500] It is not a mere theoretical possibility that digital geoblocking

1492. European Commission, Final report on the E-commerce Sector Inquiry, COM(2017) 229 final, 10 May 2017.
1493. European Commission, Final report on the E-commerce Sector Inquiry, COM(2017) 229 final, 10 May 2017.
1494. In this publication we focus on the restrictions implemented by digital tools, such as online sales restrictions and online search advertising restrictions.
1495. European Commission, decision 17 December 2018, AT.40428 (*Guess*).
1496. European Commission, press release 20 January 2021, 'Antitrust: Commission fines Valve and five publishers of PC video games EUR 7.8 million for "Geoblocking" practices'. European Commission, decision 20 January 2021, AT.40413, AT.40414, AT.40420, AT.40422, AT.40424 (*Valve – Video games*), the decisions in these cases weren't published at the time of finalising this publication.
1497. European Commission, decision 25 March 2019, AT.40436 (*Nike*).
1498. European Commission, Guidelines on Vertical Restraints, C(2022) 3006 final, 10 May 2022, para. 206.
1499. BCA, Decision of 6 May 2021, ABC-2021-P/K-09 (*Caudalie*).
1500. European Commission, decision 13 May 2019, AT.40134 (*AB InBev*).

practices will be challenged under the prohibition on abuse of a dominant position as well. Finally, it should be noted that the issue of unilateral geoblocking practices by non-dominant companies was addressed with the entry into force of the Geoblocking Regulation in December 2018.[1501]

We expect that the Commission will continue to take the lead in cases concerning cross-border sales restrictions. This not only fits the Commission's supranational profile but also has the added advantage that the same types of restrictions are not treated differently by different national authorities.

[4] Resale Price Maintenance

Table 10.8 RPM: Investigations and Decisions

	European Commission	*CMA*	*Autorité de la Concurrence*	*Bundeskartellamt*	*ACM*	*BCA*	*Total*
RPM	4[1502]	5[1503]	2[1504]	0	1[1505]	1[1506]	**13**

Virtually all authorities under investigation have looked into RPM agreements in the digital sector (*see* Table 10.8).[1507] RPM agreements aim to set a fixed or minimum resale price that must be observed by the buyer of the contract goods.[1508] RPM

1501. Regulation (EU) 2018/302 of the European Parliament and of the Council of 28 February 2018 on addressing unjustified geoblocking and other forms of discrimination based on customers' nationality, place of residence or place of establishment within the internal market. We will not discuss the implementation and enforcement of the Geoblocking here in detail as it is not competition law. However, the Commission noted in its November 2020 evaluation report on the implementation of the Geoblocking Regulation that '*the implementation process by the Member States has been held back by delays*' and '*only six Member States had adopted and notified the measures and bodies designated for the enforcement of the Regulation*'. *See*, European Commission, Report on the first short-term review of the Geoblocking Regulation, COM(2020) 766 final, 30 November 2020.
1502. European Commission, decision 24 July 2018, AT.40465 (*Asus*); European Commission, decision 24 July 2018, AT.40469 (*Denon & Marantz*); European Commission, decision 24 July 2018, AT.40181 (*Philips*); European Commission, decision 24 July 2018, AT.40182 (*Pioneer*).
1503. CMA, decision 17 July 2020, 50565-6 (*GAK, Yamaha*); CMA, decision 29 June 2020, 50565-5 (*Roland*); CMA, decision 29 June 2020, 50565-4 (*Korg*); CMA, decision 22 January 2020, 50565-3 (*Fender*); CMA, decision 1 August 2019, 50565-2 (*Casio*).
1504. Autorité de la Concurrence, decision 26 January 2017, 17-D-01 (*Sanbri*), Autorité de la Concurrence, decision 16 March 2020, 20-D-04 (*Apple*).
1505. ACM, decision 14 September 2021, ACM/20/040569 (*Samsung*)
1506. BCA, Decision of 6 May 2021, ABC-2021-P/K-09 (*Caudalie*).
1507. We have only looked at RPM cases where digital technology played a key role.
1508. On the qualification of RPM agreements in the context of online platforms, *see*: P. Akman and D.D. Sokol, 'Online RPM and MFN under Antitrust Law and Economics' (2017) 50 Review of Industrial Organization 133-151, https://doi.org/10.1007/s11151-016-9560-x and H. Bekisz, 'When Does Algorithmic Pricing Result In an Intra-Platform Anticompetitive Agreement or Concerted Practice? The Case of Uber In the Framework of EU Competition Law', (March 2021) 12(3) Journal of European Competition Law & Practice 217-235, https://doi.org/10.1093/jeclap/lpab017.

agreements are treated as hardcore restrictions by all authorities under investigation.[1509] The fixed or minimum resale price can be set directly by the producer or can be achieved indirectly, for example where a producer pressurises, intimidates or threatens its distributors when they do not follow the desired fixed resale price.[1510] Digital technology plays a role in the capacity of producers to observe the fixed or minimum resale prices set by their distributors. Digital technology can thus be seen as a facilitator of RPM agreements.[1511] For example, in the Dutch *Samsung* case, the ACM considered that Samsung used spider software and price monitoring websites to monitor the price movements of its own products (Chapter 8 ACM).[1512] Similarly, in the Commission's four *Consumer electronics* cases,[1513] the Commission noted that the use of '*sophisticated price monitoring tools*' *by manufacturers* '*allowed the manufacturers to effectively track resale price setting in the distribution network and to intervene swiftly in case of price decreases*'.[1514] Digital technology can also be the trigger to apply RPM in the first place. In France, for example, the Autorité imposed a fine in the *Sanbri* case for an RPM agreement between a producer and its distributors to directly apply the prices recommended by the producer.[1515] *Sanbri* stated that it had started RPM practice because some of its brick-and-mortar distributors feared price decreases by internet distributors: '*[nos distributeurs exploitant des points de vente physiques] craignaient que les distributeurs Internet, par exemple, cassent les prix.*' [vrij vertaald: *onze distributeurs die fysieke verkooppunten exploiteren waren bezorgd dat bijvoorbeeld internetdistributeurs de prijzen zouden onderbieden*].[1516] In addition, the French *Apple* case is the first case where a big tech company has been fined for imposing resale prices.[1517] The Autorité found that Apple's premium resellers (APRs) couldn't diverge from Apple's recommended prices in light of the strict terms and conditions under which resellers could promote their products: '*Apple strictly controls the ability of APR's to implement promotional actions due to the strong restrictions imposed by the various contractual stipulations, for the use of the brand in communication and promotional materials.*'[1518]

1509. The new EU Guidelines on Vertical Guidelines do not break with this rule, *see* European Commission, Guidelines on Vertical Restraints, C(2022) 3006 final, 10 May 2022, paras 185 ff.
1510. The 2022 EU Vertical Guidelines do clarify that the imposition of minimum advertised prices will be treated as an indirect form of RPM, *see* European Commission, Guidelines on Vertical Restraints, C(2022) 3006 final, 10 May 2022, para. 187.
1511. C. Veljanovski, 'What Do We Now Know about "Machine Collusion"', (January 2022) 13(1) Journal of European Competition Law & Practice 47-50, https://doi.org/10.1093/jeclap/lpab080.
1512. ACM, decision 14 September 2021, ACM/20/040569 (*Samsung*).
1513. European Commission, decision 24 July 2018, AT.40465 (*Asus*); European Commission, decision 24 July 2018, AT.40469 (*Denon & Marantz*); European Commission, decision 24 July 2018, AT.40181 (*Philips*); European Commission, decision 24 July 2018, AT.40182 (*Pioneer*).
1514. European Commission, Press Release 24 July 2018, 'Antitrust: Commission Fines Four Consumer Electronics Manufacturers for Fixing Online Resale Prices'.
1515. Autorité, decision 26 January 2017, 17-D-01 (*Sanbri*).
1516. *Ibid.*, para. 29.
1517. Autorité, decision 16 March 2020, 20-D-04 (*Apple*).
1518. *Ibid.*, para. 865.

The strong ideological alignment against RPM agreements among the authorities investigated makes this practice suitable for enforcement across jurisdictions, with a relatively limited risk of diverging views. We expect the authorities under investigation will continue to enforce RPM agreements vigorously and that the flood of new cases of recent years may not have ended yet. However, the *Sanbri* case shows that the EU's new permissive stance on dual pricing for offline and online sales (*see* below §10.05[A][6]) may no longer make it necessary for some companies to employ an RPM arrangement in the first place. Sanbri stated that it had implemented the RPM arrangement because some of its brick-and-mortar distributors feared price decreases by internet distributors. The new EU vertical rules now allow a supplier to charge different prices for products sold online than for products sold offline. This reduces the incentive for suppliers like Sanbri to put in place an RPM arrangement with their distributors.

[5] Exclusivity Agreements

Table 10.9 Exclusivity Agreements: Investigations and Decisions

	European Commission	*CMA*	*Autorité de la Concurrence*	*Bundeskartellamt*	*ACM*	*BCA*	*Total*
Exclusivity agreements	1[1519]			2[1520]			**3**

The Bundeskartellamt and the Commission are the only authorities with a track record in investigations of exclusivity agreements under the cartel prohibition. Interestingly, all the investigations mentioned in Table 10.9 concern exclusivity agreements between big tech companies. In two press releases on 19 January 2017, the Bundeskartellamt and the Commission each announced separately that they had terminated their ongoing investigations into agreements between Amazon subsidiary Audible.com (Audible) and Apple without the adoption of a formal decision. And, more recently, an ongoing investigation by the Bundeskartellamt focuses on so-called brand gating agreements between Amazon and suppliers that use the Amazon platform, whereby Amazon and the supplier would reserve the exclusive right to sell on the Amazon platform.

1519. European Commission, press release 19 January 2017, 'Antitrust: Commission welcomes steps taken by Amazon/Audible and Apple to improve competition in audiobook distribution'.

1520. Frankfurter Allgemeine Zeitung, 29 October 2020, 'Wettbewerbsverfahren gegen Amazon und Apple'; Bundeskartellamt, press release 19 January 2017, 'Bundeskartellamt closes proceedings against Audible/Amazon and Apple'. *See also* (not a vertical agreement): Bundeskartellamt, decision 3 December 2019, B7-25/17 (*Tax advisory software*).

Agreements between big tech companies appear to have come under closer scrutiny recently.[1521] Exclusivity arrangements between big tech companies where they operate in different parts of the distribution chain may similarly receive increased attention.

[6] Other Vertical Restrictions: Dual Distribution, Hybrid Platforms and Dual Pricing

Not all types of vertical restrictions that may occur in digital markets have thus far been subject to enforcement action under the cartel prohibition among the authorities under investigation. Nonetheless, the authors believe that such restrictions still deserve to be mentioned because they have been subject to recent policy changes that are driven by changes in the digital economy. Dual distribution and dual pricing are of particular relevance in this context. In addition, the EU's stricter approach to hybrid platforms deserves to be mentioned.

Dual distribution refers to a distribution model where a supplier not only sells its goods or services through third-party distributors but also directly to end customers. In this situation, the supplier is a supplier and a competitor of its distributors at the same time. In 2020, stakeholders responding to a public consultation on vertical rules by the Commission found that there was *'insufficient clarity as to whether information exchanges in dual distribution scenarios are to be treated as part of the vertical relationship and can thus be considered as covered by the [Vertical Block Exemption Regulation]'*.[1522] Among the respondents to the public consultation, most said that exchanges of data in the context of dual distribution can have pro-competitive effects, because pricing data or data on consumer profiles from distributors may allow suppliers to distribute their products more effectively, thereby enhancing inter-brand competition.[1523] Some respondents, however, expressed the concern that requiring distributors to pass on customer data would provide the supplier with a 'strategic advantage' and restrict the distributor's capacity to compete with the supplier.[1524] This conundrum has now been solved by the Commission in its 2022 vertical block

1521. *See, e.g.*, the recent EU investigation in the so-called Jedi Blue agreement between Google and Meta. *See*: European Commission, press release 11 March 2022, Antitrust: Commission opens investigation into possible anticompetitive conduct by Google and Meta, in 'online display advertising'.
1522. European Commission, Staff Working Document, 'Evaluation of the Vertical Block Exemption Regulation', SWD(2020) 172 final, 8 September 2020, p. 157. The concern about information exchange was just one among many concerns about dual distribution raised by stakeholders responding to the Commission's consultation. Other key concerns were the applicability of the exemption for dual distribution to wholesalers and importers (in addition to manufacturers) under Article 2(4)(a) VBER (old) and the interplay with the horizontal guidelines of the Commission.
1523. European Commission, Staff Working Document, 'Evaluation of the Vertical Block Exemption Regulation', SWD(2020) 172 final, 8 September 2020, p. 157.
1524. European Commission, Staff Working Document, 'Evaluation of the Vertical Block Exemption Regulation', SWD(2020) 172 final, 8 September 2020, p. 157.

exemption regulation.[1525] The regulation states that information exchanges in the context of dual distribution are permitted provided that the information is both '*related to the implementation of the vertical agreement*' and '*necessary to improve the production or distribution of the contract goods or services*'.[1526]

Furthermore, so-called hybrid platforms are excluded from benefiting from the block exemption for vertical agreements where they provide 'OIS' to companies, to the extent that they sell goods or services in competition with the same companies that they provide the OIS.[1527] The term 'hybrid platforms' refers to platforms that provide OIS to third-party companies and at the same time sell goods or services that are in competition with the products or services that are provided by the third-party companies that operate on the platform. Examples of such hybrid platforms would be the online marketplace of Amazon and the Apple and Google app stores. This means that hybrid platforms will need to assess individually whether any information exchange between them and the companies operating on the platform may infringe the cartel prohibition. The Commission adds that it will unlikely prioritise enforcement of vertical OIS agreements of hybrid platforms in the absence of '*restrictions by object or significant market power*'.[1528] Large hybrid platforms would therefore appear to be the primary candidates for enforcement. Now the new VBER 2022 has entered into force, it remains to be seen what enforcement action will be undertaken under the cartel prohibition in the coming years.[1529] The Computer and Communications Industry Association (CCIA), representing large online platforms and tech companies, has said that the new EU vertical rules '*mark a u-turn from the Commission's earlier insistence that what is illegal offline should also be illegal online by allowing restrictions of competition online, that are illegal offline. In particular, the new rules make it easier for big brands and suppliers to discriminate against online sales channels; notably with respect to pricing, selective distribution systems, and other restrictions of competition which were previously prohibited. In addition to increasing prices for consumers and reducing competition, the revised VBER is likely to bring greater uncertainty and harm*

1525. Regulation 2022/720, 10 May 2022.
1526. *Ibid.*, Article 2(5). The Commission Vertical guidelines include a list of examples of information that normally fulfil these conditions (whitelist) and examples of information that normally don't (blacklist). *See*, European Commission, Guidelines on Vertical Restraints, C(2022) 3006 final, 10 May 2022, paras 99-100.
1527. Regulation 2022/720, 10 May 2022, Article 2(6) and definition of OIS: '*online intermediation services' means information society services within the meaning of Article 1(1), point (b), of Directive (EU) 2015/1535 of the European Parliament and of the Council (6) which allow undertakings to offer goods or services: (i) to other undertakings, with a view to facilitating the initiating of direct transactions between those undertakings, or (ii) to final consumers, with a view to facilitating the initiating of direct transactions between those undertakings and final consumers, irrespective of whether and where the transactions are ultimately concluded*'.
1528. European Commission, Guidelines on Vertical Restraints, C(2022) 3006 final, 10 May 2022, para. 109.
1529. Concerns about the anticompetitive effects of information exchange between hybrid platforms and third parties operating on those platforms have so far only led to enforcement action under the prohibition on abuse of dominance, *see* for example the Apple and Amazon investigations opened by the Commission in cases AT.40703 (*Amazon – Buy Box*) and AT.40716 (*Apple – App Store Practices*).

to small and medium-sized merchants in Europe'.[1530] Interestingly, the draft UK vertical rules do not exclude hybrid platforms from the scope of the UK block exemption.[1531] Therefore, now Brexit is a reality, and UK legislation seems to start entering a different path at least in this respect.

Finally, the 2022 Commission's vertical guidelines and the draft UK vertical rules allow dual pricing agreements to benefit from the block exemption.[1532] Dual pricing is a distribution practice where a supplier charges different prices for products sold online than for products sold offline. Allowing dual pricing is a shift from the previous EU and UK guidelines in favour of suppliers that wish to charge a different price for their products intended for online sale and their products intended for offline sale. The Commission justifies the change in policy, because '*it may incentivize or reward an appropriate level of investment in online or offline sales channels*'.[1533] The UK legislator adds that the change '*is likely to benefit some retailers through their offline channels*' and that '*online-only retail channels could lose part of their competitive advantage relative to offline retail channels*'.[1534]

1530. Computer & Communications Industry Association, press release 10 May 2022, 'New EU Distribution Rules Will Allow Discrimination Against Online Commerce'.
1531. The Competition Act 1998 (Vertical Agreements Block Exemption) Order 2022, draft document, February 2022 and Explanatory Memorandum to the Competition Act 1998 (Vertical Agreements Block Exemption) Order 2022, draft document, February 2022. Still the UK draft vertical rules are more strict than the EU rules as they not only exclude wide parity clauses from the scope of the block exemption, but also considers these to constitute hardcore restrictions (*see* §5.01, Parity Clauses).
1532. Regulation 2022/720, 10 May 2022, The Competition Act 1998 (Vertical Agreements Block Exemption) Order 2022, draft document, February 2022 and Explanatory Memorandum to the Competition Act 1998 (Vertical Agreements Block Exemption) Order 2022, draft document, February 2022, paras 7.27-7.29 and 12.1.
1533. European Commission, Guidelines on Vertical Restraints, C(2022) 3006 final, 10 May 2022, para. 209.
1534. Explanatory Memorandum to the Competition Act 1998 (Vertical Agreements Block Exemption) Order 2022, draft document, February 2022, para. 12.1.

§10.06 CARTELS FORMED BY OR THROUGH ALGORITHMS

[A] General Remarks

New technologies are increasingly enabling companies to resort to algorithmic solutions in order to make their activities on the market more efficient. Albeit the use of algorithms may bring along various benefits for consumer welfare, some competition authorities and academic literature have expressed their concerns regarding the emergence of algorithmic collusion. First of all, the greater availability of price information and the utilisation of automated pricing mechanisms can facilitate explicit cooperation between undertakings.[1535] This is the case because algorithms make it simpler to identify and promptly react to deviations in the behaviour of the members of a cartel.[1536] Moreover, these developments can also reduce the likelihood of errors, that may occur while developing coordinated pricing systems, or accidental deviations from colluding firms' strategies. For example, if the use of a pricing algorithm is combined with access to up-to-date information on the prices of the colluding undertakings, this may facilitate price collusion between the members of a cartel and make the cartel more stable.[1537] Additionally, algorithms can make markets more transparent as a result of price monitoring and make it possible to punish deviating cartel members more quickly.[1538] Companies that come to an agreement not to undercut each other's prices may thus utilise a pricing algorithm to automatically ensure that such an agreement is followed.[1539]

Second, in case colluding undertakings use the same algorithmic system to set their prices, either by utilising the same technology provided by a third party, or by outsourcing this activity to such a third party, this may result in an algorithmic hub-and-spoke model.[1540] In that respect, it may be possible for the third party to assist the competing firms in coordinating their pricing activities by developing an algorithm for the cartel members that enables an automatic implementation of their pricing system.[1541] Accordingly, the algorithm becomes an automated executor of the hub-and-spoke cartel agreement.[1542] It should also be noted that there is a crucial difference between competitors knowingly and unknowingly using the same pricing algorithm.[1543] The scenario discussed above represents the former scenario, which is evidently covered by Article 101 TFEU. In case, however, undertakings utilise a coordinated algorithm developed by a third party without being aware that their

1535. CMA, 'Algorithms: How they can reduce competition and harm consumers' (2021) CMA p. 30.
1536. *Ibid.*
1537. Andreas Mundt, 'Algorithms and Competition in a Digitalized World' (2020) CPI Antitrust Chronicle p. 3.
1538. *Ibid.*, p. 4.
1539. Colm Hawkes, 'A Market Investigation Tool to Tackle Algorithmic Tacit Collusion: An Approach for the (Near) Future' (2021) 3 College of Europe Research Papers in Law 6.
1540. CMA, *supra* n. 1535, p. 30.
1541. Mundt, *supra* n.1537, p. 4.
1542. Hawkes, *supra* n. 1539, p. 7.
1543. *Ibid.*

competitors are also using it; this could arguably be regarded as permitted parallel market behaviour.[1544] Accordingly, this situation would not be caught by Article 101 TFEU as there may be no clear evidence of an agreement or a concerted practice.[1545]

Another negative outcome could be autonomous tacit collusion, whereby pricing algorithms are taught by the cartel members to collude with one another without the need for human intervention.[1546] This could take the form of the development of a self-learning algorithm that is capable of an independent execution of its tasks.[1547] Accordingly, algorithms can interact with each other and thus automatically cause alignment in the conduct of competitors.[1548] Nevertheless, this scenario remains highly theoretical.[1549] As in the above-mentioned algorithmic hub-and-spoke model, autonomous tacit collusion could either be caused by an algorithm explicitly developed for that purpose, or by a self-taught system the developers (and users) of which did not have an intention to facilitate collusive behaviour. Only the former case would evidently qualify as anticompetitive under Article 101 TFEU.[1550]

[B] From Theory to Practice

Cartels using algorithms have by now become a fact,[1551] albeit still a rare one: of the investigated authorities, the Competition and Markets Authority (CMA) was the first to impose fines for this in the *Online Sales of Posters and Frames* case.[1552] Two things stand out immediately in this case. First, it essentially concerned a very traditional cartel agreement: a price agreement between two competitors. This finding appears to positively answer the question of whether the existing rules were sufficient to enable effective action by the competition authority in this particular case. Second, it is noteworthy that the undertaking that wrote the algorithm at the instruction of the cartelists was not itself fined by the CMA. This despite the fact that that undertaking had been informed of the cartelists' objectives[1553] and thus knowingly *'intended to contribute by its own conduct to the common objectives pursued by all the participants and that it was aware of the actual conduct planned or put into effect by other undertakings in pursuit of the same objectives or that it could reasonably have foreseen it and that it was prepared to take the risk'*.[1554] It should be noted that, according to a footnote in the decision imposing the fine, the CMA did indeed consider investigating the role of the software supplier but decided not to give priority to such an investigation: '*The CMA considered whether to investigate further [GBE's software provider's]*

1544. *Ibid.*, p. 8.
1545. *Ibid.*, pp. 8-9.
1546. CMA, *supra* n. 1535, p. 30.
1547. Hawkes, *supra* n. 1539, p. 9.
1548. *Ibid.*
1549. *Ibid.*, p. 11; Mundt, *supra* n. 1537, p. 4.
1550. Hawkes, *supra* n. 1539, p. 10.
1551. *Ibid.*, p. 12.
1552. *Case 50223: Online Sales of Posters and Frames, supra* n. 455.
1553. *Ibid.*, paras 3.73-3.74.
1554. *Case C-194/14 P (AC Treuhand v. Commission)* [2015] European Court of Justice ECLI: EU:C:2015:717 [30].

involvement in the Infringement (including whether [GBE's software provider's] may have facilitated the agreement between Trod and GBE). However, the CMA has concluded that this is not an administrative priority.'[1555] Nevertheless, the case may have been suited for fining the software supplier as a cartel facilitator.[1556] If the CMA would have interpreted its prioritisation policy differently and would have investigated the role of the software supplier, this might have sent out a signal that software developers should take due account of competition law when developing their software (and possibly should also continue to monitor the use of the software they designed actively in the case of self-learning algorithms).

In any case, the *Online Sales of Posters and Frames* case is an example of a case where the existing tools have proved adequate to be applied to an algorithm-driven cartel situation.

The fact that algorithms can have a price-boosting effect was already made clear through an earlier example, which revolved around the sale of the book *The Making of a Fly: The Genetics of Animal Design*[1557] (also quoted by (among others) Commissioner Vestager)[1558] by two vendors on Amazon. Seller 1 had designed its algorithm to come shy of matching the price of seller 2 (0.9983), while seller 2 had designed its algorithm to ask 27% more than seller 1. As a result, the prices went into an upward spiral until the price was adjusted manually. The highest asking prices eventually became USD 18,651,718.08 (plus USD 3.99 shipping costs) and USD 23,698,655.93 (plus USD 3.99 shipping costs) respectively, until the prices were manually adjusted by seller 1.[1559] Although this was not a cartel, but an example of autonomous behaviour, it becomes clear from this situation that depending on how an algorithm is designed and instructed, it may have a profound effect on the market behaviour of the undertaking for which it operates.

[C] Regulatory Challenges

Increasingly, the question is being raised as to whether the current tools available to competition authorities are sufficient for effectively combating cartels or collusion by means of algorithms (self-learning or otherwise).[1560] For example, Ezrachi and Stucke have warned on several occasions that the computing power of self-learning algorithms

1555. *Case 50223: Online Sales of Posters and Frames*, *supra* n. 455, para. 3.76.
1556. In Spain, a distributor of cigarettes was recently fined for offering software and data to tobacco companies. The tobacco companies used the software to exchange competitively sensitive information. *See* Comisión Nacional de los Mercados y la Competencia, press release 12 April 2019, 'La CNMC sanciona a las principales empresas fabricantes de tabaco y a Logista por una infracción consistente en un intercambio de información estratégica'.
1557. Vestager, *supra* n. 281.
1558. P.A. Lawrence, *The Making of a Fly: The Genetics of Animal Design* (Blackwell Scientific Publications 1992).
1559. M. Eisen, 'Amazon's $23,698,655.93 Book about Flies' (*It Is Not junk*), http://www.michaeleisen.org/blog/?p=358; Vestager, *supra* n. 281.
1560. For a good overview article of the now numerous literature on this subject, *see* for example: R. Steppe, 'Algoritmische Prijsbepaling En Stilzwijgende Collusie Onder EU-Mededingingsrecht' (2018) 12 SEW 512-521.

combined with access to large amounts of data may result in price competition being almost eliminated.[1561] In their view, this process may arise from tacit collusion, without there being a prohibited cartel agreement.[1562] According to these authors, it is necessary to consider the regulation of tacit collusion.[1563] To effectively do so, competition authorities need to have sufficiently strong data-gathering power, so as to be able to thoroughly study how modern algorithms used by undertakings function. This will in turn require competition authorities to develop sufficient technological expertise.[1564] The CMA has argued that there should be more clear guidelines as to when the utilisation of the same or coordinated algorithms by competing undertakings should be deemed anticompetitive.[1565] For instance, the CMA stressed the importance of algorithmic transparency when it comes to explaining the functioning and decision-making of algorithms to consumers.[1566] Similarly, it noted that it is crucial to ensure that the processes behind algorithmic decision-making are fair and accurate.[1567] Accordingly, this can be accomplished by developing guidance, as exists already for algorithmic trading by investment companies.[1568] Moreover, the CMA has referenced the Data Protection Impact Assessment (DPIA) developed by the Information Commissioner's Office. In that respect, the CMA noted that the DPIA and the accompanying framework for auditing artificial intelligence (AI) can provide additional guidance for evaluation of the (pricing) algorithms.[1569] As a consequence, this would allow firms to ensure that algorithms are by design compliant with British competition law.

Other legal scholars however see lesser issues than Ezrachi and Stucke. Schrepel, for instance, has investigated whether the number of cartel cases in the US in which algorithms play a role has increased since 2007 (his answer is no) and takes the view that an effective approach to undesirable market behaviour of algorithms can be realised through a combination of review and application of the current competition rules.[1570] Additionally, Calzolari argues that algorithmic collusion should be distinguished from tacit collusion. In the case of tacit collusion, undertakings use the existing

1561. *See* for example A. Ezrachi and M.E. Stucke, *Virtual Competition: The Promise and Perils of the Algorithm-Driven Economy* (Harvard University Press 2016) 208-211.
1562. A. Ezrachi and M.E. Stucke, 'Artificial Intelligence & Collusion: When Computers Inhibit Competition' (2017) 2017 University of Illinois Law Review 1808.
1563. *Ibid.*, 1175-1809; I. Greaf, 'Algorithmic Price Fixing under EU Competition Law: How to Crack Robot Cartels?' (*CITIP Blog*, 10 May 2016) https://www.law.kuleuven.be/citip/blog/algorithmic-price-fixing-under-eu-competition-law-how-to-crack-robot-cartels/.
1564. Hawkes, *supra* n. 1539, p. 16.
1565. CMA, *supra* n. 1535, p. 43.
1566. *Ibid.*, p. 45.
1567. *Ibid.*, p. 44.
1568. *Ibid.*, p. 46.
1569. *Ibid.*, p. 44.
1570. Thibault Schrépel, 'Here's Why Algorithms Are Not (Really) a Thing' (15 May 2017, *Concurrentialiste Review*) https://leconcurrentialiste.com/2017/05/15/algorithms-based-practices-antitrust/; he has further elaborated upon this topic in Thibault Schrépel, 'The Fundamental Unimportance of Algorithmic Collusion for Antitrust Law' (10 February 2020, *Harvard Law School Antitrust Association*) https://orgs.law.harvard.edu/antitrust/2020/02/10/the-fundamental-unimportance-of-algorithmic-collusion-for-antitrust-law/; Posner already took a similar position around the turn of the century, *see* R.A. Posner, 'Antitrust in the

market conditions, whereas, in the case of algorithmic collusion, undertakings contribute to the market conditions that allow tacit collusion to take place.[1571] Algorithmic collusion should, therefore, be regarded as a concerted practice. Accordingly, when undertakings in question develop an algorithmic software that is used for autonomous collusion, they could be argued to knowingly contribute to creating a situation on the market when their rational algorithms are likely able to collude.[1572] Indeed, it could be defended that they could reasonably foresee that the algorithms may collude, even if the initial purpose of their creation was not anticompetitive under Article 101 TFEU.[1573]

Notably, in its report for the OECD, already discussed in the chapter on the Commission, the Commission stresses that if tacit collusion occurs through self-learning algorithms, three basic conditions still have to be met: (i) it must concern homogeneous products or services, (ii) there needs to be a possibility of effective retaliation, and (iii) there must be an absence of the perspective for market players to gain significant market share in case of a price reduction.[1574] It should also be noted that, in the meantime, it has become established case law (through the *Eturas* judgment) that the receipt of repeated communications from which an economic operator has not demonstrably distanced itself, may be sufficient to draw a legally valid conclusion that this economic operator was involved in a concerted practice.[1575] If this line were to be followed, it could also be argued that the current tools available to the competition authorities in this respect could be sufficient. Nevertheless, the Commission mentions three possible instruments to extend the existing competition law framework:

(1) Self-regulation by the market. However, the Commission is concerned that this may come about too late or not at all.[1576]
(2) Extending the concept of '*communication*', whereby enforcement action could be taken in situations in which – without there being any exchange of data or even *signalling* – algorithms can 'decipher' each other through repeated interaction. The Commission notes – without specifically mentioning the *Eturas* judgment cited above – that it cannot be ruled out that in certain cases such interactions may already be covered by the cartel prohibition.[1577]
(3) Prohibiting tacit collusion. The Commission does not support this, as it does not see how, without price regulation, companies can be required to set their

New Economy' (2000) John M. Olin Program in Law and Economics Working Paper, https://chicagounbound.uchicago.edu/law_and_economics/58.

1571. Luca Calzolari, 'The Misleading Consequences of Comparing Algorithmic and Tacit Collusion: Tackling Algorithmic Concerted Practices under Art. 101 TFEU' (2021) 6(2) European Papers 1193.
1572. *Ibid.*, p. 1207.
1573. *Ibid.*
1574. 'Algorithms and Collusion – Note from the European Union', *supra* n. 285, para. 30.
1575. *Case C-74/14 (Eturas and Others) Eturas' UAB and Others v. Lietuvos Respublikos konkurencijos taryba* [2016] ECLI:EU:C:2016:42.
1576. 'Algorithms and Collusion – Note from the European Union', *supra* n. 285, para. 31.
1577. *Ibid.*, para. 33.

> prices without regard to the (visible) market behaviour of their competitors. The Commission is more concerned with preventing the creation of market structures within which tacit collusion can take place (through merger control) and by acting against resale price maintenance.[1578]

However, researchers at the University of Bologna claim to have demonstrated that algorithms can also make classic cartel agreements but do not leave any evidence for such agreements.[1579] If this conclusion were to be confirmed in other investigations, this would obviously make it very difficult, if not impossible, for the competent authorities to track down such cartel agreements.

In its 2018 biennial report on competition policy, the Monopolkommission, an independent advisory body to the German government, devotes a chapter to the issue of effective competition enforcement with regard to algorithms.[1580] The Monopolkommission concludes that in data-intensive sectors, such as the internet economy, price algorithms can facilitate collusion and the emergence of a collusive outcome: '*In data-intensive sectors such as the internet economy, price algorithms can facilitate collusion by automating collusive behaviour and, thus, accelerating it technically. For example, they can stabilise collusion by collecting information on competitors' prices and sanctioning deviations from collusive market outcomes more quickly. The use of price algorithms can also make explicit agreements or agreements restricting competition unnecessary. Lastly, in the case of self-learning algorithms, the relevant business decision is already made at the time of the decision regarding the price algorithm and is not made in the price-setting process.*'[1581] The Monopolkommission notes that the discovery by competition authorities of collusion by undertakings is already difficult in general and that the use of price algorithms can increase this problem. The Monopolkommission considers that consumer organisations often receive signals of price increases as a result of collusion between undertakings. The Monopolkommission therefore proposes to give consumer organisations the right to initiate sector enquiries under competition law. If a competition authority were to reject an application for such an enquiry, it should be obliged to provide a detailed statement of the reasons for its decision. If a competition authority does launch an investigation and this investigation would then reveal a price cartel implemented by algorithms, the Monopolkommission recommends that consideration be given to reversing the burden of proof with regard to the proof of the damage caused by the infringement. Liability for financial losses resulting from the covert use of price algorithms will therefore fall on the users of these algorithms. Finally, the Monopolkommission points out that price algorithms are often not designed by their users but by companies with special expertise. '*Whether such a*

1578. *Ibid.*, para. 34.
1579. Emilio Calvano et al., 'Artificial Intelligence, Algorithmic Pricing and Collusion' (2018) CEPR Discussion Paper No. DP13405.
1580. 'XXII. Hauptgutachten Gemäß § 44 Abs. 1 Satz 1 GWB: Algorithmen Und Kollusion' (Monopolkommision 2018) https://www.monopolkommission.de/de/index.php/de/beitraege/216-xxii-algorithmen.
1581. 'XXII. Hauptgutachten Gemäß § 44 Abs. 1 Satz 1 GWB: Algorithmen Und Kollusion', *supra* n. 1580, 64.

third party is liable for violations of competition law typically depends on the responsibility of the companies using the price algorithm. This means that IT service providers can either be subject to particularly far-reaching liability or, conversely, benefit from liability gaps, depending on whether the decision on the design of the price algorithm in question lies more with the user or with the respective IT service provider. The liability of such third parties should be generally reviewed.'[1582] In the opinion of the Monopolkommission, it would therefore have been obvious for the CMA to indeed have investigated whether the developer of the software facilitating the infringement in *Online Sales of Posters and Frames* should have been imposed a fine. It does appear however that in that case, the decision in respect of the design of the algorithm in question lay with the cartelists and not so much with the software developer. According to the Monopolkommission's reasoning, this could lead to software developers being able to benefit from what is known as a 'liability gap'. The question is, of course, how such a reasoning would relate to the *Treuhand* judgment.[1583] After all, this judgment does not imply that it is necessary for a competition authority to demonstrate that an undertaking took the initiative to commit a cartel infringement in order to be able to fine that undertaking as a cartel facilitator.

Additionally, EU Commissioner Vestager has stated that a company or individual can (and should) always be held liable for the actions of algorithms: '*Whatever the algorithm, there is still a person or business responsible for it*'[1584] and '*businesses also need to know that when they decide to use an automated system, they will be held responsible for what it does. So they had better know how that system works*'.[1585] In the Commission's contribution to the OECD's market investigation, which was mentioned above on several occasions, the Commission also upholds the principle that an undertaking (or natural person) concerned can always be held liable for the prohibited behaviour of an algorithm, even in case the algorithm – unlike in *Online Sales of Posters and Frames* – came to the prohibited behaviour autonomously: '*firms involved in illegal pricing practices cannot avoid liability on the grounds that their prices were determined by algorithms. Like an employee or an outside consultant working under a firm's "direction or control," an algorithm remains under the firm's control, and therefore the firm is liable for its actions.*'[1586] The same view can be found in the opinion of Bundeskartellamt president Mundt. Mundt clearly stated in the context of the *Lufthansa* case that Lufthansa cannot hide behind an algorithm: '*Solche Algorithmen werden ja nicht im Himmel vom lieben Gott geschrieben*' [freely translated: 'such algorithms did not drop from the sky'] and that Lufthansa '*sich nicht hinter Algorithmen verstecken [könnte]*' [freely translated: '*cannot hide behind algorithms*'].[1587]

The Dutch competition authority (ACM) had a more nuanced view, at least in 2018. It states that an automated cartel between self-learning algorithms is probably

1582. *Ibid.*, 65.
1583. Case C-194/14 P *(AC Treuhand v. Commission)*, *supra* n. 1554.
1584. Vestager, *supra* n. 281.
1585. *Ibid.*
1586. 'Algorithms and Collusion – Note from the European Union', *supra* n. 285, para. 38.
1587. Busse, *supra* n. 1002.

not in conflict with current Dutch and European competition law: '*Een specifiek risico is dat zelflerende algoritmes geautomatiseerde kartels vormen. Dankzij de hoeveelheid data en de mogelijkheid om prijzen in hoog tempo aan te passen kunnen de algoritmes leren van scenario's en convergeren naar een evenwicht met hogere prijzen. De uitkomst daarvan kan vergelijkbaar zijn met de schade van klassieke kartelafspraken. Waarschijnlijk is dit niet in strijd met de huidige Nederlandse en Europese mededingingswetgeving, omdat er geen onderliggende afspraak is en geen intentie om een kartel te vormen. Daarmee is die situatie vergelijkbaar met stilzwijgende afstemming of "slim volggedrag"*' [freely translated: '*A specific risk is that self-learning algorithms form automated cartels. Due to the amount of data and the ability to adjust prices at high speed, the algorithms can learn from scenarios and converge towards an equilibrium with higher prices. The outcome may be comparable to the damage caused by traditional cartel agreements. This is probably not contrary to current Dutch and European competition law, because there is no underlying agreement and no intention to form a cartel. This makes the situation comparable to tacit collusion or "smart tracking"*'].[1588] The ACM thus implicitly seems to assume that it is in fact possible to address developed algorithms that receive a cartel instruction under the current cartel prohibition. A similar line of reasoning seems to apply to self-learning algorithms that engage in a cartel based on the exchange of competitively sensitive information and behavioural coordination by a self-learning algorithm that goes beyond mere smart tracking.

On 11 February 2020, the ACM published its Guidelines on Online Consumer Protection.[1589] In this legal instrument, the ACM also pays extensive attention to the application of consumer law to the use of algorithms by businesses.[1590] However, the competition rules fall outside of the scope of these Guidelines; thus, it remains to be seen whether the ACM will also publish a similar legal document on the application of competition law to algorithms in the future.

[D] Concluding Remarks

In summary, it appears for the time being that the authorities under review that have explicitly expressed their views on this subject expect that to a large extent the challenge of 'cartel algorithms' can be tackled under competition law with the current legal instruments. This expectation seems to be based on the fact that if an algorithm is developed with the aim of entering into a cartel, this cartel will be demonstrable under the current regulations. Of course, this becomes more difficult if there is no algorithm developed with a cartel objective from the onset, but instead, a self-learning algorithm enters into a cartel at a given moment with the objective of profit maximisation. The starting point of the Commission's and the Bundeskartelamt's reasoning in that situation appears to be that the person responsible for a self-learning algorithm that independently proceeds to cartel behaviour has a conditional intent in respect of

1588. 'Het Signaal 2018', *supra* n. 1060, p. 3.
1589. ACM, 'Guidline: Protection of the Online Consumer. Boundaries of Online Persuasion' (2020) ACM p. 6.
1590. *Ibid.*, pp. 27-28.

that behaviour since he or she failed to take measures to prevent the algorithm from displaying the prohibited behaviour. The question is whether this reasoning is always applicable in practice. If an economic operator uses in good faith a self-learning pricing algorithm that goes on to engage in cartel behaviour, who is liable? That market participant could take the view that it could not reasonably have foreseen that the algorithm was capable of the prohibited conduct (and that the conduct was also not in line with its instruction to the algorithm), while the developer could in turn argue that it could not reasonably foresee that the self-learning algorithm it developed would have been capable of a cartel infringement. In a theoretical case in which both would speak the truth - which is not inconceivable - neither of them would hold intent (conditional or otherwise). If one or both parties were nevertheless held liable for the cartel behaviour of the algorithm, this would qualify as a strict liability. Decision-making practice and case law in the coming years will have to show whether an enforcement gap or instead over enforcement could nevertheless arise in such circumstances.

To avoid this situation as much as possible, Vestager pointed out that companies should be aware of competition law when designing algorithms: '*That's also how businesses need to think when they design and use algorithms. They may not always know exactly how an automated system will use its algorithms to take decisions. What businesses can – and must – do is to ensure antitrust compliance by design. That means pricing algorithms need to be built in a way that doesn't allow them to collude. Like a more honourable version of the computer HAL in the film 2001: A Space Odyssey, they need to respond to an offer of collusion by saying "I'm sorry, I'm afraid I can't do that."*'[1591]

1591. Vestager, *supra* n. 281.

§10.07 BIG DATA

[A] Introduction

Access to (large quantities of) data is becoming an increasingly important - if not crucial - instrument to compete in the digital sector.[1592] Accordingly, it is no surprise that the activities of the authorities under review demonstrate that big data indeed plays an increasingly important role in their investigations. At the same time, none of the mergers that involved big data and fell within the temporal research scope of this book was opposed by the authorities under review, which presupposes that the authority in question did not identify any insurmountable competition issues. Several cases did however require remedies. National competition authorities have also handled some cases involving big data. However, none of these national cases raised notable objections on the basis of the (big amounts of) data involved.

Most relevant cases from a data perspective during the research period concerned merger control proceedings. Arguably, the most groundbreaking antitrust case in which big data stood central that was handled by the authorities under review during the research period and in which a final decision was reached, was the *Facebook* (now Meta) decision by the Bundeskartellamt,[1593] which is currently pending before the European Court of Justice in a preliminary ruling case.[1594]

[B] European Commission

Apart from drafting several (sections of) reports on the issue (reference is made to the chapter on the Commission), the Commission has thus far only dealt with questions involving large quantities of data in merger cases. The investigation into Amazon's dual role as a sales platform and a retailer - which was ended by the Commission accepting commitments from Amazon - and its use of business data of its users in this dual role from its independent users, may however lead to the Commission's first decision under the prohibition of abuse of a dominant position in which the collection and use of data play a pivotal role.[1595] The Commission's investigation into Facebook's[1596] (now Meta) use of advertising data (equally pending) may also spark a new landmark case under the prohibition of abuse of a dominant position. The outcome of that latter investigation is however still uncertain at the time of finalising the second

1592. For an overview of possible competition concerns of big data, *see* OECD, 'Big Data: Bringing Competition Policy to the Digital Era' (2016) https://one.oecd.org/document/DAF/COMP(2016)14/en/pdf.; Graef, *Data as essential facility, Competition and Innovation on Online Platforms*, Kluwer Law International 2016, p. 245.
1593. Bundeskartellamt, decision of 6 February 2019 in case B6-22/16 (*Facebook*).
1594. Case C-252/21.
1595. European Commission Case AT.40703. For the press release of the Commission, please refer to: https://ec.europa.eu/commission/presscorner/detail/en/ip_20_2077.
1596. Press release IP/21/2848of 4 June 2021 in case AT.40684, *Antitrust: Commission opens investigation into possible anticompetitive conduct of Facebook*, https://ec.europa.eu/commission/presscorner/detail/en/IP_21_2848.

edition of this book (May 2023). On 19 December 2022, the Commission did send a Statement of Objections to Meta.[1597]

On the basis of its decisions in merger cases so far, the European Commission appears to have been fairly flexible in clearing mergers involving large amounts of data. In the *Facebook/WhatsApp* case, for example, it concluded that access to and control over WhatsApp user data would not give Facebook a dominant position, as competitors would retain access to sufficient alternative data sources to allow them to remain in effective competition with the merged entity.[1598] The Commission reached similar conclusions in *Microsoft/LinkedIn*[1599] and *Apple/Shazam*.[1600] In *Microsoft/LinkedIn*, the Commission cleared the notified concentration subject to behavioural remedies, including the provision of services to competing platforms and accessibility for competitors to data stored in the Microsoft Cloud. In *Google/Fitbit*, Google had to commit to not use the data collected from Fitbit devices for advertising, as well as giving third-party developers free access to users' data and ensuring that equipment manufacturers have free access to the Android APIs necessary to ensure interoperability with Android smartphones. In *Meta/Kustomer*,[1601] the Commission also investigated whether the merging of the relevant data in possession of Meta and Kustomer would lead to a substantial lessening of competition. It however found that such would not be the case. The (behavioural) remedies imposed by the Commission, in this case, did not relate to the parties' respective data sets. The Competition and Markets Authority (CMA)[1602] and the Bundeskartellamt[1603] reached similar conclusions in their respective investigations of the same concentration.

Some years after the Commission's unconditional approval, it became clear that the approval of Facebook's acquisition of WhatsApp no longer enjoys unanimous support within the Commission staff. Tommaso Valetti, Chief Economist at the time of the said merger, criticised the European Commission's rapid clearance of the merger some years later. Although Valetti did not take the view that the acquisition of Facebook – and the earlier Instagram acquisition that was cleared by the CMA[1604] – should have been prohibited, he did find the markets to be defined incorrectly in both cases. Valetti also criticised the CMA's product market definition in the *Instagram* case, as a result of the identification – for example – of a separate market for camera apps rather than a broader market for (various types of) social media on which Facebook

1597. European Commission, press release of 19 December 2022, *Antitrust: Commission sends Statement of Objections to Meta over abusive practices benefiting Facebook Marketplace*, https://ec.europa.eu/commission/presscorner/detail/en/ip_22_7728.
1598. Case No COMP/M.7217 (Facebook/WhatsApp), *supra* n. 291.
1599. Case M.8124 (Microsoft/LinkedIn), *supra* n. 291.
1600. Case M.8788 (Apple/Shazam), *supra* n. 291.
1601. Case M.10262 (Meta/Kustomer).
1602. ME/6920/20, Anticipated acquisition by Facebook, Inc. of Kustomer, Inc., Decision on relevant merger situation and substantial lessening of competition.
1603. Bundeskartellamt, 'Pressemitteilung: Freigabe der Übernahme von Kustomer durch Meta (ehemals Facebook)' (11 February 2022, *Bundeskartellamt/Digitalwirtschaft*) https://www.bundeskartellamt.de/SharedDocs/Publikation/DE/Pressemitteilungen/2022/11_02_2022_Meta_Kustomer.pdf?__blob=publicationFile&v=2 p. 1.
1604. This case dates from 2012 and therefore falls outside our period under review.

and WhatsApp might have been considered as competitors. Consequently, whereas the CMA did not identify any serious competition problem, Valetti openly questioned whether a broader market definition as described would have also resulted in approval.[1605] Valetti's criticism was later seconded by then CMA chief executive Andrea Coscelli, during a forum discussion at the aforementioned CRA conference on 5 December 2018. In a keynote speech at the annual Fordham Competition Law Institute Conference, on 9 October 2020, Coscelli stressed that the CMA's approach to digital mergers has evolved considerably, including a broadening of the range of theories of harm related to access to data. Coscelli has also warned that the UK is at risk to fall behind on regulatory legislation with regards to Big Tech companies compared to the EU and that it would be hard to increase merger regulation in a later stage due to the 'undue cost' on corporates.

[C] Bundeskartellamt

In its aforementioned *Facebook* decision, the Bundeskartellamt emphasises that apart from providing market power, the possession of big data by large tech companies may also lead to privacy concerns. The Bundeskartellamt explicitly names a supposed failure by Facebook (now Meta) to comply with the privacy protection rules of the GDPR as a reason for its conclusion that Facebook's policy of combining data from its various applications constitutes an abuse of a dominant position. The decision therefore seems to be grounded in a combined application of competition law and privacy law. That raises the question of whether the Bundeskartellamt was not exceeding its powers when applying the GDPR and if the privacy authorities should not be enforcing it instead. This question is currently pending before the European Court of Justice. The advocate general has advised the Court to rule largely in favour of the Bundeskartellamt in this respect.[1606] In its decision, the Bundeskartellamt does explain why it considers itself competent to apply the GDPR. It infers that GDPR enforcement is not exclusively entrusted to the national data protection authorities since it can also be applied by the civil courts. The Bundeskartellamt also states that it consulted the various privacy authorities of the German federal states, their federal umbrella body and the data protection authorities of other EU Member States, among which the Irish privacy authority, and that none of them claimed exclusive jurisdiction. Additionally, the Hamburg state authority is explicitly mentioned as having supported the Bundeskartellamt's procedure.[1607]

As mentioned, the request for a preliminary ruling is still pending before the European Court of Justice. After the Court's judgment, the proceedings before the

1605. M. Acton, 'Facebook Got Tot Easy a Pass over WhatsApp and Instagram Purchases, Says EU's Valletti' *MLex Market Insight* (24 October 2018).
1606. Opinion of 20 September 2022 in case 252/21, https://curia.europa.eu/juris/document/document.jsf?text=&docid=265901&pageIndex=0&doclang=EN&mode=req&dir=&occ=first&part=1&cid=1992373.
1607. 'Case Summary – B6-22/16: Facebook, Exploitative Business Terms Pursuant to Section 19(1) GWB for Inadequate Data Processing', *supra* n. 945, paras 8-9.

national courts in Germany may also be expected to consume a substantial amount of time. If in the end, Meta were to lose in these main proceedings before the national courts in Germany, it would either have to apply different terms of use in Germany or adapt its terms and conditions in several jurisdictions to the requirements of the decision of the Bundeskartellamt. Since Meta is fiercely litigating the decision, the latter seems unlikely. If Meta were to ultimately prevail in the ongoing procedures, it could continue to use EU-wide (and, perhaps, even worldwide) terms and conditions, in particular in relation to combining user data from various applications.

[D] Autorité de la Concurrence

The Autorité has not yet had the opportunity in many individual cases to state its position on the importance of big data to competition (in digital markets) very prominently. The Autorité has however carried out a substantial amount of studies and has issued policy documents on the subject.[1608]

The key French big data case concerns the interplay between competition law and data privacy law concerns Autorité's investigation into the data protection policy that Apple uses on its iPhone.[1609] The complainants argue that Apple's new privacy policy is an exclusionary practice that calls into question the targeted advertising business model of app developers, '*who earn on average twice as much revenue from personalised advertising as from contextual advertising*'. Apple, however, argues that the policy aims to strengthen the privacy protection of customers. The Autorité has yet to take a position on this delicate matter that has implications for many other market players. It rejected a request to impose interim measures on Apple[1610] but is still investigating the case. The Autorité has also published studies on competition law and data[1611] (2016, with the Bundeskartellamt) and on data processing[1612] (2018) and an opinion on payment services that addresses the role of data collected by big tech companies. It also announced a market study into cloud services (2022).[1613]

1608. Autorité de la concurrence and Bundeskartellamt, The Autorité has expressed its views on data abuse by former state monopolies, *see* 'Competition Law and Data', *supra* n. 839, 31-32.

1609. Autorité de la Concurrence, decision 17 March 2021, 21-D-07 (*Apple Targeted advertising (a)*).

1610. The complainants demanded that the Autorité would order Apple not to require the use of its window to obtain user consent for tracking, until a decision on the merits of the case would be reached, or until an acceptable solution is found, following negotiations between Apple and industry stakeholders, in accordance with the second requested interim measure, and to engage in a constructive dialogue with industry stakeholders in order to find an acceptable solution for obtaining permission/consent for user tracking that complies with the requirements of European privacy legislation (in particular the GDPR and the ePrivacy Directive), and would be less disruptive to users and harmful to competition in the relevant markets.

1611. Autorité de la Concurrence and Bundeskartellamt, 'Competition Law and Data', 10 May 2016.

1612. Autorité de la Concurrence, 'Opinion on Data Processing in the Online Advertising Sector', 18-A-03, 6 March 2018.

1613. Autorité de la concurrence, press release 27 January 2022, 'The Autorité de la concurrence starts proceedings ex officio to analyse competition conditions in the cloud computing sector'.

[E] Competition and Markets Authority

The CMA also acknowledges that data can lead to market power. In a keynote speech, delivered on 9 October 2020,[1614] the then-chairman Coscelli noted that analysis of a broad range of theories of harm, including those related to access to data, has become a key element of the development of the assessment of digital mergers. In 2015, Alex Chisholm, Coscelli's predecessor at the CMA, had already identified a number of indicators for possible competition problems in markets where (personal) data is collected and used, such as:[1615]

- the extent to which data is a key element for a company's business model;
- whether data is made available exclusively;
- whether there already exists significant market power, which will also make the parties with market power the first to have market data;
- the existence of alternatives for which less data needs to be collected.

According to Chisholm, the decisive factor will have to be assessed on a case-by-case basis. The efficiencies for firms and/or consumers resulting from the use of data originating from consumers will need to be balanced against collusion or abuse of a dominant position (as a result of exclusion or exploitative behaviour) resulting from the use of those data on the other hand. Chisholm argues that this is closely related to the structure and functioning of the market in question and how these factors affect the lasting value of data: '*When looking at any specific market, or case, it would also be important to think about the value of data. Some data loses value over time, so it is hard to see how persistent, unmatchable competitive advantage could be maintained. However, some data has persistent value – for example, in relation to customer transaction history on auction sites – and it is easier to see how the control of this data could become a barrier to entry.*'[1616]

The CMA has also applied such theories of harm in various cases or is currently in the process of doing so. First of all, the CMA started investigating whether Facebook (currently: Meta) might be, through its collection and use of advertising data, abusing a dominant position in the social media or digital advertising markets. Meta collects data through its digital services, such as its advertising services but also the Facebook Login, the single sign-on option that allows users to sign into other websites using their Facebook account. The CMA will assess in particular whether Meta has used such data to benefit its own services.[1617] However, no investigation results, in this case, have been published yet. The same applies to the CMA's investigation into Amazon for

1614. Speech: *Digital Markets: using our existing tools and emerging thoughts on a new regime*, CMA, 9 October 2020, https://www.gov.uk/government/speeches/digital-markets-using-our-existing-tools-and-emerging-thoughts-on-a-new-regime.
1615. Chisholm, 'Speech at the UEA Centre for Competition Policy Annual Conference in Norwich: Alex Chisholm Speaks about Data and Trust in Digital Markets'.
1616. *Ibid.*
1617. https://www.gov.uk/government/news/cma-investigates-facebook-s-use-of-ad-data.

marketplace concerns.[1618] In this case, the CMA investigates whether Amazon abuses a possible dominant position by giving an unfair advantage to its own retail business or sellers that use its fulfilment services when compared to other sellers that do not use such services.

In the field of merger control, in *Nielsen/Ebiquity*,[1619] the CMA conducted an elaborate (phase II) investigation into the merging entities' combined 'AdIntel' data resources, but eventually issued an unconditional clearance decision since that investigation indicated that the parties were not (close) competitors. In *Google/Looker Data Sciences*, the CMA investigated a theory of harm under which Google would make it difficult for its competitors to access the necessary data generated by Google from online advertising and web analytics services but, however, found that there was no compelling evidence that Google would have the incentive to do so.[1620]

On 19 May 2021, the CMA and the Information Commissioner's Office (ICO) published a joint statement on competition and data protection in digital markets.[1621] The report concludes that the objectives regarding competition and data protection in the context of the digital economy are strongly aligned and complementary. The main conclusions of the report are as follows:

- *'First, more competitive markets will deliver the outcomes that consumers care about most, which increasingly include enhanced privacy and greater control over personal data.*
- *Second, we have concluded that this relationship is mutually reinforcing. Well-designed regulations and standards that preserve individuals' privacy and place individuals in control of their personal data can promote positive competitive outcomes. In turn, with appropriate and targeted regulation, competitive pressures can be harnessed to incentivise responsible innovations that protect and support users.*
- *Third, the creation of a level playing field is fundamental for enabling effective competition to thrive. Data protection law helps to achieve a level playing field with regards to data access, by ensuring that processing of personal data by all parties is fair and lawful and individual rights are upheld.'*

Both authorities declare their commitment to consulting one another to ensure the synergies identified in this statement can be maximised, and any tensions overcome.

1618. https://www.gov.uk/government/news/cma-investigates-amazon-over-suspected-anti-competitive-practices.

1619. ME/6733/18, *Anticipated Acquisition by Nielsen Holdings PLC of the AdIntel Division of Ebiquity PLC* (Competition and Markets Authority).

1620. ME/6839/19, Completed acquisition by Google LLC of Looker Data Sciences, Inc., paras 119 ff.

1621. CMA and ICO, *Competition and data protection in digital markets: a joint statement between the CMA and the ICO*, 19 May 2021, https://assets.publishing.service.gov.uk/government/uploads/system/uploads/attachment_data/file/987358/Joint_CMA_ICO_Public_statement_-_final_V2_180521.pdf.

[F] ACM

The Dutch competition authority (ACM) has not yet dealt with the issue of (big) data and its impact in antitrust cases, but the subject has been of relevance in two of its merger decisions. In addition, the ACM has briefly touched on the subject in one of its policy documents.[1622] Also of relevance is an article published by, *inter alia*, Freek Bruggert, head of the Digital Taskforce of the ACM (though the article is published in a personal capacity).[1623] In this article, Bruggert and his colleague Jan Tichem speak out against a general duty to share data. They see no automatic link between market power and innovation, in the sense that greater market power by definition leads to less innovation. They likewise reject the opposite, Schumpeterian theory (a certain degree of market power is necessary for markets to innovate). They therefore argue that the effect of data-driven market power on competition should be assessed on a case-by-case basis. Accordingly, they do not consider *ex ante* regulation to be a good instrument. They do see competition law as appropriate for carrying out this assessment on a case-by-case basis. One may question whether the authors still hold this opinion with the advent of the DMA and the data-sharing obligations for gatekeepers that can be imposed under the DMA. They see no issue in the fact that competition law (in particular the prohibition of abuse of a dominant position) only intervenes if the data are indispensable and sharing would lead to more innovation (essential facility):

> '*D[ie] hoge bewijslast sluit aan bij de gepaste voorzichtigheid bij een ex post ingrijpen. Het is namelijk lang niet zeker dat data tot marktmacht leiden en dat verplichte datadeling in alle gevallen tot meer innovatie leidt*' [freely translated: '*That high standard of proof is in line with the appropriate caution in the event of ex post intervention. It is far from certain that data will lead to market power and that mandatory data sharing will lead to more innovation in all cases*'].

This is in line with the overall policy vision of the ACM that, in principle, it wants to have a very thorough understanding of digital markets before proceeding to enforcement. The same attitude can be found in its publication *Het Signaal 2018*, although the ACM does not rule out an obligation to share data in cases where the data cannot be duplicated from other sources (and would therefore qualify as an essential facility):

> '*Door het bevorderen van (open) standaarden en goed werkende interfaces en het wegnemen van wettelijke belemmeringen of onduidelijkheden over bijvoorbeeld eigendom van data kan het delen van data een verdere impuls krijgen. Als consumenten controle hebben over hun data kunnen zij die ook voor concurrerende aanbieders beschikbaar maken. (...) In andere gevallen kan een verplichting tot openstellen van datasets nodig zijn. Bijvoorbeeld als ondernemingen data die een*

1622. 'Het Signaal 2018', *supra* n. 1060, 5.
1623. Bruggert and Tichem, *supra* n. 1076, 306-308.

> *cruciale input zijn voor nieuwe diensten of producten niet kunnen of willen delen. In de systematische verkenning moet worden vastgesteld welke data voor welke toepassingen belangrijk zijn of worden. Criteria als omvang en variëteit van de dataset, exclusiviteit, de waarde van de data en het eventuele belang van wederkerigheid (niet alleen profiteren, maar ook bijdragen) spelen mee bij de afweging of verplichte openstelling nodig is. Waar meerdere marktpartijen zelf vergelijkbare of alternatieve data kunnen verzamelen ligt een verplichting minder voor de hand dan wanneer er sprake is van een unieke dataset. In het publieke domein ziet die afweging er waarschijnlijk anders uit dan in het private*' [freely translated: '*By promoting (open) standards and well-functioning interfaces and removing legal obstacles or ambiguities about, for example, ownership of data, data sharing can be given a further boost. If consumers have control over their data, they can also make it available to competing providers.* (...) *In other cases, an obligation to provide access to data sets may be necessary. For example, when companies are unable or unwilling to share data that are crucial input for new services or products. A systematic exploration should determine which data are or will be important for which applications. Criteria such as the size and variety of the data set, exclusivity, the value of the data and the possible importance of reciprocity (not only benefiting, but also contributing) play a role in the consideration of whether mandatory opening up is necessary. Where several market parties can collect comparable or alternative data themselves, an obligation is less obvious than in the case of a unique data set. In the public domain, this consideration probably looks different than in the private domain*'].[1624]

Actual decisions of the ACM in which data power played an important role have thus far remained limited to merger control cases. In its investigation relating to the creation of a joint venture by Pon Netherlands and NS Groep, which would operate an app that allows consumers to plan, book and pay for their trips, combining different modes of transportation (i.e., Mobility as a Service, or 'MaaS'), the ACM assessed the potential exclusion of other (potential) providers of integrated mobility services through an app by offering them the relevant inputs (train and public transport bicycles) at higher prices or (other) less favourable conditions than the joint venture.[1625] By committing, amongst other remedies, to provide competitors with the relevant inputs under FRAND conditions, the concerns of the ACM were satisfactorily addressed by the parties. Similarly, the ACM investigated the potential shielding of data in Sanoma/Iddink.[1626] However, the concentrating parties offered remedies pursuant to which competitors would continue to have access to certain crucial data, which took away these and other concerns of the ACM. Reference is made to the chapter on the ACM for a more elaborate description of these remedies.

1624. 'Het Signaal 2018', *supra* n. 1060, 5.
1625. Autoriteit Consument & Markt, decision 20 May 2020, ACM/20/038614 (*NS Groep N.V./Pon Netherlands B.V./JV*).
1626. Autoriteit Consument & Markt, decision 28 August 2019, ACM/19/035555 (*Sanoma Learning B.V./Iddink Holding B.V.*).

[G] Belgian Competition Authority

In its priorities announcements for 2021 and 2022, the BCA announced that it will focus mainly on the use of (personal) data and algorithms to facilitate antitrust infringements.[1627] This policy has, however, not (yet) resulted in any concrete decisions.

The BMA's only decision in which it dealt with data as a potential source of dominance was *Great Circle/IRM*.[1628] In that case, the BCA rejected a request from Great Circle for access under the *essential facilities* doctrine to Belgian meteorological data owned by IRM, since on an at least European-wide market for commercial meteorological information, IRM held no dominant position because the meteorological data obtained in other EU Member States can also be used in Belgium and vice versa.

[H] Analysis and Future

Although there are now various precedents regarding the competitive importance of (big) data, the picture drawn by these decisions is still highly fragmented. In addition, most precedents relate to merger control cases – none of which turned out to be very problematic (with the observation that several cases did require remedies). Under the prohibition of abuse of a dominant position, the Bundeskartellamt's *Facebook* decision is arguably the most important landmark precedent thus far. Most definitely, the interest of competition authorities for data as a potential source of market power and even market dominance has increased over the research period.

When it comes to mergers, it is noteworthy that the remedies imposed by the authorities under review in data-driven cases were predominantly behavioural. This is also understandable since data-related market power can be reduced through obligations granting third parties access to such data or on the contrary by preventing the merging entities to start sharing or combining certain data. In the available precedents dating from the research period, only obligations to share data have been imposed and no prohibitions to merge data. However, theories have of harm pursuant to which the merging of data by the parties to a concentration could give rise to a substantial lessening of competition have been tested by (in particular) the Commission and the CMA. It is perfectly conceivable that in future cases, also remedies prohibiting the merger of data could be imposed or at least considered (with the observation that of course, it is eventually up to the case parties to propose remedies).

More precedents will undoubtedly follow in the coming years. The European Commission's (ongoing) investigation into Meta is among the most interesting cases to follow in this context. In addition, the German *Facebook* case is not over yet, with the

---

1627. *Het prioriteitenbeleid van de Belgische Mededingingsautoriteit voor 2021* (Belgische Mededingingsautoriteit/Autorité belge de la Concurrence 2021) and *Het prioriteitenbeleid van de Belgische Mededingingsautoriteit voor 2022* (Belgische Mededingingsautoriteit/ Autorité belge de la Concurrence 2022).

1628. BCA, Decision of 15 February 2019, ABC-2019-V/M-10 (IRM), section VI, para. 51.

European Court of Justice's preliminary ruling underway and most likely two further instances of national litigation underway.

The entry into force of the DSA and DMA may be expected to give rise to (even) more attention for data as a source of market power. The DSA obliges very large platforms to share essential data with authorities and researchers so that the latter can track how online risks (may) develop. Under the DMA, gatekeepers designated as such are under an obligation to offer business users insight into the data they generate on their platforms. This could reduce the market power yielded by the data in question since rival firms in dual distribution models (such as Amazon's business users who compete with Amazon at the retail level) will have access to the same data as the gatekeeper – thus reducing or even eliminating the advantage the gatekeeper can achieve from the data in question.

In conclusion, a certain pattern appears to reveal itself, pursuant to which the authorities under review consider data as an instrument to create and abuse dominance in certain markets – and the authorities do not seem to shy away from investigating this possibility in both abuse of dominance and merger control investigations. It seems a reasonable expectation that (for the time being) the authorities will continue to follow a casuistic approach and there will thus remain considerable differences between the different authorities' policies and even from one case dealt with by the same authority to another. After all, data itself comes in very different manifestations in terms of form and content – and therefore also in terms of economic value – as former CMA chairman Chisholm also acknowledged.[1629] Nevertheless, the competition authorities (if possible working together within the European Competition Network (ECN), under the leadership of the Commission) should be encouraged to attempt to develop guidance for identifying circumstances in which (large amounts of) data may place the owner thereof in a dominant position and what types of conduct may constitute an abuse of such a data-driven dominant position. Input here can come from the ongoing and accrued experience (both positive and negative) in abuse and merger cases.

1629. Chisholm, 'Speech at the UEA Centre for Competition Policy Annual Conference in Norwich: Alex Chisholm Speaks about Data and Trust in Digital Markets', *supra* n. 1615.

§10.08 NON-COMPLIANCE

It appears to become a cautious trend that some very large (tech) companies appear to prefer paying a fine imposed by a competition authority rather than changing their behaviour in the way that authority orders them to. For example, after the acquisition of WhatsApp by Facebook, Facebook had provided the Commission with misleading information on the technical possibilities of combining data and was fined for that infringement.[1630] Reference is made to the chapter on the Commission. An even clearer concern is Apple, which decided to pay the full amount of EUR 50 million of conditional penalty payments for abuse of dominance to the ACM, for not effectively changing its App Store terms and conditions for the providers of the dating apps.[1631] In that respect, the ACM has further specified that Apple must pay EUR 5 million each week until it either adjusts its terms and conditions or pays the entire EUR 50 million fine.[1632] Eventually, however, Apple did amend its terms and conditions in a way that the ACM considered satisfactory.[1633] Reference is made to the chapter on the ACM. In the French Google Neighbouring Rights, Google was fined by the Autorité for not complying with the interim measures that the French competition authority had imposed.[1634] Reference is made to the chapter on the Autorité. Outside the tech world, the acquisition of GRAIL by Illumina (relating to the pharmaceutical market) is another case in point. In that case, Illumina decided to close the transaction before the Commission's approval, thus choosing to risk a fine (which the Commission indeed imposed) for infringement of the standstill obligation.[1635] Illumina denied that a standstill obligation existed since the EU notification thresholds were not exceeded and the case had come under the Commission's (alleged) jurisdiction through a referral under Article 22 EU Merger Regulation (EUMR).[1636] After all, on 6 September 2022, the Commission prohibited the merger as

1630. European Commission, decision of 17 May 2017 in case M.8228, *Facebook/WhatsApp* (fining decision), *see also, e.g.*: Jennifer Rankin, 'Facebook fined £94m for 'misleading' EU over WhatsApp takeover' (*The Guardian*, 18 May 2017) https://www.theguardian.com/business/2017/may/18/facebook-fined-eu-whatsapp-european-commission.
1631. ACM, Press release 14 February 2022, 'Developing a new app is an unnecessary and unreasonable condition that Apple imposes on dating-app providers'.
1632. ACM, 'Apple fails to satisfy requirements set by ACM' (*ACM*, 24 January 2022) https://www.acm.nl/en/publications/apple-fails-satisfy-requirements-set-acm.
1633. ACM, 'ACM: Apple changes unfair conditions, allows alternative payments methods in dating apps' (*ACM*, 11 June 2022) https://www.acm.nl/en/publications/acm-apple-changes-unfair-conditions-allows-alternative-payments-methods-dating-apps.
1634. Autorité de la concurrence, 'Rémunération des droits voisins: l'Autorité sanctionne Google à hauteur de 500 millions d'euros pour le non-respect de plusieurs injonctions' (*Autorité de la concurrence*, 13 July 2021) https://www.autoritedelaconcurrence.fr/fr/article/remuneration-des-droits-voisins-lautorite-sanctionne-google-hauteur-de-500-millions-deuros; David Tayar and Jalil El Khanchoufi, 'The Neighbouring Rights Saga (France): Google Fined €500 million for Breaching Interim Order to Negotiate in Good Faith With News Agencies and Publishers' (2021) 13(5) *Journal of European Competition Law & Practice* 2-3.
1635. Elise Reuter, 'Illumina Vows to Fight EU Efforts to Block $8B GRAIL Merger' (*MedTechDive* 1 August 2022) https://www.medtechdive.com/news/illumina-vows-to-fight-eu-efforts-to-block-8b-grail-merger/628590/.
1636. European Commission, 'Press Release: Mergers: Commission adopts interim measures to prevent harm to competition following Illumina's early acquisition of GRAIL' (2021) IP/21/5661 Press Corner p. 1.

it found it restrictive to innovation and detrimental to consumer choice on the new market for blood-based early cancer detection tests.[1637] It also found the remedies proposed by Illumina insufficient.[1638]

These examples raise the question of whether the fines as currently imposed are sufficiently deterrent. The maximum fines that can be imposed would certainly appear to be. At the EU level, fines imposed on the basis of Council Regulation 1/2003 can reach up to 10% of the annual turnover of a company.[1639] National fines can be even higher. In the Netherlands, for example, the ACM can impose fines up to 80% of the undertaking's annual turnover (in cases of recidivism where the infringement lasted four years or more). It can be argued that these fines should certainly be high enough to demotivate an undertaking to break competition law. Actual fines that are imposed, however, tend to be much lower than these maximum amounts. It could be debated whether the actual fines imposed on big tech companies are always sufficiently high to deter them from breaking the rules. Some have argued whether there is a justifiable concern as to the effectiveness of the present regime on fines and whether it is time to revisit the guidelines on fines calculation.[1640]

If too many large (tech) companies would choose the path of 'paying off' their anticompetitive behaviour, this could undermine the effectiveness of competition law enforcement. However, the magnitude of a fine is just one of the elements that an undertaking will take into account when deciding whether to comply with an order or a threat to impose a fine from a competition authority. A second important factor is an order's or threat's perceived legitimacy, specifically taking into account the fact that tech markets are changing, which allows us to explore the borders of what can theoretically be allowed. If an undertaking believes that a competition authority errs in law, it may be inclined not to comply with what that authority tells it to do. In such a situation, the undertaking in question may also expect to overturn any wrongfully imposed fines in court – which would imply not having to pay such fines eventually or at least being reimbursed. Third, an undertaking may in practice be expected to always balance the damage incurred by complying with a competition authority's wishes (e.g., because it may need to make undesired changes to its business model which may also have consequences in other jurisdictions than the one in which the fine was or shall be imposed) against the damage incurred because of the fine itself. The latter can be the reputational damage an undertaking suffers after the fine has been made public, such as a decrease in its stock prices.[1641] Many customers can also choose to switch to the

1637. European Commission, 'Press Release: Mergers: Commission prohibits acquisition of GRAIL by Illumina' (2022) European Commission pp. 1-2.
1638. *Ibid.*, 2.
1639. European Commission, 'Fines for breaking EU Competition Law' (2011) European Commission p. 1; Council Regulation 1/2003 of 16 December 2002 on the implementation of the rules on competition laid down in Articles 81 and 82 of the Treaty OJ L 1 [2003] art 23(2c).
1640. *See, e.g.*: Éric Barbier de La Serre and Eileen Lagathu, 'The Law on Fines Imposed in EU Competition Proceedings: Still Time for a Refresh of the Guidelines' (2020) 11(9) *Journal of European Competition Law & Practice* 540.
1641. Stijn van den Broek et al., 'The Reputational Penalties to Firms in Antitrust Investigations' (2012) 8(2) *Journal of Competition Law & Economics* 231-258.

undertaking's competitors.[1642] Moreover, a company in question can face civil claims for damages from its customers.[1643] If the anticompetitive behaviour continues, an undertaking does not only risk facing periodic penalty payments but, in some instances, a company director can be disqualified from acting as such for a significant period of time (e.g., up to fifteen years in the UK).[1644] Of course, this third factor does imply that in the case that there is no doubt of a certain conduct's illegality (e.g., in the case of classic hardcore infringements), the amount of any fine (or penalty payment) should always be such as to render the outcome of this balancing act in favour of compliance. However, in cases where a competition authority's standpoint is more controversial, it may very well be justified for that authority to take this into account when calculating the fine or the penalty payment. This is especially true for tech-related cases, where important explanations for the company's behaviour justify it. Nonetheless, that should of course not lead to a scenario in which the deterrent effect of fines for (alleged) competition law infringements on the biggest market players would become insufficient. Therefore, authorities as well will need to perform a careful balancing act when setting fines.

To conclude, it will remain to be seen whether the cautious trend that large (tech) companies may choose to pay rather than comply will continue in the years to come. Should this be the case, then this may in turn incite competition authorities to impose higher fines and penalty payments. At the same time, competition authorities should always be aware of the novelty of some of the cases they deal with in rapidly changing markets such as tech markets. That novelty may also be a reason for cautiousness when setting the amount of fine or penalty payment.

1642. Georgina Laverack, '5 Consequences of Breaking Competition Law' (*GOV.UK Blog*, 2 March 2020) https://competitionandmarkets.blog.gov.uk/2020/03/02/5-consequences-of-breaking-competition-law/.

1643. Torben Toft, 'Consequences of Non-compliance: The EU Experience' (2011) 2 AML Competition Week: Competition Law and Policy & the Business Community 15.

1644. Laverack, *supra* n. 1642; Okeoghene Odudu, Periodic Penalty Payment, Global Dictionary of Competition Law (*Concurrences* 2022), https://www.concurrences.com/en/dictionary/periodic-penalty-payment#part-jurisprudence.

§10.09 COOPERATION BETWEEN AUTHORITIES

[A] Introduction

Digital markets are often larger than national or at least have an international dimension. Reference is made in this respect to Chapter 3 above on the definition of markets involving multisided platforms. This implies that in cases involving the digital sector, there will often be a need for authorities to cooperate across borders. It is therefore appropriate to provide an overview of the various forms of formal and informal cooperation in which the authorities under review engage among each other and with other competition authorities.

Competition authorities around the globe cooperate with each other in order to both increase efficiency of antitrust and merger control investigations and to learn from each other's experiences.[1645] The manner in which national competition authorities and the European Commission cooperate is regulated at national, European, and international levels and can take place on either a binding or a voluntary basis. This subchapter describes the various forms of cross-border cooperation between competition authorities of the EU Member States, the UK and the European Commission ('Commission') when it comes to enforcement in digital markets. Furthermore, it will discuss the relevant legal frameworks that regulate the international cooperation between competition authorities and summarise the already existing cooperation initiatives between competition authorities, focusing primarily on the six authorities under review.

First, the cooperation of competition authorities within the EU shall be described. The next section of this subchapter deals with EU-UK relations. A subsequent section discusses international relationships. This subchapter ends with a few concluding remarks and an outlook for the future.

[B] Cooperation Within the EU

Cooperation between competition authorities in the EU is primarily regulated by Council Regulation (EC) No. 1/2003.[1646] Accordingly, this Regulation specifies that competition law instruments must be applied by both the Commission and the Member States in close cooperation and sets a clear framework as to what information can or must be shared between the Commission and the national competition authorities of the Member States.[1647] This rule especially covers the exchange of evidence-related information between the parties, including confidential documents.[1648] Moreover, a

1645. OECD, 'Challenges of International Co-operation in Competition Law Enforcement' (2014) OECD p. 21.
1646. Council Regulation (EC) No. 1/2003 of 16 December 2002 on the implementation of the rules on competition laid down in Articles 81 and 82 of the Treaty OJ L 1 [2003] (Regulation 1/2003), Chapter IV.
1647. *Ibid.*, Article 11(1).
1648. *Ibid.*, Article 11(2), Article 12(1), and Article 12(2).

national competition authority should inform the Commission and, if deemed necessary, other national competition authorities, about the start of a formal investigation and its final decision on the case in question.[1649] If needed, a competition authority can consult with the Commission on any matters related to EU competition law.[1650] On the other hand, in case the Commission has started a formal investigation, national competition authorities should, in principle, refrain from initiating a parallel investigation.[1651] For instance, the Apple App Store dating apps investigation by the ACM is conducted in close coordination with a similar investigation conducted by the European Commission. This arrangement was possible due to the fact that the Dutch competition authority looks into the conditions imposed by Apple on the app providers that are not in direct competition with Apple apps.[1652] By contrast, the Commission is analysing whether Apple App Store terms and conditions are creating barriers to entry for the app providers that do compete with the apps provided by Apple itself.[1653] In that respect, it should be noted that Apple has eventually (after forfeiting penalty payments for non-compliance up to the maximum of EUR 50 million) changed its terms and conditions regarding payments involving dating apps. In the end, however, the ACM was satisfied with the outcome (reference is made to the chapter on the ACM for an elaborate description of the case).[1654]

When it comes to digital matters in particular, the European Competition Network (ECN) launched an important initiative in its joint statement regarding how national competition authorities can strengthen the Digital Market Act (DMA).[1655] The ECN has stated that there is a need for close cooperation between national competition authorities to ensure the *effet utile* of the DMA implementation and enforcement.[1656] Accordingly, the statement advocates that the DMA is applied by the Commission's Directorate-General for Competition, together with its complementary enforcement by and support from the national competition authorities.[1657] It also underlines that

1649. *Ibid.*, Article 11(3) and Article 11(4).
1650. *Ibid.*, Article 11(5).
1651. *Ibid.*, Article 11(6); for more information on this topic, *see*: Pieter Van Cleynenbreugel, 'Sharing Powers Within Exclusive Competences: Rethinking EU Antitrust Law Enforcement' (2016) 12 CYELP 49.
1652. ACM, 'ACM can continue its investigation into the Apple App Store'(*ACM*, 22 June 2021) https://www.acm.nl/en/publications/acm-can-continue-its-investigation-apple-app-store; ACM, 'Apple has adjusted its policy for dating apps; ACM, 'ACM obliges Apple to adjust unreasonable conditions for its App Store' (*ACM*, 24 December 2021) https://www.acm.nl/en/publications/acm-obliges-apple-adjust-unreasonable-conditions-its-app-store; ACM, 'ACM to assess these adjustments' (ACM, 17 January 2022) https://www.acm.nl/en/publications/apple-has-adjusted-its-policy-dating-apps-acm-assess-these-adjustments.
1653. European Commission, 'Press Release – Antitrust: Commission opens investigations into Apple's App Store rules' (2020) European Commission 1.
1654. ACM, 'ACM: Apple changes unfair conditions, allows alternative payments methods in dating apps' (ACM, 11 June 2022) https://www.acm.nl/en/publications/acm-apple-changes-unfair-conditions-allows-alternative-payments-methods-dating-apps.
1655. European Competition Network, 'Joint paper of the heads of the national competition authorities of the European Union: How national competition agencies can strengthen the DMA' (2021) ECN 2.
1656. *Ibid.*, pp. 3, 5.
1657. *Ibid.*, p. 12.

competition law as a whole is crucial when it comes to maintaining a smooth functioning of dynamic and fast-moving digital markets and thus should also align with technological development.[1658] In that respect, there is a necessity for antitrust watchdogs to be able to conduct quick and efficient interventions and cross-border cooperation undoubtedly helps to achieve this goal.[1659] The ECN report adds that the DMA and the competition law *acquis* are deeply intertwined as the latter is one of the main legal instruments that can effectively, and sometimes *ex ante*, scrutinise the activities of Big Tech.[1660] It is, however, unclear whether this approach would be effective in practice. As a result, the statement strongly advocates close cooperation and consistency between the DMA and competition law enforcement on both European and national levels.[1661] This approach, however, must take account of the rules on competences of the Commission and national competition authorities.[1662] Specifically, the joint statement of the national competition authorities recommends allowing national competition agencies to use the DMA as a basis to initiate proceedings against the gatekeepers and, where necessary, to assist the Commission with its own investigations.[1663] One can expect that this statement expressed a concrete approach to how they envisage their involvement in DMA enforcement.[1664] However, no concrete steps were taken in that regard yet and it remains unclear how the Statement's signatories will address the DMA enforcement. It should also be noted that a similar statement was also issued by France, Germany, and The Netherlands, where a separate place was given to cooperative enforcement of rules on merger control.[1665] Nevertheless, it is arguable that this claim is not in line with the enforcement mechanism of the DMA and that the national competition authorities are trying to get a place in a system that did not foresee their involvement. Indeed, the only authority with the power to enforce the DMA as such is the Commission.[1666] Reference is made to the relevant national chapters.[1667]

All of the above reflects the fact that the EU is generally in favour of cooperation between national competition authorities, specifically when it comes to digital matters.

1658. *Ibid.*, p. 2.
1659. *Ibid.*, p. 3.
1660. *Ibid.*, p. 5.
1661. *Ibid.*, pp. 6, 8.
1662. *Ibid.*, p. 9.
1663. *Ibid.*
1664. Autoridade da Concorrencia, 'The European Competition Network publishes a joint paper addressing the issue of the involvement of national competition authorities in the Digital Markets Act' (*AdC*, 1 July 2021) https://www.concorrencia.pt/index.php/en/articles/european-competition-network-publishes-joint-paper-addressing-issue-involvement-national.
1665. France, Germany, and the Netherlands, 'Strengthening the Digital Markets Act and Its Enforcement' (2021) BMWI Point 7; EU Law Live, 'Germany, France and The Netherlands call for the strengthening of the Digital Markets Act and its enforcement' (*EU Law Live*, 27 Mau 2021) https://eulawlive.com/germany-france-and-the-netherlands-call-for-the-strengthening-of-the-digital-markets-act-and-its-enforcement/#.
1666. Foo Yun Chee, 'EU Commission to be sole enforcer of tech rules, EU countries agree' (*Reuters*, 8 November 2021) https://www.reuters.com/technology/eu-commission-be-sole-enforcer-tech-rules-eu-countries-agree-2021-11-08/.
1667. *See* Chapter 4 on the European Union.

It recognises the fact that due to the cross-border nature of the tech markets, it can be of the utmost importance for the competition agencies to be able to exchange their experience with each other and thus better safeguard the smooth functioning of the internal market.

[C] EU-UK Cooperation

As was discussed in the UK Chapter, the post-Brexit relations on competition law between the EU and the UK are primarily governed by the Trade and Cooperation Agreement (TCA).[1668] This treaty seeks to safeguard the cooperation between the Competition and Markets Authority (CMA), the Commission, and the national competition authorities of EU Member States.[1669] The cooperation primarily involves an exchange of information between the parties and occurs on a voluntary basis.[1670] Moreover, the TCA gives the CMA, the Commission, and the EU Member States' national competition authorities the right to initiate parallel investigations and to conclude separate coordination and cooperation agreements between each other.[1671] A clear example of such a parallel investigation is the Facebook Marketplace parallel investigation by the Commission and the CMA (*see* the chapters on the Commission and the CMA, respectively).[1672]

The CMA sees a necessity for increased cooperation between competition authorities in order to successfully tackle anticompetitive practices of tech companies. Hence, it has placed this goal high on its agenda. This is clearly reflected by the fact that international cooperation is one of the key priorities of the CMA's new Digital Market Strategy.[1673] Accordingly, the UK competition authority is keen to cooperate with other antitrust watchdogs worldwide, including those in the EU, when it comes to regulating digital markets.[1674] It further stated that as the activities of tech businesses are often cross-border, all competition authorities are confronted with similar regulatory challenges.[1675] Close cooperation would therefore facilitate the manner in which the CMA and other competition authorities solve these complex cases by allowing them to exchange their experiences.[1676]

1668. Trade and Cooperation Agreement between the European Union and the European Atomic Energy Community, of the one part, and the United Kingdom of Great Britain and Northern Ireland, of the other part [2021] OJ L 149 (Trade and Cooperation Agreement) Article 361.
1669. *Ibid.*, Article 361(1) and Article 361(2).
1670. *Ibid.*, Article 361(3).
1671. *Ibid.*, Article 361(4); Emily Craig, 'CMA Warns of Parallel Investigations after Brexit Transition Period' (*GCR*, 2 December 2020) https://globalcompetitionreview.com/brexit/cma-warns-of-parallel-investigations-after-brexit-transition-period.
1672. Jon Porter, 'EU and UK Open Antitrust Investigations into Facebook Marketplace' (*The Verge*, 4 June 2021) https://www.theverge.com/2021/6/4/22456313/facebook-marketplace-european-commission-formal-antitrust-investigation-eu-uk.
1673. CMA, 'The CMA's Digital Markets Strategy' (2021) CMA p. 13.
1674. *Ibid.*
1675. *Ibid.*
1676. *Ibid.*; CMA, 'Policy Paper: Competition and Markets Authority's digital markets strategy' (*GOV.UK*, 9 February 2021) https://www.gov.uk/government/publications/competition-and-markets-authoritys-digital-markets-strategy.

It follows from the above that the CMA takes a similar approach to the Commission when it comes to cooperation between competition authorities, advocating cooperation and the exchange of information. Nevertheless, the level of cooperation provided for by the TCA does not as far as within the EU and is primarily based on voluntary commitments. The CMA thus remains at complete liberty in its own approach towards the manner in which it deals with tech-related cases and is free to decide the type of information and approaches it is going to share or incorporate into its own practice.

[D] International Level

Finally, it should also be noted that cooperation between competition authorities with regard to enforcement (policy) in digital markets is also discussed at the level of international organisations. Specifically, during the G7 Summit of 2021, fourteen antitrust authorities, including the CMA, the Commission, the Bundeskartellamt, and the Autorité, have contributed to a joint report on how competition in digital markets can be improved.[1677] The report emphasises the pivotal importance of cross-border cooperation between the competition authorities to successfully safeguard competition in digital markets.[1678] It also outlines that the challenges different antitrust authorities face are similar due to the borderless character of the activities of tech firms.[1679] Well-organised international cooperation would additionally allow the authorities to learn from each other's practices and improve the way they tackle anticompetitive cases of tech companies domestically.[1680] The cooperation in question implies the exchange of information regarding digital cases and practices, together with the possible production of joint outputs (such as research reports) by the authorities.[1681] Finally, the report highlights the continuous cooperation between competition authorities through already established competition networks on the international level.[1682] A good illustration of such international cooperation is the Multilateral Mutual Assistance and Cooperation Framework between the British CMA and the Australian Competition and Consumer Commission, the Competition Bureau of Canada, the New Zealand Commerce Commission, the US Department of Justice, and the Federal Trade Commission of the United States of America.[1683] This latter Framework is based on the

1677. CMA, the Commission, the Bundeskartellamt, and the Autorité de la Concurrence, 'Compendium of approaches to improving competition in digital markets' (2021) G7 9, Compendium of approaches to improving competition in digital markets - GOV.UK (www.gov.uk).
1678. *Ibid.*, p. 31.
1679. *Ibid.*, p. 35.
1680. *Ibid.*
1681. *Ibid.*, pp. 35-36.
1682. *Ibid.*, p. 36.
1683. CMA, 'Corporate report Multilateral Mutual Assistance and Cooperation Framework between the CMA, ACCC, CBC, NZCC, USDOJ and USFTC' (*GOV.UK*, 2 September 2020) https://www.gov.uk/government/publications/multilateral-mutual-assistance-and-cooperation-framework-between-the-cma-accc-cbc-nzcc-usdoj-and-usftc.

memorandum of understanding and model agreement between the authorities involved.[1684]

Other international organisations, such as the International Competition Network (ICN) and the OECD, have also emphasised the need for close cooperation between competition authorities worldwide.[1685] Indeed, to ensure that competition authorities around the world are able to adjust their practices and policies to the rapidly evolving markets, they have to cooperate and exchange their knowledge and experiences with each other.[1686] Moreover, the ICN has planned to start a so-called Third Decade organisational review to successfully prepare its institution for the upcoming technological challenges coming from international tech giants.[1687] This review will be performed by the ICN together with the US Federal Trade Commission.[1688] Accordingly, the ICN seeks to conduct a network-wide top-to-bottom assessment of its procedures to see whether it can effectively tackle new developments on the markets.[1689] It is expected to cover the ICN's working methods and to present substantive recommendations to adapt them to the new realities faced by competition authorities.[1690] Undoubtedly, this initiative will also have a considerable impact on how the ICN members cooperate with each other on cross-border digital cases.

The need for enhanced collaboration between competition authorities in the digital age was also emphasised during the International Federation of European Law (FIDE) Congress 2021 in the Hague.[1691] Coordination may either take the form of codified bilateral and multilateral mechanisms, or informal memoranda between the authorities in question.[1692] The report has further concluded that digitalisation had a dual impact on competition, by creating new market participants as well as completely new markets.[1693] This has led various countries' competition authorities to change their enforcement policy and/or their governments to adopt new rules and legislation.[1694] This search for new enforcement priorities and new legislation has further increased the level of cooperation between competition authorities.

1684. Multilateral Mutual Assistance and Cooperation Framework for Competition Authorities: Memorandum of Understanding.
1685. For more details, *see*: OECD, 'OECD Handbook on Competition Policy in the Digital Age' (2022) OECD p. 57; Federal Trade Commission, 'International Competition Network Addresses Enforcement and Policy Challenges of the Digital Economy at United States-Hosted 19th Annual Conference' (*FTC*, 17 September 2020) https://www.ftc.gov/news-events/news/press-releases/2020/09/international-competition-network-addresses-enforcement-policy-challenges-digital-economy-united.
1686. OECD, *supra* n. 1685, p. 57.
1687. Federal Trade Commission, *supra* n. 1685.
1688. *Ibid.*
1689. ICN, '2020 Virtual Annual Conference' (ICN, 2020) https://www.internationalcompetitionnetwork.org/2020vac/.
1690. *Ibid.*
1691. D. Mândrescu (ed.) 'EU Competition Law and the Digital Economy: Protecting Free and Fair Competition in an Age of Technological (R)evolution' (2021) 3 The XXIX FIDE Congress 51, FIDE_OA_vol_3.pdf (fide2020.eu).
1692. *Ibid.*
1693. *Ibid.*, 1.
1694. *Ibid.*, 2.

Finally, the Stanford Computational Antitrust project deserves mentioning in the context.[1695] This initiative was started by Dr Thibault Schrépel at CodeX, The Stanford Centre for Legal Informatics which established a network of sixty-five antitrust agencies around the world.[1696] Notably, the Dutch ACM, the British CMA, and the French Autorité are members of the project.[1697] Accordingly, the project discusses the opportunities various computational tools can bring to the competition authorities to tackle trends in newly emerging and dynamic markets. The competition authorities are therefore sharing their experience regarding the topic in order to learn from each other's practices and how automation of the antitrust legal reasoning helps to tackle new complex markets. This project is also briefly discussed in the respective chapter by Teodora Groza in the Game Changers section of the book.

[E] Conclusion

In conclusion, cooperation between competition authorities is regulated quite extensively at the EU level and actual cooperation in digital cases (both between the Commission and national authorities as well as between national authorities among themselves) can also be observed within the EU. The coordination of the Commission's and the ACM's investigations into the Apple App Store forms a good example. At the international level, most cooperation between authorities takes place on a purely voluntary basis. When it comes to dealing with digital cases, international cooperation is also still in its early stages of development and is most advanced when it comes to EU-UK relationships. In view of the fact that the UK was until recently part of the EU, this comes as no surprise. All other international cooperation initiatives discussed above are not (yet) based on a strong cooperation framework and can be seen more as forums for discussion and a search for best practices rather than actual fully operational mechanisms designed to tackle cross-border competition law issues and infringements. However, there is a clear trend towards enhanced collaboration, which is reflected by the increased amount of recommendations from such organisations as the OECD pushing for closer and more far-reaching cooperation approaches.

With the ever-continuing growth of the digital sector and the related increase of competition cases relating in whole or in part to digital markets, the need for international cooperation between competition authorities may also be expected to continue to grow. It is therefore likely that international cooperation initiatives shall also continue to develop and gradually become less obligation-free. A further question is whether cooperation will – or should – remain limited to only competition authorities. Competition cases in the digital sector often also have privacy and consumer law-related angles. For instance, such collaboration is already happening in the

1695. Thibault Schrépel, 'Computational Antitrust: An Introduction and Research Agenda' (2021) 1 Stanford Computational Antitrust 4.
1696. Computational Antitrust, 'Agencies' (*CodeX: The Stanford Center for Legal Informatics*, 2022) https://law.stanford.edu/codex-the-stanford-center-for-legal-informatics/computational-antitrust-agencies/.
1697. *Ibid.*

Netherlands between the ACM and the Autoriteit Persoonsgegevens (the national privacy authority entrusted with the enforcement of the GDPR in the Netherlands) with the aim of achieving a more comprehensive approach regarding the regulation of tech markets.[1698] Similarly, the British CMA has taken its first steps towards closer cooperation with the Information Commissioner's Office (British privacy and data protection authority), when it comes to investigations of digital markets.[1699] The German Facebook user data case constitutes a very good example of a case where in particular competition law and privacy law – but also less prominently consumer law – interact. In cases like this – which are highly likely to pop up more and more frequently as tech giants continue to increase their influence on all walks of life – international coordination of all three of these legal disciplines may well become a necessity for effective and harmonised enforcement.

Currently, such coordination does not exist at all at the international level and moreover is equally lacking at the EU and national levels.[1700] Indeed, when it comes to the EU, the enforcement of both the cartel prohibition and the prohibition of abuse of dominance is divided between the Commission and national authorities. The EU Merger Regulation (EUMR) is enforced primarily by the Commission, as will also be the case with the DMA.[1701] By contrast, the enforcement of the GDPR, the various directives on consumer law, and in the future the Digital Services Act (DSA) lies exclusively with national authorities.[1702] At the national level, only the CMA and the ACM are entrusted with the enforcement of both competition and consumer law. The other authorities under review enforce only competition law and none of the authorities under review has been entrusted with the power to enforce the GDPR. To this, it must be added that in the Facebook user data case, the Bundeskartellamt in fact applied the GDPR, an action on the legality of which the ECJ must now – together with various other points of law – pass judgment in the pending preliminary ruling procedure.

With coordinated enforcement of competition, privacy and consumer law lacking even within every single jurisdiction under review, European and international interdisciplinary enforcement of these three fields of law seems a very distant perspective. Perhaps, bundling enforcement of competition, privacy and consumer law in the hands of one authority at the national level would be a useful first step towards a genuinely coordinated enforcement policy. Such a step was advocated by Marc Wiggers, one of the authors of this book, during the *iTech* conference that took place in Lisbon on 10 November 2021. Once harmonised enforcement at the national level has been accomplished, coordination across borders may very well evolve organically.

1698. ACM, 'National Cooperation' (*ACM*, 2022) https://www.acm.nl/en/about-acm/collaboration/national-cooperation.
1699. CMA, 'Press Release: ICO and CMA set out blueprint for cooperation in digital markets' (*GOV.UK*, 19 May 2021) https://www.gov.uk/government/news/ico-and-cma-set-out-blueprint-for-cooperation-in-digital-markets.
1700. K. Cseres, 'Comparing Laws in the Enforcement of EU and National Competition Laws' (2010) 3(1) European Journal of Legal Studies 8-13.
1701. European Commission, 'Sneak peek: how the Commission will enforce the DSA & DMA – Blog of Commissioner Thierry Breton' (*European Commission*, 5 July 2022) https://ec.europa.eu/commission/presscorner/detail/en/STATEMENT_22_4327.
1702. *Ibid.*

CHAPTER 11
Game Changers

§11.01 INTRODUCTION

Our research as authors into the decision practice of six competition authorities in Europe is retrospective by nature. It covers the past and the present, although the future is reflected in our recommendations (*see* §12.03). In this penultimate chapter of our book, we look towards the future and the potentially big changes that lay ahead. Which developments that we can currently observe may be expected to shape the competitive landscape of tomorrow?

This chapter takes a peek at five major developments that are bound to change the competitive landscape, described by external authors who are each thought leaders in their respective fields of law. As main authors, we are confident that their contributions will add depth to this book and will increase its relevance.

Thibault Schrépel kicks off with a contribution on the impact of blockchain on antitrust. His contribution explains how blockchain introduces new competition issues, but may also bring solutions for better monitoring of compliance. On the one hand, it can facilitate collusion. On the other hand, undertakings can infringe competition law within the blockchain by manipulating its validation system for anticompetitive gain.

The second contribution is written by Giuseppe Colangelo and focuses on self-preferencing by (near-) monopolists. Giuseppe explains how monopolists and 'moligopolists' can give preferential treatment to their own products and services, thus entrenching their power in core markets and also extending it into associated markets. Acting as gatekeepers and regulators within their ecosystems, these platforms can constitute unavoidable trading partners and may therefore be in a position to pick winners and losers in the marketplace. How can competition law cope with this?

Up next is Ai Deng who discusses the impact of the development of machine learning on the competitive process. Ai explains how new technologies in the development of machine learning and artificial intelligence constitute a risk to facilitate or even provoke competition law infringements, whilst at the same they also help to ensure compliance with the competition rules and policy.

Wolf Sauter of the Dutch competition authority (ACM) subsequently shines a light on green antitrust and digital competition. Do technological developments help us in reaching a greener world or do they make this more difficult? What role can competition law play in making digital technologies work for a greener world?

Fifth and finally, Teodora Groza gives us an insight into computational antitrust. She explores how algorithms can help competition authorities make their enforcement more effective.

We believe that in conjunction, these five excellent contributions constitute an appropriate ending to our journey through the landscape of digital competition law in Europe.

§11.02 AN INTRODUCTION TO BLOCKCHAIN ANTITRUST

Thibault Schrépel

[A] Overview

Blockchain is to transactions what the Internet is to information. To the extent that antitrust law regulates transactions between companies, it should come as no surprise that blockchain has important antitrust implications.[1703]

Blockchain raises new competition issues. On the one hand, blockchain can be used to infringe competition law in the 'real world'. For example, two companies can collude by means of automated transactions on the blockchain (also known as 'smart contracts'). Once recorded on-chain, smart contracts are immutable which creates trust between colluders that code will enforce the terms of their illegal agreement.[1704] On the other hand, companies can infringe competition law within the blockchain. For example, miners (intermediaries who validate blockchain transactions) can divide the market among themselves to take turns validating transactions. If they do so, validation fees will rise to a level high enough level to compensate for revenue sharing.

But blockchain is also pro-competitive. When a blockchain is 'public' and 'permissionless', access to and use of the blockchain is free. All participants govern the blockchain horizontally. Such a mode of governance makes it difficult to implement anticompetitive practices that violate Article 102 TFEU, as no single blockchain participant can implement an abuse on its own. The technical architecture of these blockchains frees economic transactions from a potential coercive power. For example, blockchain developers are guaranteed that no single user at the Ethereum (a popular blockchain) layer 1 can decide to exclude their application or impose unfair terms and conditions for access to the blockchain. In short, applications running on top of a public permissionless blockchain (e.g., decentralised metaverse) escape most leveraging practices. So much for the legal solutionists.[1705]

[B] Cases

The following section provides the first comprehensive overview of the most important blockchain cases to date:

1703. For an in-depth analysis, *see* Thibault Schrépel, *Blockchain + Antitrust: The Decentralization Formula* (Edward Elgar, 2021).
1704. *See* Thibault Schrépel, *Collusion by Blockchain and Smart Contracts* (2019) 33 Harvard Journal of Law & Technology 117, 124.
1705. Thibault Schrépel, *Law + Technology*, Journal of Law and Technology at Texas (2023) (describing legal solutionism as 'the recasting of all complex social situations in neatly defined problems legal rules can solve').

Direct Effects / *Implementation*	*Anticompetitive Practice Producing Direct Effects Inside Blockchain*	*Anticompetitive Practice Producing Direct Effects Inside the 'Real Space'*
Anticompetitive Practice implemented *Inside of a Blockchain*	*United American v. Bitmain* (2021); *Leibowitz v. iFinex* (pending)	Still waiting (e.g., smart contracts automating collusion)
Anticompetitive Practice implemented *Outside of Blockchain*	Still waiting (e.g., a tech company cutting access to its cloud solution used by blockchain nodes)	*Gallagher v. Bitcointalk.org* (2019); National Association of Cryptocurrencies and Blockchain (2022); *BSV v. cryptocurrency exchanges* (pending)

'Blockchain antitrust' includes everything blockchain and antitrust related, regardless of whether the practices are implemented inside or outside the chain, and regardless of where their most direct effects materialise.[1706] The field is growing slowly, and while new cases are emerging, they remain limited to half of what blockchain antitrust could be. That said, recent litigation is targeting increasingly important groups and features of blockchain ecosystems.

The first blockchain antitrust case, *Gallagher v. Bitcointalk.org* (2019), involved a practice implemented outside the chain whose direct effects manifested in the so-called 'real space'.[1707] A developer sought compensation after being banned from a popular forum run by the Bitcoin Foundation. He railed against a strategy implemented to allegedly prevent him from accessing other developers and introducing a competing blockchain. The case, brought under section 2 of the Sherman Act, was ultimately dismissed because, according to the court, 'it [was] highly unlikely that, given the opportunity, he [Gallagher] could allege cogent and viable legal claims'.[1708]

In *United American v. Bitmain (2021)*, a group of Bitcoin Cash ABC users sought relief under section 1 of the Sherman Act.[1709] The group complained that other users had 'forked' the blockchain, i.e., duplicated the blockchain and assigned different operating rules to the new version. The group alleged that the forking diminished the value of the original chain and because it resulted from concerted behaviour, infringed Sherman Act section 1. The suit also targeted Bitmain Technologies, which redirected its mining power to the forked chain. The court ultimately dismissed the case for lack of evidence showing coordination with anticompetitive intent between the defendants.

In a case investigated in Brazil, the National Association of Cryptocurrencies and Blockchain (NACB) asked the Administrative Council for Economic Defense (CADE) to

1706. The definition derives from the mindset of complexity science: including practices implemented outside the chain and/or producing their direct effects outside the chain proves crucial to understand blockchain dynamics that are *not* simply defined by on-chain practices.
1707. *Gallagher v. Bitcointalk.org et al.*, 3:18-cv-05892-EMC (N.D. Cal. 2018).
1708. *Gallagher v. Bitcointalk.org et al.*, 3:19-cv-01151-N-BK (N.D. Cal. 2019).
1709. *United American Corp. v. Bitmain, Inc.*, 1:18-cv-25106-KMW (S.D. Fla. 2018).

investigate the refusal of several banks to provide banking services.[1710] The NACB argued the refusals were anticompetitive strategies aimed at reducing the competitive pressure created by decentralised finance. The case was initially closed in December 2018 by the CADE, but the agency's tribunal requested it be reopened. The agency finally closed the case in July 2022 in favour of the banks, which justified their practice on the grounds of security and customer protection.

In *Leibowitz v. iFinex* (pending), a class action lawsuit was filed in 2020 to challenge the practices of Tether, a blockchain, and Bitfinex, an exchange.[1711] Tether's creators are accused of infringing section 2 of the Sherman Act in the alleged stablecoin market (coins or tokens whose value is tied to an asset outside the blockchain). The plaintiffs allege that Tether released new tokens to falsely 'signal to the market that there was rapidly growing demand for cryptocurrencies' and inflate prices, while not backing those tokens with sufficient reserves. Bitfinex allegedly contributed to the scheme by allowing Tether's tokens to be exchanged for other cryptocurrencies, in violation of section 1 of the Sherman Act. The plaintiffs are seeking compensation amounting to three times the alleged harm, i.e., approximately USD 1.4 trillion.

In a new case brought before the Competition Appeal Tribunal in August 2022 against four exchanges (Binance, Bittylicious, Kraken and Shapeshift), the plaintiff (BSV Claims Ltd.) is seeking GBP 9.9 billion in compensation for the coordinated delisting of the Bitcoin Satoshi Vision cryptocurrency. According to BSV, these exchanges colluded to damage the cryptocurrency created by Craig Wright, who has publicly claimed to be Satoshi Nakamoto – a claim he has never been able to substantiate, thus creating distrust in his other endeavours.

[C] Lessons

Several lessons emerge from these early cases. First, there are no past or ongoing cases of anticompetitive practices implemented outside a blockchain but producing their effects inside the chain. Such practices could include, for example, a tech company restricting access to a cloud solution that is heavily used by blockchain nodes. Similarly, there is no mention of cases involving anticompetitive practices implemented inside a blockchain but producing direct effects inside the so-called real space. With tens of millions of smart contracts running on public chains, the field calls for agencies to use advanced computational tools to increase detection levels.

Smart contracts pose a new challenge to law enforcement, transforming collusion from a non-cooperative to a cooperative game. Collusive agreements that do not rely on immutable code are non-cooperative, i.e., one colluder cannot force other colluders to abide by the terms of their illegal agreements. Smart contracts are different because even though they may be legally void – e.g., if they automate an illegal cartel – they will

1710. CADE, National Association of Cryptocurrencies and Blockchain (2018).
1711. *Leibowitz et al. v. iFinex et al.*, 1:19-cv-09236-KPF (S.D.N.Y. 2019).

still execute when the conditions embedded in their code are met.[1712] In so doing, smart contracts make illegal agreements between companies more cooperative than before.[1713] The result is a stronger, fundamentally new type of collusion in which companies have greater confidence that other colluders will abide by their agreement.[1714] Deviations from collusive terms and leniency applications are expected to be less frequent for this very reason.

The trust that blockchain creates among users requires enforcement agencies to be more proactive in pursuing competition law infringements. One way of proceeding is to start from the so-called real space, where collusion often manifests itself (e.g., with high prices). Scanning blockchains and smart contracts in the hope of identifying illegal behaviours affecting the real space will prove more difficult, as the purpose behind blockchain transactions and smart contract code is not represented on-chain.[1715]

Second, technical knowledge is required to understand the ins and outs of antitrust cases in the ecosystem. Cases involving anticompetitive practices that are implemented and have direct effects within blockchains, such *as United American v. Bitmain* and *Leibowitz v. iFinex*, are particularly challenging from a technical standpoint. At a minimum, attorneys need to understand the basics of blockchain to be able to communicate with the technical experts assisting them in cases.

Third, current cases involve so-called layer 1 blockchain, i.e., decentralised, distributed, and encrypted databases. Antitrust litigation has – so far – had little to do with blockchain applications such as smart contracts or Web3. One can expect litigation to increase due to exciting technical developments and increasing competition in the metaverse's space. Public enforcement may focus on the application layer, which is easier to understand and has a significant impact on consumers.

Fourth, current cases provide a glimpse into the economic significance of blockchain-related antitrust claims. Tens of millions of blockchain transactions are ordered every day.[1716] Agencies should want blockchains to remain free of anticompetitive practices that would affect all transactions ordered at higher levels. Given the current inability to detect the majority of anticompetitive practices in the real space, agencies may want to encourage blockchain adoption as a complement to antitrust. Both blockchain and antitrust seek to eliminate market coercion, i.e., decentralisation. But blockchain can only contribute if antitrust agencies supplement code where it is ineffective against anticompetitive practices. It is a great mistake to be afraid of technology when it can also contribute to our legal systems.

1712. Thibault Schrépel, *Blockchain + Antitrust: The Decentralization Formula* 164 (Edward Elgar, 2021) (explores the role of oracles in executing smart contracts).
1713. *Ibid.*, 165 (discusses the cooperative nature of smart contract-based collusions).
1714. *Ibid.*, 138 (argues that smart contract-based collusions are more worrisome than algorithmic collusion that do not rely on blockchain, precisely because smart contract-based collusions are fundamentally new).
1715. *Ibid.*, 170 (discusses concrete screening strategies for agencies).
1716. For an overview of Ethereum transactions, *see* https://etherscan.io/.

§11.03 SELF-PREFERENCING

Giuseppe Colangelo

Self-preferencing is the symbol of the current competition policy *zeitgeist* in digital markets. By giving preferential treatment to their own products and services, large online companies are deemed to be entrenching their power in core markets and extending it into associated markets. Acting as gatekeepers and regulators within their ecosystems, these platforms represent unavoidable trading partners and may pick winners and losers in the marketplace. Furthermore, they often also perform a dual role, acting as both an intermediary and a trader operating on the platform, hence they may be tempted to influence results in their own favour.

As a result, to ensure a level playing field the legislative initiatives undertaken around the world to tame digital gatekeepers include provisions targeting different forms of self-preferencing. However, self-preferencing is also emerging in Europe as a theory of harm before courts and antitrust authorities.

The birth of self-preferencing is usually associated with the European Commission's investigation against Google for having positioned and displayed, in its general search results pages, its own comparison shopping service more favourably compared to rival comparison shopping services.[1717]

However, a similar issue was addressed a few months before by the High Court of England and Wales in the dispute between Streetmap and Google, which involved the interaction of competition between online search engines and online maps.[1718] It is worth noting that the UK Court held that the complaint should have been appropriately characterised as an allegation of discrimination. Further, in order to establish whether Google's conduct determined an anticompetitive foreclosure, the Court concluded that it was necessary to prove its effects, which cannot be simply assumed and should be appreciable in affecting competition. Following this line of reasoning, Mr Justice Roth found that the introduction of the Maps OneBox with no shortcut hyperlinks to Streetmap (and other online maps) did not in itself have an appreciable effect in taking custom away from Streetmap, therefore it was not reasonably likely to give rise to anticompetitive foreclosure. Moreover, even if it was likely to have such an effect, Google's conduct was objectively justified because the way in which it implemented the technical efficiency of presenting a thumbnail map on the Search Engine Results Page (SERP) was not disproportionate.

In *Google Shopping* the European Commission reached a different conclusion and, by promoting its own comparison shopping service in its search results and demoting those of competitors, in 2017 Google is held to have engaged in a strategy of leveraging the dominance of its flagship product (i.e., the search engine) in the adjacent market for comparison shopping services. According to the Commission's findings, Google's strategy is articulated in two interlinked practices aimed at ensuring prominent placement for its own comparison shopping service and demoting rival

1717. European Commission, 27 June 2017, Case AT.39740, *Google Search (shopping)*.
1718. *Streetmap.EU Ltd. v. Google and others*, [2016] EWHC 253 (ch).

comparison shopping services in its search results, respectively. The Commission concluded that the conduct fell outside the scope of competition on the merits and was capable of extending Google's dominant position in the national markets for general search services to the national markets for comparison shopping services (offensive leveraging), and of protecting Google's dominance in the former (defensive leveraging). Rather than illustrating the new theory of harm under the practice concerned, the Commission is interested in describing the latter as belonging to the well-known category of leveraging. Accordingly, there is no need to look for a new legal test, since self-preferencing constitutes a well-established, independent, form of abuse.

As a result, the case spurred the debate on the legal test applied to impose upon Google a principle of equal treatment to rival comparison shopping services and its own service, namely whether it fell more within exclusionary than discriminatory abuses and, in the first hypothesis, whether tying or the essential facility doctrine were the proper framework to assess such self-preferencing abuse.

Indeed, in May 2020, in a litigation between a real estate association (VBO Makelaars) and the association of real estate agents (Nederlandse Vereniging van Makelaars (NVM)), the Amsterdam Court of Appeal did not follow the European Commission approach.[1719] By founding that Funda did not abuse its dominant position favouring the listings of NVM members over those of rival agents, the Dutch court framed self-preferencing as a discriminatory abuse and argued that the complainant failed to demonstrate that the discrimination concerned distorted its competitive position leading to a competitive disadvantage on the downstream market for real estate services.

Conversely, in June 2021, the French Competition Authority (AdlC) instead followed the path of the European Commission investigating practices implemented by Google in the online advertising sector.[1720] Like the European Commission, the AdlC did not refer to self-preferencing, deciding instead to describe Google's conduct as favouring. Furthermore, regarding the leveraging strategy, the AdlC referred to *Google Shopping* and quoted the very same case law mentioned by the Commission in that decision.

However, the AdlC is also currently running an investigation into Apple's privacy policy where self-preferencing is explicitly mentioned and seems to be framed in a different way.[1721] According to the AdlC, the existence of a differential process between the collection of the user's consent for Apple's advertising services and that of third-party advertising services might result in a form of discrimination if Apple applied, without justification, more binding rules on third-party operators than those it applies to itself for similar operations.

Against this backdrop, the judgement of the General Court in *Google Shopping* was much awaited.[1722] Although the Court upheld the Commission's decision, it

1719. Gerechtshof Amsterdam, 26 May 2020, Case C/13/528337, *VBO Makelaar v. Funda*.
1720. Autorité de la concurrence, 7 June 2021, Decision 21-D-11, *Google*.
1721. Autorité de la concurrence, 17 March 2021, Decision 21-D-07, *Apple*.
1722. General Court, 10 November 2021, Case T-612/17, *Google LLC and Alphabet Inc. v. European Commission*, EU:T:2021:763.

framed self-preferencing as discriminatory abuse. Further, the Court outlined four criteria that differentiated Google's self-preferencing from competition on the merits. Notably, the Court underlined the universal vocation and openness of Google's search engine, the superdominant position held by Google on the market for general search services (which allowed it to act as a gateway to the Internet), the presence of high barriers to entry in the market for general search services, and the abnormal conduct undertaken by Google.

While the Commission's approach appeared unprecedented because it revolved around the idea of characterising favouring as a specific form of leveraging, the Court advanced a clearer legal qualification of the conduct concerned. Nonetheless, the definition of the conduct is still unclear and the listed criteria apparently define a pretty narrow framework. Such approach is apparently at odds with the wide application of self-preferencing as a stand-alone abuse instead supported by the European Commission and some national competition authorities (NCAs).

Indeed, a few weeks after the General Court's ruling, the Italian Competition Authority (AGCM) issued a monster fine against Amazon for the preferential treatment granted to third-party sellers who use its own logistics and delivery services (i.e., Fulfilment by Amazon (FBA)), which confirmed that *Google Shopping* is anything but conclusive about self-preferencing as an antitrust offence.[1723] The conduct is merely described by the AGCM as an unequal and unjustified preferential treatment granted by a dominant player to its own services pursuing a leveraging strategy, hence falling outside the scope of competition on the merits. Therefore, rather than reflecting the qualification and the criteria set out by the General Court, the Italian decision is clearly inspired by the Commission's approach in *Google Shopping* and, in line with the idea of describing self-preferencing as a new form of leveraging abuse, Amazon's practice is characterised in terms of tying. In summary, the AGCM endorsed an expansive approach towards the scope of self-preferencing, which is at odds with the legal qualification and the narrow criteria set out by the General Court in *Google Shopping*. Indeed, self-preferencing is not framed as a discriminatory abuse and the particular context depicted by the General Court to assess the circumstances under which the preferential treatment is missing.

Finally, as self-preferencing can be implemented through different means, the preferential provision of data and information may also be considered abusive according to a broad interpretation of this prohibition. Along this line of reasoning, in November 2020, the European Commission sent a statement of objections informing Amazon of its preliminary view that it has infringed antitrust rules by systematically using non-public business data from independent retailers who sell on its online marketplace in order to benefit its own retail business, which directly competes with those retailers.[1724]

1723. Autorità Garante della Concorrenza e del Mercato, 30 November 2021, Decision No. 29925, *FBA Amazon*.

1724. European Commission, 10 November 2020, Case AT.40462, *Amazon Marketplace*. *See* European Commission, *Commission sends Statement of Objections to Amazon for the use of non-public independent seller data and opens second investigation into its e-commerce*

A similar allegation has been made by the European Commission and the UK Competition and Markets Authority (CMA) against Facebook for using advertising data gathered from advertisers in order to compete with them in markets where it is active, such as classified ads.[1725] Moreover, within the investigation opened by the European Commission on Apple's App Store rule requiring developers to use Apple's in-app purchase mechanism for the distribution of paid apps and/or paid digital content, a specific focus relates to the concern that the conduct in question may disintermediate competing developers from important customer data, while Apple may obtain valuable data about the activities and offers of its competitors.[1726]

Such high level of enforcement of self-preferencing appears at odds with the uncertainties surrounding the alleged new theory of harm. As mentioned, these uncertainties have not been completely addressed by the General Court in *Google Shopping*. Indeed, rather than articulating a legal test for a new antitrust offence, the criteria pointed out by the Court appear extremely fact-specific, namely, strictly related to the strategy and business model concerned, and to the role of a search engine within the Internet.

The legal challenge posed by self-preferencing reflects the very advantage it may bring to antitrust authorities. Because preferential treatment may result from a wide range of practices, self-preferencing potentially covers different types of behaviour, subject to different legal standards and essentially connotated by their exclusionary nature, although they may also include exploitative elements. Therefore, in advancing such a new theory of harm, antitrust enforcers would benefit from significant leeway bypassing legal standards required to prove traditional anticompetitive practices. As a result, self-preferencing would provide antitrust authorities with a powerful tool to compete with recent regulatory interventions in digital markets.

Besides its potential as an enforcement shortcut, self-preferencing is functional for imposing a neutrality regime over online gatekeepers. The aim is to ensure a level playing field vis-à-vis competitors, which appears uneven because of the bottleneck and intermediation power exerted by large online platforms, and neutralise conflicts of interest raised by their dual mode intermediation. Such dual role performed by some platforms refuels the never-ending debate over vertical integration and the related concerns that, by giving preferential treatment to its own products and services, an integrated provider may leverage its dominance from one market to related markets. Indeed, the circumstances that may give rise to a conflict of interests and the circumstances that can give rise to leveraging strategy can be similar. From this perspective, self-preferencing is a by-product of the emergence of ecosystems. By

---

business practices, (2020) Press release, available at https://ec.europa.eu/commission/presscorner/detail/en/ip_20_2077.

1725. European Commission, 4 June 2021, Case AT.40684, *Facebook leveraging*; UK Competition and Markets Authority, *CMA Investigates Facebook's Use of Ad Data*, (2021) Press release, available at https://www.gov.uk/government/news/cma-investigates-facebook-s-use-of-ad-data.

1726. European Commission, 16 June 2020, Case AT.40716, *Apple – App Store Practices*.

integrating complementary products and services, a platform that controls and operates at all levels of the value chain is able and may have the incentive to favour its own offers.[1727]

However, as recognised by antitrust authorities, self-preferencing conduct is 'often benign'.[1728] Furthermore, since the value generated by the ecosystem depends on the activities of independent complementors, thus it is not completely under the control of the platform owner, the latter is required to deal with the governance regulating access to and interactions around the ecosystem. Although the variety of legal, technological, and informational measures that could be adopted to this aim may limit and disadvantage firms operating on the platform and competing with the platform owner, there may be legitimate justifications that would need to be carefully considered in each instance. In addition, it cannot be disregarded that platforms implement different business models, hence they are driven by different incentives, which in turn affect their strategies.

Against this backdrop, an outright ban on self-preferencing may question the very existence of ecosystems, challenging their design and monetisation strategies. The fact that preferential treatment can take different forms and may have different impacts because of the different business models adopted by platforms should support instead a differentiated, case-by-case, and effects-based assessment.

Finally, and more importantly, antitrust law does not impose a general duty to ensure a level playing field by sharing competitive advantages with rivals and a competitive advantage cannot be automatically equated with an anticompetitive effect. This is even more evident in the aftermath of the recent Court of Justice (CJEU) ruling in *Servizio Elettrico Nazionale*, which confirmed the effects-based approach to the assessment of the abusive nature of practices arising from the recent European case law and clarified its main principles.[1729] Notably, the CJEU definitively stated that competition law is not intended to protect the competitive structure of the market, but rather consumer welfare, which represents the ultimate goal of the antitrust intervention. Accordingly, as illustrated in *Intel*, not every exclusionary effect is necessarily detrimental to competition:[1730] competition on the merits may, by definition, lead to the departure from the market or the marginalisation of competitors that are less efficient and so less attractive to consumers from the point of view of, among other things, price, choice, quality or innovation. In particular, given that an exclusionary effect does not necessarily undermine competition, a distinction must be drawn between a risk of foreclosure and a risk of anticompetitive foreclosure, since only the latter may be penalised under Article 102 TFEU. If any conduct having an exclusionary effect were

1727. Colomo, *Self-Preferencing: Yet Another Epithet in Need of Limiting Principles* (2020) 43 World Competition 417.

1728. Australian Competition and Consumer Commission, *Updating competition and consumer law for digital platform services*, (2022) Discussion Paper for Interim Report No. 5, 85.

1729. CJEU, 12 May 2022, Case C-377/20, *Servizio Elettrico Nazionale SpA v. Autorità Garante della Concorrenza e del Mercato*, EU:C:2022:379.

1730. CJEU, 6 September 2017, Case C-413/14 P, *Intel v. Commission*, paras 133-134, EU:C:2017:632.

automatically classed as anticompetitive, such provision would become a means for protecting less capable, less efficient undertakings and would in no way protect the more meritorious undertakings, which can serve as a stimulus to a market's competitiveness.

By and large, these well-settled principles do not support the claim that antitrust rules are aimed at ensuring platform neutrality. Rather, given that, as acknowledged by the General Court in *Google Shopping*, self-preferencing cannot be considered prima facie unlawful and therefore as such outside the scope of competition on the merits, its assessment revolves around the demonstration of anticompetitive effects, taking account of the circumstances of the case, the relevant legal and economic context.

Against this background, the recent European case law on self-preferencing revolves instead essentially around the competitive advantage benefitted by a platform because of its dual role. However, a competitive advantage does not amount to an anticompetitive foreclosure, which should not only be proved but also assessed against potential advantages for consumers in terms of price, quality, and choice of new goods and services. It is even more questionable how NCAs' expansive approach towards self-preferencing as stand-alone abuse may fit into this legal framework. Being informed by the Commission's approach in *Google Shopping*, both the AdlC's decision in *Google AdTech* and the AGCM's decision in *Amazon Logistics*, indeed, do not appear consistent either with the legal qualification and the criteria defined by the General court. Similar doubts are raised by the investigations on the preferential access to and use of non-public business data.

Therefore, in the aftermath of the *Google Shopping* ruling and despite the intense level of enforcement by courts and antitrust authorities, doubts about characteristics and boundaries of self-preferencing are still on the table, and a legal test distinguishing such purported new antitrust offence from other practices aimed at pursuing leveraging strategies and already addressed by antitrust rules is still missing.

The entry into force of the Digital Markets Act (DMA) will not clarify these doubts. By introducing a long list of per se prohibitions which includes different forms of self-preferencing, the DMA will definitively facilitate the enforcement against some practices when implemented by firms designated as gatekeepers. Notably, with regard to self-preferencing, the DMA prohibits gatekeepers from: engaging in any form of self-preferencing in ranking services and products offered by themselves; using in competition with business users any data not publicly available which is generated through activities by those business users; preventing the uninstallation of preinstalled applications; giving preferential access to hardware, operating system and software features to their own ancillary services; and refusing to grant FRAND access to app stores, search engines, and social networking services.

However, even if such prohibitions have been inspired by antitrust investigations, the DMA represents a regulatory intervention aimed at protecting a different legal interest from antitrust rules (i.e., to ensure that markets, where gatekeepers are present, are and remain contestable and fair, independently from the actual, likely or presumed effects of the conduct of a given gatekeeper). Accordingly, the relevant legal basis is represented by Article 114 TFEU, rather than Article 103 TFEU, which is intended for the implementation of antitrust provisions pursuant to Articles 101 and 102 TFEU. Therefore, in light of the purported complementarity, traditional antitrust rules remain applicable, although their application should not affect the obligations imposed on gatekeepers under the DMA.

§11.04 MACHINE LEARNING AND ANTITRUST: A CONCISE INTRODUCTION

Ai Deng

[A] Introduction

Heralded as the impetus of the fourth industrial revolution, machine learning (ML) and artificial intelligence (AI) are increasingly becoming an integral part of our daily lives in both the physical and virtual worlds. Not surprisingly, as these technologies become ubiquitous in our society, the implications of ML and AI on competition and antitrust have received much attention in the global community. But what are ML and AI? Why are ML and AI relevant to competition and antitrust? What complications and opportunities, if any, do ML and AI bring to antitrust policymaking and enforcement? In this chapter, we briefly address each of these questions. As one of the most dynamic areas of global antitrust with an ever-evolving landscape and rapid innovations, understanding the basic issues and the latest ideas will help us better prepare for what the future will bring.

[B] What Is ML? What Is AI?

Computer scientist Tom Mitchell gave a widely quoted formal definition of an ML *algorithm*: 'a computer program is said to learn from experience *E* with respect to some class of tasks *T* and performance measure *P* if its performance at tasks in *T*, as measured by *P*, improves with experience *E*'.[1731] To put it simply, ML algorithms are computer programs that *learn* from and improve with experiences.[1732] In practice, 'experience' almost always comes from various forms of data, which can be numeric, text, and even images. In ML parlance, 'training' an ML algorithm refers to the process of building an algorithm using data. This 'training' phase is when the algorithm learns. Artificial neural network (ANN), a buzzword in the tech world, is one such ML algorithm and hence needs to be 'trained' using data in a given application.

AI is a different concept. At a basic level, the difference between AI and ML can be understood as the difference between *learning* and *intelligence*: learning is not intelligence but rather a way to achieve intelligence. In fact, ML has become one of the most popular approaches to AI (hence ML-based AI). More formally, the definitions of AI focus on the question of what intelligence is.[1733] Despite the difference, we will use

1731. T. Mitchell, *Machine Learning* 2 (McGraw-Hill Education 1997).

1732. Consider a (linear) regression model economists often use in merger and conduct cases to quantify damages and estimate post-merger prices. These regression models can be thought of as a type of ML algorithm that 'learns' from the data. For a user-friend but more in-depth introduction to ML, *see*, Ai Deng, 'An Antitrust Lawyer's Guide to Machine Learning' (2018) 33 Antitrust 82.

1733. In the book *Artificial Intelligence: A Modern Approach*, the authors listed eight definitions of AI in four categories along two dimensions: (1) thinking and acting humanly, and (2) thinking

AI and ML interchangeably in this chapter as the antitrust implications typically do not hinge on the technical distinctions between the two.

Despite AI's well-documented success, we often do not know exactly how a particular AI/ML algorithm worked. This is especially true for some traditionally highly complex algorithms such as ANN. The black-box nature of some of these ML algorithms limits our understanding of the algorithmic decision-making process and arguably their adoption. To address this limitation, the field of explainable AI (XAI) has emerged and is now an active research area. I will return to XAI in a later section to discuss its role in antitrust compliance.

[C] Why Is ML Relevant to Competition and Antitrust?

The relevance of ML to antitrust largely centres around the following questions:[1734]

Market Power. Does big data, as an input to ML algorithms, present an entry barrier and therefore enhance market power?
Anticompetitive Conduct. Does using ML/AI algorithms to set prices lead to (tacit) collusion? What implications do ML/AI algorithms have on pricing and competition more broadly? Do ML/AI algorithms facilitate overt anticompetitive conduct such as exclusionary conduct?
Mergers. What are the implications of pricing algorithms in a horizontal merger context? How should one analyse a merger with a significant algorithmic component?
Antitrust Enforcement and Compliance. Can we leverage the power of ML/AI to better combat anticompetitive conduct? If so, how?

We touch on each of these topics below.

[1] Market Power

For ML algorithms to work, we need data, often a lot of data. In fact, many would attribute ML's success in the past decade, to a large part, to the availability of these 'big data', and the necessary computing power to process them. To the extent that data is a critical input to ML and ML-based AI, does having data present a barrier to entry and hence a source of market power? This seemingly simple question does not have a simple answer. Below, I lay out some basic principles to keep in mind when assessing big data and market power.[1735]

---

and acting rationally. Although there are other approaches to obtaining AI, machine learning has become the dominant one in recent years.

1734. AI and ML also have implications on other issues such as intellectual property and privacy, among others. We focus on the key implications on antitrust and competition in this chapter.

1735. This topic has wide-ranging implications on competition well beyond what we can cover in this chapter. For example, we do not specifically discuss the policy and regulatory implications of big data and whether and when interoperability may be an appropriate policy instrument.

First, we need to clarify whether the big data in question is the output of an industry or a type of input. If the big data is an industry output, then the entry barrier question will be relatively straightforward to analyse using standard tools. But if the big data is an input, then the analysis becomes more nuanced.

In this case, the first step is to further clarify the relevant characteristics of the data in question. To that end, let's start with a formal definition of big data. Big data is often defined by four Vs: Volume, Velocity, Variety, and Veracity.[1736] It is important to recognise that in a given industry, not all four Vs are equally relevant. Consider a standard ML task, say, image recognition, where an algorithm tells you whether the animal in a picture is a cat or a dog. Traditionally, this kind of application requires a lot of data, in which case, volume is an important characteristic. Now consider user targeting in the context of online advertising. For targeting to work, firms need 'fresh data' about the user's browsing history and behaviour. In this case, data volume at an individual user level would be less relevant than the 'freshness' and the velocity of the data. Understanding the most relevant characteristics of the big data in question will help us properly assess the difficulty of procuring such data. Some data may be readily available through inexpensive collection or through data vendors while others may be much harder to obtain without significant investment.[1737]

Identifying the most relevant characteristics of the data also cannot be done in a vacuum. As an input, the value of big data ultimately relies upon the ML algorithms they are used to train. This means that, for example, a blanket data-sharing requirement may not be the right approach to fight potential market power brought about by big data. Indeed, advances in ML have started alleviating traditional ML methods' reliance on a huge amount of data.[1738,1739]

[2] Collusion

The infamous *Topkins* case in the US and the *Trod* case in the UK involve the use of pricing algorithms to implement human-collusive agreements.[1740] Although we do not

1736. Some define big data with an additional V: Value.
1737. I am abstracting away from the precise definition of an entry barrier. For a formal discussion, *see* Preston R. Fee, Hugo M. Mialon and Michael A. Williams, 'What Is a Barrier to Entry?' (2004) 94(2) American Economic Review 461-465.
1738. Transfer learning and closely related one- and even zero-shot learning are the types of ML that leverage algorithms already trained using data often in other domains.
1739. It is sometimes stated that data have decreasing rate of returns. As Hal Varian, chief economist at Google put it, 'your first million observations are generally worth a lot more than your last million'. Hal Varian, 'Recent Trends in Concentration, Competition, and Entry' (2019) 82(3) Antitrust Law Journal 832. However, it is also important to recognise that this argument hinges on at least two implicit assumptions that (1) both batches of the data are of the same quality and (2) they are drawn from the same population, hence contains largely similar information.
1740. Press Release, US Dep't of Justice, Former E-Commerce Executive Charged with Price Fixing in the Antitrust Division's First Online Marketing Prosecution (6 April 2015), https://www.justice.gov/opa/pr/former-e-commerce-executive-charged-price-fixing-antitrust-divisions-first-online-marketplace:According to the charge, Topkins and his co-conspirators agreed to fix the prices of certain posters sold in the United States through Amazon Marketplace. To

yet have real-world examples of autonomously colluding pricing algorithms, there is growing theoretical and experimental evidence showing that certain algorithms could lead to tacit coordination.[1741] Empirical indications of softened competition by the use of pricing algorithms have also started to emerge.[1742]

Deng (2020) surveys both the ML and the economics literature on algorithmic tacit collusion.[1743] The main lessons from the ML literature are (1) designing algorithms that can learn to tacitly collude is challenging but not impossible at least in experimental settings where the complexity of the market and the type of interactions between competitors is substantially limited *and* when the algorithms are given a sufficient amount of time to learn and (2) there are several algorithmic features that can facilitate coordination, including the ability to communicate, use of a central planner to coordinate cooperation, among others.[1744] Therefore, companies and antitrust enforcers concerned about the risk of algorithmic collusion should watch out for these algorithmic features in the pricing algorithms.

The lessons from the economics literature are two-fold. First, similar to the findings in the ML literature, economists have shown that at least in certain experimental settings, algorithmic (tacit) collusion is achievable under various assumptions. For example, the study by Calvano et al. (2021, 2022) shows that the so-called *Q*-learning, a popular ML algorithm, leads to supracompetitive prices in their simulated markets through what appears to be a reward-and-punishment scheme, a hallmark feature of a cartel.[1745] Even though recent studies have called some of their conclusions

---

implement their agreements, the defendant and his co-conspirators adopted specific pricing algorithms for the sale of certain posters with the goal of coordinating changes to their respective prices and wrote computer code that instructed algorithm-based software to set prices in conformity with this agreement.

Trod is a similar case. The UK CMA found that Trod Ltd and GB eye Limited conspired to not undercut each other's prices. The agreement was also implemented by automated repricing tool. *See* Online Sales of Posters and Frames, Competition & Mkts. Auth. Cases (4 December 2015), https://www.gov.uk/cma-cases/online-sales-of-discretionary-consumer-products. Note also the recent OFGEM UK's decision to fine energy suppliers for a market allocation agreement facilitated by software programs. U.K. Gas & Elec. Mkts Auth., Infringement by Economy Energy, E (Gas and Electricity) and Dyball Associates of Chapter I of the Competition Act 1998 with Respect to an Anti-Competitive Agreement (26 July 2019), https://www.ofgem.gov.uk/publications-and-updates/decision-impose-financial-penalties-economy-energy-e-gas-and-electricity-and-dyball-associates-following-investigation-infringement-chapter-i-competition-act-1998.

1741. Emilio Calvano et al., 'Artificial Intelligence, Algorithmic Pricing and Collusion', (October 2020) 110(10) American Economic Review; Emilio Calvano et al., 'Algorithmic Collusion with Imperfect Monitoring' (December 2021) 79 International Journal of Industrial Organization. J.M. Sanchez-Cartas and E. Katsamakas, 'Artificial Intelligence, Algorithmic Competition and Market Structures' (2022) 10 IEEE Access 10575-10584.

1742. S. Assad et al., 'Identifying Algorithmic Pricing Technology Adoption in Retail Gasoline Market' (2020) 112 AEA Papers and Proceedings 2022, 457-460.

1743. Ai Deng, 'Algorithmic Collusion and Algorithmic Compliance: Risks and Opportunities' (2020) 27 The Global Antitrust Institute Report on the Digital Economy.

1744. Deng (2020) also flagged another type of algorithms known as *leader* and *builder* algorithms that could lead to (tacit) coordination, *ibid.*

1745. *Supra* n. 1741. For why this study does not suggest that algorithmic tacit collusion is already a genuine threat to competition, *see* Ai Deng, 'Algorithmic Tacit Collusion is a Limited Threat to Competition' (10 December 2019) Law360, available at https://www.law360.com/articles

into question, *see*, *e.g.*, den Boer et al. (2022), more elaborate collusive algorithms have been developed in theoretical settings.[1746] Second, the economics literature has identified a set of market structural characteristics that facilitate collusion. Examining the impact of pricing algorithms on these structural characteristics, therefore, gives us a principled way to assess the risk of algorithmic collusion. Interested readers are referred to Deng (2020) for a detailed discussion. In this section, I discuss only two such characteristics to highlight the intricacies of a proper analysis.[1747]

Transparency about market demand and supply conditions (e.g., costs, prices) is one structural factor that has been argued to facilitate tacit collusion and can be enhanced by the use of algorithms. However, the recent literature has shown that under certain conditions, market transparency, especially transparency about demand, can make collusion more difficult to sustain. The key insight is that market transparency may, in some instances, increase firms' incentive to 'cheat'.[1748]

Some have also argued that an algorithm's speed could prevent cartel members from cheating because any deviation from a tacitly or explicitly agreed-upon price could be detected and potentially retaliated against immediately.[1749] The observation that faster reaction reduces the incentive to deviate in the first place under *perfect* monitoring has been recognised in the economic literature as well. But economists have also shown that faster responses can be a double-edged sword when it comes to cartel stability under *imperfect* monitoring. A seminal article in this literature (Sannikov & Skrzypacz, 2007) shows that under some conditions if market information is monitored continuously and firms can react to it quickly, collusion becomes very

---

/1226694/algorithmic-tacit-collusion-is-a-limited-threat-to-competition. More recently, Asker et al. (2022) show that whether the pricing algorithm learns to set supracompetitive prices depends critically on the algorithm design, among other factors. *See*, John Asker, Chaim Fershtman and Ariel Pakes, 'Artificial Intelligence, Algorithm Design, and Pricing' (2022) 112 AEA Papers and Proceedings 452-456.

1746. Arnoud V. den Boer, Janusz M. Meylahn, and Maarten Pieter Schinkel, *Artificial Collusion: Examining Supracompetitive Pricing by Q-learning Algorithms*, Amsterdam Law School Research Paper No. 2022-06, December, 2022. Arnoud V. den Boer and J. M. Meylahn, 'Learning to Collude in a Pricing Duopoly', (2022) 24(5) Manufacturing & Service Operations Management 2577-2594. For a More In-Depth Survey of the Recent Economic Literature, *see* Ai Deng, *Algorithmic Collusion: A Progress Report*, Working Paper, 2023.

1747. Deng (2020), *supra* n. 1743.

1748. This was formally studied by Sugaya and Wolitzky (2018) who provided an economic theory to explain why privacy (less transparency) can be beneficial to a cartel. Takuo Sugaya and Alexander Wolitzky, 'Maintaining Privacy in Cartels' (2018) 126(6) Journal of Political Economy. Miklos-Thal and Tucker (2019) explained in their study on the implications of algorithm-enhanced market demand prediction, while 'better forecasting allows colluding firms to better tailor prices to demand conditions, it also increase each firm's temptation to deviate to a lower price in time periods of high predicted demand.' Therefore, the authors concluded that 'despite concerns expressed by policy makers, better forecasting and algorithms can lead to lower prices and higher consumer surplus.' Jeanine Miklós-Thal and Catherine Tucker, 'Collusion by Algorithm: Does Better Demand Prediction Facilitate Coordination Between Sellers?' (2019) 65(4) Management Science.

1749. Michal S. Gal, *Algorithmic-Facilitated Coordination: Note by Michal Gal* 26 (Bkgd. Note to Competition Cmte., 22 June 2017), https://one.oecd.org/document/DAF/COMP/WD(2017)26/en/pdf. OECD, Algorithms and Collusion: Competition Policy in the Digital Age 22 (2017), www.oecd.org/competition/algorithms-collusion-competition-policy-in-the-digital-age.htm.

difficult.[1750] The basic intuition is that as firms continuously monitor the market to detect and punish cheating, market noise, due to imperfect information, would generate too many false signals of cheating ('false positives'). Consequently, when firms can also punish the perceived cheating quickly (e.g., through lowering prices), theory shows that a cartel becomes hard to sustain. The takeaway for the antitrust community is again that algorithmic pricing requires a more nuanced approach to assess.

[3] Horizontal Merger

While the possibility of algorithmic collusion has been extensively discussed in the global antitrust community in recent years, there has been much more limited discussion in the context of mergers. Given the increasing adoption of ML in businesses, we will soon need to confront the algorithmic component in a horizontal merger review.

ML has implications on at least the following four aspects in a horizontal merger review.[1751]

Market Definition. There are at least two implications regarding market definition. First, we need to recognise that sophisticated pricing algorithms can potentially segment the market into a massive number of customer groups with different willingness-to-pay by leveraging detailed customer data.[1752] This is closely related to algorithmic pricing discrimination, a topic we return to in the next section. In a merger investigation, granular customer segmentation can lead to narrow relevant antitrust markets defined by targeted customers, which could lead to a higher likelihood of finding a group that may be harmed by the transaction. Second, the use of algorithms may also present an opportunity to better delineate these markets. In fact, regardless of how firms use pricing algorithms to segment the customer base, information on customer segmentation is likely available in ordinary-course business documents or may be recovered through clever backward engineering.[1753]

Unilateral Effects. Standard tools for evaluating mergers are still valid for evaluating the likely competitive effects of mergers when prices are set by pricing algorithms. However, by basing the analysis (say, a merger simulation) on the merging parties' own pricing algorithms, it might be possible to better predict the merger effects. Of course, to conduct a full-blown merger simulation using one of the merging parties'

1750. Yuliy Sannikov and Andrzej Skrzypacz, 'Impossibility of Collusion under Imperfect Monitoring with Flexible Production' (2007) 97 American Economic Review 1794, 1814.

1751. For an in-depth discussion of these issues, *see*, Ai Deng and Cristián Hernández, 'Algorithmic Pricing in Horizontal Merger Review: An Initial Assessment,' (Spring 2022) 36(2) Antitrust.

1752. *See*, for example, Terrell McSweeny and Brian O'Dea, 'The Implications of Algorithmic Pricing for Coordinated Effects Analysis and Price Discrimination Markets in Antitrust Enforcement' (Fall 2017) 32(1) Antitrust.

1753. In addition to ordinary-course documents, interviews with companies' pricing teams can be particularly helpful to understand how the firms define customer segments. Even if such information is not already documented, data analysis can be used to infer patterns of price discrimination. For more details, *see*, Deng and Hernández (2022), *supra* n. 1751.

pricing algorithms, it is likely necessary to modify the algorithm's objective to maximise the joint post-merger profit. How difficult (or feasible) it is to modify the algorithm's objective will depend on the specifics of the case. Another important point to keep in mind is that the combined firm might have a unilateral incentive to change certain important features of their pricing algorithms and consequently post-merger pricing and customer segmentation post-merger. This type of uncertainty regarding the post-merger conduct, however, is present with or without an algorithmic component in a merger.

Coordinated Effects. Unlike unilateral effects, coordinated effects analysis in a merger does not typically lend itself to a common quantitative procedure because the theory of collusion does not offer a unique prediction about the market outcomes. Still, many lessons we draw above on algorithmic tacit collusion apply in the merger context. For example, one should assess the impact of post-merger use of algorithms on various structural characteristics and specifically whether algorithms make the market more or less conducive to tacit coordination while understanding that a certain degree of uncertainty is unavoidable.

One perhaps subtle but important observation is whether the disclosure of the pricing algorithm itself may lead to softened competition and the risk of tacit coordination even if the merger does not eventually consummate. This is a plausible concern as prices and pricing strategies are among the most competitively sensitive information. This means that both the antitrust enforcers and the merging parties should be mindful of such disclosure. For a more in-depth discussion, *see* Coutts (2022).[1754]

Remedies. The goal of divestitures is to preserve the premerger competition. To the extent divesting merging parties' pricing algorithms is contemplated in a merger review, several important nuances, including data compatibility issues and the risk of collusion, should be kept in mind. The considerations involved are necessarily complex. Consider a situation where both merging parties (Firm A and Firm B) use pricing algorithms and it has been determined that preserving competition requires divesting a set of overlapping products from Firm B and the pricing algorithm for those products. Suppose further that instead of using the algorithm as is, the divestiture buyer 're-trains' the divested algorithm using its own data, which does not include Firm B's products that were not divested. In such a case, it is not immediately clear what effect re-training the algorithm would have on the prices of the divested products. The answers would be case-specific.[1755]

1754. Michael David Coutts, Mergers, Acquisitions and Merger Control in an algorithmic pricing world, Journal of Competition Law & Economics, 2022, 00, 1-59.

1755. In addition, a divestiture typically involves an entire business unit which would include not only physical assets but also the personnel. To the extent that a divestiture also involves the personnel who has intimate knowledge about the inner workings of the divested pricing algorithms, one complication both the antitrust agencies and the merging parties need to wrestle with is what happens if these personnel is also be involved in the firm's other analytical capabilities. *See* Deng and Hernández (2022), *supra* n. 1751.

[4] Other Ways in Which Algorithms Affect Prices

The broader question of how algorithms affect pricing beyond algorithmic tacit collusion has also captured the attention of antitrust practitioners, scholars, and enforcers. Algorithmic price discrimination (PD) is one such topic. It is important at the outset to emphasise that the welfare effect of PD is ambiguous. In fact, under certain conditions, the ability to price discriminate could lead to increased competition and lower prices for consumers.[1756]

It should not be surprising that consumer data again become front and centre in the context of algorithmic PD. This is also where algorithmic pricing and privacy legislation such as GDPR and California Consumer Privacy Act (CCPA) intersect. *See* Gautier et al. (2020) for a detailed discussion.[1757] The interaction between PD and algorithmic collusion, especially in the context of the gig economy is discussed by Mehra (2021). He argues that PD may interact with tacit collusion in such a way as to sustain a cartel and calls for reviving some enforcement against PD.[1758] *See also* MacKay and Weinstein (2022).[1759]

Other novel ways by which pricing algorithms affect pricing have also been identified. For example, Hansen et al. (2020) show that pricing experiments run by certain algorithms could lead to supracompetitive prices when a firm behaves as if it is a monopolist (i.e., ignoring the impact of competitors' prices on its own profit). Brown and MacKay (2020) show that if firms can choose their pricing frequency, then each firm has a unilateral profit incentive to choose a frequency different from those of their competitors. This again could lead to higher prices.[1760] Harrington (2022) studies the effect of third-party pricing algorithms on competition and finds that 'outsourcing the pricing algorithm does not reduce competition but does make prices more sensitive to the demand variation'. He further shows that in his theoretical model, outsourcing decreases consumer welfare and increases industry profit. Cheng and Nowag (2022)

1756. This is related to the concept of price response asymmetry. *See* Mark Armstrong, '*Recent Developments in the Economics of Price Discrimination*', *Advances in Economics and Econometrics: Theory and Applications: Ninth World Congress: Volume II* (Cambridge University Press, 2006), pp. 97-141.
1757. On the technical front, the authors discussed the existing scientific studies developing PD approaches as well as technical challenges, some of which mirror those in the developing of autonomous colluding pricing algorithms I alluded to above.
1758. Salil K. Mehra, 'Price Discrimination-Driven Algorithmic Collusion: Platforms for Durable Cartels' (2021) 26 Stanford Journal of Law, Business & Finance 171.
1759. Alexander J. MacKay and Samuel N. Weinstein, 'Dynamic Pricing Algorithms, Consumer Harm, and Regulatory Response', HBS Working Paper (2022).
1760. Zach Y. Brown and Alexander MacKay, 'Competition in Pricing Algorithms' (2023) 15(2) American Economic Journal: Microeconomics. The basic intuition is that 'a superior-technology firm commits to "beat" (best respond to) whatever price is offered by its rivals ... The rivals take this into account, softening price competition.' Obviously, this result is true under their assumptions regardless of whether the price is set by algorithms or humans. But the authors argue that the use of pricing algorithms makes firms' commitment to respond at given frequencies credible.

discussed ways in which algorithms may be used to engage in predation and exclusion.[1761] Finally, MacKay and Weinstein (2022) argue that pricing regulation can be considered a feasible solution to the challenges non-collusive algorithmic pricing poses.[1762]

[D] Leverage ML to Combat Anticompetitive Conduct

As is with any powerful tools, a natural question is whether we can leverage ML and AI to better combat anticompetitive conduct. In what follows, I discuss several promising paths forward.[1763]

[1] Monitoring and Detection

The first approach is to use algorithm-automated monitoring as an active antitrust compliance tool. These tools monitor the behaviour of humans as well as algorithms. The main advantage of this approach is that it does not attempt to open the black box of complicated algorithms; it focuses instead on the relevant firm behaviours that can be observed and interpreted.

Directly monitoring the 'symptoms' of an antitrust violation is the most straightforward starting point. These 'symptoms' are often referred to as plus factors or collusive markers in the context of collusion.[1764] The emergence and increasing popularity of Regulatory Technology (RegTech) where ML and AI are deployed to screen for non-compliant conduct give us a glimpse of the value of this approach. Indeed, a recent survey by the Stanford Computational Antitrust Project shows that several antitrust agencies have started implementing a variety of automated and/or ML tools.[1765] Despite the tremendous promise ML holds, it is important to understand that they also present technical pitfalls, so a blind application is not recommended. *See* Deng (2017) for a critical discussion.[1766]

1761. Thomas K. Cheng and Julian Nowag, 'Algorithmic Predation and Exclusion' (2023) 25 University of Pennsylvania Journal of Business Law.
1762. MacKay and Weinstein (2022), *supra* n. 1759.
1763. Compliance by design is another related concept. It is a more complex topic, so I do not discuss it in this chapter. Interested readers are encouraged to consult Deng (2020), *supra* n. 1743.
1764. A number of plus factors have been identified in the economics and law literature. In addition to the 'traditional' plus factors (*see* William E. Kovacic et al., 'Plus Factors and Agreement in Antitrust Law' (2011) 110 Michael Law Review 393, 393), plus factors tailored to algorithmic pricing are also proposed. *See*, Michal Gal, 'Algorithms as Illegal Agreements' (2019) 34:67 Berkley Technology Law Journal.
1765. The Adoption of Computational Antitrust by Agencies: 2021 Report, 2, 78 Stanford Computational Antitrust, 2022, available at https://papers.ssrn.com/sol3/papers.cfm?abstract_id=4142225.
1766. Ai Deng, 'Cartel Detection and Monitoring: A Look Forward' (2017) 5 Journal of Antitrust Enforcement 488.

[2] Explainable AI

XAI, a concept I introduced above, can be another powerful tool in algorithmic antitrust compliance.[1767] To see why, let us abstract from the technical aspects of XAI and assume that an XAI algorithm can 'explain' its decision-making process by answering *why* and *what-if* type questions.

Imagine that your pricing algorithm is setting a price that you think might be too high. A helpful *what-if* question could be, 'What if we lower the price?' or 'Would we generate higher immediate profit if we lower the price?' The answer might be, 'Based on demand forecasts and our customers' price elasticity, this is the optimal price we should set' or 'We have no reason to lower our price because we know that the competitor's algorithm is not going to lower theirs, and we know that because we have determined that this is the best course of action that benefits both of us in the long term', or even 'We should not lower our price because the last time we lowered our price, the competitor started a price war.' Putting aside the question of whether or not the last two responses suggest problematic algorithmic conduct, having this knowledge can be extremely helpful. While this above example is currently hypothetical, recent advances in XAI give us reason to be optimistic that it will not remain so for too long.[1768]

[3] Market Design

The compliance tools that we have discussed so far, arguably except for XAI, are passive in nature because *detection* is their primary objective while *deterrence* is merely a desired by-product. Exciting ideas for more proactive approaches have emerged recently. One example is the idea of carefully designing the marketplace to discourage collusion and promote competition. Consider a platform marketplace, such as Amazon and eBay. Johnson et al. (2020) show that under some conditions, platform design rules involving steering consumer demand towards a subset of the sellers could achieve that objective.[1769] In the authors' words, their dynamic price-directed

1767. The AI research community has proposed several ideas to help achieve interpretability and explainability of AI. Two common approaches, rooted in the technical aspects of AI, are (1) the use of inherently interpretable algorithms (known as 'white-box algorithms') and (2) the use of clever backward engineering (also known as post hoc methods). Naturally, there is not a single definition of explainability, and different domains may find different definitions acceptable.

1768. An AI study published in 2018 titled 'Contrastive Explanations for Reinforcement Learning in Terms of Expected Consequences' is a step toward achieving the type of explainability discussed here. The researchers of the study developed a method that enables an algorithm to precisely answer the what-if questions similar to those we posed above. Another study titled 'Explainable Reinforcement Learning Through a Causal Lens', first published in 2019, proposed yet another approach to answering why and why-not type questions.

1769. Justin Johnson, Andrew Rhodes and Matthijs Widenbeest, Platform Design when Sellers Use Pricing Algorithms, Working Paper 2021.

prominence (PDP) policy does so 'by steering additional demand to a firm not just in the period in which it cuts prices but also in some later periods, subject to the firm not raising prices and not being undercut by more than a "cushion" set by the platform. The net effect is that it is more difficult to punish a firm that has cut prices, and therefore incentives to deviate are amplified, reducing cartel stability'. Brero et al (2022) extended the idea to also equip the platforms with ML capabilities to *learn* rules that prevent collusion.[1770]

[4] Other Ideas

The ideas discussed above are not without their challenges. Some may be expensive to implement, and some are inspirational at this point. Are there 'easier' ways to counteract the risks of anticompetitive algorithmic conduct? The answer is yes. For example, because ML algorithms need to learn and correct their 'mistakes' along the way as a natural part of learning, even the simple protocol of documenting the learning process of the (pricing) algorithms can be helpful.[1771] For example, if an algorithm is able to figure out on its own to use reward and punishment to elicit and sustain tacit collusion after the training phase, the learning process should reflect that, allowing *ex post*, if not real time, discovery.

Relatedly, some AI researchers have also proposed to label algorithms in much the same way as we label the nutrition facts on food items. These labels, or 'model cards' as some researchers call them, would give information about the algorithms' performance characteristics. For example, the label for a pricing algorithm could clearly state whether the algorithm is equipped with communication or negotiation capabilities, both of which are shown to facilitate collusion, and whether there is experimental evidence that the algorithm learns to tacitly collude with one another. Because implementing model cards is not costless for private firms, proper incentives need to be offered.

[E] Conclusion

For antitrust-policy makers who strive to design policies that deter anticompetitive conduct and promote competition and innovation, for antitrust enforcers who need to assess the pro-and anticompetitive effects of certain algorithmic conduct *before* deciding to bring an enforcement action, and for private counsels who want to advise their clients on the antitrust implications of adopting and integrating ML algorithms in the clients' businesses, a good understanding of the interaction between ML and competition is a necessity, especially as the case laws are still being developed. In this ever-changing and non-stationary world, technologies are never going to be static, and

1770. Brero Gianluca et al., Learning to Mitigate AI Collusion on Economic Platforms, 2022, available at //dagcmkpagjlhakfdhnbomgmjdpkdklff/enhanced-reader.html?openApp&pdf=https%3A%2F%2Farxiv.org%2Fpdf%2F2202.07106.pdf.

1771. Formally, learning by trial and error is the main feature of the so-called reinforcement (machine) learning. *See* Deng (2018) for an introduction, *supra* n. 1732.

only one thing is certain: when it comes to ML and antitrust, we need to keep abreast of the developments of the technologies and continue to refine and improve our understanding of their impact on the competitive process.

§11.05 DIGITAL MARKETS AND SUSTAINABILITY IN THE CONTEXT OF EU COMPETITION LAW

Wolf Sauter[*]

[A] Introduction

At first sight, the three categories of digital markets, sustainability and EU competition law are only tenuously connected, as illustrated by this simple triangle on a dotted base (Figure 11.1).

[B] Competition Law

Figure 11.1 The Relationship Between Competition Law, Digitalisation and Sustainability

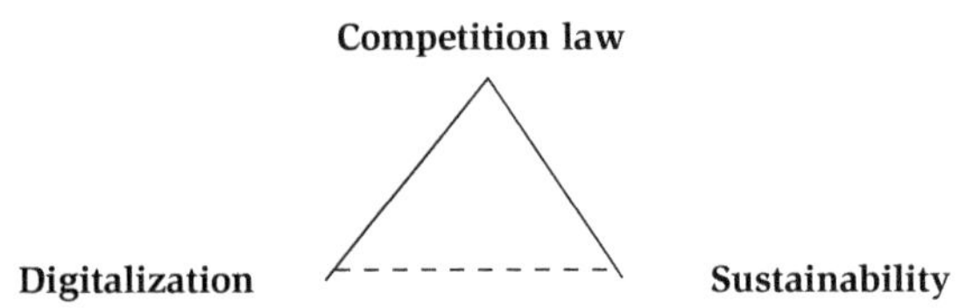

Source: Figure by the Author.

By itself of course, digitalisation as a subject of EU competition law by now has an impressive track record dating back at least to the Microsoft Case,[1772] and more recently including, for instance, the *Google Shopping* Case[1773] that is amply covered in the present volume, alongside proposed regulation covering the Digital Markets Act, the Digital Services Act, Data Governance Act and the Data Act that are now at various stages of adoption. Sustainability has come back into focus following cases such as CECED,[1774] Der Grüne Punkt[1775] and more recently AdBlue,[1776] notably with the March 2022 draft of revised Horizontal Guidelines that include a new chapter on sustainability.

* This section was written in a private capacity and all opinions expressed here are my own.

1772. Case T-201/04, *Microsoft Corp. v. Commission*, Judgment of 17 September 2007, ECLI: EU:T:2007:289.

1773. Cae T-612/17, *Google LLC, formerly Google Inc. and Alphabet, Inc. v. Commission*, Judgment of 10 November 2021, ECLI:EU:T:2021:763.

1774. 2000/475/EC: Commission Decision of 24 January 1999 relating to a proceeding under Article 81 of the EC Treaty and Article 53 of the EEA Agreement (Case IV.F.1/36.718.CECED), OJ 2000, L187/47.

1775. Case C-385/07 P, *Der Grüne Punkt – Duales System Deutschland GmbH v. Commission of the European Communities*, Judgment of 16 July 2009, ECLI:EU:C:2009:456.

1776. CASE AT.40178 – CAR EMISSIONS. Commission Decision of 8 June 2021, based on Article 7 of Regulation (EC) 1/2003.

So, two of the three legs of the above triangle appear in rude health. However, digital markets and sustainability have much less in common, making the exercise of examining their relationship in the context of EU competition policy necessarily at least partly a speculative one. Nevertheless, on closer reflection, some evidence of links all around can be found, and these will be the topic of this necessarily brief contribution. First, I will clarify the links covered. Next, I will sketch the framework for sustainability under the EU competition rules. Finally, I will set out some first reflections on how this may affect digital markets.

[C] The Link Between Digitalisation and Sustainability

At an everyday level it is already possible to think of instances of digitalisation that may enhance sustainability – such as working from home aided by an internet connection; having videoconferences instead of travelling for face-to-face meetings with a much larger carbon footprint; or connecting electronic devices and appliances to the Internet in order to optimise their efficient use. At the same time trends such as the electricity-intensive mining of cryptocurrencies points to digitalisation as a burden on the environment. There is already a link with antitrust here. For instance, Artificial Intelligence and the Internet of Things are inaugurating a new era where human intervention is avoided altogether, facilitating collusive outcomes while enabling new ways of market interaction that can have an impact on sustainability.

Think of digitalisation and artificial intelligence in agriculture. They may on the one hand make resource use and energy consumption more efficient and by implication potentially also more sustainable by improving logistics and monitoring.[1777] On the other hand, they may promote the concentration of farm data in the hands of a small set of multinational enterprises enjoying increasing market power at the expense of farmers and their independence as entrepreneurs.[1778] And they may do so without promoting sustainability, or at least shift the locus of decision-making to entities that have their own profitability as the overriding concern, to the exclusion of much else, as is witnessed by the new entity formed by the Bayer/Monsanto merger in (*inter alia*) digital agriculture which also featured the innovation theory of harm.[1779]

Looking at these issues in a more structured way requires a definition of sustainability. Sustainability is a broad concept that has been defined by the United

1777. Beatrice Gaske, Antonio Bau and Felix Ekardt, 'Digitalization and AI in European agriculture: A strategy for achieving climate and biodiversity targets?', (2021) 13 Sustainability 4652.
1778. Can Atik and Bertin Martens, 'Competition Problems and Governance of Non-personal Agricultural Machine Data: Comparing Voluntary Initiatives in the US and EU' (2021) 12 Journal of Intellectual Property, Information Technology and E-Commerce Law 370-396; Can Atik, 'Understanding the Role of Agricultural Data on Market Power in the Emerging Digital Agriculture Sector: A Critical Analysis of the Bayer/Monsanto Decision', in David Bosco and Michal S. Gal (eds) *Challenges to Assumptions in Competition Law* (Edward Elgar, 2021) 41-78; Tom Verdonk, 'Planting the Seeds of Market Power: Digital Agriculture, Farmers' Autonomy, and the Role of Competition Policy', in Leonie Reins (ed.), *Regulating New Technologies in Uncertain Times* (Springer, 2019) 105-132.
1779. Case M.8084 – Bayer/Monsanto. Commission Decision of 21 March 2018, based on Article 8(2) Regulation (EC) 139/2004.

Nations in the context of human social and economic development as comprising seventeen sustainable development goals and their respective targets and indicators. This includes protection of the environment, biodiversity and climate, public health, animal welfare and fair trade, as well as working conditions and human rights.

The impact of digitalisation and artificial intelligence on sustainability has been studied as part of the concept of digitainability.[1780] Just as our common sense examples illustrate, it highlights that there may both be positive and negative interdependencies between digitalisation and sustainability. This concept in turn has led to the emergence of a digitainability assessment framework focused on the UN sustainable development goals.[1781] For present purposes, we will leave aside the UN development goals as such but retain the UN definition of sustainability.

[D] The Emergence of Green Antitrust in the EU

In recent years the debate on competition law and sustainability has heated up, especially in the EU.[1782] Promoters of green antitrust believe that urgency requires decentralised action here, including by undertakings acting jointly, concluding what might otherwise be seen as anticompetitive agreements that should be accommodated within competition law. They face off against some with a more utopian view who believe such issues are best left to the self-enforcing decrees of a benign world government while firms are inherently untrustworthy and likely to abuse sustainability concerns for their own illicit purposes.[1783] As is often the case, the perfect here seems to be the enemy of the good,[1784] and it may take a while for the world government to step in effectively, while time is precisely of the essence especially where climate change is concerned.

Over the past few years, the EU's several national competition authorities and governments have looked for ways to accommodate sustainability concerns in competition law and prodded the European Commission to follow their lead.[1785]

1780. Ulrich Lichtenthaler, 'Digitainability: The Combined Effects of the Megatrends Digitalization and Sustainability' (2021) 9 Journal of Innovation Management 64-80.
1781. Sivan Gupta and Jacob Rhyner, 'Mindful Application of Digitalization for Sustainable Development: The Digitainability Assessment Framework' (2022) 14 Sustainability 3114.
1782. Seminal: Suzanne Kingston, *Greening EU Competition Law and Policy* (Cambridge University Press 2011). *See* Anna Gerbrandy, 'Solving a Sustainability-Deficit in European Competition Law' (2017) 40 World Competition 539-562. For a recent overview *see* Simon Holmes, Dirk Middelschutte and Martijn Snoep (eds), *Competition Law, Climate Change and Environmental Sustainability* (Concurrences 2021).
1783. Pro: Simon Holmes, 'Climate Change, Sustainability, and Competition Law' (2020) 8 Journal of Antitrust Enforcement 354-405; contra Maarten Pieter Schinkel and Leonard Treuren, 'Green Antitrust: Friendly Fure in the Fight Against Climate Change', in Simon Holmes, Dirk Middelschutte and Martijn Snoep (eds), *Competition Law, Climate Change and Environmental Sustainability* (Concurrences 2021), 91-104.
1784. Voltaire, *Contes en vers* (1772), in 'La Bégueule' stated 'Dans ses écrits un sage Italien/Dit que le mieux est l'ennemi du bien'. https://fr.wiktionary.org/wiki/le_mieux_est_l%E2%80%99ennemi_du_bien.
1785. Viktoria Robertson, 'Sustainability: A World-First Green Exemption in Austrian Competition Law' (2022) 13 Journal of European Competition Law & Practice, https://doi.org/10.1093/

Fortunately, the European Commission has meanwhile come down decisively on the side of green antitrust. After a trial balloon in its September 2021 Competition Policy Brief,[1786] by March 2022 the Commission published its draft revised Horizontal Policy Guidelines with a new chapter on sustainability.[1787]

This aims to set out its methods of assessment of agreements between competitors that pursue one or more sustainability objectives. Sustainability fits in with the EU's attempt to create a new economic model with the European Green Deal and the Fit For 55 legislative programme.[1788]

The draft revised Horizontal Guidelines highlight sustainability development as a core principle of the Treaty on European Union and a priority objective of the EU's policies, with the European Commission being committed to implementing the UN's abovementioned sustainable development goals.

The draft revised Horizontal Guidelines incorporate two main developments.

In the first place they create a soft safe harbour for sustainability standardisation agreements that are unlikely to appreciably restrict competition if they meet the following cumulative conditions: (i) they are transparent; (ii) they do not impose an obligation to comply on those who do not wish to participate; (iii) undertakings remain free to adopt a higher standard; (iv) there is no exchange of commercially sensitive information; (v) there is effective non-discriminatory access to the features of the standard; (vi) it does not lead to a significant increase in price or reduction in choice; and (vii) there is a monitoring system for compliance.

Second, the Commission also takes a new approach to the fair share for consumers under the second condition of Article 101(3) TFEU by defining three types of benefits that can be considered both separately and cumulatively:

- Individual use benefits: such as in terms of directly experienced price and quality – this is the classic approach.
- Individual non-use benefits: in terms of willingness to pay for increased sustainability that is not directly experienced by consumers – this is an innovation.
- Collective benefits: sustainability benefits enjoyed collectively can count towards a fair share to the extent there is a significant overlap between the consumers enjoying the benefits and the consumers enjoying the relevant market.

---

jeclap/lpac092; Jurgita Malinauskaite, 'Competition Law and Sustainability: EU and National Perspectives' (2022) 13 Journal of European Competition Law & Practice, https://doi.org/10.1093/jeclap/lpac003.

1786. European Commission, 'Competition policy in support of Europe's Green Ambition', *Competition Policy Brief* 2021/1.

1787. Communication from the Commission – Guidelines on the applicability of Article 101 of the Treaty on the Functioning of the European Union to horizontal co-operation agreements – Draft. https://ec.europa.eu/competition-policy/public-consultations/2022-hbers_en#view-the-consultation-document.

1788. On the broader EU ambitions *see* Editorial comment, 'The European Climate Law: Making the Social Market Economy Fit for 55?' (2021) 58 Common Market Law Review 1321-1340.

The sum of these three sources of benefits would then have to lead to a fair share for consumers. This fair share is however still defined as full compensation – or at least 'net neutrality' for consumers within the relevant market. This reflects the approach taken in the famous CECED Decision of 2000, which pioneered the concept of individual and collective benefits in relation to CO_2 emissions caused by domestic appliances.[1789]

Exactly how these concepts will be applied in practice after the final version of the Guidelines is adopted remains to be established. However, appears that following the Commission's readoption of the use of comfort letters to provide guidance on the application of the competition rules during the COVID-19 Crisis,[1790] it now intends to resort to informal guidance more frequently in future.[1791] It may even be looking for a good example to exercise its powers under Article 10 of Regulation 1/2003 to make a formal finding of non-applicability in an Article 101(3) TFEU setting.

In any event green antitrust is not just a more tolerant approach towards sustainability agreements. Greenwashing, or disinformation disseminated by a firm in order to falsely present an environmentally responsible public image, will be discouraged. And the recent AdBlue cartel Decision under Article 101 TFEU in relation to the restriction of technological development regarding environmental measures in the automotive sector shows that green antitrust can bite.[1792] There was no obvious digital dimension in AdBlue – as it concerned the coordination of tank sizes and distance between refills for liquids designed to limit diesel vehicle emissions of NO_x. However, Dieselgate – triggering the first cases of enforcement against the digital gaming of environmental rules and cheating software in the automotive sector – suggests there might well have been.[1793]

[E] Conclusion: Implications for Digitainability

We are moving toward a new model of European society which will simultaneously be Greener and more Digital. In both areas, we see important legislative efforts with the Digital Market Act, Digital Services Act, Data Governance Act and Data Act on the one hand and the Green Deal and Fit for 55 legislation on the other that are so far largely independent of each other. At the same time, crossovers are increasingly appearing in

1789. *Supra* n. 1774.
1790. Communication from the Commission: Temporary Framework for assessing antitrust issues related to business cooperation in response to situations of urgency stemming from the current COVID-19 outbreak, OJ 2020, C116 I/7. *See* https://ec.europa.eu/competition/antitrust/medicines_for_europe_comfort_letter.pdf https://ec.europa.eu/competition/antitrust/comfort_letter_coronavirus_matchmaking_event_25032021.pdf.
1791. On 24 May 2022 the Commission launched a consultation to revise its informal guidance notice https://ec.europa.eu/competition-policy/public-consultations/2022-informal-guidance-notice_en#reference-documents-and-other-related-consultations.
1792. *Supra* n. 1774.
1793. Edin Mujkic and Donald Klingner, 'Dieselgate: How Hubris and Bad Leadership Caused the Biggest Scandal in Automotive History' (2019) 21 Public Integrity 365-377.

practice, such as in the area of digital agriculture and also in the automotive sector and more widely everywhere the Internet of Things[1794] interacts with the energy transition.

What does all this imply for the convergence between digitalisation and sustainability in an antitrust context? Where the Green and Digital trends touch, antitrust may play a role in providing a framework to determine the legal constraints that apply. After all, the application of the Treaty rules on antitrust and therefore competition policy is bound to take account of and accommodate other objectives of Union Policy,[1795] in order to ensure the coherence and consistency of EU law.[1796] Antitrust offers the necessary flexibility to navigate uncharted territory while referring to established principles. The sustainability dimension offers a mixture of enhanced freedom and increased guidance within the antitrust framework. Time will tell what this means for digitainability as we await the first cases.

1794. COM(2022) 19 final, Report from the Commission to the Council and the European Parliament Final report - sector inquiry into consumer Internet of Things, Brussels, 20.1.2022.

1795. Holmes, *supra* n. 1783.

1796. Wolf Sauter, *Coherence in EU Competition Law* (Oxford University Press 2016); Jurian Langer and Wolf Sauter, 'The Consistency Requirement in EU Law' (2017/18) 24 Columbia Journal of European Law 39-73.

§11.06 COMPUTATIONAL ANTITRUST: KEEPING UP WITH DIGITAL MARKETS

Teodora Groza

As this volume shows, digital markets have become the focal point of antitrust enforcement. The rapid digitalisation of the economy has required antitrust agencies and policymakers to adapt to new business models.[1797] Nonetheless, the increasingly data-intensive nature of antitrust investigations[1798] challenges resource-constrained competition authorities, raising worries not only about the duration of proceedings[1799] but also about their precision.[1800] Furthermore, the antitrust rules and standards developed to tackle anticompetitive conduct in analogue markets are often inadequate for the digital environment. The current framework cannot aptly capture the realities of data-driven markets,[1801] from the role of data as a competitive asset[1802] to the disruptive potential of new entrants.[1803] Computational antitrust offers a solution to these ills: using digital tools to address digital harms. This chapter (1) explains what is computational antitrust, (2) shows what computational tools are currently used by antitrust agencies, and (3) introduces future potential uses of computational antitrust.

1797. *See, inter alia,* 'Antitrust: Commission opens investigation into possible anticompetitive conduct by Google in the online advertising technology sector' (European Commission, 22 June 2021) available at https://ec.europa.eu/commission/presscorner/detail/es/ip_21_3143, accessed 22 July 2022; Mike Scarcella, 'Uber, Lyft Drivers Claim Price-Fixing in Lawsuit Against Companies' (Reuters, 21 June 2022) available at https://www.reuters.com/business/autos-transportation/uber-lyft-drivers-claim-price-fixing-lawsuit-against-companies-2022-06-21/, accessed 23 July 2022.

1798. In the *Google Shopping* case, the European Commission had to analyse 1.7 billion search queries. Thibault Schrépel, 'Computational Antitrust: An Introduction and Research Agenda' (2021) 1 Stanford Computational Antitrust 1, 7.

1799. The *Google Shopping* proceedings were opened in 2010. As of July 2022, the decision of the General Court issued in November 2021 was appealed to the European Court of Justice. *See* 'Competition Policy: AT.39740 Google Search (Shopping)' (European Commission) available at https://ec.europa.eu/competition/elojade/isef/case_details.cfm?proc_code=1_39740, accessed 20 July 2022.

1800. Antitrust agencies, most notably the European Commission, have routinely fined market players for the provision of inadequate or insufficient information. In the future, the flip-side of this scenario might catch ground: companies subject to antitrust scrutiny appealing antitrust decisions on the basis of incomplete analyses of the data provided.

1801. In response to this, the preferred approach of the European Commission has been to enact new tools fit-for-purpose. However, these tools run the same risks as traditional antitrust instruments: being rendered outdated by developments in the industry. *See,* for instance, Proposal for a Regulation of the European Parliament and of the Council on contestable and fair markets in the digital sector (Digital Markets Act) [2020] COM/2020/842 final.

1802. For an analysis, *see* Jan Eeckhout and Laura Veldkamp, 'Data and Market Power' (May 2022) NBER Working Paper 30022 available at https://www.nber.org/papers/w30022, accessed 15 July 2022.

1803. *See, inter alia,* Nicolas Petit, *Big Tech and the Digital Economy: The Moligopoly Scenario* (Oxford University Press 2020).

[A] What Is Computational Antitrust?

Computational antitrust refers to the use of legal informatics for the automation of antitrust procedures and the improvement of antitrust analyses.[1804] Common examples of legal informatics tools are document management systems, text analysis tools based on natural language processing, and algorithms predicting legal outcomes based on machine learning. Such tools are widely deployed in other fields of law, from the popular legal databases of Westlaw and LexisNexis to the US government's application for assessing compliance with building codes.[1805] Whilst these programs have existed for decades, the implementation of computational tools in antitrust enforcement and compliance has lagged. Computational antitrust has been put on the agenda of the antitrust community only in recent years, most notably by the 'Computational Antitrust' project hosted by Codex, The Stanford Center for Legal Informatics.[1806]

Despite being in its infancy, computational antitrust has transformative potential. This is largely due to a series of characteristics of antitrust law which render it particularly well-suited for computation. First, antitrust procedures are highly protracted[1807] and require the collection, submission and analysis of large bodies of documents. Computational tools have the potential to fully automatise document submission and post-submission document management, clearing up substantial resources for both law firms and competition agencies. Second, antitrust investigations, particularly in digital markets, are increasingly data-intensive. The capacity to process large data sets is crucial not only for ensuring that decisions are rendered in a timely manner but also to safeguard their accuracy. Natural language processing can help analyse sizeable datasets by filtering out key facts, identifying patterns and trends,[1808] and spotting anticompetitive intentions through sentiment analysis.[1809] Third, antitrust investigations rely heavily on measurable inputs, such as market shares or price effects.[1810] In the short term, computational tools can automatise the calculation of these inputs. In the long term, they can lead to more dynamic antitrust analyses that capture a wider array of proxies for market power and look beyond short-term effects.

1804. Thibault Schrépel, 'The Computational Antitrust Project' (Computational Antitrust, Codex: The Stanford Center for Legal Informatics, 2021) https://law.stanford.edu/codex-the-stanford-center-for-legal-informatics/computational-antitrust-project/, accessed 5 July 2022.
1805. 'Building Energy Codes Program' (Office of Energy Efficiency and Renewable Energy) available at https://www.energycodes.gov/rescheck > .
1806. Schrepel, *supra* n. 1798.
1807. Article 102 investigations are currently extremely protracted, with an average duration of more than five years. *See* Frances Dethmers and Jonathan Blondeel, 'EU Enforcement Policy on Abuse of Dominance: Some Statistics and Facts' (2017) 38(4) European Competition Law Review 147, 161.
1808. For an illustration, *see* Felix B. Chang et al., 'Doctrinal Implications of Computational Antitrust' (2021) 1 Stanford Journal of Computational Antitrust 118.
1809. For an application of sentiment analysis to antitrust, *see* Fabiana Di Porto et al., 'I See Something You Don't See: A Computational Analysis of the Digital Services Act and the Digital Markets Act' (2021) 1 Stanford Computational Antitrust 85.
1810. Computational tools can also be leveraged to better understand *how* courts and agencies measure these inputs. *See* Chang et al., *supra* n. 1808.

Computational tools have the potential to revamp antitrust enforcement. However, there are certain limitations to their uses. To begin with, computational tools will never lead to the full automation of antitrust enforcement – and rightly so. Notwithstanding the calculable elements of market shares and the existence of per se rules, antitrust laws are open-ended and require the careful balancing of pro- and anticompetitive effects.[1811] In the foreseeable future, algorithms will not have the power to exhaustively predict and calculate the effects of business conduct in a way which would enable a black-or-white competitive assessment.[1812] This means that a human element will continue to be necessary to assess the data that we have and to decide on the competitive merits of market behaviour. Furthermore, and relatedly, algorithms can only optimise the achievement of clearly established goals. Antitrust laws currently operate with vague standards such as 'substantially lessen competition' or 'significant impediment to effective competition'.[1813] The discussion on goals is also ongoing, and despite the prevalence of the consumer welfare standard, there is still no agreement as to its precise meaning.[1814] Lastly, scholars have raised concerns about the impact of algorithmic law enforcement on due process rights.[1815] Whilst these issues are not specific to computational antitrust, algorithmic decision-making can run afoul of the principles of non-discrimination, transparency, and the duty to give reasons. Nonetheless, these can be avoided through careful programming.[1816] Algorithmic biases are the by-product of human ones, and, contrary to human reasoning, algorithmic decision-making follows a clear structure which can be explained and publicised.[1817]

[B] What Computational Tools Are Currently Used in Antitrust Enforcement?

Computational antitrust is already a reality. Building on a survey carried out by the Stanford Computational Antitrust project in the first quarter of 2022, this section explains what computational tools are currently used by antitrust agencies.[1818] The existing tools can be grouped along three axes: (1) document management systems; (2)

1811. Daniel Crane, 'Antitrust Antitextualism' (2021) 96(3) Notre Dame Law Review 1220.
1812. *See* Schrepel, *supra* n. 1798, 13: 'computational tools (as others) are poorly suited for predicting all forces in the economy'.
1813. *See, inter alia,* Stefan Thomas, 'The Known Unknown: In Search for a Legal Structure of the Significance Criterion of the SIEC Test' (2017) 13(2) Journal of Competition Law & Economics 346.
1814. For a discussion, *see* Herbert Hovenkamp, 'On the Meaning of Antitrust's Consumer Welfare Principle' (Network Law Review, 2020) available at https://www.networklawreview.org/herbert-hovenkamp-meaning-consumer-welfare/, accessed 20 July 2022.
1815. *See, inter alia,* Pedro Rubim Borges Fortes, 'Paths to Digital Justice: Judicial Robots, Algorithmic Decision-Making, and Due Process' (2020) 7(3) Asian Journal of Law and Society 453. For an antitrust-specific account, *see* Cary Coglianese and Alicia Lai, 'Antitrust by Algorithm' (2022) 2 Stanford Computational Antitrust 2.
1816. Schrepel, *supra* n. 1798, 11: 'the process of computation does not have to be a black box (...) after all, computational tools are what we decide to build'.
1817. *Ibid.*
1818. Thibault Schrépel and Teodora Groza, 'The Adoption of Computational Antitrust by Agencies: 2021 Report' (2022) 2 Stanford Computational Antitrust 78.

instruments for the detection of anticompetitive practices; and (3) tools for the enhancement of merger control.

First, competition authorities worldwide are moving towards fully digital archives, as agencies from Argentina to the United Kingdom have digitised their file records. Taking a further step, the Competition Protection Commission of Armenia has integrated its electronic platform with the databases of other state registries, including the tax registry and the business register.[1819] The UK Competition and Markets Authority (CMA) has similarly developed a 'data pipeline' which incorporates the records of all the registered companies from the Companies House.[1820] Alongside integrating external registries, agencies are optimising the management of their records through computational tools. The Australian Competition and Consumer Commission leverages its electronic records by using natural language processing techniques combined with vectorisation and clustering in order to spot groups of similar documents.[1821] The agency has implemented pattern-matching algorithms in order to identify key facts such as phone numbers and credit card numbers across data sets. The switch to electronic records of internal documents is a welcome development which gives case handlers superior access and command of large case files. For the future, agencies are investing in switching to fully digital file submission systems. This development would benefit not only the agencies themselves, but also the law firms representing companies subject to antitrust scrutiny.

Second, antitrust agencies are relying on computational tools in order to detect anticompetitive practices. Solid progress is visible in the area of detecting bid-rigging, where agencies are using data mining and screening techniques in order to detect signs of collusion. Notably, the Brazilian Administrative Council for Economic Defense has already started an investigation that relies entirely on data identified through its mining and screening algorithms.[1822] In the future, we will witness more and more bid-rigging investigations fully reliant on algorithmic data, precisely since the Catalan, Colombian, Czech, and Singaporean agencies have also implemented similar detection tools. Alongside bid rigging, agencies are also leveraging computational tools in order to monitor online prices. The Colombian Superintendence of Industry and Commerce gathers information on pricing practices through bots that mimic the interaction of consumers with online stores.[1823] A similar tool is also used by the Australian agency, enabling the collection of extensive pricing data which can be used both for the detection of collusion and excessive and predatory pricing practices.[1824]

Moving beyond traditional anticompetitive practices, the CMA has targeted its dedicated Data, Technology and Analytics Unit (DaTa) towards understanding novel types of business conduct.[1825] The DaTa unit invests heavily in understanding the role of data in digital advertising, the impact of mobile devices' choice architecture on

1819. *Ibid.*, 81.
1820. *Ibid.*, 112.
1821. *Ibid.*, 82.
1822. *Ibid.*, 83.
1823. *Ibid.*, 86.
1824. *Ibid.*, 82.
1825. *Ibid.*, 112.

consumer behaviour, and the moderation of online reviews by tech platforms like Google and Amazon. In a similar vein, the French Competition Authority has created an algorithm to keep track of the evolution of the terms of service of the main online platforms in order to help case handlers check the compliance of these terms with existing regulations and with any commitments previously made to the agency.[1826]

A notable development in the detection of anticompetitive practices is the increasing reliance on data on ownership structures. In this context, the French and the Czech authorities are jointly developing a program for assessing the risk of collusion on the basis of firms' ownership structures.[1827] The move towards the integration of data on corporate ownership and the analysis of incentives following from ownership patterns is remarkable, as it aligns antitrust enforcement with the recent scholarship on the anticompetitive risks of common ownership and the importance of corporate governance for antitrust compliance.[1828]

Moving on to the final axis, ownership data is also relied on in the field of merger control. The Brazilian agency has developed tools for analysing graphs showing corporate relationships between companies and assessing levels of control.[1829] However, as compared to anticompetitive practices, the implementation of computational tools in merger assessment is underdeveloped. The CMA's DaTa unit offers case support for mergers by assessing technology-focused theories of harm and has also helped streamline the process from document submission to document review.[1830] Nonetheless, given the insular nature of these developments, there is yet no breakthrough progress in merger control.[1831]

[C] What Does the Future Hold?

Existing tools prove that legal informatics have the potential to transform antitrust enforcement and compliance. Whilst current instruments are targeted towards improving the detection of anticompetitive practices and the management and review of file records and data sets, the future of computational antitrust will likely bring improvements in substantive antitrust rules. In the field of merger control, the current system relies on the market shares of the merging parties in order to filter out transactions which do not raise competitive concerns. Furthermore, for the transactions that do meet the relevant thresholds, the competitive analysis draws heavily on static price

1826. *Ibid.*, 93.
1827. DATACROS, 'Developing a Tool to Assess Corruption Risk Factors in Firms' Ownership Structure' available at https://www.transcrime.it/datacros/, accessed 20 July 2022.
1828. *See, inter alia,* José Azar et al., 'Anticompetitive Effects of Common Ownership' (2018) 73(4) Journal of Finance 1513; Florence Thèpot, *The Interaction Between Competition Law and Corporate Governance: Opening the 'Black Box'* (Cambridge University Press 2019).
1829. *Ibid.*, 83.
1830. *Ibid.*, 112.
1831. Albeit undocumented in the report, competition agencies have historically also relied on simulations in merger control. For an overview, *see* Oliver Budzinski and Victoriia Noskova, 'Prospects and Limits of Merger Simulations as a Computational Antitrust Tool' (2022) 2 Stanford Computational Antitrust 57.

effects.[1832] The calls to fine-tune merger control and render it more dynamic might find an answer in computational tools. For instance, Casey and Niblett envisage a future in which the existing merger control regime will be replaced by micro-directives, i.e., highly tailored laws that leverage the predictive power of machine learning algorithms in order to forecast the competitive consequences of proposed transactions.[1833] In order to train the algorithms, developers can rely on data from past transactions – including mergers that did not trigger any notification or review. The inclusion of acquisitions that were not reviewed has game-changing potential, as it can reveal the inadequacy of a system overly reliant on data on market shares. Such analyses of past acquisitions can reveal that large transactions were competitively neutral or even beneficial, whilst mergers that went under the radar have harmed consumers through price increases or reductions in quality.

There are potential improvements in the laws governing unilateral conduct, too. In this field, again, market shares are the main proxies for market power and ultimately dominance. Yet, in data-driven digital ecosystems, access to data on consumer behaviour and control of data bottlenecks can amount to market power, even if these are not reflected in market shares. Whilst traditional market share calculations cannot capture corporate data control, it is envisageable that in the future computational tools will be able to gauge the anticompetitive potential of outsized datasets. Mahari et al. advocate for the introduction of a new proxy for market power: 'data power'.[1834] Once adequate measuring tools will be developed, it is well possible that access to and control of data will become a novel metric of market power.

Ultimately, the purpose of computational tools is to render antitrust faster, more accurate, and more predictable. As more and more data about markets become available – and reviewable by agencies equipped with adequate tools – we will have more and more clarity about which kinds of conduct are anticompetitive. Furthermore, simulation tools will enable the modelling of the effects not only of business conduct but also of antitrust remedies and regulatory interventions.[1835] Given these trends, we can envisage a future in which competition agencies will develop algorithms for screening the bulk of business behaviour and will license them to law firms. In this optimistic scenario, antitrust compliance will become largely a do-it-yourself business, enabling lawyers and law enforcers to dedicate their resources to understanding the most novel and complex types of market behaviour.

1832. This is slowly changing. For instance, in the Dow/DuPont merger decision, the European Commission relied heavily on an innovation theory of harm, moving beyond static price effects. Case M.7392 *Dow/DuPont* (2017). For an analysis, *see* Mats Holmström et al., 'Killer Acquisitions? The Debate on Merger Control for Digital Markets' (2018) Yearbook of the Finnish Competition Law Association available at https://papers.ssrn.com/sol3/papers.cfm?abstract_id=3465454, accessed 20 July 2022.
1833. Anthony J. Casey and Anthony Niblett, 'Micro-Directives and Computational Merger Review' (2021) 1 Stanford Computational Antitrust 132.
1834. Robert Zev Mahari et al., 'Time for a New Antitrust Era: Refocusing Antitrust Law to Invigorate Competition in the 21st Century' 1 Stanford Journal of Computational Antitrust 53.
1835. Jay Himes et al., 'Antitrust Enforcement and Big Tech: After the Remedy Is Ordered' (2021) 1 Stanford Computational Antitrust 65.

CHAPTER 12
Conclusion

Our tour of six competition authorities in Europe is slowly coming to an end. The journey has been varied and fascinating. It might even entail the risk of seducing the authors and readers into becoming eternal travellers. It is good that we have made this journey together, but it is also now time to bring matters to a conclusion. However, the ending can be no more than a snapshot: the digital landscape is constantly changing and enriching itself. The technological, legal and social developments in the digital sector have undeniably gained momentum and we have an interesting future ahead of us. The differences in the situation in the various jurisdictions at the time of finishing the first edition of this book in the second half of 2019 and at the time of finishing the second edition three years later are significant: the number of precedents in all six jurisdictions has grown very substantially since (although Belgium is still lagging behind), and many jurisdictions have introduced specific legislation or are considering this.

The central question in our investigation was how six European competition authorities view and are dealing with digital competition, particularly in their own jurisdictions. In order to answer this question, we have formulated a number of sub-questions which will be answered first below (§12.01). We will then discuss the main bottlenecks identified in our investigation (§12.02). Recommendations will then be given on how to deal with these bottlenecks or how to resolve them (§12.03).

§12.01 ANSWERING RESEARCH QUESTIONS

This book aims to answer the following sub-questions:

(a) How active were the investigated competition authorities in the digital sector during the period under review?
(b) Which regulatory styles and which enforcement instruments were used by the competition authorities investigated during the period under review?

(c) On which companies and topics did the competition authorities focus during the period under review?
(d) What are the similarities and differences in the enforcement action of these competition authorities during the period under review?

Questions (a) and (b) have been answered in §10.01 and §10.02 of the Analysis (Chapter 10respectively. The remaining subchapters of the Analysis have dealt with the various subjects that the authorities under review have investigated. Below, the remaining questions (into the undertakings that were subject to investigations and the similarities and differences in the enforcement action of the various authorities under review) shall be discussed and answered.

[A] On Which Companies and Topics Did the Competition Authorities Focus During the Period under Review?

[1] GAMA Only Received a Minority of the Fines, but the Lion's Share of the Fining Amount

In the previous edition of this book, we noted that national competition authorities fined small companies and that only the Commission fined tech giant Google (the only GAMA (Google, Apple, Meta, Amazon) company fined at the time). Three years later, the Commission has not imposed any additional fines on tech giants while the Dutch competition authority (ACM) and the Autorité have (*see* Figure 12.1). It is no longer only the Commission that challenges the tech giants. Apple has now incurred substantial fines in both the Netherlands and France, no longer making Google the only GAMA company to have been fined during the investigation period.

Figure 12.1 Number of Fining Decisions per Authority (January 2013-July 2022)

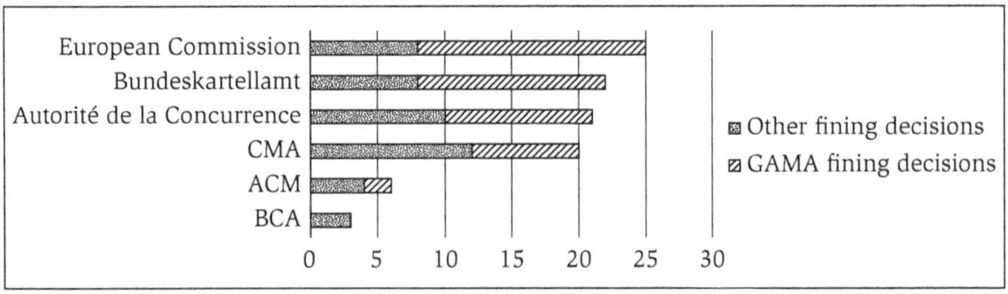

The growing importance of the role of national competition authorities in comparison to the Commission's level of activity is confirmed by the number of investigations opened. All but one of the national competition authorities have opened at least two investigations into conduct by GAMA (*see* Figure 12.2). Many of these investigations are still ongoing. It is therefore not unlikely that the number of fines imposed by national competition authorities will exceed the number of fines on big tech companies imposed by the Commission within the next few years.

Figure 12.2 Number of Investigations Opened per Authority (January 2013-July 2022)

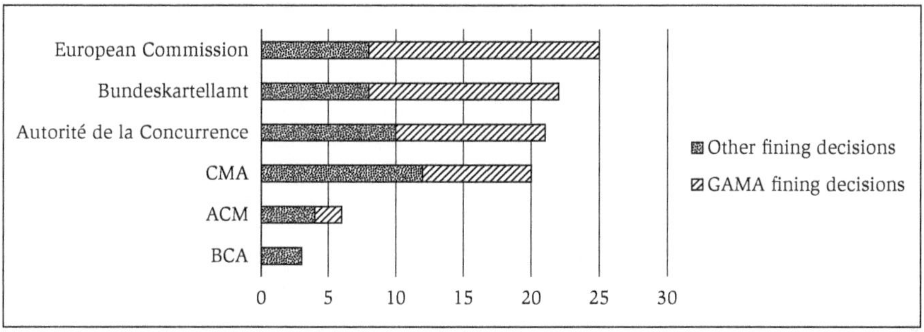

Whether the same will be true in terms of the fining amount, is however much more unlikely. The Commission is responsible for the highest total fining amount by far (Figure 12.3). Only the Autorité has a somewhat similar track record with a total fining amount of more than EUR 2 billion. The other authorities have thus far imposed substantially lower fines or – in the case of the Bundeskartellamt – no fines at all. None of the CMA, BCA, ACM and Bundeskartellamt has a total fining amount that surpasses EUR 0.1 billion (*see* Figure 12.3). GAMA received 95% of the total fining amount.

Figure 12.3 Total Fine Amounts per Authority (GAMA Versus non-GAMA) (January 2013-July 2022)

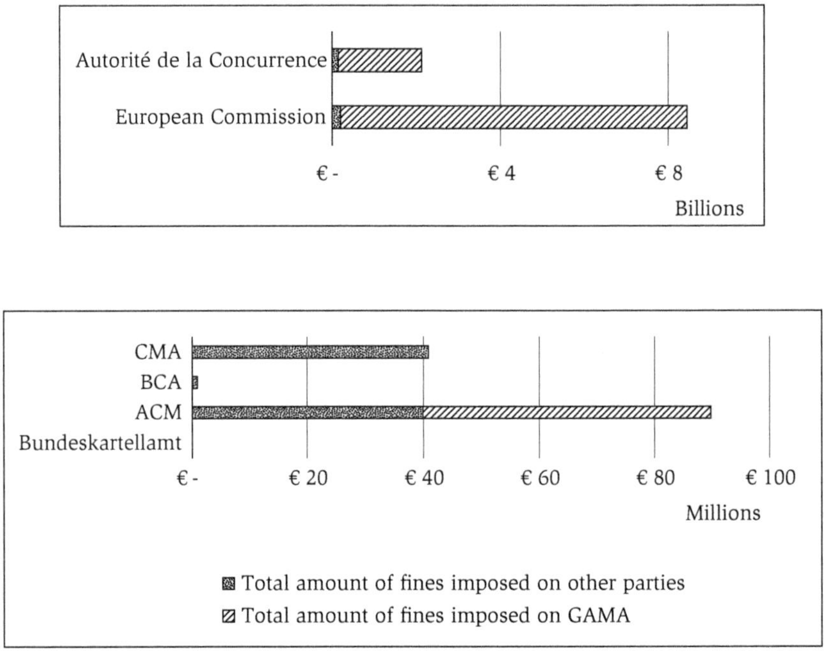

[2] 'Big Tech' Is Still in (Almost) Everyone's Sights

In the previous edition, we noted that big tech was clearly in the sights of the competition authorities under review. This is still true three years later, with the number of yearly decisions addressed to GAMA increasing from only one in 2015 and 2016 to five in 2021 and halfway through 2022 (Figure 12.4). In addition, we count twenty-six pending investigations into GAMA that have been initiated since 2019, showing increased enforcement action against GAMA among the authorities under investigation (Figure 12.5).

Figure 12.4 Decisions Involving GAMA (2013-July 2022)

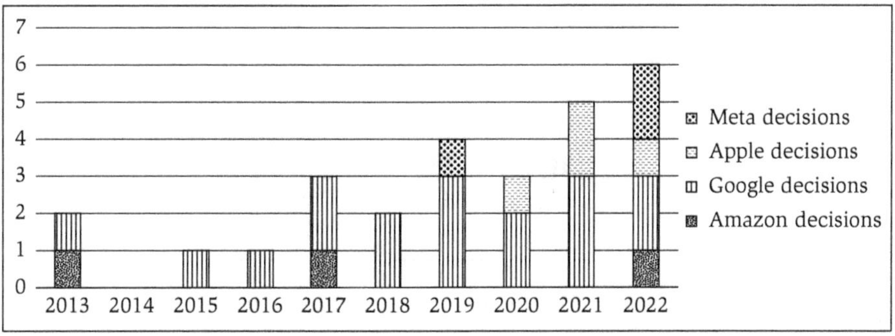

Figure 12.5 Pending Investigations Involving GAMA, by Year of the Start of Investigations (2018-July 2022)

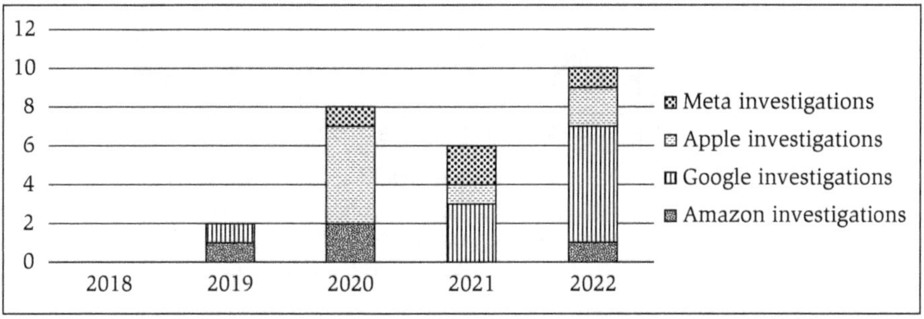

[3] Specific Attention to Certain Online Activities

In the previous edition of this book, we noted that the hotel booking sector and e-commerce received specific attention from the authorities under investigation. This is still true if we look at enforcement action against vertical restrictions, where twenty-two investigations concerned e-commerce, seven online hotel bookings and two audiobooks (*see* Figure 12.6). There was also one investigation into online video games and one into online video. Looking at the number of decisions per year, we see an upward trend from 2013 until 2021 (*see* Figure 12.7). The majority of the decisions relate to e-commerce, while the online hotel booking sector was mostly a priority in the early years under investigation (2013-2015).

Figure 12.6 Top Three Investigations per Activity: Vertical Restrictions (2013-July 2022)

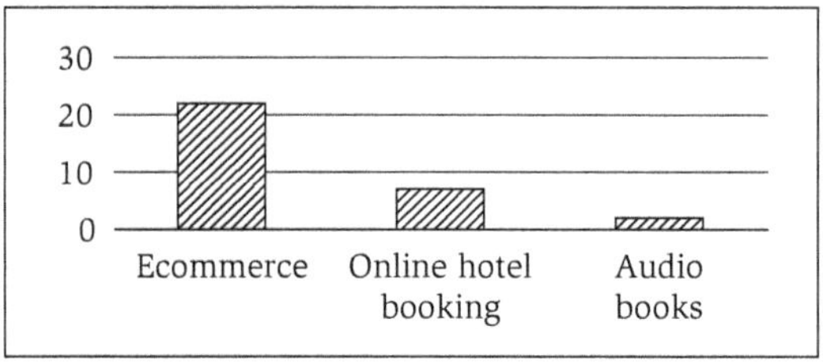

Figure 12.7 Number of Vertical Restrictions Decisions (2013-July 2022)

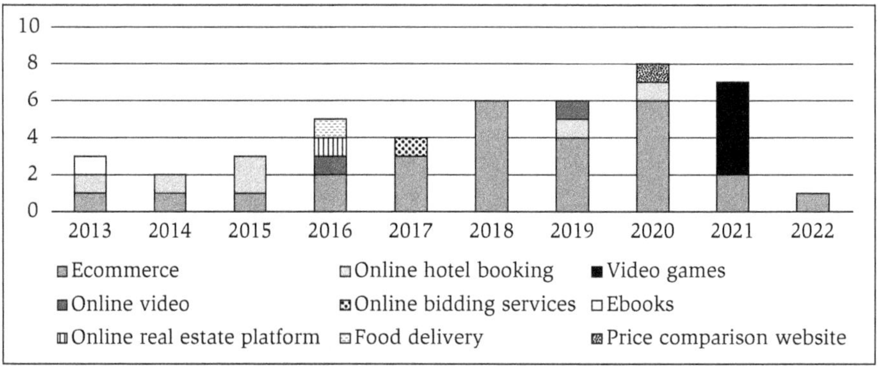

Abuse of dominance investigations has focused on different aspects of the digital economy, mostly targeting online advertising, app stores and software-related practices (Figure 12.8).

Figure 12.8 Top 7 Investigations per Activity: Abuse of Dominance (2013-July 2022)

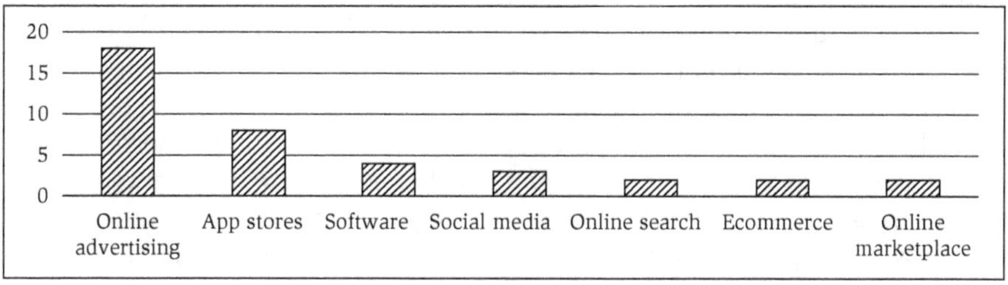

[4] Focus on Digital Platforms and Online Retail Has Led to Renewed Focus on Vertical Agreements

Online digital platforms played a role of at least some importance in almost all cases where the competition authorities took enforcement action during the period under review. Pretty much until the start of the various investigations into the hotel booking sector, competition authorities mainly left the application of vertical competition law to the civil courts, focusing instead on detecting and fining horizontal cartel agreements. The major role that vertical competition law plays in the markets in which digital platforms (including online retailers) operate has, it seems, changed this.

Initially, regulatory action focused on parity clauses (*see* analysis §10.05[A][1]), but in the meantime, the range of subjects has broadened considerably. Platform bans, geoblocking and digital cross-border sales restrictions and resale price maintenance have also been a major concern of the investigated authorities (*see* analysis §10.05[A][2]-§10.05[A][4]).

[5] Big Data

All the authorities investigated have looked into the value of data and the importance of data for the competition process (*see* analysis §10.07). What stands out here is that the thinking about this is becoming much more critical, with the main exponent of this being the Bundeskartellamt's Facebook (now Meta) decision. In that case, the combining and sharing of data between different applications were qualified as an abuse of a dominant position. Officials of the Competition and Markets Authority (CMA) and the Commission have already openly expressed reservations about the relative ease with which they successively approved the acquisitions of two of these applications, Instagram and WhatsApp. More generally, it is clear that the role and value of data are increasingly subject to critical scrutiny in the context of merger control.

[6] Algorithms Are on Everyone's Mind, Actual Cases Are Rare

Possible violations of competition law by or with the help of algorithms remain a hot topic. However, the enforcement harvest during the investigated period is relatively limited. The most important precedent is still the CMA decision in Online Sales of Posters and Frames from 2016, which is extensively discussed in the UK chapter of this book and in which a fine was imposed for a cartel that was implemented using an algorithm. Although perhaps understandable in the light of the fact that the undertakings concerned in this case were rather small, the policy choice not to examine the role of the software supplier as a cartel facilitator for reasons of prioritisation may be a less fortunate one from the perspective of legal development.

The Commission's decisions imposing fines on consumer electronics suppliers are also interesting. The relevant press release states that algorithms were used to monitor the vertical price agreements, and it follows from the Commission's decisions that software and price comparison websites indeed played an important role in strengthening the effective operation of resale price maintenance in these cases. It also follows from the decisions that the manufacturers' intervention in the commercial practices of the most competitive retailers had an impact on the prices of other retailers because of the widespread use of pricing algorithms among retailers.

The third case in which algorithms took centre stage was the Bundeskartellamt's short-lived investigation into Lufthansa. The Bundeskartellamt investigated whether Lufthansa, using algorithms, abusively increased ticket prices following the bankruptcy of its competitor Air Berlin. Mundt argued in the context of this case: '*Solche Algorithmen werden ja nicht im Himmel vom lieben Gott geschrieben*' [freely translated: 'Such algorithms did not drop from the sky'] and that Lufthansa '*sich nicht hinter Algorithmen verstecken [könnte]*' [freely translated: '*cannot hide behind algorithms*'].

In 2022, ACM chairman Snoep said that algorithmic collusion was the ACM's biggest concern and that they're behind the pace of developments set by market players: '*So far, we haven't come across actual algorithmic collusion in the marketplace but [that's] probably the area of biggest concern to us, that that will happen and also because it will be so ... incredibly difficult to detect [...] We are ... a little bit behind the development[s]. I don't think that is bad. I think it's good to let market forces and the markets develop first freely and then see whether there is a need for intervention into the market rather than the other way around.*'[1836]

In its 2021 decision regarding Samsung, the ACM paid attention to the fact that algorithms were used for monitoring retailers' prices (*see* the chapter on the ACM).

In view of the broad attention that the subject is currently receiving and despite the difficulty of detecting algorithmic collusion, it seems likely that the number of precedents in which algorithms play a crucial role will increase in the coming years. The successful development of technology will undoubtedly also contribute to this.

1836. MLex, 'Algorithmic collusion 'biggest concern' for Dutch competition enforcer, Snoep says', speech of M. Snoep at 'Blockchain + The Law' conference, Amsterdam Law & Technology Institute, 3 February 2022.

[7] *Written Policy Rules Are Scarce but Shaping Up*

Written policy rules were barely discernible at the time of writing the first edition of this book. This has changed, as competition authorities have updated their policy guidelines for vertical and horizontal agreements. The Bundeskartellamt and the European Commission have issued four individual guidance letters regarding cooperation between companies active in digital markets. In the field of abuse of dominance, there still is a lack of guidance for the tech sector. This will be discussed in more detail when discussing the bottlenecks.

[B] What Are the Similarities and Differences in the Enforcement Action of These Competition Authorities During the Period under Review?

The main similarities and differences in the policies of the authorities under investigation that have been found are the following.

[1] *Enforcement Styles Vary Considerably from Authority to Authority and the Level of Enforcement Is Increasing*

As indicated above, the enforcement styles of the various European competition authorities vary widely, in terms of content, method and frequency of enforcement. The main similarity is that the level of enforcement is still growing. Most enforcement precedents date from 2018 and onwards. The Belgian Competition Authority (BCA) is the only authority that has not taken any enforcement action against a big tech company (situation September 2022). The CMA and the ACM, who have often expressed hesitation to enforce and relied on the market's ability to regulate itself, have now also started several investigations into big tech companies' behaviour and – in the case of the ACM – also imposed fines. The Bundeskartellamt is unique in only prohibiting conduct without imposing fines.

[2] *Few Cartel Decisions and Fines*

Cartel enforcement against traditional cartels has thus far lagged behind enforcement against vertical restrictions and abuse of dominance infringements. During the research period, there have been only four cartel decisions against thirty abuse of dominance decisions and forty-five vertical restrictions decisions. The reasons behind these statistics are far from evident. There could be various causes for this finding, which are not mutually exclusive. Tech markets are typically dynamic markets, while cartels tend to occur more often in rigid, mature markets. Therefore, there simply may be relatively few cartels in the tech sector. On the other hand, there could also be some level of underenforcement. As becomes evident from this book, enforcement has had a strong focus on abuse of dominance cases throughout the research period (and in particular in the last few years thereof). Abuses of dominance investigations are directed against the largest and most powerful undertakings on the market and usually involve substantial consumer interest and (potential) harm. It is therefore very well conceivable that competition authorities may have prioritised enforcement of dominance cases over tracking down potential cartels. In this respect, it is also likely that the substantial number of complaints (*see* §12.01[B][5] below) is partially responsible for the large number of dominance investigations in the tech sector that the authorities under review have launched over the research period. The number of strong leads for cartel cases that competition authorities received over the research period has undoubtedly been much smaller, also because competition law enforcement has witnessed a substantial decline in the number of leniency applications (most likely due to the simultaneous rise of a civil damages claims culture) in the past years. The renewed interest in agreements between big tech companies, as evidenced by the European Commission's and CMA's investigation into the 'Jedi Blue' agreement between Google and Meta, may however mark the start of more enforcement relating to horizontal agreements.[1837]

[3] Relatively Few Fines Compared to the Number of Enforcement Precedents

With regard to the above, it is interesting that – apart from the billions in fines for Google and Apple in the EU and France – the investigated authorities have remained relatively mild in the use of fines against other Big Tech (GAMA) companies. In many cases, bans or the acceptance of commitments or informally induced behavioural changes were sufficient and no fine was issued. Only 26% of the abuse of dominance decisions led to a fine, while 69% of vertical restrictions decisions led to a fine. It should be noted, however, that an enforced change in behaviour can indeed already be painful and costly for a company, even if the enforcement order is not accompanied by a(n) unconditional penalty. For example, a cease and desist order can also call into question similar behaviour from the same or other undertakings, and thus cause a 'radiation effect'. In that respect, there is much to be said in favour of a cautious use of fines in complex cases in rapidly developing and innovative digital markets. The strongest exponent of this view is of course the Bundeskartellamt, which has so far made the policy choice not to impose any fines in digital markets at all (at least in abuse of dominance cases).

[4] Authorities Are Studying Hard, but Remain Searching

Apart from the BCA, all the investigated authorities have set up special teams for digital competition, which include data scientists. The CMA is the frontrunner in this respect, with its Data, Technology and Analytics unit consisting of almost fifty people led by

1837. European Commission, Google-Meta (Open Bidding) agreement (2022); CMA, Google/Meta – header bidding (Jedi Blue) (2022).

Stefan Hunt.[1838] Apart from (once again) the BCA, all the investigated authorities have also invested in market studies, in particular – although certainly not exclusively – in the earlier years of the research period. This has led to follow-up enforcement action on many occasions and to new guidelines for vertical and horizontal agreements, but guidelines for digital platforms are still lacking. This is probably due to the fact that the authorities' role is to follow the fast-moving digital markets and therefore inherently they are a little behind the curve. Enforcement of new gatekeeper rules in the EU and Germany will compel the authorities in these jurisdictions to look ahead, requiring even more knowledge of digital markets.

In the latter respect, it can already be observed that authorities are increasingly engaging in joint studies and publications, best practices and conferences – both inside and outside formal networks such as the European Competition Network (ECN). If they were to increase these efforts, this development could become a game changer, possibly enabling the authorities to really get 'on top of things'. Most likely, that would require a less obligation-free approach. For example, it may be possible for the authorities to achieve substantial efficiencies by pooling resources and dividing focus areas and individual cases between them.

[5] Complaining Pays Off, but Unclear How Many Complaints Are Rejected

Complaints have played an important role in the initiation of investigations by the authorities under investigation. The majority of the abuse of dominance enforcement procedures described in this book was initiated by complaints. Complaints thus appear to be a good means for market players to steer authorities to some extent in their search described above and to focus attention on what they consider to be the problems in the digital market. Authorities are, however, not very transparent about the number of complaints they receive and about the reasons for rejecting complaints. The Autorité is an exception, as it has published the largest number of rejection decisions among the authorities under investigation.

[6] Merger Control Is Not (Yet) the Tool of Choice to Tackle Digital Competition Problems, but This May Change

There are significant differences in the number and types of merger control decisions (with competitive concerns) taken by each authority (*see* Chapter 10, Analysis, Introduction). It is no coincidence that most merger reviews have been conducted in the UK (24 until July 2022), where the rules for claiming jurisdiction over a merger are more flexible than in jurisdictions on the continent. The EU's new Article 22 EU Merger Regulation (EUMR) referral policy as described in §10.04[D] above might be a turning point but has so far not led to any digital competition mergers being called in that did

1838. CMA, 'The technology-led transformation of competition and consumer agencies: The Competition and Markets Authority's experience', discussion paper, 14 June 2022.

not meet the thresholds in any EU country (although the Bundeskartellamt only claimed jurisdiction over the *Meta/Kustomer* case after that case had already been referred to the Commission by various other national competition authorities; *see* §10.03[E]). Only the CMA has blocked mergers,[1839] four authorities have imposed behavioural remedies and five have conducted an in-depth (phase II) investigation into a digital competition merger. The CMA (4),[1840] the Commission (5)[1841] and the Bundeskartellamt[1842] have investigated acquisitions made by GAMA during the investigation period, but this is only a fraction of the hundreds of acquisitions that GAMA made during the period under investigation.[1843] A noticeable parallel in merger cases is that the authorities are critically investigating the value of data, interoperability standards and service quality concerns as well as the harm a merger may do to innovation. There is, however, neither an upward trend in behavioural remedies decisions (eight in total, spread out over five years) to address these concerns nor a steep upward trend in prohibition decisions during the investigation period (three in total, spread out over three years). The behavioural remedies that were imposed served to ensure access to the services or data of the merged entity after the merger or to ensure that the merged entity continued the supply of services on fair and reasonable terms after the merger.

§12.02 BOTTLENECKS

Our investigation leads us to identify nine bottlenecks:

(1) lack of uniformity in enforcement;
(2) uncertainty about technological developments and insufficient understanding and consensus regarding the key problems and challenges;
(3) inherent knowledge gap of competition authorities in the tech sector;
(4) lack of precedents and case law;

1839. During the investigation period these were: ME/6806/19, 9 April 2020 (Sabre/ Farelogix); ME/6752/18, 25 April 2019 (Sainsbury/Asda); ME/6891/20, 30 November 2021 (Facebook/Giphy). After the cut-off date of our research, the CMA also prohibited the acquisition of Activision Blizzard by Microsoft on 24 April 2023, *see* press release: https://www.gov.uk/government/news/microsoft-activision-deal-prevented-to-protect-innovation-and-choice-in-cloud-gaming.

1840. ME/6839/19, 13 February 2020 (Google/Looker Data Sciences); ME/6836/19, 4 August 2020 (Amazon/Deliveroo); ME/6891/20, 29 March 2022 (Facebook/Giphy); ME/6920/20, 27 September 2020 (Facebook/Kustomer).

1841. M.10262, 27 January 2022 (Facebook/Kustomer); M.9660, 11 May 2021 (Google/Fitbit); M.8788, 12 November 2018 (Apple/Shazam); M.7217, 3 October 2014 (Facebook/WhatsApp); M.7290, 7 August 2014 (Apple/Beats).

1842. Bundeskartellamt, 'Pressemitteilung: Freigabe der Übernahme von Kustomer durch Meta (ehemals Facebook)' (11 February 2022, *Bundeskartellamt/Digitalwirtschaft*) https://www.bundeskartellamt.de/SharedDocs/Publikation/DE/Pressemitteilungen/2022/11_02_2022_Meta_Kustomer.pdf?__blob=publicationFile&v=2 p. 1.

1843. Digital Competition Expert Panel, 'Unlocking Digital Competition' (Furman Report), March 2019 and G. Parker, G. Petropoulos and M. Van Alstyne, 'Platform Mergers and Antitrust', Bruegel Working Paper, 15 June 2021.

(5) competition law in itself does not offer solutions for all problems; the relationship with other fields of law (in particular privacy law) and the competent authorities for these fields of law is insufficiently clear and there is an insufficient interdisciplinary cooperation between authorities;
(6) no harmonisation of new legislation and additional enforcement instruments;
(7) lack of guidance;
(8) lack of sufficient cooperation on a global scale; and
(9) lack of balance in opinions about 'big tech'.

We will discuss each of these bottlenecks below.

[A] Lack of Uniformity in Enforcement

The numerous differences in the area of competition enforcement in terms of content and style are the first major bottleneck. A lack of uniform enforcement can lead to legal uncertainty and unequal treatment of companies. This is all the more pressing in the digital economy, where, as a rule, undertakings operate in several countries or worldwide. Digital markets call for a more harmonised approach. During the period under review, this was often absent, both in substantive terms and in the manner and degree of enforcement.

Compared to the previous edition, new guidance for vertical agreements between companies has been published in the EU and the UK, as well as new draft guidance for horizontal agreements. This is an important development that may be expected to lead to more uniformity in enforcement. However, numerous difficulties remain.

When it comes to vertical agreements, the Bundeskartellamt however remains out of step with other European authorities. It is still applying a one-to-one transposition of its traditionally restrictive policy on vertical agreements to digital markets. The discrepancy between the Bundeskartellamt's approach to narrow parity clauses and those of the other authorities is significant, potentially giving rise to serious issues for platforms operating across borders (*see* §10.05[A]). To take the concrete example of the online hotel booking business, the Bundeskartellamt's win at the Federal Supreme Court means that online hotel booking platforms operating in Germany need to remove their narrow parity clauses or, at least, bring them in line with the judgment. This will quite conceivably also affect the online hotel booking platforms' position outside Germany. Moreover, unlike the other investigated authorities, the Bundeskartellamt has, even after the ECJ's *Coty* judgment, continued to espouse the position that there is never any real justification for platform bans. It seems almost inevitable that the Bundeskartellamt will have to nuance its policy, especially in light of the 2022 Commission guidelines for vertical agreements. These guidelines consider (paragraph 335) that platform bans are not hardcore restrictions unless the ban aims at preventing online sales altogether.

The European Commission appears to be reluctant to bring an exploitative abuse of dominance case, or at least has not pursued any in the digital economy. However, the Bundeskartellamt has pursued an exploitative abuse case. The Meta decision, in which combining and sharing user data was considered an exploitative abuse of a dominant position, shows that the Bundeskartellamt is not afraid to take controversial decisions where other authorities may be hesitant. Whether the decision will be upheld, remains to be seen, as the Higher Regional Court of Düsseldorf referred several questions to the ECJ that will be answered most likely some time in 2023. The ECJ's and the subsequent Düsseldorf court's rulings are highly likely to become important precedents. In the UK, there is also more belief in the merit of enforcing against exploitative abuse cases. Meta faces a GBP 2.3 billion standalone claim in the UK Competition Appeal Trial for exploiting personal data of UK citizens.[1844] This is however a case that was initiated by private enforcement and therefore falls outside the scope of this book. The CMA has thus far not pursued any exploitative abuse cases in the digital sector.

Third, in the previous edition, there were no examples of parallel abuse of dominance investigations into the same conduct by different competition authorities. This has changed in a bit more than three years' time. The unprecedented increase in abuse of dominance investigations in most of the jurisdictions under investigation holds a risk that different authorities reach different conclusions about the same conduct. The Apple investigation in the Netherlands coincides with a parallel (pending) EU investigation that may eventually lead to differences in interpretation of the law. From the publicly available information, it appears that these national investigations have been carefully coordinated with the European Commission. It's too early to draw any conclusions, but the European Commission seems to have learned its lesson from the online hotel booking cases ten years ago, where it arguably acted too late to play a meaningful enforcement role and enforcement in this case was exclusively in the hands of the national authorities (which at the time also still included the CMA). The European Commission needs to ensure that national competition authorities within the EU apply the EU competition rules uniformly and may therefore be expected to proactively coordinate antitrust investigations. The introduction of different gatekeeper regimes in the EU, Germany and (possibly) the UK has the risk of contributing to a further lack of uniformity in enforcement (*see also* Bottleneck §12.02[F] below).

The lack of uniformity causes a drag on the operation of tech companies and on the functioning of the EU internal market, and this will only increase if more differences in enforcement policy arise in the various EU Member States. Booking.com has, of course, experienced this first hand in the context of parity clauses and has called the intervention of European competition authorities regarding these parity clauses 'unfortunate' and 'a clear example to avoid'.[1845] Booking.com recommended: 'it is essential that close cooperation between authorities takes place but also that there is a uniform interpretation and application of the competition rules when it comes to digital markets/platforms'. In practical terms, this means that authorities need to coordinate with each other on issues relevant to digital markets, such as distinguishing different

1844. BBC, 'Meta faces billion-pound class-action case', 14 January 2022.
1845. Booking.com, A contribution to 'Shaping competition policy in the era of digitisation', 2018, https://ec.europa.eu/competition/information/digitisation_2018/contributions/booking.pdf.

types of multisided platforms, distinguishing and defining the different markets affected by platforms, the way in which markets are defined, the determination of market power (including the role of multi-homing, single-homing and tipping effects), foreclosure effects, efficiencies and vertical restraints. Authorities should do this at the earliest possible stage, coordinating their market monitoring and sector inquiries.

[B] Uncertainty about Technological Developments (Collingridge Dilemma) and Insufficient Understanding and Consensus about the Main Problems and Challenges

With the rapid development of technological progress, it is not entirely clear to what extent and in which direction technological developments will change our society, at what rate, and to what extent these developments will have positive and negative effects on (among other things) competition and the structure of the market. European competition authorities currently have different views on competition issues and different priorities in the digital sector, and this may increase as technological developments evolve. This in turn may result in an enforcement deficit (authorities do not see that there is a problem and therefore do not act or act too late) or an enforcement surplus (authorities 'hunt' for problems that simply do not exist or may solve themselves without intervention). The former situation leads to undesirable distortions of competition (and thus, according to economic theory, to a loss of wealth), while the latter carries the risk of curbing innovation.

For example, in §10.06, the chapter of the analysis devoted to algorithmic collusion, a brief overview is given on the range in which the views of experts differ about what algorithms can and will not be able to do, now and in the near and more distant future. As mentioned in subchapter §10.06[C] of the Analysis on algorithmic collusion, Ezrachi and Stucke have taken the position that algorithms already encourage the flattening of price competition (and this effect will take on ever greater proportions), but Schrépel on the other hand objects that there is no empirical evidence for this. He therefore takes the view that an effective approach to undesirable market behaviour of algorithms can be realised through a combination of review and application of the current competition rules. More recently, Calzolari has likewise argued that algorithmic collusion should be distinguished from tacit collusion. In the case of tacit collusion, undertakings use the existing market conditions, whereas, in the case of algorithmic collusion, undertakings contribute to the market conditions that allow tacit collusion to take place. Algorithmic collusion should, therefore, be regarded as a concerted practice. Accordingly, as undertakings develop algorithms, they would knowingly contribute to creating a situation on the market in which their rational algorithms are likely able to collude (and thus be caught by Article 101 TFEU and its national counterparts).

Other competition issues that are closely related to technological progress – and that the Digital Markets Act (DMA) is meant to regulate at the EU level – relate to self-preferencing and interoperability. In subchapter §11.03 of this book chapter on Game Changers, Colangelo observes in relation to the former topic that, in the aftermath of the *Google Shopping* ruling and despite the intense level of enforcement by courts and antitrust authorities, doubts about characteristics and boundaries of self-preferencing are still on the table, and a legal test distinguishing such purported new antitrust offence from other practices aimed at pursuing leveraging strategies and already addressed by antitrust rules is still missing. He further believes that the upcoming entry into force of the DMA will not clarify these doubts. He observes in this respect that the DMA represents a regulatory intervention aimed at protecting a different legal interest from antitrust rules (i.e., to ensure that markets, where gatekeepers are present, are and remain contestable and fair, independently from the actual, likely or presumed effects of the conduct of a given gatekeeper). He therefore sees the DMA as complementary to traditional antitrust rules and believes these shall remain applicable and relevant, although their application should not affect the obligations imposed on gatekeepers under the DMA.

If there is no broad consensus on the current state of the art, how can competition authorities be expected to adapt their policies to future developments? This is a diabolical dilemma as described by David Collingridge.[1846] He indicates that efforts to control technology are facing two problems: one of information and one of control. The information problem is that the impact of technology (and thus the need for regulation) only becomes clear once its use becomes widespread. The control problem is that control or regulation of technology becomes more difficult as its use becomes widespread. David Collingridge has expressed the dilemma as follows: 'When change is easy, the need for it cannot be foreseen; when the need for change is apparent, change has become expensive, difficult and time-consuming.'

It could be argued that a sensible competition authority should wait for technological developments to materialise before intervening. The BCA seems to be an outspoken exponent of this thinking, which we also found in a more nuanced form with the ACM at the time when Chris Fonteijn was still its chairman. However, since Martijn Snoep took the helm in 2018, the ACM has clearly become more interventionist. At the same time, competition authorities are increasingly afraid of intervening late or insufficiently, as many digital technologies are now widespread and widely used and are causing the structure of the market to change. The notion appears to be: if we wait too long, it might be too late. Then the harmful effects of certain digital technologies may have already taken hold and have become difficult to undo. This is the best way of describing the attitude of the Autorité, the Commission, the Bundeskartellamt and increasingly the CMA, who did not hesitate to act (and to act toughly) against big tech. The latter two authorities have (or soon will have) also been given additional tools to strike swiftly, with the introduction of Article 19a GWB in Germany and the DMA in the EU. Still, enforcement of new gatekeeper rules in the EU and Germany will not make all things easier from a technological perspective as it compels the authorities to look ahead, requiring them to gather even more knowledge of digital markets.

1846. D. Collingridge, *The Social Control of Technology* (Frances Pinter 1980).

[C] Inherent Knowledge Gap of Competition Authorities in the Tech Sector

The next bottleneck flows seamlessly from the previous one. Although competition authorities are increasingly hiring technology specialists and are investing in increased cooperation and the sharing of best practices, they are not – and never will become – technology companies themselves. The CMA is the frontrunner in this respect, but its Data, Technology and Analytics unit still consists of 'only' fifty people. Generally speaking, successful technology companies are able to offer their staff top-of-the-market conditions and challenging work and are thus well placed to attract the top of the skills market. This is something that competition authorities cannot do or can only do to a significantly lesser extent, in particular in terms of remuneration. Large tech companies also have large, often increasing amounts of technical and commercial knowledge and valuable data. Of course, the competition regimes of the jurisdictions under investigation do not automatically give competition authorities access to all this technology, knowledge and data. The proportionality principle requires that they can only demand the surrender of this information if there is a legitimate interest (such as a concrete suspicion of a breach of competition law, a merger notification or a sector investigation). We would certainly not wish to call this principle into question.

However, this situation does present a challenge for authorities (and, in a more general sense, society at large). By definition, big tech has a head start in terms of knowledge. Technology companies themselves know best what technology, data and users they have and what they can do with these resources. Therefore, they possess an inherent lead in knowledge over the authorities. Technology companies will always be earlier in knowing what is coming and what will be technically possible in the (near) future. In principle, competition authorities can 'merely' study and observe the market and are therefore forced to play a reactive role. Competition authorities are to some extent dependent on information from others. For the time being, complaints and market research are usually the starting point for enforcement action in digital markets.[1847]

The course of events surrounding Facebook's (currently Meta) acquisitions of WhatsApp and Instagram illustrate how competition authorities appear to lag behind. During the notification procedure for its intended acquisition of WhatsApp, Meta informed the Commission that it was not technically possible to reliably and automatically link Facebook and WhatsApp accounts (and thus share data between both applications). However, some three years later, that statement turned out to be incorrect: linking accounts was already technically possible at the time of the notification in 2014, although it would take until 2016 before Meta would actually proceed to do so. The Commission imposed a fine on Facebook when it discovered this. However, this infringement procedure had no consequences for the clearance granted, since the Commission's clearance decision also addressed the scenario that accounts would be

1847. Of course, leniency applications can also give rise to an enforcement procedure (during the investigation period, this was the case in the CMA's Online Sale of Posters and Frames case).

linked and where the Commission still saw sufficient room for competition. However, the combining of data has caused competition problems in the eyes of other authorities. The Bundeskartellamt subsequently prohibited the combination of user data from (among others) WhatsApp with Facebook on account of abuse of a dominant position. In the US, the Federal Trade Commission (FTC) demands the divestiture of Instagram and WhatsApp in a lawsuit against Meta introduced in 2020. The CMA also appeared to have second thoughts about its rapid clearance of the acquisition of Instagram by Facebook, yet another application in respect of which the Bundeskartellamt prohibited the combination of user data and Facebook data. Irrespective of the question of whether the decision of the Bundeskartellamt is legally sound and will ultimately stand up in court, one could argue that Facebook could not have merged user data to the same extent (and thus, in the eyes of the Bundeskartellamt, probably could not have abused its dominant position to the same extent) if it had not been allowed to successively incorporate Instagram and WhatsApp. The Bundeskartellamt explicitly takes the perspective of the consumer into account in its conclusion that the abuse consists of the exploitation of consumers.

The Facebook case is perhaps the clearest example of developing insights (and perhaps even doubts or regret of earlier decisions) among competition authorities after gaining more knowledge about the functioning of companies and digital markets. Nonetheless, it is certainly not the only example, nor will it be the last one. The Autorité has, for example, addressed self-preferencing by Google in the market for ad servers for publishers of websites and mobile apps. Google's dominance in this market traces back to the European Commission's 2008 clearance decision in Google/DoubleClick, which a former top executive later described as a 'total game changer' and is generally considered a key step in Google's global dominance in online advertisement.[1848] Keeping (as far as possible) up-to-date with the technology sector in terms of technological and market knowledge is thus clearly one of the biggest challenges (if not the biggest challenge) that competition authorities will face in the coming years. Compared to the first edition of this book, authorities now have a more technological capacity to analyse digital markets and are investing in increased cooperation and the sharing of best practices. For example, the CMA conducted an in-house big data analysis of all of the search events (more than 3 billion) seen by Google and Bing in a one-week period in the UK in the context of their market study into digital advertising.

[D] Lack of Precedents and Case Law Is Diminishing, but There Are Still Many Unclarities

In total, only twenty-two enforcement decisions and twenty relevant merger decisions were taken by the investigated European competition authorities during the period under investigation at the time of finishing the first edition of this book. At the time of

1848. The New York Times, '*This Deal Helped Turn Google into an Ad Powerhouse. Is That a Problem?*', 21 September 2020 and The Wall Street Journal, '*How Google Edged out Rivals and Built the World's Dominant Ad Machine: A Visual Guide*', 7 November 2019.

finishing the second edition, the number of precedents has increased substantially to seventy-nine enforcement decisions and fifty-five relevant merger decisions. Nonetheless, the precedents that have been established are not unambiguous and many legal questions remain unexplored. Companies in the digital sector as well as their trading partners and consumers are therefore still faced with uncertainty about what behaviour is or is not permitted. This may put a brake on innovation by giving rise to hesitation about cooperating with other undertakings. It may also give rise to competition law infringements out of ignorance (*see also* more in detail bottleneck §12.02[G] below).

Although our investigation has focused on the enforcement by competition authorities (and the – as yet still fragmented – case law resulting from litigation against these decisions) and has not looked systematically at the other (particularly civil law) case law involving digital competition, it would appear that the case law that does exist is limited and insufficiently uniform. There now exists domestic case law in various countries on parity clauses and platform bans, and differences are becoming apparent between (*inter alia*) the case law in the Netherlands and the case law in Germany (*see* analysis §10.05 on platform bans). There is still relatively little European case law, although the judgments of the Court of Justice of the European Union (CJEU) in Eturas[1849] and Coty[1850] may contribute to uniform enforcement of competition law in the digital sector, also in the Member States. For example, the Autorité refers to Coty in substantiating its decision to impose a fine on Stihl and allowing a total ban on online sales via third-party websites. It is worth noting that both these judgments were delivered because of preliminary ruling procedures. By asking preliminary questions, a national court thus seems to be (able to) partly fill the gap left by the competition authorities (although it is important to note that the preliminary questions in Eturas were asked following a decision by the Latvian competition authority to impose a fine, the Coty judgment originated from civil proceedings). A highly anticipated judgment relating to a request for a preliminary ruling will come with the answering of the BGH's questions to the ECJ in the preliminary ruling to be delivered regarding the Facebook case.

The number of enforcement cases in the jurisdictions investigated has increased exponentially, particularly since 2018. The bottleneck of there being insufficient precedents and case law could therefore probably be the only identified bottleneck that might resolve itself (to a certain extent) with the passage of sufficient time. However, as technological developments continue to move at an enormous pace, it would appear inevitable that new uncertainties will continue to pop up, with precedents and case law inevitably lagging behind. As indicated, this process is already starting to occur up to a certain extent.

1849. Case C-74/14 *'Eturas' UAB and Others v. Lietuvos Respublikos konkurencijos taryba* [2016] ECLI:EU:C:2016:42.

1850. Case C-230/16 *Coty Germany GmbH v. Parfümerie Akzente GmbH* [2017] ECLI: EU:C:2017:941.

[E] Competition Law Does Not Offer Solutions for All Problems, the Relationship with Other Fields of Law (in Particular Privacy Law, Platform-Specific Regulation, and Consumer Law) and the Competent Authorities for These Fields of Law Is Insufficiently Clear

Competition law is not a panacea for the digital sector, just as it is not for more traditional sectors. Competition authorities are not equipped to deal with all harmful effects of digital technologies. Sometimes other authorities are better positioned, and other fields of law are more appropriate for tackling certain undesirable behaviour – even with the advent of new, sector-specific legislation in various investigated jurisdictions and debate about introducing such legislation in others. This, of course, is more of a blessing than a curse, and certainly not a problem as such. However, it may become a problem if other fields of law produce outcomes that are conflicting with the outcome under competition law, thereby causing authorities to take conflicting decisions, contest each other's jurisdiction and cause double enforcement or no enforcement at all because the one authority is waiting for the other to act and vice versa.

Data protection law plays a role of at least equal importance as competition law when it comes to, for example, the management and sharing of large amounts of personal data. Legislation and regulations on liability for AI, consumer protection and protection of small- and medium-sized enterprises are also often highly relevant in this context. The initiatives for adopting such legislation are on the rise. In this context, the European Parliament's recommendations on civil law rules on robotics and the Commission's policymaking on AI and platform-to-business commercial practices are the first to deserve mentioning.[1851] Moreover, the Commission has published a proposal for a Regulation on Artificial Intelligence, *aka* the AI Act.[1852] This legislative proposal seeks to harmonise the EU Member States' approach regarding the use of artificial intelligence. It should be noted that the AI Act Proposal is partially based on the Commission White Paper on Artificial Intelligence and codifies the principles of trustworthy and secure AI development enshrined in this white paper.[1853] The Commission Staff Working Document 'Liability for emerging digital technologies',[1854] the Commission Regulation 'Promoting Fairness and Transparency for Business Users of

1851. European Parliament resolution of 16 February 2017 with recommendations to the Commission on Civil Law Rules on Robotics 2015/2103(INL) [2017]; for more information regarding this legal instrument, *see*: Aida Ponce, 'A Law on Robotics and Artificial Intelligence in the EU?' (2017) 2 ETUI Research Paper – Foresight Brief 4.
1852. Proposal for a Regulation of the European Parliament and of the Council Laying Down Harmonised Rules On Artificial Intelligence (Artificial Intelligence Act) And Amending Certain Union Legislative Acts COM(2021) 206 final 2021/0106(COD).
1853. White Paper On Artificial Intelligence – A European Approach to Excellence and Trust COM(2020) 65 final [2020].
1854. Commission Staff Working Document Liability for emerging digital technologies Accompanying the document Communication from the Commission to the European Parliament, the European Council, the Council, the European Economic and Social Committee and the Committee of the Regions Artificial intelligence for Europe SWD/2018/137 final.

Online Intermediation Services',[1855] the Commission communication 'Artificial Intelligence for Europe'[1856] and the creation of the European Alliance for AI as part of the Commission AI Strategy also require mentioning.[1857] However, as these initiatives are mainly still in their infancy, it is too early to judge their (potential) ability to mitigate the harmful effects of digital technologies.

Still, the interplay of competition law and privacy law has become particularly clear during the period under review. The Bundeskartellamt's Meta decision, which – after various stages of domestic litigation – led to a request for a preliminary ruling that is still pending, was one of the landmark cases in this respect. The Bundeskartellamt applied not only competition law but also, so it avers, finds that an infringement of the GDPR amounts to an abuse of a dominant position. The final conclusion that the GDPR was indeed infringed was drawn by the Bundeskartellamt itself and not by the privacy authorities (who, nonetheless had been informed and consulted in the decision-making process up to a certain extent). In doing so, did the Bundeskartellamt not interfere in the jurisdiction of the data protection authorities? The summary decision states that all German data protection authorities and apparently also several foreign authorities (it is unclear which and how many) were informed. However, only the authorities of the federal state of Hamburg and Ireland appear to have given their opinion on the matter. As regards the other authorities, the Bundeskartellamt seems to have applied the adage 'silence means consent'. This state of affairs does raise questions. What information did the Bundeskartellamt provide on its investigation and to whom? Were the competent data protection authorities given sufficient time to respond? Were they also in a position to comment on the preliminary findings of the Bundeskartellamt (insofar as they relate to their policy area)? If so, did they agree (by a majority)?

[F] No Consensus on the Nature of Additional Enforcement Instruments and No Harmonisation of New Legislation

Another issue that emerges from the investigation is the question of whether competition authorities need new powers to deal with technological developments and the inherent knowledge deficit identified under bottleneck 3. When we published the first edition of this book, this discussion was just getting started and the outcome of the debate was highly uncertain. At the time of finishing the second edition of this book in the spring of 2023, there appears to be a consensus that indeed, new enforcement tools are required to cope with the particularities of digital markets – in particular where large online platforms are concerned.

1855. Communication from the Commission Artificial Intelligence for Europe {SWD(2018) 137 final} COM(2018) 237 final [2018].
1856. *Ibid.*
1857. European Commission, 'The European AI Alliance' (*European Commission*, 2018) https://digital-strategy.ec.europa.eu/en/policies/european-ai-alliance#: ~ :text = The%20European%20AI%20Alliance%20is,consultations%20and%20online%20forum%20exchanges.

As described in detail in subchapter §10.03 of the Analysis, new legislation targeted directly at the digital sector has been introduced in the EU (the DMA and the DSA) and Germany (Article 19a GWB). The French and Belgian rules on economic dependence are also of particular relevance for the tech sector. In the UK and the Netherlands, the introduction of new legislation is being anticipated.

As also described in subchapter §10.03 of the Analysis, there are however important differences in the legislation. The DMA enables the Commission to impose a fixed set of rules on large gatekeeper platforms. The German rules under Article 19a GWB provide more flexibility, both with regard to the undertakings that may be subjected to their application as well as with regard to the remedies that may be imposed. On the other hand, the designation of companies subject to Article 19a GWB is more complex in comparison to the DMA. The French and Belgian rules apply only in a situation of economic dependence, and not exclusively to the digital sector. Time will tell eventually which system will be most successful in dealing with the various challenges of competition law and policy enforcement in the digital sector if at all it will prove possible to give a clear answer to that question.

In short, there is now a clear consensus that indeed, competition authorities need new enforcement instruments. On the other hand, different solutions are being chosen in the various jurisdictions under review. However, this need not be a problem from the competition authorities' perspective. In procedural terms, competition law in the various EU Member States has never been harmonised and nor is this an objective. On the other hand, if the applicable rules deviate in a material respect from one jurisdiction to another, this could become a nightmare for those companies that are subject to them. Even where tech companies operate on national markets, there will inherently always be some international element to their operations. If they would increasingly be confronted with rules that differ from country to country, that could seriously hamper their operations.

Hence, it is important that these different systems shall not lead to contradictory enforcement measures or double jeopardy situations in the same or similar cases in the various jurisdictions under investigation. As the first bottleneck, we already identified a lack of uniformity in enforcement when it comes to enforcement of the regular competition rules. Now that the various jurisdictions under investigation are introducing specific legislation that differs significantly, the risk of conflicting enforcement policies or decisions will only increase.

[G] Lack of Guidance

Finally, there is too little (joint) guidance on which types of market cooperation and behaviour in digital markets are permitted and which types are not. However, the Commission and the CMA both have updated guidelines for vertical agreements and guidelines for horizontal agreements are in the making. These guidelines cover key aspects of the digital economy, including parity clauses, platform bans, geoblocking and data-sharing. The Bundeskartellamt and the European Commission have issued four individual guidance letters regarding cooperation between companies active in digital markets.

Still, there are many areas where there is no or very little guidance. This applies to individual guidance on cooperation agreements between companies, self-preferencing, interoperability standards, the use of pricing algorithms and data access standards. It also applies to how data privacy, security and intellectual property considerations may justify anticompetitive practices by dominant companies. Finally, it applies to which mergers will be scrutinised under the Commission's Article 22 referral policy or the CMA's merger control regime.

This can lead to companies shying away from economically advantageous forms of cooperation or (if they have reason to suspect that they have a dominant position) from implementing a certain economically advantageous one-sided market behaviour. Such under the motto 'err on the side of caution', as companies in such a position of (relative) ignorance have insufficient certainty as to whether the behaviour in question is permitted. This is all the more true where there might be different interpretations of the competition rules in different Member States. This means that a lack of guidance can, on the one hand, slow down innovation: economically desirable market behaviour is impeded by fear and ignorance. On the other hand, such a shortcoming may lead to unnecessary infringements through ignorance.

An important cause of the lack of guidance seems to be the fact that there is only a fairly limited number of precedents. Unsurprisingly, the clearest and most comprehensive guidance that has been issued, on vertical agreements, is also the subject of most of the decisions of the authorities under investigation (forty-five out of seventy-eight decisions concern vertical restrictions). It is in several respects easier and more attractive for authorities to write policy rules by the codification of existing precedents than by writing policies that have not yet been tried and tested in practice. This also prevents subsequent court rulings from showing that competition authorities applied false positive or false negative qualifications to a certain type of behaviour in their policy rules. The downside of such an attitude is that companies 'have to work out for themselves' what is and is not allowed over a period of years. This legitimate interest of companies in knowing what is and what is not allowed is in danger of being overlooked if authorities delay adopting policies for too long because they are of the view that certain doctrines have not yet been sufficiently crystallised in their decision-making practice and case law.

Competition law compliance has clearly become 'top of mind' for most companies. It can therefore be expected that if it has been made sufficiently clear to undertakings that a competition authority qualifies certain conduct as prohibited, that undertaking will be more likely to comply with that prohibition. As mentioned in discussing the previous bottleneck, this process requires the rules in various jurisdictions to be more or less uniform in all (European) jurisdictions, at least in a material sense. The greater the extent to which the rules differ from one jurisdiction to another, the more difficult such 'compliance by default' will become for the companies involved. In the digital sector, however, clarity is still lacking on (too) many points and uniformity does not appear to be governments' greatest concern when introducing new sector-specific regulatory legislation.

[H] Lack of Sufficient Cooperation on a Global Scale

The cooperation on digital competition cases among the competition authorities under investigation appears to have intensified since the previous edition of this book (2019). However, there are notable differences in the European approach to mergers and anticompetitive behaviour and the approach of other large enforcement agencies, such as the US Federal Trade Commission and the US Department of Justice, the Australian Competition & Consumer Commission, the Japan Fair Trade Commission, the Competition Bureau of Canada, the South African Competition Commission and the Competition Commission of India.

From the section on Cooperation Between Authorities in the Analysis, it becomes clear that while the number of cooperation initiatives between competition authorities worldwide is on the increase, these initiatives are generally without many obligations – in particular where it concerns cooperation initiatives outside the EU. Most of the initiatives amount to the sharing of knowledge and best practices. Outside the EU, there are however no cooperation initiatives that are more far-reaching such as making joint decisions on the allocation of cases or focus areas. Only within the ECN can such further-reaching initiatives currently be observed.

Tech giants are however global players and neither their activities nor the effects thereof are limited to the EU's borders. In addition, also within the EU enforcement policies are not always homogeneous and conflicting outcomes have been reached in different EU Member States (*see* bottleneck §12.02[A] above). Such conflicting outcomes can be harmful not only to the undertakings under scrutiny (double jeopardy issues, obstacles to pursuing one uniform commercial policy across borders) but also to consumers and other undertakings (competitors, suppliers, customers and consumers).

[I] Lack of Balance in Opinions about 'Big Tech'

General opinions about 'big tech' have changed just as rapidly as technological developments have progressed. As already mentioned in the preface of this book, until approximately 2017 the general sentiment was that, despite some concerns, 'tech was good'. Gradually, the sentiment started to change and may now be described as the exact opposite: '(big) tech is bad'.[1858]

1858. Compare, e.g., *New York Times*, 'Why Is Big Tech under Assault? Power.', 21 April/14 June 2021, https://www.nytimes.com/2021/04/21/technology/big-tech-power.html, *Questrom Magazine*, 'Is It Time to Break Up Big Tech?', https://www.bu.edu/questrom-magazine/fall-2019/is-it-time-to-break-up-big-tech/, *Harvard Business Review*, 'Can Big Tech Be Disrupted?; A Conversation with Columbia Business School Professor Jonathan Knee by Alison Beard', January-February 2022, https://hbr.org/2022/01/can-big-tech-be-disrupted, *Poole Thought Leadership (NC State University)*, 'Big Tech's Dark Side: Killer Apps, Abs, and

Arguably, both positions lack nuance. The initial positive view may be said to have disregarded some inherent risks attached to platforms and network technology, whereas the current mood may be said to lose sight of the obvious benefits of digital technologies and the substantial innovative power of big tech companies. In case legislation and decision-making depart from a negative bias towards large tech companies (as seems currently the case), such legislation and administrative decisions run the risk of becoming equally biased. While being critical is generally good, being biased usually leads to poor policy and legislative choices. It is therefore a big challenge for competition authorities and legislatures – in Europe and around the globe – to avoid any (positive or negative) bias fuelled by public opinion and to instead carry out their work truly objectively.

§12.03 RECOMMENDATIONS

The following recommendations are made in response to the bottlenecks identified above.

[A] Ensure Coherent Guidance with Supranational Scope Through Cooperation

An important bottleneck that was identified is the fact that the tech sector is asking for more guidance on various subjects. In a very simplified way, the authorities used the period up to 2017 for study purposes and then started enforcement. The challenge now facing the authorities is to translate the results of this study into concrete – where possible and desirable, joint – policy (while of course respecting the autonomy of the Member States). The European competition authorities already share their knowledge of the digital sector in the ECN and the Commission, as a supranational authority could introduce a mechanism to raise inconsistency issues or encourage the use of case teams consisting of officials from different authorities. Authorities could also increase cooperation earlier on in the process, including on market investigations, market monitoring and priority setting. But we recommend that they would not stop at that. There are many conceivable initiatives that would neither require new legislation nor enormous efforts in terms of resources and human resources. Authorities could for example consider setting up joint centres of excellence or research pools on certain topics that are 'hot' issues in multiple jurisdictions. They could also consider seconding staff with experience in working on a particular subject or theory of harm to a fellow competition authority that is also dealing with a similar issue, or even establish floating pools of highly specialised personnel that could serve as 'A-Teams' to be deployed in the jurisdiction where the need is greatest at a given point in time. This could resolve the

Acqs', 25 August 2021, https://poole.ncsu.edu/thought-leadership/article/big-techs-dark-side-killer-apps-abs-and-acqs/, *Trouw*, 'Europarlementariër Paul Tang: "We moeten techbedrijven opbreken door ze open te breken"', 30 September 2021, https://www.trouw.nl/economie/europarlementarier-paul-tang-we-moeten-techbedrijven-opbreken-door-ze-open-te-breken~bea80603/.

problem of inconsistency between the policies of the various authorities and reduce the risk of overlapping or parallel investigations, which have been identified. It could also lead to more speed, both when it comes to enforcement in particular cases as well as with respect to the process of drafting and formalization of policy (rules). It may furthermore be expected to yield higher-quality decisions that have a greater chance to stand in court. In general terms, the policy should ideally be even broader than European. Tech companies are often active worldwide, so the best approach is also worldwide, at least wider than European.

We have identified an urgent need for clear, consistent policies in the following areas:

- application of competition law to digital platforms, in particular with regard to self-preferencing and data-sharing (refusals);
- clear rules for market definition for markets revolving around (big) data and an answer to the question in which cases these do or do not constitute an essential facility;
- admissibility of and liability for anticompetitive behaviour of algorithms (self-learning or otherwise).

[B] Transparency about Joint Action and Involvement of Market Parties and Experts

It is also important that international cooperation and consultation on international cooperation should, where possible, be transparent. For an outsider, the ECN, for example, is often a black box. Such a black box can quickly become an ivory tower. Legislation and regulations should be developed in dialogue with the market, the scientific community and other stakeholders with relevant knowledge. The practice of the Commission (and others) of organising conferences and public consultations is to be commended in this respect. We call on competition authorities to join forces with other competition authorities, academia and market parties and increasingly communicate about this so that market parties know which directions authorities are thinking of, they can better assess the consequences thereof and, if necessary, anticipate them.

[C] Learn from Each Other's Enforcement, Including the Resulting Case Law, and Continue to Closely Monitor and Evaluate the Impact of Enforcement

Cooperation in the development of policy alone is not enough. That policy must then be applied to concrete cases. In order to ensure that uniformity is also maintained in the concrete application of policies, competition authorities should closely monitor and evaluate each other's enforcement and its consequences (including case law) and thus learn from each other.

[D] Keep an Eye on Innovation and the Business Climate: Be Proportional

It is important that competition authorities, on the one hand, act against anticompetitive behaviour, but, on the other hand, do not go so far in their actions that innovation and business location policy suffer. In concrete terms, this can be done to, for example:

- act proportionately, using the appropriate enforcement instruments;
- examine whether the market can solve problems on its own and consider self-regulation as a possible solution to problems identified;
- be generously open to issuing concrete guidance in individual cases.

[E] Continue to Invest in Research and Sufficient Experts

A major bottleneck is a lack of understanding of technological developments and an inherent knowledge gap of competition authorities in respect of the technology sector. In order to solve these bottlenecks, competition authorities should continue (or as far as the BCA is concerned, start) to invest in research and experts. This should also certainly include sufficient data specialists. Links with the market, academia and other knowledge-based stakeholders are also very important in this context.

[F] Ensure Coordination with Complementary Fields of Law and Their Competent Authorities by Means of Protocols

It is undesirable to have an unclear delineation of competition law with other fields of law (such as privacy law and consumer law) and the mutual delineation of powers between competition authorities on the one hand and authorities that supervise the laws and regulations in those other fields of law on the other hand. It is recommended that competition authorities should, where possible, set down their cooperation with other authorities in protocols: who will act when? How are conflicting outcomes handled? Protocolling increases the transparency of supervision. Both with regard to the content of the supervision and the way in which supervision is exercised. It is in the interests of the European technology sector that uniform enforcement is carried out as soon as possible and in a uniform manner.

Perhaps, it could be worth considering bringing the enforcement of competition law, privacy law and consumer law into one hand. That would substantially reduce the chance of conflicting outcomes At present, of the jurisdictions under investigation, only in the UK and the Netherlands are competition and consumer laws enforced by the same authority. In none of the jurisdictions under review is enforcement of privacy law (in particular the GDPR) currently in the same hands as enforcement of competition law.

Another - not necessarily mutually exclusive - solution could be to create a separate sectoral tech authority that could enforce competition law, privacy law and consumer law - along with specific sectoral legislation such as the DMA, the DSA and the German Article 19a GWB – for the tech sector. Of course, the introduction of such an authority would require a thorough delimitation of its powers vis-à-vis those of the regular competition, privacy and consumer authorities. Both arrangements further to such a tech authority would absorb all of the latter's powers in tech-related cases, as well as solutions pursuant to which the regular authorities would retain certain powers alongside the new tech authority.

[G] National Courts: Do Not Hesitate to Refer Questions for a Preliminary Ruling

A lack of precedents could be less of a problem if, in appropriate cases, national courts have no hesitation to ask the CJEU for a preliminary ruling on the interpretation of EU competition law. This also offers a solution where uniform policy is lacking in a substantive sense. If the ECJ gives a clear ruling on a particular issue, the uniform application of that ruling throughout the EEA is in principle ensured.

[H] Be Independent and Consider the Facts and Circumstances of Each Case Carefully

It is important that the political establishment confines itself to adopting laws and regulations, which the competition authorities can then apply to concrete cases in full independence. This avoids undesirable direct political influence in specific cases. It is crucial that competition authorities investigate the facts of each specific case properly and weigh them appropriately. As indicated above, sufficient technical knowledge and expertise are crucial in this respect.

[I] Take a Leading Role in the World by Providing a Coherent and Uniform Vision of the Impact of Technology on Competition

The first recommendation is that European competition authorities should provide more uniform guidance on various subtopics. That should be a starting point rather than an endpoint. The next step should be developing a uniform and coherent vision of competition and technology as a whole. This is the only way of avoiding both an enforcement deficit, resulting in a lack of competition, and a surplus of enforcement that will stifle innovation and worsen the business location environment.

This last 'task' facing competition authorities is also the greatest challenge. But this challenge should be taken up. The need for this has become pertinently clear during this survey of the various European competition authorities.

With this final recommendation, our (second, revisited) journey through the European landscape of digital competition has indeed come to an end. But of course, that end is only very relative. The pace at which legal and technological developments shall continue may be expected to accelerate even further. In reality, this journey is only just starting!

Table of Cases

Note: Only cases that feature in the national chapters 4-9 are included.

Belgium

EU: European Court of Justice

EU: General Court

France

Germany

The Netherlands

United Kingdom

Competition Appeal Tribunal, *Ping v CMA [2018] CAT 13*, 7 September 2018, 126, 127, 324
Competition Appeal Tribunal, *Facebook, Inc. and Facebook UK Limited v. Competition and Markets Authority*, 1366/4/12/20, 26 August 2020, 162
Competition Appeal Tribunal, *CMA*, 1366/4/12/20, 13 July 2021, 251, 260, 265, 353
Competition Appeal Tribunal, *CMA*, 1429/4/12/21, 15 July 2022, 396
Competition Appeal Tribunal, *CMA*, 1429/4/12/21, 14 June 2022, 163

United States

United States District Court Northern District of California San Francisco Division, *Plea Agreement: United States of America v. David Topkins*, 30 April 2015, 380
United States District Court Northern District of California San Francisco Division, *Plea Agreement: United States of America v. Trod Limited, d/b/a Buy 4 Less, d/b/a Buy For Less, d/b/a Buy-For-Less-Online*, 11 August 2016., 380, 381
S District Court for the Southern District of New York, *Spencer Meyer v. Travis Kalanick 1:15 Civ. 9796 ECF Case Jury Trial Demanded*, 2016, 34

Table of Decisions

Note: Only decisions that are quoted in the national chapters 4-9 are quoted in these tables

Antitrust decisions

European Commission

CMA

Autorité de la Concurrence

BCA

Merger decisions

European Commission

CMA

Autorité de la Concurrence

Bundeskartellamt

ACM

Index

I

L

M

N

O

P

U

V

www.ingramcontent.com/pod-product-compliance
Lightning Source LLC
Chambersburg PA
CBHW071236230926
51849CB00001B/117
9789403511672